THE ROYAL TOMBS OF EGYPT

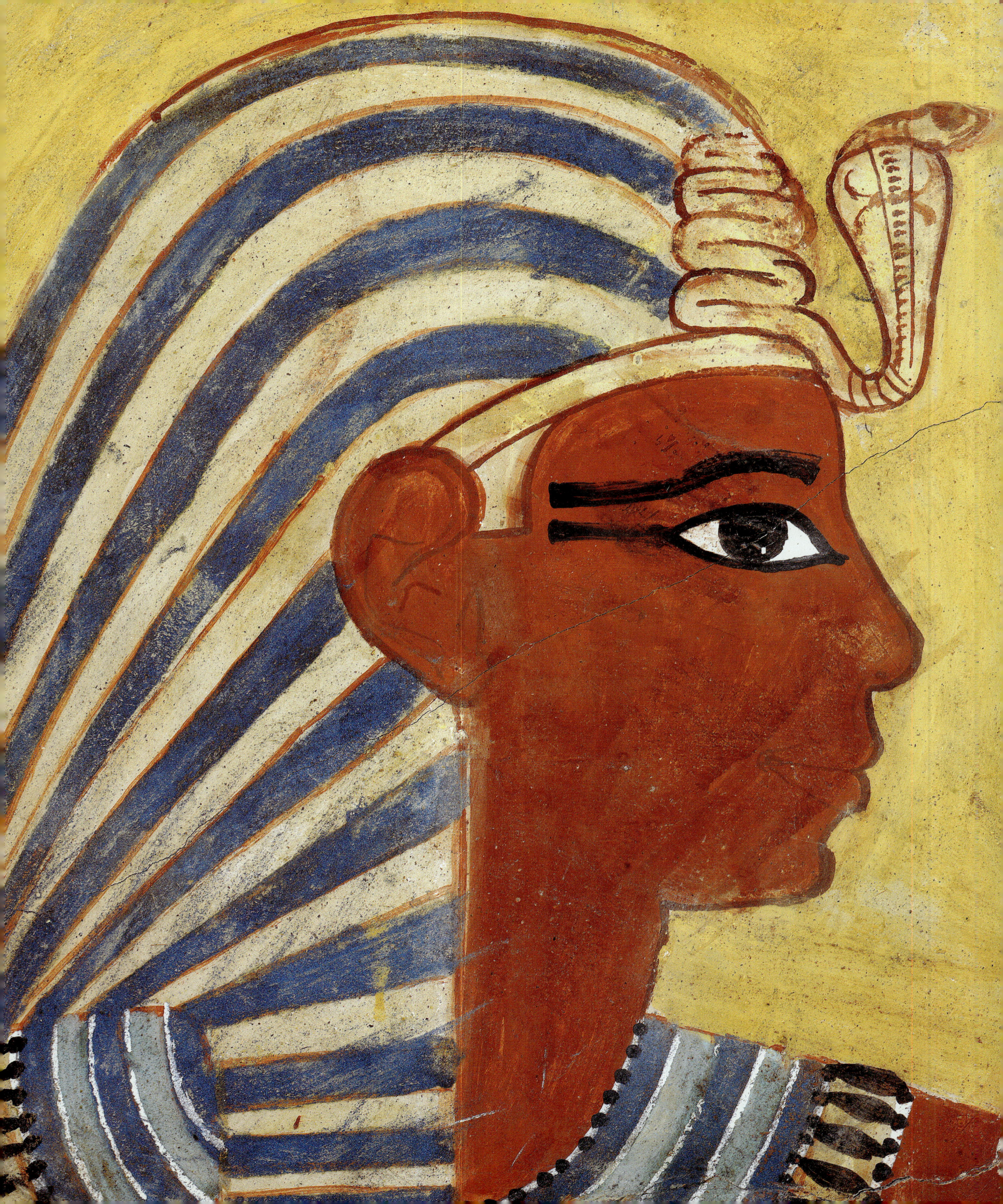

ZAHI HAWASS
PHOTOGRAPHS BY SANDRO VANNINI

THE ROYAL TOMBS OF EGYPT

THE ART OF THEBES REVEALED

WITH OVER 300 COLOUR ILLUSTRATIONS

Thames & Hudson

To my dear friend Ali Radwan
for his love of Egyptology.

Zahi Hawass

TUTHMOSIS IV
(page 2)
This image of Tuthmosis IV from his tomb in the Valley of the Kings shows the pharaoh in the *nemes* headcloth, his forehead protected by a uraeus (hooded cobra).

PREFACE

In 1977, I was working in the Valley of the Kings as an archaeologist. During this time, two important things happened. The first was that I climbed the Qurn, the peak that stands sentinel over the Valley. The night that I made this climb, the moon was full, and the silence was absolute. I will never forget this night. The small chambers that once held the treasures of King Tut, the beautiful scenes in the tombs, illustrating the books that tell us about the ancient Egyptian Netherworld: all could be smelled and seen under the full moon. I found myself dreaming of all the magnificent royal tombs, and slept in the Valley until dawn.

The second thing that happened was that I met a man named Sheikh Ali Abd el Rassoul at El-Marsam Hotel. He was the last living member of the Abdel Rassoul family, the shepherds who found the first cache of royal mummies. Sheikh Ali told me about the secret tunnel, 300 feet long, in the tomb of Seti I, which some think leads to the burial chamber of Seti I. I recently explored the first half of this tunnel, which is cut into fragile rock and is quite dangerous, and plan to go back soon. These are the two stories I always remember, which have made a special place in my heart for the Valley of the Kings, my second love after the pyramids.

When I was asked to write this book, I thought it would be a good opportunity to learn about the secret books that help the deceased king on his journey to eternity. It was very interesting to write each chapter on my famous yellow lined legal pads, and give it to Janice Kamrin to type and edit. At the same time, Sandro Vannini was working in the Valley, taking his beautiful photos and sending them to us for review so that we could make a great and unique book.

This book comes at a time of great excitement in the Valley, with the discovery, for the first time in over 80 years, of a new tomb. As the Tomb of Tutankhamun is numbered KV 62, this new discovery has been officially named KV 63. As I write this preface, KV 63 (see page 34) is yielding new artifacts. Only last week, a beautiful gilded coffinette, probably for a funerary figurine (*shabti*), was found inside one of the coffins, which also contained a number of ancient pillows! There are still several coffins left to open and conserve, and then a great deal of debris—at least half a meter—still covering the floor to sift through. The finds here have already been fascinating, and the next months will reveal more of this intriguing story.

Zahi Hawass

CONTENTS

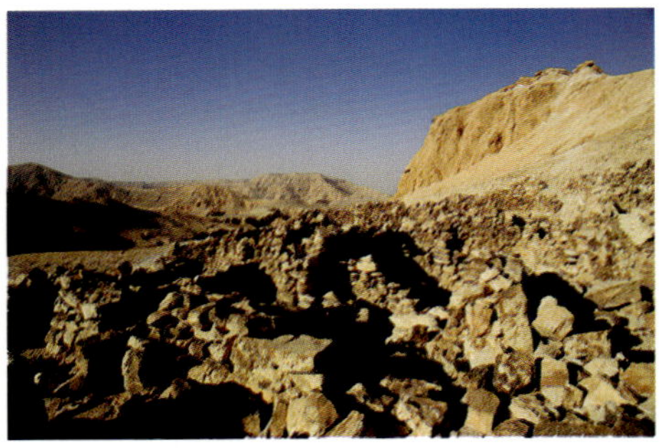

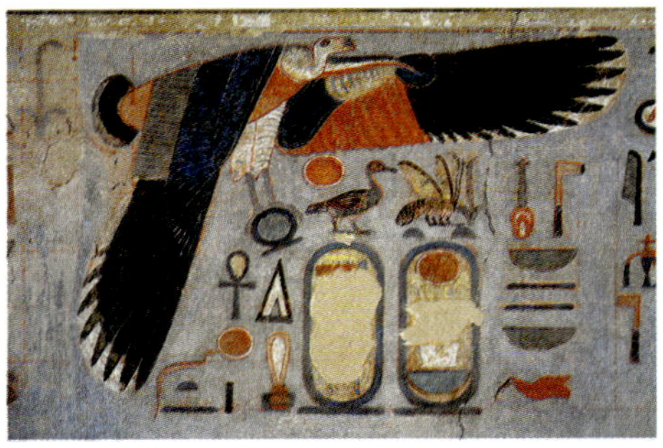

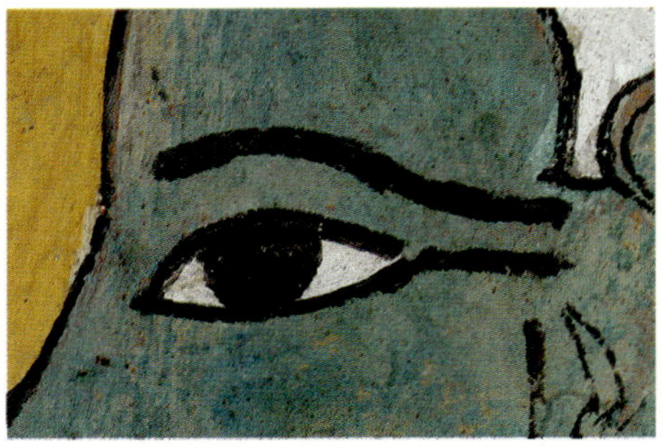

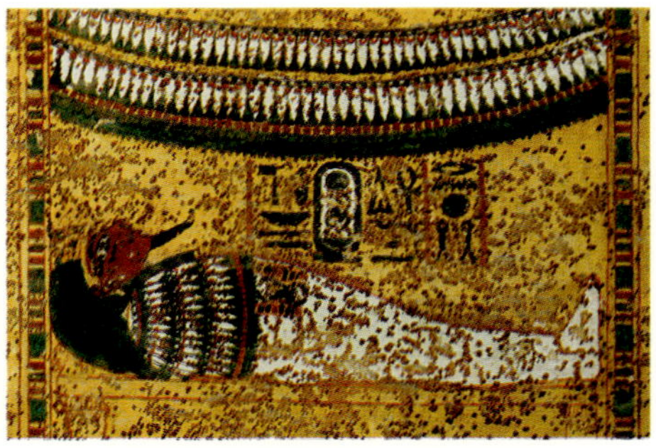

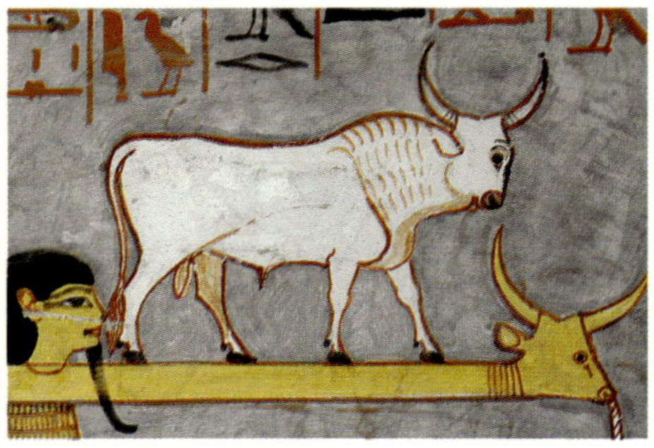

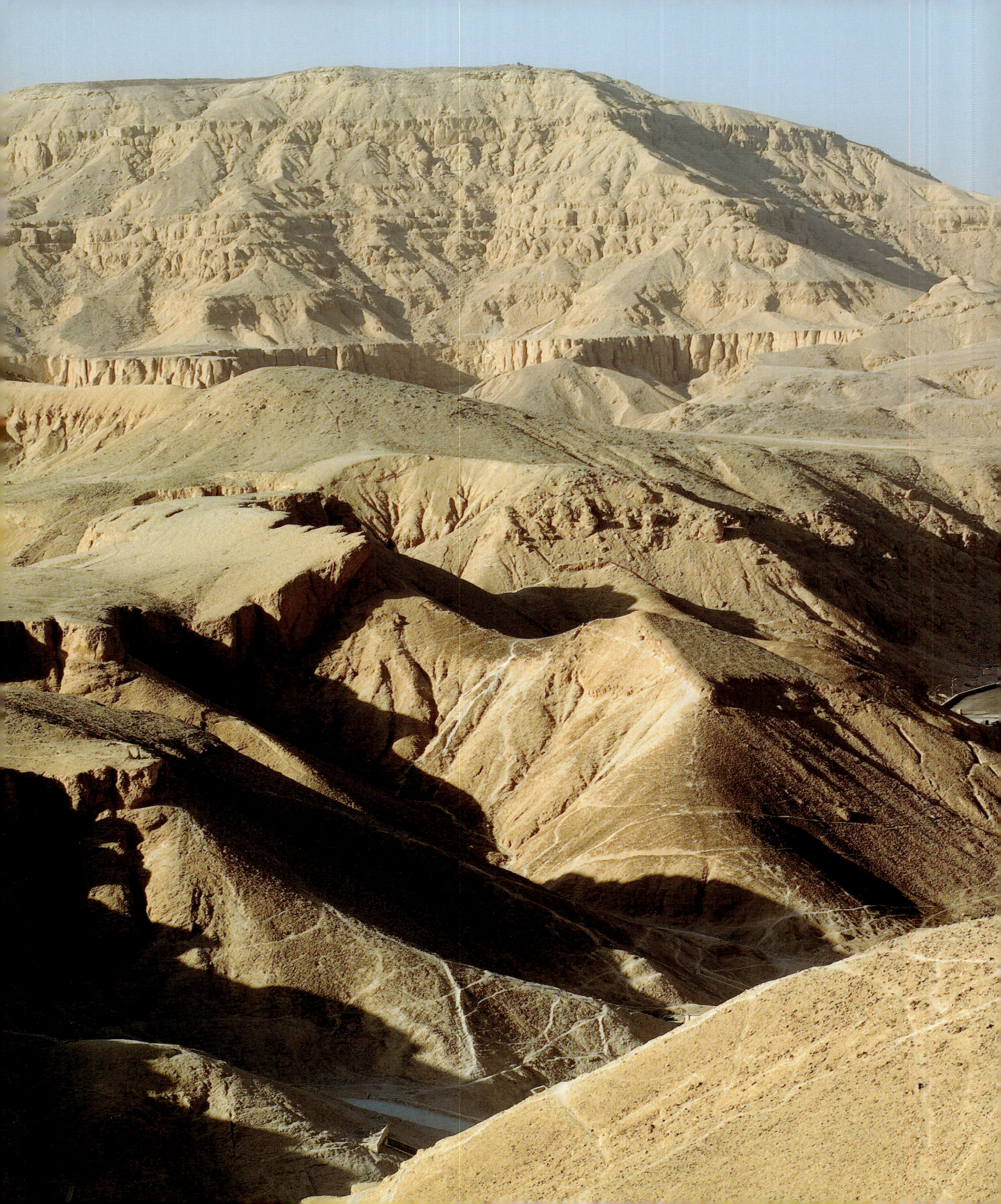

INTRODUCTION

THE ROYAL TOMBS OF ANCIENT EGYPT

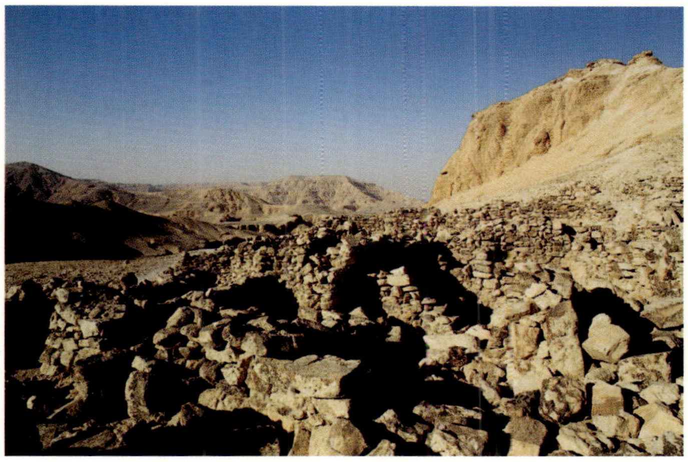

Deep in the rocky hills on the west bank of modern Luxor lie a series of wadis—the dry beds of ancient rivers and streams—known collectively today as Biban el-Maluk, or the Valley of the Kings. Most of the pharaohs of the New Kingdom were buried here, in tombs tunneled into the walls and desert floors of these canyons.

The choice of this remote location, the architecture of the tombs, and especially their decoration, provide a window into the religious beliefs of the ancient Egyptian kings. The tomb was not a final prison, but a sacred place where the king's resurrection would be effected, a gateway to eternity, and an eternal dwelling for the royal soul. Once he had made the transition from death to resurrection, the king became equal to the gods.

The vast number of ancient tombs and the significant number of temples discovered in Egypt, compared to the relatively few remains of houses, palaces, and cities, can be attributed in part to the vagaries of preservation. The houses of the living, including the royal palaces, were meant to be temporary, to last only for a lifetime. Monumental palaces and private houses of all sorts were of mud brick, and lay on the floodplain. They have therefore, with few exceptions, decayed, washed away, or been buried beneath modern habitation.

Temples and tombs, on the other hand, were designed as permanent houses for the gods and the dead. The immense resources poured into their construction and decoration bears witness to the importance of religion and the Afterlife in the lives of the ancient Egyptians. Study, development, and carefully controlled dissemination of religious dogma, carried out by priests, was essential to the proper functioning of the Egyptian world. This dogma changed over time, and is reflected in the architecture and decoration of the royal tombs.

THE WEST BANK AT THEBES

The low desert on the west bank at Luxor was the land of the dead, host to thousands of tombs dating to the pharaonic era, especially the New Kingdom. The rocky foothills here give way rapidly to the higher peaks of the Theban massif, identified by the ancients as the womb of the great goddess.

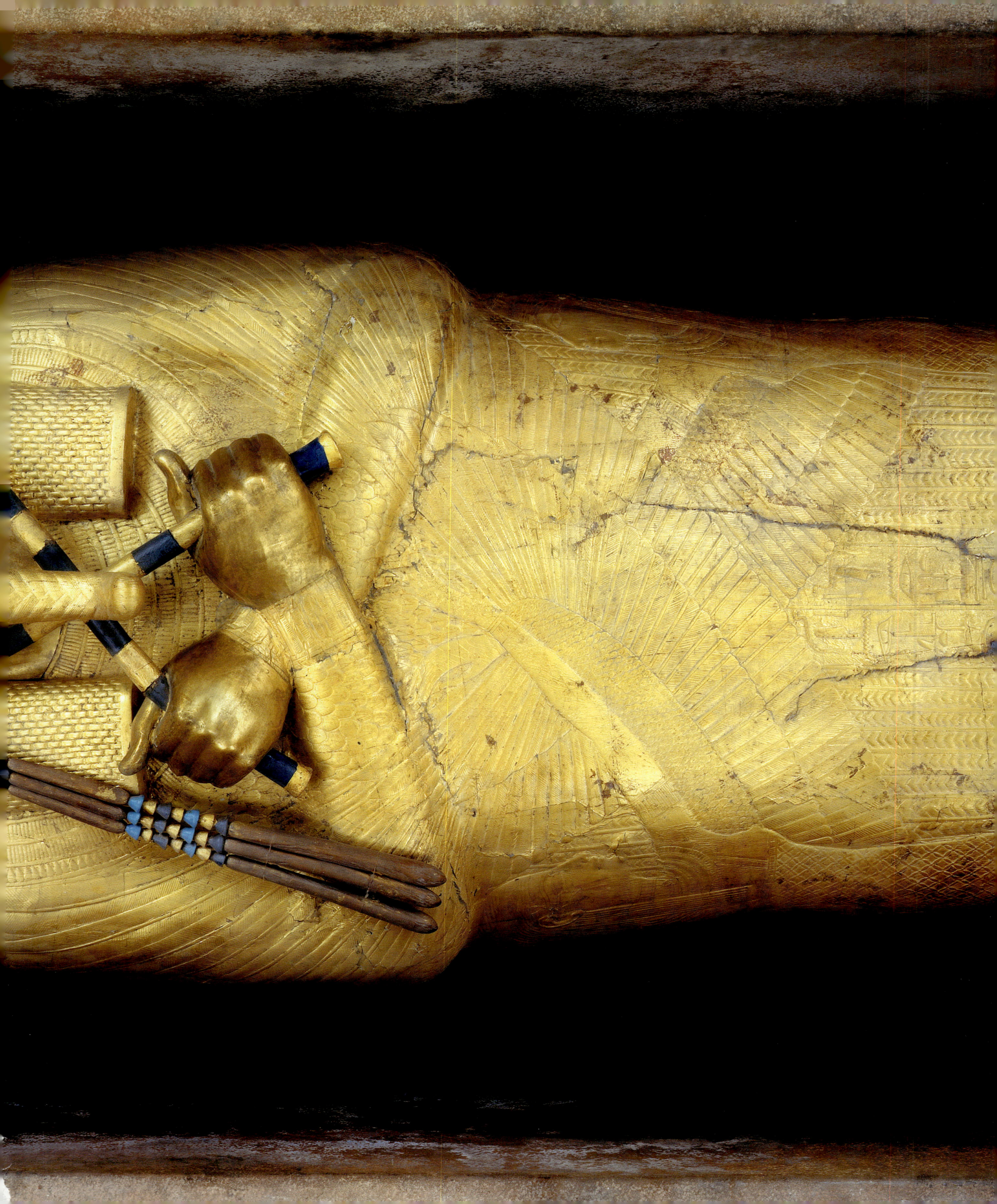

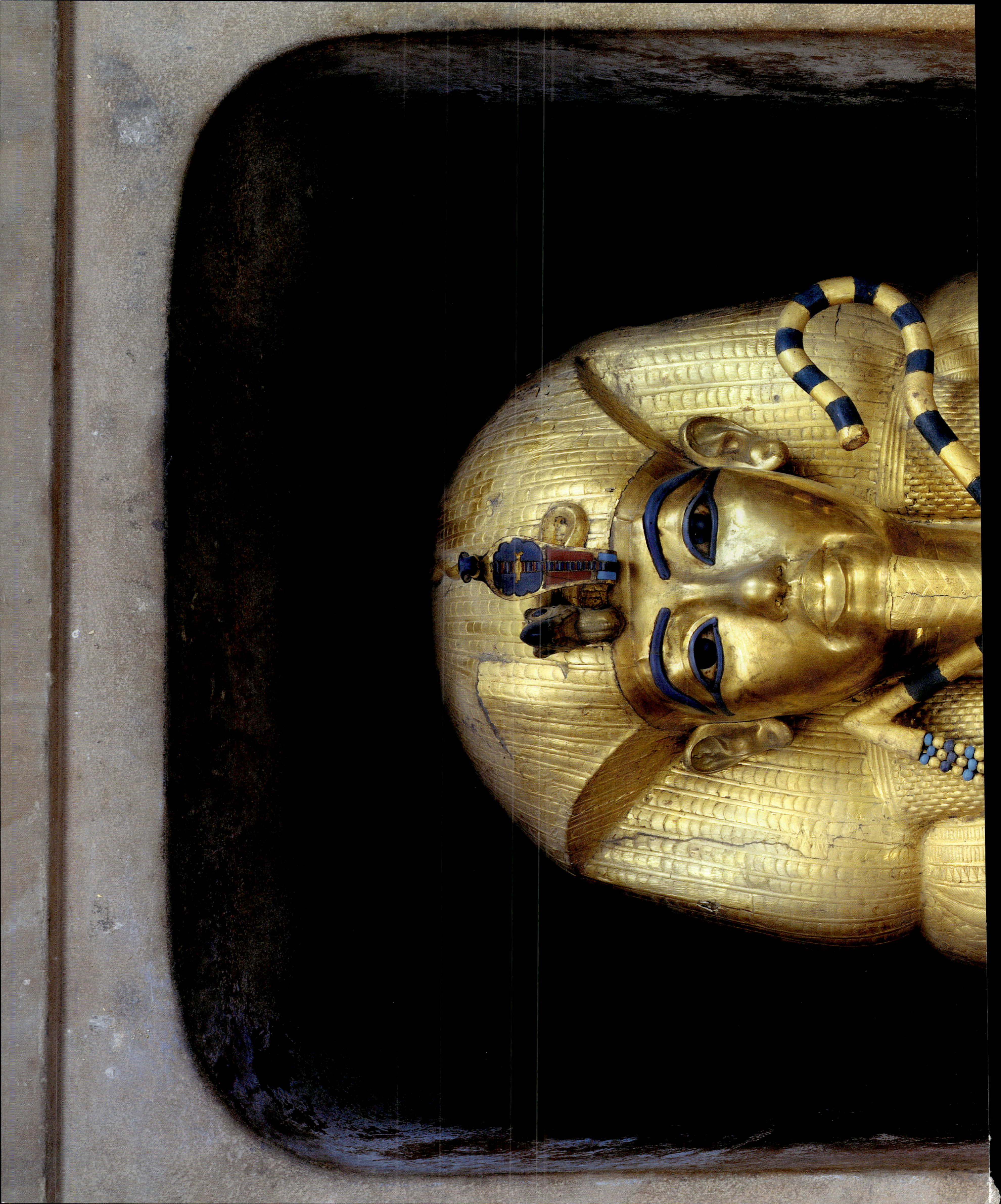

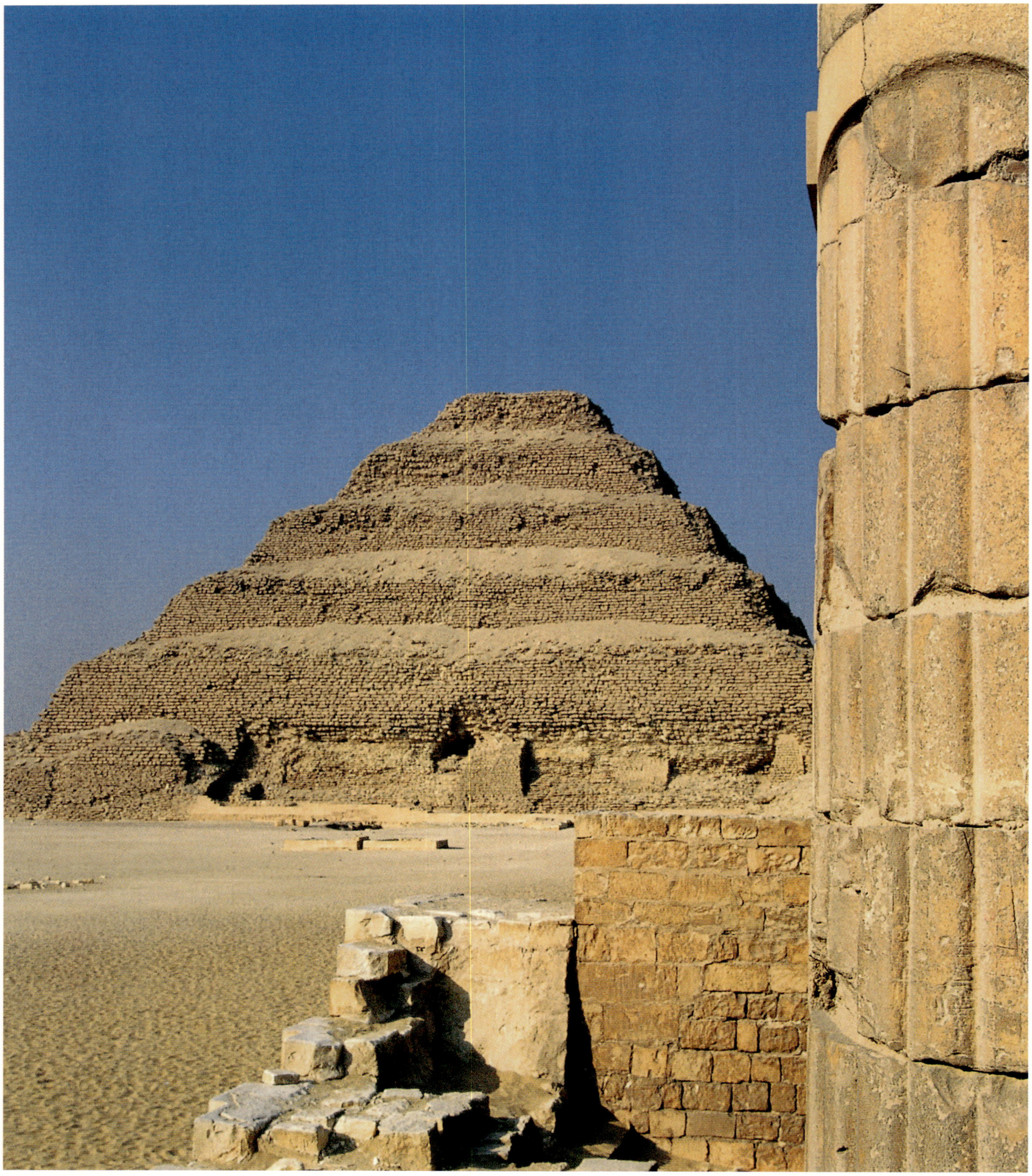

THE STEP PYRAMID OF DJOSER AT SAQQARA

This pyramid (ca. 2687–2668 BC) is both the first pyramid and the first monumental stone structure in the world. Its pyramidal shape makes reference to the *benben*, the sacred stone of the sun god, which was both a representation of the primeval mound of creation and a solar image. The Step Pyramid provided a ladder on which the deceased king could mount to join his fellow gods in the sky.

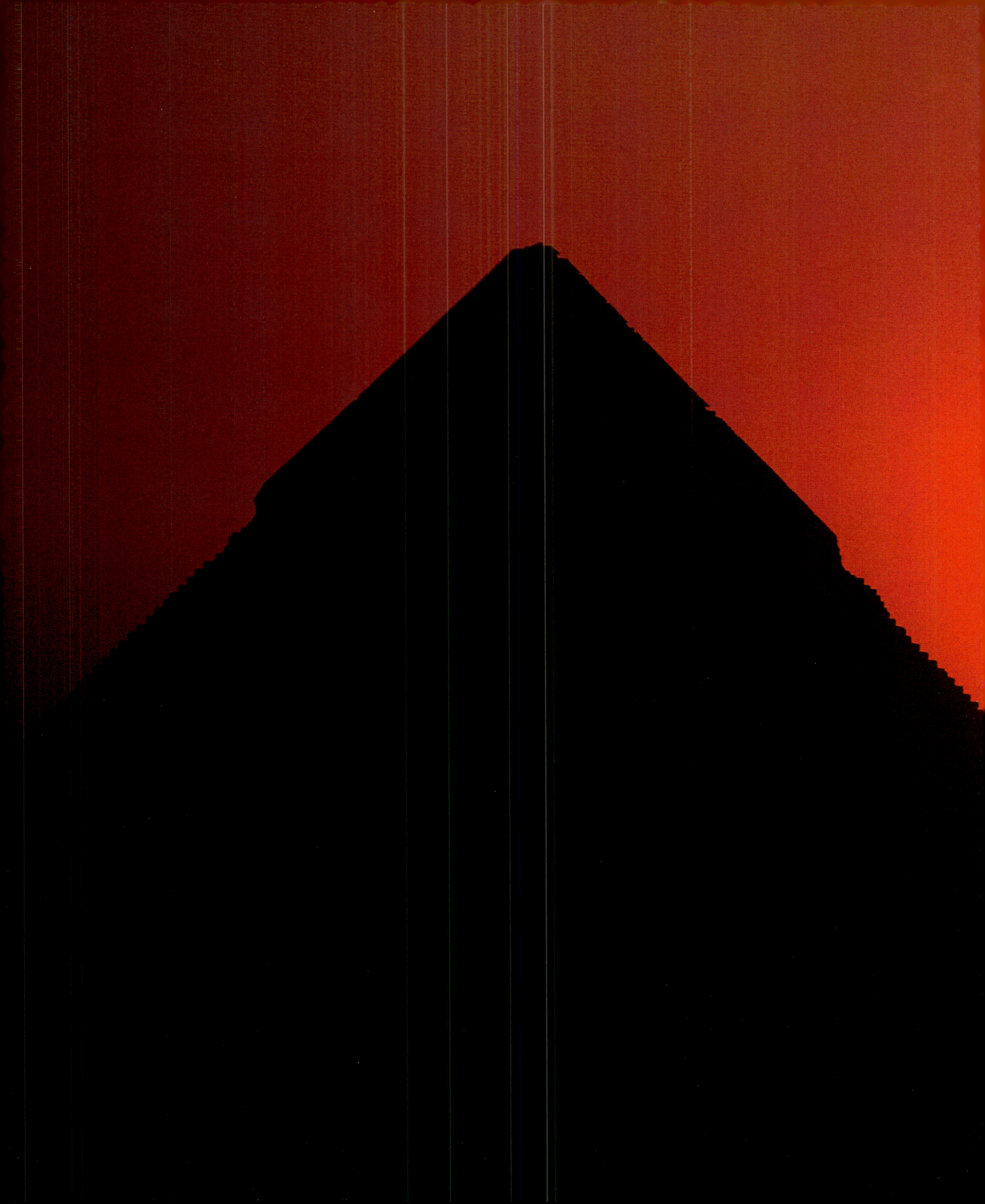

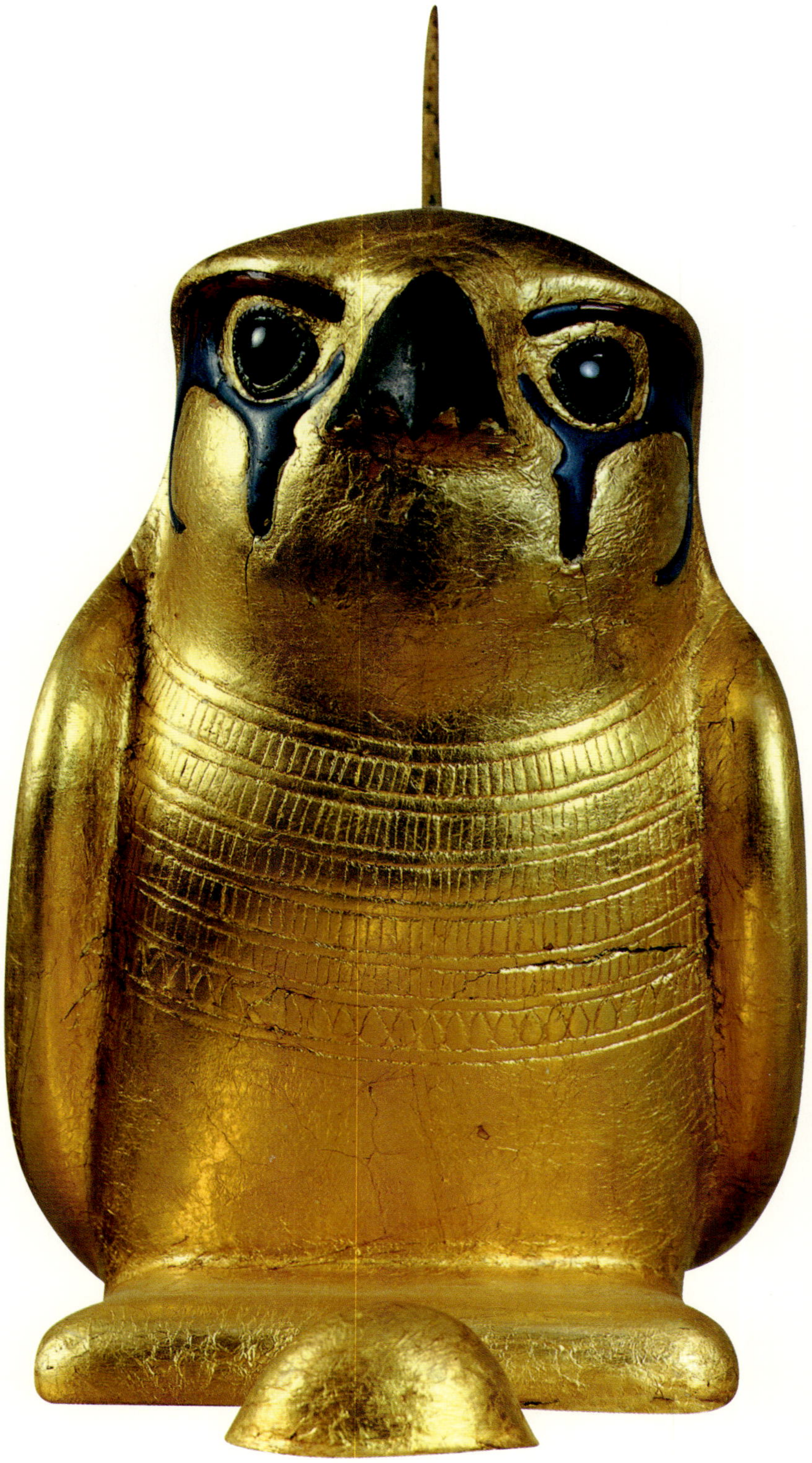

SOPDU STANDARD
Found in the tomb of Tutankhamun, this gilded wooden image represents Sopdu, god of the desert that lay beyond the borders of Egypt, in the form of a falcon. A number of divine statues were buried with Tutankhamun, to protect him and guide him in the Afterlife.

OUTER COFFIN OF TUTANKHAMUN
Tutankhamun's mummy was protected by a nest of coffins and shrines. Shown here is the outermost coffin, made of cedarwood cased with gold. The king is shown in an unusual headdress, his forehead protected by the cobra and vulture, and a divine beard. In his hands he holds the crook and flail, insignia of kingship in general and identified especially with the king of the gods, Osiris. Traces of black on the coffin show where oils and unguents were poured during the funeral ceremonies. The mummy of the king still lies within this coffin in the Valley of the Kings.

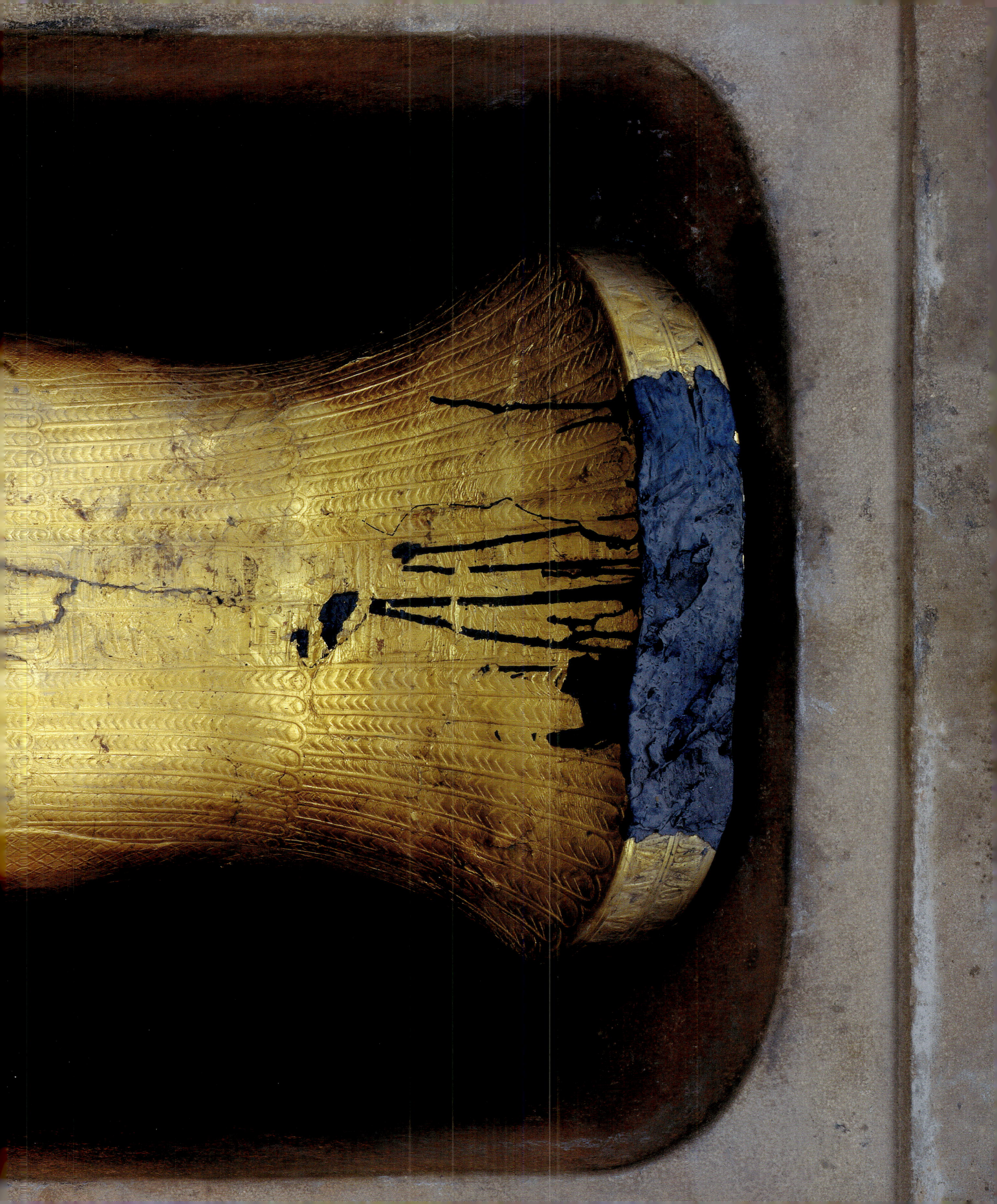

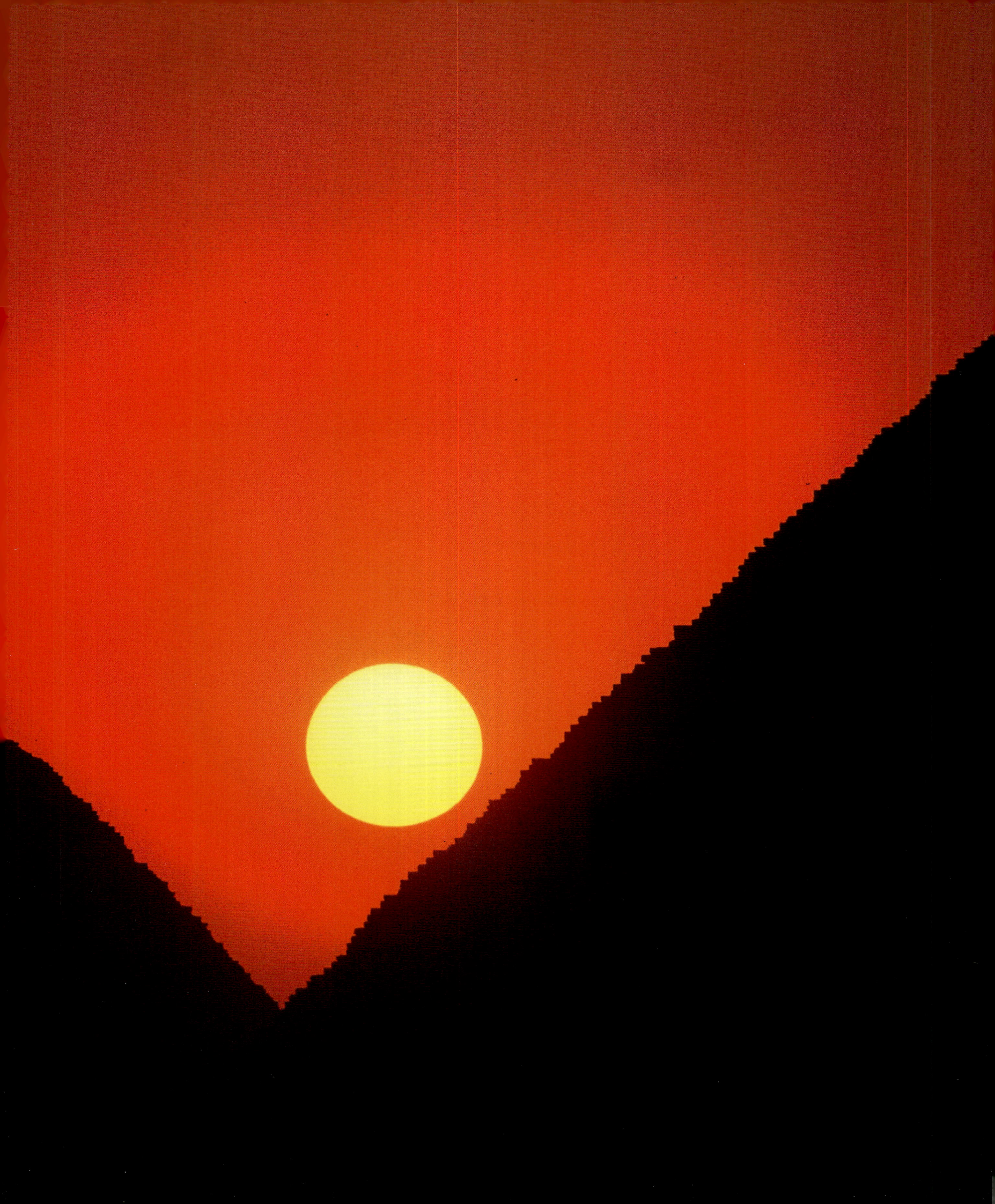

THE ANCIENT EGYPTIAN WORLDVIEW

Thousands of years ago, the ancient Egyptians lived in what must have seemed to them a strange, mysterious, and savage environment. They were buffeted by forces beyond their control, afraid of the capriciousness of nature, and bound by the external world around them. We can only guess that they soon began to ask themselves who had created their universe, and how? Who was controlling their environment?

In an attempt to answer these unanswerable questions, the Egyptians invented hidden gods who had power over everything. Whenever a feature of the universe appeared that they could not understand, they invented a new deity, often associating him or her with one of the animals that shared their world. They could not stand against the will of these gods, but worshipped them, making offerings to appease their anger and gain their favor.

As this fledgling religion developed, the Egyptians began to conceptualize a creator god, greatest among the gods, who had made the universe. In their most basic creation myth, the universe before this creation consisted of limitless darkness and water. Inherent in this chaotic realm, known in later times as "Nun," was a hillock of earth, the primeval mound. At the moment of creation, the creator god appeared on this mound and brought the ordered universe into being. This creator god was known by different names, but was linked early on with the sun god, because the sun defined their world, rising and setting regularly. Linking these two primordial powers, the Egyptians invented a sky god who had created the universe through the disk of the sun.

In the earliest periods of Egyptian religion, the heavens were the primary focus. The cult of the sun god, named Re at least by the mid-Old Kingdom, was paramount. After death, the king was thought to travel to the sky to join the unchanging circumpolar stars. Later, the god Osiris, king of the dead, who had been murdered by his brother and then resurrected by his wife, Isis, became more important. By the New Kingdom at the latest, the cults of Re and Osiris had been joined into an integrated system.

The journey of the sun was seen as a metaphor for death and resurrection, as it died (set) each evening in the west and was reborn (rose) each morning in the east. After death, both the sun and the deceased king traveled through a world beyond the visible earth. This world was populated by demons, monsters, and gods, and survival here was a matter of knowledge and skill. In the darkest hours of the night, the king and sun god would rejoin Osiris, who lay in the depths of the Netherworld, and thus gain the power to be reborn. This resurrection of the king, which happened both once, when he traveled from death to the Afterlife, and also daily, as he journeyed with the sun, helped to guarantee the continuance of the cosmos.

The names, attributes, powers, and mythologies associated with the various gods changed over time, although much remained constant. For example, the sun god, Re, first appeared as a fisherman, rowing in a small boat across the marshes. This simple idea caused the Egyptians to wonder why this god could not take them with him in his boat across the sky. This concept was linked with the north, with the marshy land of the Delta. In the south, at his cult site of Edfu, the sun god took the shape of a hawk, soaring across the sky.

These two concepts joined, and Re became a hawk-headed man who crossed the day sky in his morning bark, called *mandjet*, which means "become strong," and traveled through the night in his evening bark, called *mesketet*, which means "become weak." When the sun rose, it was also called Khepri, and was represented as a scarab beetle. At noon, when the sun was high in the sky, it was Re, represented as a man with the head of a hawk crowned with the sun disk. When the sun set, he was Atum-Re, an old man leaning on his staff. In the morning, he was Khepri again, or the child Nefertem, appearing on the opening blossom of a lotus.

Each human being, including the king was believed to consist of three principal parts: the body (*khet*), the soul (*ba*), and the lifeforce (*ka*). After death, these three parts of the human were divided; the goal of a proper funeral and mortuary cult was to reunite them. The body was mummified and placed in the substructure of the tomb. The *ba* was imagined as a bird with a human head, which could travel down the burial shaft to re-enter the body, or travel in the world of the living. The *ka* was imagined as the unseen twin of the person, to whom offerings were made after death, and who functioned in the eternal Afterlife. If the body deteriorated, it was important to have other images of the deceased, such as statues or reliefs, which the *ka* could recognize and enter. If the body or image of the deceased, the *ka*, and the *ba* did not rejoin, the eternal Afterlife would be lost.

SUNSET AT GIZA
Set in the western desert in the north of Egypt, near where the Nile Valley and the Delta meet, the site of Giza hosts the greatest pyramids ever built. On the right is the Great Pyramid of Khufu; on the left is the pyramid of his son Khafre. Between the two, the sun sets, creating an earthly image of the ancient Egyptian hieroglyph for "horizon."

THE ROYAL TOMB THROUGH THE AGES

The ancient Egyptians began burying their dead at least as early as the Predynastic Period. During this era, the deceased were simply placed in pits in the sand, in some cases with offerings of food, drink, or valued items from life. This was the time before the invention of writing, before the unification of Egypt and the beginning of pharaonic history.

The first kings of Egypt were buried at Abydos, in a cemetery that stretched back for centuries. Increasing complexity over time can be seen here, from the egalitarian burials of the earliest periods, to the larger, more elaborate tombs of early chieftains, and finally to the tombs of the first kings of Egypt.

The earliest tomb identified as the burial place of a ruler, perhaps even a king (U-j at Abydos), is in the form of a palace for the Afterlife, with a series of subterranean rooms, including areas identified as storerooms, private apartments, and a kitchen, arranged around a central hall. Slits in the walls are thought to represent windows or doors through which the deceased king's soul could travel.

Continuing the sequence represented by tomb U-j are the burials of the first kings of a united Egypt, designated by Egyptologists as Dynasty 0. The earliest of these are far out in the desert, and consist of double chambers containing wooden shrines. Although no superstructures remain, it is likely that these were simple mounds of sand, perhaps held back by retaining walls, or mastabas (bench-like structures) of mud brick. These might have symbolized the mound of creation. The tomb of the first king of the 1st Dynasty consists of three large subterranean chambers and about 36 smaller pits. Some of the smaller pits seem to have been for the burials of young men and of seven young lions, evidently sacrificed to accompany the king to his Afterlife. The remaining tombs of this dynasty followed a similar pattern, of one or more chambers—the burial chamber approached in later graves by a staircase—with a wooden shrine (perhaps in the form of a palace) inside and subsidiary burials (mainly of humans

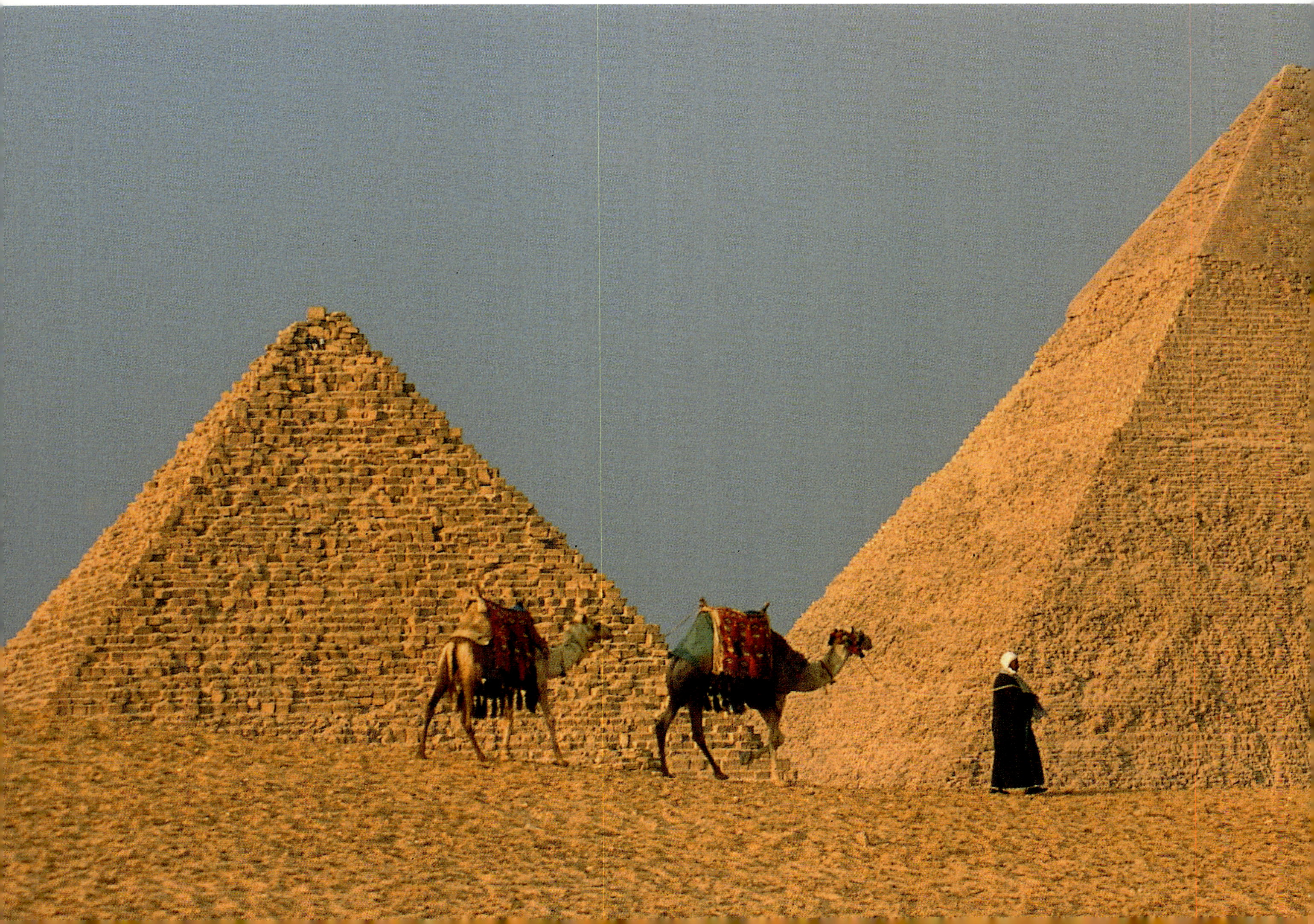

and dogs) arranged around the outside. Most have a gap in the line of retainer burials at the southwest corner, facing a large canyon cutting through the cliffs that cradle the site. Both royal and subsidiary burials had stelae associated with them.

At the edge of the floodplain were mud-brick enclosures where the royal cults were celebrated. Aha had three of these enclosures, all relatively small. The subsequent kings each appear to have had one enclosure (although not all of these have been securely identified), most surrounded, like the tombs, with subsidiary burials. There is little interior architecture, thus the assumption is that the cult structures were of perishable materials. The walls of the enclosures are elaborated with niches. This is thought to imitate the walls of the enclosure of the principal royal residence, which lay, from the reign of Aha on, at Memphis.

Several kings of the 2nd Dynasty were buried at Saqqara, in the desert west of Memphis, in labyrinthine tombs tunneled into the bedrock of the plateau. These consist of roughly-carved corridors and chambers without decoration, perhaps echoing either the layout of the royal palace or what we see later as the winding ways of the Netherworld (although from what we can tell, the mortuary religion seems to have been oriented more toward the heavens at this time). Strange features in these structures include odd knobs on some of the walls, the function of which is unknown. The superstructures that must once have surmounted these mazes are completely gone, presumably removed when the area was reused by later kings and nobles. Also at Saqqara, at the north end of the site, are a series of large tombs with rectangular superstructures of mud brick, their walls niched like the royal cult enclosures at Abydos. These belonged to high courtiers, and perhaps queens, of the 1st and 2nd Dynasties. The last two kings of the 2nd

The Pyramids of Giza
Built in the mid-4th Dynasty (ca. 2609–2523 BC), these towering solar symbols served to guard the burials of the kings who built them.

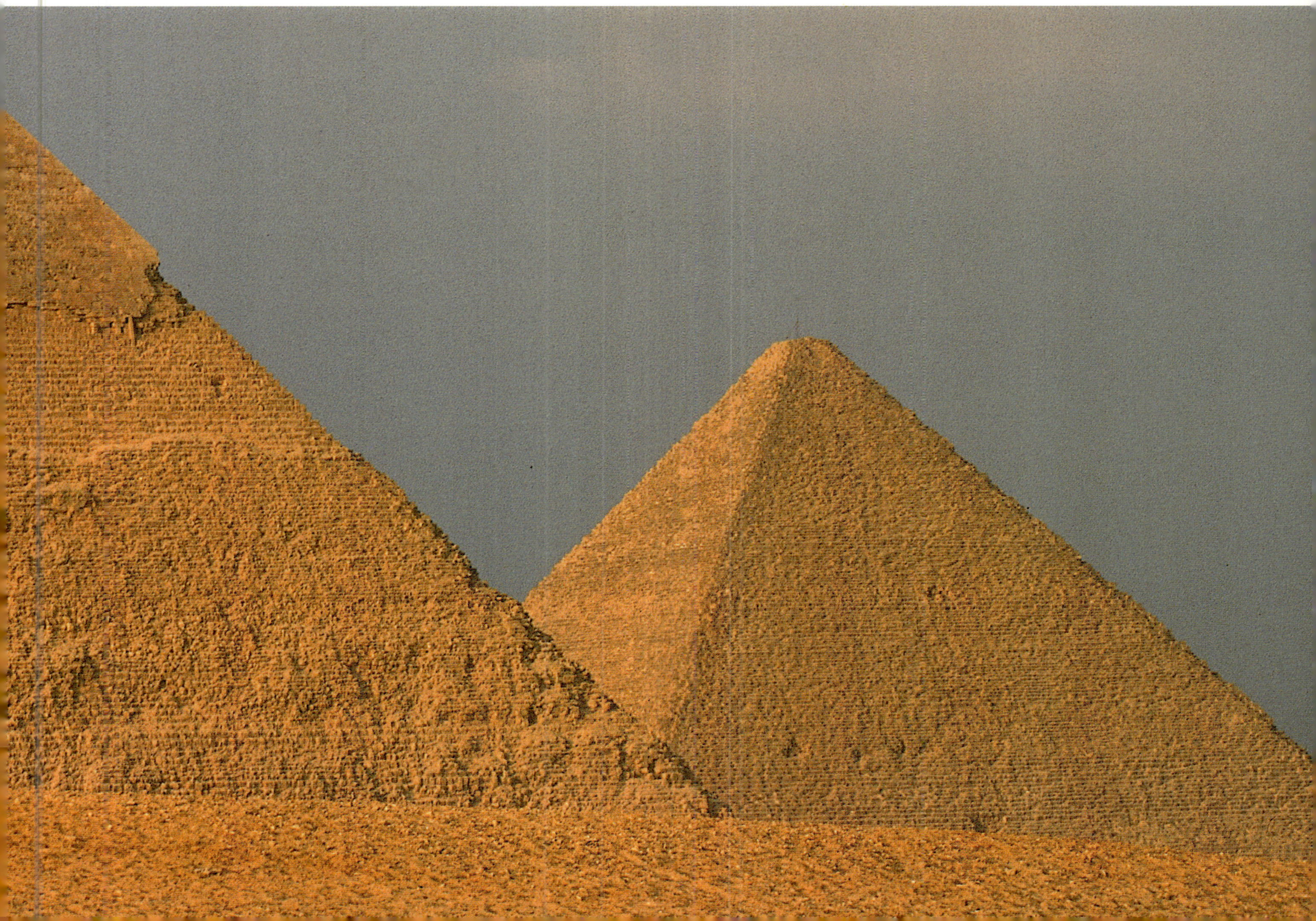

Dynasty were buried at Abydos, with tombs in the desert and immense cult enclosures near the floodplain.

A major change in royal funerary architecture took place in the 3rd Dynasty with the creation of the Step Pyramid of King Djoser at Saqqara by his chief advisor, Imhotep. From this point until the end of the Old Kingdom, all kings were buried in the Memphite western desert, in a series of necropolei that stretched from Abu Rawash in the north to Meidum in the south.

Set in a vast complex (almost 45 acres) of stone cult structures and magazines within a niched wall of limestone blocks, Djoser's pyramid was a towering stepped structure, a ladder to the sky. Underneath the pyramid was a maze of corridors and chambers, some of which held the burials of the king's relatives and others of which contained goods for the Afterlife. The king's own burial suite was decorated with faience tiles imitating reed mats bordering reliefs carved in limestone of the monarch performing his earthly ceremony of rejuvenation, the Sed Festival. In the enclosure wall is a second tomb dedicated to Djoser, not large enough for a burial, known as the South Tomb; the function of this structure is still debated by scholars.

One dynasty later, the true pyramid was invented, its four sides smooth and flat, meeting in a point at the apex. The most famous of these is the Great Pyramid of Khufu, which towers to a height of over 145 meters (480 feet). Although this is only the third true pyramid ever built (the first two, both at Dahshur, having been constructed for Khufu's father, Sneferu), it is the largest and best-engineered of all the Egyptian pyramids.

Khufu's pyramid was surrounded by a complex that included two temples (a pyramid temple and a valley temple), a causeway, a satellite pyramid (linked in some way with the cult of the king), subsidiary pyramids for his queens, and boat pits, either in reality or symbolically containing barks for the king's travel in the Afterlife. Most of these components appear in the succeeding complexes of the Old Kingdom, becoming more standardized over time. As the succession of dynasties continues, from 4th to 5th to 6th, the pyramids themselves become smaller, and the decoration of the temples becomes more elaborate.

The function of the pyramid is elucidated by the Pyramid Texts, long inscriptions carved in the burial chambers of pyramids from the last reign of the 5th Dynasty until the end of the Old Kingdom. According to these spells, the king hoped to use the rays of the sun to climb up to the sky after his death, finally reaching the imperishable circumpolar stars. Thus the tomb was built in the shape of a pyramid and cased with shining white limestone to mirror these rays and also reflect the sun, turning the pyramid itself into a source of light. On top was placed a pyramidion cased with electrum, to capture the gleam of the solar orb. At the same time, since the Egyptians were capable of holding two complementary or even seemingly contradictory concepts at the same time, this shape also symbolized the primeval mound of creation. Both this mound and the solar rays were associated with a symbol of the sun god known as the *benben*, thought to be a sacred stone kept in the solar temple of Re at Heliopolis. The shape may in addition be taken from nature, from the pyramidal piles of sand or shaped rock seen in the desert.

All Old Kingdom pyramids were entered from the north. These entrance passages are straight and lead to a series of one or more rooms. This orientation enabled the king to travel from his burial chamber directly to the circumpolar stars. After the reign of Khufu, who built two chambers high in the body of the pyramid, burial suites are at the base of the pyramid or below the surface, carved into the rock of the plateau.

The spells of the Pyramid Texts, in addition to guaranteeing the ascent of the king to the heavens, guided him through all of the rituals necessary for a successful funeral and burial. They also gave him the information that he needed to face the dangers of the beyond. Once the king had joined the gods, he went even further and became the supreme creator god, eating the other gods and their magical powers to provide himself with the strength he required. The king is also associated in these spells with Osiris, lord of the dead.

The monarchs of the Middle Kingdom were also buried under pyramids. The first several of these are clearly based on their Old Kingdom predecessors, but soon new layouts begin to appear. In contrast to the late Old Kingdom pyramids, which are quite standardized in terms of their layout and decoration, the Middle Kingdom pyramids vary a great deal in their internal structures, construction techniques, and surrounding complexes. Pyramid Texts are no longer found carved in the burial chambers.

From the reign of Senwosret II on, the north-facing entrance of the Old Kingdom pyramid was abandoned. The substructures beneath subsequent Middle Kingdom pyramids are mazes of corridors and chambers, perhaps partly designed to foil tomb robbers, but mainly meant to mimic the winding ways of the Netherworld. The Pyramid Texts that had once been found in royal burial chambers are seen instead during the Middle Kingdom on the coffins of the elite. The content of these spells also shifts. References to the sky and the stars disappear, and the focus becomes Osiris, King of the Dead.

According to later mythology, Osiris was a member of the fourth generation of gods, the great-grandson of the creator god, Atum-Re. Married to his sister, Isis, he succeeded his father, the earth god Geb, as king of Egypt. Osiris had a jealous brother, Seth, who murdered him, had his body cut to pieces, and then usurped his throne. Isis collected the scattered fragments of her husband, reassembled them (making the first mummy), then brought him back to life long enough to become pregnant with a son, Horus. Osiris descended to the Netherworld, where he became king of the dead.

During the Second Intermediate Period, the rulers who maintained native control in the south built their tombs with pyramidal superstructures. Beneath each was a tunnel extending from the north side of the pyramid to a small room and then to the burial chamber.

THE VALLEY OF THE KINGS

At the end of the Second Intermediate Period, Egypt was reunited by princes from the town of Waset, now known by its Greek name of Thebes and its modern name, Luxor. Thebes became, for a time, the capital of Egypt. The political capital soon moved north again to Memphis, but Thebes remained an important administrative center and, as the cult site of the god Amun-Re, one of the principal religious cities in the land. The ancestors of the New Kingdom monarchs had been buried on the west bank of Thebes, so it was here that the first kings of the 18th Dynasty founded a new royal necropolis.

We do not know exactly where the first kings of the New Kingdom were buried. Their ancestors had been laid to rest at Dra Abu el-Naga, a site on the desert slopes between the mountains and the floodplain at the north end of the Theban necropolis. The first king of the 18th Dynasty, Ahmose I, had an additional mortuary complex at Abydos, where most kings of the Early Dynastic Period had been buried, but his mummy was found in Thebes, so he must have been buried in this area.

The complex of wadis that form the Valley of the Kings had become the official burial ground of the New Kingdom monarchs by at least the reign of Hatshepsut. Many scholars believe that the first tomb in the valley was carved by Tuthmosis I, whose architect boasts that he supervised the construction of his monarch's sepulcher, "none seeing and none hearing." This king is also credited with the foundation of the village of Deir el-Medineh, where the artisans who cut and decorated the royal tombs lived. However, Tuthmosis I's original tomb has not yet been securely identified, and at least one scholar believes that it may still lie hidden in the Theban hills. The king's body was most likely moved at some point, first into the tomb of his daughter, Hatshepsut (KV 20), and then into a new tomb built for him by his grandson, Tuthmosis III (KV 38).

DEIR EL-BAHARI
The bay of cliffs at Deir el-Bahari shelter two major mortuary temples. The earlier is the temple and tomb of Mentuhotep II (ca. 2061–2011 BC), founder of the Middle Kingdom. The later, and larger, was built by Hatshepsut, powerful female pharaoh of the early 18th Dynasty (ca. 1502–1482 BC).

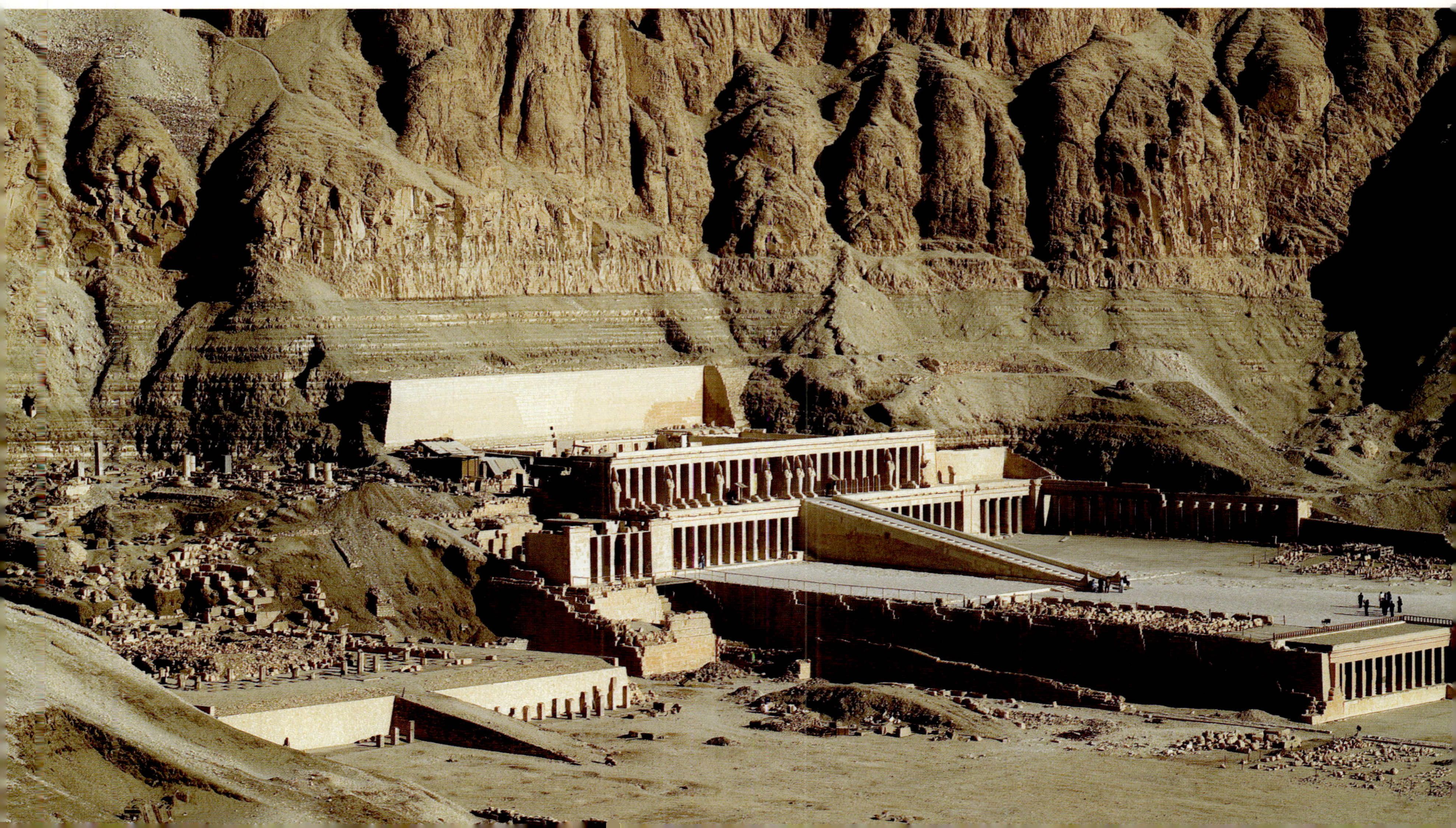

From this point onward, the Valley of the Kings was used by all but one of the monarchs of the 18th, 19th, and 20th Dynasties. The sole exception was the late 18th-Dynasty king Akhenaten, who rejected the principal state god of his forefathers, Amun, in favor of the sun disk, the Aten. He abandoned Thebes, then the religious capital of the country, for a virgin site in Middle Egypt known today as el-Amarna, and it was there that he cut his tomb.

Despite the military might of the New Kingdom pharaohs, their tombs were still vulnerable to tomb robbers. They had seen that neither the huge pyramids of the Old Kingdom nor the maze-like substructures of the Middle Kingdom pyramids had saved the ancient kings and their treasures. Thus, these kings chose instead to hide their tombs deep in the Theban hills. Carving the tombs here did help to protect them, as the valley could be guarded, and the tombs themselves were hidden from view. If one visits the Valley of the Kings today, it is easy to imagine how difficult it would have been to find these tombs in ancient times. Some are high up in the cliffs, nestled into crevices and reachable now only by stairs. Others, protected by modern entrances, are hidden in the valley floor. Several lie in the remote western arm of the Valley, and are hard to find even today.

The royal valley had an important symbolic meaning as well, superceding even issues of security. The entire Theban massif was seen as the land of the dead. The western mountains here have roughly the shape of a recumbent cow, linked with the great goddess Hathor, long worshipped in the bay of cliffs at Deir el-Bahari. In Egyptian mythology, Hathor was thought to receive the setting sun and carry him in her body to be reborn each morning. A separate but connected myth concerns the Celestial Cow (Mehetweret, "the Great Flood"), who appeared from the waters of the primordial ocean and bore the sun god up to the heavens. Thus, by burying their dead under these hills and inside the womb of the great cow the Egyptians magically provided for their own rebirth and for the continuous daily creation and passage of the sun. The landscape beneath these hills was seen as a reflection on earth of the Netherworld that lay beyond the land of the living.

The Valley of the Kings is surmounted by a pyramidal peak, known today as el-Qurn. This peak dominates the skyline, and is a reference to the sacred *benben* shape under which kings were traditionally buried. It was thought to be protected by a goddess named Meretseger, "she who loves silence."

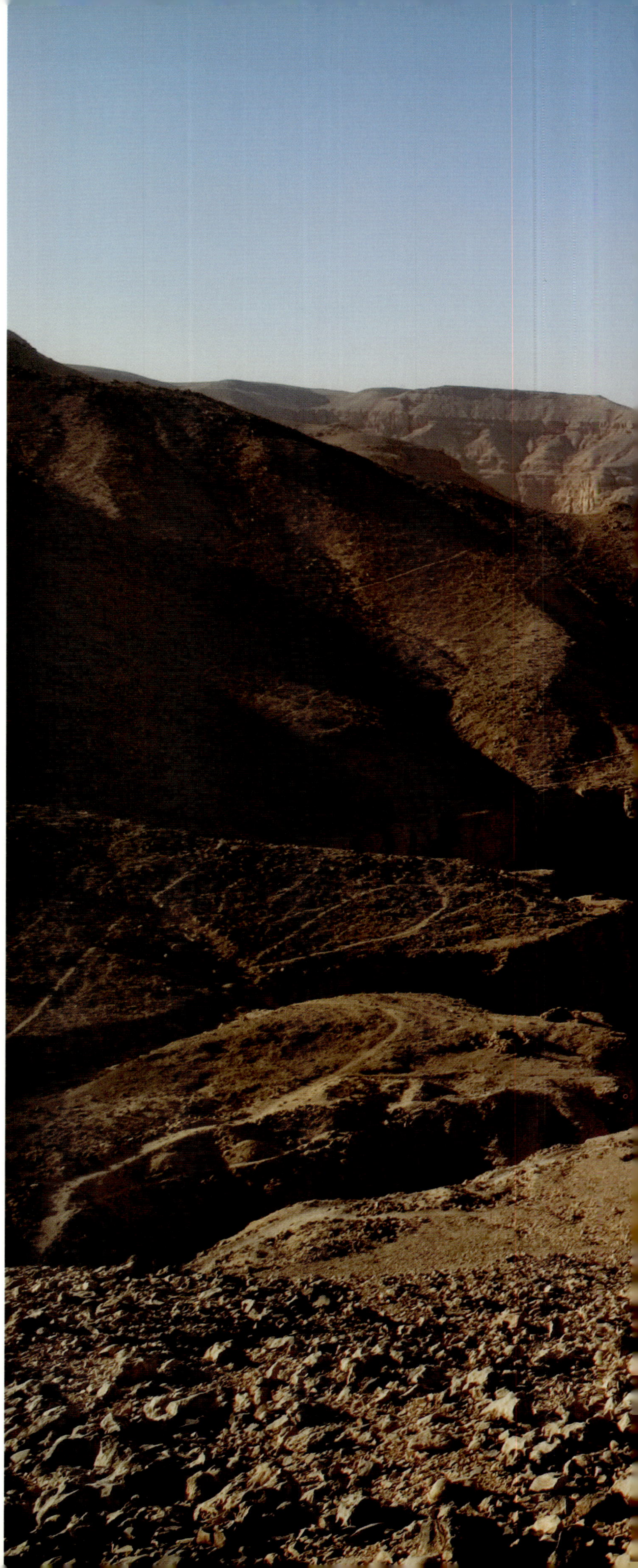

VALLEY OF THE KINGS
The Valley of the Kings is really a series of interconnected wadis, cutting through the barren landscape of the Theban hills. This side wadi houses three smaller tombs, none of which were cut for kings.

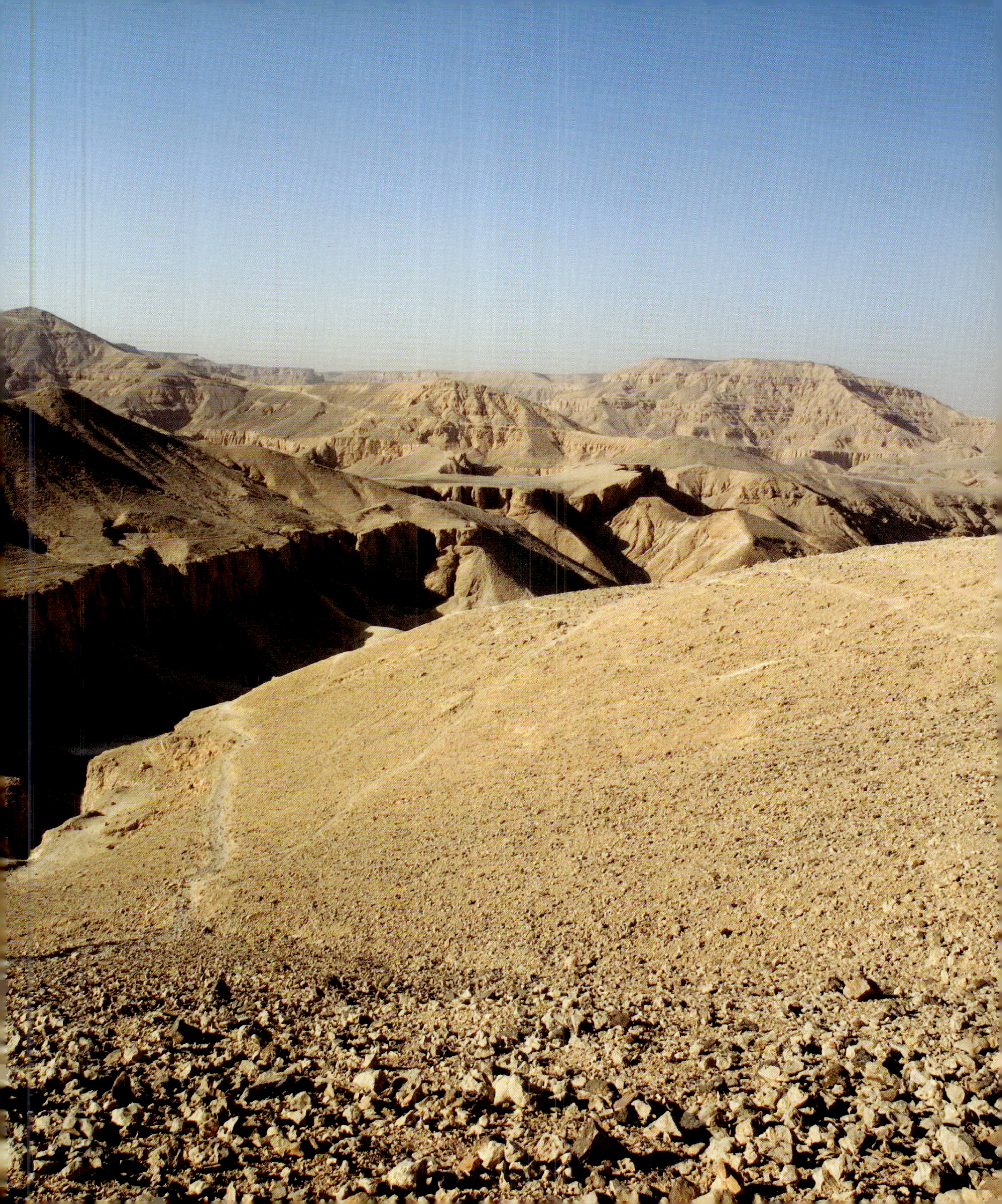

The tombs here, therefore, lie in a hidden place, linked with the unknowable land where the sun spent the hours of the night. The deceased king would travel through this land with the sun, to join with Osiris in the deepest depths of the night and then be reborn with him at dawn. In a parallel conception, this journey also symbolized the king's eternal resurrection, the transition from death to rebirth that was re-enacted each day.

The pyramids of the Old and Middle Kingdom were only one component of an entire complex dedicated to the cult of the deceased king. The New Kingdom monarchs returned to the concept seen in the 1st and 2nd Dynasties, of separating the burial itself from the place where the mortuary cult was celebrated. The sepulchers in the Valley of the Kings were complemented by mortuary temples in the low desert at Luxor, one for each king, at the edge of the floodplain. Taken together, the mortuary temple and tomb created a machine for the resurrection and eternal life of the deceased king.

The Valley of the Kings contains 63 tombs, 26 of which were for the burial of kings. The others, many of which are still anonymous and were completely empty when discovered in modern times, were cut for royal relatives and retainers. Most scholars have long believed that the royal valley had long ago given up all its secrets. But only recently, eighty-three years, 3 months, and 6 days after the discovery of Tutankhamun (KV 62), a new tomb was added to the King's Valley roster. KV 63, being excavated as I write this book, is a small chamber tomb, not carved for a king. Inside are seven coffins, six for adults and one for a child. So far, no mummies have been found, and it is most likely that this tomb, perhaps prepared originally for burial and then robbed, was used in the late 18th Dynasty as a storage chamber or cache for embalming materials. Who knows what else might still lie hidden in the Theban hills?

This book focuses on the royal tombs in the Valley of the Kings. Through the exquisite photographs provided by Sandro Vannini, the reader will be taken on a tour of the Egyptian Netherworld, and provided with the keys and tools developed by the ancient priests to ensure the eternal Afterlife of the deceased monarch and the proper order of the Egyptian cosmos.

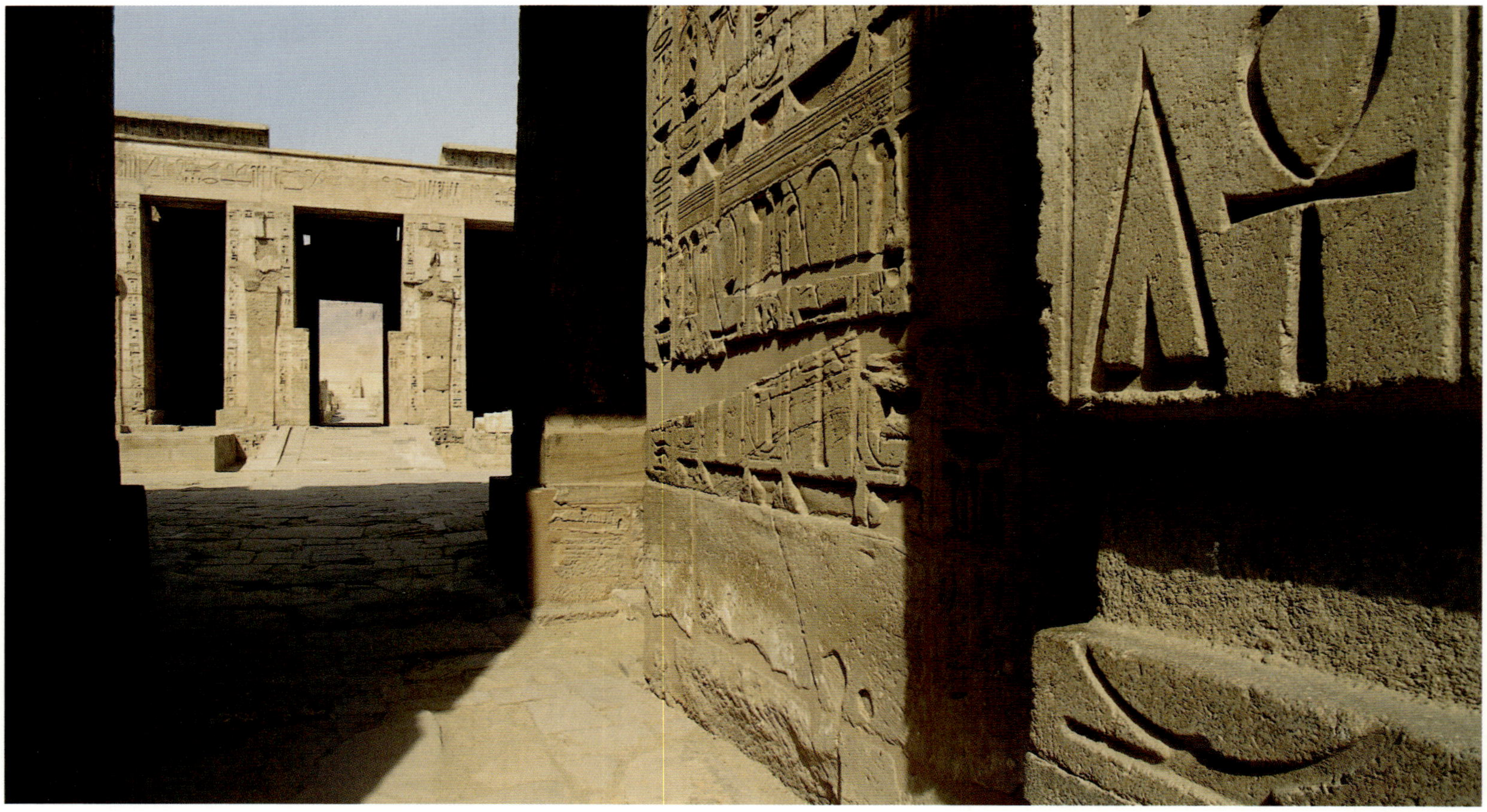

THE MORTUARY TEMPLE OF RAMSES III
Like the other kings of the New Kingdom, Ramses III built a mortuary temple at the edge of the floodplain on the west bank at Thebes. Known today as Medinet Habu, this massive complex, with multiple pylons, courts, and chambers, is the best-preserved of its kind.

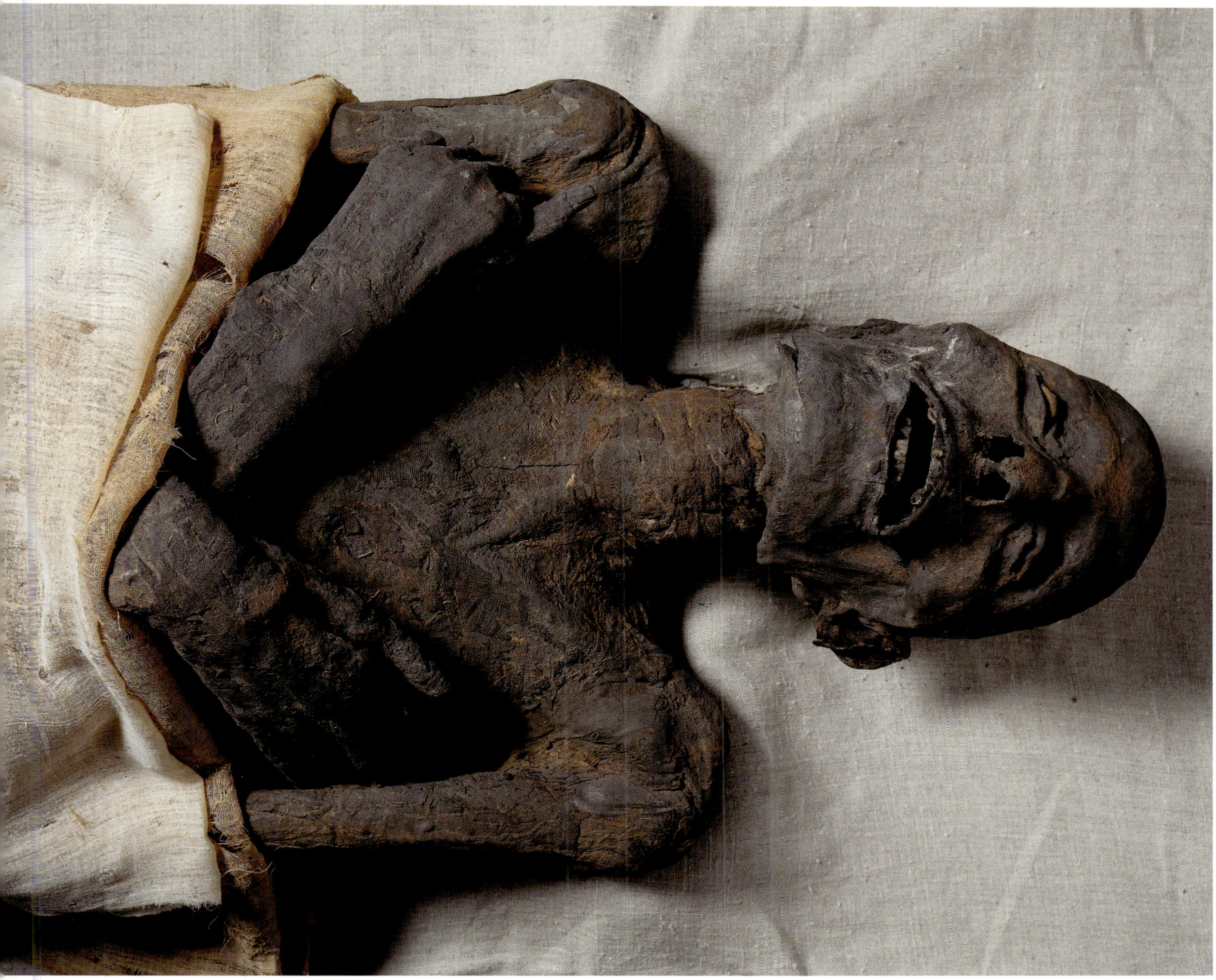

MUMMY OF RAMSES I (?)
Recently returned to Egypt by the Michael C. Carlos Museum of Atlanta, Georgia, this royal mummy had been in a small museum in Canada for over a century before it was noticed by Egyptologist Arne Eggebrecht. It is thought to be Ramses I (ca. 1315–1314 BC), founder of the 19th Dynasty.

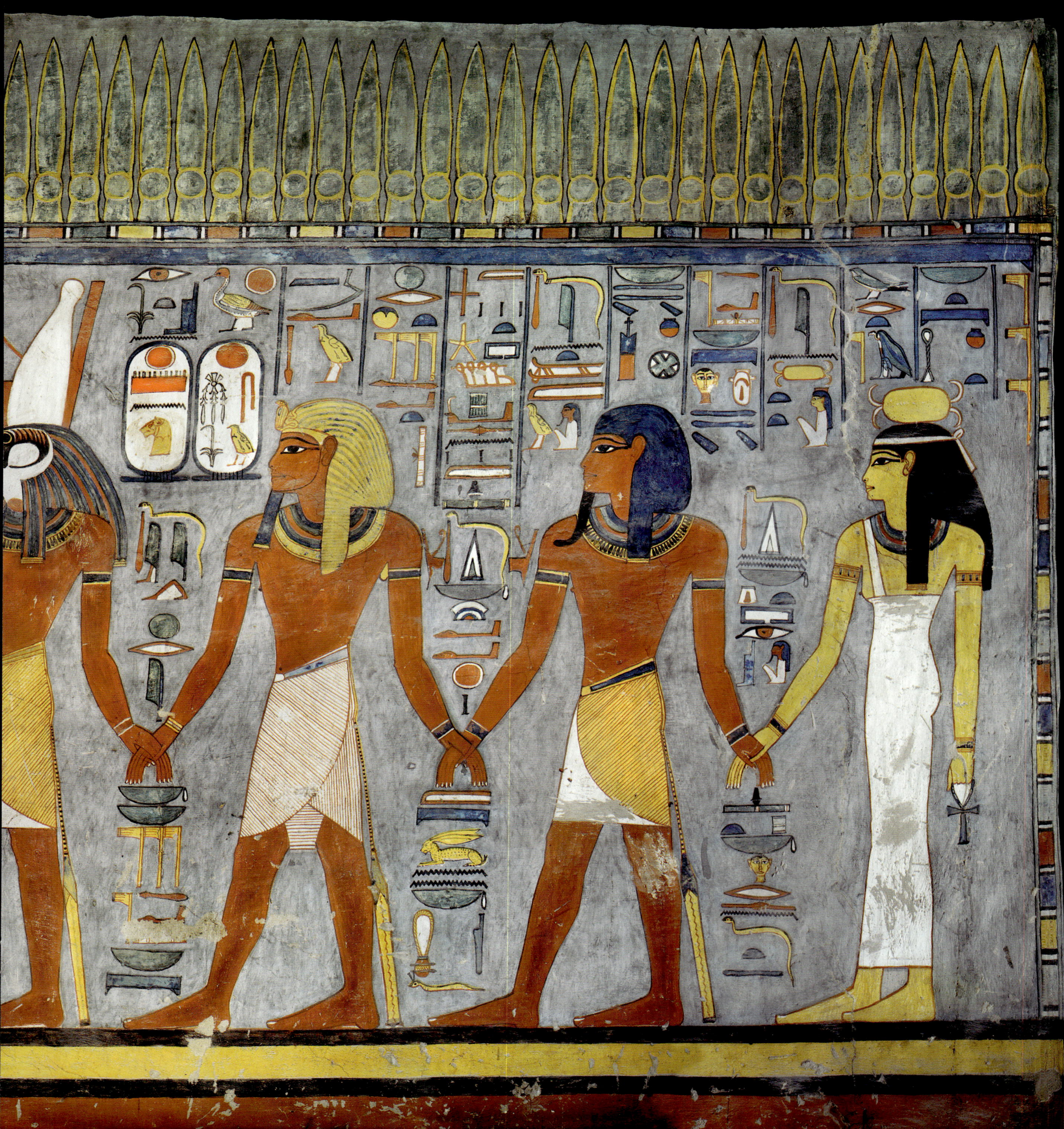

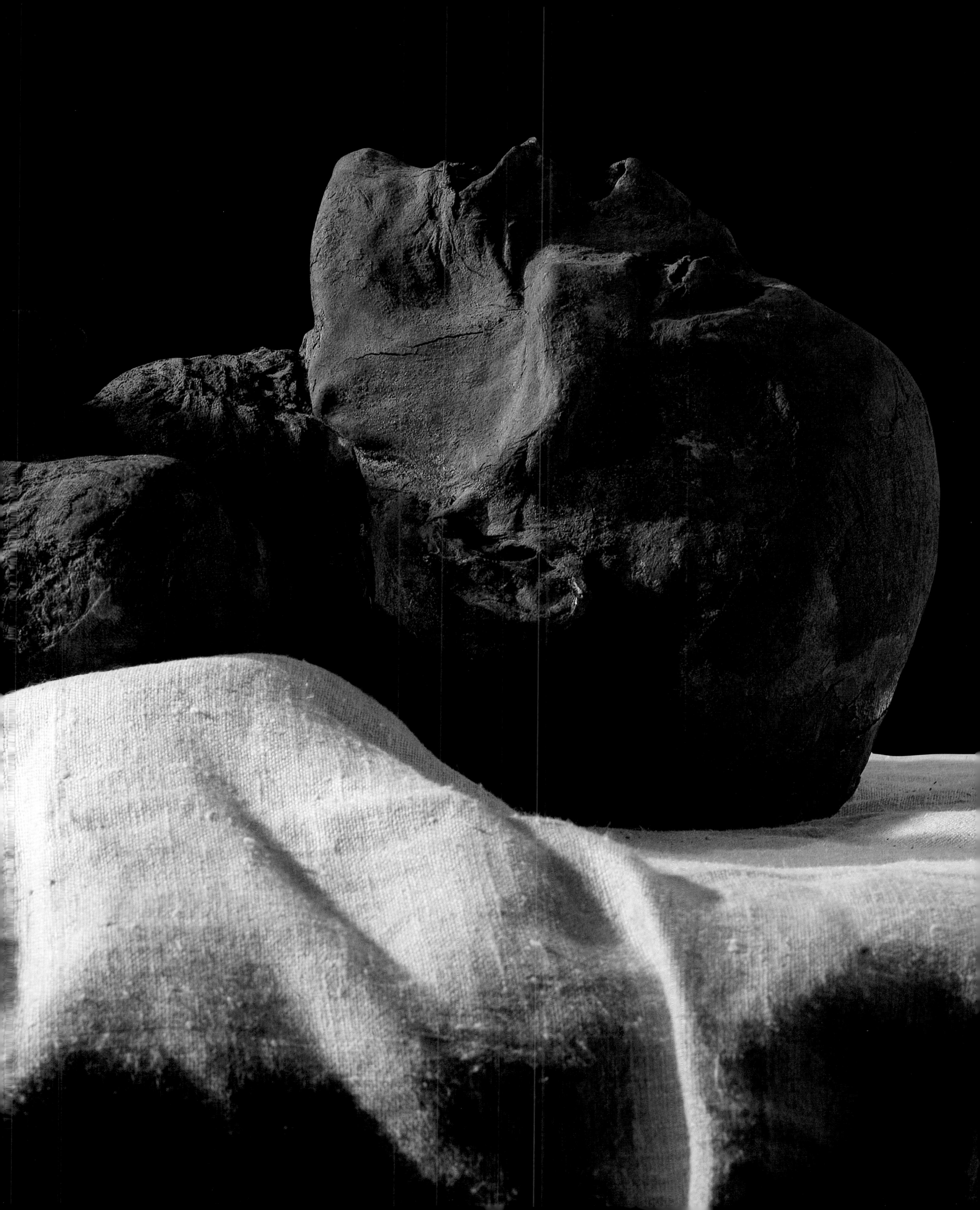

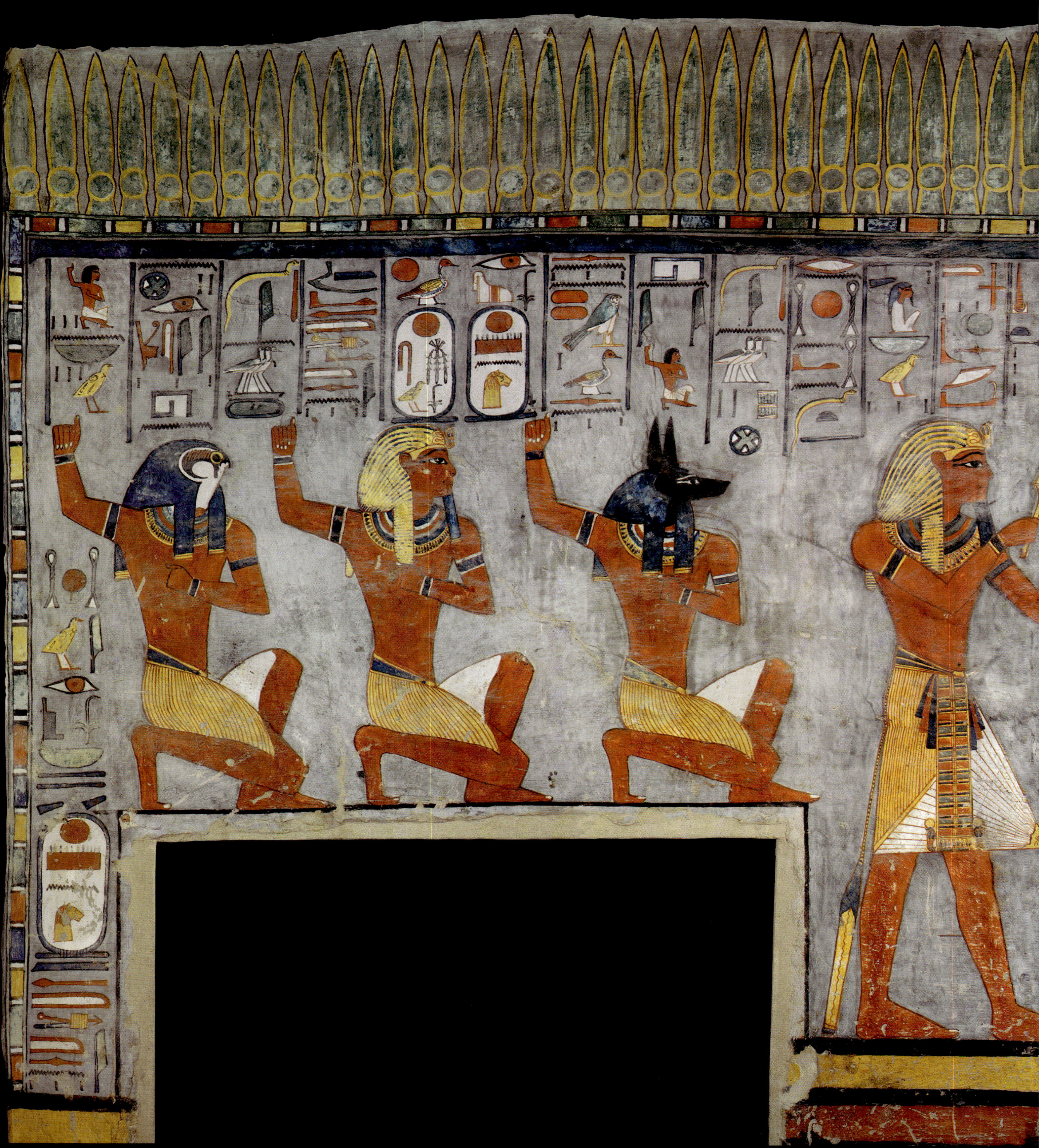

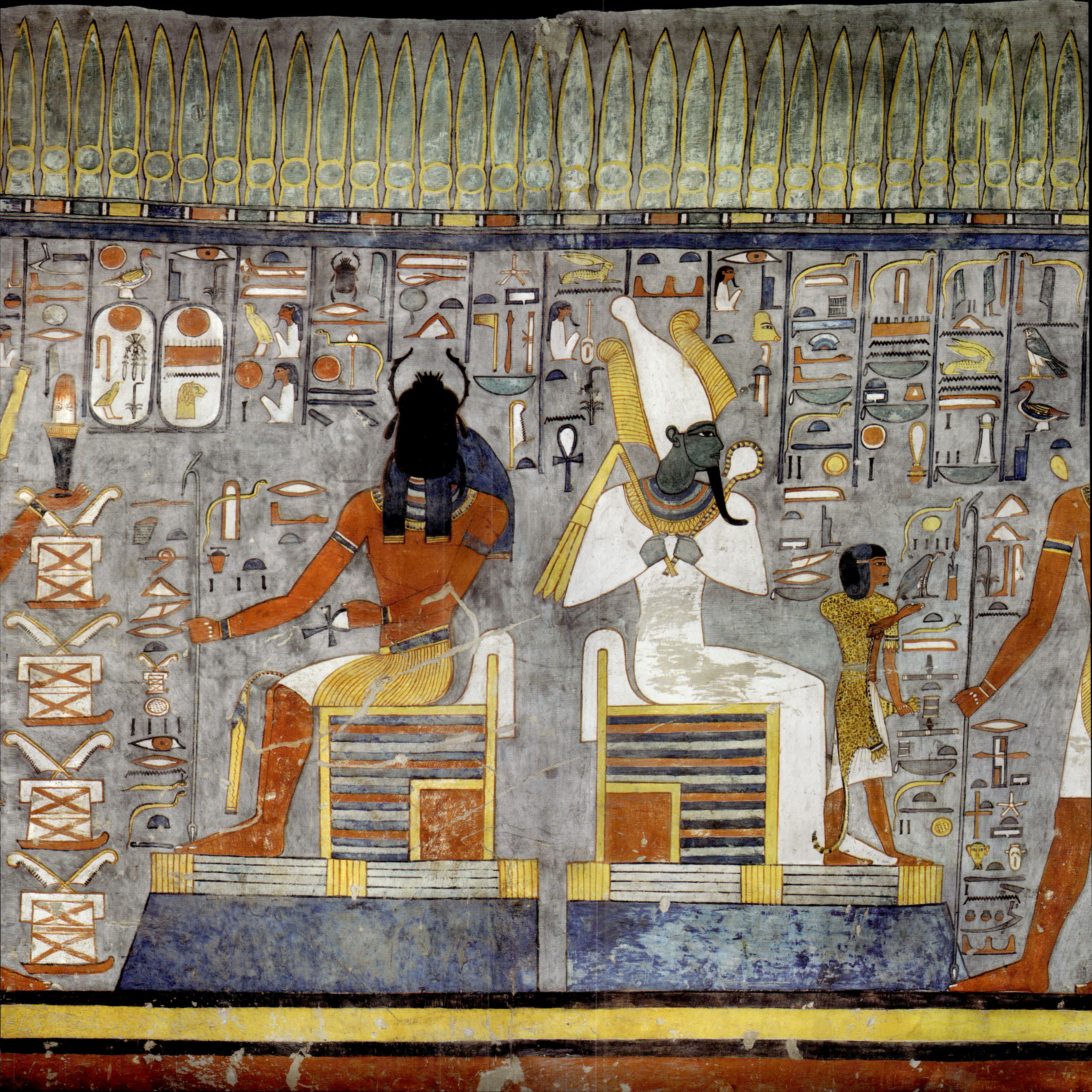

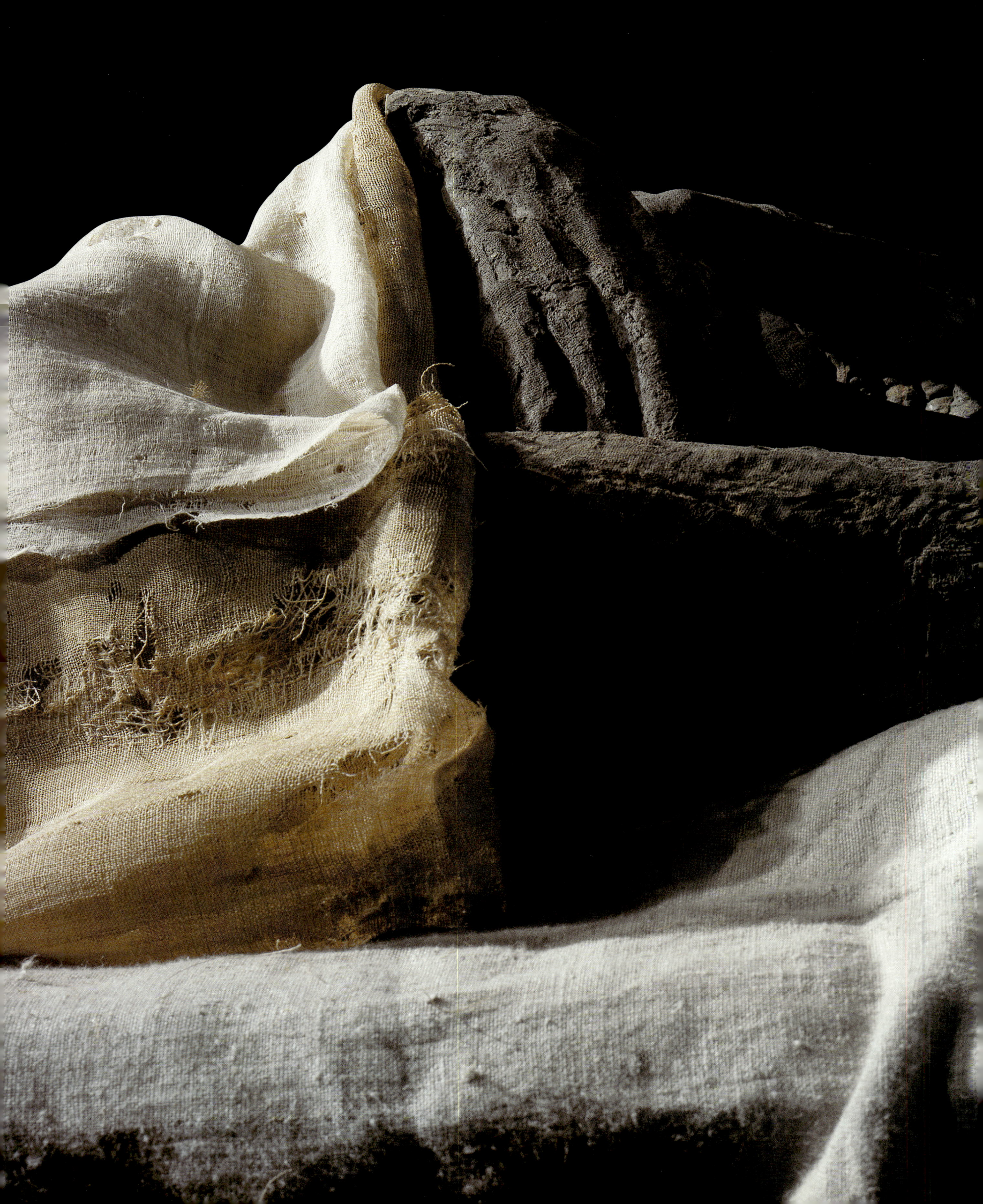

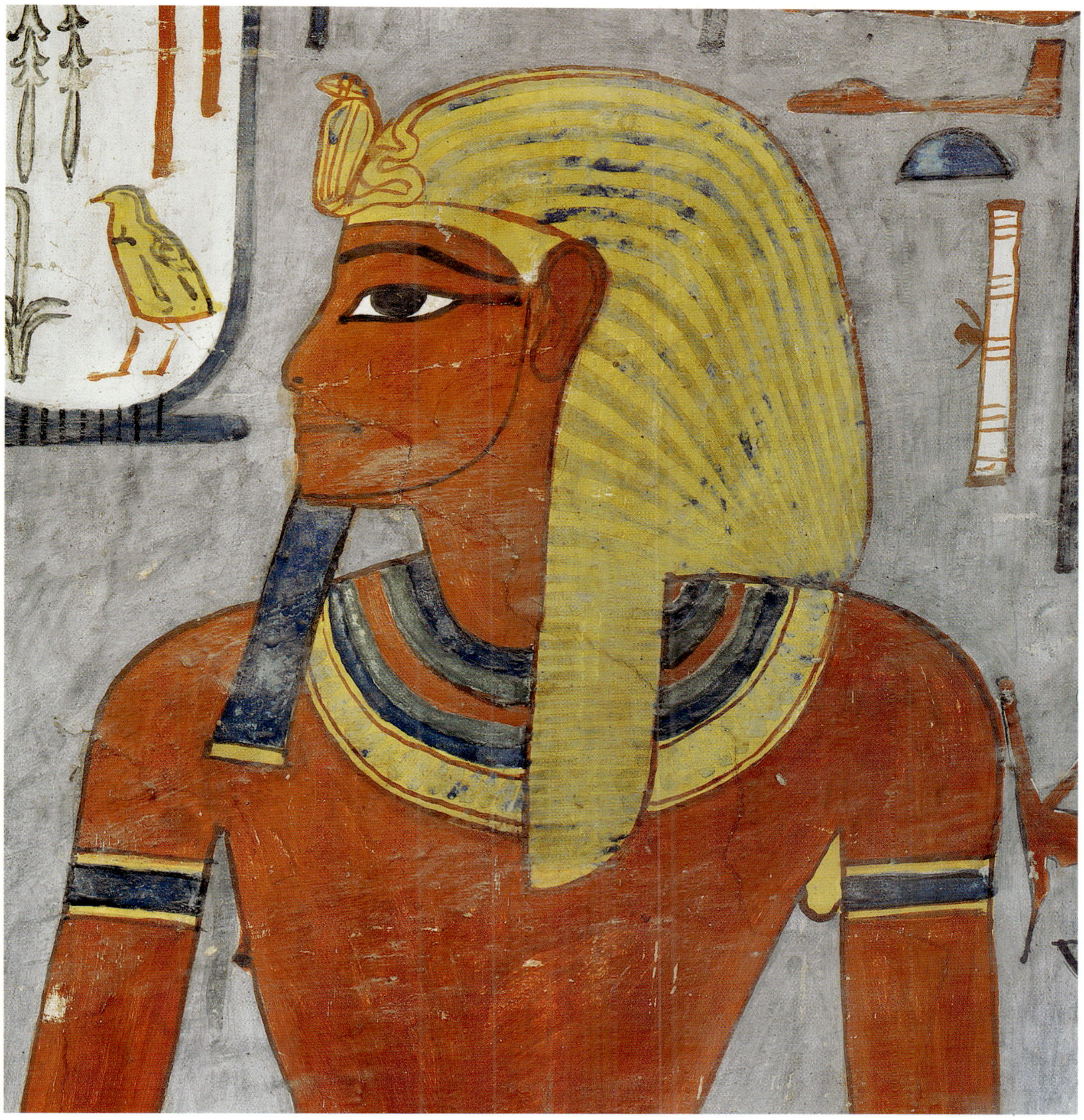

RAMSES I WITH THE GODS
(Preceding pages)
This scene from the tomb of Ramses I depicts the king before the two most important mortuary gods: Re, the sun god, in his guise as the scarab beetle Khepri, and Osiris. The king is led into the presence of Osiris (right) by the falcon-headed god Horus, the primordial god Atum, and Neith, and welcomed by a small figure of an Iunmutef priest, who would have presided over the funeral ceremonies. A second figure of the king approaches Atum-Re-Khepri alone. Behind this figure, a third representation of Ramses kneels and makes a gesture of jubilation and worship, flanked by figures of the souls of Pe and Nekhen, two important cult centers from the earliest periods of Egyptian history.

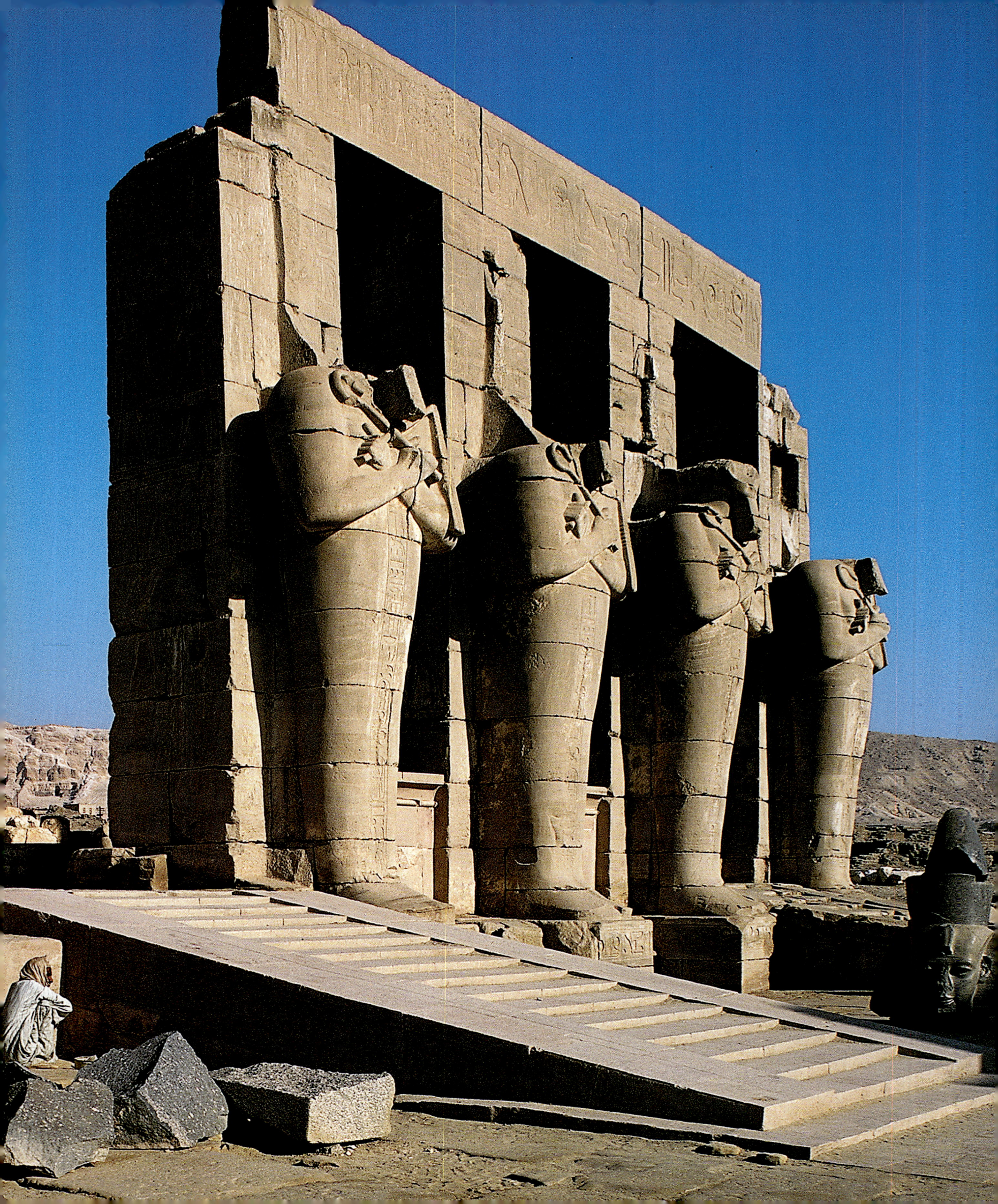

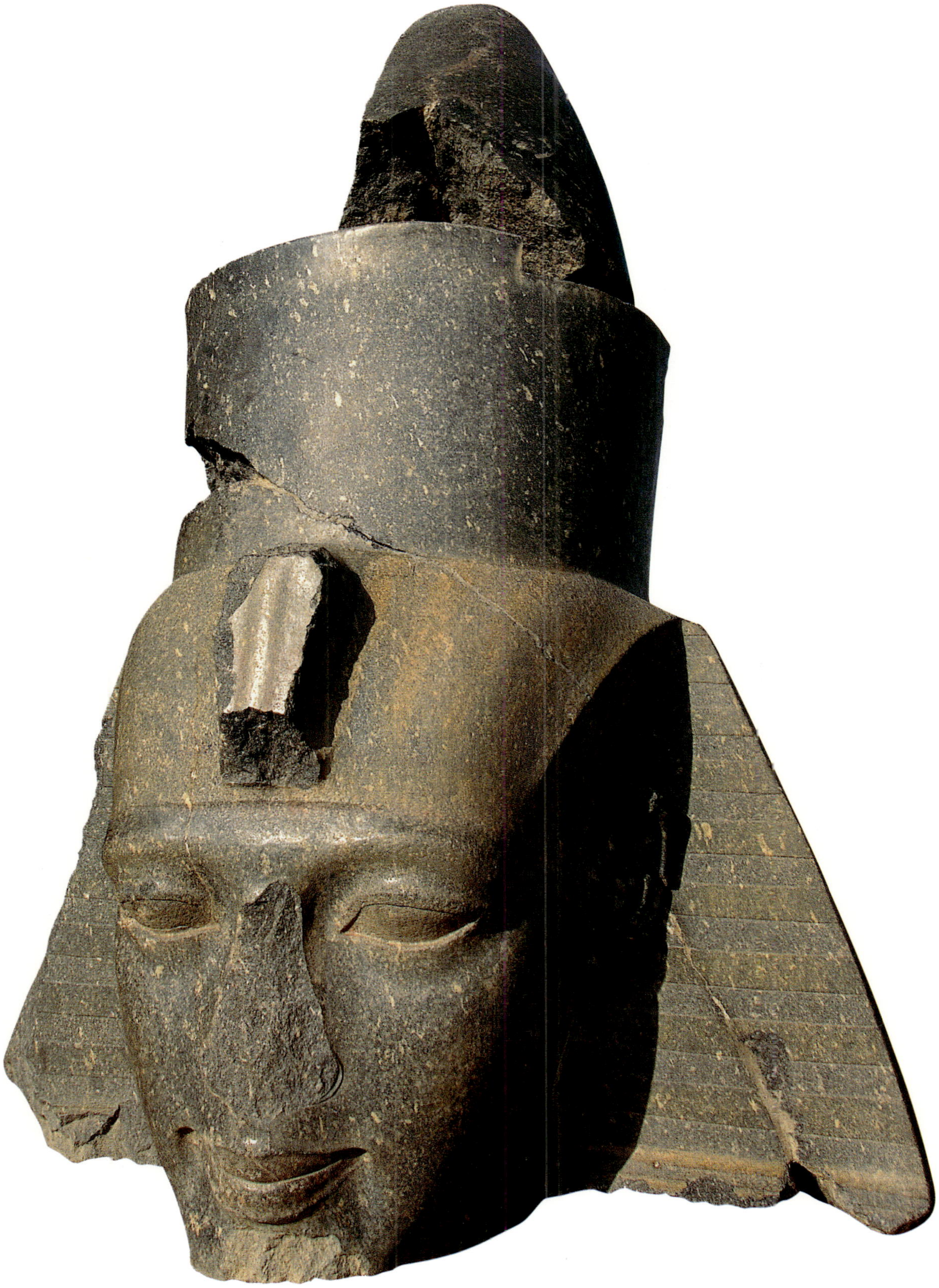

THE RAMESSEUM
Each New Kingdom pharaoh had a mortuary temple, built where the low desert meets the cultivated land. One of the largest and best-preserved is the Ramesseum, constructed for the great warrior king Ramses II (ca. 1304–1237 BC). Here we see the back of the second court, lined with colossal statues of the king as the god Osiris. This granite head came from another royal statue, one of many that graced this temple in antiquity.

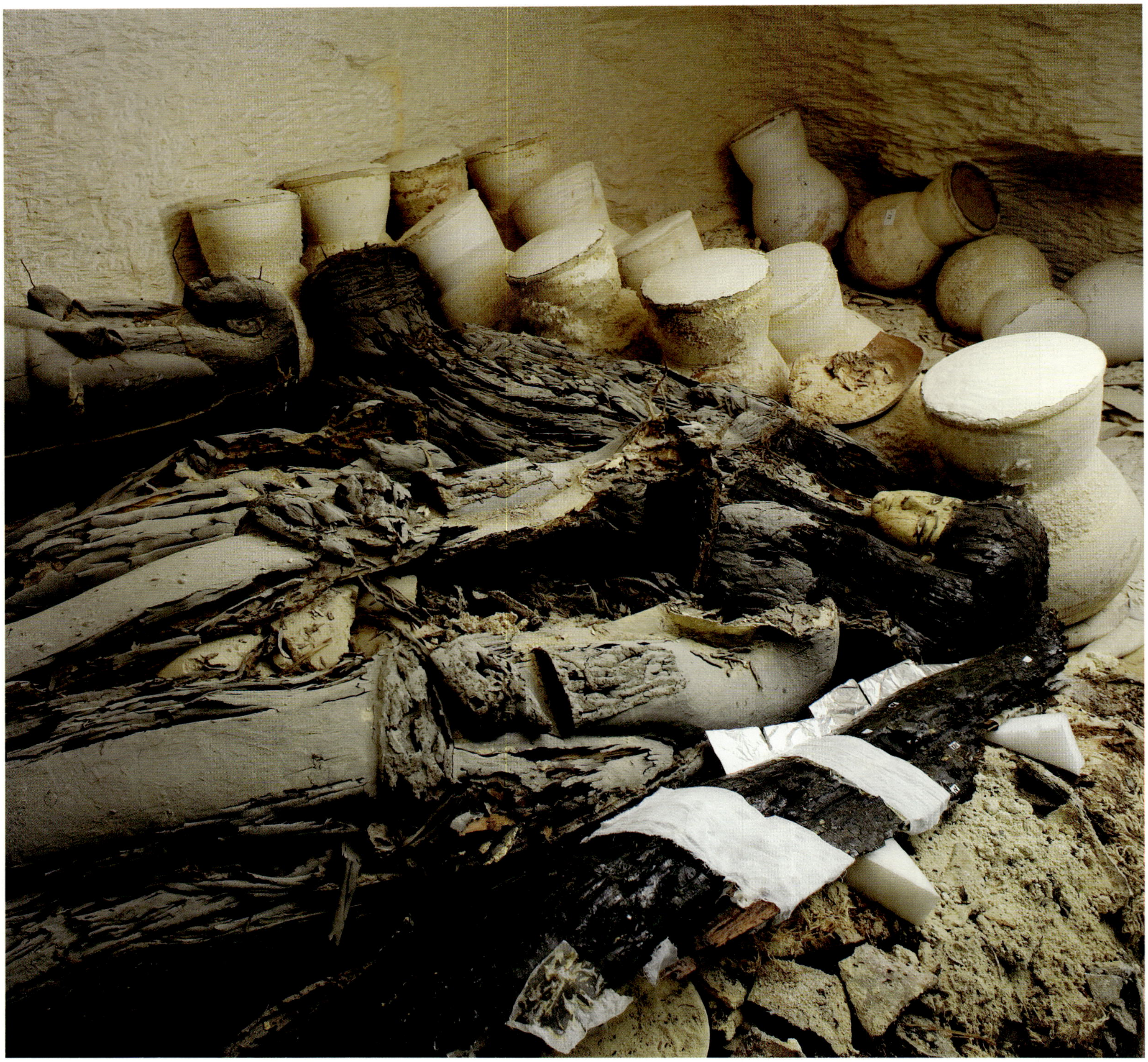

THE INTERIOR OF KV 63
Recently discovered and still being excavated, KV 63 is the first new tomb found in the Valley of the Kings for decades. This simple chamber holds seven coffins and many pottery jars. However, to date no mummies have been found, and the best guess of the archaeologists is that it is an embalming cache, used to hold extra mummification materials.

MEDINET HABU
The decoration of the temple of Ramses III at Medinet Habu is still wonderfully preserved in many places. A great deal of color can still be seen, giving at least a faint impression of the pigments that covered the walls in antiquity.

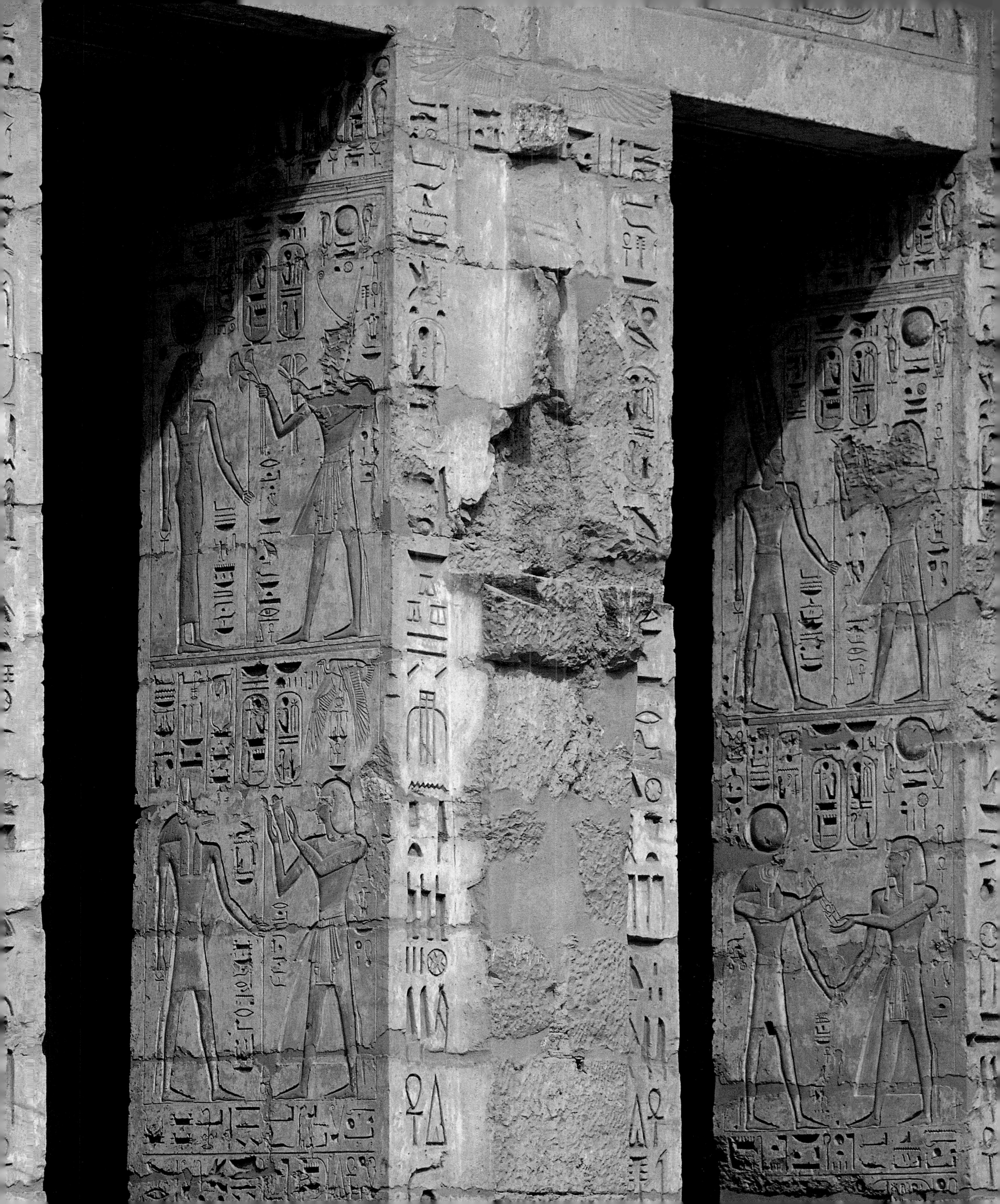

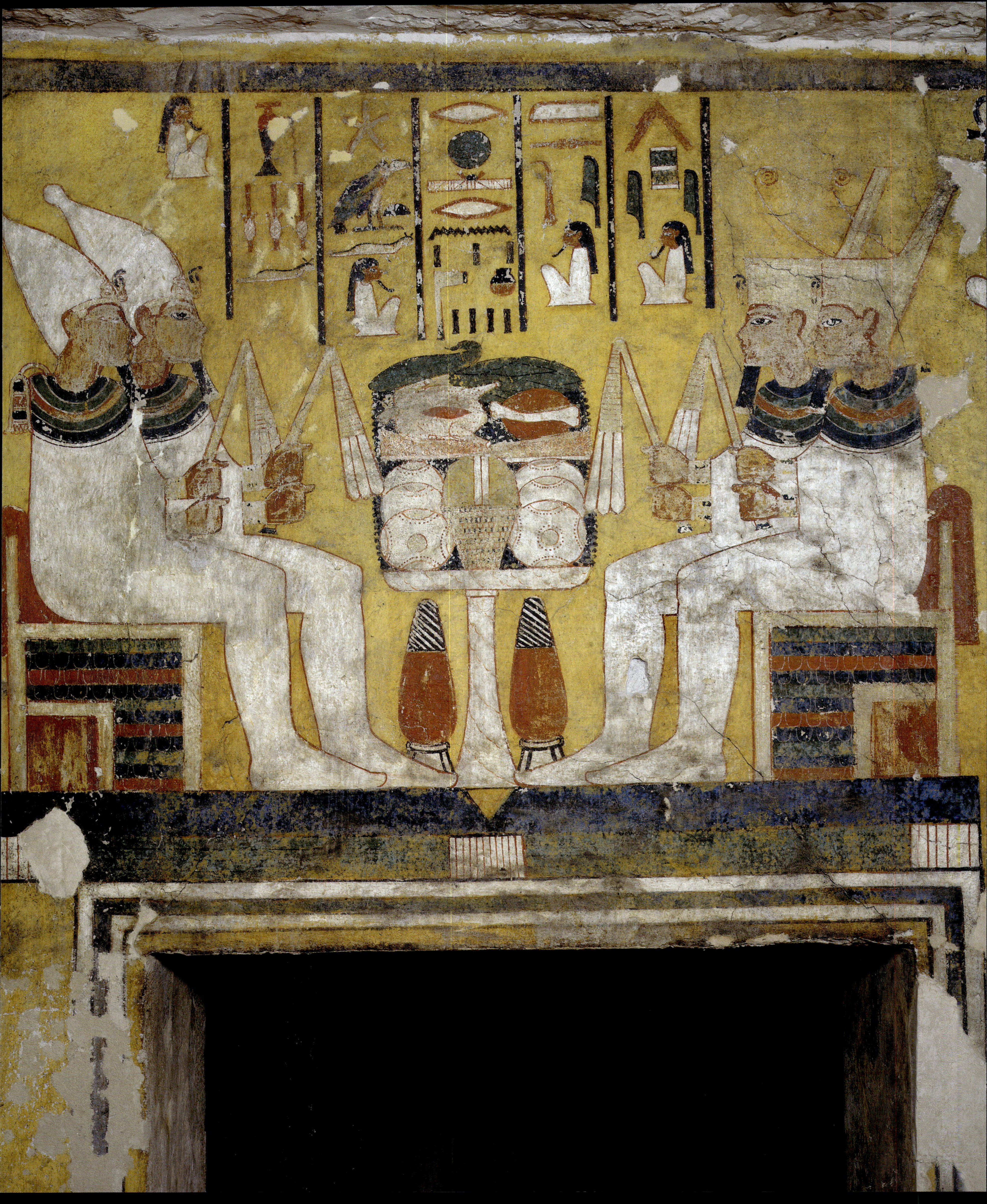

CHAPTER 1

BUILDING AND EQUIPPING THE ROYAL TOMB

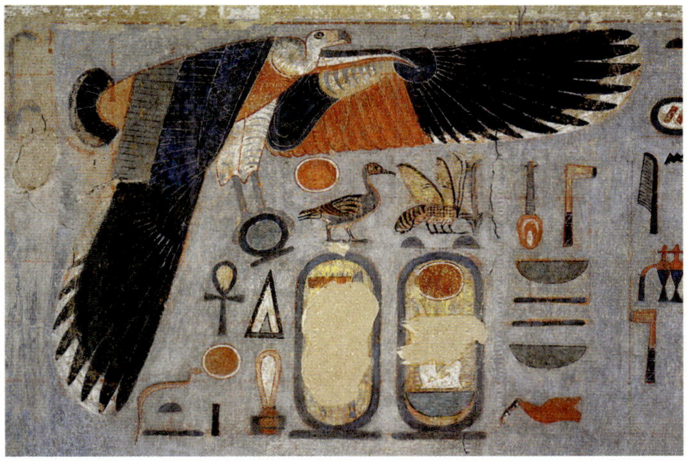

Both the architecture and the decoration of each royal tomb in the Valley of the Kings served to enhance its identification as the king's gateway to eternity. Each tomb was built as a series of tunnels and chambers, acting as a terrestrial map of the Netherworld through which the king traveled each night to be reborn with the dawn. The scenes and texts on the walls served as guides for this journey.

Egyptologists believe that it was the ancient priests who detailed the plans of the tombs, handing down the information to the architects and artisans to execute. Decisions could be made to omit or add chambers, change the axis, and make other modifications according to the religious beliefs paramount at the time, and according to the geography and geology of the site chosen. Erik Hornung, one of the greatest scholars of the Valley of the Kings, and pre-eminent living expert on the scenes and texts decorating the walls of the tombs, has dubbed some of the changes that are seen from one reign to the next the "extension of the existing." According to this concept, it was the king's role to re-establish the world as it had been at the moment of creation, but also to outdo his predecessors, to make something bigger, more elaborate, or more perfect than what had come before.

Each architecturally-defined area of the tomb had a specific purpose, and each detail of the layout and decoration was carefully designed. Work on reconstructing these meanings, to a large extent through study of the scenes and texts on the walls, is a relatively new science. The first great scholar to tackle these compositions was Alexandre Piankoff, who served as a mentor to Erik Hornung. Also active in this field is Friedrich Abitz. Egyptologists Elizabeth Thomas and John Romer have done significant studies of the architecture. Kent Weeks, who is currently excavating KV 5, the tomb of the sons of 19th Dynasty pharaoh Ramses II, knows the valley extremely

THE FOUR SONS OF HORUS

Only the burial chamber of the tomb of Aye was decorated, painted in flat colors against a golden ground. Above the door from the burial chamber to a side room, evidently for the king's viscera, sit the Four Sons of Horus, guardians of the separately mummified internal organs.

well, and is actively involved in our efforts to protect and conserve it.

No two royal tombs were exactly the same, but there are basic precepts that were followed throughout most of the history of the Valley of the Kings. All of the tombs are tunneled into the rock, either on the floor of the valley or in the cliff faces high above. Each is entered through one or more descending staircases and/or corridors that lead to a series of additional passages and chambers. Although the actual orientations of the tombs differ, the basic flow was symbolically from east, the direction of the rising sun, to west, the realm of the setting sun. The walls of the tomb—at first only of the burial chamber, but later of all the halls and rooms—were adorned with scenes and texts from a group of religious compositions: the Books of the Netherworld, the Litany of Re, and later, a variety of Books of the Heavens and the Earth.

There are certain basic changes in layout and decoration that can be traced over time, and scholars have divided the history of the tombs into several main phases.

ENTRANCE TO KV 20
The tombs in the Valley of the Kings were tunneled into the rock, creating man-made caverns. KV 20, most likely the earliest tomb in the valley, descends in a long arc deep into the earth. At the end is a burial chamber, the only part of the tomb to be decorated.

THE TOMBS OF THE 18TH DYNASTY

The 18th Dynasty was a period of experimentation, with no real standardization of plan evident. The basic concept expresses the nighttime journey of the sun through the Netherworld, with the main content of the decoration derived from the Book of the Amduat (the Book of What is in the Netherworld). The focus is on Osiris and the other Netherworld gods.

In the early 18th Dynasty, only the burial chamber is decorated. In the tomb of Tuthmosis III (fifth ruler of the dynasty), images of gods appear for the first time on the walls of the room preceding the burial chamber. Until the reign of Horemheb at the end of the dynasty, only the burial chamber and perhaps one other room are adorned. With Horemheb decoration begins to cover more and more of the tomb.

The tomb believed to be earliest in the Valley is KV 20, thought by some to have been built by Tuthmosis I and usurped by his daughter Hatshepsut and by others to have been built originally by Hatshepsut, who later moved her father's body to join hers. This consists of a very long descending corridor, curving in an arc deep into the earth and ending in a rectangular burial chamber, with several roughly carved and undecorated chambers along the way and three storerooms to the sides. Fifteen slabs bearing scenes from the Book of the Amduat were once set up around the walls of the burial chamber.

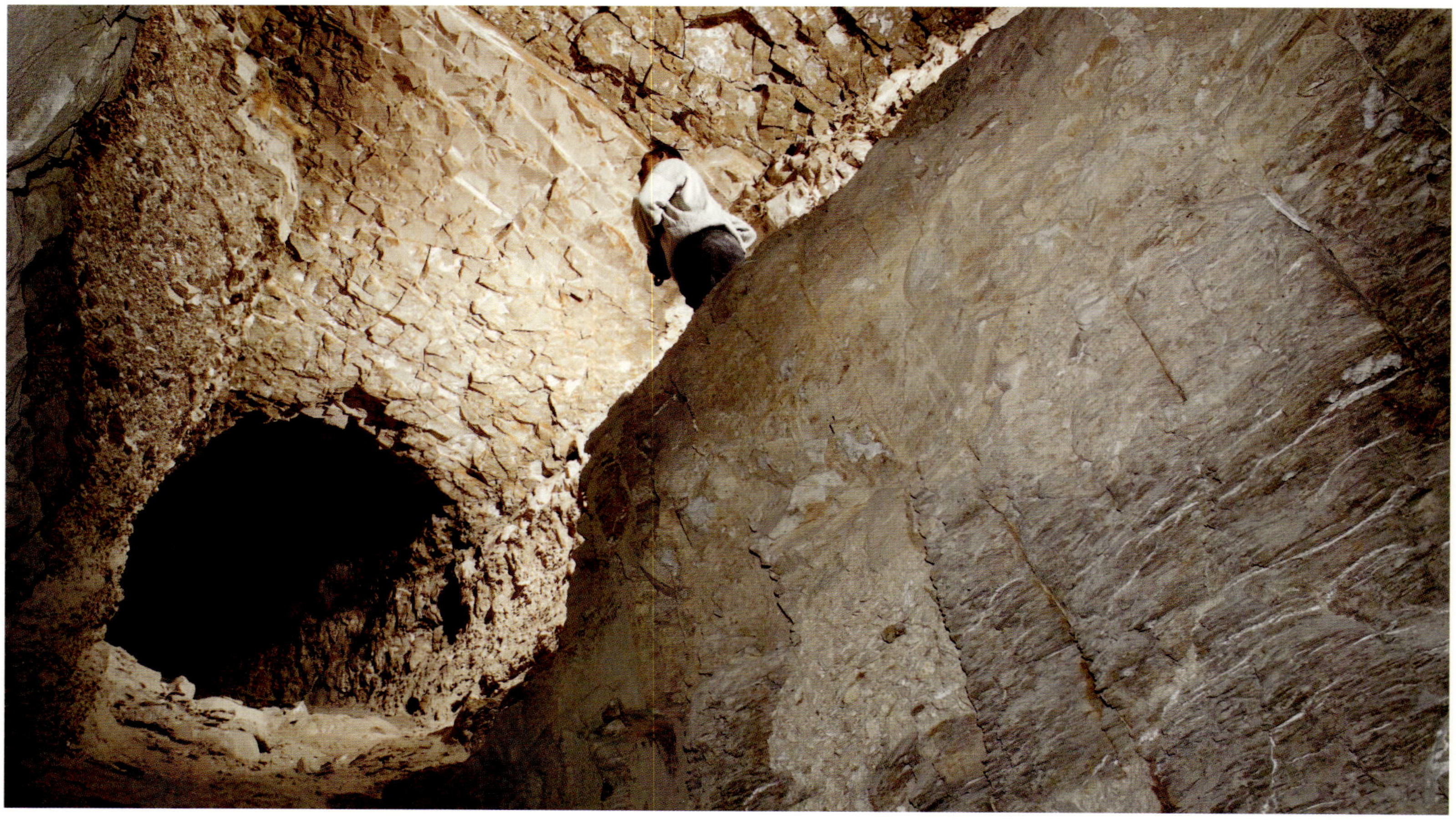

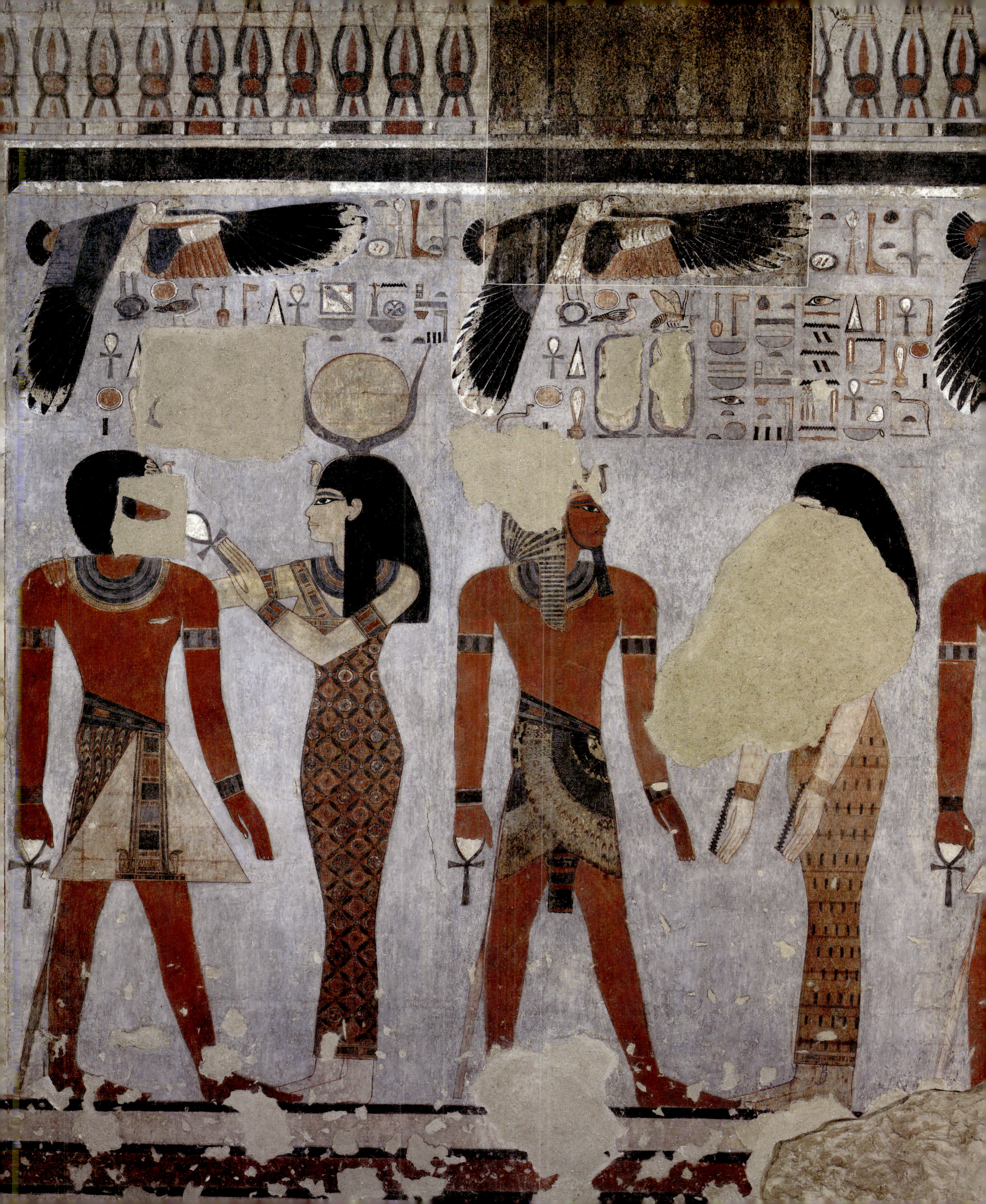

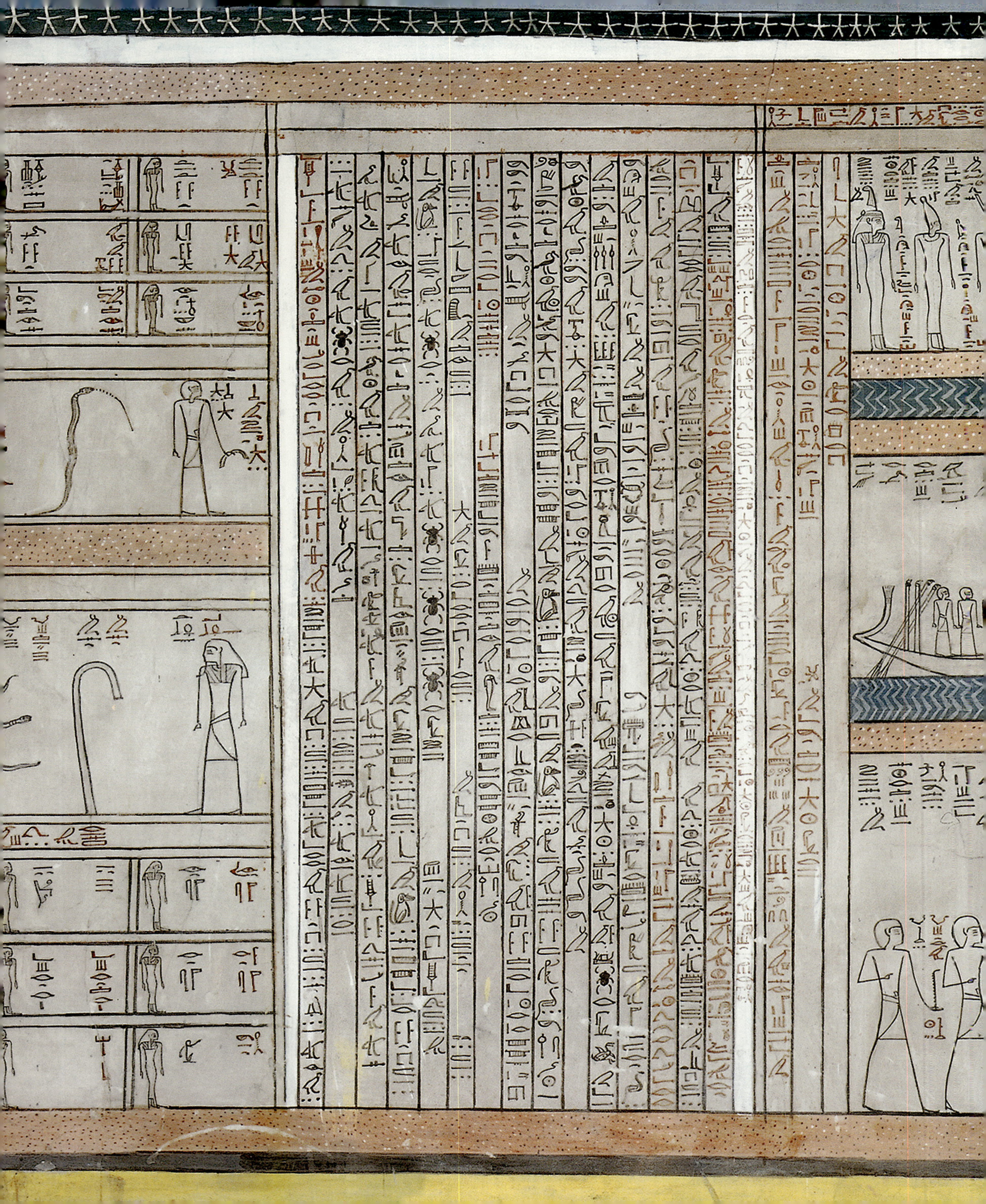

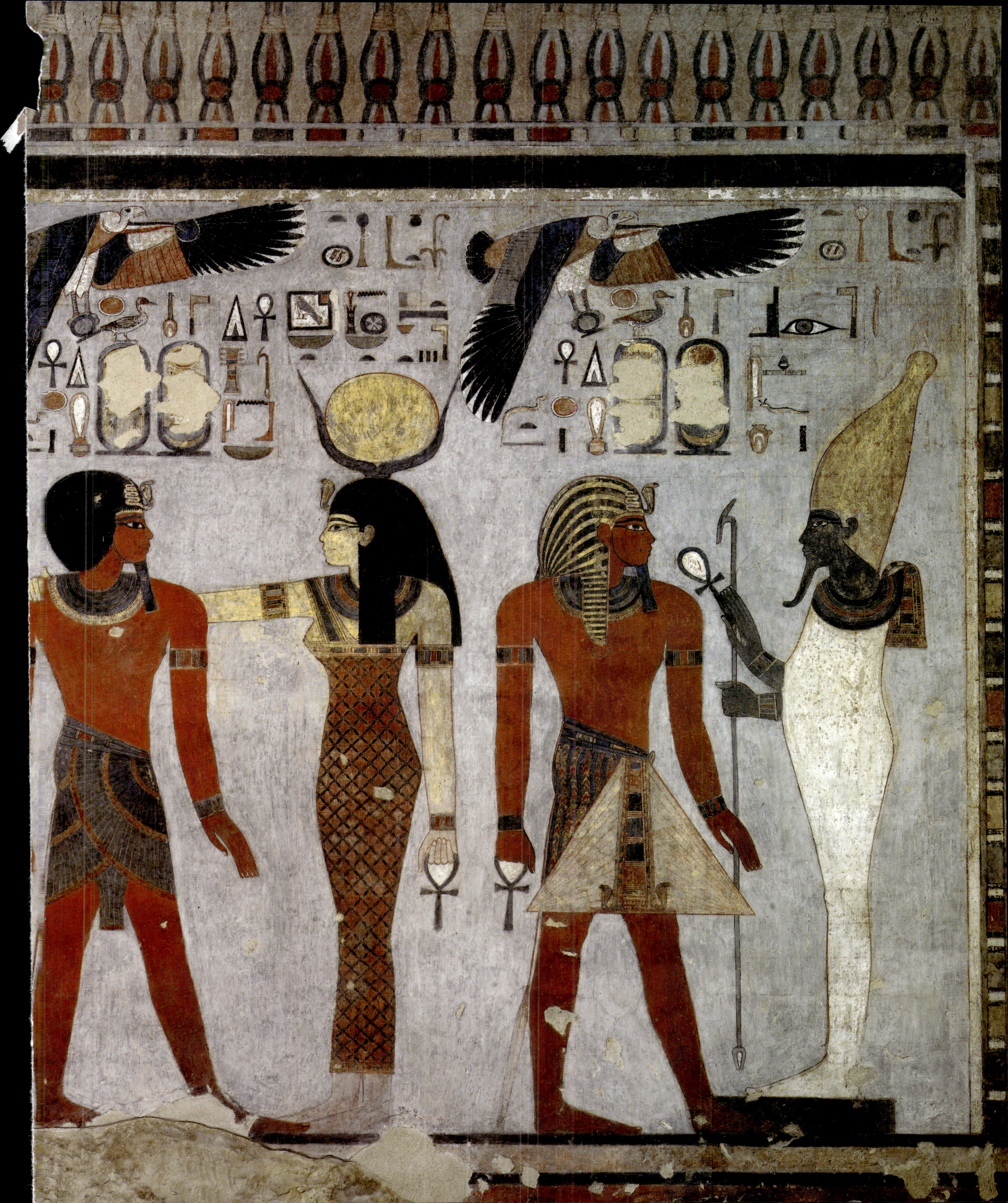

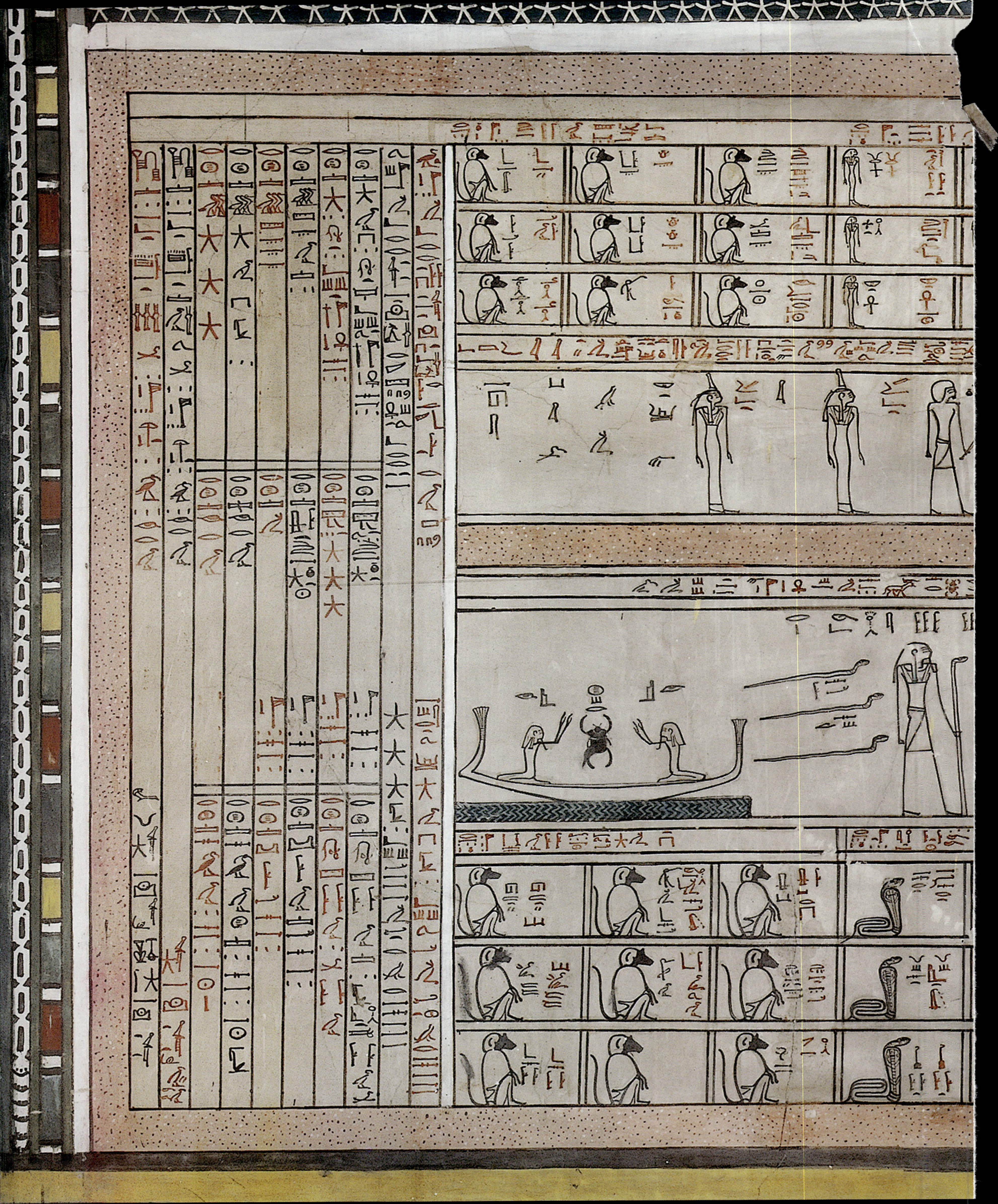

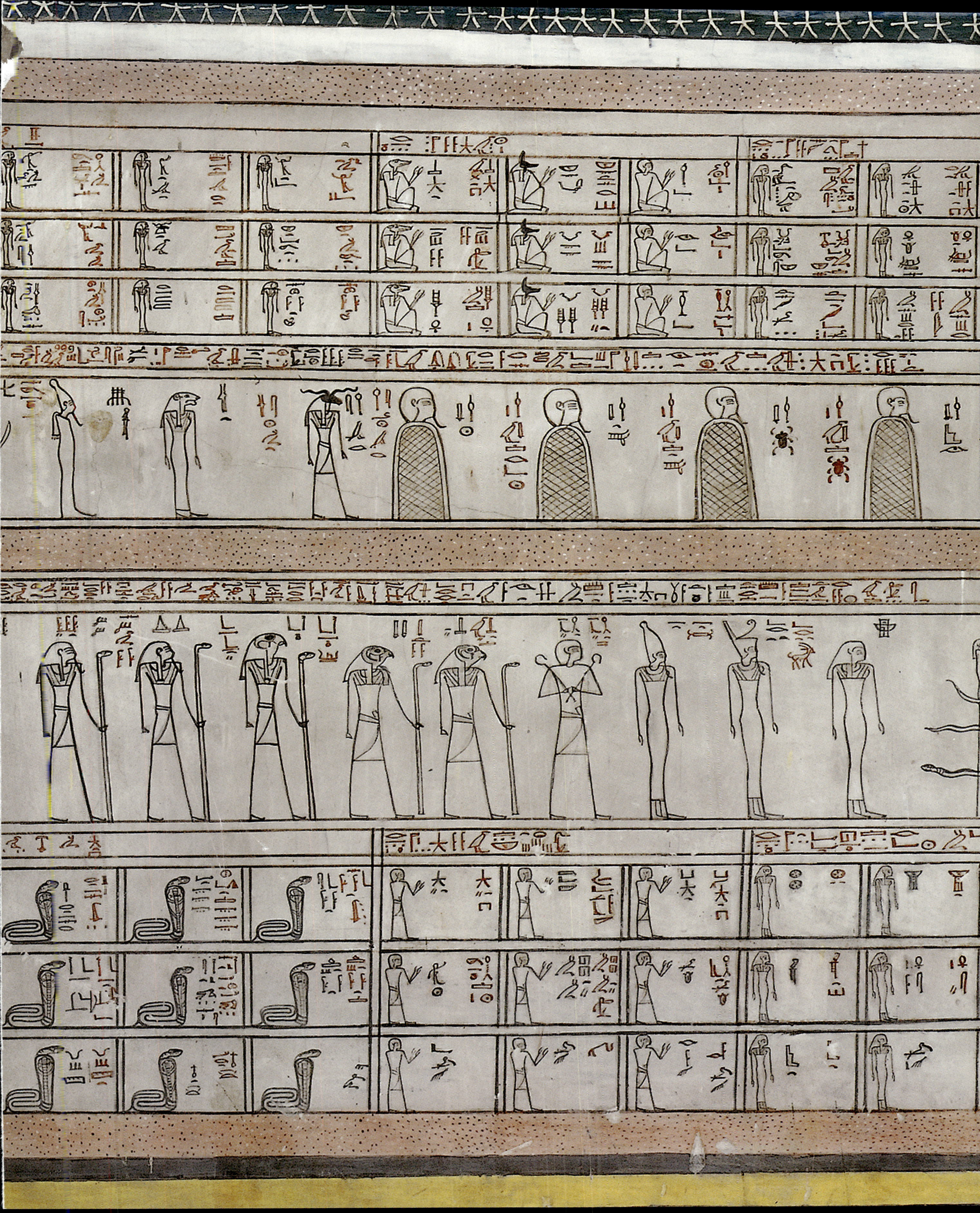

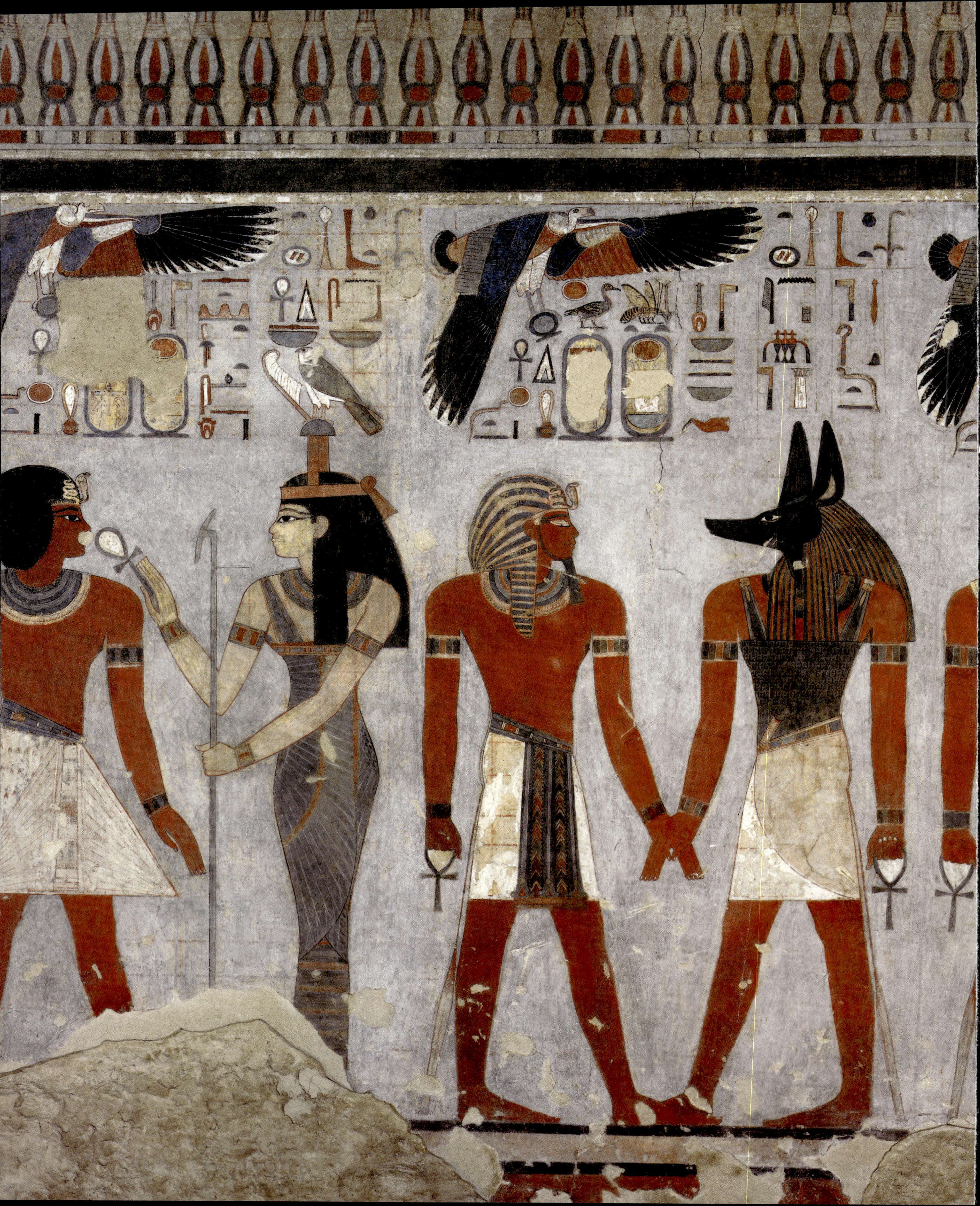

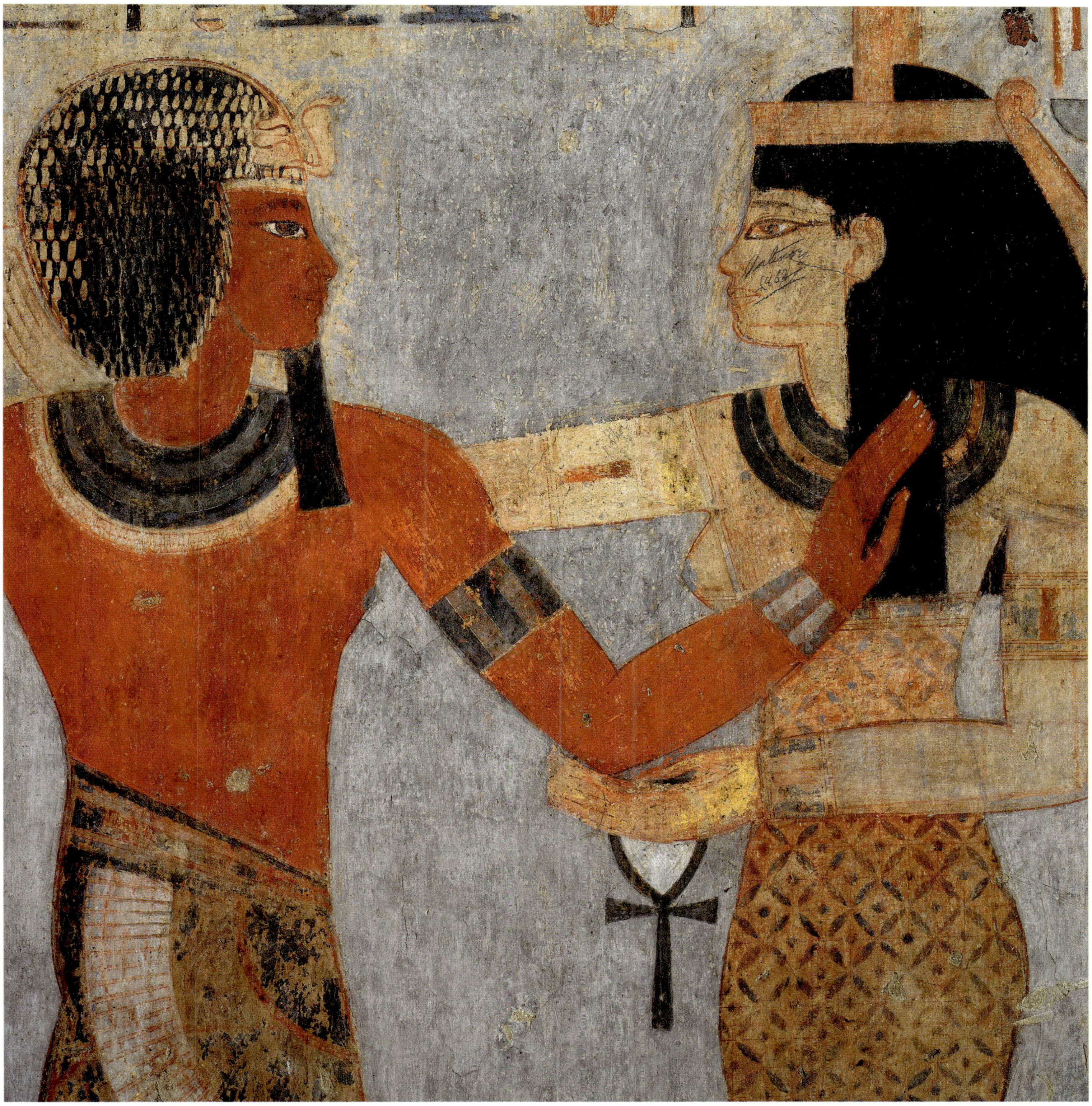

AMENHOTEP III AND HATHOR

The king, wearing a short wig and royal beard, embraces and is embraced by Hathor, great goddess and mistress of the land of the dead.

BURIAL CHAMBER OF AMENHOTEP II

(Preceding pages)

The earliest scenes and texts used to decorate the royal tombs of the New Kingdom came from the Book of the Amduat. This was divided into the twelve hours of the night; two hours, with their accompanying texts, are visible here.

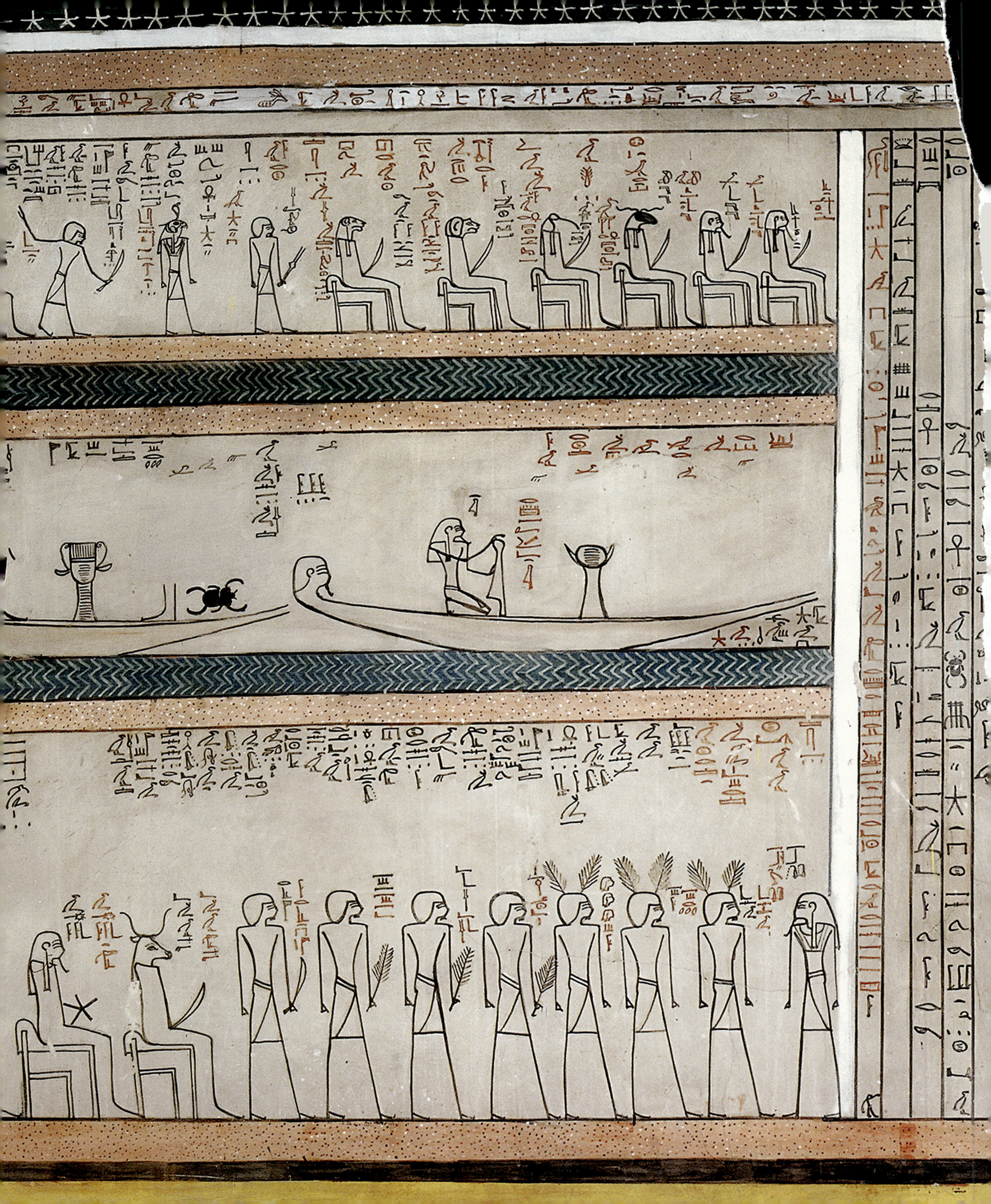

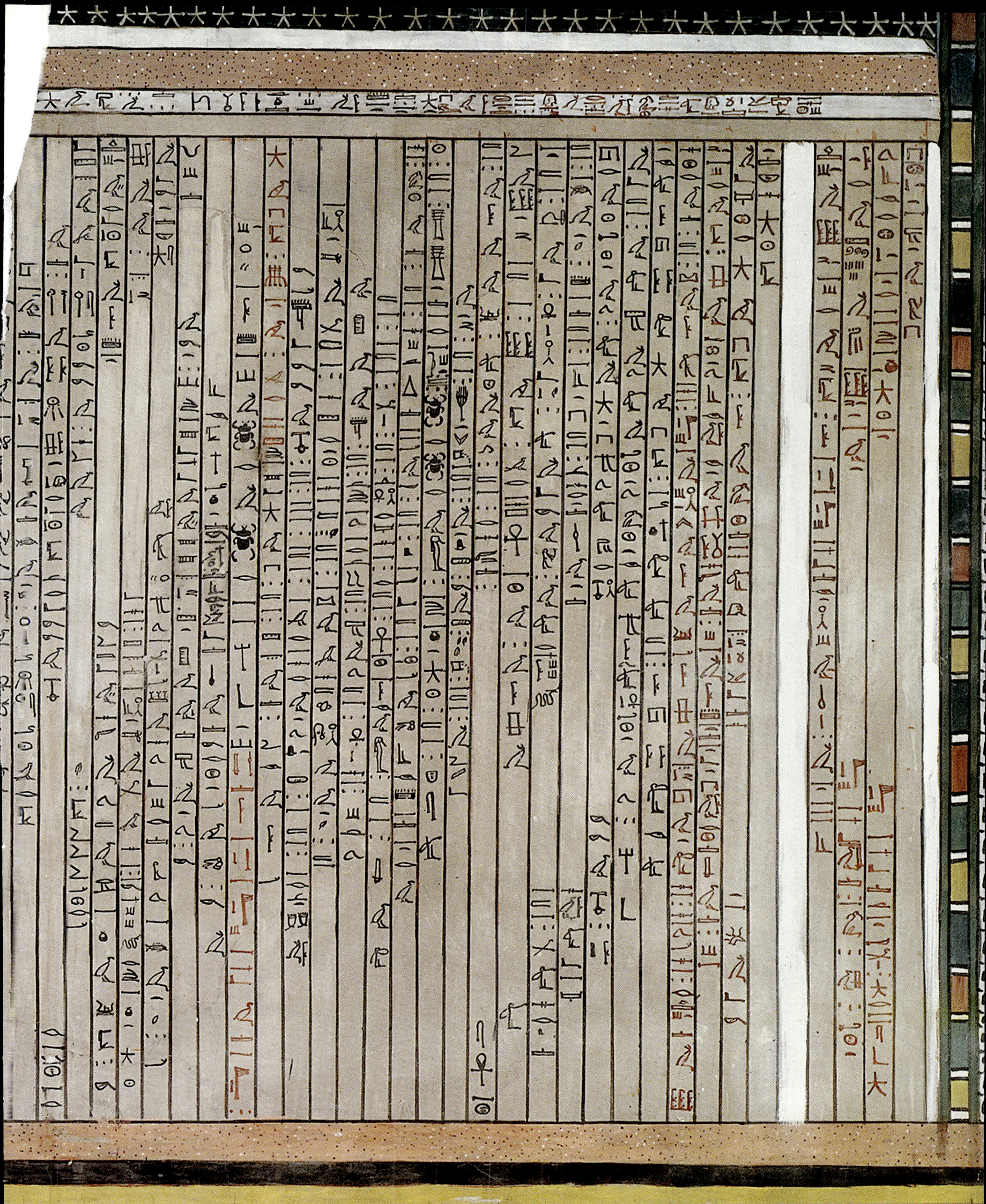

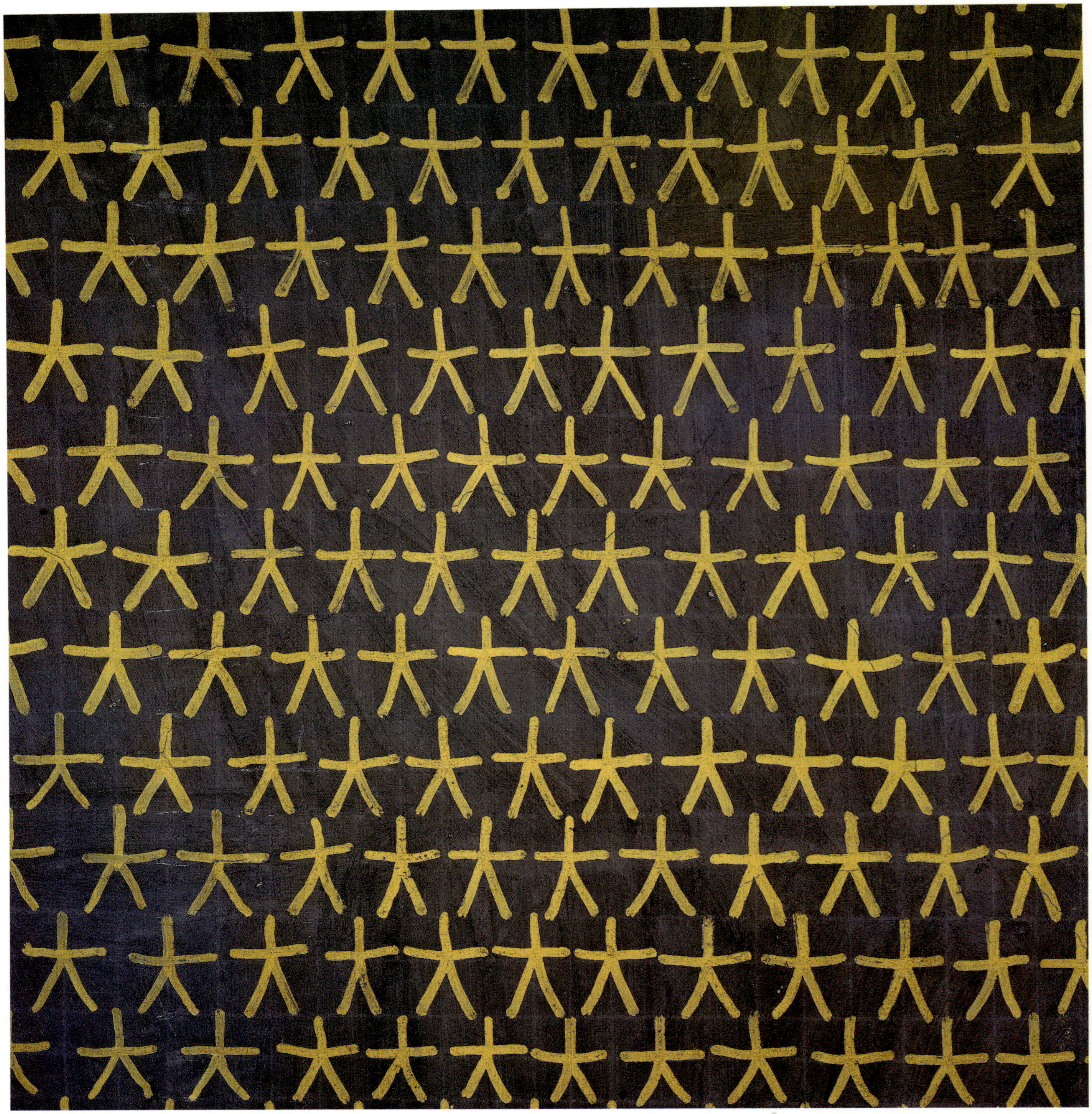

The Starry Sky

Many ceilings in the royal tombs were decorated with fields of golden stars on a blue ground, reinforcing the identification of the sepulcher as a miniature cosmos.

Gods and King

(pp. 39–41)

The great underworld gods Osiris, Anubis, and Hathor greet the deceased king and offer him life in this scene from the tomb of Amenhotep III.

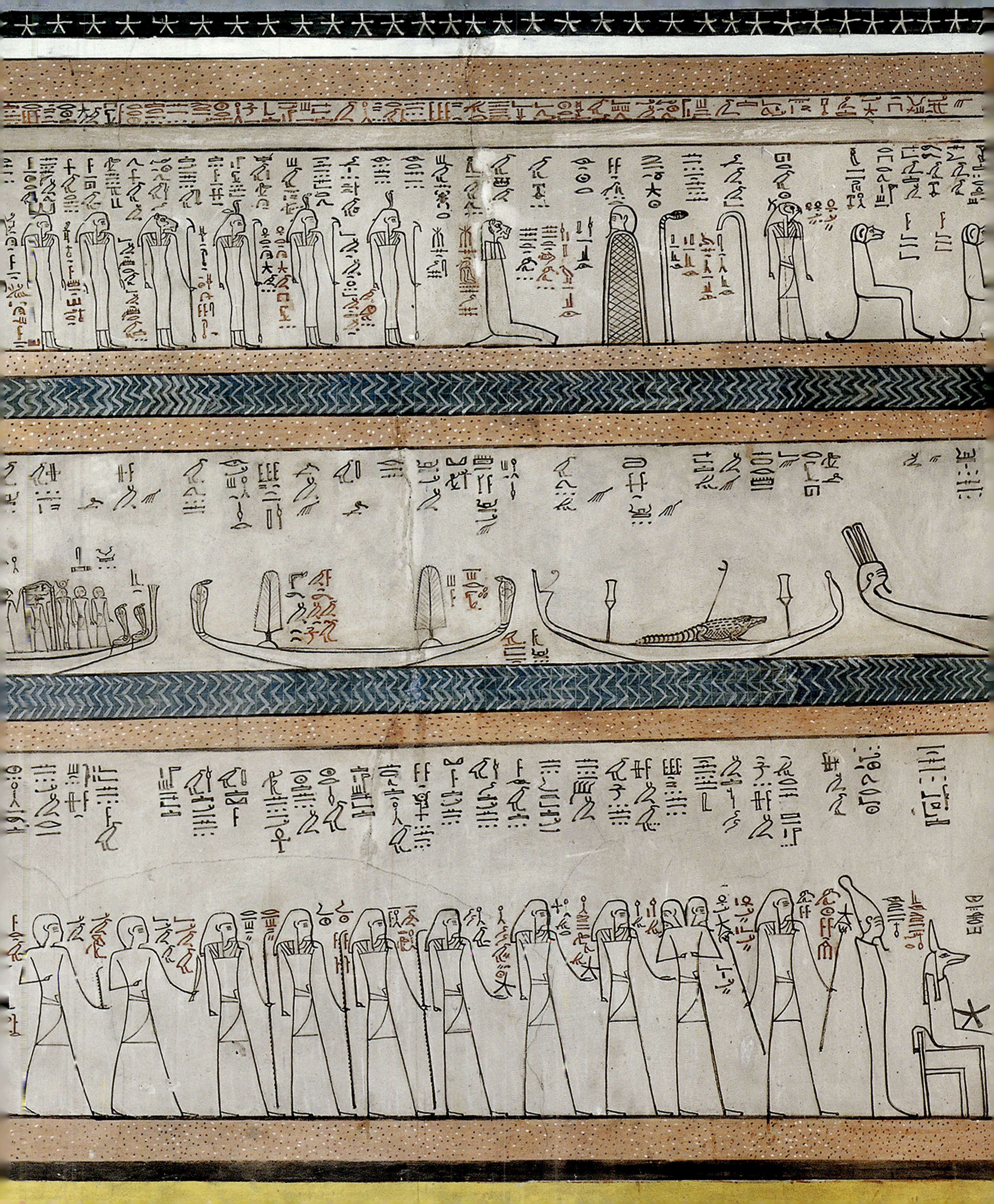

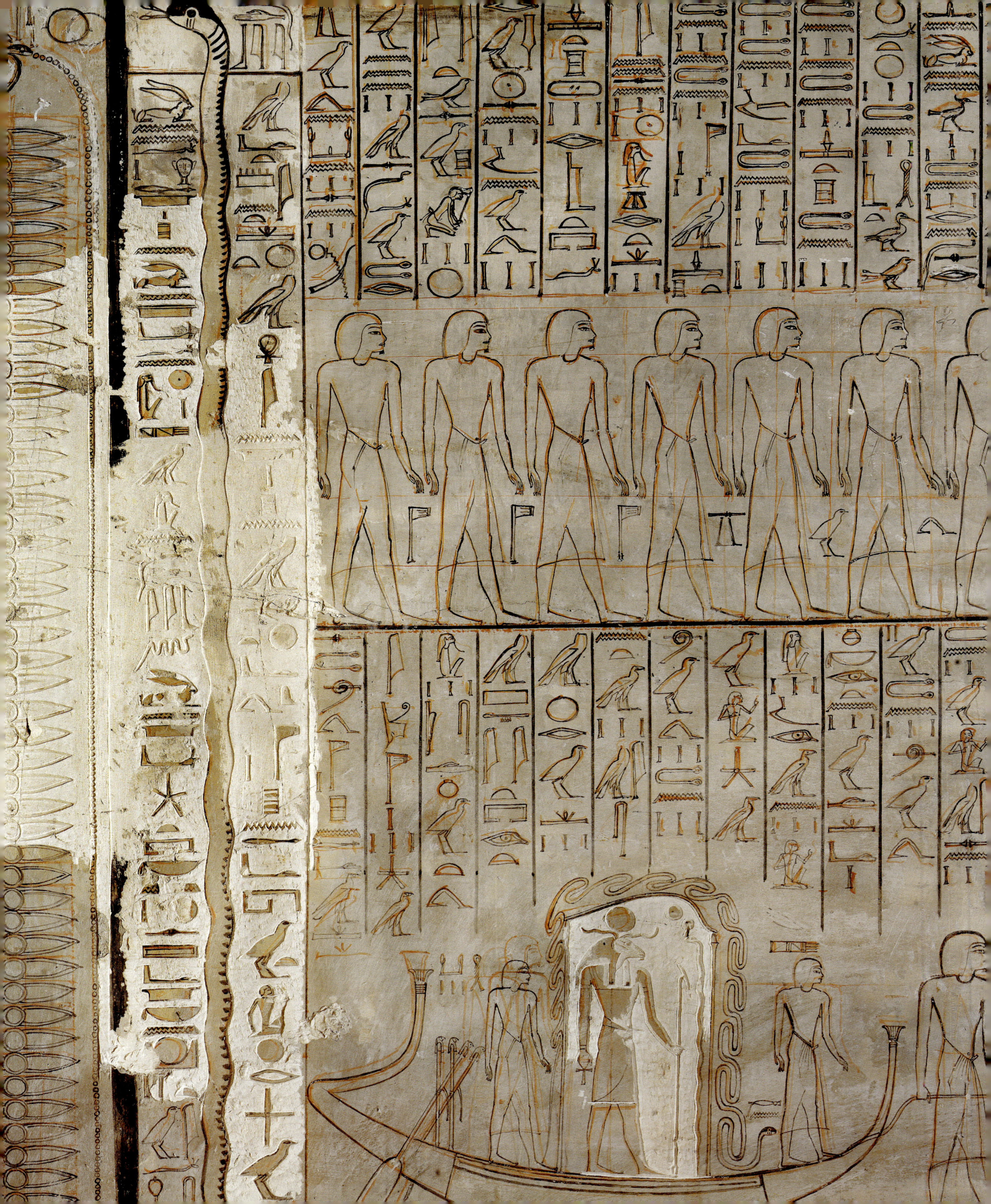

Scholars are still divided on the question of which tomb belonged to Tuthmosis II, the direct successor of Tuthmosis I and husband of Hatshepsut. The next tombs securely placed in the sequence are KV 38, the final resting place of Tuthmosis I (built for him by his grandson, Tuthmosis III), and KV 34, the tomb of Tuthmosis III himself. KV 38 is a small tomb, its descending corridor cut steeply into the rock at the base of a cliff, with a square antechamber and an oval burial chamber. This shape is that of the royal cartouche, the ring symbolizing the circuit of the sun inside which the king's name was written. Hornung also links this shape with the form of the Netherworld, or Duat. Like KV 20, the decoration (from the Amduat) was carved onto limestone blocks which were then set against the roughly carved walls

KV 34 was carved high into the face of a cliff, and consists of a descending corridor leading to a new feature, a deep "well shaft." A pillared hall lies at right angles to the well shaft, its walls adorned with images of underworld deities set into small boxes and labeled with their names. From here, steps lead down into an oval burial chamber, with a cartouche-shaped sarcophagus of yellow quartzite set at the far end. The walls of this chamber bear the first complete example of the Book of the Amduat. Each of the 12 hours of the night is depicted here, drawn with stick figures in black and red on a beige, pink, and green ground, as if a papyrus had been unrolled to cover the walls. On the pillars are images from another book, the Litany of Re. The ceiling in this tomb is decorated with yellow stars on a blue background, reminiscent of the burials chambers of the Old Kingdom.

The tomb of Tuthmosis III's son, Amenhotep II (KV 35), is a more regularized version of his father's, with some new features. A chamber has been added off the bottom of the well shaft (undecorated here). The first pillared hall is undecorated, and the burial chamber is rectangular, with six pillars rather than two. The floor at the far end of the burial chamber is sunken, so that the sarcophagus lies on a lower level. The decoration of the walls here is very similar in both content and decoration to that in the tomb of Tuthmosis III: the pillars show the king before the underworld deities Osiris, Anubis (jackal-headed god of embalming), and Hathor.

Architecturally, the next tomb in the sequence, that of Tuthmosis IV (KV 43), is a slightly expanded version of its direct predecessor, with longer corridors and a separate antechamber set at a right angle between the first pillared hall and the burial chamber. Only the well shaft and antechamber are decorated, both with images of the king before underworld divinities. The style here is new: the background is golden, the color of the divine realm, and the figures are fully formed and colorfully painted.

Dug into the rock of the western wadi of the Valley of the Kings, the tomb of Amenhotep III (KV 22) is even larger and more elaborate than Tuthmosis IV's, with two additional burial suites, intended to receive the bodies of the great queen Tiye and the king's daughter-consort Sitamun, added off the main burial chamber. The well shaft, antechamber, and burial chamber are decorated here, with elegantly-drawn figures against a blue-grey background; the themes are the king with various gods and the Book of the Amduat.

After the anomalous tomb of Akhenaten at el-Amarna, Tutankhamun returned to the Valley of the Kings, but was buried in a tomb (KV 62) that was probably originally meant for a private person and hastily adapted at the young king's premature death. The only decoration here is in the burial chamber where the scenes, executed with oddly foreshortened figures on a golden ground, include the funeral procession, the Opening of the Mouth (a ceremony performed on the mummy to enable it to function in the Afterlife), the king with various funerary gods, and a vignette from the Book of the Amduat.

The next king, Aye, took over a large tomb in the western wadi most likely begun by Tutankhamun (KV 23). For the first time in the Valley of the Kings, the axis is straight from the entrance directly to the burial chamber, evidently due to the influence of Akhenaten's straight-axis tomb at Amarna. This is thought to have allowed the light to enter, thus acting as a link to the sun. The decoration here is in the same style as Tutankhamun's, perhaps even executed by the same artists. An unusual feature here is a large canopic chamber off the square burial chamber.

The architecture of the tomb of Horemheb, last king of the 18th Dynasty, follows the earlier pattern, with its single axis displaced slightly as it leads forward from the first pillared hall. The sunken area of the burial chamber was expanded into what amounts almost to a separate room, the "crypt." The decoration includes a number of innovations: First a new text, the Book of Gates, was introduced. Second, the scenes and texts were carved first, then painted. Many areas were not completed, and the procedure followed by the ancient artisans can be clearly traced here.

UNFINISHED WALL FROM THE TOMB OF HOREMHEB
The walls of the tomb of Horemheb were the first to be carved as well as painted. This was never completed, so the steps followed by the artists are clear: first the images were sketched in black, then corrected by the master artisan in red.

THE 19TH DYNASTY: THE PERIOD OF CHANGE

The entrances to the 18th Dynasty tombs were hidden, but the kings of the 19th Dynasty no longer tried to hide the access to their burials. From the reign of Aye on, the straight axis, at first with a jog and later without, had become the norm, and this is the style seen throughout the era.

During the 19th Dynasty's main phase of development, the entrance stairs and corridors plunge less steeply into the rock, becoming almost horizontal by the end of the period. The second king, Seti I (KV 17), was the first to have a vaulted ceiling, on which was painted an astronomical chart, in his burial chamber. Also during this reign, side rooms appeared for the first time off the first pillared hall. In the reign of Seti I's son, Ramses II (KV 7), a new style was introduced for the burial chamber: rather than lowering the area at the back to form a crypt, the center of this chamber was dropped.

The biggest changes in the 19th Dynasty had to do with decoration. Following the lead of Horemheb, Seti I had his entire tomb carved and painted with scenes and texts. The repertoire continues to expand: in this tomb, the Book of the Amduat and the Book of Gates are joined by the Book of the Heavenly Cow.

A mysterious tunnel leads from the back wall of Seti I's crypt deep into the rock. This has not been fully explored in modern times, as the rock is friable and it is dangerous to enter. Some have speculated that this leads to the real burial chamber of the king, perhaps still containing treasures. However, it is likely that this is instead a symbolic passage to the Netherworld, heading into the realm of Osiris.

In the tomb of Ramses II the sun disk, representing the sun god at dawn, is carved above the entrance to the tomb; this motif occurs in all subsequent kings' tombs. The sun here is yellow; elsewhere in the tomb, when sunset and the nighttime sun are represented, the disk is red. Also for the first time in the tomb of Ramses II, there are images of the goddess Ma'at, daughter of Re, flanking the tomb entrance. On the south wall she holds the lotus, heraldic plant of Upper (southern) Egypt, and on the north wall she clutches papyrus, symbol of Lower (northern) Egypt. In most of the tombs of this dynasty, the king was shown saluting the sun god Re-Horakhty in the first descending corridor. The Litany of Re became the standard decoration in the entrance corridors, elaborating on the many shapes of the sun god during his daily journey.

Another innovation of this dynasty is the Osiris Shrine or Chapel. This is part of the first pillared hall, and shows the king meeting with Osiris and the gods of the Netherworld.

During the 19th Dynasty, the tomb can be viewed in two main sections. In the front are scenes and texts relating to the sun god, Re. In the back, beginning in the Osiris Chapel, the emphasis is on Osiris and his domain and on the king's identification with this god.

LATE 19TH DYNASTY AND 20TH DYNASTY: THE PERIOD OF SIMPLICITY

During the last part of the New Kingdom, the plan of the royal tombs was simplified. The entrance corridors became increasingly wider and shallower: the last six royal tombs in the Valley of the Kings contain tunnels wider than 3 meters (10 feet), with ceilings 4 meters high (23 feet). The tombs of this period were blocked with huge stones. Another change occurred in the sarcophagus chamber. The traditional direction of the sarcophagus had been symbolic north–south, perpendicular to the symbolic east–west axis of the tomb. Now the sarcophagus was placed parallel to the tomb axis, with the head of the sarcophagus to the west so that the king was looking east in the direction of the rising sun. The number of storage rooms also increased, with a maximum of 10 rooms in the tomb of Ramses III.

During the 20th Dynasty, the connection between the deceased king and Re became stronger, superseding in some ways the link with Osiris. New books were added to the repertoire: the Book of the Caverns; the Book of the Earth; and the Books of the Heavens, including the Books of the Day and Night. The lower parts of the tomb now showed the whole cycle of the sun during the day and night, with the addition of scenes and text from the Book of the Earth to help the deceased monarch reach the Netherworld.

The most elaborate tomb of this sequence is that of Ramses III (KV 11). The axis of this tomb had to be shifted to the right soon after the entrance passages, because the architects broke through into the nearby tomb of Amenmesse (KV 10). There are some beautiful and unique scenes here, in side rooms off the upper descending passages, illustrating the types of objects that might have been stored inside.

With the sepulcher of Ramses V/VI (KV 9), we reach the final phase of the New Kingdom royal tomb. There is a return

RAMSES VI AND MA'AT
The burial chamber of Ramses VI, like the other tombs of his era, was decorated with scenes from the Afterlife Books. The pillars bear figures of the king and various gods. Here, the pharaoh presents a small figure of Ma'at, goddess of the cosmic order.

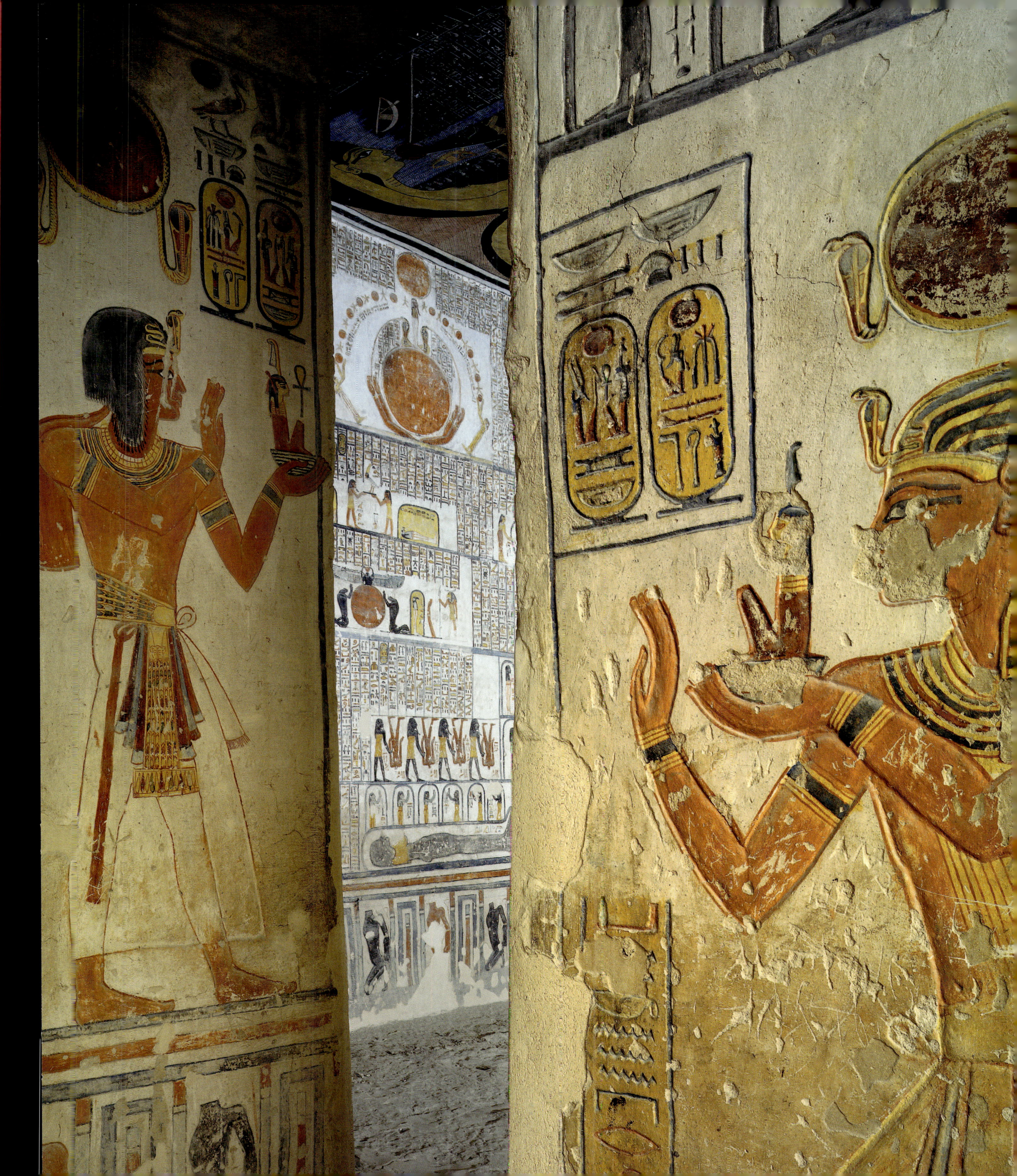

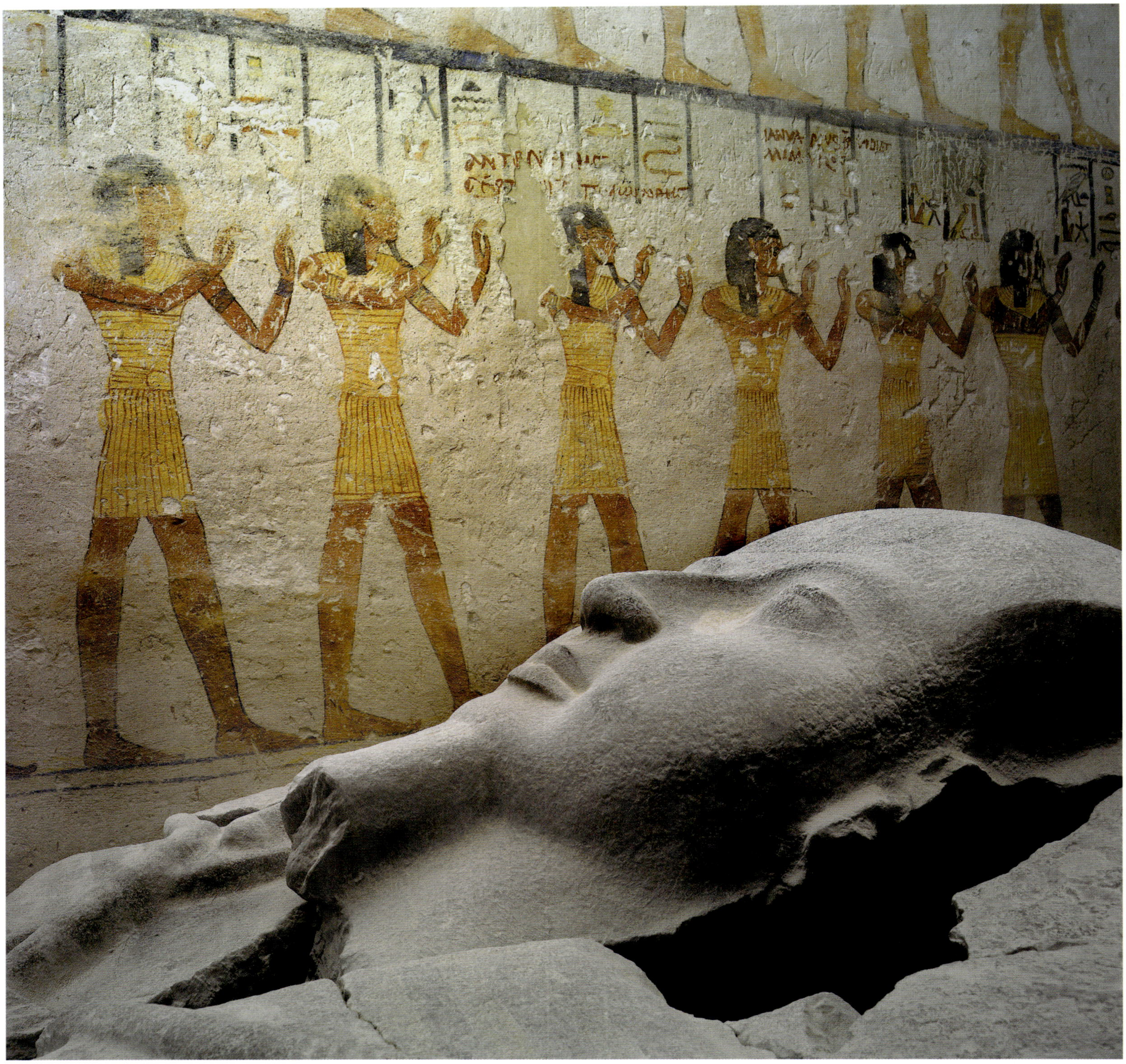

Sarcophagus of Ramses VI

Ramses VI's inner anthropoid sarcophagus of green stone was found smashed into pieces, and the mask was taken to the Louvre Museum; a cast has been reunited with the rest of the sarcophagus, which was recently reconstructed.

A Miniature Cosmos

The rear wall of the burial chamber of Ramses VI is adorned with scenes and texts from the Book of the Earth, while above the ruined sarcophagus stretches the vault of the heavens bearing an image of the sky goddess, Nut, and texts from the Books of the Day and Night.

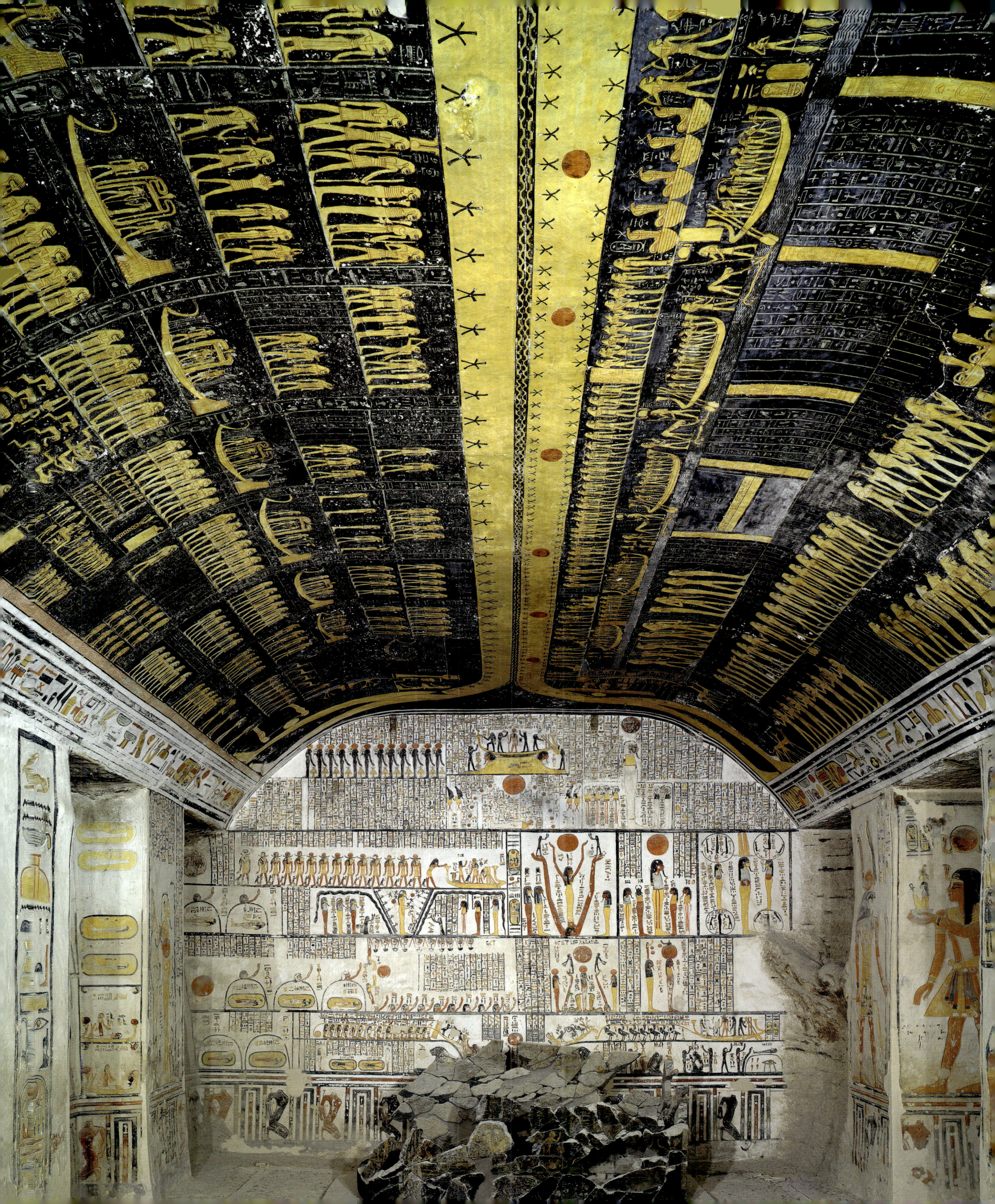

to the halls with pillars and large chambers seen in the 19th Dynasty but an avoidance of the side rooms. Decoration also reached its peak here, with almost all of the Netherworld Books represented.

Ramses XI built the last tomb in the royal valley (KV 4), but did not live to complete it. After his death, the Valley was abandoned. The next kings, assigned by historians to the Third Intermediate Period (Dynasties 21 and 22), moved their burials north to Tanis, the new capital of Egypt.

Names and Purposes of the Architectural Features

The royal tomb was the gate or the road that made possible the transition from life to the Afterlife, and it was essential for the king to know how to traverse it successfully. Every detail was laid out in the architecture and decoration, so that the monarch would not lose his way or encounter a situation with which he was not equipped to deal. Within the overall purpose of guiding and safeguarding the passage of the deceased king and sun god through the Netherworld, and ensuring their union with Osiris so that they would be reborn, each of the architectural areas of the tomb had a specific function. These details could change over time, but the basic concepts remained similar throughout the New Kingdom.

Information on the Egyptian names of the areas of the tomb comes from a papyrus, known as the Lepsius Papyrus and now in the Turin Museum. This bears an image of the tomb of 20th-Dynasty king Ramses IV, labeled with the names of the various chambers and corridors. Another source of information is an ostracon, a large flake of limestone, bearing a plan of the tomb of Ramses IX. These ancient names can help in some cases to clarify the function of the various areas.

The entrance passage to the tomb was called the road of Shu, god of the air. Before the reign of Tuthmosis IV, this entrance was open to the sky.

The first corridor was the passage of Re, often decorated with the Litany of Re, a recounting of the names of the sun god. This was the part of the tomb into which the rays of the sun might still reach; more importantly, it was the tunnel through which the deceased king, in the company of the sun god, would emerge and thus be reborn each morning.

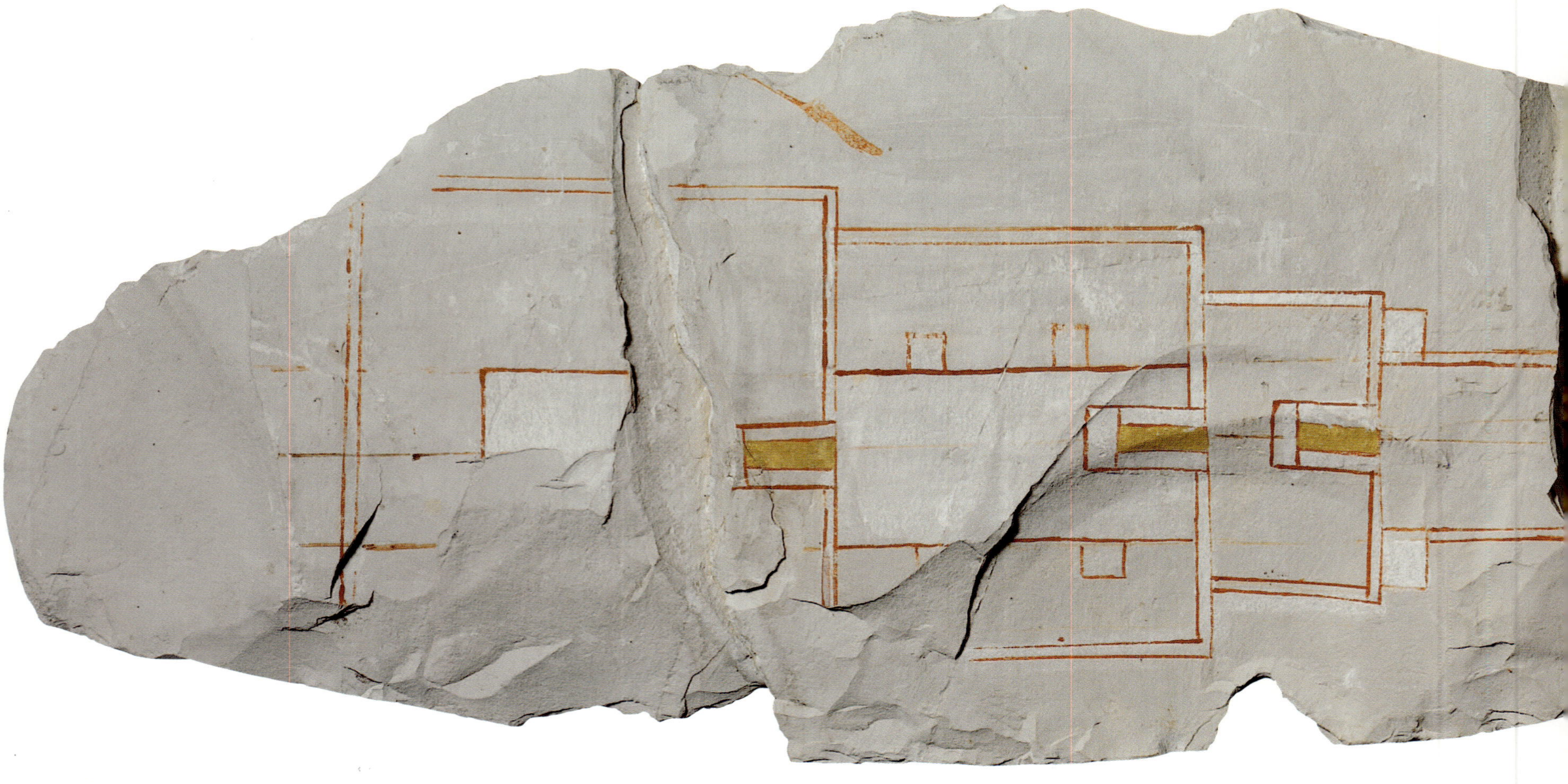

The next corridor, which begins the main descent into the rock, was equipped with wide niches at each side, known later as the "Chapels where the Gods Rest." Here Shu and Re joined the other gods, and rested before beginning their journey.

The ancient name for the well shaft was the "Hall of Waiting" or the "Hall of Stopping." Scholars have suggested that this was meant to keep the floods that periodically wash through the valley from reaching the burial chamber, or to hinder tomb robbers, who would have had to find a way across. However, Friedrich Abitz argues that a shaft to stop floods would be more usefully placed at the entrance to the tomb, and that tomb robbers would not be long delayed by the well, which can easily be crossed on a plank of wood or with ropes. The royal architects also had the example of the maze pyramids of the Middle Kingdom, and had seen that this sort of device was a poor deterrent to robbery. Through study of the decoration on the walls above these shafts from the reign of Horemheb on, Abitz has concluded that the shafts are connected with the fifth hour of the night as it appears in the Book of the Amduat. This hour is linked to the mortuary god Sokar, and the transformation of the king from the earthly Lord of the Two Lands to the ruler of the Netherworld, Osiris. Thus Abitz believes that this is a symbolic shaft for the deceased king as Osiris-Sokar.

The first pillared hall has been nicknamed by modern scholars the "Chariot Hall," because the remains of a chariot were found in this hall in the tomb of Tuthmosis IV. Especially from the 19th Dynasty on, when the Osiris shrine appeared in this area, this hall can be seen as transitional to the lower part of the tomb, the entrance to the Netherworld itself, where the true journey to the Afterlife began. The next passages have no special names, and their decoration can vary.

The burial chamber was known as "The Hall of Rest," or "The House of Gold." The latter name probably refers to the nest of gilded shrines that would have been set up around the royal sarcophagus. (The only complete example of these was found in the tomb of Tutankhamun.) In most of the tombs in the Valley, the burial chamber is surrounded by small side rooms, two for storage of food and drink and two for storing statues and funerary equipment.

PLAN OF A ROYAL TOMB

This ostracon (flake of limestone) was found in the tomb of Ramses VI, and represents the plan of the tomb of Ramses IX. Evident here are the main features of a late New Kingdom royal tomb: an entrance corridor with stairs flanking a ramp; more passages flanked by side rooms; a series of halls; an antechamber; the upper, pillared part of the burial chamber, and the lower crypt, containing the sarcophagus.

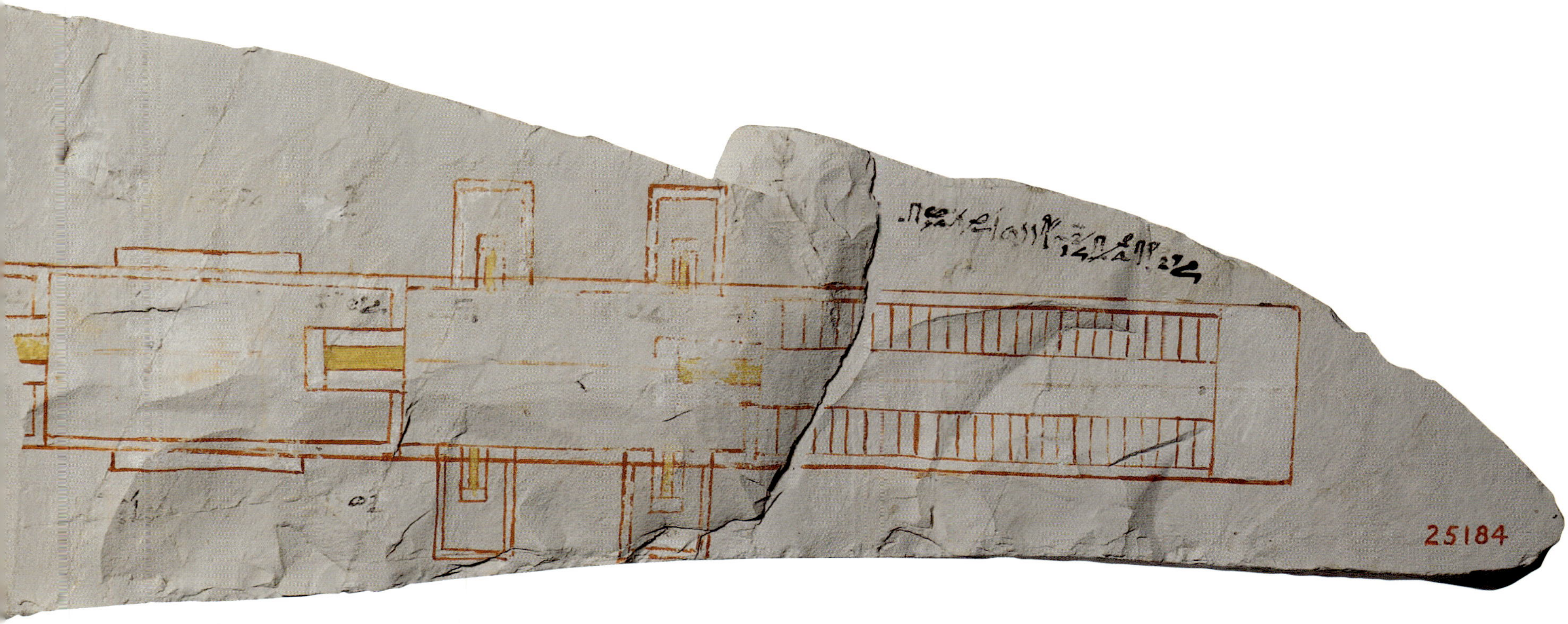

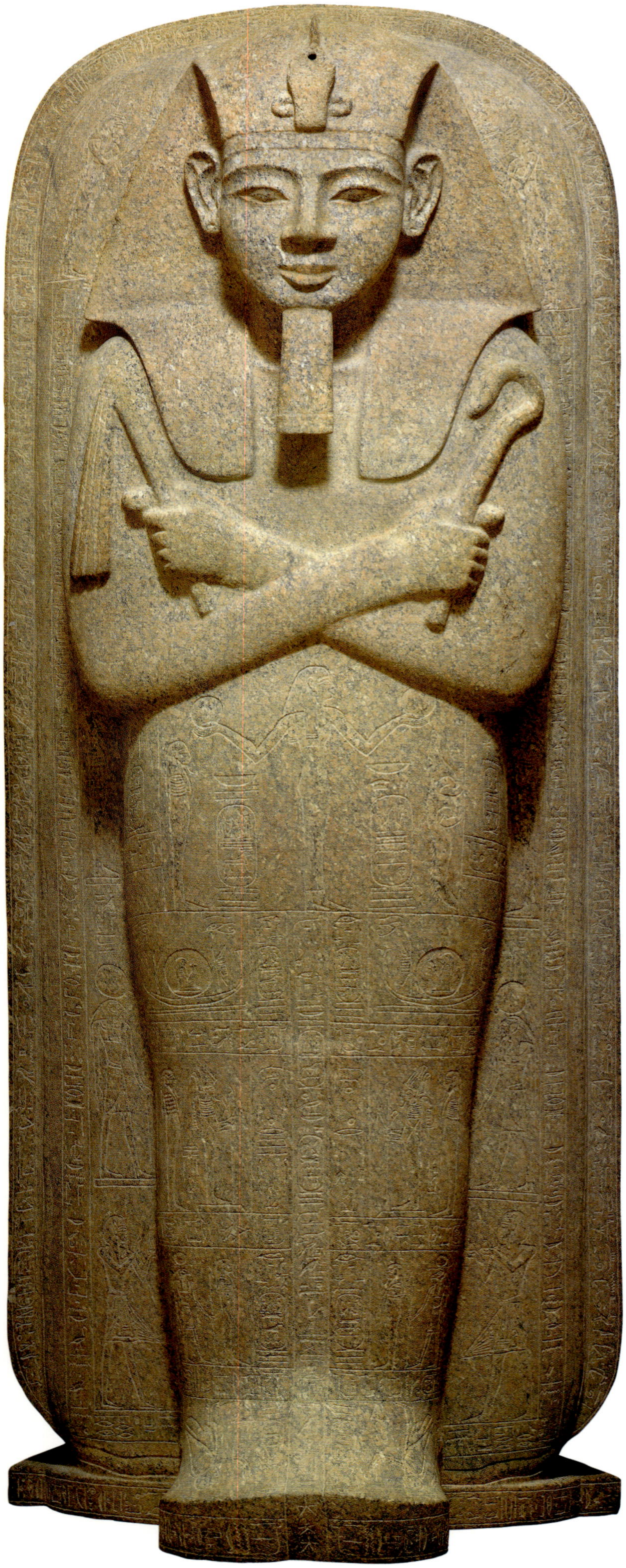

Equipping the Tomb

It was essential to equip each tomb properly with items for the funeral and materials for the Afterlife. The tomb of Tutankhamun (KV 62) gives us the only relatively complete assemblage of royal funerary equipment from the New Kingdom, although bits and pieces from other tombs provide additional information about the items essential to the king's Afterlife.

Mummy, Coffins, and Sarcophagi

Certainly, the most important item was the body itself, properly mummified and thus preserved for eternity. The process of mummification was already finely developed by this time, although it reached its peak later, during the 21st Dynasty. After death, the body was laid on a special embalming table, washed and anointed. Then an incision was made in the left side of the abdomen, through which the viscera (stomach, liver, lungs, and intestines) were removed. These were mummified individually and placed in containers known as canopic jars or chests. The heart, considered the seat of both intellect and emotion, was either removed, desiccated, and placed back in the body, or simply left in place. The brain was taken out, either through the nose or the back of the head (or, as was shown by the recent CT-scan of Tutankhamun, by a combination of the two methods), and thrown away.

Powdered natron, a naturally-occurring blend of salt and sodium bicarbonate, was heaped around the body to draw out the moisture. This was changed frequently for a period of 40 days. The desiccated body was then cleaned and anointed again and wrapped in linen bandages. Wound into these bandages, in religiously significant and carefully prescribed positions, were amulets, jewels, and weapons, all designed to protect the deceased king and provide essential items for the Afterlife.

Sarcophagus of Merenptah
This, the outer sarcophagus of Merenptah, still lies in his tomb; the inner stone sarcophagus was taken by the priests of the 21st Dynasty and reused for Psusennes I in his burial at Tanis.

Innermost Coffin of Tutankhamun
(Following pages)
Made of solid gold and inlaid with carnelian, turquoise, lapis lazuli, and glass, this coffin held the mummy of Tutankhamun. It is in the form of the king as Osiris, his body wrapped in bandages and protected by Isis and Nephthys, who stretch their wings to enfold him. This was the first of three coffins, which were nested inside a stone sarcophagus and surrounded by four gilded wooden shrines.

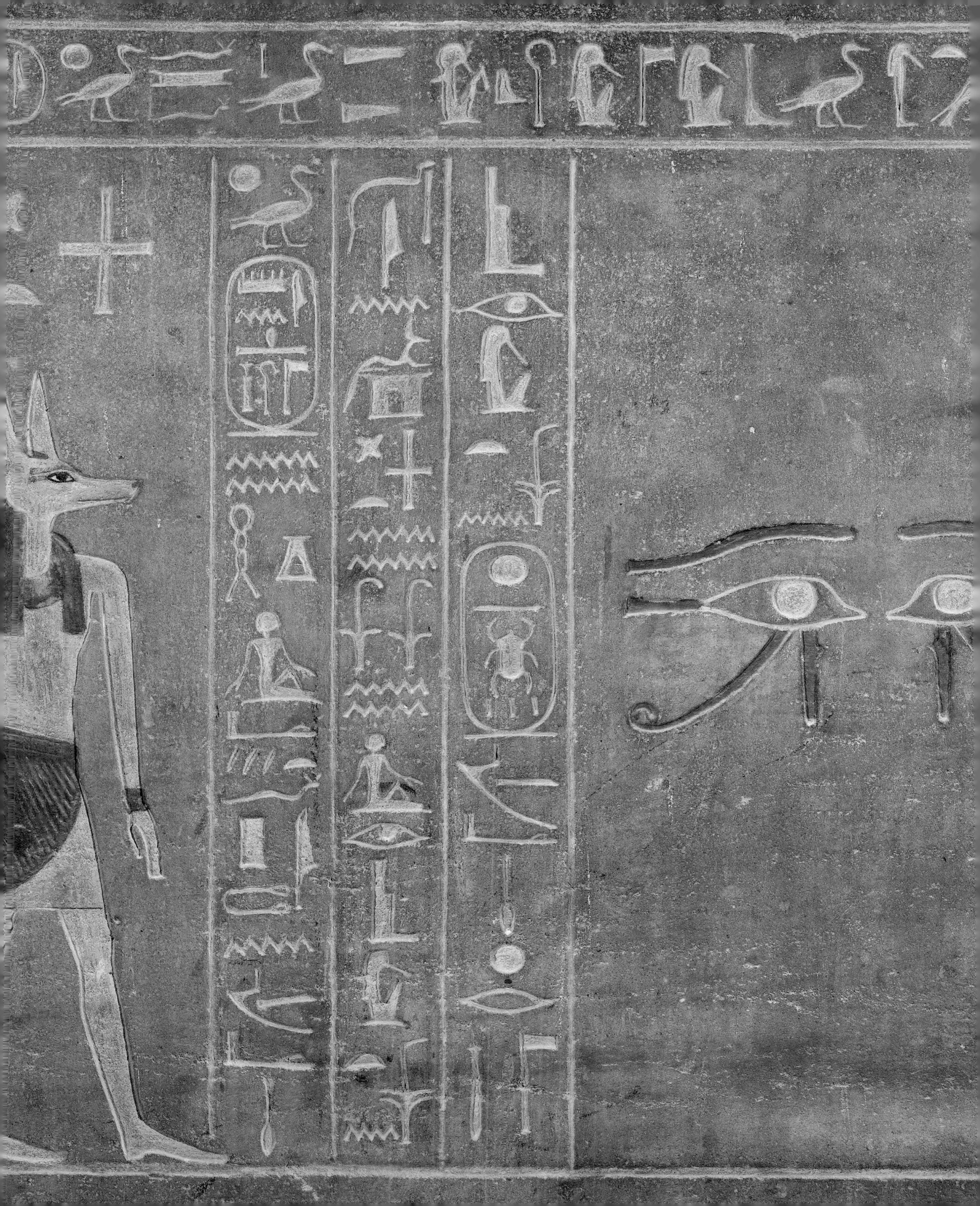

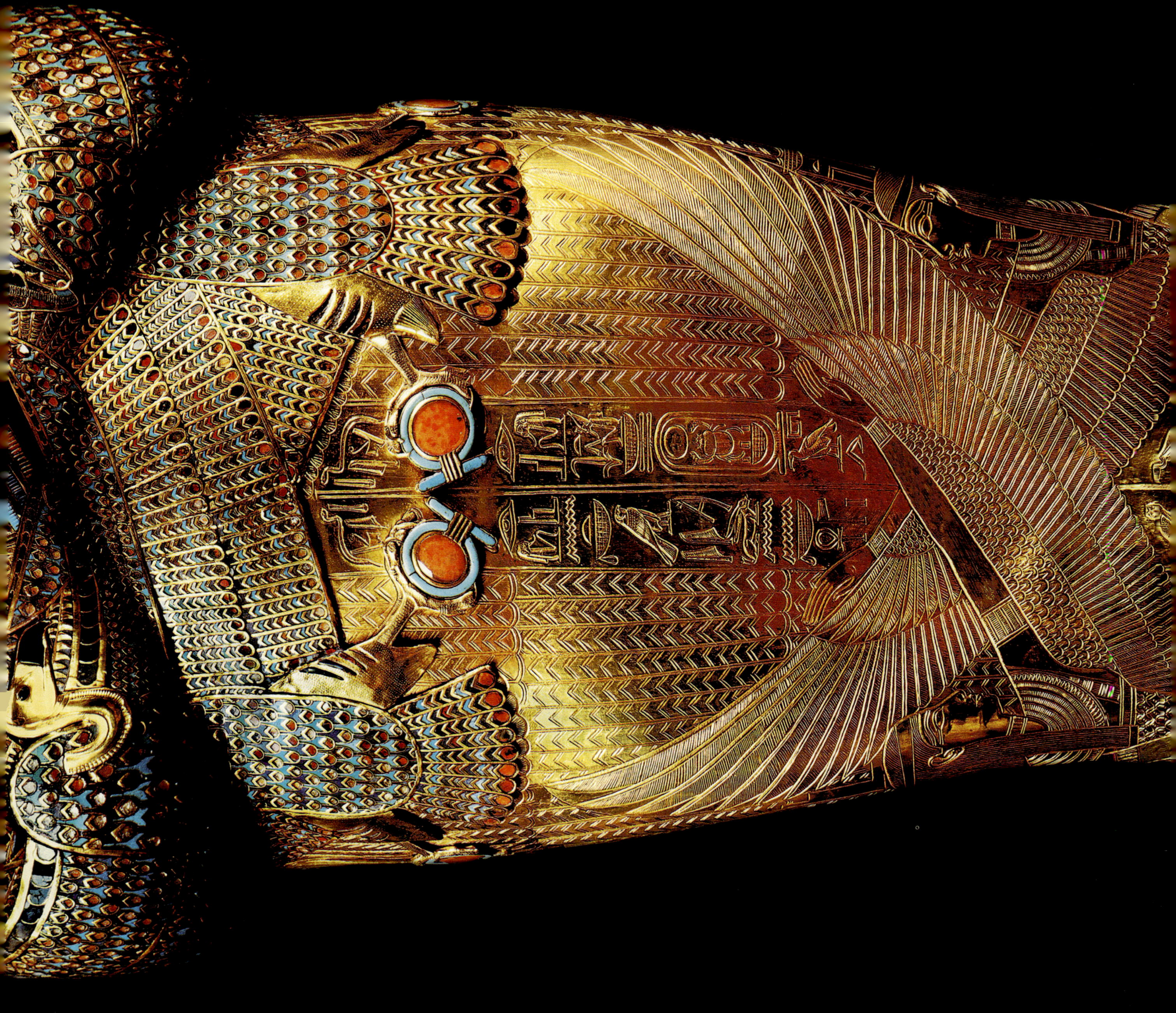

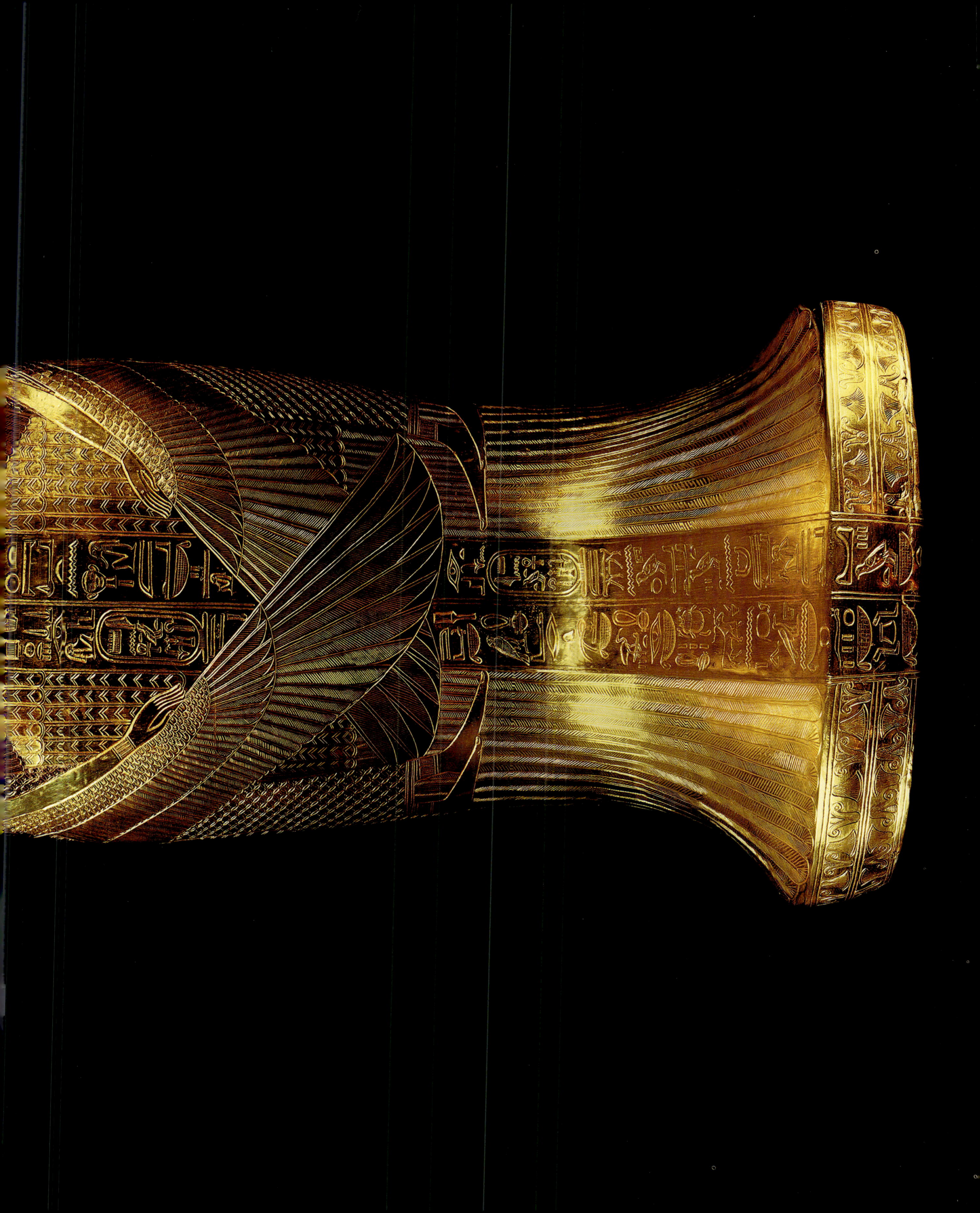

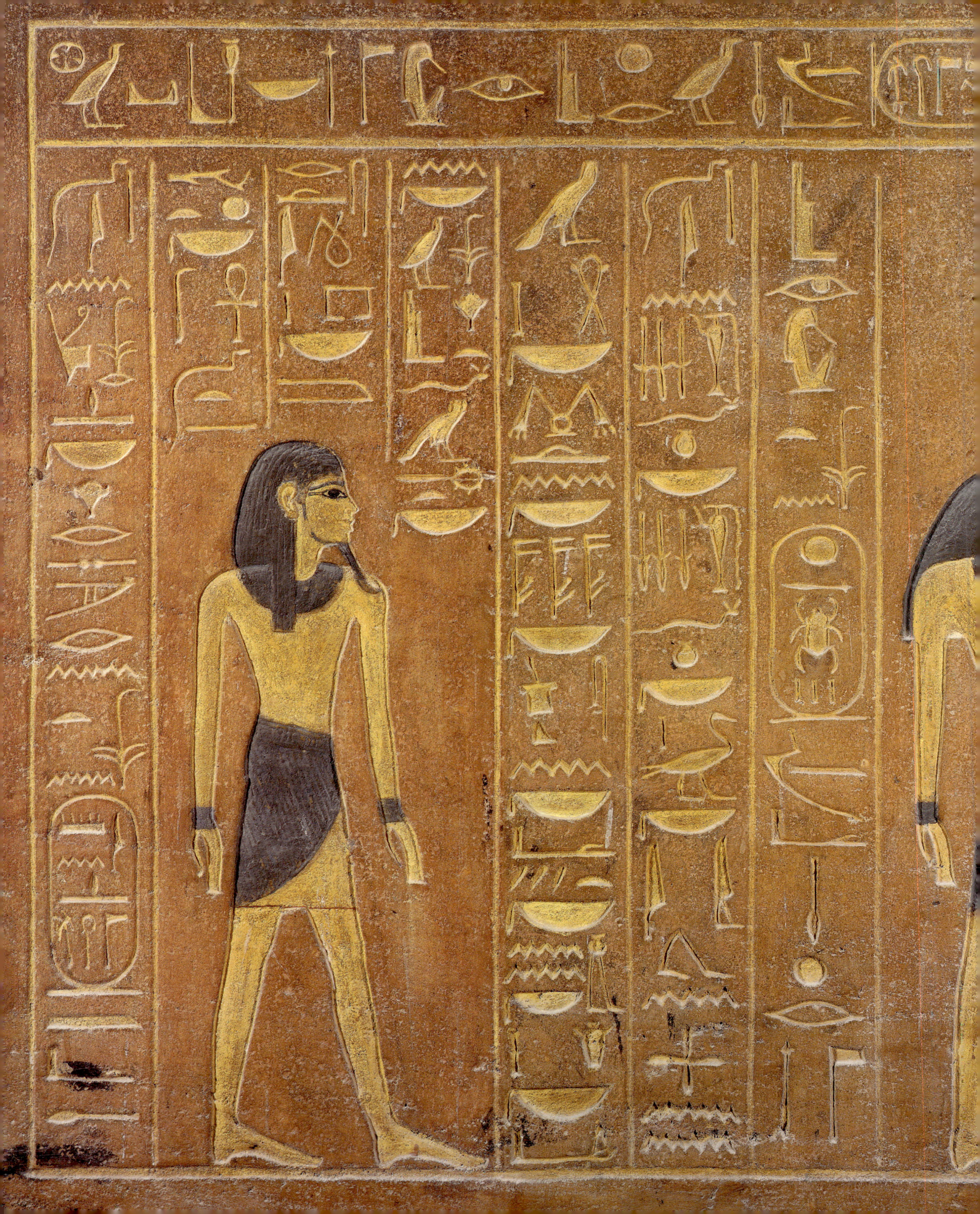

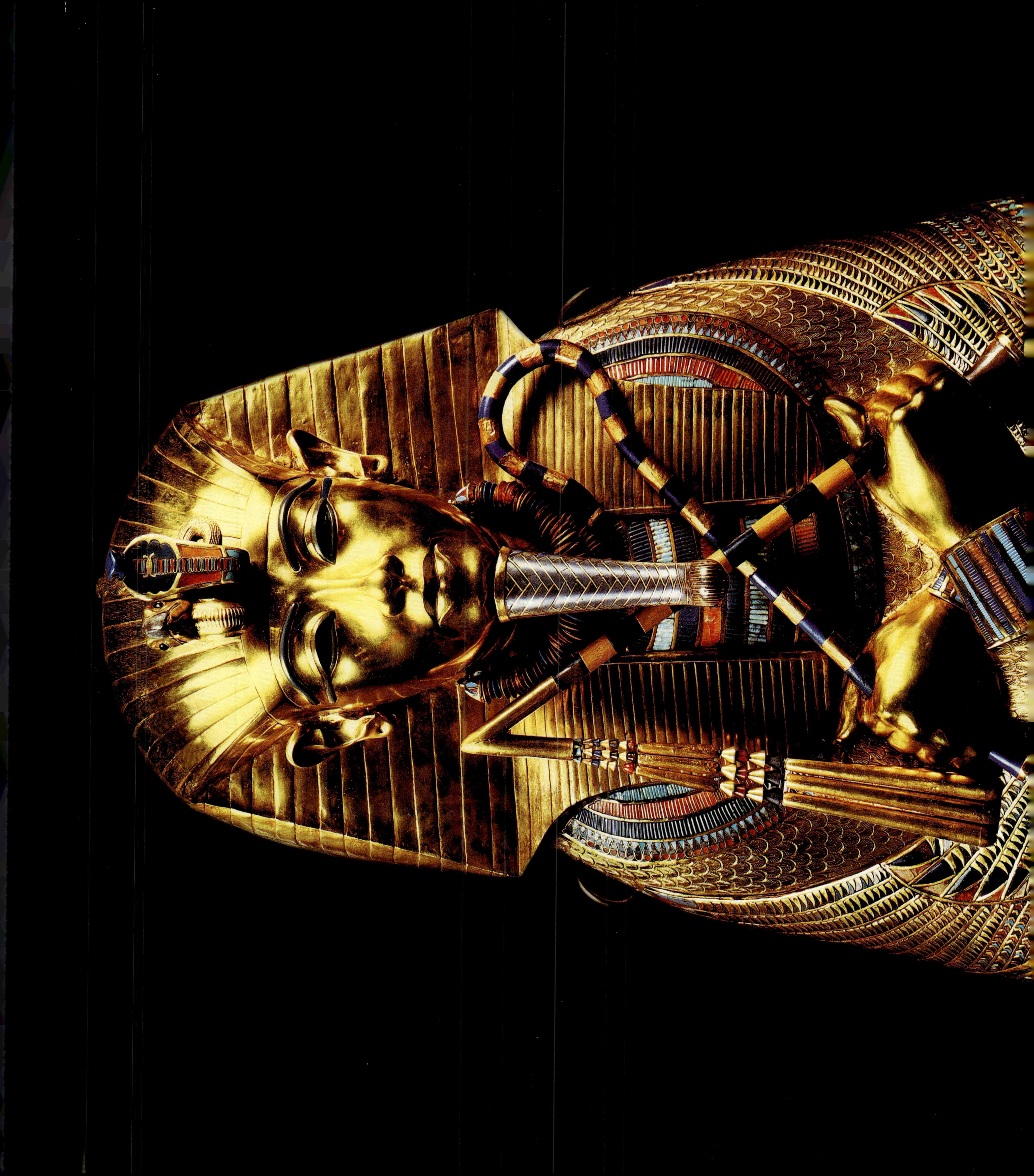

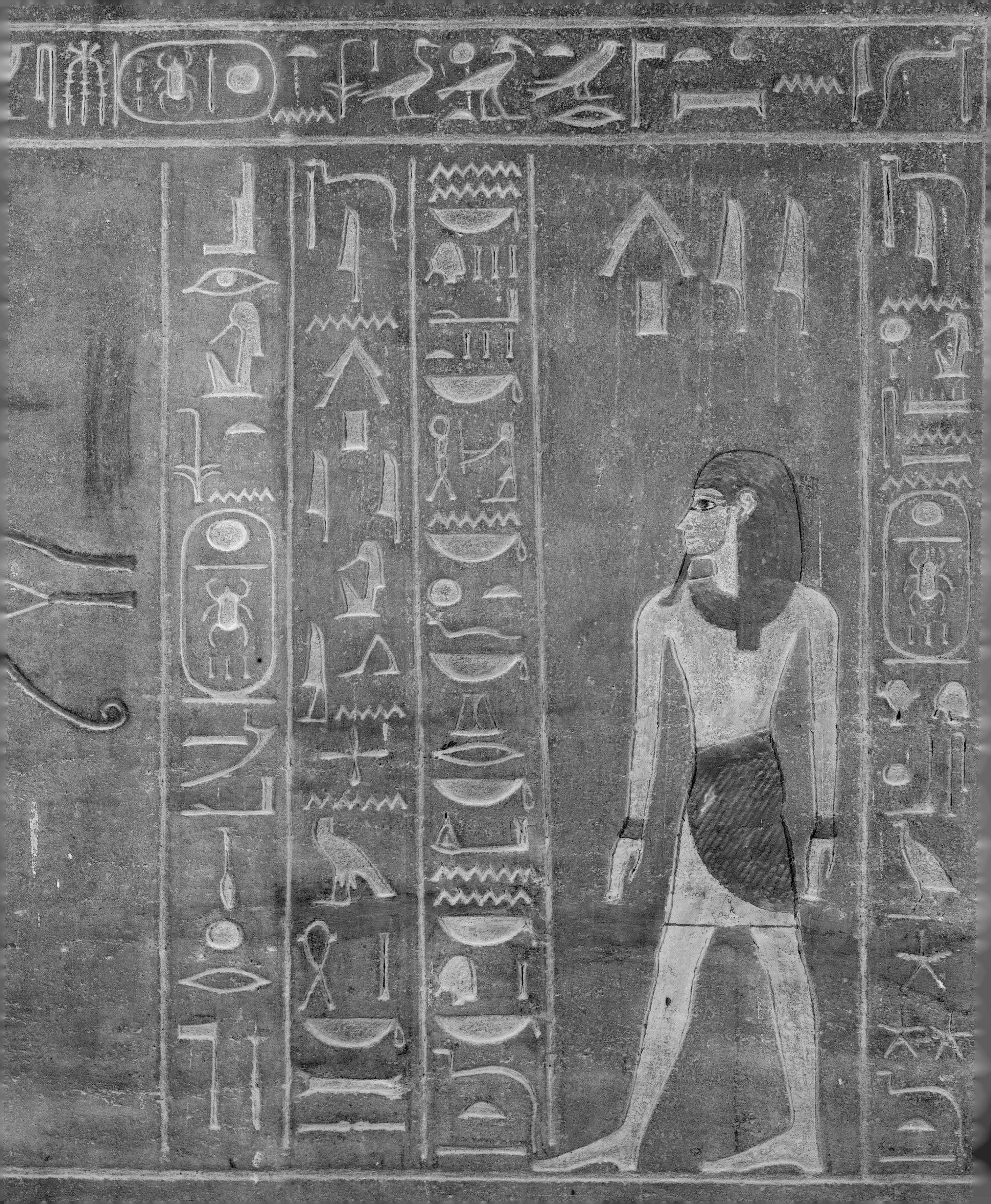

Through a twist of fate, many of the mummies of the New Kingdom pharaohs have been preserved for us and are now for the most part in the Egyptian Museum, Cairo. These had been stripped in antiquity of all but a few scraps of their amulets and jewels, and some of the bodies had been badly damaged by tomb robbers. The mummies were found in a series of two caches, one high in the cliffs near the mortuary temple of Hatshepsut at Deir el-Bahari and the other in the tomb of Amenhotep II (KV 35). They had been hidden there by priests and scribes of the early Third Intermediate Period who, acting on orders from their rulers, had entered each of the royal tombs and taken away any remaining valuables. They had then unwrapped each mummy (both kings and queens), removed any jewels or amulets left behind by robbers, then piously rewrapped and labeled the bodies before secreting them in a series of caches.

Thus, when they were discovered in the late 1800s, the royal mummies were no longer protected by their full complement of funerary equipment. Amulets, jewels, and weapons were gone, and most mummies were in replacement coffins or the least valuable of their original containers (or the original coffins stripped of their gold). Only Tutankhamun was found where the ancient priests had left him, nestled safely inside a series of coffins, a sarcophagus, and gilded wooden shrines. It is likely, from bits and pieces found in the other tombs, that the other kings were similarly protected, although the materials and decoration of the specific elements would have differed.

A helmet-like mask was placed over Tutankhamun's head, echoing the royal features so that the soul could recognize its body in the Afterlife. On his head was the royal *nemes* headdress, crafted of gold and colored glass, and protecting his brow were Nekhbet (the vulture) and Wadjet (the cobra), tutelary goddesses of Upper and Lower Egypt respectively. Chapter 151 from the Book of the Dead, identifying the various parts of the mask with specific deities who were to protect the king, was inscribed on its back. Bands of gold inlaid with colored glass and semi-precious stones were wrapped around the body, imitating the external bandaging that would, for other people, have been in linen. The mummy, with its mask, was anointed with some sort of liquid resins, then placed inside an anthropoid coffin of solid gold, inlaid with glass and engraved with the protective wings of Nekhbet and Wadjet. Echoing the mask within, the king wears here the *nemes* protected by cobra and vulture.

The inner coffin, covered with linen shrouds and again anointed with liquid resin, was placed inside a second and then a third gilded wooden coffin, each of similar although not identical form and decoration to the first. This entire assemblage then was lowered into a rectangular sarcophagus of red-yellow quartzite, with the protective goddesses Isis, Nephthys, Serket, and Neith carved in relief at the four corners, their winged arms outstretched to protect the king. Around this sarcophagus, which is in the center of the burial chamber, were erected four shrines of gilded wood decorated with religious scenes and texts.

Although Tutankhamun's is the only full set discovered, a number of the coffins and stone sarcophagi that housed other royal bodies have been found. The coffins are all anthropoid in shape, and were found, some still containing their original owners, in the royal mummy caches. The coffin of Tuthmosis III was there, for example, but had been completely stripped of its original gilding. The inner container of Amenhotep II was crudely made of cartonnage. One of the most beautiful examples held the body of Ramses II, but was probably originally made for his grandfather, Ramses I. It was designed to be gilded, like Tutankhamun's, but was finished instead in plain wood, perhaps because of the short reign of its original owner.

THE EYES OF TUTANKHAMUN

Found on the head of Tut's mummy was this exquisite mask of solid gold, bearing the features of the king. Making it all the more lifelike are the eyes, inlaid with obsidian and calcite and outlined with lapis lazuli.

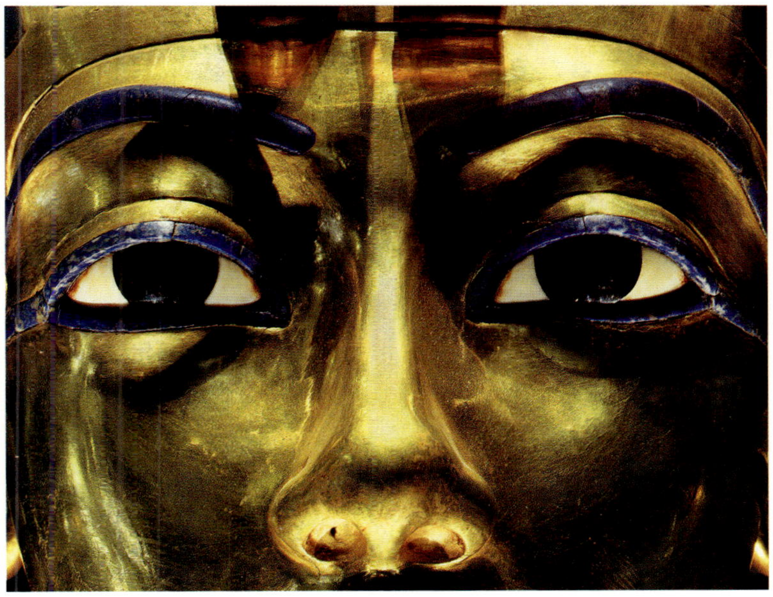

SARCOPHAGUS OF AMENHOTEP II

(*Preceding pages*)

Carved of yellow quartzite, the sarcophagus of Amenhotep II is beautifully decorated with protective spells spoken by important funerary gods. Visible here are the jackal-headed Anubis, and two of the Four Sons of Horus, responsible for guarding the viscera. The mummy of the king, stripped of its coffins and jewels, was found inside the sarcophagus.

The earliest sarcophagus known from the New Kingdom is an unfinished example, made for Tuthmosis II and found in KV 42. From the reign of his widow Hatshepsut come two royal sarcophagi, both of quartzite, one for the queen-regnant and the other re-inscribed for her father, Tuthmosis I. These are rectangular, and carved with images of and protective spells spoken by Isis and Nephthys (who guarded the foot and head, respectively), the canopic genii (the four sons of Horus), and the embalming god Anubis. The lid was carved with a cartouche shape and an image of the sky goddess Nut. This goddess also appears on a larger scale on the floor of the trough and the inside of the lid. On the sides are *wedjat* eyes, the sacred eyes of Horus, through which the deceased (although he or she was now laid on their back rather than their side, as had been the case earlier) could look out into the world.

The 18th Dynasty kings through Amenhotep III followed much the same pattern in terms of material and decoration; the shape is modified, beginning with Tuthmosis III, into a cartouche. The most beautiful of these sarcophagi is Tuthmosis IV's, on which the figures were elegantly carved and then painted in still-vibrant colors. In the sarcophagus of Amenhotep III, the *wedjat* eyes were moved onto the underside of the lid, so that the king could look out directly. The size of the sarcophagus also increased significantly over time.

Amenhotep IV/Akhenaten introduced a new style of sarcophagus, going back to the rectangular shape but with figures of his great wife Nefertiti carved in high relief at the four corners to protect her husband. This pattern is followed by the remaining kings of the 18th Dynasty, who changed the figures at the corners from the queen to Isis, Nephthys, Serket, and Neith.

Seti I and Ramses II introduced a new type of anthropoid outer coffin, now of stone instead of wood. Rather than protective deities and spells, these were carved with vignettes from the Books of the Netherworld. These were used at least into the reign of Ramses VI, made of alabaster in most cases and of greywacke for Ramses VI. Remains of rectangular sarcophagi, in some cases nested, were also found for several kings of the 19th and 20th Dynasties, including Merenptah (the innermost of whose sarcophagi was taken to Tanis and reused by a later king) and Ramses III. These bear mummiform figures of their respective kings carved in very high relief on the lids, and are decorated with images from the Netherworld Books.

Thus coffins, sarcophagi, and outer shrines were all designed, regardless of the era, to protect the king buried within. Like the tomb itself, the Netherworld guides, carved in some cases on the outer shrines (as in Tutankhamun's case) and beginning in the reign of Seti I on the containers themselves, helped to guarantee the king's successful transition to the Afterlife.

Canopic Chests

The royal viscera were mummified individually, and identified with the four sons of Horus: the liver with Imsety, the intestines with Qebehsenuef, the stomach with Duamutef, and the lungs with Hapy, each protected by a goddess (Isis, Serket, Neith, and Nephthys respectively). Based on Tutankhamun's example, the only complete set available, the viscera were then wrapped and placed in coffinettes, miniature versions of the coffins containing the body. These were then put into canopic chests. Tutankhamun's canopic chest was carved from a single block of Egyptian alabaster. During the New Kingdom, many private people had canopic jars topped with the heads of these deities: the human-headed Imsety, the falcon-headed Qebehsenuef, the jackal-headed Duamutef, and the baboon-headed Hapy. However, royal canopic chests were always stoppered with the head of the king himself. At the end of the 19th Dynasty, the kings switched from chests to large canopic jars.

Tutankhamun's canopic chest was placed inside a shrine of gilded wood. At each side was placed a gilded statuette of one of the tutelary goddesses, and a frieze of cobras with sun disks on their heads was placed around the top. The sides were inscribed with protective spells. In other tombs, the chest was set into an emplacement at the foot of the coffin, or put into a separate niche.

Shabtis

Funerary figures originally appeared in the First Intermediate Period, made of wax, wrapped with linen, and put in miniature coffins. These began to be made of stone in the Middle Kingdom, with only a few in each burial. By the New Kingdom, these figures, meant to perform onerous duties in lieu of the owner in the Afterlife, were made of a variety of materials and included with most burials. Often inscribed on them was Spell 6 from the Book of the Dead, which mentions the various agricultural tasks that are to be carried out.

A full complement of 413 *shabti*s was found in the tomb of Tutankhamun, in stone, faience, and wood, and in a variety of sizes and styles. There were 365 for the days of the year, plus one overseer for each ten-day week and a supervisor for each of the twelve months.

GOLDEN DIADEM
This golden diadem, inlaid with semi-precious stones, was found on the head of Tutankhamun's mummy. When he wore this in life, the streamers of beaten gold would have cascaded down his back. His forehead would have been protected by the cobra, tutelary goddess of Lower Egypt, and the vulture, protectress of Upper Egypt.

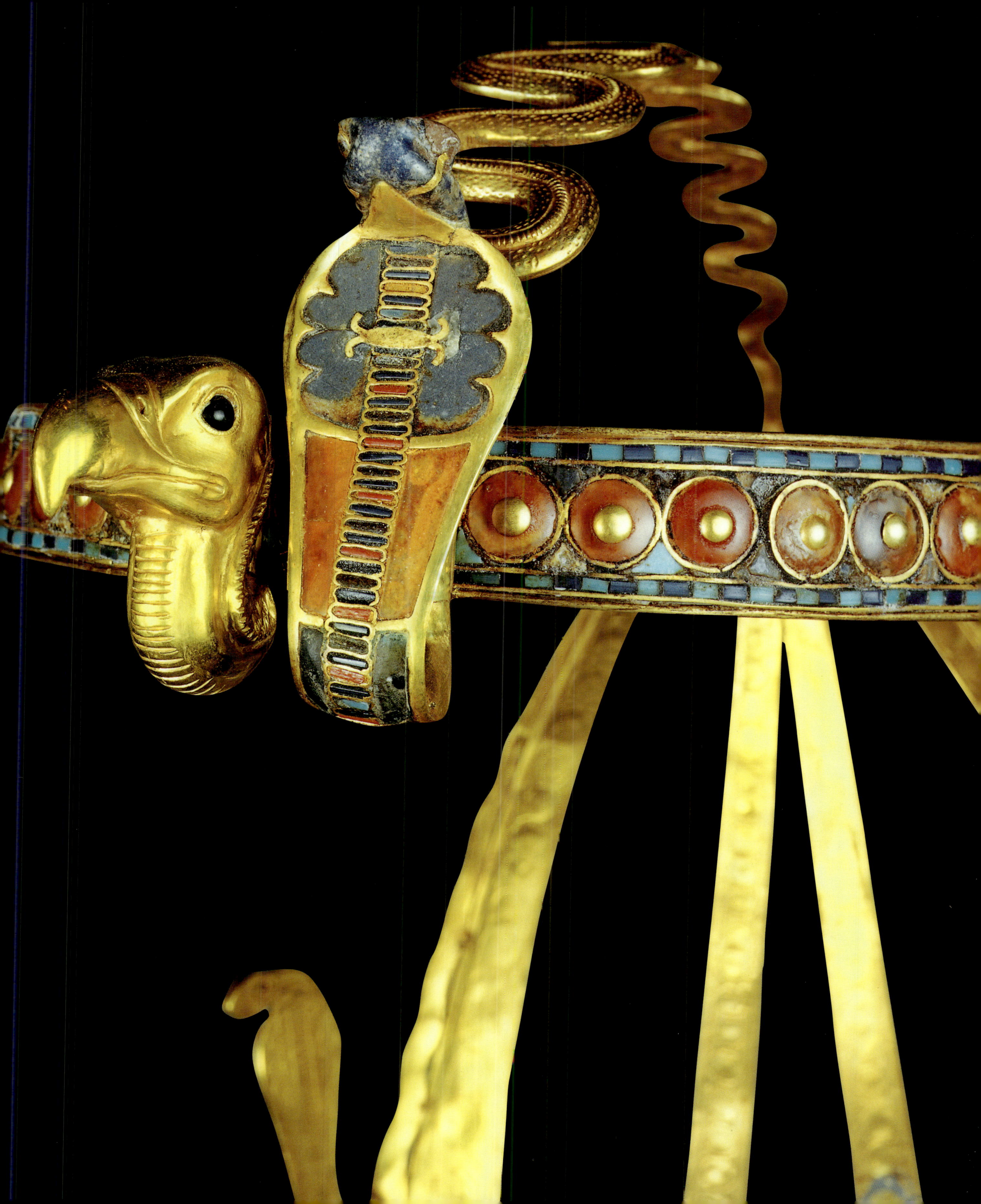

Jewels and Amulets

Again, it is only Tutankhamun's equipment that can inform us about the essential jewels, amulets, and other items meant to be placed on the royal body. Private examples tell us that each king would have had a heart scarab, inscribed with chapter 30B from the Book of the Dead; Tutankhamun's heart scarab was found in a box in the Treasury, while around his neck was instead a scarab of black resin, inscribed with a different spell from the Book of the Dead. Below this was a pair of golden hands clutching a crook and flail.

Bound into the royal wrappings were a total of 150 objects, many of pure gold. Much of this was jewelry: pectorals, broad collars, bracelets, finger-rings, an apron, and a girdle. Along the royal thighs were two daggers, one of gold and the other of iron, at that time an exotic material. Much of the jewelry served amuletic functions. For example, there were vulture and cobra collars, representing Nekhbet and Wadjet, bracelets and necklaces with scarabs (representing the sun god at dawn), and *wedjat* eyes. There were also amulets in the shape of *djed* pillars, the hieroglyph for stability that represented the backbone of Osiris, a miniature iron headrest (raising the head of the deceased was associated with rebirth, and headrests could symbolize the horizon, with the head on top taking the role of the sun), and other amulets in various shapes. A beaded cap decorated with cartouches and cobras had been placed on the king's head. On his toes and fingers were golden caps to keep the nails in place, and on his feet were golden sandals.

Ritual Objects

Other important items of the royal funerary equipment were ritual figures, generally between one-third and fully life-size. There were 35 of these in the tomb of Tutankhamun, most distributed in 22 shrines found in the Treasury. Two life-size guardian figures representing the king were found flanking the sealed entrance to the burial chamber. Guardian and ritual figures were also found in the tombs of Amenhotep II, Tuthmosis IV, Horemheb, Ramses I, and Seti I, and depictions of similar figures were painted on the walls of the tomb of Seti II. Some of these figures were of the king himself in various guises (such as harpooning hippos, an image which symbolized his triumph over chaos), and others were of different underworld deities.

Guarding the entrance to the Treasury beyond the burial chamber was Tutankhamun's Anubis Shrine, a large box of gilded wood with the figure of a recumbent jackal on top. In addition to various jewels, this shrine contained objects thought to relate to mummification or the ceremonies of the Opening of the Mouth.

In the antechamber of Tutankhamun's tomb were three ritual couches. Fragments of such objects had been found in other royal tombs, and such objects were also depicted on the walls of the tomb of Seti II. These are larger than a normal bed, and are in the shape of magical animals: a lion, a cow with the solar disk between the horns on her head, and the devourer Ammut, with a hippopotamus head, feline legs and feet, and a crocodile tail. The purpose of these beds is still not completely clear, but probably has to do with the funeral rites.

There are other objects from the royal tombs that had magical functions. For example, there were Osiris beds, large silhouettes of the god Osiris that were filled with seeds that would sprout after the funeral, symbolizing eternal fertility and resurrection. In niches set into the walls of the burial chambers were magical figures placed on clay bricks inscribed with protective spells.

"Daily Life" Items

In addition to clearly religious and protective items, objects used in daily life and needed for the eternal Afterlife were also placed in the tombs. Beds, headrests, chairs, boxes full of clothing and jewelry, jars containing precious oils and unguents, staffs of office, writing implements, cosmetic items, games, musical instruments, weapons such as bows and arrows, throwsticks, full-size chariots, and model boats, among other necessities, were buried with the kings. Tutankhamun took a large amount of food with him to the beyond: bread as well as unprocessed grain to make more, meat and poultry, chickpeas and lentils, spices, honey, and a variety of fruits. Although beer was a staple of the Egyptian diet, Tutankhamun was not buried with any; instead, he may have had some fruit juice, and certainly took with him a quantity of wine.

Thus, equipped with everything he might need for the eternal life beyond the grave, the king was ready for his journey to the Beyond. The funeral itself would have been an elaborate affair, when the mummified body was anointed, the ceremony of the Opening of the Mouth was performed, and the nest of coffins was placed inside the sarcophagus and surrounded with the gilded shrines. The tomb was then filled with its equipment and sealed by the necropolis police, who would stand guard over the monarch's sacred eternity.

ROYAL JEWELS

Even though his tomb was robbed in antiquity, and some of the portable items carried away, Tutankhamun was discovered with over 200 individual pieces of jewelry. Shown here is a pendant in the shape of one of the king's names, Nebkheperure: a scarab beetle (*kheper*), between a basket (*neb*), and a sun disk (*re*). The three amulets below are in the form of the gods Thoth, Horus, and Anubis.

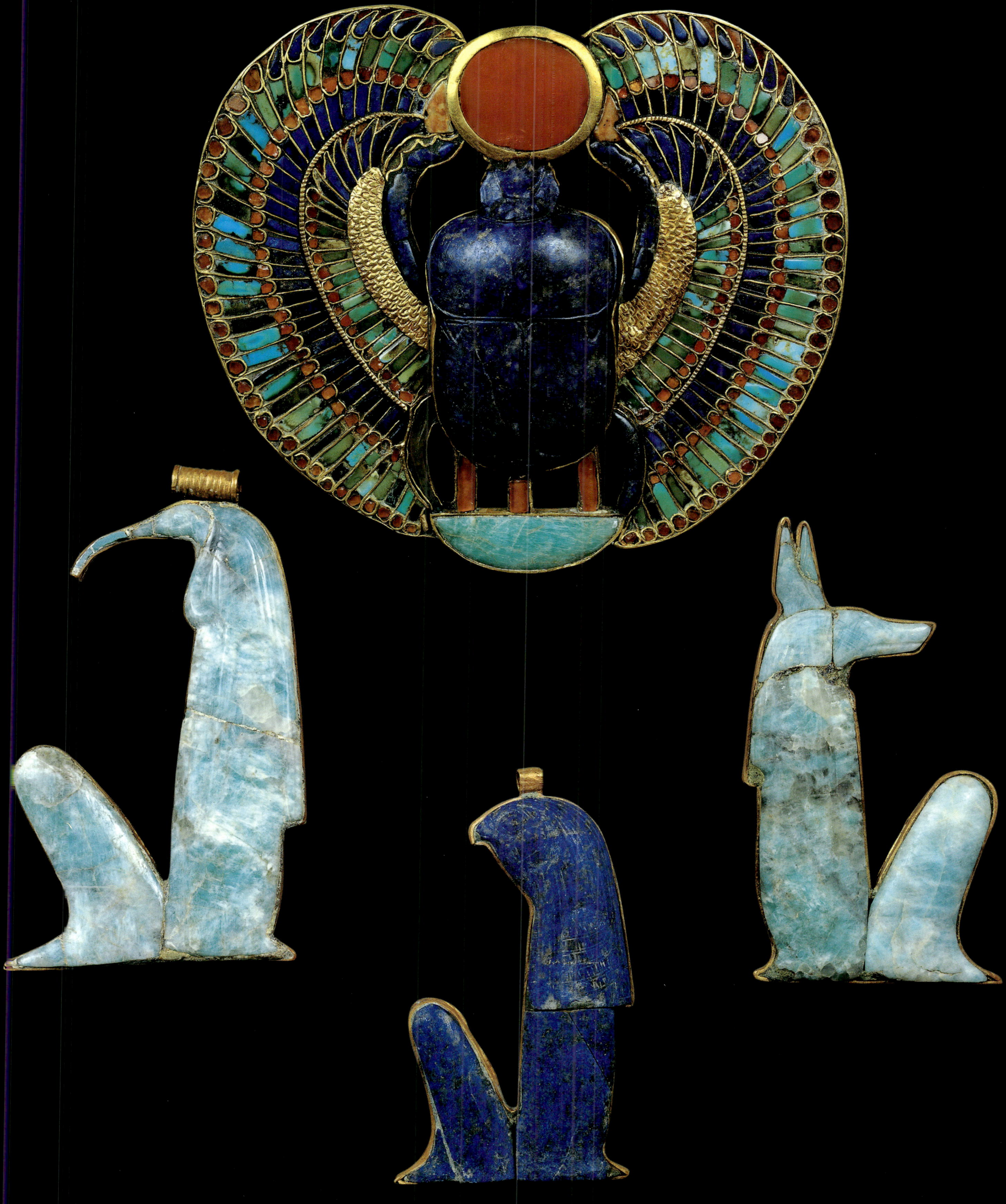

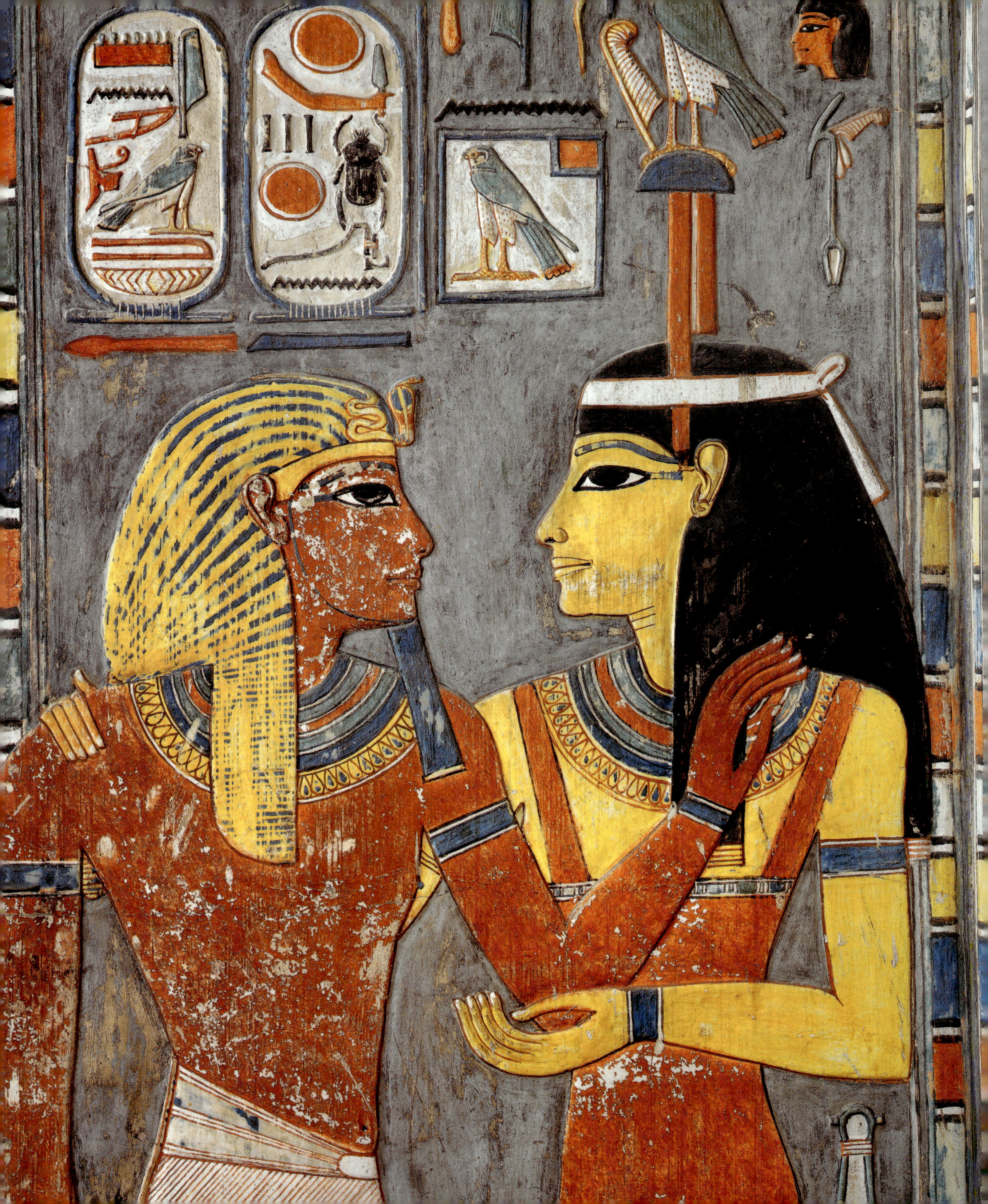

Chapter 2

Images of the King with the Gods

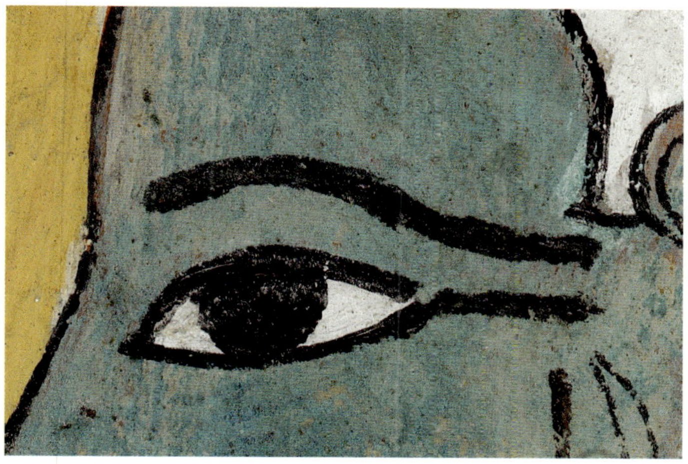

Beginning in the tomb of Tuthmosis III and then in almost every subsequent sepulcher, the repertoire of scenes in the royal tombs includes images of the king with various gods. These are distinct from the more complex Afterlife books, in which these same divinities, and many others, are woven into elaborate scenes illustrating the journey through the Netherworld or sky. The images discussed in this chapter are fairly simple: for the most part they consist only of a figure of the king with one god, although series of such paired figures can be arranged in friezes. Generally, both are standing and facing one another; the king either stands passively or actively makes offerings to the god, and in return the god offers protection and eternal life to the king.

The icon of king and deity, although in less formulaic form, dates back to the Old Kingdom, seen, for example, in the royal pyramid complexes. This was an important part of the decorative program of the mortuary complex, and aided the king in his transition to divinity. By the New Kingdom, single images of king and god facing one another had become essential to the decoration of the divine temple, where the king is shown caring for the god and being given the tools he needs to rule in return.

In the earliest examples from the New Kingdom royal tombs, the gods are the chief Netherworld deities, shown welcoming the pharaoh to the beyond and promising him eternal life. In these, the king is passive, receiving without giving in return. Later scenes are similar to those found in divine temples, where ruler and deity are shown in a reciprocal relationship: the king makes an offering to the god, and is granted in return protection and eternal life. The principal purposes of all of these scenes is for the gods to offer protection to the deceased king against the dangers of the Netherworld, and to ensure his rebirth in the Afterlife.

Horemheb and Hathor

In this scene from the antechamber of Horemheb's tomb, the deceased king is shown in an embrace with Hathor, great goddess of the West. Her name can be seen clearly here, just above and in front of her head: the Horus falcon (*Her*) is shown inside an enclosure wall (*Hut*), making *Hut-her* (Hathor), the house/womb of Horus.

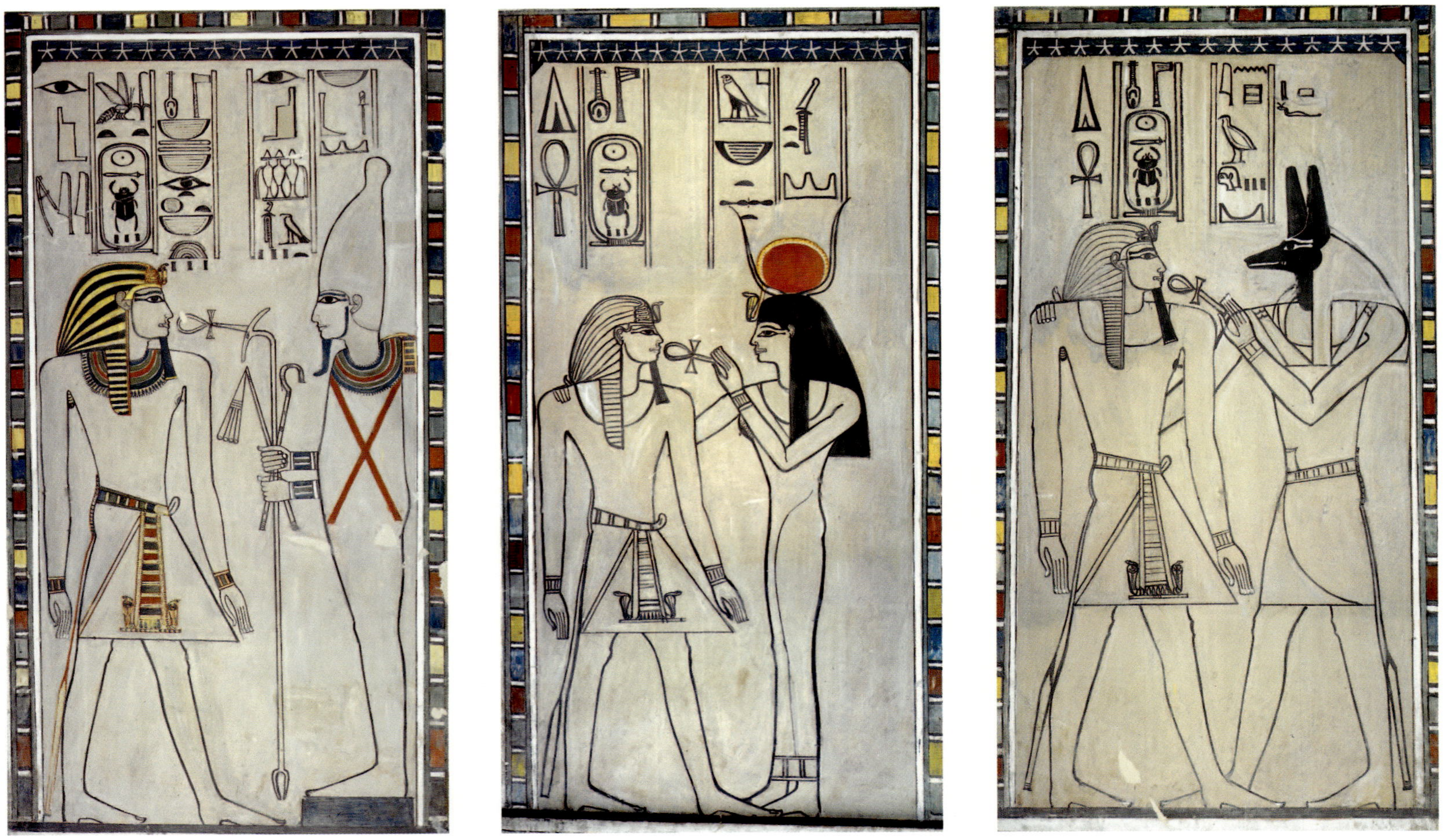

Amenhotep II with Osiris, Hathor, and Anubis

In the tombs of the earlier 18th Dynasty the king is passive, receiving life from the god. The deities that appear in these tombs are Osiris, king of the Netherworld; Hathor in her guise as Mistress of the western desert; and the god of embalming, Anubis, as the guardian of the desert landscape. These gods are shown here on pillars from the tomb of Amenhotep II: Osiris, wrapped as a mummy, wearing the white crown of Upper Egypt; Hathor with cow's horns and a sun disk on her head; and the jackal-headed Anubis. The king in each instance wears the royal *nemes* headdress.

The earliest scene of the king with a god appears on a pillar in the burial chamber of Tuthmosis III. Here the monarch is shown being suckled by Isis in the form of a tree goddess. Although Isis was a great divinity in her own right, in this particular instance, the deity is probably to be identified as Hathor, who frequently takes this form (Isis does not). She is given the name of Isis here because this was the name of Tuthmosis III's mother. On the same pillar, Isis/Hathor is depicted in a papyrus skiff, crossing the fields of the world beyond the earthly realm.

Almost all of the royal tombs from this time until the end of the New Kingdom contain scenes of the king with gods that fall outside of the larger Netherworld books. In the tombs of the earlier 18th Dynasty, these images appear on the pillars of the burial chamber, the antechamber, and/or the upper walls of the well shaft. The most frequently depicted deities are Osiris, Anubis, and Hathor, the three most important gods of the Netherworld.

Osiris, Hathor, and Anubis

The chief of these gods, Osiris, was the ruler of the world below the earth. In his earliest guise, he was a fertility god, linked with the annual flooding of the Nile and the fecundity of the soil that was deposited as the waters receded. As such, he was intimately associated with death and resurrection. His principal cult throughout Egyptian history was at Abydos, a site in Upper Egypt where the first kings of a united country were buried. He was essential to mortuary religion beginning at the latest in the Old Kingdom, featuring predominantly in the offering prayers inscribed in the cult chapels of the elite. He is one of the three principal gods, along with Re and Horus, mentioned in the Pyramid Texts.

Osiris is traditionally depicted in the form of a mummy, standing or sitting with his legs wrapped tightly together. His hands emerge from the bandages to grasp a crook and a flail, fundamental elements of the royal regalia.

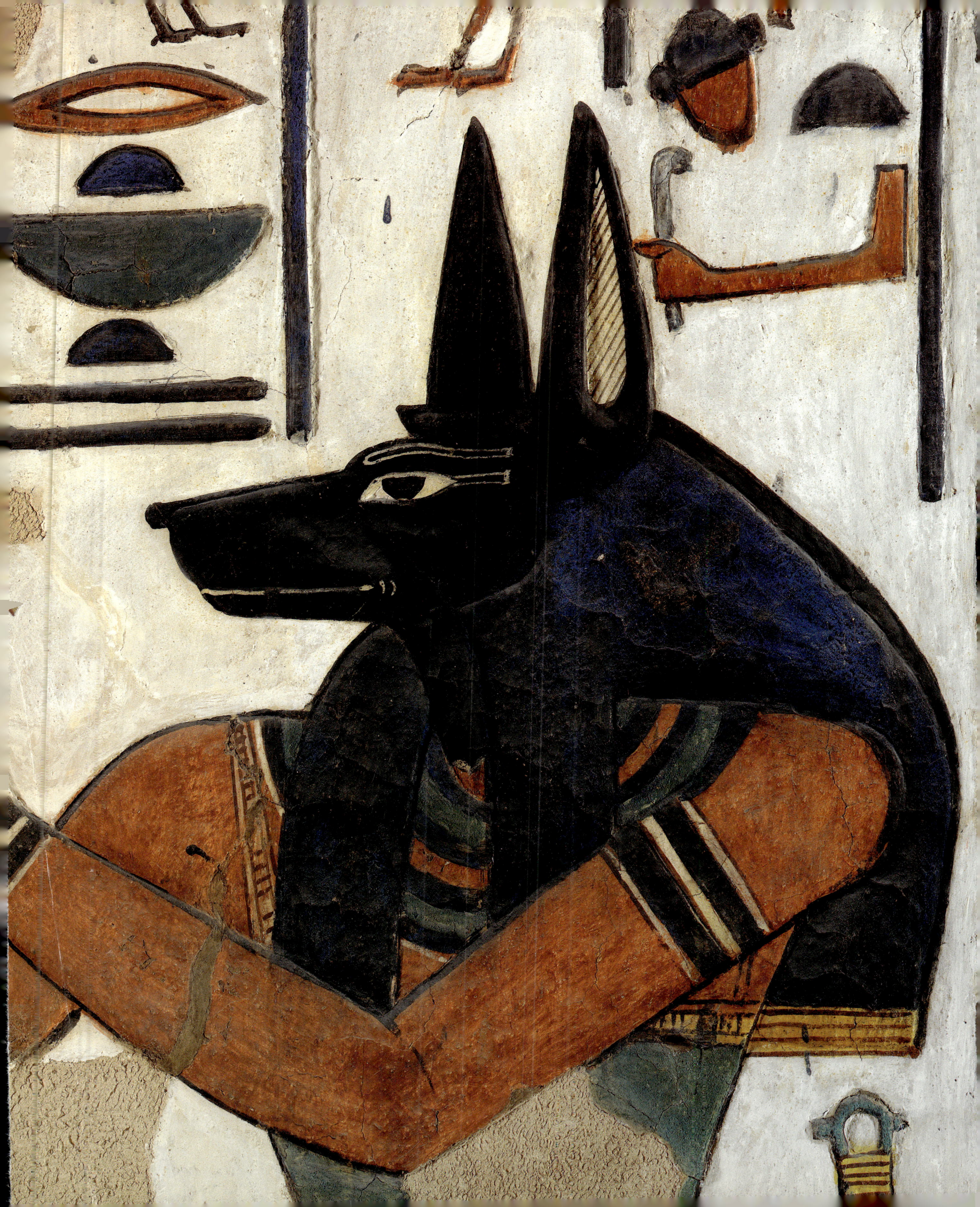

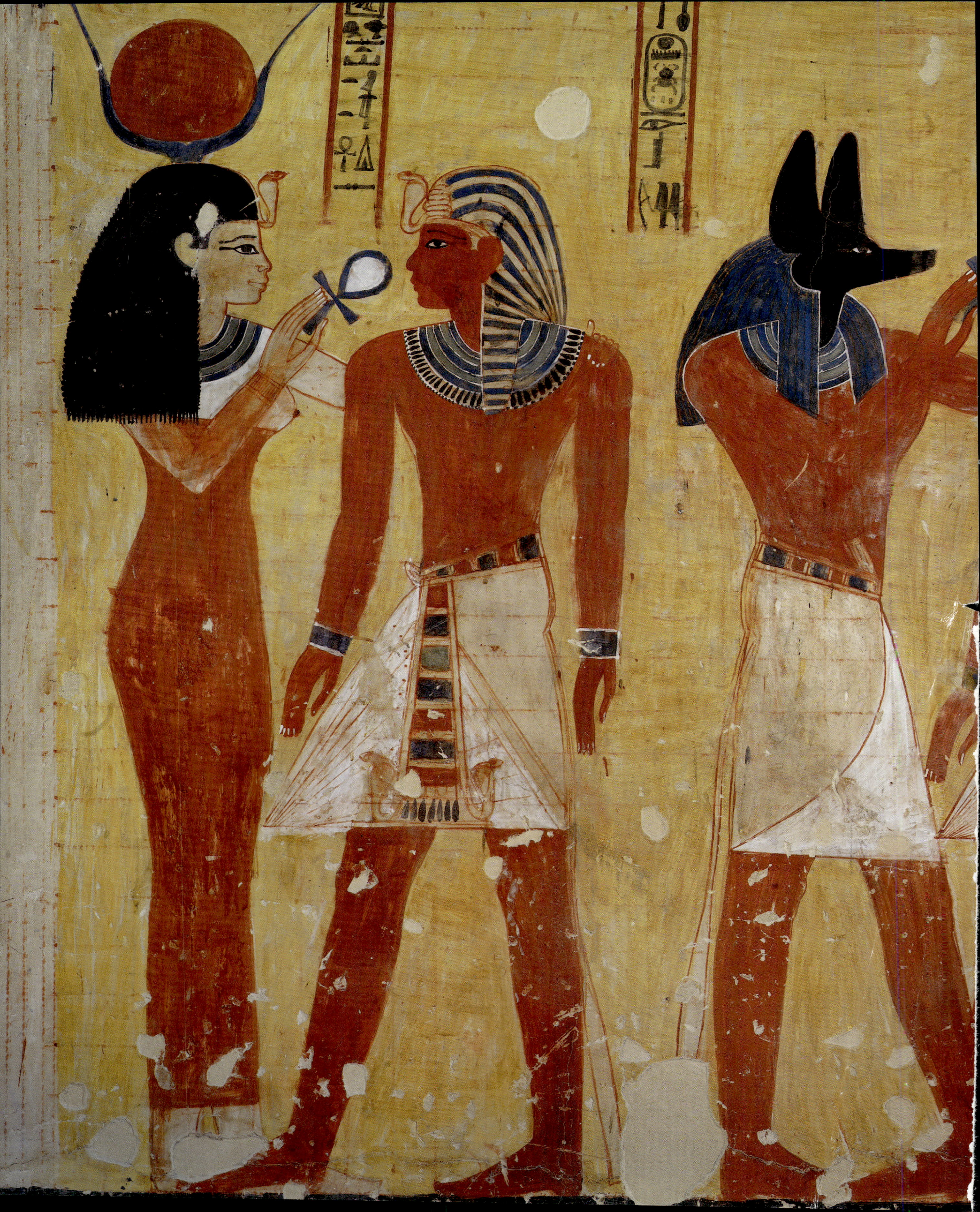

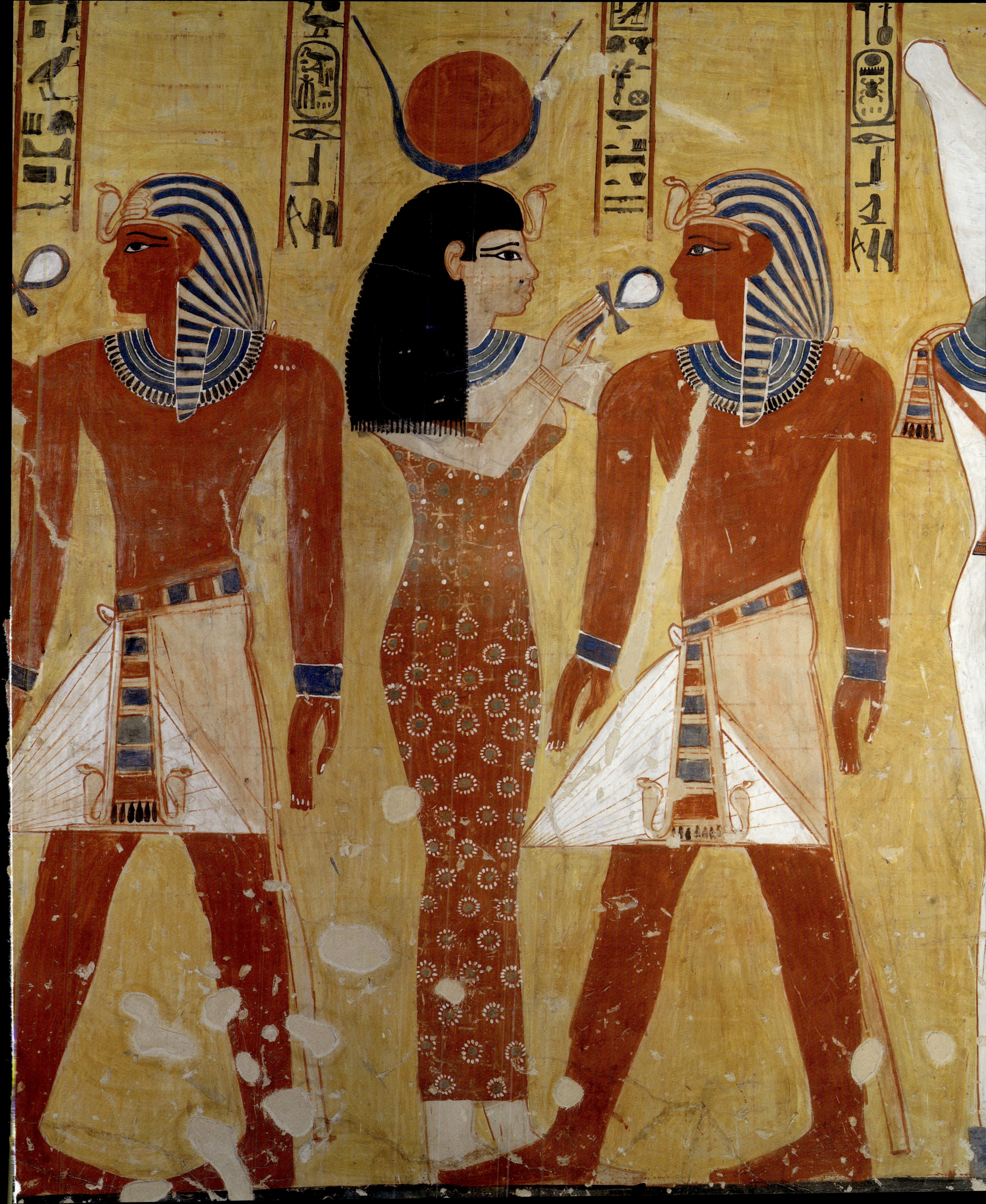

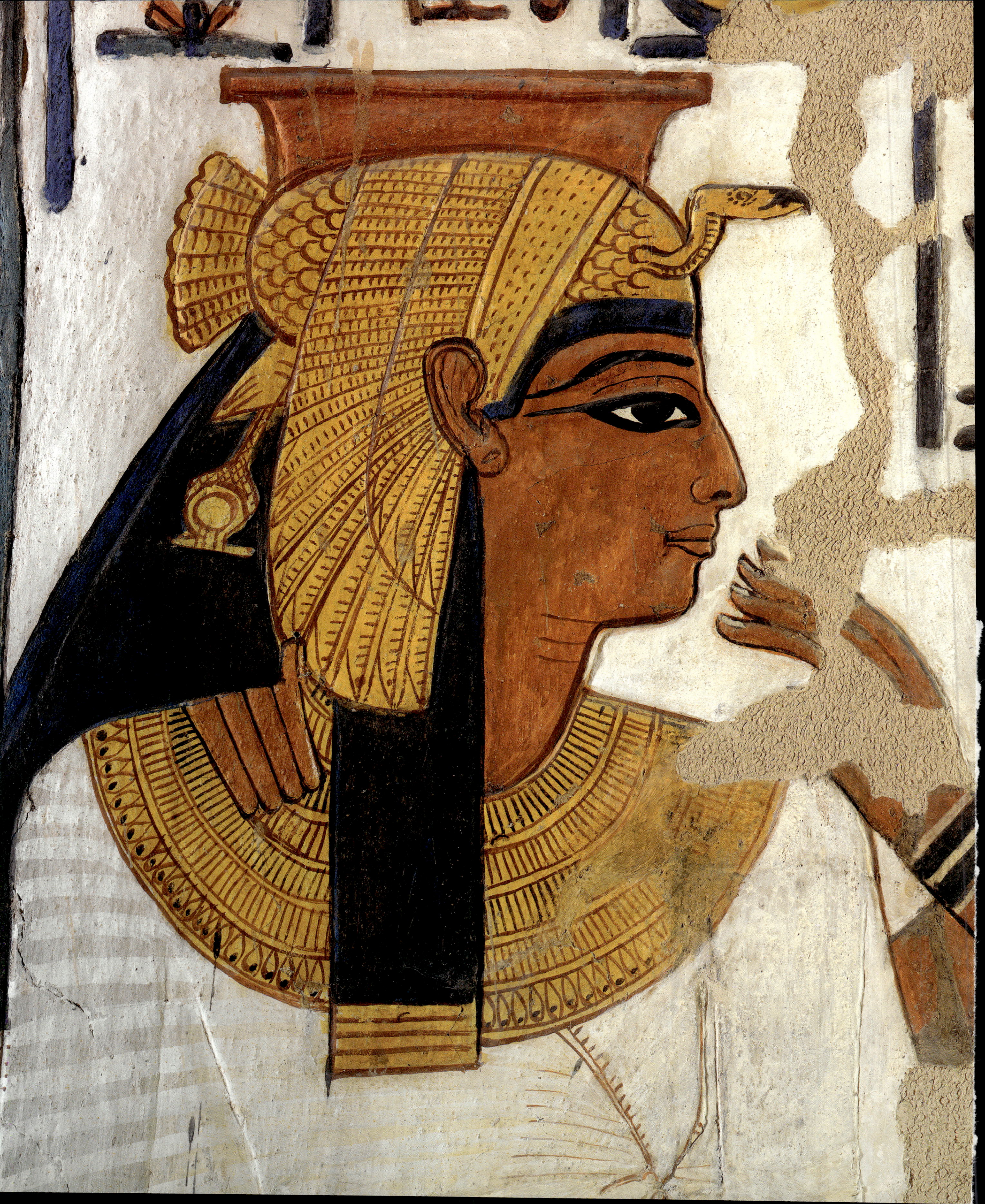

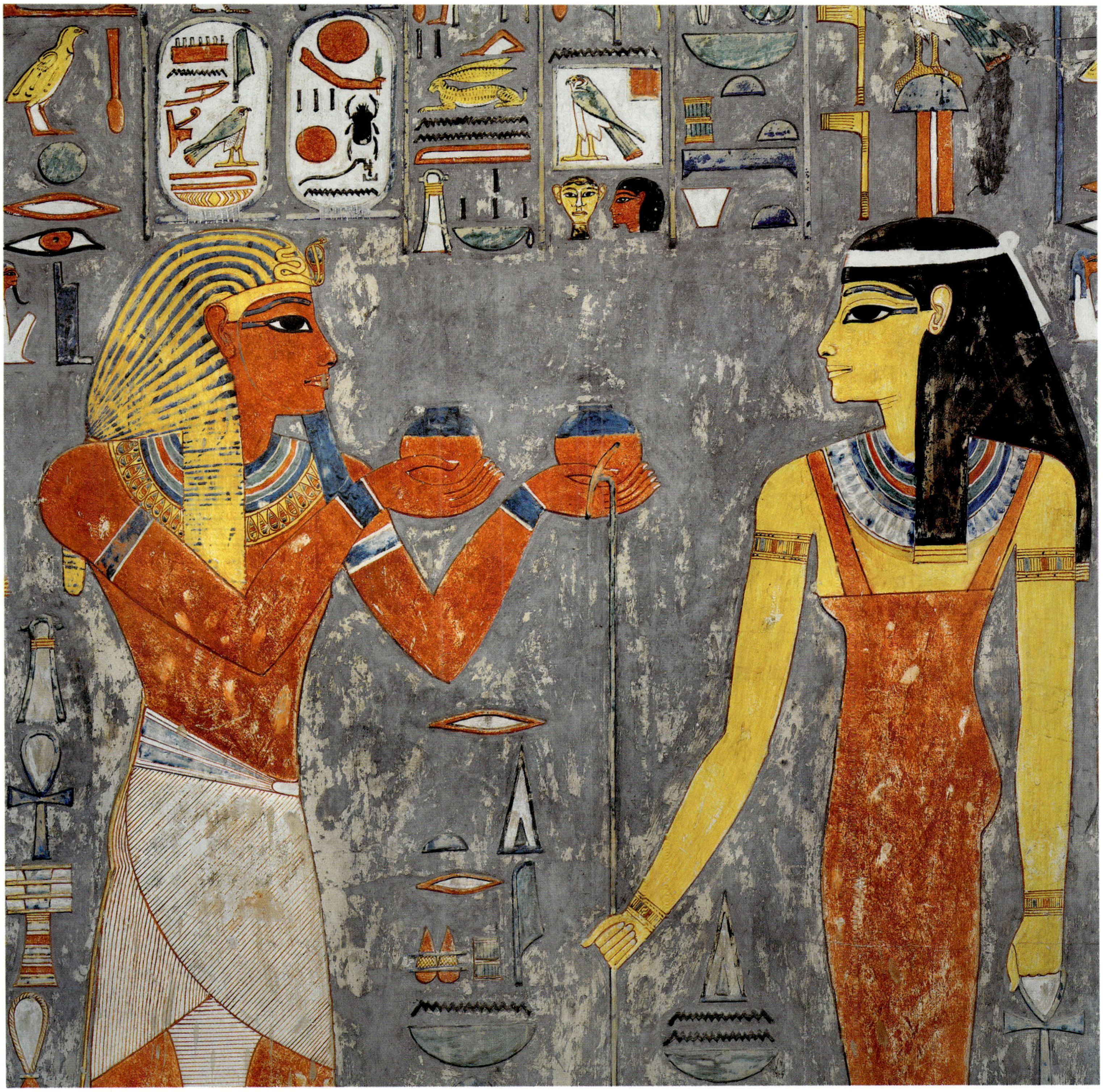

HOREMHEB WITH HATHOR
Horemheb is the first king to be shown as active in the presence of the gods. Here he offers wine to Hathor. Hathor is shown with the symbol for the west, the land of the dead, on her head to identify her in this detail from the tomb of Horemheb.

QUEEN NEFERTARI WITH ANUBIS
(pp. 73–74)
This scene from the tomb of Nefertari shows the jackal-headed Anubis, "who is in the place of embalming," welcoming the queen to the Afterlife.

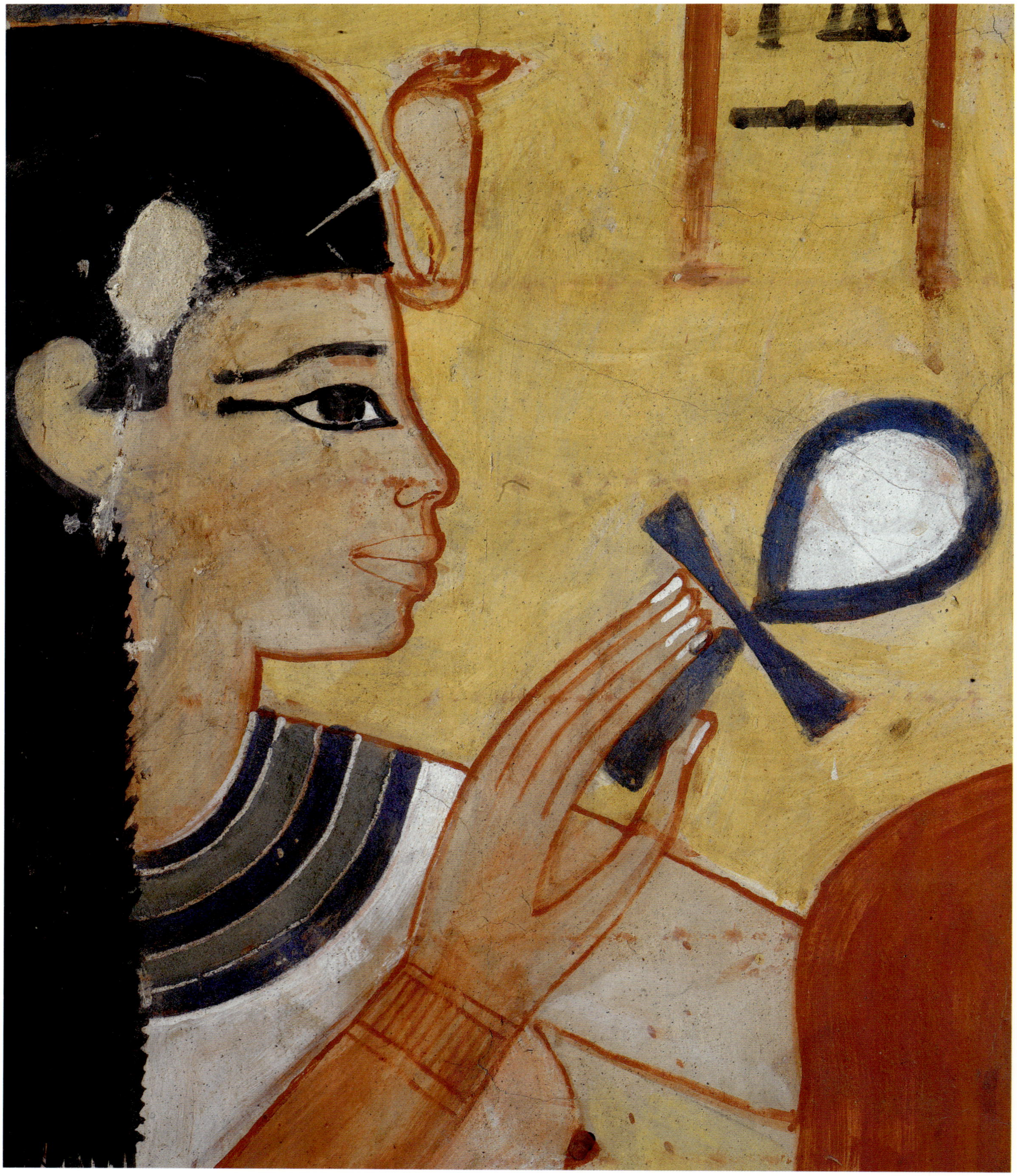

Tuthmosis IV with the Gods

Tuthmosis IV is shown here in a passive stance, receiving eternal life from the major mortuary deities. From left to right are Hathor, Anubis, Hathor, Osiris, and Hathor once again.

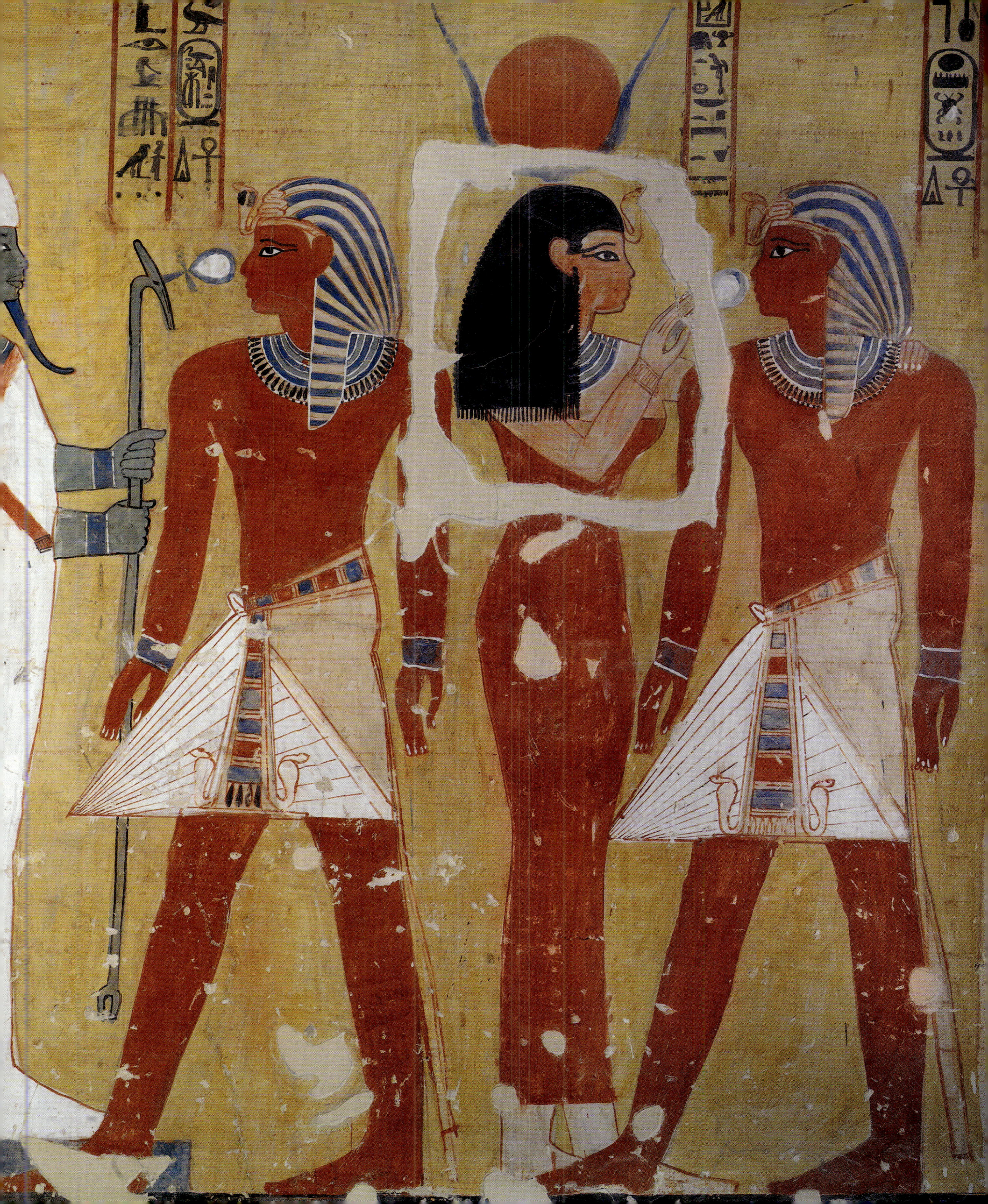

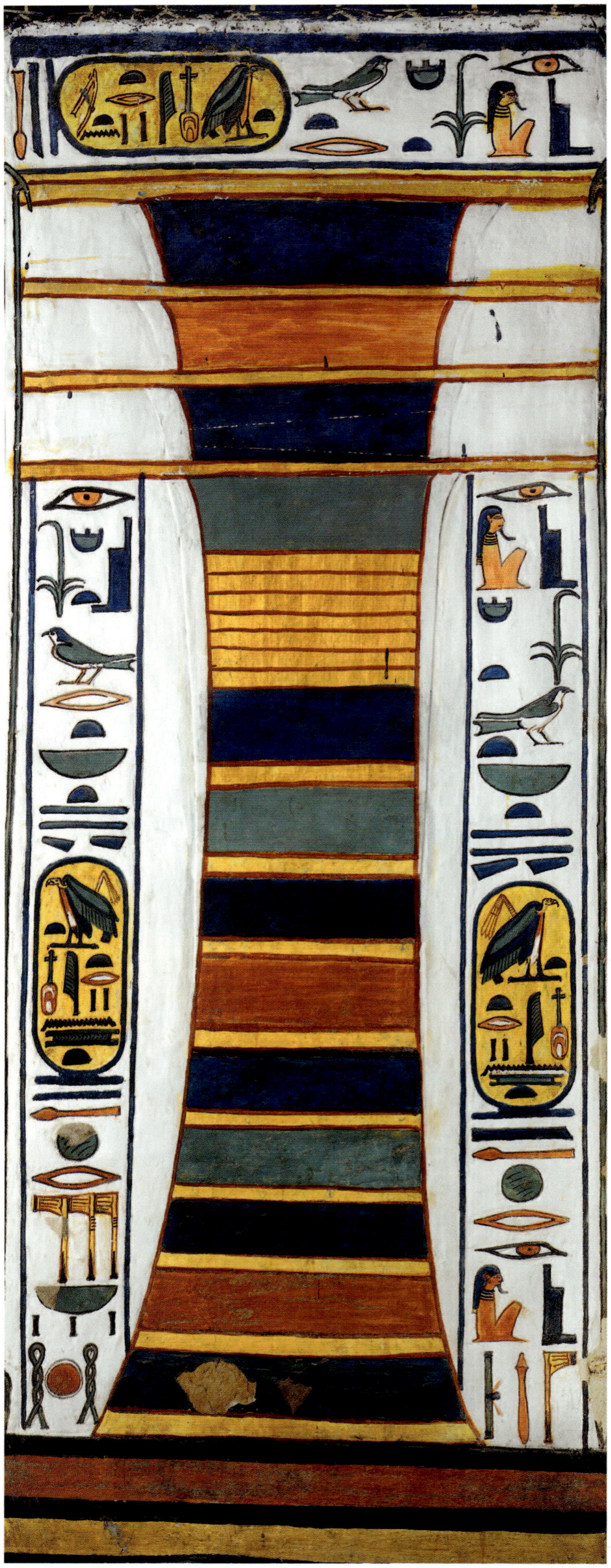

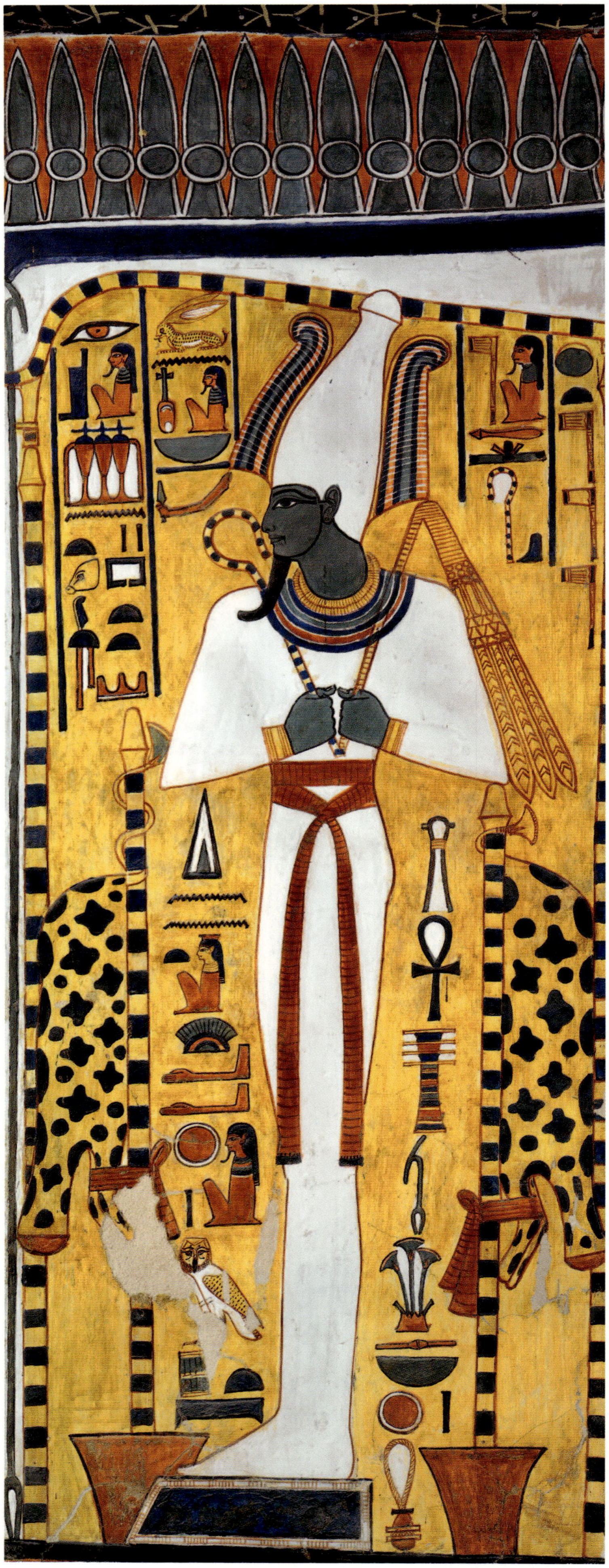

On his head is the white crown of Upper Egypt, often flanked by ostrich plumes and/or surmounted by a solar disk and horns. His skin is usually either black or green, both colors which make reference to fertility.

Known as the Lady of the West and the Mistress of the Western Desert, Hathor is first attested in the Early Dynastic Period, but her worship may date back to prehistoric times. She has many different forms and roles, which shift according to place, time, and context. Her name is written with a falcon, the hieroglyph for the name of Horus, inside a courtyard, a sign for house (here to be interpreted also as womb), thus emphasizing her role as mother of Horus. This name also identifies her as a sky deity, since Horus was a sky god and his realm was the air. She is linked with the night sky, and thus with the Netherworld, as the night sky was viewed as belonging to the territory below the earth.

Hathor is seen in the company of the sun god, Re, as early as the Old Kingdom. She is both his daughter and his wife. She features heavily both in the Pyramid Texts and in the sun cult of the later Old Kingdom. The most common title for elite women of this era was Priestess of Hathor. The queen was closely identified with this goddess.

In one mythic cycle, Hathor is seen as the "Eye" of the sun god. According to this legend, Re was angry with humankind and sent out Hathor (in her guise as both Eye and lioness-goddess Sekhmet) to destroy all the inhabitants of the earth. When he saw what havoc she was wreaking, he repented, and tried to call her back. But she was filled with bloodlust, and could only be stopped by a trick: the gods flooded the fields with beer colored red; believing this to be blood, Hathor drank it and then fell asleep. In another myth, when her father Re was sulking, leaving the earth in darkness and cold, she made him laugh by exposing herself to him. She was considered a goddess of sexuality and thus fertility, and helped to ensure the royal resurrection.

In addition to her anthropomorphic form, Hathor is depicted in the guise of a cow. In both cow and human shape, she can be depicted suckling the king. She is linked with the myth of the Celestial Cow, in which she gives birth to the sun god. As a cow, she is particularly connected with the Theban area, and is shown in tomb art emerging from a papyrus thicket at the foot of the Theban hills, welcoming the dead into the land of the setting sun. Evidence from as early as the Old Kingdom also identifies Hathor as a tree deity, the Mistress of the Sycamore, producing food and drink for the benefit of the deceased and thus guaranteeing eternal life.

Hathor was worshipped in many places throughout Egypt, and also had cult centers outside the country's borders, most prominently in the Sinai and at Byblos. She had a major temple at Dendera, where she was worshipped as the consort of Horus of Edfu. Another important locus for her cult was at Deir el-Bahari, on the West Bank at Thebes.

Anubis preceded Osiris as the chief mortuary god of the ancient Egyptians. Depicted as a hybrid of jackal and dog (or a human with the head of this animal), his early association with the dead may be connected with the canine scavengers who violated the shallow desert tombs of the Egyptians. His coat is usually black, reflecting his connection to both death and decay and to the fertility essential for resurrection.

Old Kingdom offering prayers are very often addressed to Anubis, and he appears regularly in the Pyramid Texts in association with the royal funeral. One of his chief epithets was "he who is in the place of embalming," referring to his role as principal deity of mummification. He was also known as "lord of the sacred land," the desert in which the dead were buried, and as "he who is upon his sacred mountain," an image perhaps of the jackal roaming the desert mountains that shielded the ancient necropolei.

The parentage of Anubis varies from one myth to another. In later times, the cults of Anubis and Osiris were merged, and Anubis became known as the latter god's son. In the Coffin Texts, he is alternatively the son of a cow goddess named Hesat or the feline deity Bastet. He was the principal deity of an area of Middle Egypt whose capital was known as Cynopolis (city of the dogs) by the Greeks, but he was worshipped throughout Egypt. He had his own chapel in the temple of Hatshepsut at Deir el-Bahari.

Djed Pillar

(p. 80)

The *djed* pillar, seen here in the tomb of Nefertari, is thought originally to represent some sort of vegetation. Later, it was identified as the backbone of the great god Osiris. It is a hieroglyph, meaning "stability."

Osiris

(p. 80)

Also from the tomb of Nefertari, Osiris appears here in his mummy wrappings with the white crown of Upper Egypt flanked by plumes on his head. He stands on a dais in the shape of the hieroglyph for *ma'at*, flanked by two Anubis fetishes, animal skins mounted on poles.

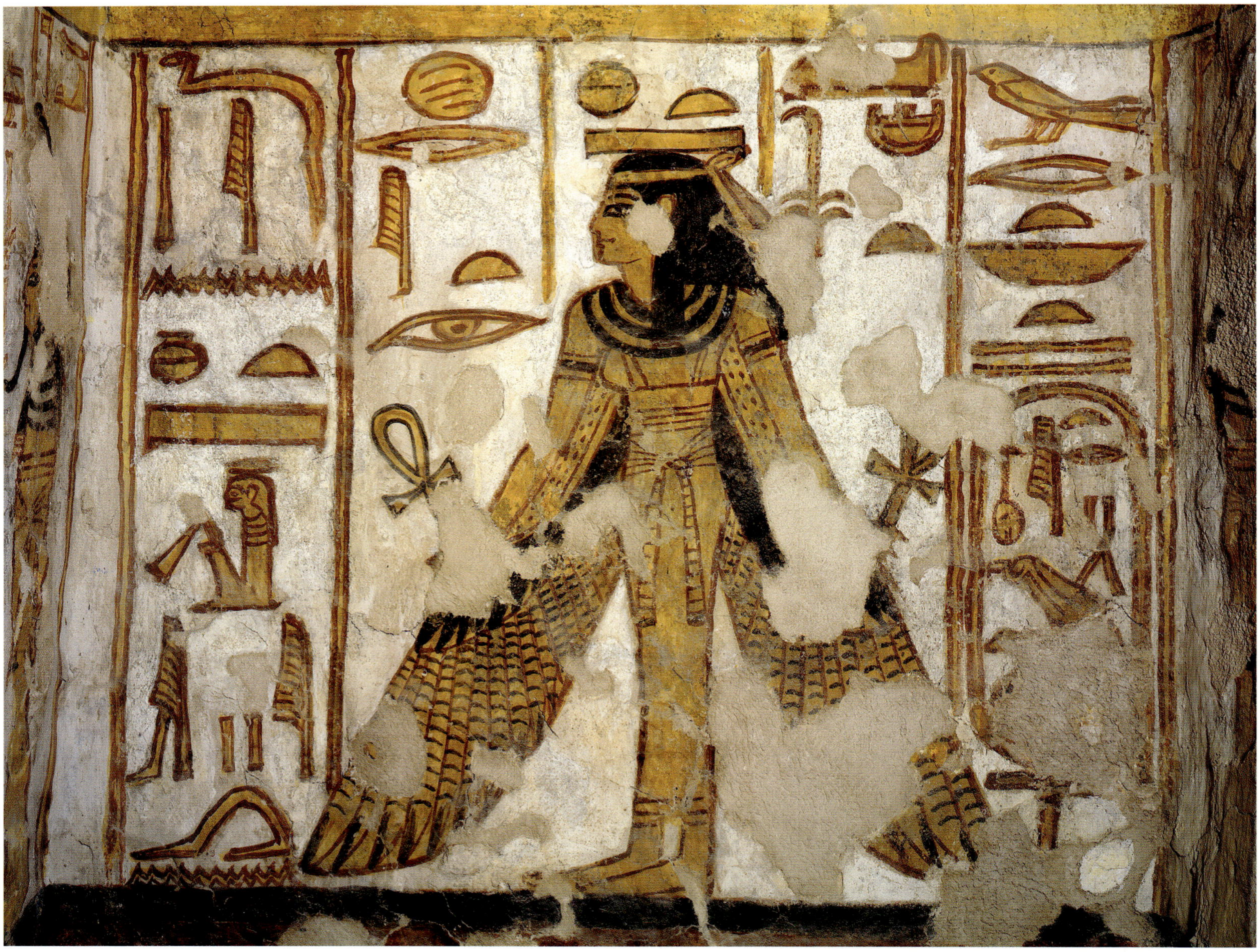

NUT, GODDESS OF THE SKY
The sky goddess, Nut, is frequently shown on the inside lids of coffins, her wings outstretched to protect the deceased. In this image from the tomb of Nefertari, queen of Ramses II, Nut says: "May you come before my father, the Osiris, great royal wife, Mistress of the Two Lands, Nefertari."

NUT

The tomb of Amenhotep III introduces the sky goddess Nut into the repertoire of scenes, dominating one side of the well shaft while Nut heads the divinities on the other. Both goddesses embrace the king and welcome him to the rejuvenating Netherworld.

Nut was the principal goddess of the sky, the personification of the celestial vault. She was the daughter of the second generation of the gods: the creator god, Atum-Re, bore a daughter, Tefnut (moisture) and a son, Shu (air); Nut and her brother Geb, the god of the earth, were the offspring of this pair. Nut and Geb coupled and gave birth to Osiris, Isis, Nephthys, and Seth.

Nut was the goddess most closely associated with resurrection and rebirth. In a myth that reaches its fullest form in the Books of the Heavens, she was imagined to swallow the sun disk each evening and give birth to it again each morning. Some Egyptologists believe that Nut was an incarnation of the Milky Way, mentioned in Spell 176 of the Book of the Dead. She is most often depicted in the form of a woman with her arms and legs outstretched, and one scholar has pointed out that the sky before dawn at the winter solstice during the Predynastic era would have taken this form. Like Hathor,

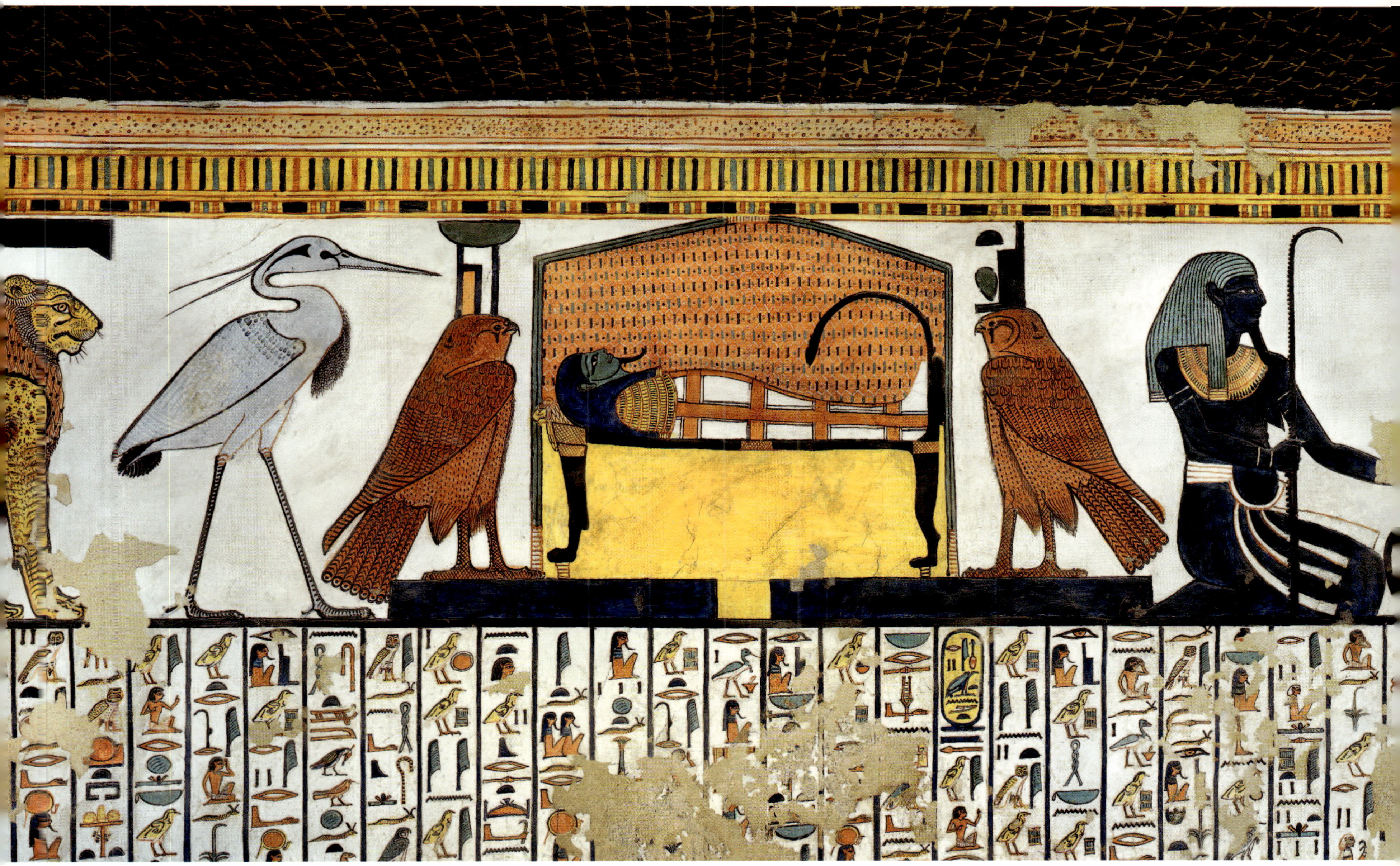

Osiris Mummified
Nepthys (*left*) and Isis (*right*) are shown here, in the tomb of Nefertari, in the form of kites (a type of bird of prey) flanking a shrine containing the lion-headed funerary bed couch on which lies the mummified Osiris.

Nut can be identified with the Celestial Cow. She is often depicted on the inner lid of coffins and sarcophagi, representing the sky and guaranteeing the resurrection of the dead, who will pass through her body to be reborn.

Isis

The decoration of the tomb of Tutankhamun is anomalous, as only the burial chamber is painted, and this mainly with scenes connected with the funeral. On one wall, Nut and Osiris welcome the king; on the opposite wall, the deities who escort Tutankhamun into the Afterlife are Anubis and Isis.

Isis appears again in the tomb of Horemheb, along with her son Horus (in his guise as Harsiese, the Greek form of *Hor sa Iset*, or Horus son of Isis). These two gods join Osiris, Anubis, and Hathor on the walls of the well shaft. Here, for the first time the king is active, offering wine to several of these deities.

Depicted either with a throne (a shorthand version of her name in hieroglyphs) on her head or, like Hathor, in a long wig surmounted by a horned sun disk, Isis is given some of the same epithets as Hathor, such as Lady of Heaven and Mistress of Western Thebes. It is often difficult to distinguish these two goddesses without an associated hieroglyphic text containing their names.

Isis does not appear in the historical record before the 5th Dynasty, and no birth or burial site for her was identified in Egypt's cultic landscape. However, it is apparent that she was extremely important from early on, as she is named over eighty times in the Pyramid Texts, and in later times became one of the most valued and beloved of the Egyptian gods, syncretized with many other female deities.

In her principal guise, Isis was the sister and wife of Osiris, and the mother of Horus. During her child's minority, she hid with him in the papyrus thickets of the Delta, protecting and healing him when he was injured. Through the association of the living king with Horus, Isis became seen as mother and protector of the monarch. As her name is written with the image of a throne, it has been suggested that she personifies the royal power inherent in the position of king. One of Isis's principal attributes was her ability to do magic.

Along with her sister Nephthys, Isis was responsible for collecting the scattered pieces of her murdered husband's body and reconstituting them so that he could receive proper burial. Thus, she is seen often with Nephthys flanking Osiris's bier or standing behind his throne. Near the entrances to Ramesside tombs, these two goddesses are shown flanking the sun god in the form of a disk, in part an allusion to the union of Osiris with the sun god.

Horus, Ptah, and Ma'at

Another god depicted for the first time in the tomb of Horemheb was Harsiese, the son of Isis and Osiris. This Horus is one aspect of the falcon-headed sky god, the principal deity associated with kingship. Originally a sky and sun god, his name means "the distant one" or "the one on high." His right eye was the sun and his left the moon; his wings were the sky and the spots on his feathers the stars. One of the earliest cult sites in Egypt, Hierakonpolis, was sacred to this god.

At some point, Harsiese was merged with the sky god Horus. He is represented either as a child or as a falcon-headed man. Harsiese often wears the double crown, symbolizing his role as ruler of a united Egypt. In the decoration of the royal tombs, he is often shown guiding the pharaoh to meet his mother or father in the Netherworld.

Horus had four sons, who appear first in the Pyramid Texts helping the deceased king ascend to the sky. By the New Kingdom, their principal role was to protect the viscera of the deceased. They do not appear often in the decoration of the royal tombs, but are seen in the tomb of Aye, which dates to the late 18th Dynasty.

Ptah, patron of craftsmen and tutelary god of Memphis, appears in the tomb of Horemheb along with his son Nefertem. Due most likely to his association with creativity and the production of objects such as statues and reliefs, Ptah became an important creator god, provided with an entire mythology in which he was said to have brought the world into being through thought and word. Not originally a mortuary god, Ptah took on aspects of Tatanen, an earth god worshipped at Memphis, and Sokar, a funerary deity also from the Memphite region. As Ptah-Sokar or Ptah-Sokar-Osiris, he aids in ruling the realm of the dead. He is also essential to the ritual of the Opening of the Mouth, performed at the funeral to prepare the mummy or statue of the deceased to function in the Afterlife.

It is significant that Ptah is represented wrapped in mummy bandages, from which only his head and hands emerge. He wears a close-fitting skull cap on his head, and holds a *was* scepter, symbol of dominion, a *djed* pillar, meaning stability or eternity, and an *ankh*, sign for life.

Nefertem, son of Ptah and his consort Sekhmet, is represented as a child or as a man with a lotus blossom on his head. The lotus, especially the blue lotus, was an important symbol of resurrection and rejuvenation, as its blossoms close to dusk and open again with the sunrise. In creation mythology, the lotus blossom was said to have risen from the primeval waters and given forth the sun god. Thus Nefertem is seen as an incarnation of the sun god at dawn. Perhaps due to the natural fragrance of this flower, Nefertem was also known as the god of salves and pleasant fragrances.

Another important goddess who appears first in the tomb of Horemheb is Ma'at, who greets the king on either side of the passage into the burial chamber. Depicted as a woman with an ostrich plume (one hieroglyph for her name) on her head, Ma'at represented the proper order of the universe. She is attested in the Old Kingdom, especially in the Pyramid Texts, where she is said to stand behind Re. By the New Kingdom, she had become the daughter of Re and thus the sister of the reigning king (who is the son of Re). She is also associated with Osiris and Ptah (who is often shown standing on a plinth that is another form of her name), and is identified as the wife of Thoth, god of scribes. One of the principal roles of the king was to maintain *ma'at*, to rule justly and wisely and keep balance in the cosmos; Ma'at was the personification of this concept.

Khepri, Atum, Neith, and the Souls of Pe and Nekhen

The tomb of Ramses I, although hastily cut and containing limited decoration, continues to expand the repertoire of scenes involving the king and various gods. On the entrance wall are representations of the king with Ma'at, Ptah, and Nefertem. An adjacent scene shows the king embraced by Harsiese and Anubis.

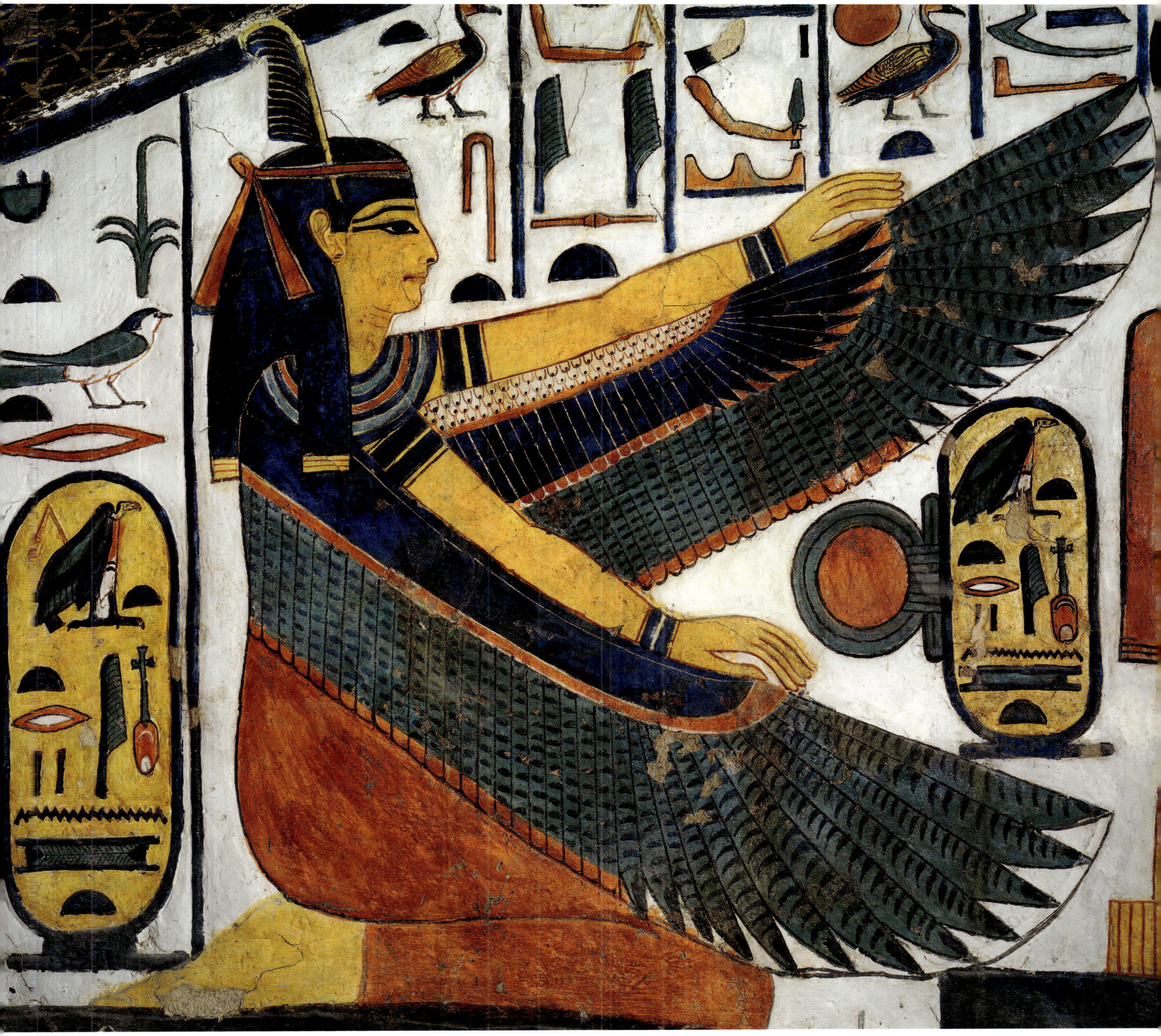

The Goddess Ma'at
Ma'at, goddess of the properly balanced and ordered Egyptian cosmos, is shown in this image from the tomb of Nefertari. Her wings serve to protect the name of the queen.

The back wall is dominated by Osiris and the scarab god Khepri, seated back to back on thrones. Khepri is an image of the sun god specifically associated with the dawn; thus, this is an icon of the union of Osiris with a form of Re. Two new gods appear here, helping Harsiese lead Ramses I to greet Osiris. One of these is Atum, an ancient god identified as the creator in the theology of Heliopolis. Shown as a man with the curled beard of divinity, he is often seen wearing the double crown of a united Egypt. The other is Neith, a very important prehistoric goddess, identified primarily as a warrior deity. Her name is written with crossed arrows and bows, and some of her epithets were Mistress of the Bow and Ruler of Arrows. Like Hathor, she could appear as the vengeful Eye of Re. She was also linked with the primeval waters of Nun, and could be associated with Mehetweret, a bovine creator deity connected with the flood. Neith was also a mother goddess, and had a role in mortuary religion as early as the Old Kingdom: in the Pyramid Texts, she joins Isis, Nephthys, and the scorpion goddess Serket to guard Osiris.

In the tomb of Ramses I, the king is depicted also with the souls of Pe and Nekhen, all in poses of jubilation. These semi-divine beings—the jackal-headed souls of Pe and the hawk-headed souls of Nekhen—represent the Predynastic rulers of Upper and Lower Egypt, and are thus symbolic ancestors of the New Kingdom monarchs. Their role was to serve both living and deceased kings, and to celebrate the daily rising of the sun and thus the resurrection of the dead.

Re-Horakhty, Shu, Geb, and Thoth

The tomb of Seti I has a greatly expanded repertoire of scenes, which include a number of new gods. The reciprocal relation between king and god becomes more evident here, for example in a scene that shows the king offering incense and libations to Osiris. In the first entrance passage, the icon of the king making offerings to Re-Horakhty appears for the first time; this is included in royal tombs for the remainder of the New Kingdom. Re-Horakhty, an amalgam of the sun gods Re and Horus of the Two Horizons, represents the morning sun. This was only one of the many forms in which Re appears in the royal tombs, as he, along with Osiris, was essential to the king's resurrection.

The first pillared hall had fourteen columns, providing surfaces on which representations of many gods could be carved and painted. Hathor, Isis, Nephthys, Serket, Ma'at, and Neith are present, along with Atum, Ptah-Sokar-Osiris, Nefertem, Khepri, and Re-Horakhty. Shu, son of Atum and god of the air, is seen here for the first time, as is his son Geb. Shu was the son of the creator god Atum, married to his sister Tefnut. Together they had Geb, the earth, and Nut, the sky. Father, son, and daughter are often depicted together in Egyptian art, with Shu standing between Geb and Nut, separating them. One myth has husband and wife coming together only during the five epagomenal days that rounded out the year, during which time they conceived Osiris and his brother and sisters.

Shu is depicted either as a lion or as a man with a feather, the hieroglyph for his name, on his head. He appears in both the Pyramid and Coffin Texts, but otherwise he is not attested often before the New Kingdom. The principal cult center for both Shu and his consort Tefnut was Leontopolis (modern Tell el-Muqdam). Geb is mentioned frequently in the Pyramid Texts, often associated with Re, or used to represent the tomb in which the king will be buried. As the father of Osiris, primeval king of Egypt, he was also linked to the monarchy. Usually represented as a man, his sacred animal was the goose (the hieroglyph for his name); in the tomb of Ramses VI, he is shown with a hare's head. His skin is usually green, symbolizing his close links to fertility; his body can be adorned with plants. In images showing him lying down with Nut arched above him, his phallus is usually erect.

The ibis-headed Thoth, god of scribes and wisdom, is depicted for the first time in the tomb of Seti I. His function was often one of conciliation or healing, and he could intervene in quarrels between the gods. Originally a moon deity, he was shown most often as an ibis or ibis-headed man, but could also be depicted as a baboon. He was already important in Predynastic times, and appears often in the Pyramid Texts, where he accompanies or assists Re in his journey across the sky. His parentage is uncertain, as he is called the son of Re, Horus, or even Seth.

Thoth's importance in the New Kingdom is reflected in the name Tuthmosis ("born of Thoth"), which is carried by four of the pharaohs of the 18th Dynasty. The main temple of Thoth was in Middle Egypt, at Hermopolis. Catacombs and pits filled with mummified ibises from the later periods of Egyptian history, found at various sites around Egypt, attest to the high regard in which this god continued to be held.

Anubis, unusually, appears with a ram's head, as he did previously in the tomb of Ramses I. The ram was originally associated with Amun, and was later subsumed into the New Kingdom cult of the syncretized sun god Amun-Re.

Re-Horakhty
One incarnation of the morning sun is Re-Horakhty, a syncretization of the ancient Heliopolitan sun god Re and Horus of the Two Horizons, one of several Horuses that formed part of the Egyptian pantheon.

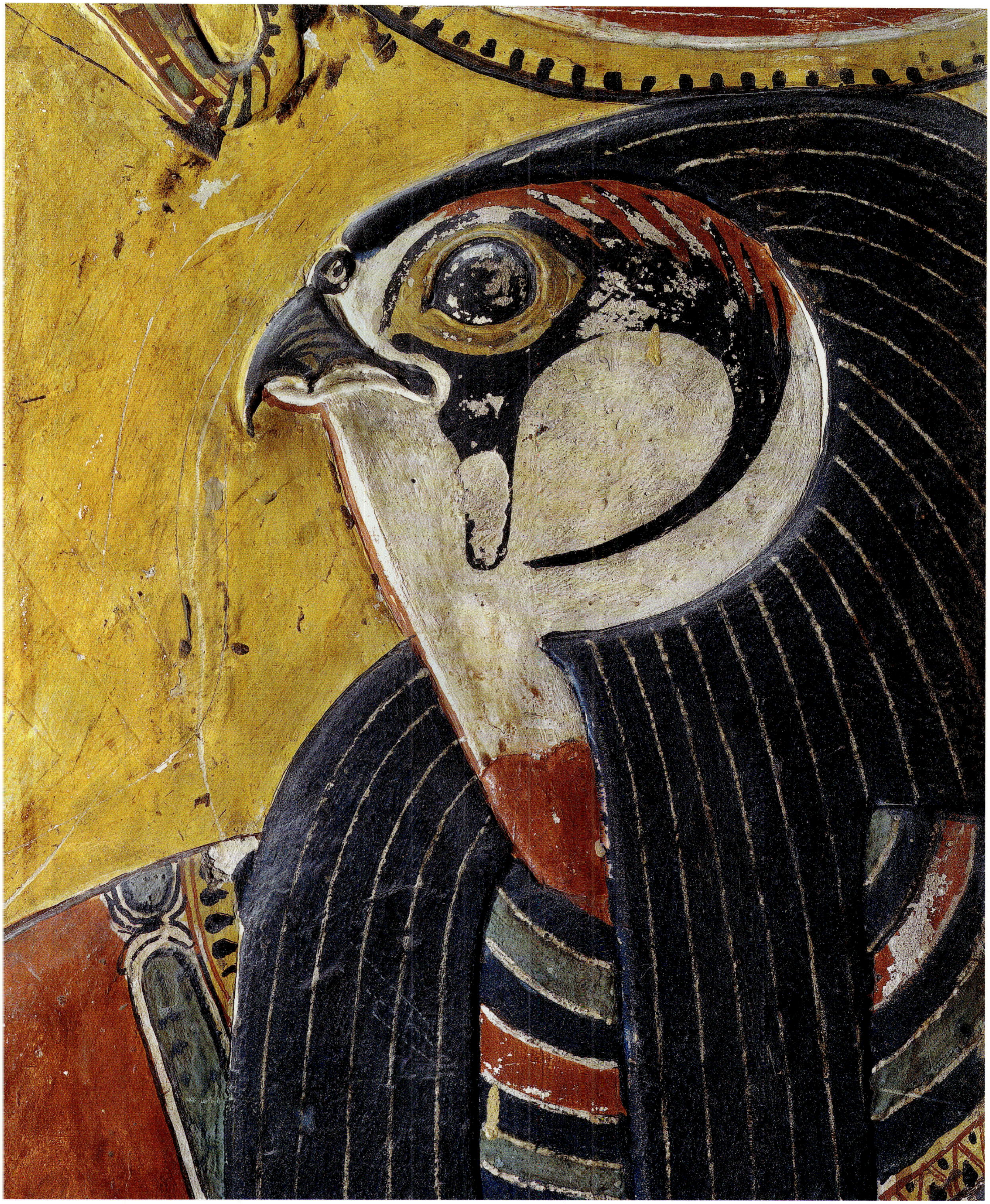

Local and Household Gods

The repertoire of gods shown with the king remains fairly constant throughout the remainder of the 19th Dynasty. It is in the tomb of Ramses III, second king of the 20th Dynasty, that new gods are introduced. In the decoration of the royal tombs from this point forward, the major gods are depicted less often, while less important gods become more prominent. For example, an obscure god named Shepsy, a provincial god from Hermopolis, joins Ptah, Re-Horakhty, Khepri, Atum, Thoth, Nefertem, and Geb on the pillars of one chamber. Meret, a goddess of music linked with the cosmic order, also appears, as does Horus-Khentekhtai from the Delta site of Athribis. The desert gods Sopdu and Onouris are represented here. In the antechamber, Bes, a household god shown in the form of a grotesque dwarf with a lion's tail, is depicted.

Beginning with the tomb of Rameses V/VI, the iconic scene in the entrance passage of the king before Re-Horakhty is joined by another image of the king, this one with Osiris. A new goddess who appears in this tomb is Meretseger, "she who loves silence," the patron deity of el-Qurn, the peak that looms over the Valley of the Kings. Meretseger is generally represented as a hooded cobra, sometimes with a woman's head. She can also be shown, although less frequently, as a snake-headed woman or as a scorpion with a female head.

Many other gods, goddesses, demons, and spirits are also included in the decoration of the royal tombs at Thebes. These, along with many of the gods discussed above, are integrated into scenes related to the various Netherworld and Sky books, or take part in vignettes associated with the Book of the Dead. We shall meet many of these fascinating creatures as we accompany the pharaoh on his journey to the beyond.

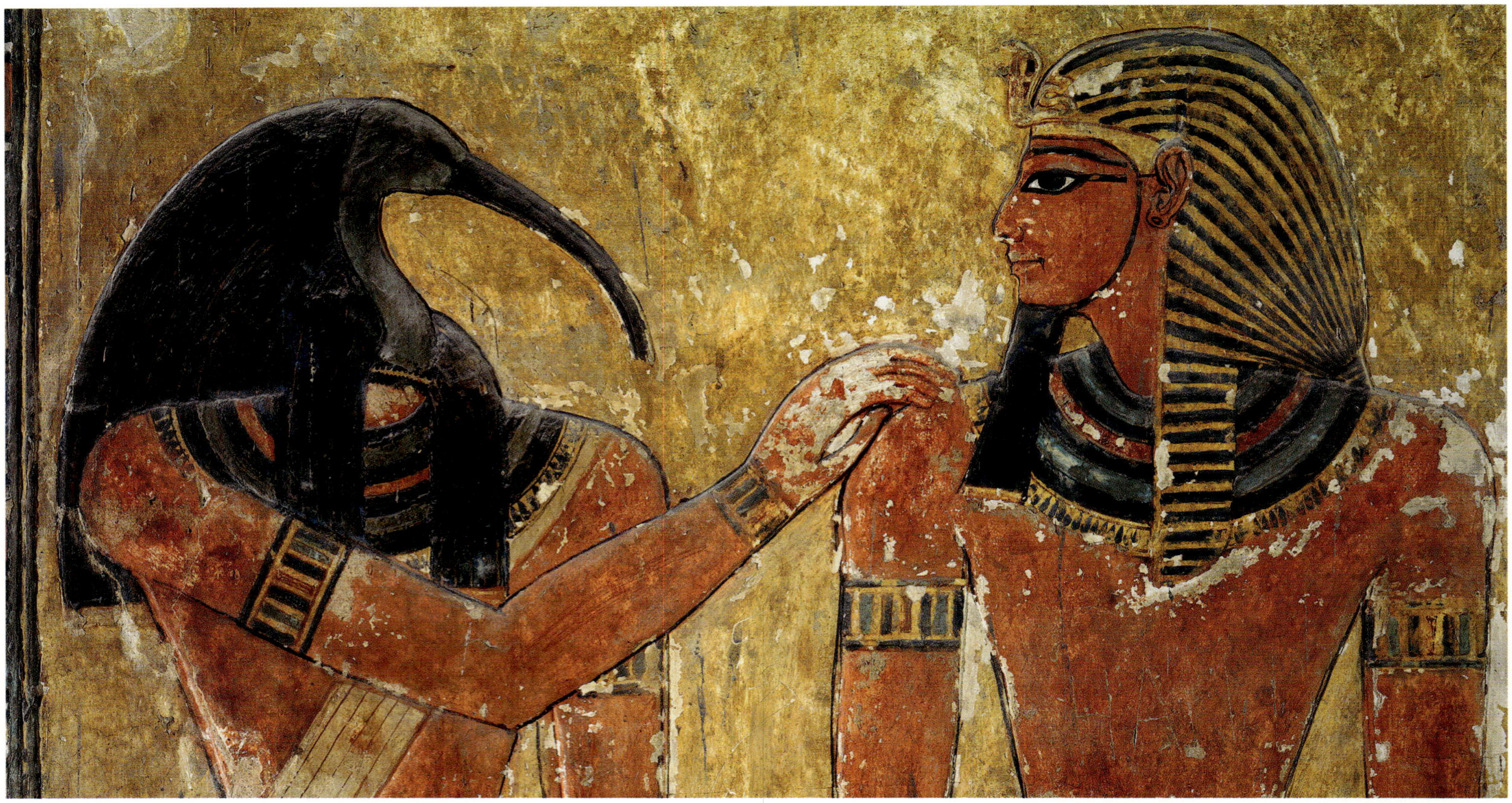

Thoth and Seti I

Thoth, patron of scribes and god of wisdom, makes an appearance here in the tomb of Seti I. Shown with the head of an ibis, one of his animals, Thoth embraces the king and welcomes him to the realm of the blessed.

Horemheb and the Gods

(Following pages)

This image from the well shaft of Horemheb's tomb in the Valley of the Kings shows the king with Osiris, Hathor, and, accompanied by Harsiese, with Isis.

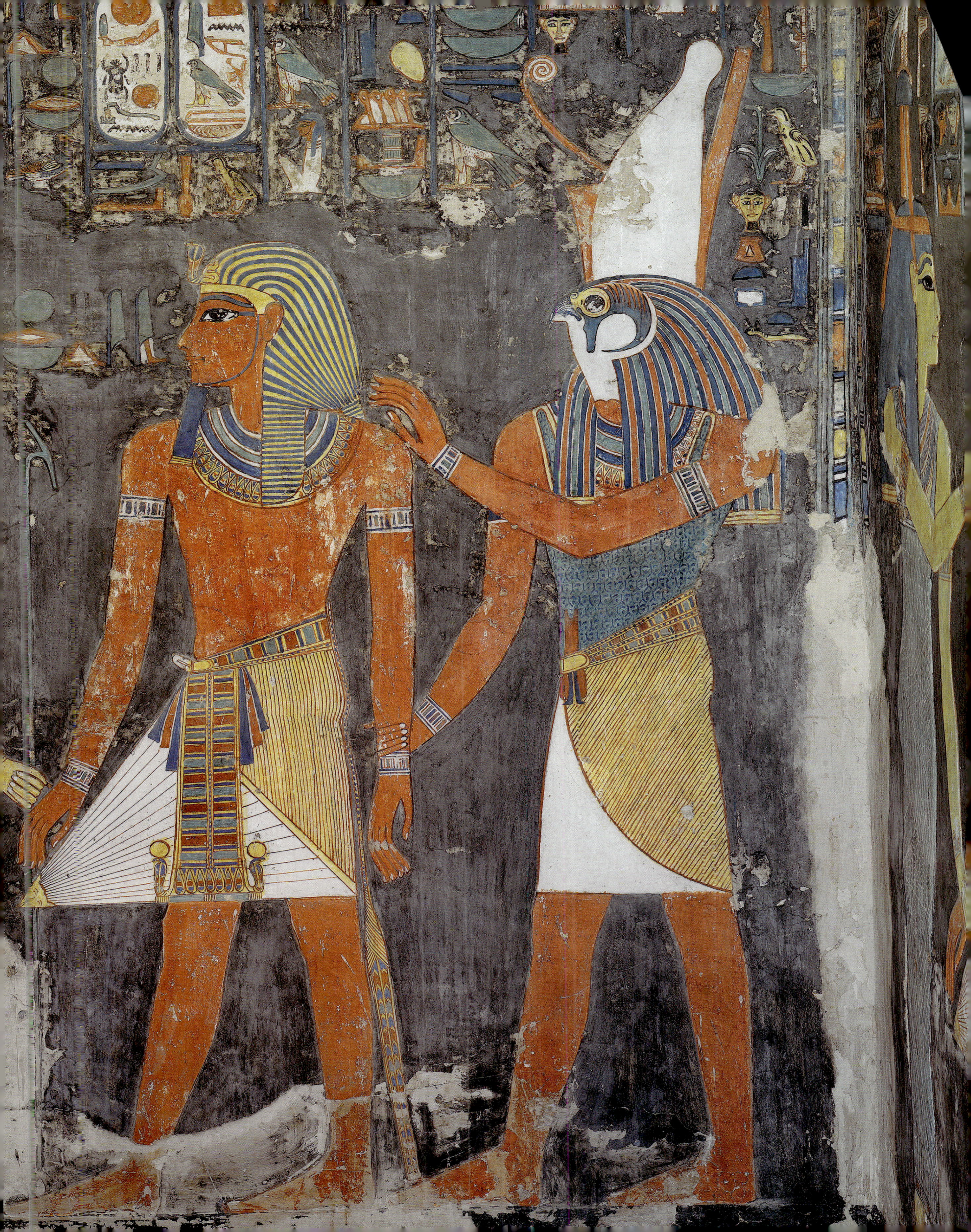

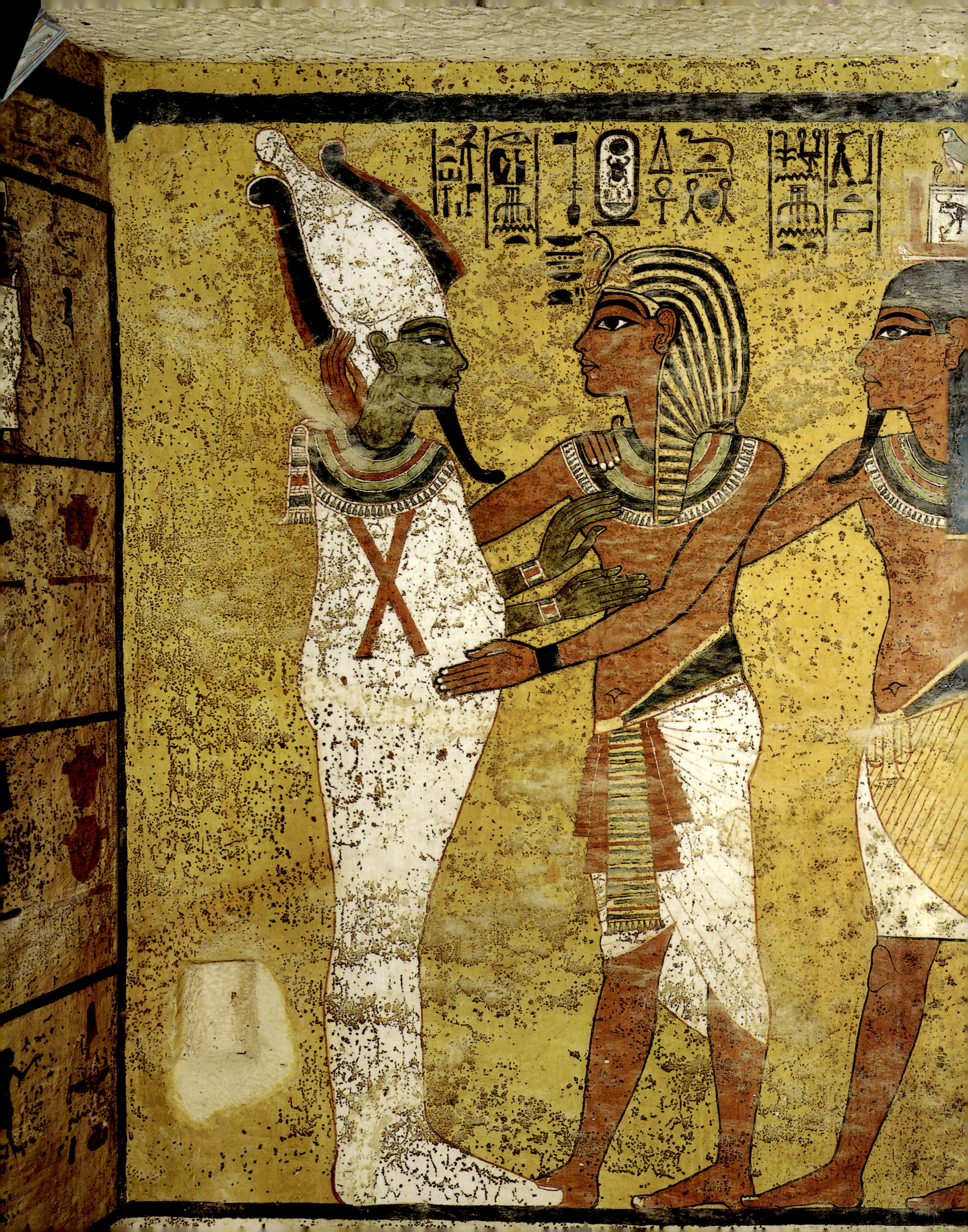

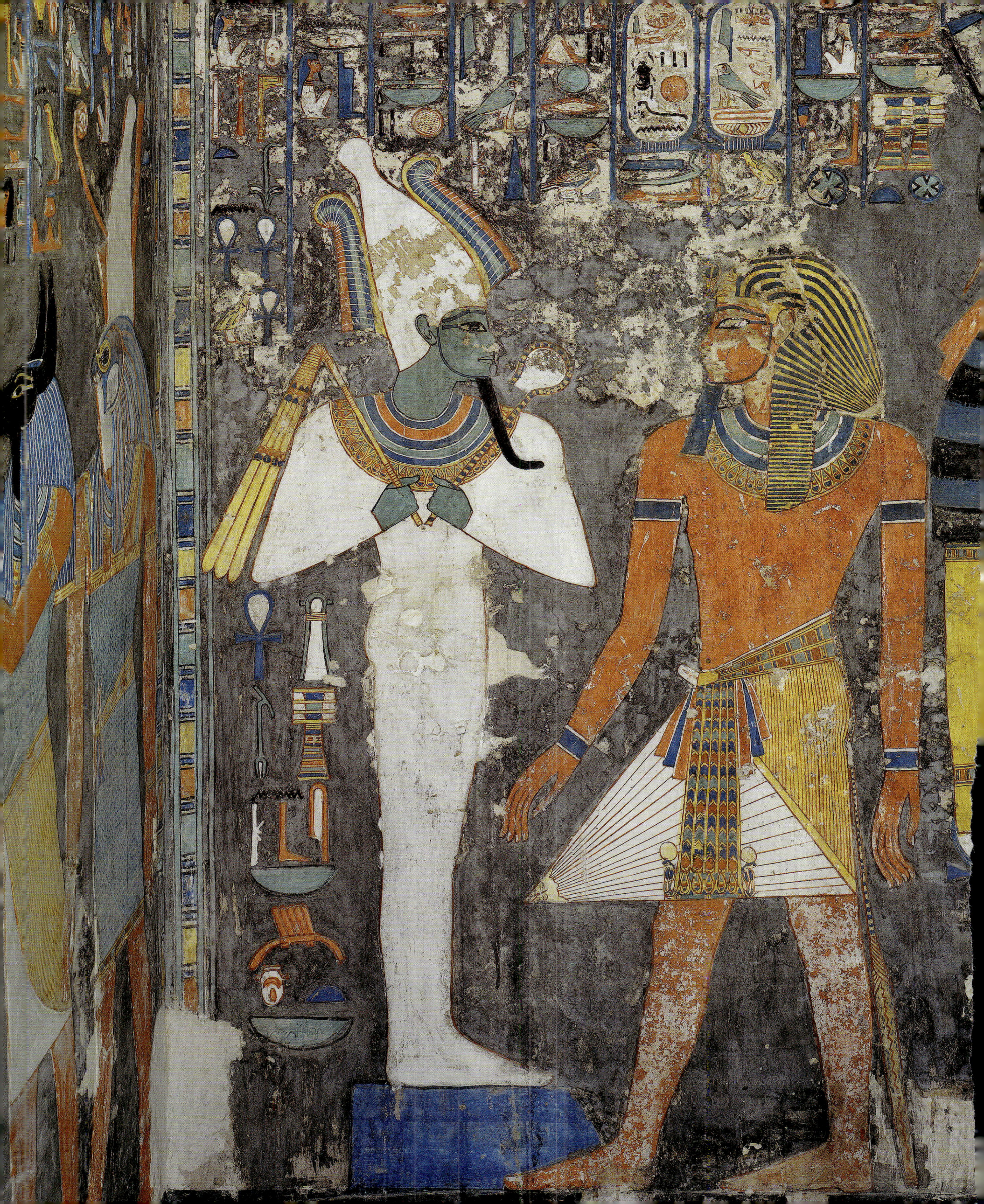

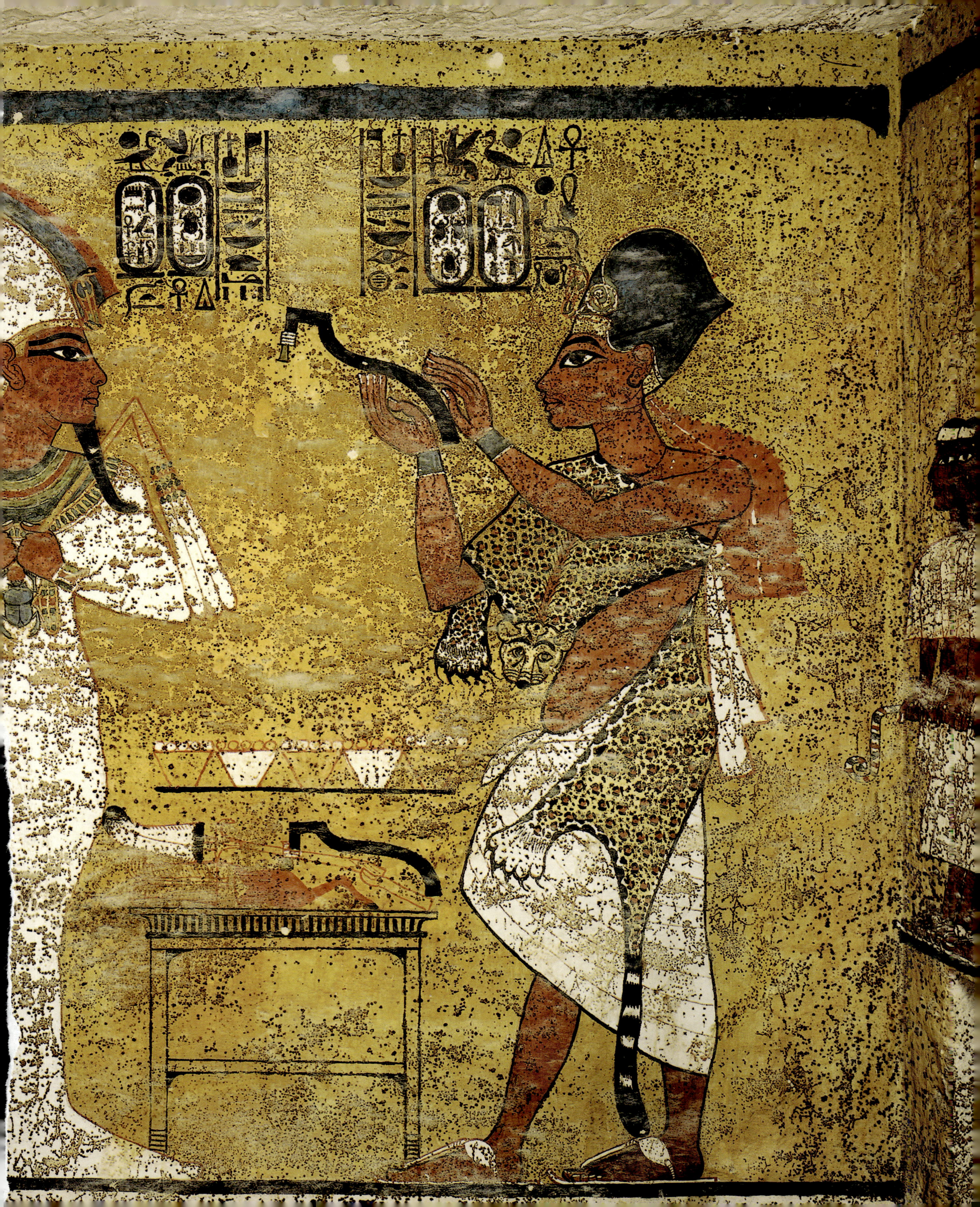

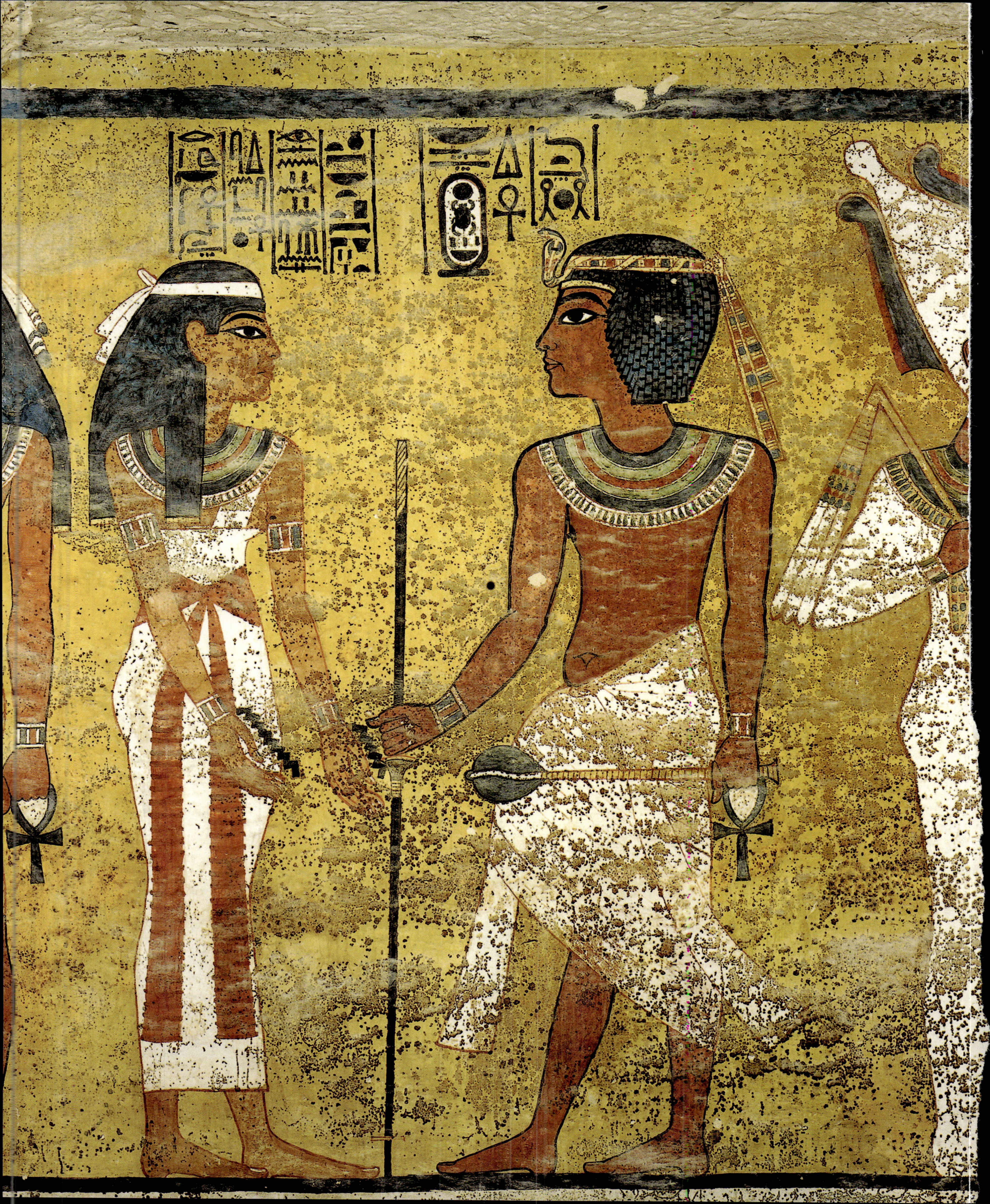

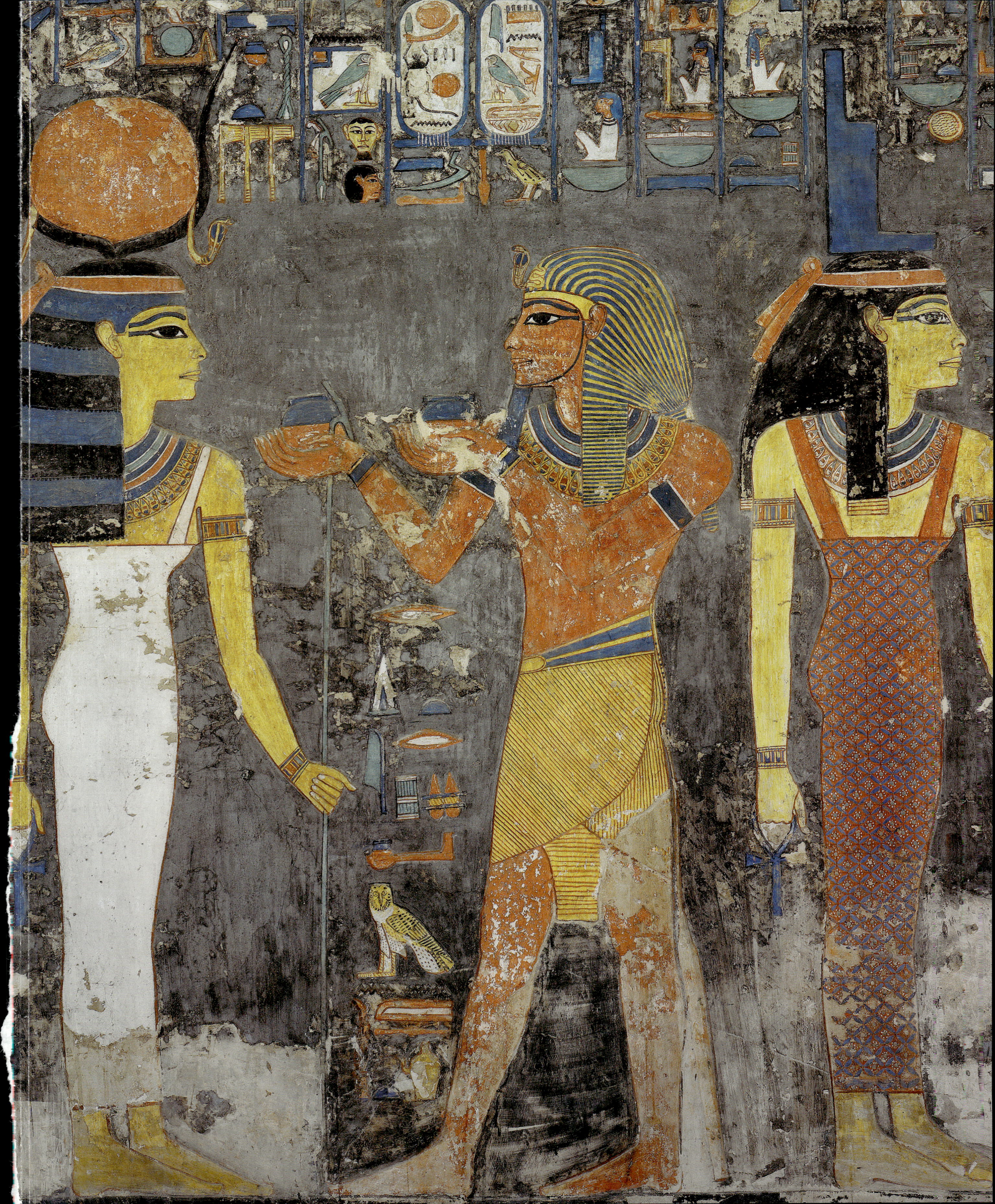

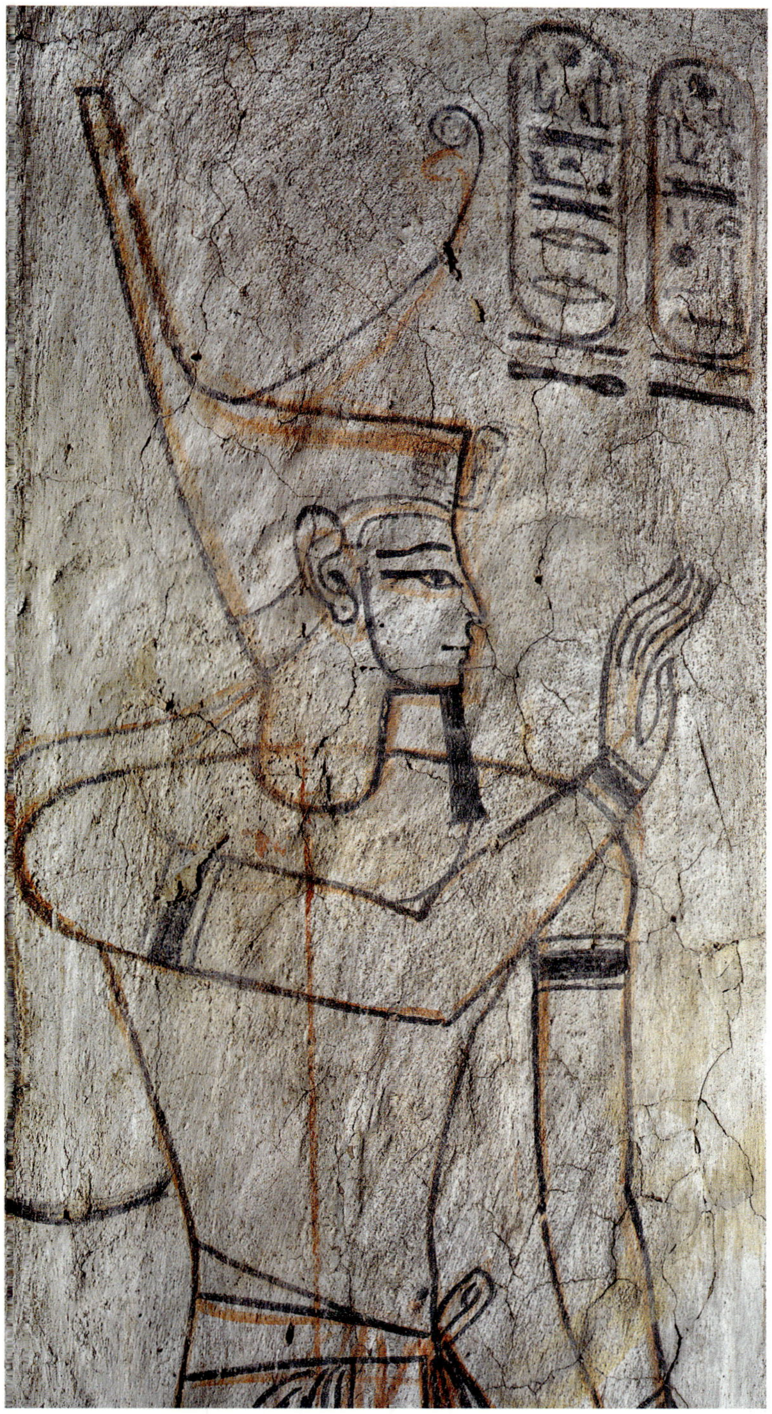

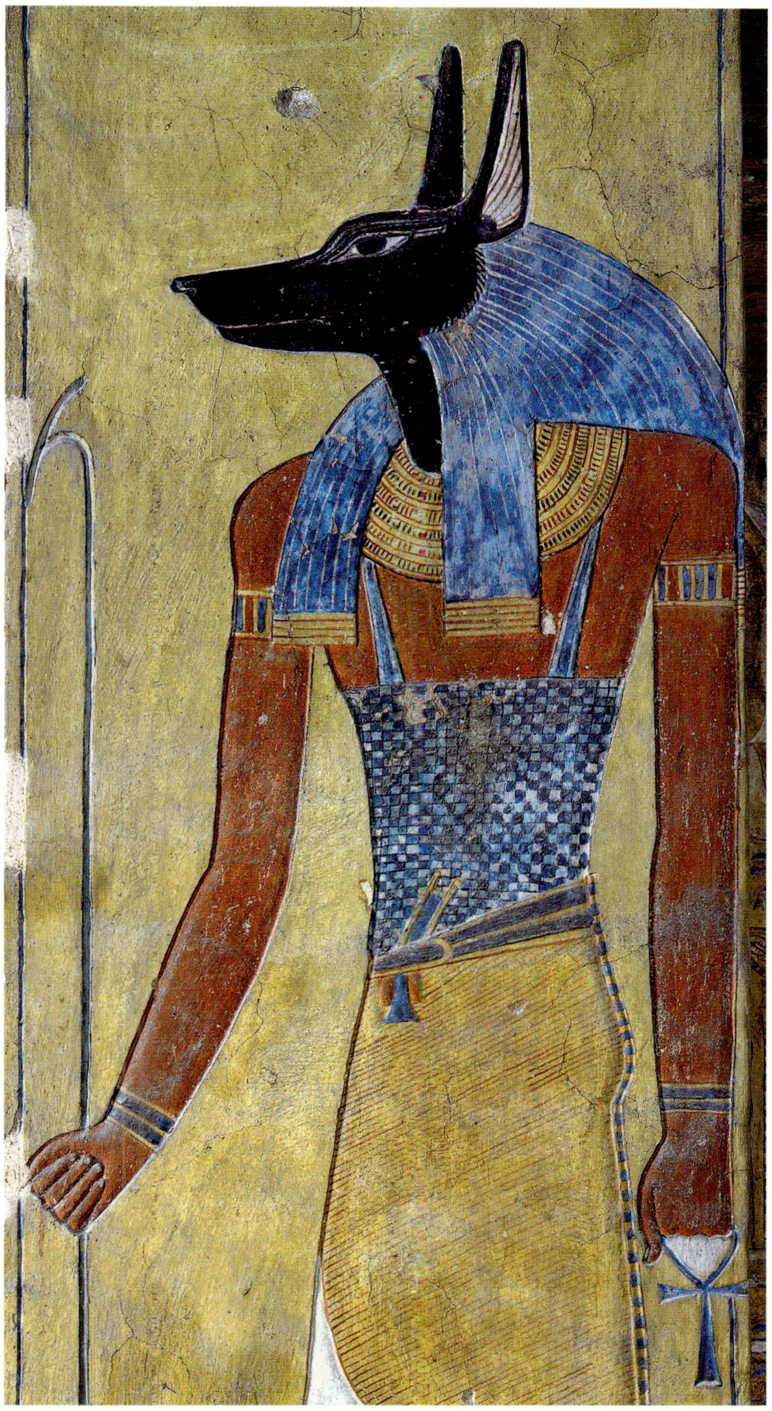

Tomb of Tausert/Sethnakht

Pillars continued to be decorated with images of god and king throughout the history of the Valley of the Kings. Earlier scenes have king and god facing one another on one side of the pillar. Beginning in the tomb of Tausert/Sethnakht, each major figure is given a complete side of one pillar to his or herself, so that it takes two pillar faces to complete a scene. Here, for example, are two pillars from the tomb of Tausert/Sethnakht: on one is an unfinished royal figure; on the other, Anubis stands, facing an image of the king on the adjacent side of the pillar.

Tutankhamun Enters the Afterlife

(Preceding pages)

On one wall of the burial chamber of Tutankhamun, the king is seen with the goddess Nut, who welcomes him with a gesture known as the *ny-ny*, in which she offers him water. Behind Nut, another figure of Tutankhamun, accompanied in this case by his *ka*, is embraced by Osiris.

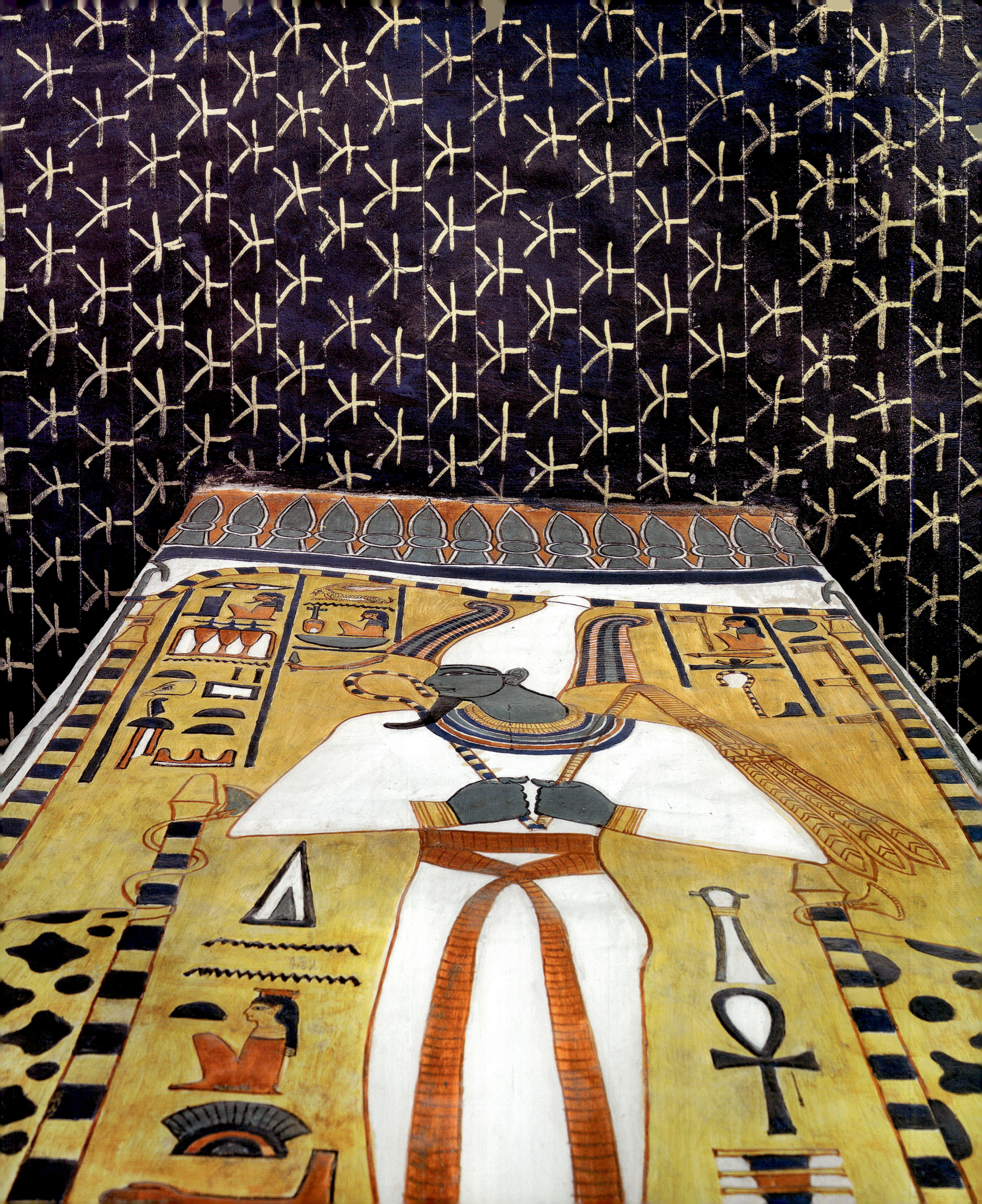

Chapter 3

The Book of the Amduat

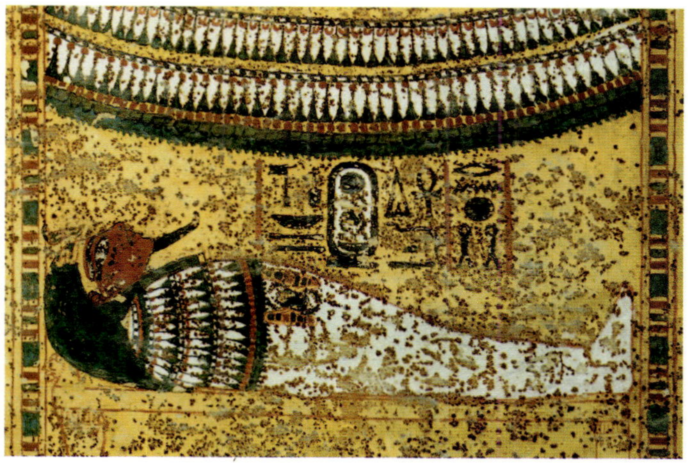

The priests and scholars of the New Kingdom imagined the beyond (known in ancient Egyptian as the Duat) to be similar to the earthly land of Egypt. Flowing through a narrow valley in the center were rivers, and mountainous deserts lay to the east and west. The denizens of this landscape included gods, demons, magical animals, and the souls of the dead. The scale here was colossal: beings could be 12 to 15 feet tall, and distances were enormous.

Played out here was the eternal cycle of death and rebirth, tied closely to the regular setting and rising of the sun. The principal goal of the journey of the sun god through the Duat was so that he could unite with Osiris in the depths of the night and receive the power to be reborn each morning. The soul, or *ba* of the deceased king was identified with the sun god, and his body linked with Osiris. Thus the reunion of Re and Osiris was paralleled by the union of royal *ba* and mummy, leading to the resurrection of the king.

The location of the Duat is often assumed to be beneath the earth, beginning at the western horizon and ending in the east where the earth meets the sky. However, texts from the 19th Dynasty suggest that the Duat was somehow behind our world, or perhaps in the sky, near where the gods lived.

The great Netherworld Books illustrate the land of the beyond in both words and images, woven together into beautiful tapestries that cover the walls of the royal tombs. The oldest of these to form part of the decoration of New Kingdom royal tombs was the Book of the Amduat, or What is in the Netherworld, whose actual title in ancient Egyptian can be translated as the Book of the Hidden Room (the burial chamber). The origins of this book, which seems to form the basis for many of the other Netherworld texts, seem to reach back into the Middle Kingdom, to a composition called the Book of the Two Ways that is found inscribed on elite coffins of the 12th Dynasty. This earlier text provides a map for the

The God Osiris
This image of Osiris graces one of the pillars in the burial chamber of Nefertari, chief consort of Ramses II, in the Valley of the Queens.

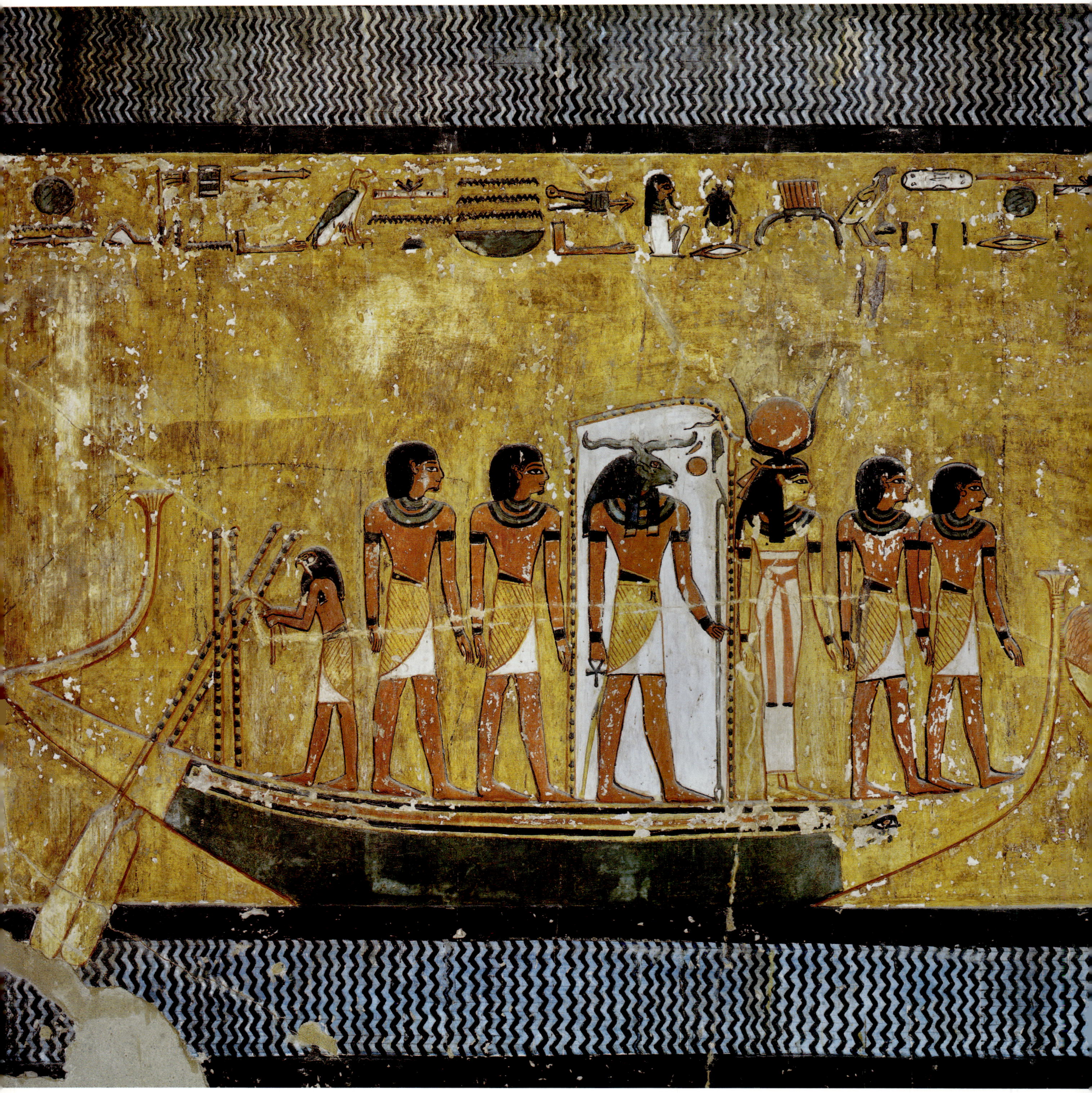

deceased to aid him in his journey through the Netherworld, pointing out to him the roads he should avoid and providing him with information about the roads he should follow. It was important that the soul know exactly what to expect, so that he could successfully pass all obstacles and reach eternal life. The New Kingdom priests clearly had access to this and other texts, from which they developed new versions.

These scholars of the New Kingdom organized the world according to lists. For example, the bases of colossal statues of kings often bore long lists of lands considered to be under the control of the Egyptians. Long onomastica, naming, for example, all the known towns along the length of the Nile, have survived and been translated by modern scholars. The Netherworld Books are likewise based on lists, primarily of the beings, both friendly and hostile, whom the king would meet during his journey.

Although it was most likely the priests of Amun-Re (a syncretism of Amun and Re) who authored the Books of the Netherworld, it is interesting to notice that the sun god is never called by his name in the texts. Instead, he is called *iuf*, which means "body." In the earliest New Kingdom texts, he is depicted in the form of a human with a ram's head. The ram is a reference to the *ba*, an aspect of the soul of the deceased: The word for ram in ancient Egyptian was spelled "*ba*," thus the use of the ram's head is something of a rebus. The ram was also the sacred animal of Amun. In later tombs, the sun god is shown in the form of a red disk.

The earliest appearance of the Amduat is in KV 20, the tomb of Hatshepsut/Tuthmosis I. Fifteen limestone slabs with drawings and texts from this book in red and black were found here, evidently meant to be placed against the walls of the burial chamber. Fragments of scenes and texts from the Amduat were also found in KV 38, the tomb of Tuthmosis I carved by Tuthmosis III; these are now in storage in the Cairo Museum.

It is in the burial chambers of Tuthmosis III and Amenhotep II that the Book of the Amduat is seen in its fullest form. This composition is divided into twelve hours, each accorded its own section of the wall. In the tomb of Tuthmosis III, it is interesting to note that the hours are not arranged in chronological sequence. Instead, they are placed according to the cardinal directions indicated in the texts themselves. Amenhotep II, on the other hand, has placed the hours in sequential order.

The burial chamber of Amenhotep III is also decorated with a full version of the Amduat. It is not seen at Amarna, but the first hour, in abbreviated form, is found in the burial chambers of Tutankhamun and Aye. Vignettes from two additional hours are represented on the golden shrines surrounding the sarcophagus of Tutankhamun. In the burial chambers of the tombs of Horemheb and Ramses I, the Amduat is replaced with the Book of Gates; it is possible that the Amduat was represented on the walls of these kings' shrines, but none of these have been preserved. From the tomb of Seti I on, various hours of the Amduat are represented again, most often in the sarcophagus chamber and the second and third corridors.

The Amduat outlines, in great detail, the journey of the sun god (in whose company the deceased king travels) through the twelve hours of the night. Each of these hours is distinct, given an individual title, its own space on the wall, and is marked off by a vertical inscription. The scenes are arranged most often in three horizontal registers. At the outset of the first hour, the sun sets over the western horizon, paralleling the death of the king. During the succeeding hours, the sun god travels through the Duat in his boat, accompanied by a select group of gods: Sia, who represents the mind and thought; the jackal-headed Wepwawet, literally the Opener of the ways; the Mistresses of the bark, a series of twelve goddesses, one of whom appears in the form of Hathor or Isis in each hour; Kherepwia, the captain of the boat, and Horus Hekenu (Horus who calls), its pilot; the destroyer god Nehes, who protects the boat from its enemies; Kashu; and the god Hu, manifestation of divine utterance.

For the first five hours, the god and his entourage descend deeper and deeper into the earth, encountering both friendly and inimical denizens of the Duat as they pass through the various landscapes of this realm. In the sixth hour, the

THE SOLAR BARK

The sun god, in his night form as a ram-headed man, is typically seen inside a shrine, accompanied by five to seven divinities: Sia; Wepwawet (not shown here); the Mistress of the Bark; the captain, Kherepwia; Nehes; Kashu; Hu; and the pilot, Horus Hekenu.

THE FIRST HOUR

(Following pages)

The west wall of Tutankhamun's tomb is decorated with an abbreviated version of the first hour of the Amduat. In the upper register is Khepri in his morning bark, preceded by five deities: Ma'at; the Mistress of the Bark, Horus, Kashu, and Nehes. Below are twelve baboons, rejoicing at the appearance of the sun. These animals were sacred to Thoth in his guise as a moon god, and were connected with the sun through their well-documented habit of turning to face the morning sun.

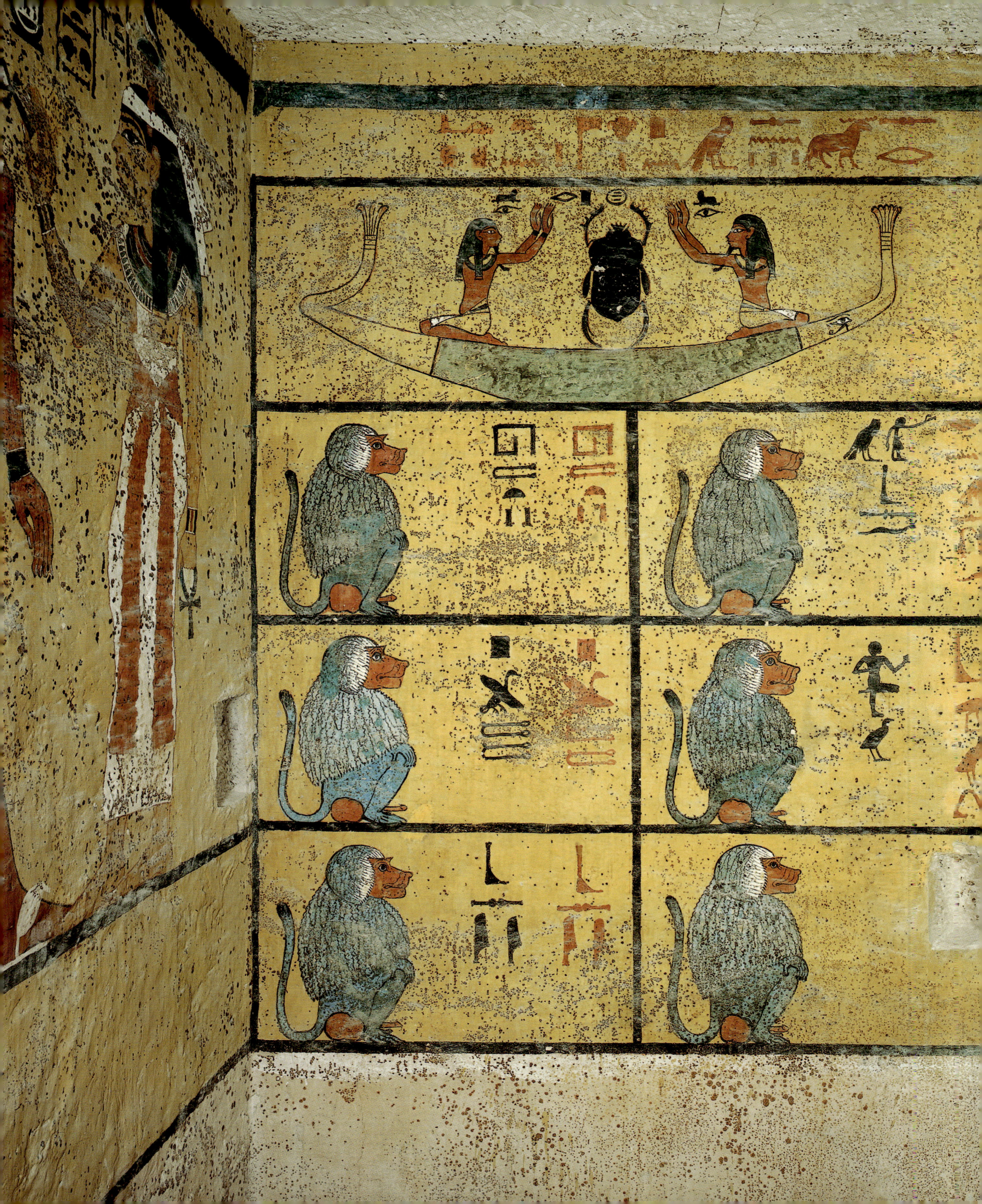

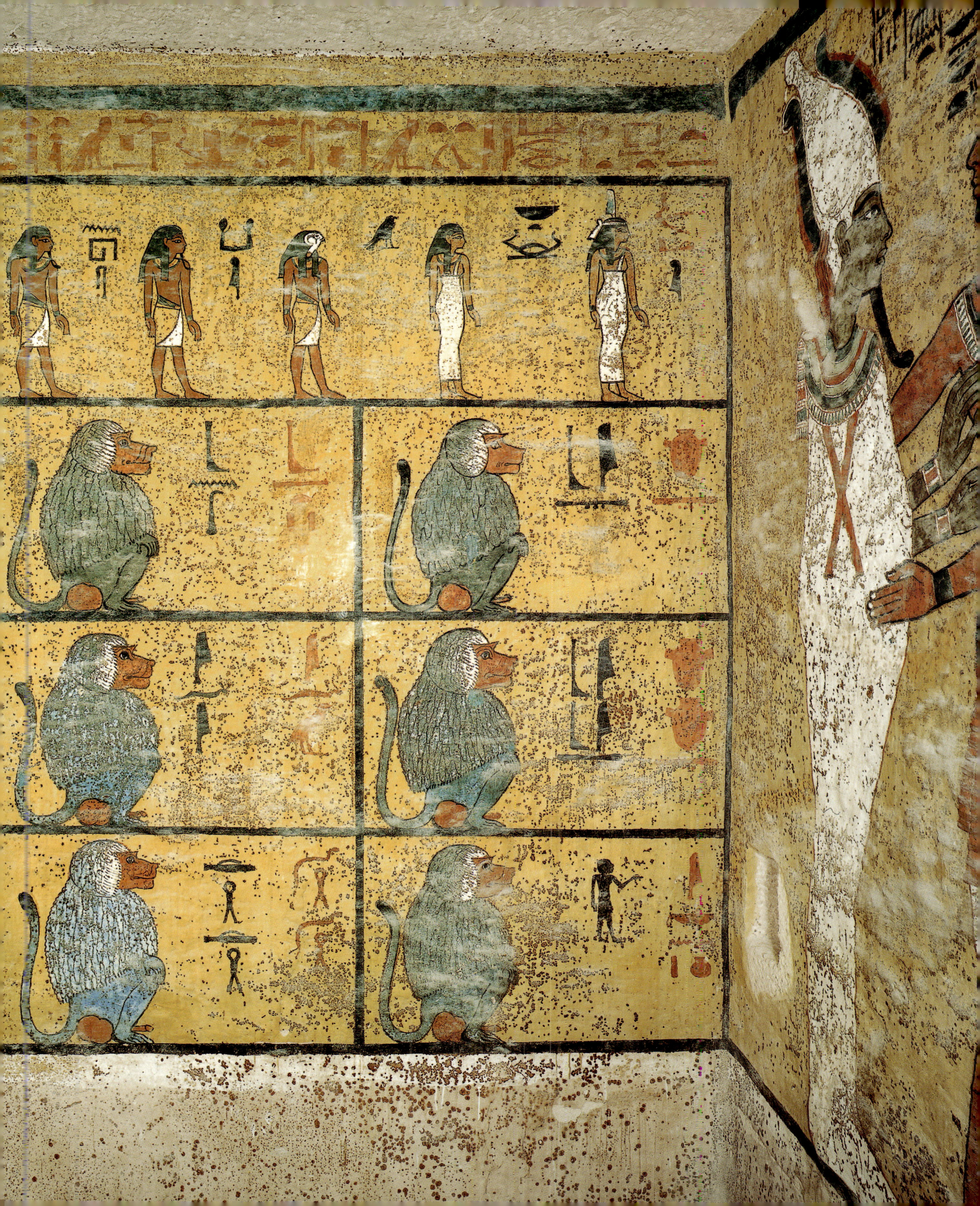

travelers reach the deepest, darkest part of the Netherworld, where the sun god is united with Osiris and receives the energy and magical power required for resurrection. The next hour is the moment of greatest danger, when the snake Apophis, who tries to swallow the sun, attacks and is defeated. During the remainder of the night, the solar bark travels in a long upward arc, until it reaches the eastern horizon at the end of the twelfth hour. At this moment, the sun is reborn in the form of the scarab beetle, and begins his daily journey through the sky; at the same time, the deceased king is resurrected, and enters eternal life.

The Egyptians believed in representational magic: by depicting something, they could ensure that it would happen. Thus, by illustrating the successful journey of the sun god, they were magically ensuring that it would take place. Throughout the journey, the rebirth of the sun at dawn is frequently referenced, guaranteeing that it would occur. It is also important to notice that each figure is labeled. By knowing the names of the companions and guardians of the sun god and Osiris, the deceased could stand with them and follow the gods. Identifying the enemies of order helped the deceased to face and defeat them.

In order to understand the images shown on the walls of the royal tombs, it is important to have a grasp of Egyptian "perspective." Egyptian art does not function like western realistic art, which attempts to show the world as it is seen through a viewer's eyes. The Egyptian artisan's primary purpose was to convey the most information possible, and a number of conventions were adopted to achieve this end. For example, human figures are generally rendered in a combination of profile and frontal views, so that the most salient features are visible. Containers, such as boxes, are shown with their contents, which would not actually be visible to the observer, above them.

When studying the images in the royal tombs, the viewer must imagine that the registers are side by side, as if they have been pushed flat. For a wall with three registers, the top register can be imagined as farthest away, with the middle register next to it and the lowest register closest. Thus in the first hours of the Amduat, for example, the bands of speckled pink at top and bottom, representing the desert, should be thought of as flanking the river in the center, just as in the real landscape of Egypt.

Hour One: "The One who Destroys the Enemies of Re"

The first hour, also known as "the beginning of the western horn, the far borders of thick darkness," illustrates the passage of the god through a transitional zone, the Valley of Re, and ends with his arrival in the Duat proper. During this hour, the sun god crosses 120 *iru* (Egyptian miles, equaling 700 English miles). His night bark (*mesketet*) travels alongside a second vessel, the day bark (*mandjet*), in which he appears in his morning form as the scarab beetle Khepri. Both boats are preceded by various Netherworld inhabitants who clear the way for the god. In the upper and lower registers are divine beings who rejoice at the start of the journey of rebirth.

Hour One (*following pages*). The day bark (not visible here), with a matt curtain at its prow, is normally depicted at the left end of the central register. Standing inside a small shrine in the center of the bark would be Amun-Re, with a ram's head to indicate that he is functioning as his *ba*, the aspect of the soul that must reunite with the body so that rebirth can take place. With the sun god is his usual entourage. Leading the procession in front of the bark (far right of this register) is the knife-wielding Guardian of the Hours followed by an upright snake that embodies the entire Netherworld, then four human-headed stelae to represent the jurisdiction of Re, Atum, Khepri, and Osiris over the realm beyond the earth. Next to these stelae is a ram-headed figure whose name is perhaps to be translated as "the great one who makes light," the lioness-headed Sekhmet, Osiris in his guise as Foremost of the Westerners (the dead), Neken, who wields a knife to protect Re from his enemies, and two figures of the goddess Ma'at.
The third register is dominated at the left by the day bark inside which Khepri, whose name means "to create, come into being," is flanked by two figures, both labeled as Osiris, who raise their arms to him in a gesture of adulation. By representing Khepri, the morning sun and thus the successful result of the journey, the king is ensuring that he will survive the twelve hours of the night to be reborn. Directly in front of the day bark are three snakes, symbolizing the variety of serpents that inhabit the Egyptian countryside. The rest of the register is filled with Netherworld divinities, all holding snake-shaped scepters, a reference perhaps to their chthonic natures.
The top register, representing the west bank, is filled with four groups of beings, all inhabitants of the Duat. Each is in its own box, which possibly stands for some sort of shrine. To the right are twelve standing goddesses, representing the 12 hours of the night. These are the goddesses that will take turns accompanying the god in his night bark. To their left are nine kneeling gods (three human-headed, three jackal-headed, and three with crocodile heads), whose job is to greet the god during his passage through the Duat. Next are twelve more standing goddesses, perhaps the hours of the day, and nine baboons, who served to open the doors of the west so that the boat of the god could enter the Duat.
The lowest register, or east bank, is organized in a similar fashion, with twelve goddesses, nine gods, twelve cobras (also representing goddesses), and nine baboons.
In this case, the baboons are present to recite a hymn to the sun god.

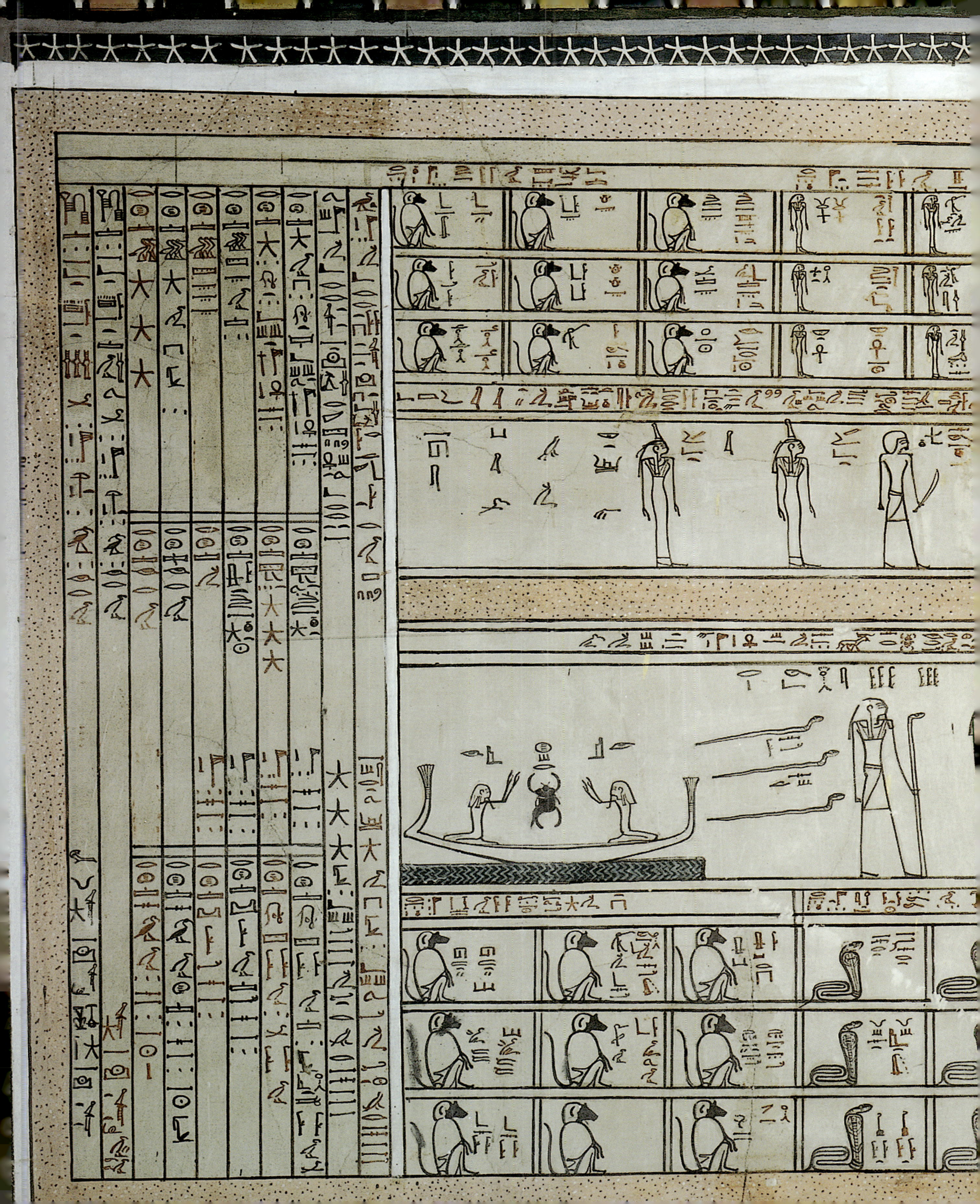

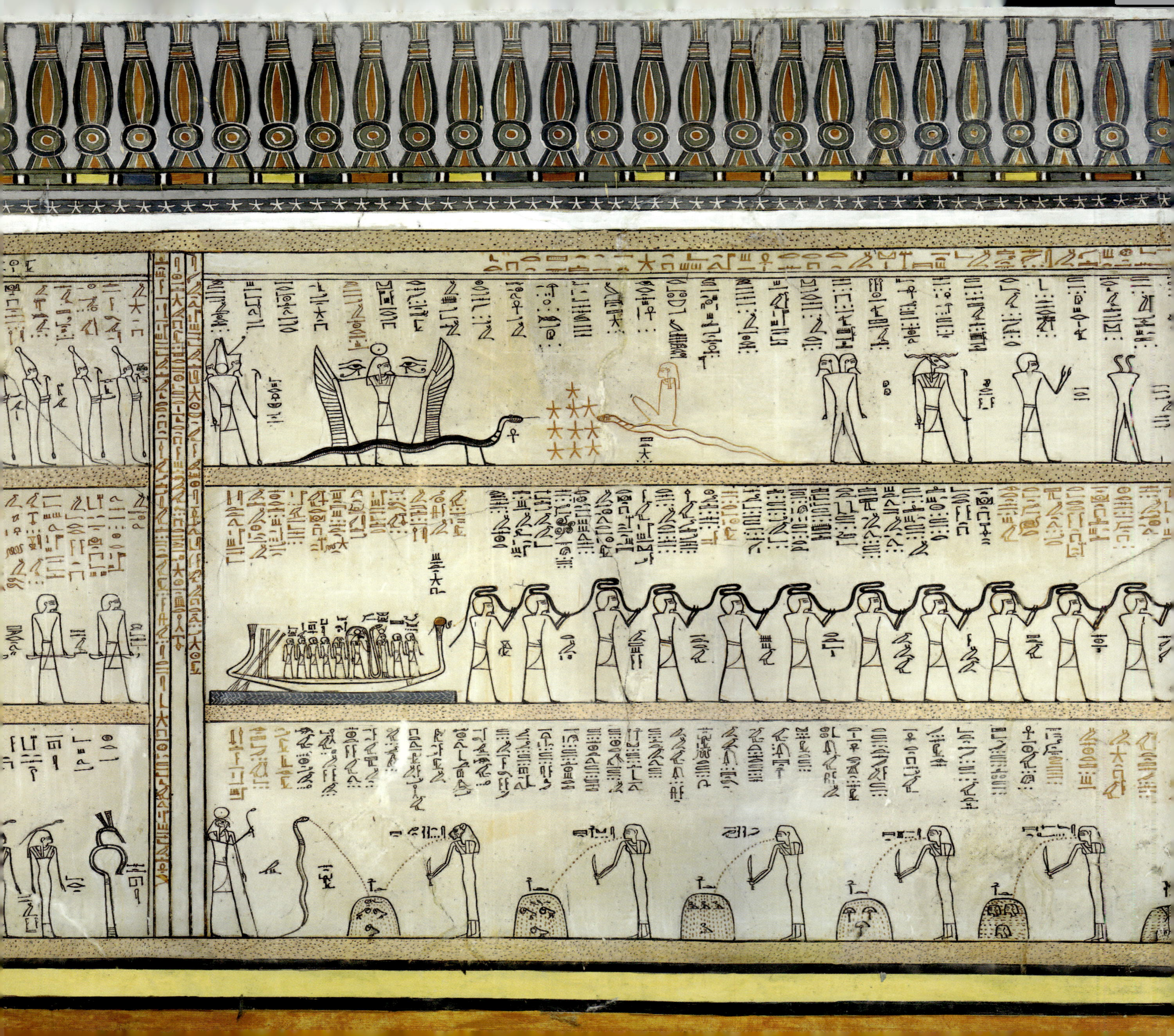

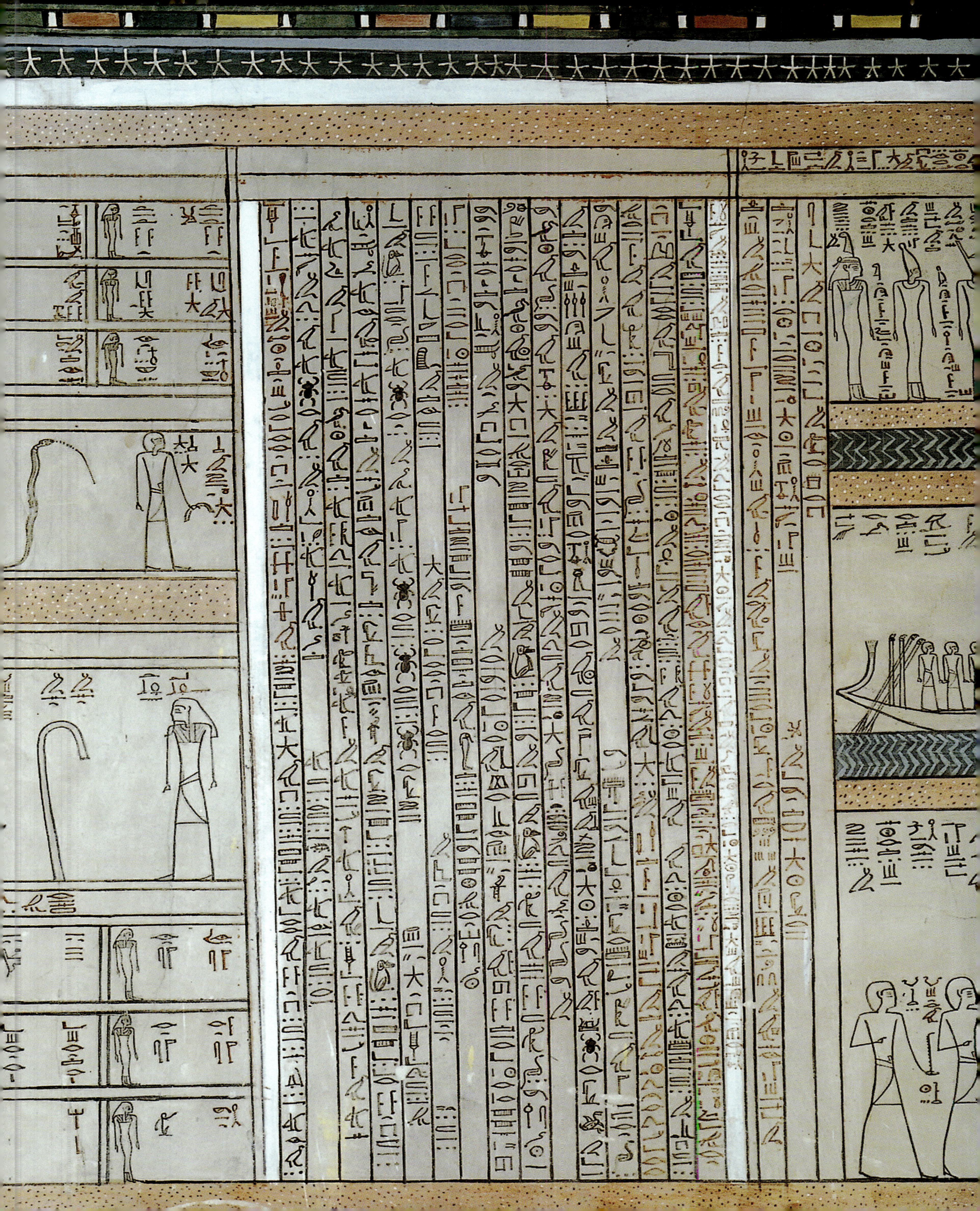

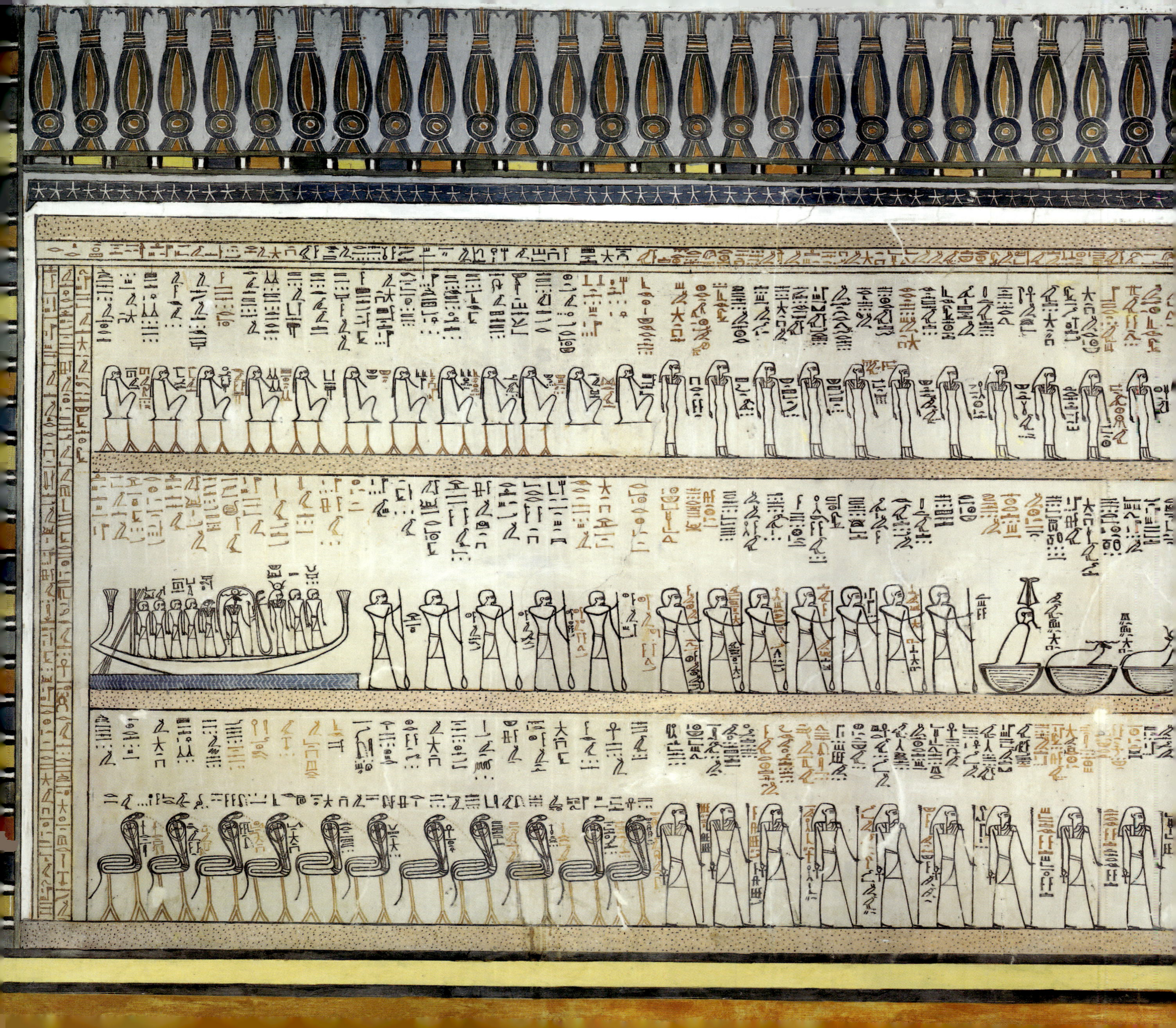

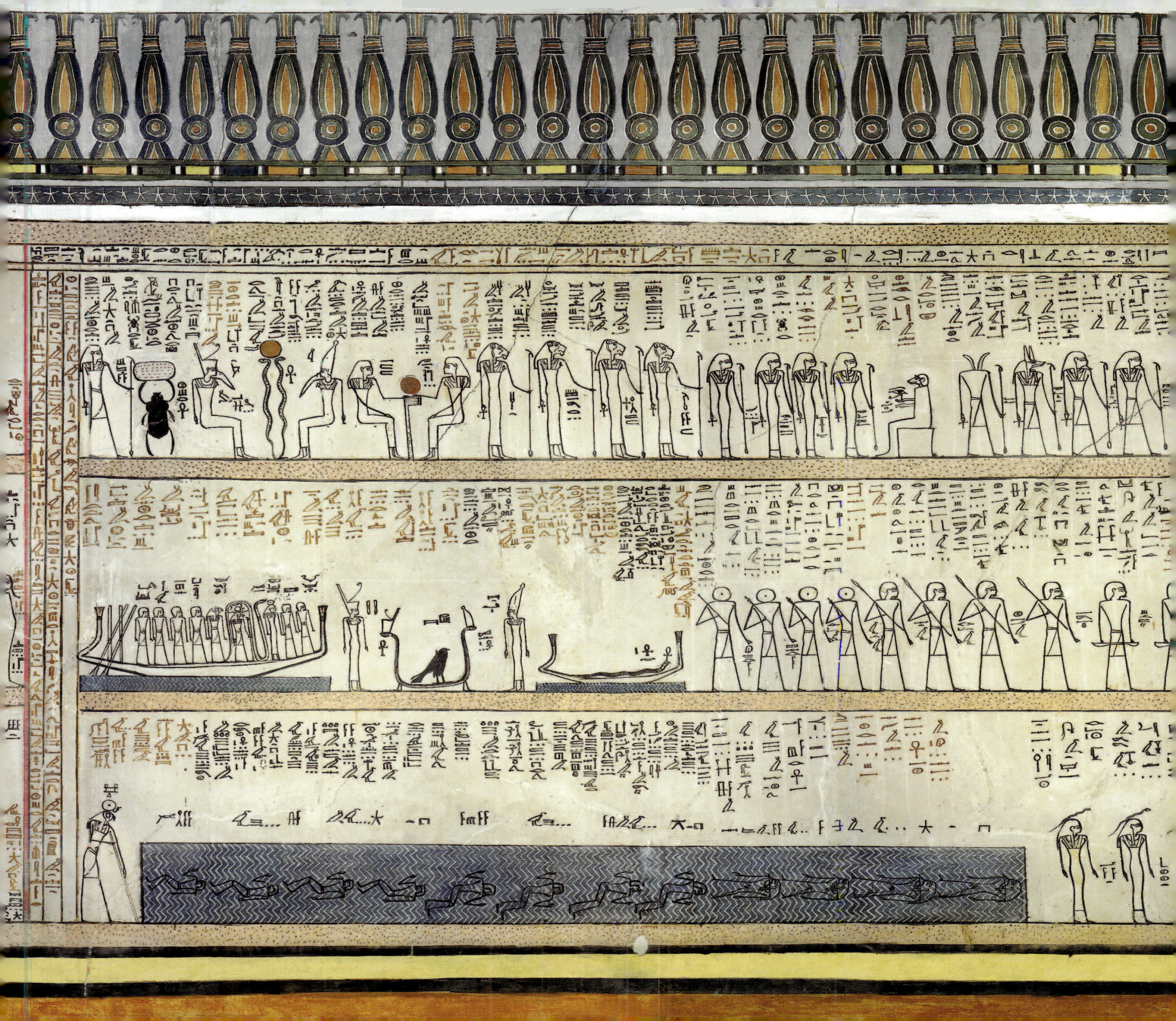

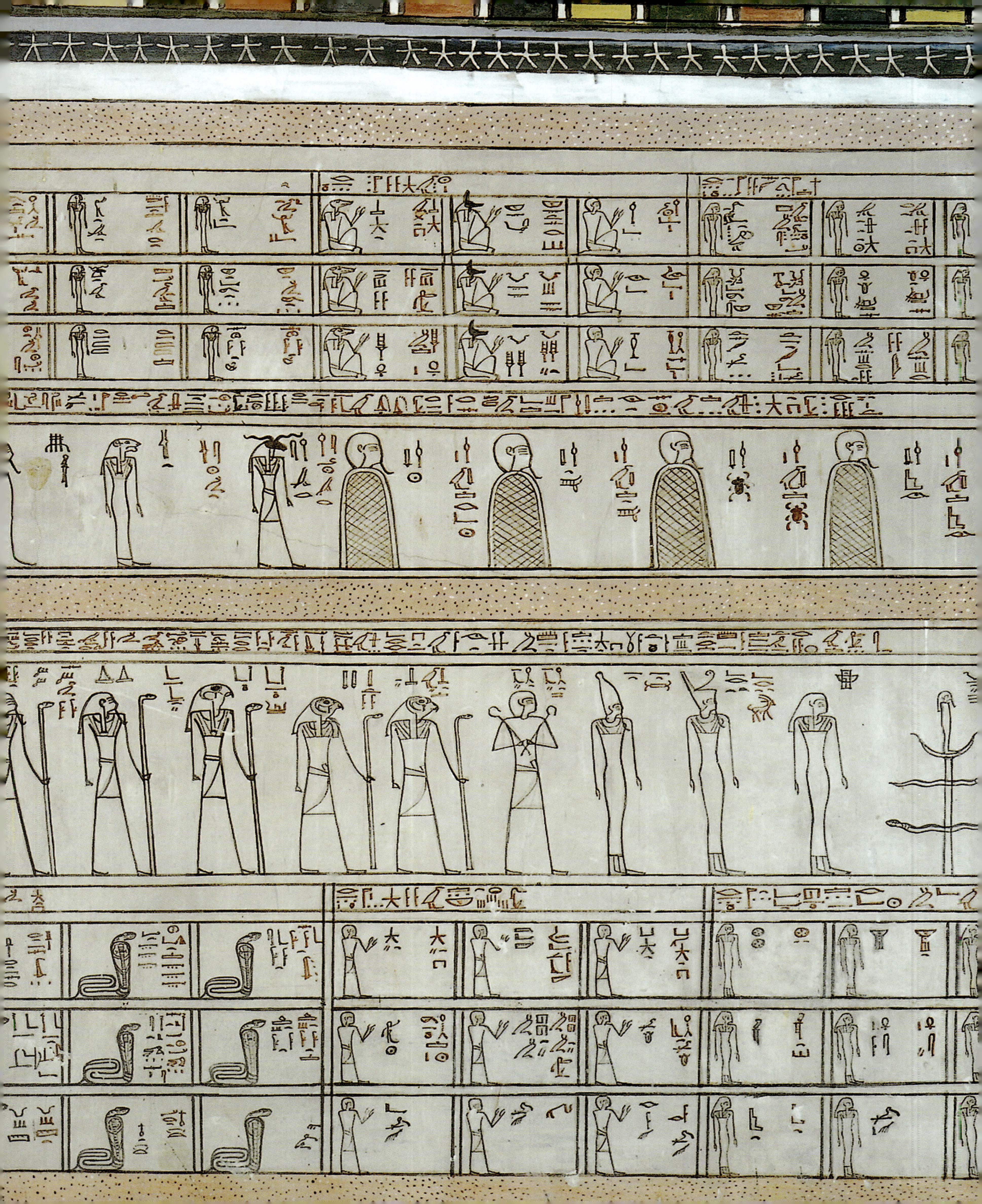

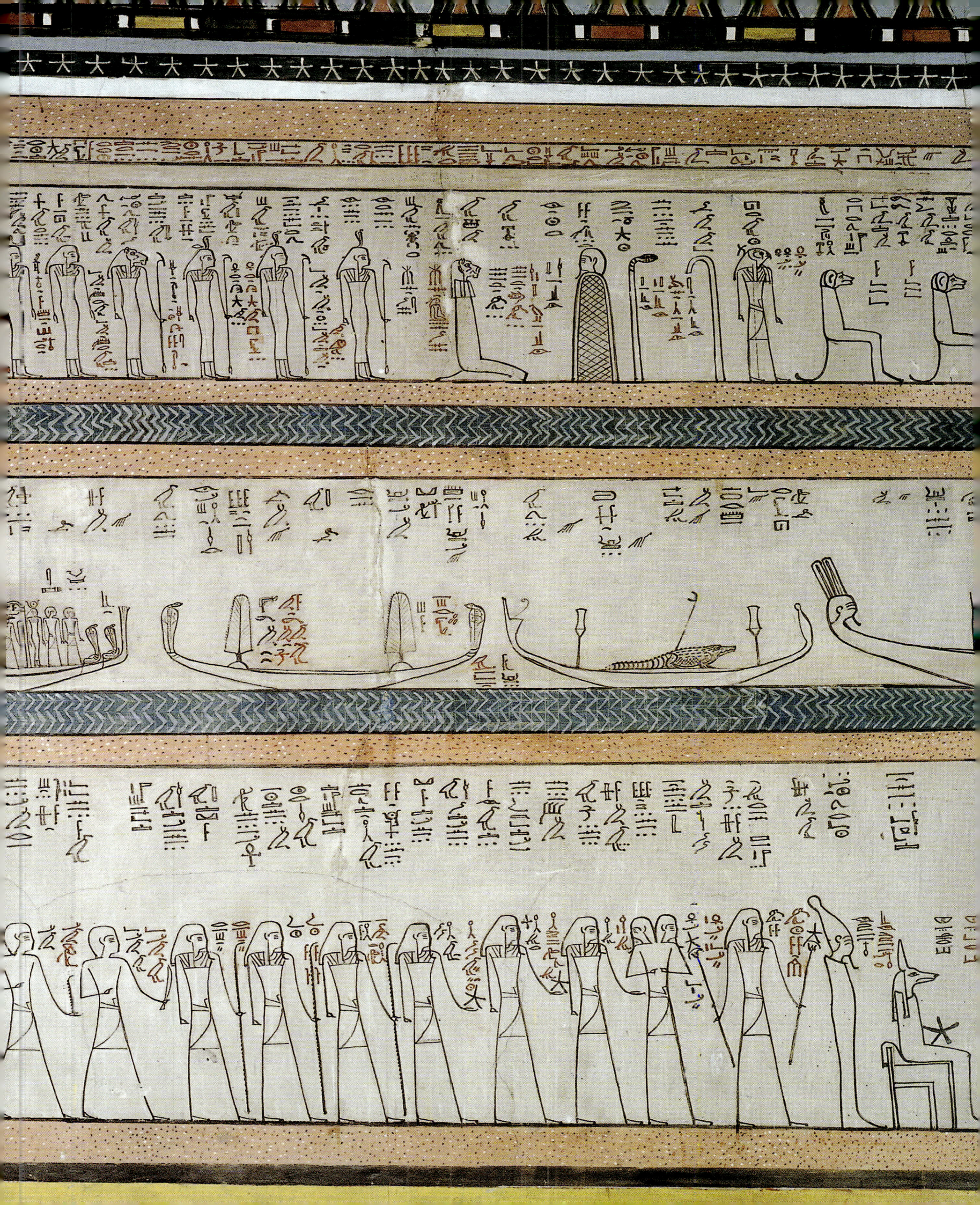

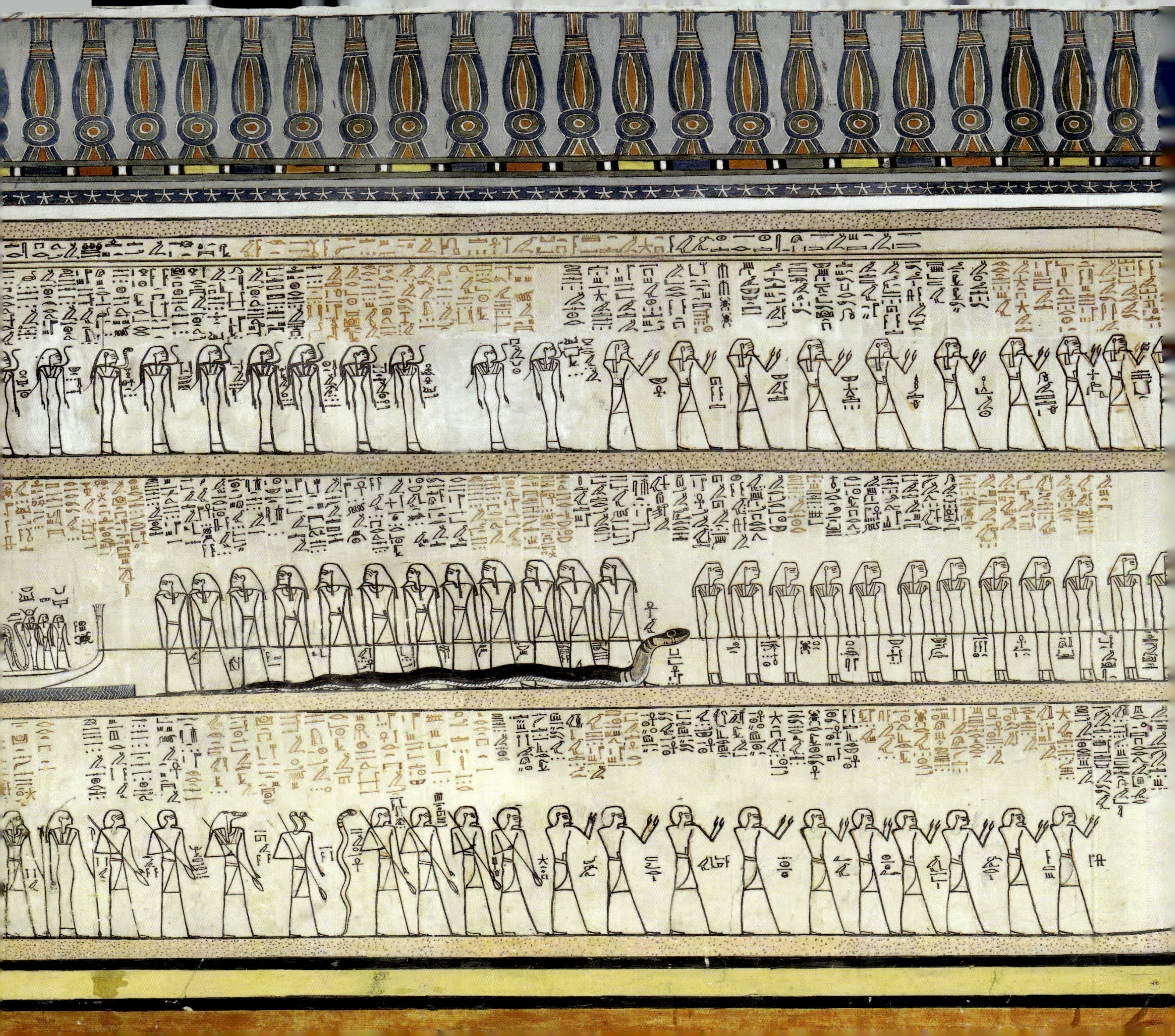

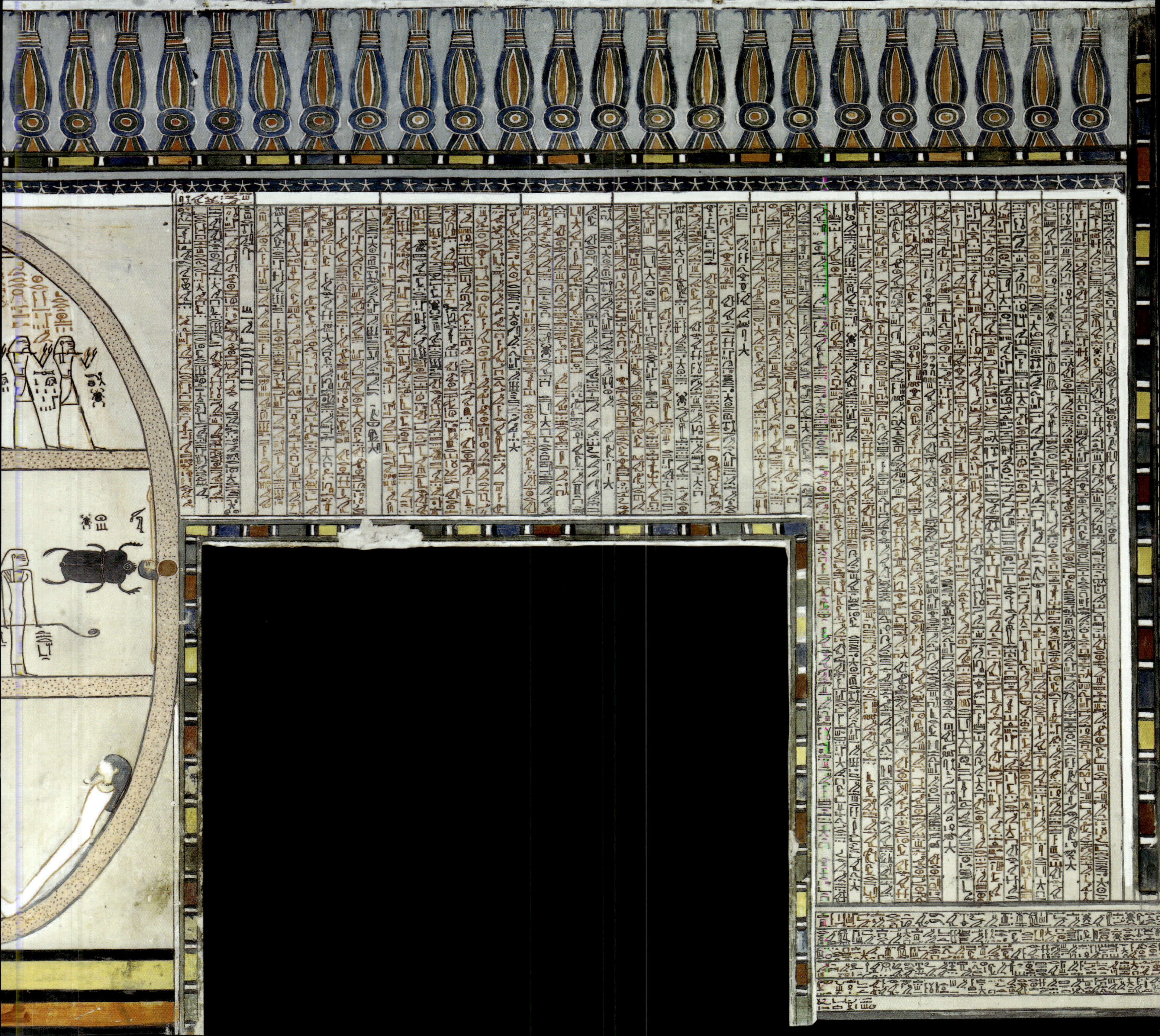

Hour Two. This hour is dominated by water, which fills the lower border of the top two registers. The ram-headed sun god in his bark can be found at the left of the second register; with him are his usual companions and protectors, with the addition at the prow of Isis and Nephthys in the form of cobras.

The bark of the sun god is accompanied here by four additional boats. First (far right) comes the bark of Thoth, its prow and stern in the form of human heads, with a moon symbol on its deck. Kneeling before this is a man with a beard, holding the feather of *ma'at*; he is the "one who supports the truth." Next is the boat of Hathor, with the Khepri beetle in its prow and a Hathor symbol flanked by two goddesses on its deck. The front and back of this boat are also human-headed, crowned with plumes. The third boat has crowned human heads at prow and stern. On its deck is a crocodile with the head of Osiris emerging from its body; this makes reference to the crocodile's role as the one who found Osiris's head after his dismemberment at the hands of Seth. Flanking the crocodile are two scepters, one for the north and the other for the south; these belong to Wepwawet as Opener of the ways. In the fourth boat, which has cobras at bow and stern, is the god of wheat, Neper. The bark of the sun god is last in the procession.

The top register, representing the west bank of the river, is filled with protective gods and goddesses. To the far right are six seated deities wielding knives, then two standing gods. In front is "the one with a strong hand who destroys enemies"; behind is Horus of the Duat.

Leading the next group is a figure clad in the royal kilt, wielding a knife; he is called "Seben who cuts the shadow." Behind him are two sacred baboons, leaning on their tails, then a strange being called Herherfy. This creature has two heads: one a falcon, the god Horus; and the other a composite canine, the head of his uncle Seth. Next are a crook and a snake scepter, and then a human-headed stela, "the words" and "the command of Osiris." The kneeling lioness goddess is "one who terrifies the blessed spirits." Following her are three goddesses with uraei on their heads, all of whom play distinct roles, the goddess Sekhmet, then five personifications, including "the first goddess of *ma'at* in the valley," who brings up the rear. All of these gods sing hymns to welcome the sun god when he arrives and cry when he leaves.

The lower register, the "east bank," is led by male figures holding sheaves of wheat: these are the "farmers of Wernes," men who have died and been welcomed into the fertile land beyond the earth. Some hold reeds in their hands to salute the god; according to the accompanying text, they offer green plants, carry water to the faithful followers of Re, and burn his enemies with fire. They also represent the growth of the wheat and thus the fertility of the land. The last figure in this series is Osiris, who holds a knife to wield against the foes of the sun god. Behind him are three seated figures, the last of whom is Anubis in his form as Lord of the sacred land. Next stands Osiris, wrapped as a mummy and called "Wennefer," indicating that he has been resurrected, and several groups of figures who are linked with time.

The Final Hours

(Preceding pages)

This wall is decorated with the ninth, tenth, eleventh, and twelfth hours of the Book of the Amduat, with the short version of the text, without illustrations, at the far right.

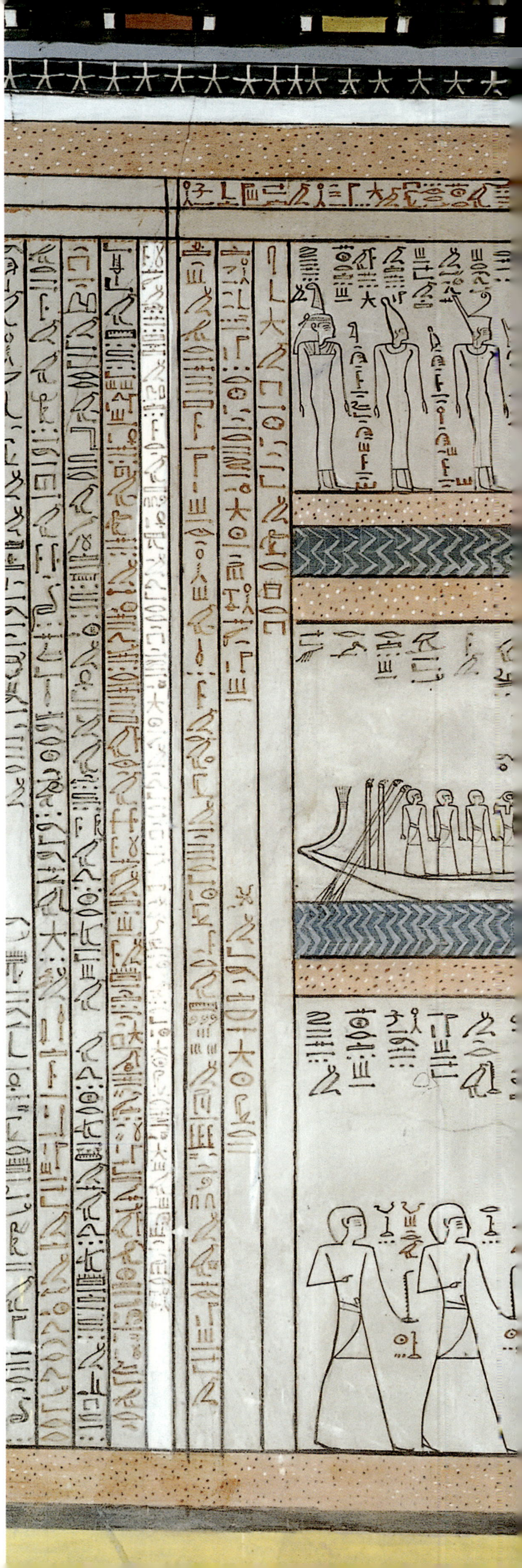

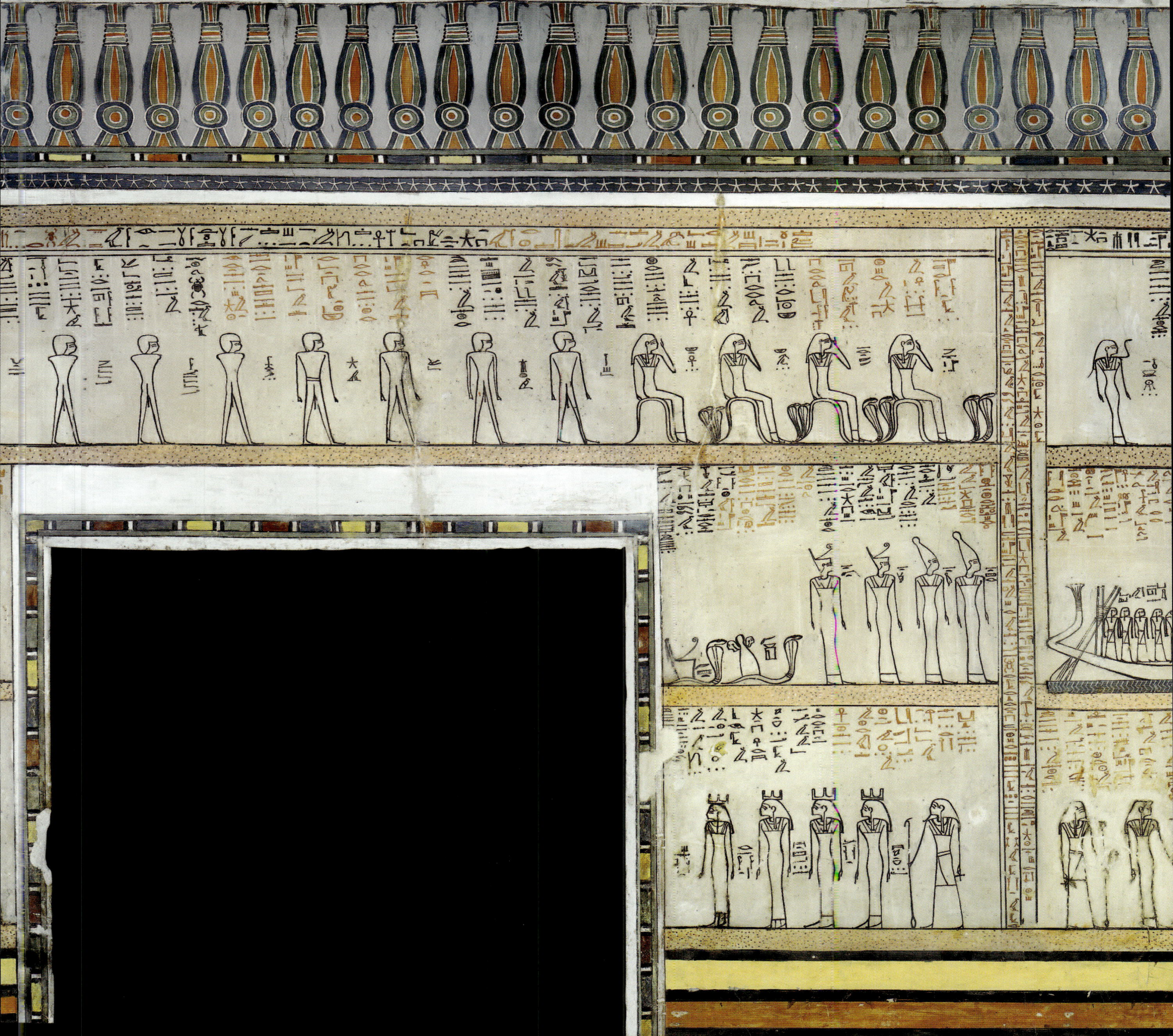

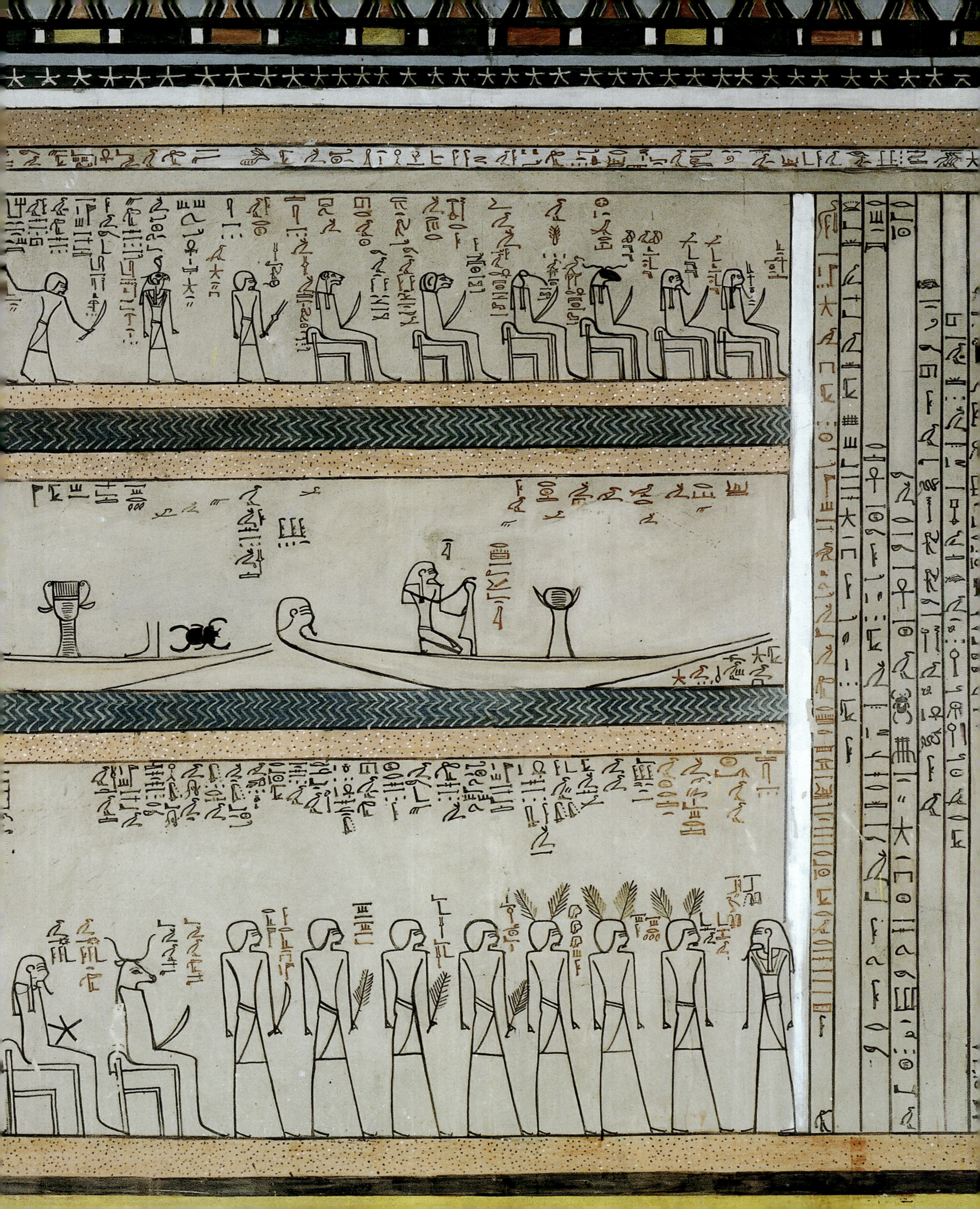

Hour Two: The Fertile Land of the Underworld

During the second hour, the solar bark, in the company of a small fleet of other vessels, travels for 309 *iru* (Egyptian miles) through the watery landscape known as the Wernes. This fertile area is similar to the Fields of the Blessed known from the Book of the Dead, a funerary book used mainly by the elite. The followers of Osiris dominate this hour: the upper and lower registers in particular are filled with deities linked with this god. Chief among them are the farmers of Wernes, responsible for the stability and security of the land and rewarded for their actions with fields to cultivate.

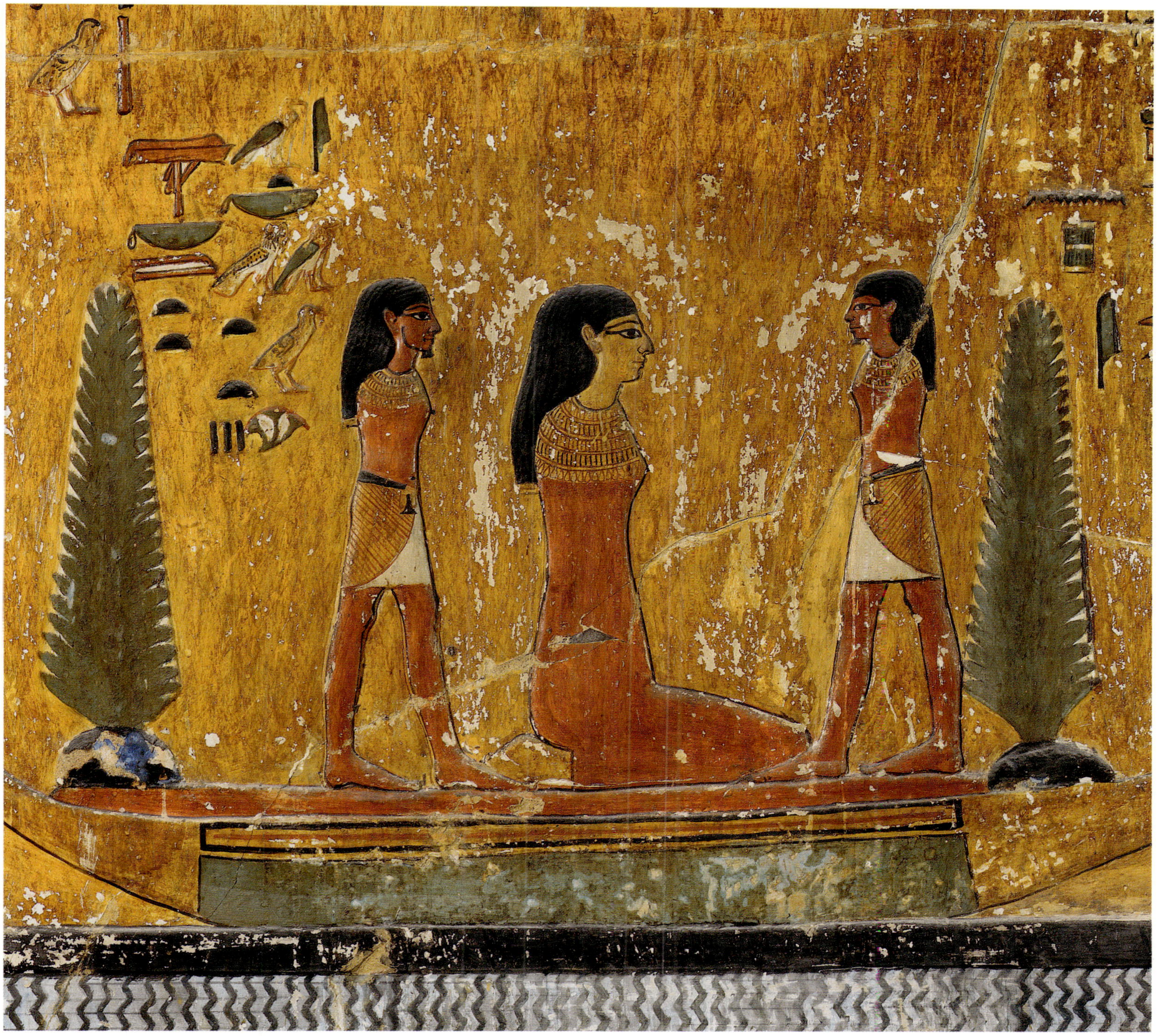

Detail from Hour Two
One of the vessels that accompanies the sun god on his journey through the Wernes bears the god of wheat, flanked by two armless figures and two sheaves of wheat.

HOUR THREE: THE WATERS OF OSIRIS

The watery landscape continues through the 309 Egyptian miles spanned by this hour, but in this case, the river is called the "waters of Osiris." The gods who follow and protect Osiris appear here, many wielding knives to keep his enemies at bay. According to the text associated with this hour, Re faces Osiris and speaks to him directly. The solar bark is again accompanied here by additional vessels.

Hour Three. The solar bark is again at the left end of the middle register, where the sun god sails with his usual companions. The divine procession here is led (far right of register) by four male figures. The first boat, the "boat of equipment," is lotus-shaped, and carries, in addition to the sailors, a snake called "the one with the tired face," and three hawk-headed figures. The third of these stands on a snake, perhaps representing the triumph of Horus the hawk over his uncle Seth in the guise of a serpent. The second boat, the "boat of comfort," has baboon heads at prow and stern, and bears a mummiform figure linked with Osiris and a headless goddess known as "the brilliant one." The third vessel, with ram prow and stern, serves to defend the bark of the god. Other than the sailors at front and back, the occupants of the boat include a god known as the "Lord of the scepter," a deity with ram's horns, enveloped in a cloak which resembles that worn by the king at his festival of rejuvenation, and the mummiform "one who is on the ground."

In the upper register are many of Osiris's servants, known as the "hidden souls," here to protect the god from his enemies. In return, they are rewarded with plots of land. The register begins with three standing male figures and the god Henu in the form of a mummified hawk seated on a standard. Behind him are three groups of deities: four weeping goddesses, four mummies, and four walking gods. Next comes a seated god, "one who brought the eye to pacify the gods," (a reference to the myth of the destruction of mankind) kneeling before a papyrus plant topped by a piece of meat; then various deities. At the far left are two baboons, one on a mound of sand and the other in a small shrine.

The lower register, representing the west bank, begins at the right with the god Khentry, guardian of the area, and the goddess Bakhet holding the eyes of Re, then three gods bent over in a strange position, looking at the ground. The rest of the register is occupied by eight figures of Osiris on thrones, four with the red crown of the north and four with the white crown of the south, followed by the gods Khnum and Nerta (linked with earthquakes). Between the two sets of Osiris figures are nine deities: two human-headed gods and two human-headed goddesses, then five ibis-headed figures, all holding knives.

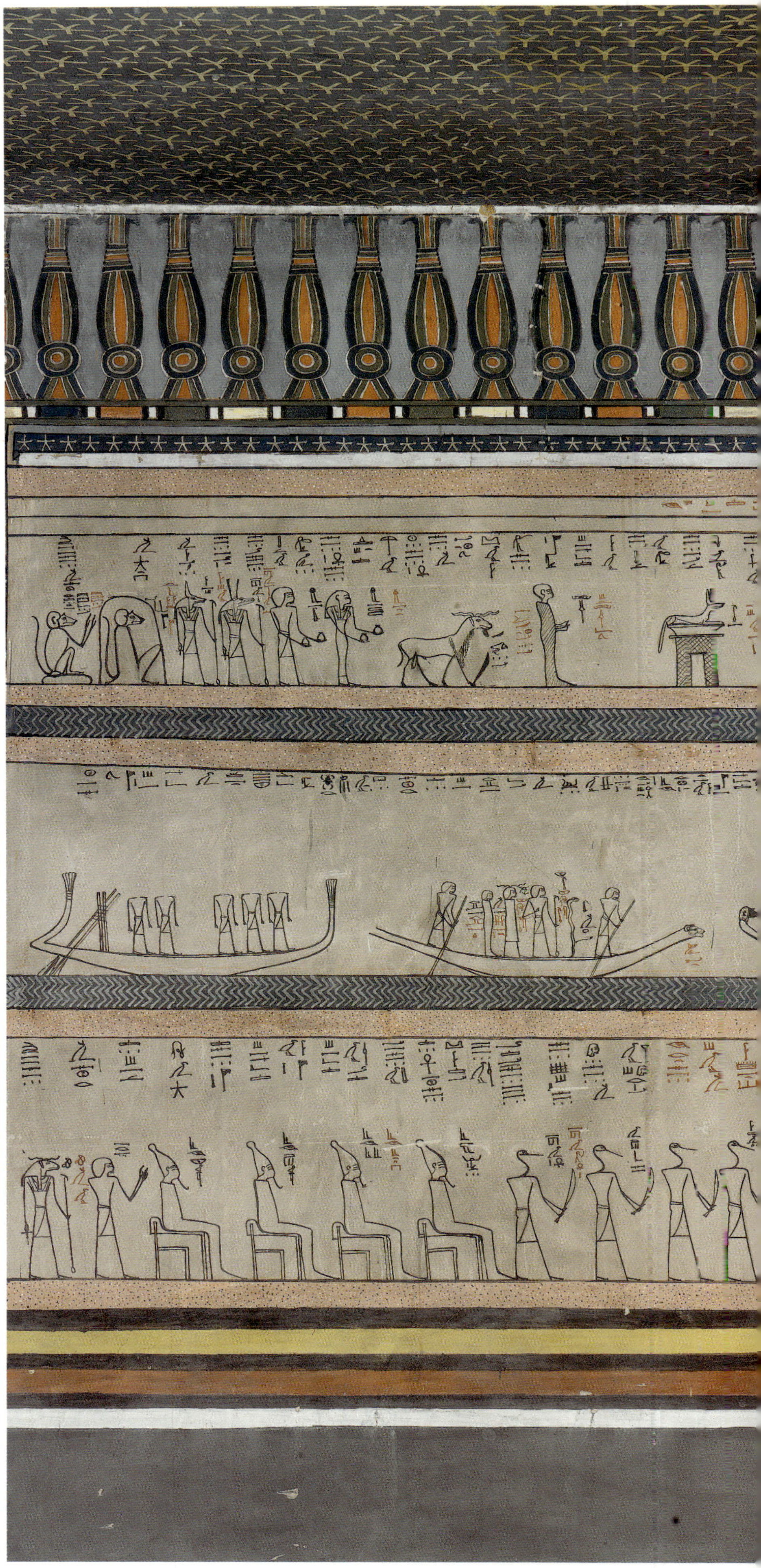

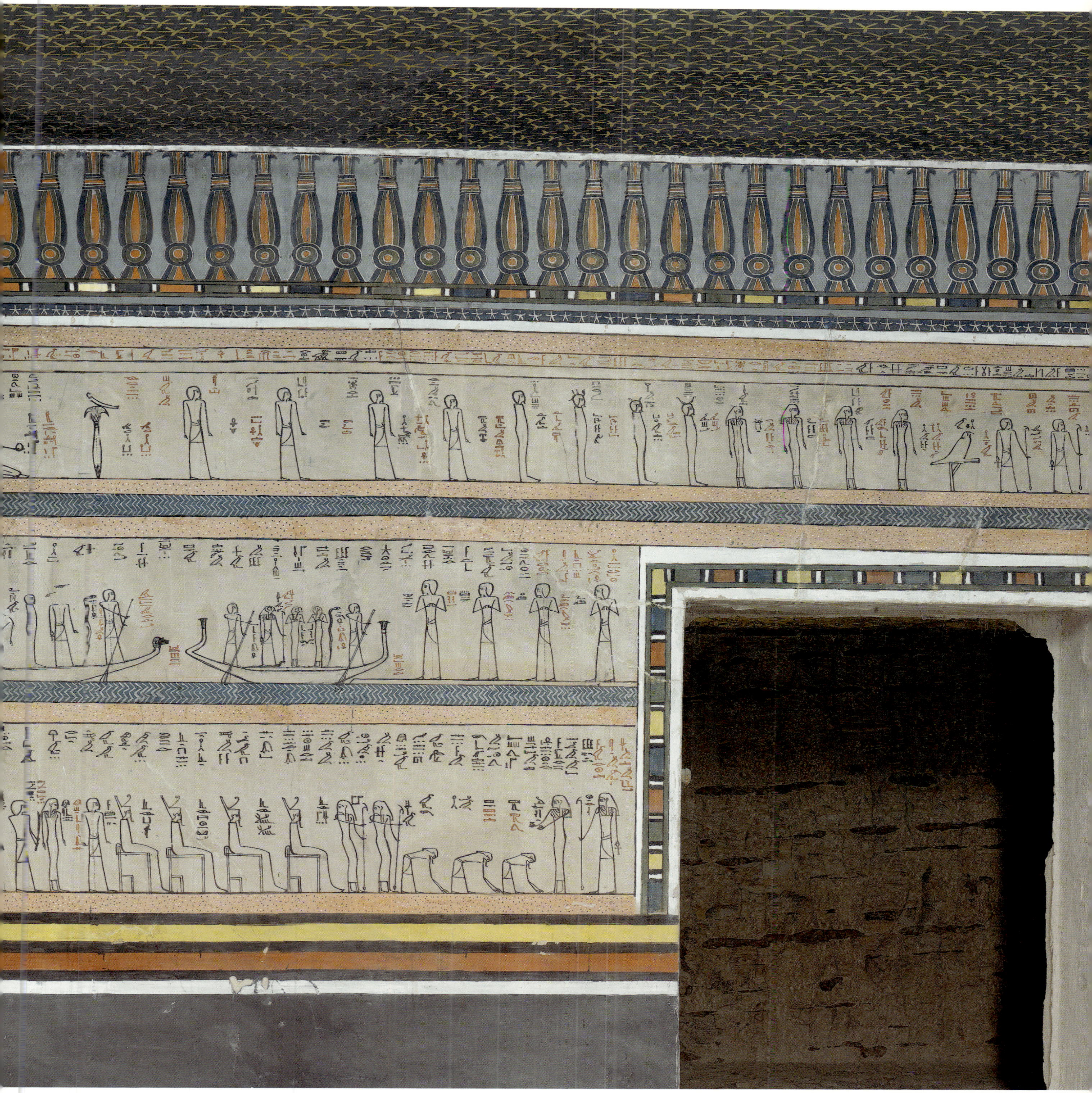

Hour Four: The Hill of Sokar

The fourth hour takes the sun from the watery world of hours two and three into the severe desert landscape of Rostau, realm of the Memphite mortuary god Sokar, who was closely associated with Osiris. The text tells us that this is a guide to the secret tunnels and hidden gates of the Memphite necropolis. The successful journey ends with a great reward, including the eating of bread in the palace of the god Atum. Scholars believe that this hour, and the next, were adapted from a religious text composed in Memphis known as the Memphite Theology.

The registers are cut through by a "path of fire," which slants across the horizontal registers in a series of steps; this path is blocked at intervals by doors. The realm of Sokar is dominated by images of snakes in many forms. The solar boat can no longer sail on the water; it takes the form of a serpent so that it can be pulled through the sand. During this hour, the wounded eye of the sun god is healed by Thoth and Sokar. At the end of the hour is seen a door guarded by a figure of the goddess Ma'at.

There are many interesting and unusual inhabitants of the Netherworld depicted here. For example, one figure has no head, but instead has what have been identified as mummy bandages sprouting from his neck. There is also a two-headed snake named Nehebkau, the guardian of this desert.

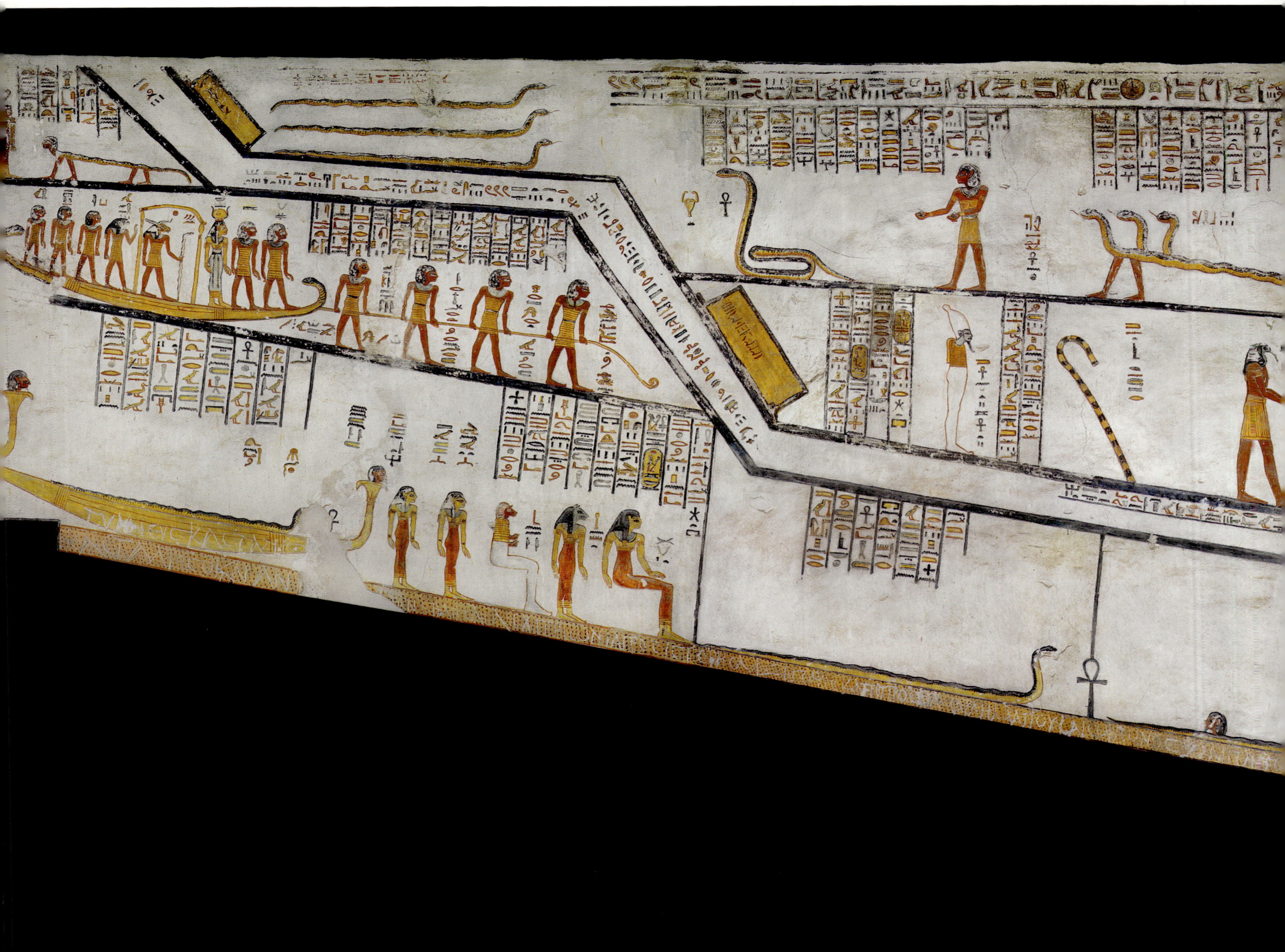

Hour Four. The solar boat, in its new serpent form, occupies its usual place at the left side of the middle register. One of the roles of the serpent boat was to throw fire and light before the god, to illuminate the complete darkness through which he traveled. The bark is towed by four human figures, followers of Osiris and Ptah. The slanting tunnel of fire separates the boat from the other gods who occupy this register. The first group of four deities faces left; there are three gods and one goddess here, each holding an *ankh* sign in his or her hand. The second group faces right and includes a strange figure with mummy bandages instead of a head. All of these gods served to protect the sun god and his crew. In the center of the register is a vignette that shows Horus and Thoth healing the eye of the Sokar, which is associated with the eye of Re. Just before the tunnel of fire is a mummiform figure of Osiris.

Leading the list of divinities in the upper register are the goddesses of north and south in their red and white crowns respectively. Behind them is a vignette showing the hawk-headed "ruler of the underworld," a crocodile-headed figure holding a rope, and Seth (here identified as the one who opens the underworld) with a large two-headed snake named Nehebkau, who is a guardian of this desert. To their right is another snake, "the great god who lives by the wind," with three heads, four human legs, and wings. A figure of a god holding the eyes of Horus in his hand comes next, facing left over the figure of a hooded cobra labeled as the scorpion goddess Serket, who also served to guard the path. Facing her are three snakes, then the tunnel cuts through the register. At the far left, under the path of fire, is another goddess in the red crown, "the one who guards the one who rises," facing a guardian snake on four legs with a human face.

In the lower register is another boat, with human heads on prow and stern. On deck is the "white snake," guard of the god Sokar and of the cemetery of Imyhat. In front of the boat are more deities, including a mummiform baboon on a throne. Crawling in front of them are male and female snakes. On the other side of the path of fire is a three-headed snake called Menmennu, who has fourteen human heads with sun disks and stars above him. These heads represent the first fourteen days of the lunar month, when the moon waxes. The royally-clad "one in the sky" is next, raising his arm beneath the winged solar disk, symbolizing the newly-born Khepri. Ending the register is the goddess Ma'at guarding the gate to the next hour.

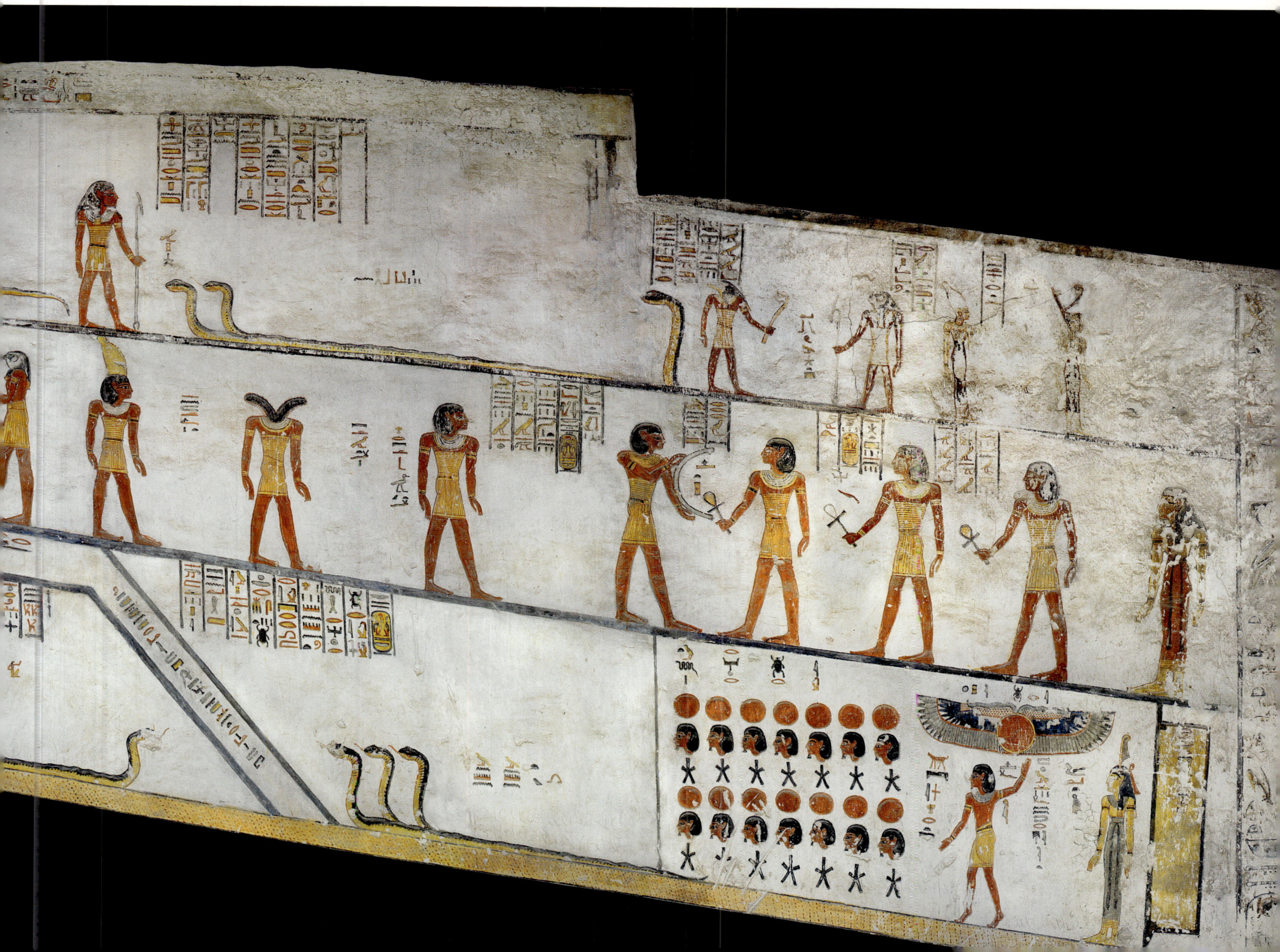

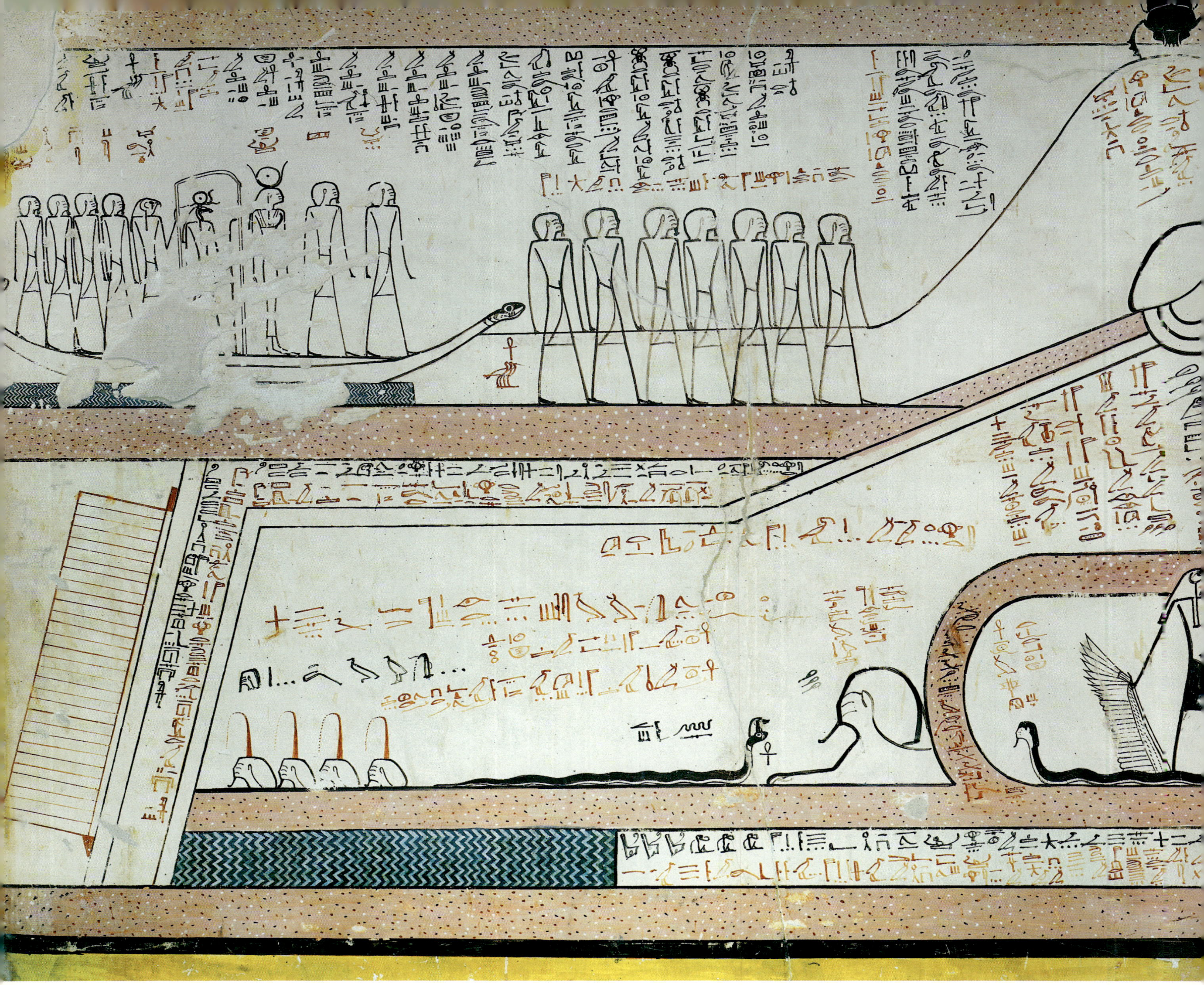

Hour Five: The Cave of Sokar

In the fifth hour, which continues through a desert landscape, the solar bark approaches the "cavern of Sokar," an oval area in which Sokar stands, holding the wings of a quadruple-headed serpent. Below the cavern is the Lake of Fire, where damned souls suffer eternal torture, but the blessed can find water. Above the cavern, the strip of desert culminates in a human head, personification of the desert, and in the top register is the burial mound of Osiris, with Isis and Nephthys in the form of birds perched on either side. The sun god is reborn from this mound, again in the form of the scarab beetle, who aids in his own rebirth by holding the tow rope of the solar bark.

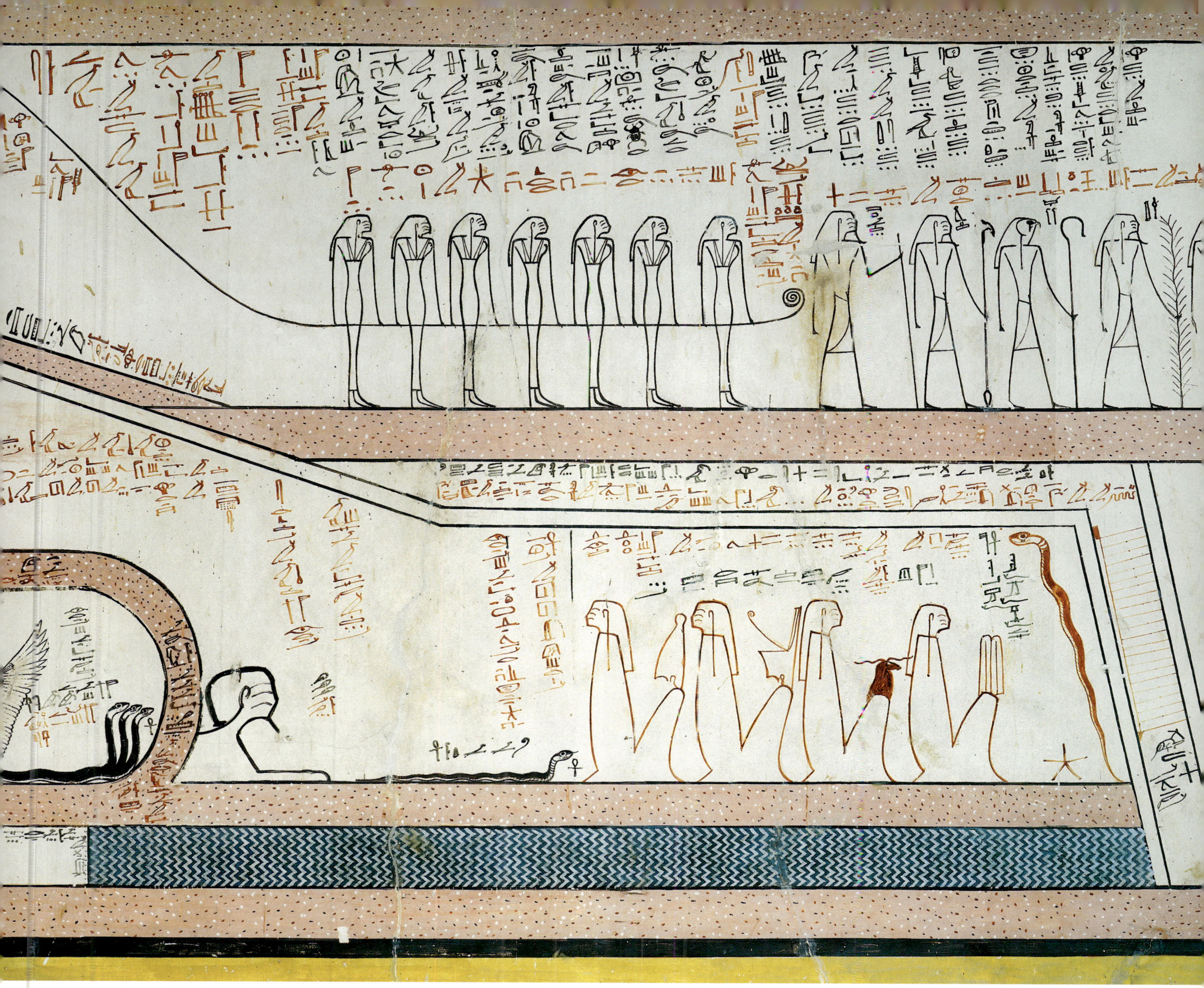

Hour Five. This image shows the lower two registers of the fifth hour. The top register here (the central register of the hour) is dominated by the solar bark, drawn in this case by fourteen figures, seven male and seven female, again representing the days when the moon grows larger. Before them are five additional gods, including Isis of the west, the "one who commands," the hawk-headed 'ruler of the road," and the "one who brings peace." The scarab beetle Khepri can be seen in the center of this register, reaching his front legs forward to grasp the tow rope. He emerges from the hill of Sokar, not visible here, from which he is reborn. In the center of the bottom register is the cave of Sokar, also known as the "egg that holds life." The cave is an oval surrounded by sand, with no door. Inside is Sokar with a hawk's head holding a snake that is called the "great god." This snake has no tail, instead he has three serpents' heads looking right and a bearded human head looking left. The snake is itself an incarnation of Sokar. Above the cave, the upper border of the register forms a pyramidal shape with the head of a woman; the accompanying inscription says that this is Isis come to protect her brother Osiris in the land of Sokar. Flanking the cave are human-headed sphinxes, representing the earth god Aker. To the right is a snake on its belly, then four seated mummiform gods, two facing forward and the other two with their heads turned to look back. To the left is another snake, then four human heads. Beneath this register is a watery band, the Lake of Fire. According to the text, the wicked are punished here by fire, but the blessed receive the waters of eternal life.

HOUR SIX: THE UNION OF RE AND OSIRIS

The sixth hour, the middle of the night, is when the solar bark reaches the waters of the Nun. According to Egyptian creation myths, the limitless Nun, swathed in darkness, existed at the beginning of time. It was from these waters that the universe was created; after the creation, the Nun, embodiment of chaos, surrounded and continually both threatened and nourished the world and its inhabitants. The sun god is seen twice here: once in his bark (which has been restored to its usual form), and once in the form of a corpse, resting inside the coils of a five-headed snake. Osiris is here, in the powerful form of a lion whose name is "bull with the voice of thunder." This is the moment when Re and Osiris unite, providing the sun god with the magical energy he needs to continue his journey and be reborn at dawn.

Osiris is the most important god in this hour, as it was his business to take care of the souls in the Duat. He was the one who could call them by their names. Without his knowledge and power, Re would not be able to resurrect at dawn. Thus this hour is crucial, the hour of greatest importance to the successful journey.

HOUR SEVEN: THE DEFEAT OF APOPHIS

The seventh hour takes place in the Cavern of Osiris. There is no water here because a great snake has drunk it all. The solar bark, however, remains in its waterborne form, and is propelled by the magic of Isis. After the successful union of Re and Osiris, this is the moment of greatest danger. Before the sun god begins his ascent to the eastern horizon, he must face his archenemy, Apophis. This great serpent lies on his sandbank directly in front of the solar bark, attempting to swallow the sun and return the world to primeval darkness. Apophis was the symbol of chaos, the embodiment of the forces of entropy, and the enemy of Creation. Of course, the gods who protect and fight for Re capture and dismember Apophis and the sun god is able to continue, triumphant, on his journey.

HOUR EIGHT: THE COFFINS OF THE GODS

In the eighth hour, the bark of the god reaches the cemetery where the mummified dead reside. No enemies of Re lurk in this land, only the blessed, who eagerly await the arrival of the sun god. The beings shown here sit on hieroglyphs for linen within caverns closed by doors that can be opened only by the call of the sun god. This emphasizes one important purpose of this hour: to provide clothing and jewels as part of the celebration of the cult. The accompanying text reveals that the speech of the *ba*s of the gods and the deceased as they rejoice in answer to the sun god is distorted so that it is heard by the living as various sounds of nature.

HOUR NINE: THE RESTHOUSE OF RE AND HIS CREW

The ninth hour is the point at which Re and his crew have a moment of rest. This is still a desert landscape, with only a small pool of water on which the solar bark can travel. The area in which the solar bark rests is secret, hidden from its enemies, and is a quiet place filled with welcoming gods. The theme of provisioning the dead continues to be important here.

Hour Six (*following pages*). Part of the top two registers of the sixth hour can be seen here. The body of the god appears at the lower left, lying prone within the curled coils of a five-headed snake, his arm raised to his head, where a figure of the Khepri beetle has been placed. This is the Mehen snake, which appears in later hours of this book protecting the god within his bark, and also features in the Book of Gates. The body of the god here also stands in for the body of the deceased king within his tomb. This scene represents simultaneously the return of the soul to the body and the unification of the body of Osiris with the soul of Re. Facing the god are twelve of the sixteen mummiform figures who occupy this register. The first four (not shown here) wear the white crown of Upper Egypt; then come four "pacified ones," four kings of Lower Egypt, and four "blessed spirits."

It is important here that the ancient kings of Egypt have come to witness and participate in this momentous event. In the register above, we see six of nine scepters, three with the white crown (not shown), three with the red crown, and three with the protective uraeus. Each holds a knife, in preparation for the dangers of the hours to come. Facing the scepters is the lion called the "bull with the voice of thunder." Next comes Isis, seated on an invisible throne, two gods, and three divine graves, guarded by fire-breathing serpents, for the head, wing, and hindquarters of the solar beetle. Facing these rooms is the goddess "who guards the head that is in the palace."

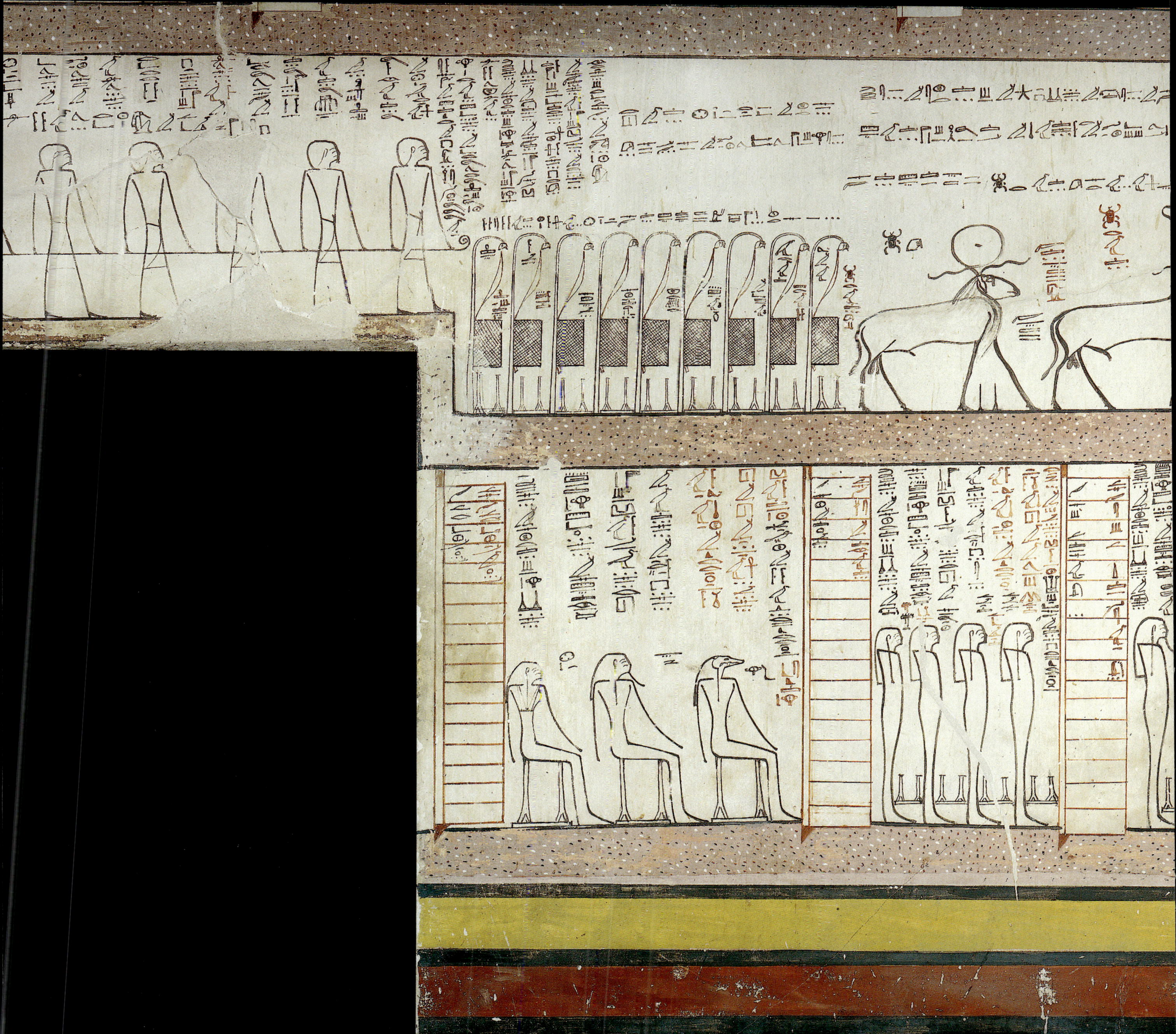

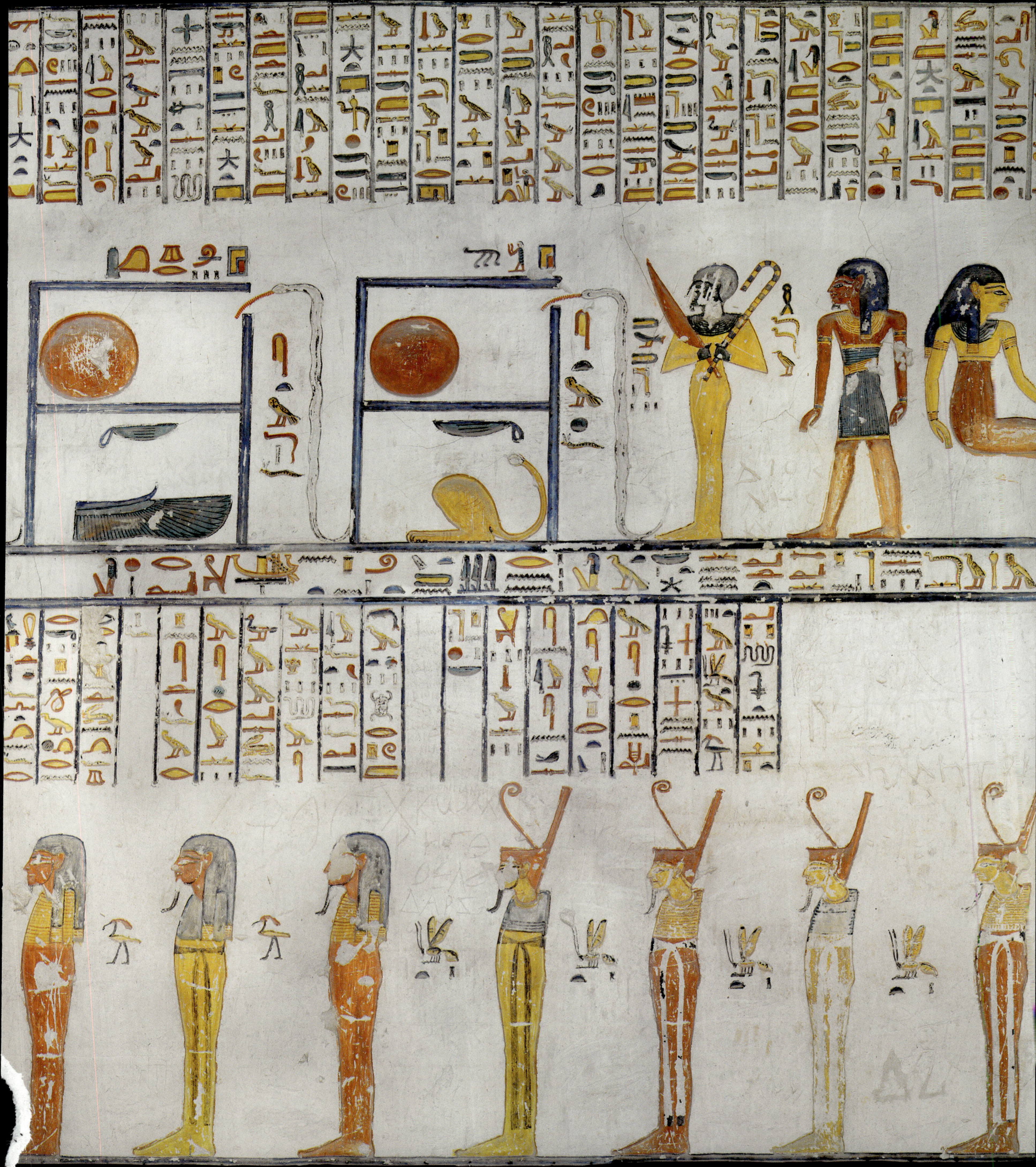

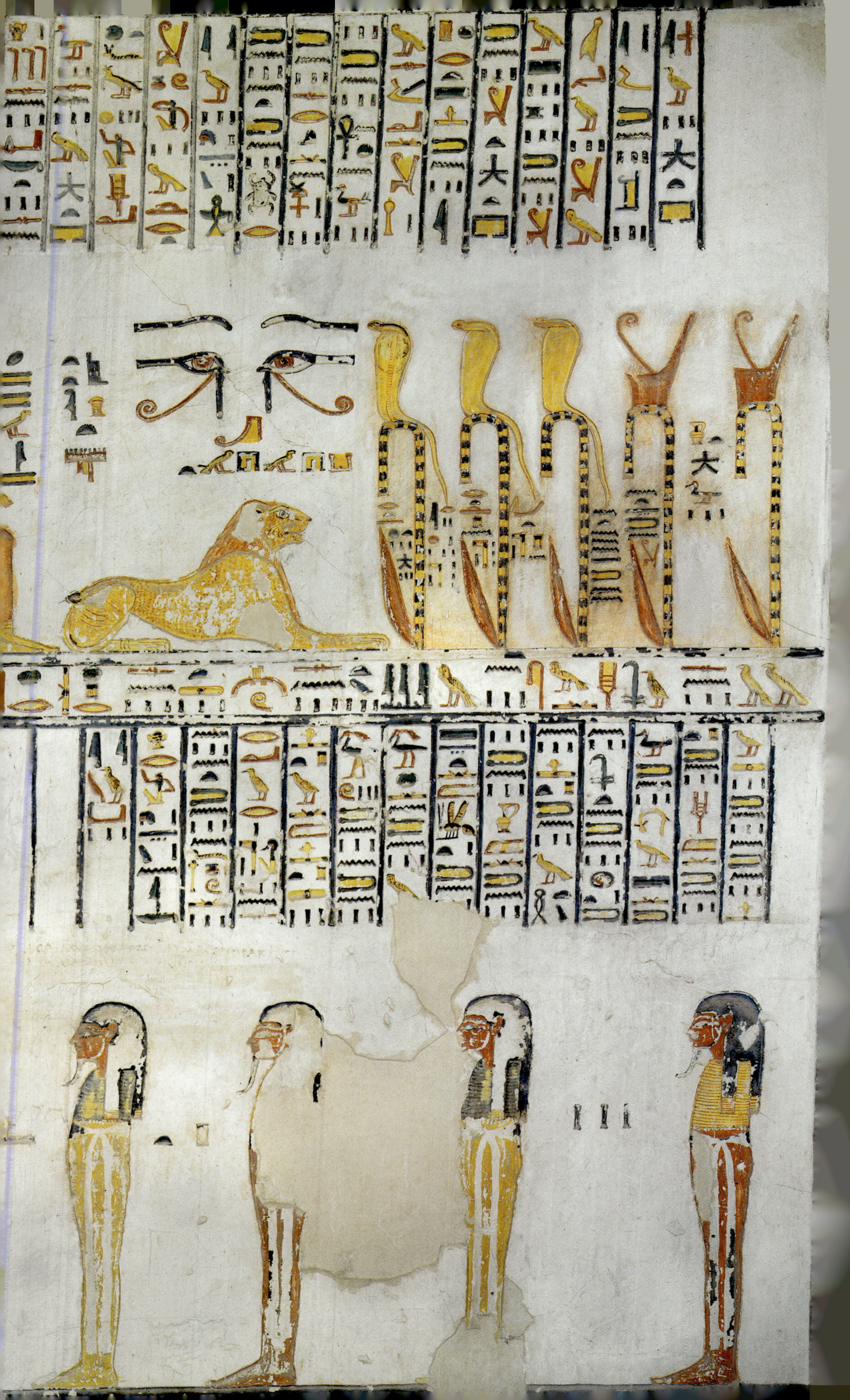

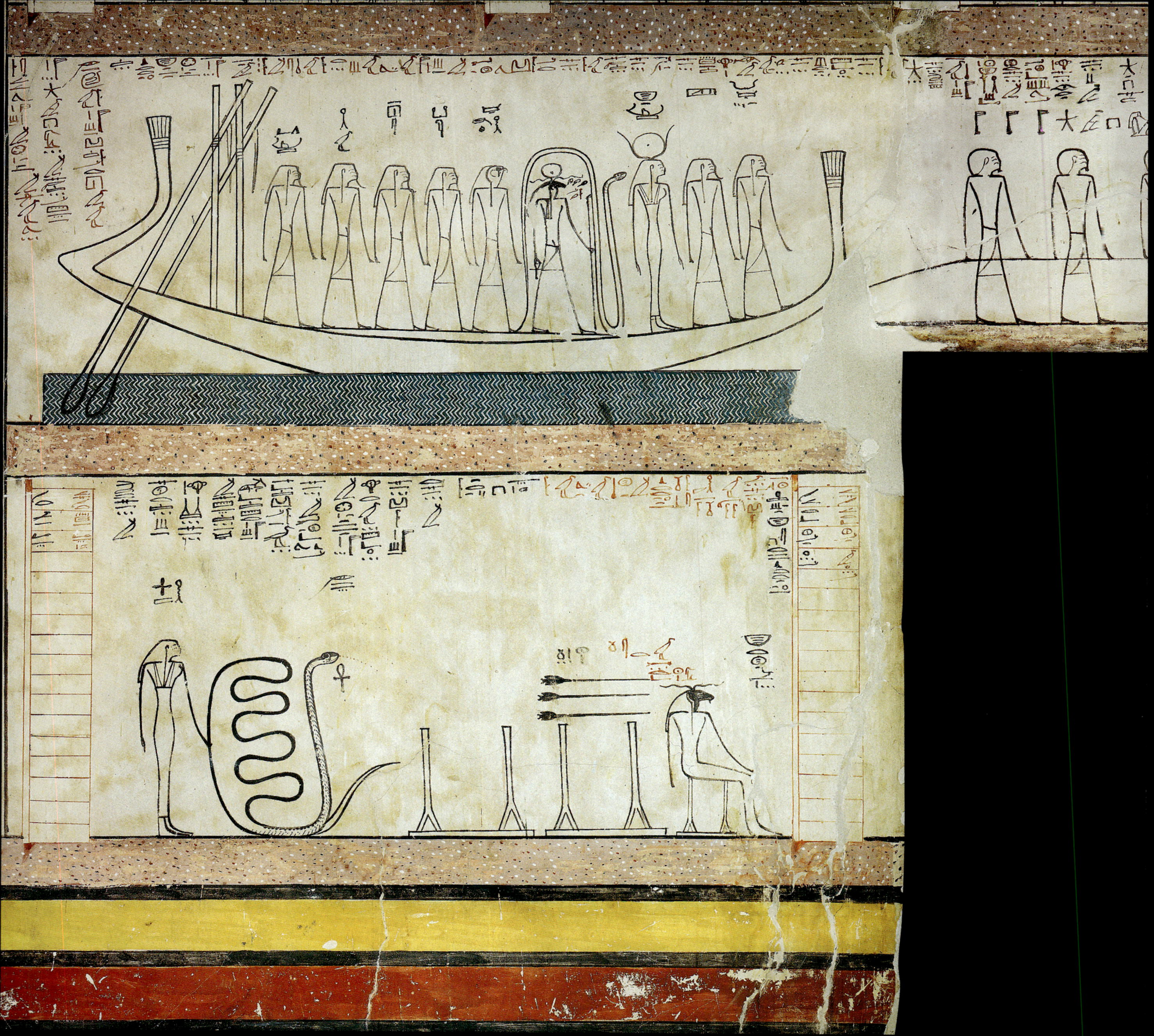

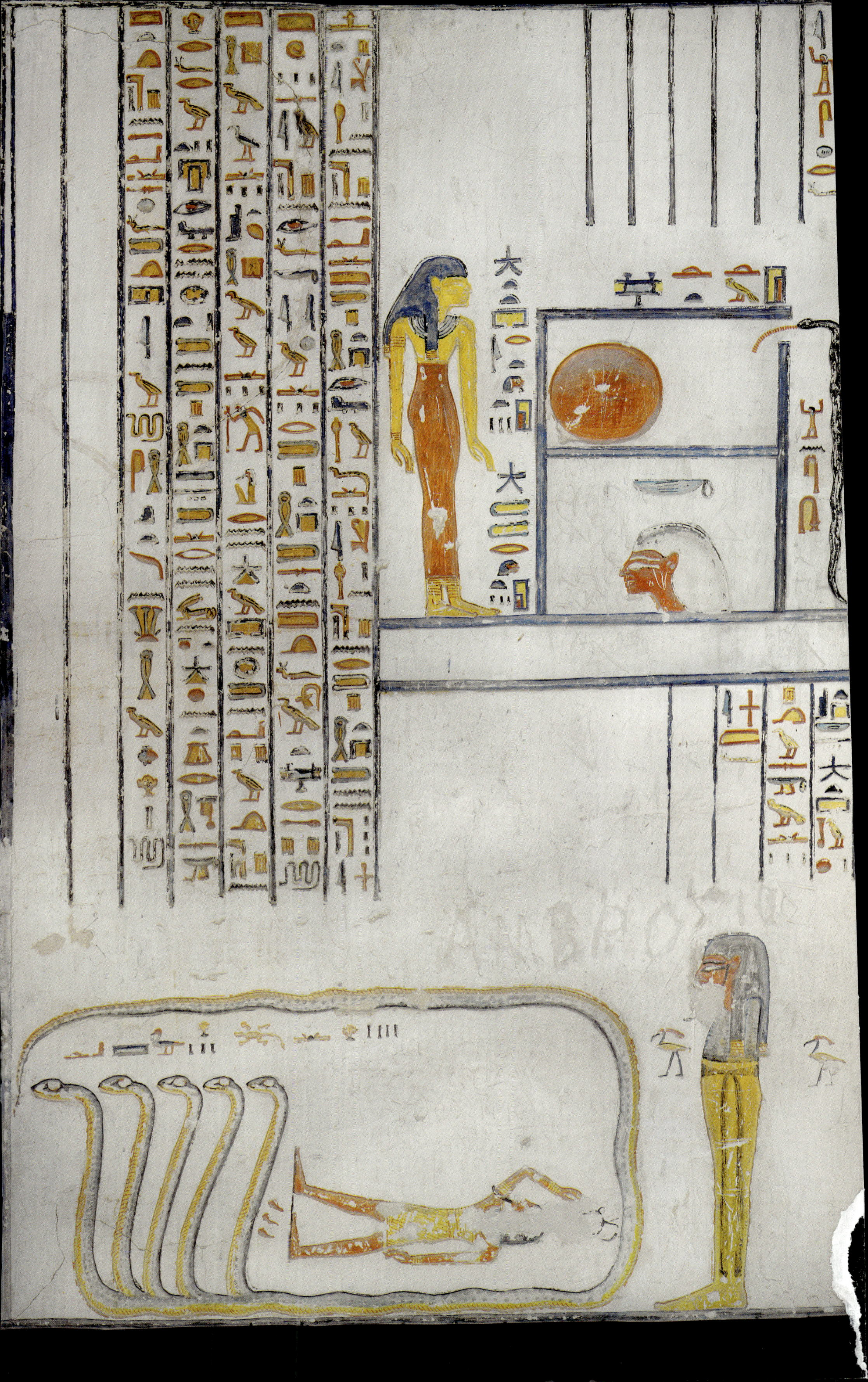

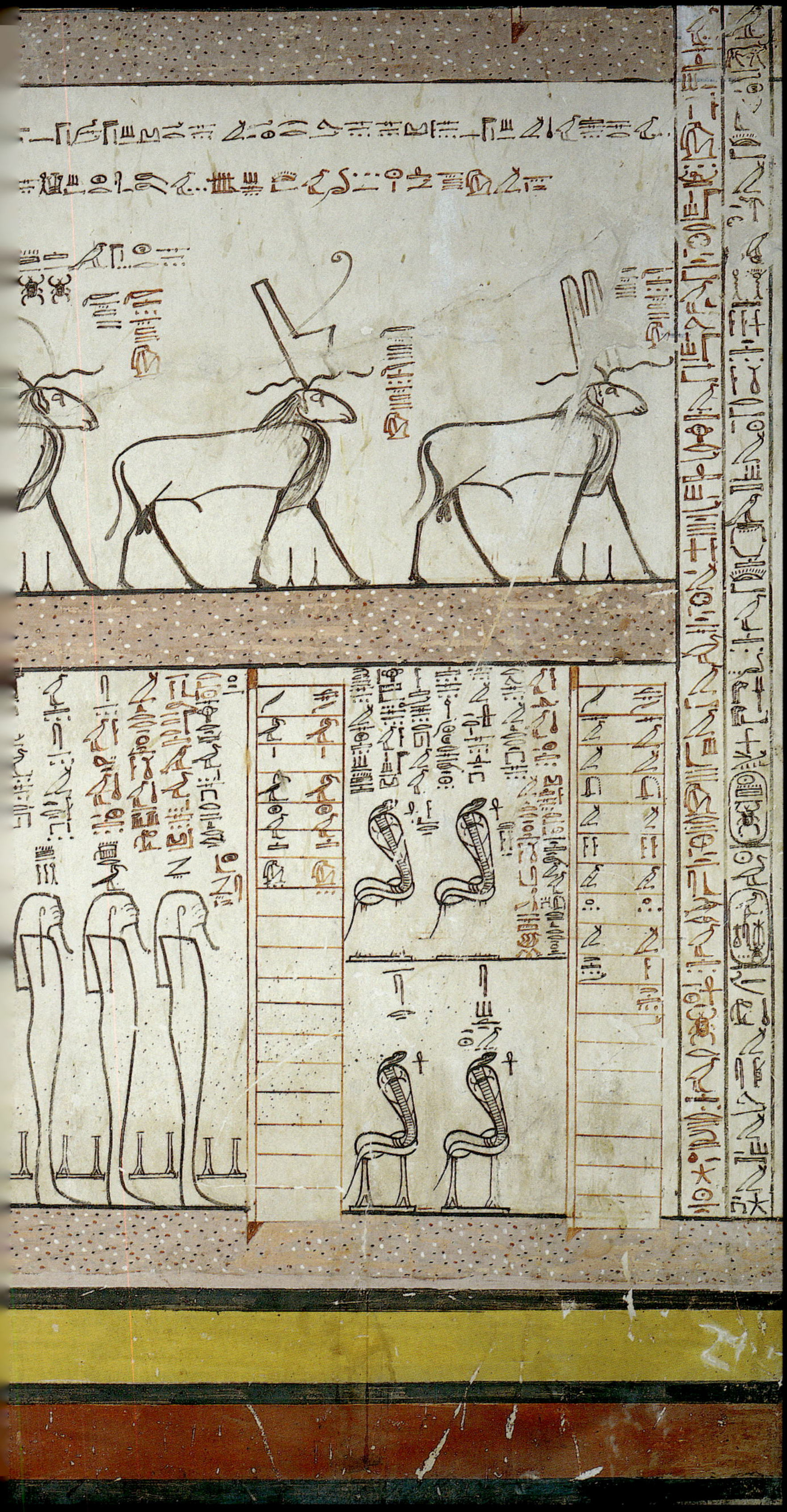

Hour Eight. The solar bark is in the middle register, in its usual place at the left. The Mehen snake continues to protect the sun god. The boat is towed here by eight gods. Before the tow men are nine personified hieroglyphs for "follower," each on the sign for cloth. These signs, apparently meant to represent the god's entourage, are preceded by four rams, each with a distinct name and crown, but all linked with the great earth god Tatanen, who represents the deepest bowels of the earth. Both the upper and lower registers of the eighth hour are divided into five caverns by a series of closed doors. Within each room in the upper register is a group of three gods, all seated on the sign for cloth. Many of the major gods are represented here: in the last room on the left are Atum, Khepri, and Shu; in the next are Tefnut, Geb, and Nut; then Osiris, Isis, and Horus. The lower register is more complex, with various groups of deities in each cavern. The texts are cryptic, as is the case throughout the Netherworld Books, which are meant to be understood only by the initiated. All of these gods will be resurrected at the moment when the bark of Re arrives, and it is the duty of the deceased to know all of their names.

Hour Nine (*following pages*). Important figures here include the sailors who row the solar bark, arranged in the middle register with their oars in their hands; the number of these varies from tomb to tomb according to the space available. Before them are the three basket signs, each topped by a different figure: first from the left is a human-headed bird with a false beard and the plumes of Amun; next is a ram; and third is a cow with the sun disk between her horns. The job of these three gods is to provide plentiful things, the bounty of Re, to the inhabitants of this land. Leading this register is a mummiform figure called the "offering of the gods." Some have suggested that this is an image of Re. In the upper register are two groups of deities: twelve standing goddesses and twelve gods seated on cloth signs. The duty of these divinities is to guard Re, although no enemies are in sight, and the nine seated males form the court of law that "brings down the enemies of Osiris." The lower register is headed at right by another mummiform figure ("the overseer of the roads of the Duat"), then nine gods holding grain stalks to provision the deceased, and twelve cobras (not visible here), seated on cloth signs and throwing fire from their mouths to light the way for the solar bark.

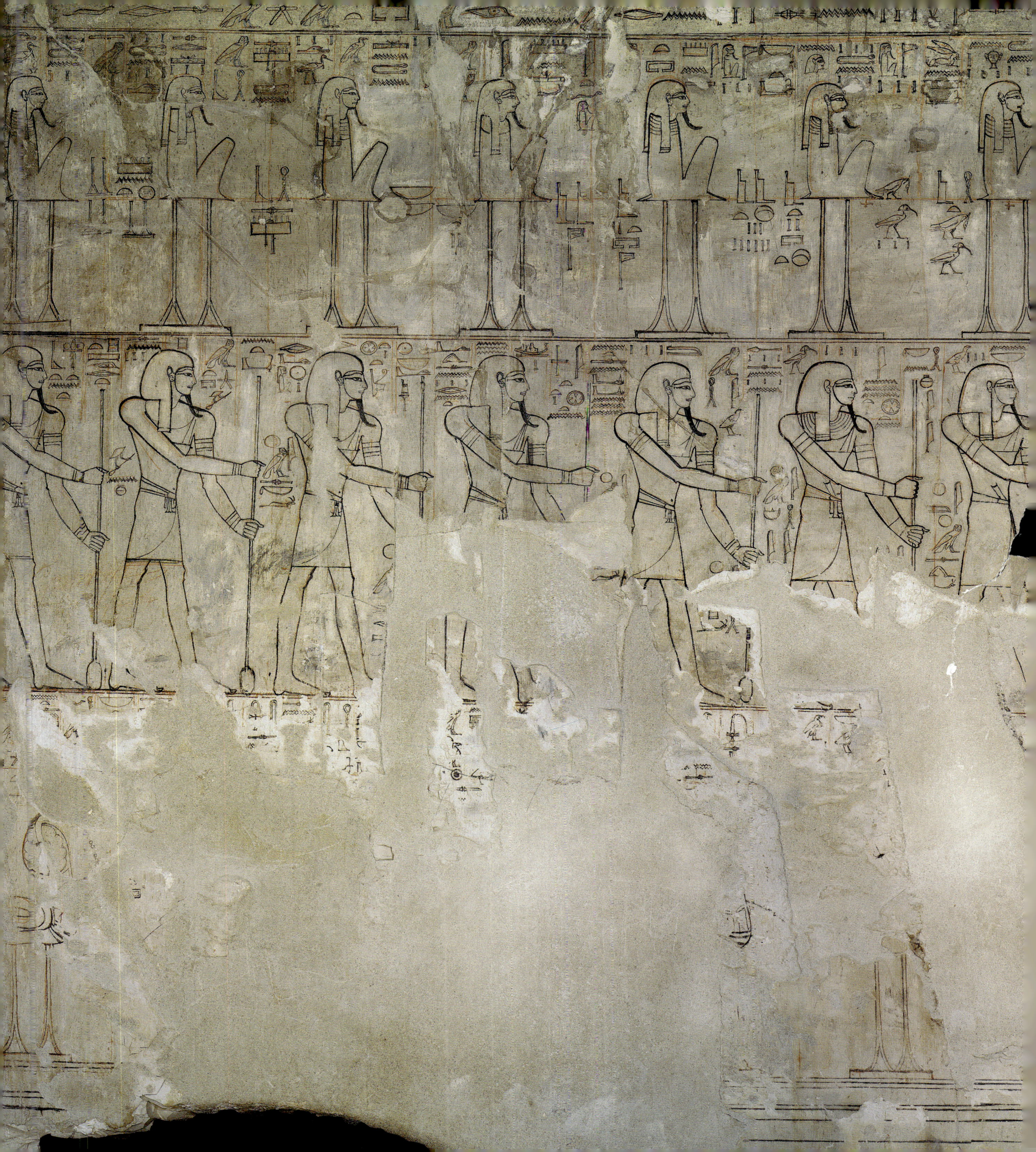

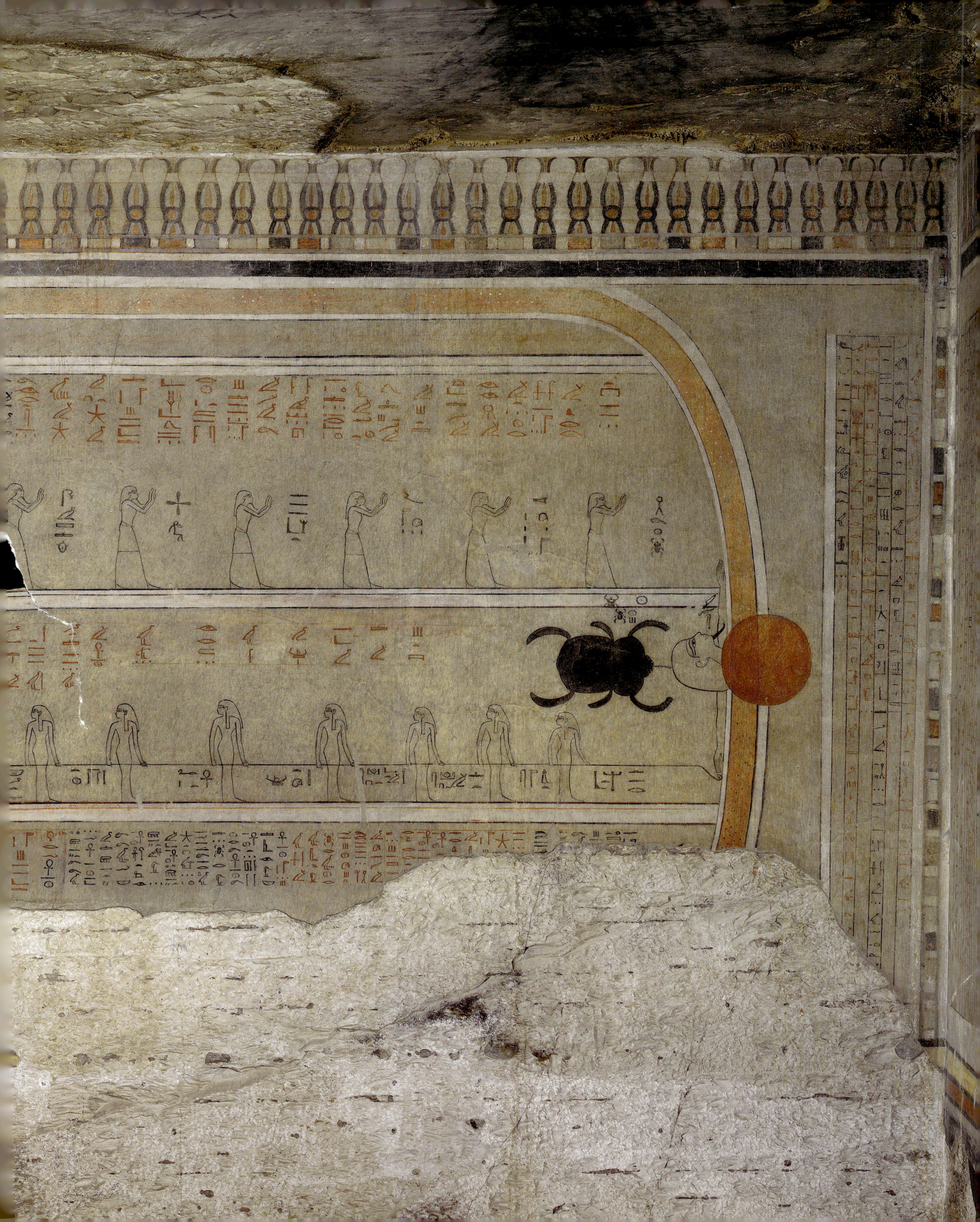

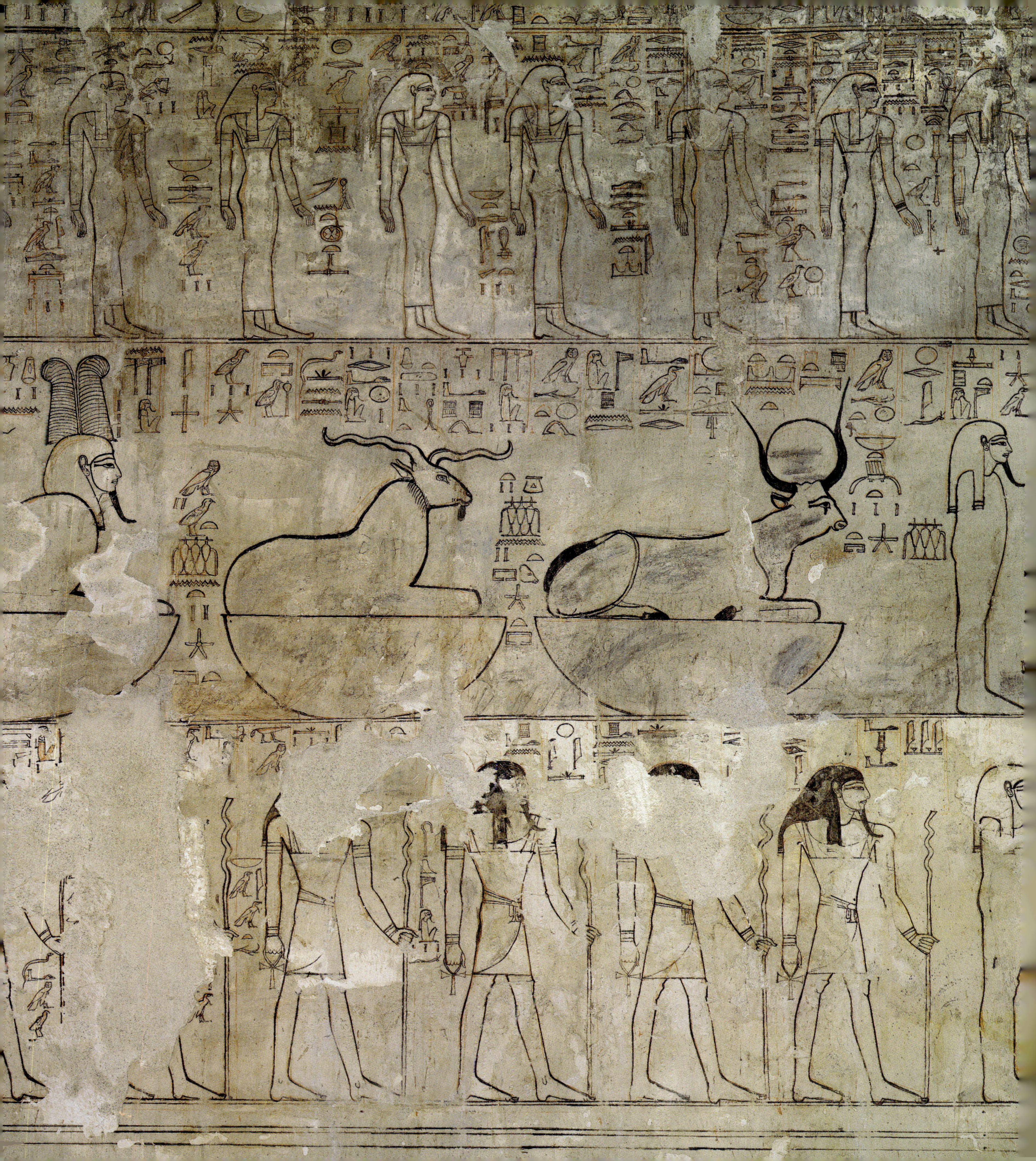

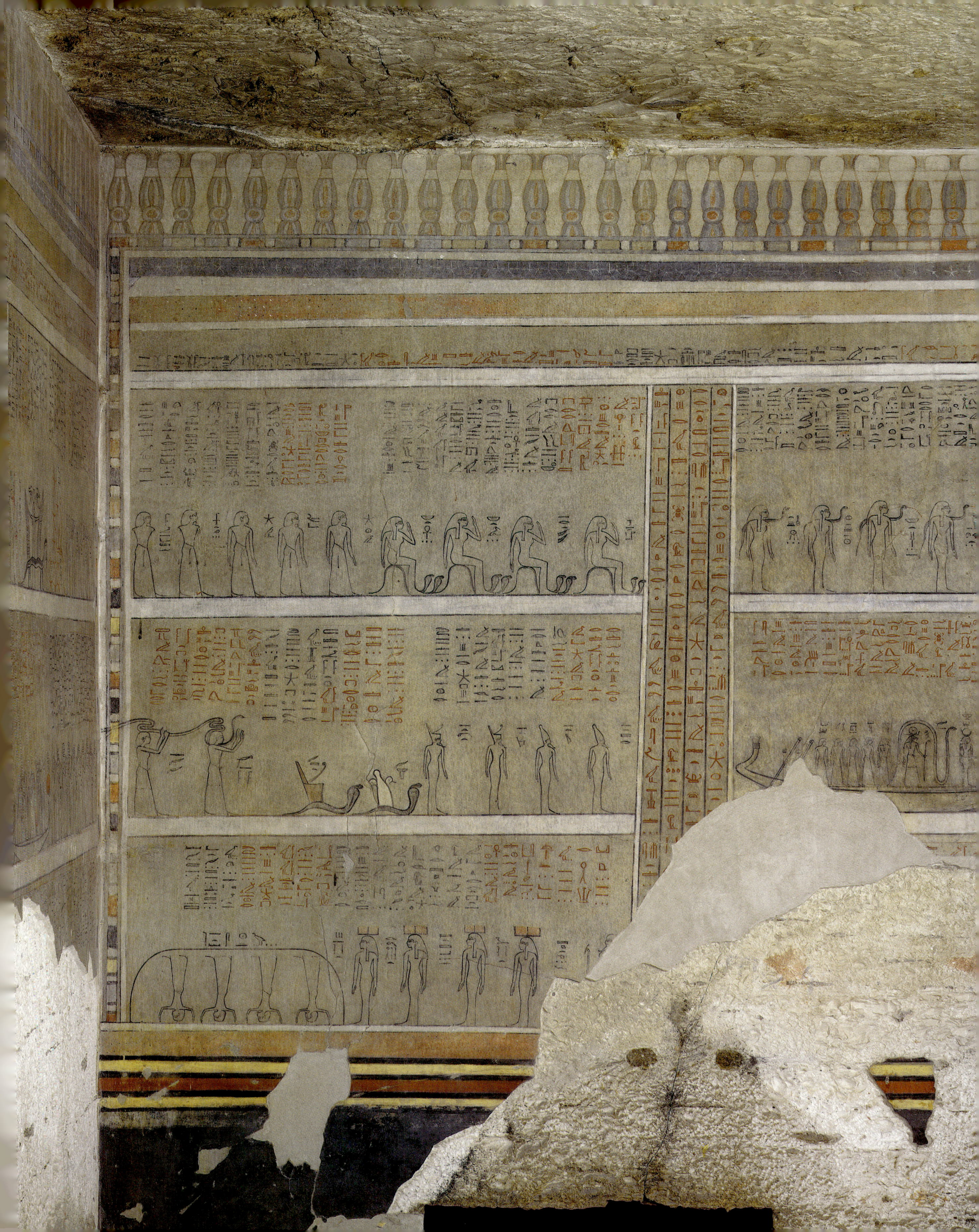

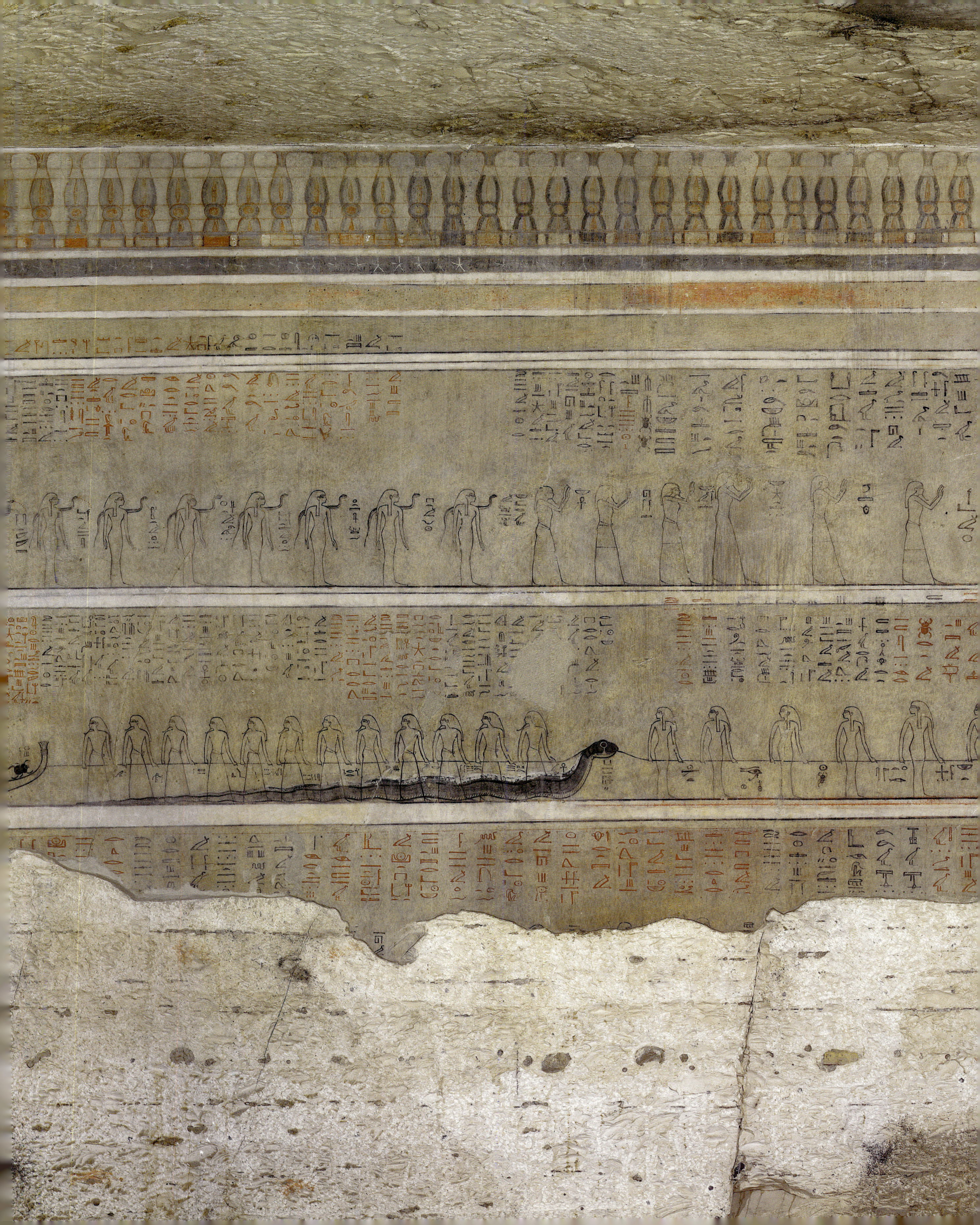

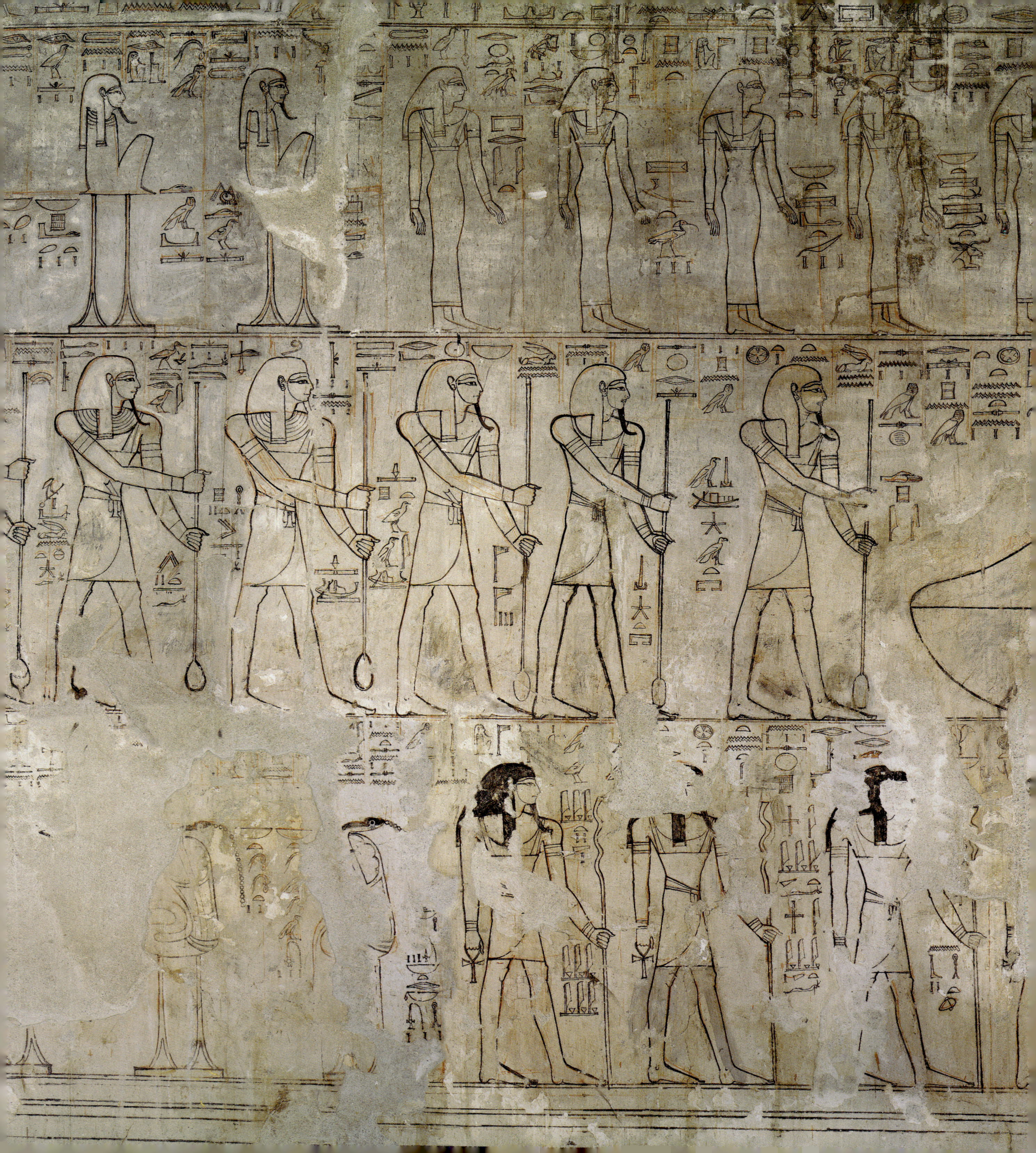

HOUR TEN: THE DEEP WATER WITH HIGH BANKS

Again, no enemies of Re appear in this hour, whose landscape of deep water and high banks is filled with protective deities. Prominent here is a long rectangle of water filled with the bodies of the drowned, who have not been given proper burial. However, the primeval water is rejuvenating, and the drowned have been prevented from decomposing by Horus the Elder (at far left with a sun disk on his head, leaning on his staff) so are later able to join the blessed. The darkness is dispersed by four goddesses with fire-spitting snakes on their foreheads, who stand behind a scepter topped by the head of Seth.

In addition to processions of divinities, a number of interesting vignettes appear in the tenth hour. In front of the solar bark is the figure of a hawk, the *ba* of Sokar, standing on a snake with two crowned heads and four legs; this image is flanked by goddesses in the northern and southern crowns. Nearby is a skiff containing a hawk-headed snake, representing yet another form of Osiris. The upper register focuses on the healing of the solar eye, shown as two red disks. One is held by two goddesses atop the sign for "god"; the other, also protected by two goddesses (shown as children with their hands to their mouths), is raised by two upright snakes. Left of these is Khepri as a beetle, holding aloft an oval ball called "the living Khepri." The remainder of this register is filled with eight Sekhmets, four with lioness heads and four with human heads, being offered the *wedjat* (eye of Horus) by a Thoth in the form of a baboon seated on a throne. The Sekhmets are entrusted with the eye so that they can keep it safe from Seth.

HOUR ELEVEN: THE FIRE AND THE TORTURE

The main purpose of this hour was to prepare for the rising of this sun, the "emergence from the eastern mountain of heaven." The solar bark, with its usual crew, bears a solar disk on its prow to light its way. The bark is led here by twelve men carrying the coils of the "world-encircling" snake on their heads. The final rejuvenation will take place within this serpent, which, according to Hornung, could not touch the ground until the final hour of the night. The men are preceded by Isis and Nephthys in the form of cobras, who carry the crowns of Upper and Lower Egypt to the Eastern Gate of Sais, as well as the goddess Neith (patron of Sais) in four of her guises.

The upper register of this hour is dedicated to signaling the moment of the sunrise and the birth of the hours. At far left is a double-headed man, the "lord of time." Next to him is a scene similar to that found inside the cavern of Sokar in the fifth hour, but here the winged snake is identified as the body of Atum, and the god who stands above it as Atum's soul. To the right of this is Osiris seated on an ascending snake surrounded by stars, then twelve gods in various forms, and finally four goddesses on double-headed cobras. These goddesses sit with their hands before their mouths, breathing fire to destroy the enemies that are seen buried within mounds of sand in the lowest register. These mounds are attacked by knife-wielding goddesses and contain, from left to right: the bodies of the enemies, again the bodies, their *bas*, their shadows (represented by the hieroglyph for this word); and their decapitated heads. No goddess attacks the sixth mound, which contains four figures turned on their heads. The hawk-headed Horus, leaning on his staff and holding a snake, and an upright snake "who burns millions" stand at the left, facing these mounds, and a series of four goddesses and one god watch the action from the right. Thus any final threat to the still-vulnerable sun god is averted, so that he can proceed safely to the final hour of the night.

HOUR TWELVE: THE REBIRTH OF THE SUN

This hour represents the successful completion of the arduous journey, when the sun god, and with him the deceased king, is reborn. The action is imagined to take place within the world-encircling snake seen in Hour Eleven, which can be linked with either the land beneath the earth or the sky above, or both simultaneously. According to the texts, movement inside this snake is from the tail, where the elderly enter, to the head, where small children emerge, to show that time is reversed in the Duat.

Hour Twelve *(preceding pages)*. The landscape in the twelfth hour is represented in an oval shape, personified with the head and arms of the god of the air, Shu. The solar bark in the central register, with Khepri resting near its prow, is towed by twelve gods and thirteen goddesses, all of whom look back toward the figure of Re. The gods stand on a large snake, but the goddesses are on the ground, with the image of Khepri above the heads of the last figures to the right. The upper and lower registers of this hour are filled with processions of primeval gods, here to protect the sun god from Apophis and raise him to the sky, aiding the sky goddess Nut to give him birth. The presence of a full complement of primordial divinities emphasizes the link between the daily rising of the sun and the perpetual re-enactment of the original moment of creation. At the far right of the lower register is the mummified body of Osiris, traveling upward against the curve of the oval horizon. Osiris is here to be united with the body of the deceased, remaining in the other world until the sun returns once more. The moment of sunrise is represented in the middle register, where Khepri, the morning sun, pushes the solar disk across the horizon, personified as Shu. For a moment, the Duat is open, then it is closed again, and the cycle of the day begins.

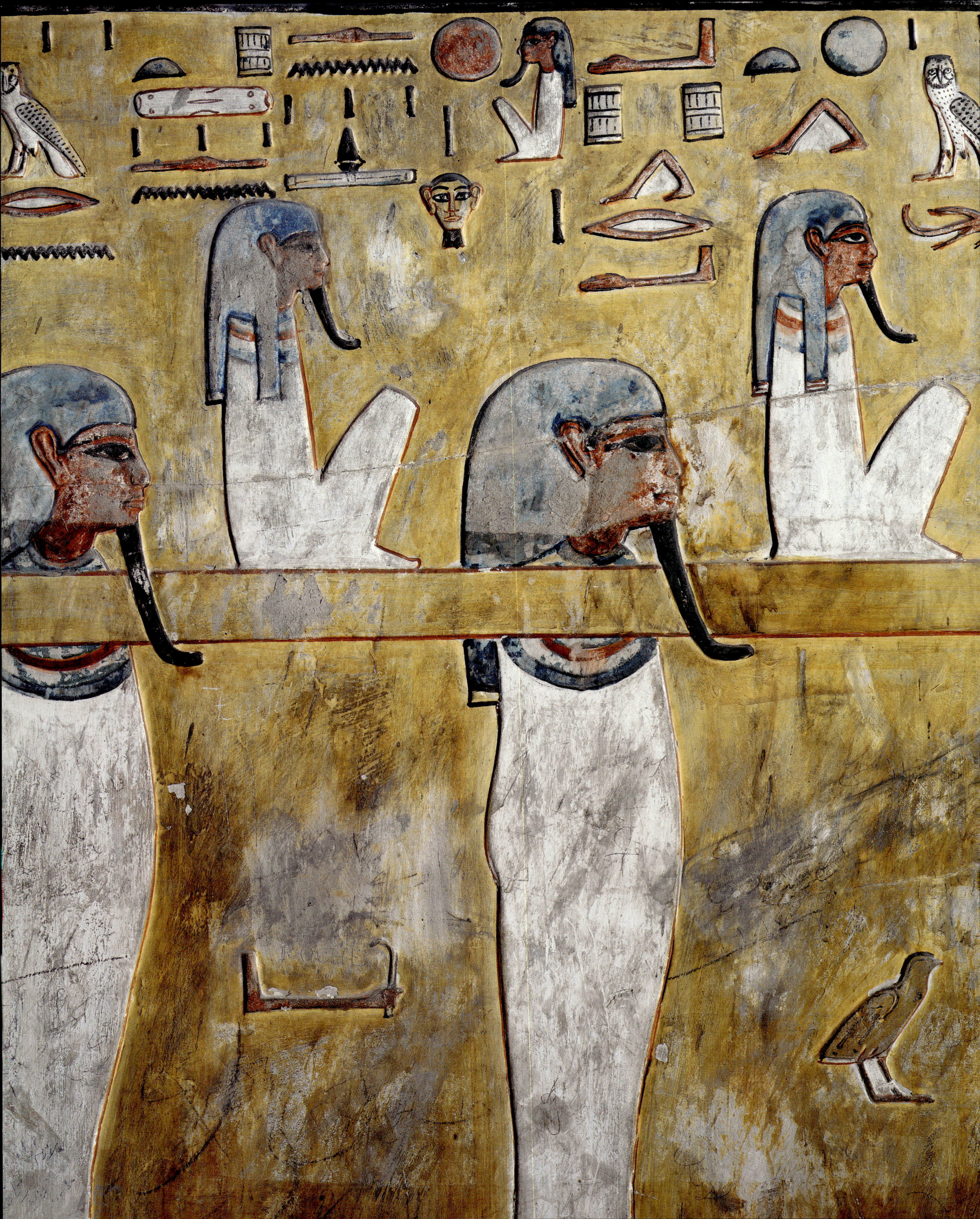

CHAPTER 4

THE BOOK OF GATES

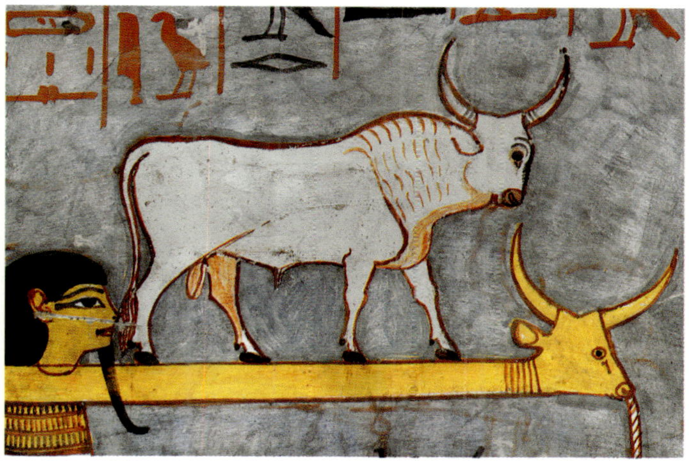

The Book of Gates is seen first in the 18th Dynasty, just before the Amarna era. The first king to use this composition in the decoration of his tomb was the post-Amarna monarch Horemheb, who chose Hours Two, Three, Four, Five, and Six for the walls of his burial chamber. Ramses I followed his example, and adorned his sarcophagus crypt with the new book. Beginning in the reign of Seti I, the Amduat and the Book of Gates appeared side by side in many royal tombs; Ramses II was the only king to inscribe the entire sequence in his tomb, although the Osireion and the tomb of Ramses V/VI also have continuous scenes. Selections from this composition also appeared on several royal sarcophagi.

Why did the Egyptians create a second Netherworld book? Was the Amduat not sufficient to guide the king safely into the Afterlife? Some Egyptologists believe that the Book of Gates was offered by the priests of Amun-Re as an alternative to the Amduat. The focus of the earlier book is on Osiris and his kingdom; it was designed to ensure that he is the great god. The Book of Gates seeks to preserve the primacy of Amun-Re, and was perhaps composed to expand the control of this god over all the earth, in the sky, and even in the Netherworld. Here Osiris's power is limited to the land of the beyond.

The general outline of this book bears many similarities to the Amduat. It is also divided into twelve hours, although in this case, the chapters are introduced by high gate-like

TOWING THE BARK OF THE SUN GOD
This detail from the third hour of the Book of Gates shows the pole to which the tow rope of the sun god's bark has been attached. This is held up by eight mummiform figures, two of which are visible here. An additional seven deities sit on the pole; two of these are shown in this photograph.

THE BARK OF THE SUN GOD
(Following pages)
Throughout the Book of Gates, the sun god appears in the form of a ram-headed male, his shrine protected by the Mehen snake. He is accompanied by the herald Sia, and the god of magic, Heka.

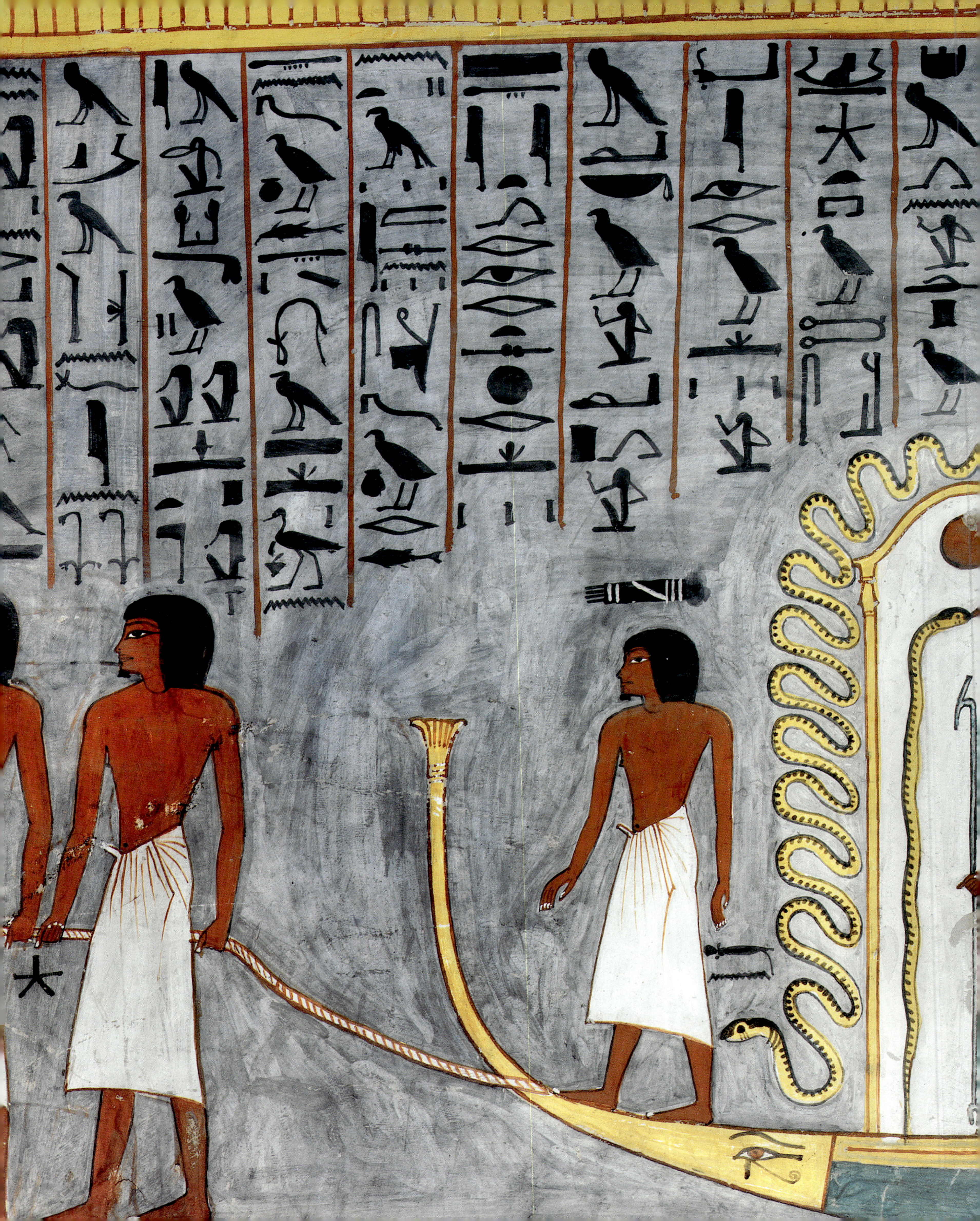

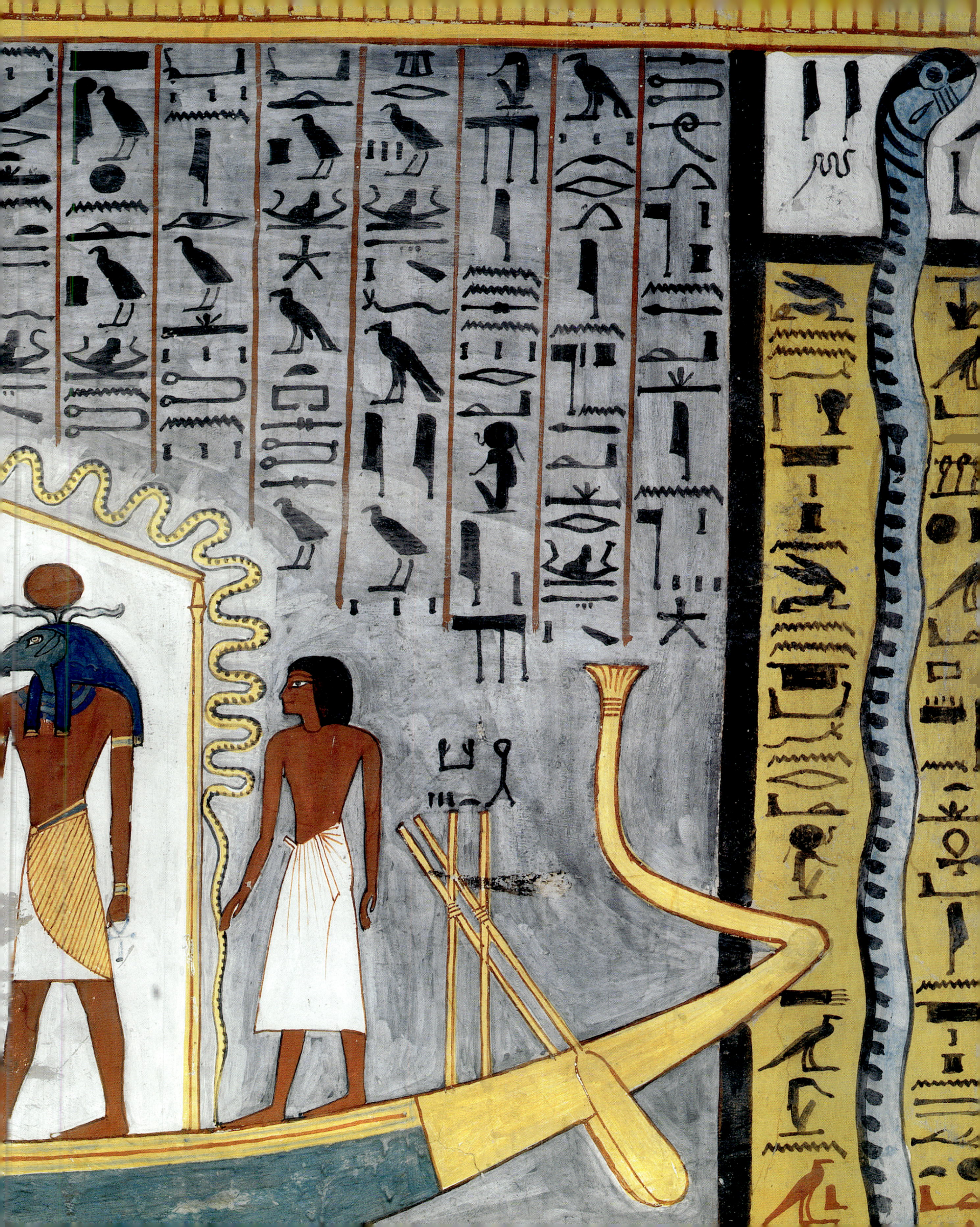

structures (from which Egyptologists took the modern name of the book). These are guarded by snakes and remain closed to the enemies of order, but open to let the solar bark pass. The concept of gates in the beyond appears as early as the Pyramid Texts, and such structures are mentioned in the Amduat, but it is only in this composition that they are given such prominence. It has been observed that the Amduat is organized more around the concept of time, while the Book of Gates is defined by space.

The sarcophagus of Seti I, which is decorated with a complete version of this composition, shows the Duat in the shape of the arched body of Osiris, bending from the west, where the sun sets, then north, then finally to the east toward the sunrise. If all the sections in the Book of Gates are considered to be equal in length, then the first six hours are set in the north, where Osiris was worshipped at Mendes, a cult site thought by some to represent the Duat on earth.

A major difference between the Book of the Amduat and the Book of Gates appears in the sixth hour, when the Cave of Sokar is replaced with the Judgment Hall of Osiris. Another is the final scene, in which the god Nun, manifestation of the primeval waters, raises the sun boat from the primordial mound into the sky.

There are far fewer denizens of the Netherworld represented in the Book of Gates, and they have been organized into groups, as if in an attempt to emphasize the importance of order. The guardians of the gates are given terrifying names, such as "he whose eyes spew fire." Passing through the gates unharmed is a difficult task, and knowledge of the names of the guardians is required. The book consists of exactly 100 scenes, separated from one another by texts dealing with the material care of the deceased.

In contrast to the Amduat, where the sun god is accompanied regularly by a larger group of gods, only two deities travel in the solar bark. In the prow is the god Sia, divine herald, whose job it is to call out instructions and open the gates. In the stern is Heka, god of magical speech. From beginning to end, the cabin of the boat is protected by the Mehen serpent. There are four humans at hand to haul on the tow rope in situations where oars will not suffice.

Another difference between the Amduat and the Book of Gates is that the king is given more prominence. He is seen in the last hour, being reborn with the sun, and there are modifications to the accompanying texts throughout the book that make more direct reference to the king.

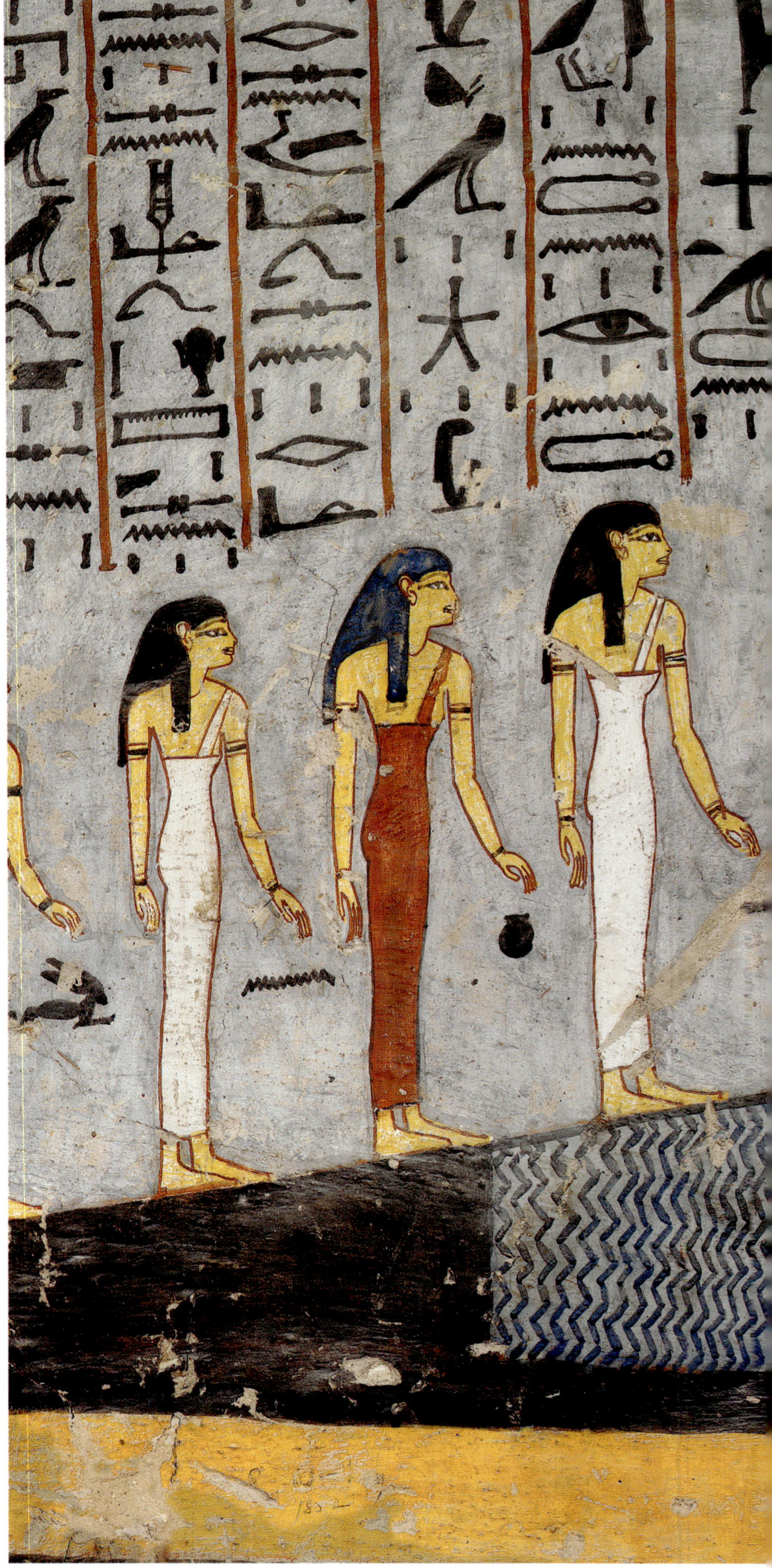

The Snake of Time.
Many serpents appear in the Book of Gates; this one is the snake of time, coiled upon itself and lying in a watery pit surrounded by a mound on which stand the goddesses linked with the twelve hours of the night.

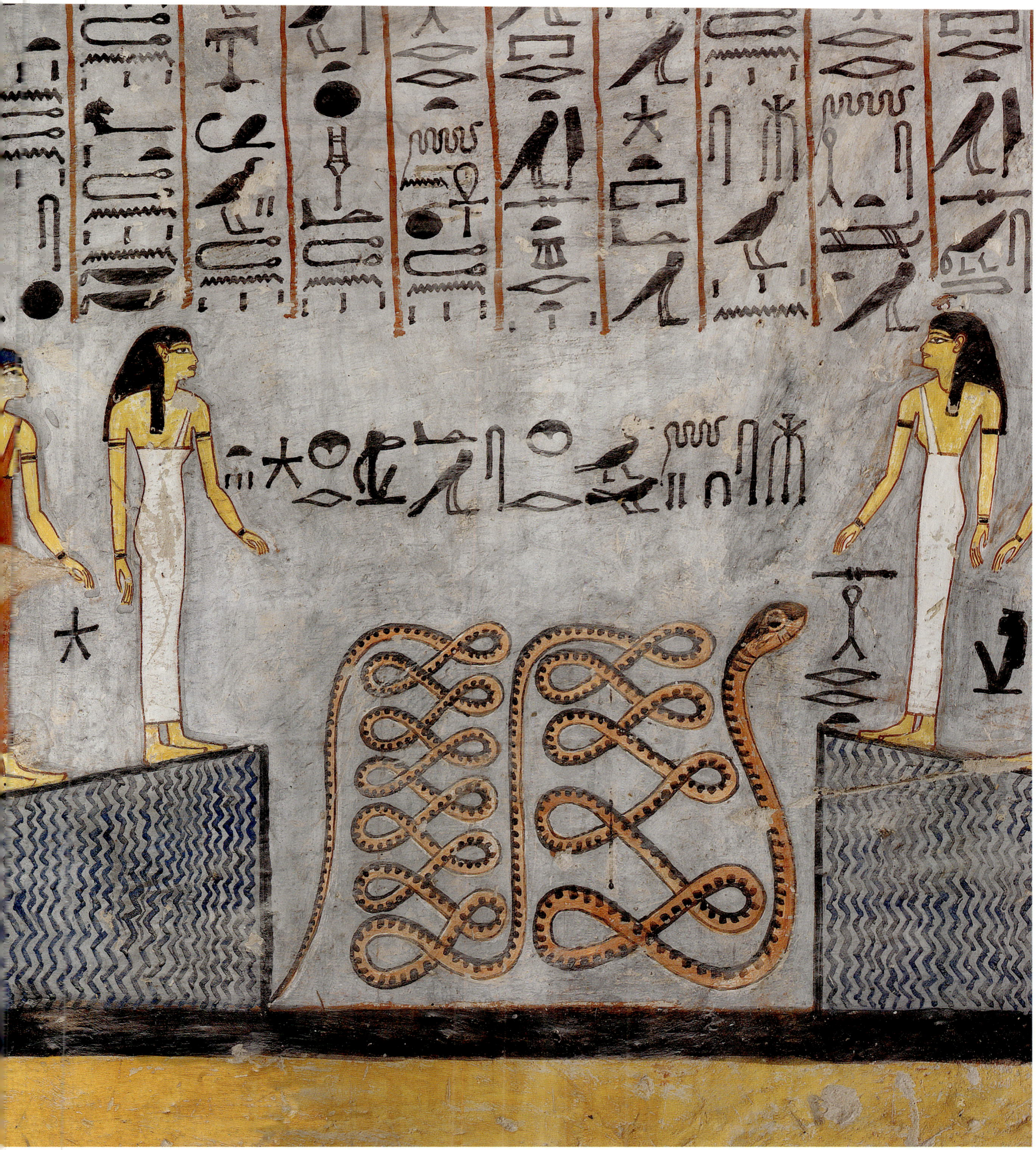

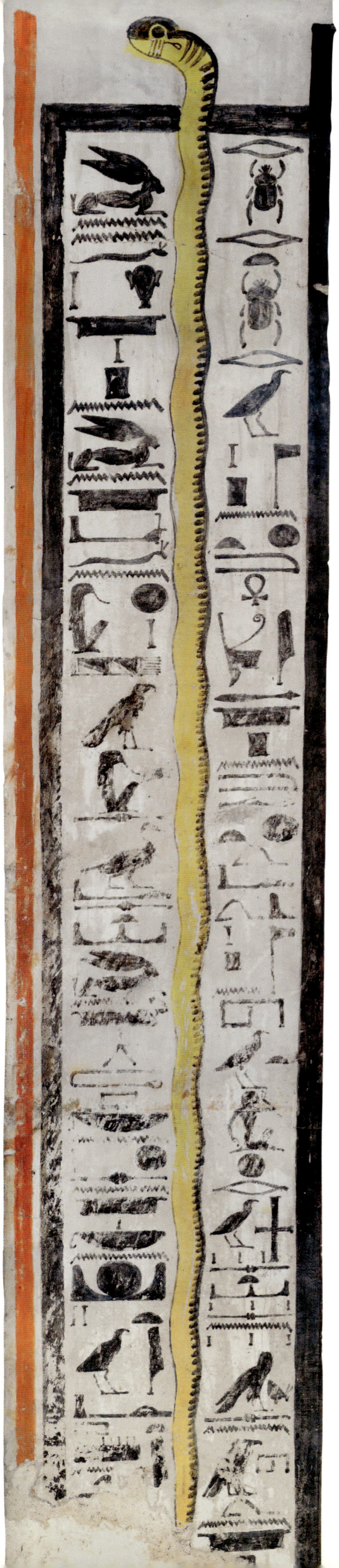

Hour One

As was the case in the Amduat, the first hour of the night deals with the transition from the earth to the Netherworld. The sun boat enters the Duat from a doorway in the tomb, perhaps in the burial chamber, depicted as a double mountain. The sun god is shown here as Khepri, the scarab beetle, with a solar disk, alluding to the successful completion of his journey. The Egyptians observed the scarab emerging from the ground, pushing a ball of dung before him; thus they associated it with the rising sun, who pushes the boat through the gates at the twelfth hour to be born anew.

The boat passes between two stakes (represented above and below) flanked by kneeling figures. One stake has a jackal's head, above which are the twelve gods of the west, here to greet the sun and welcome him into the beyond. The second stake bears a ram's head, symbol of Amun-Re, accompanied by twelve more gods.

Hour Two

One important theme of this hour is the punishment of enemies. The sun god here takes his usual form as a ram-headed man, the cabin in which he stands protected by the Mehen snake, and is found, as was usual in the Amduat, at the left end of the middle of three registers. The bark is received by twelve gods, including the ram-headed Khnum and hawk-headed Horus. At the far right is a larger figure holding a staff. In the register above are the blessed dead, who speak truth and live in *ma'at*. In contrast, the lower register is inhabited by the damned, their arms tied behind their backs to render them ineffective and harmless. The text reports that these are enemies of Re, the ones who have cursed him. At the far left is a figure of Atum leaning on a staff. Before him are the four "weary ones"; these may represent the cardinal directions, who are confused in the topsy-turvy world of the Duat.

The Gates Between the Hours

Each hour in the Book of Gates is preceded by a "gate," guarded by a snake such as the one seen here. The deceased king was required to know the name of each guardian in order to pass and proceed to the following hour. Some scholars believe that the gates were clusters of stars that moved across the sky, marking the hours of the night.

The Second Hour

(Following pages)

Atum dominates this hour, with the "weary ones," perhaps representations of the four cardinal directions, and enemies of the sun god, captured and their arms tied behind their back, before him. Above is the sun god in his bark, received by a group of divinities.

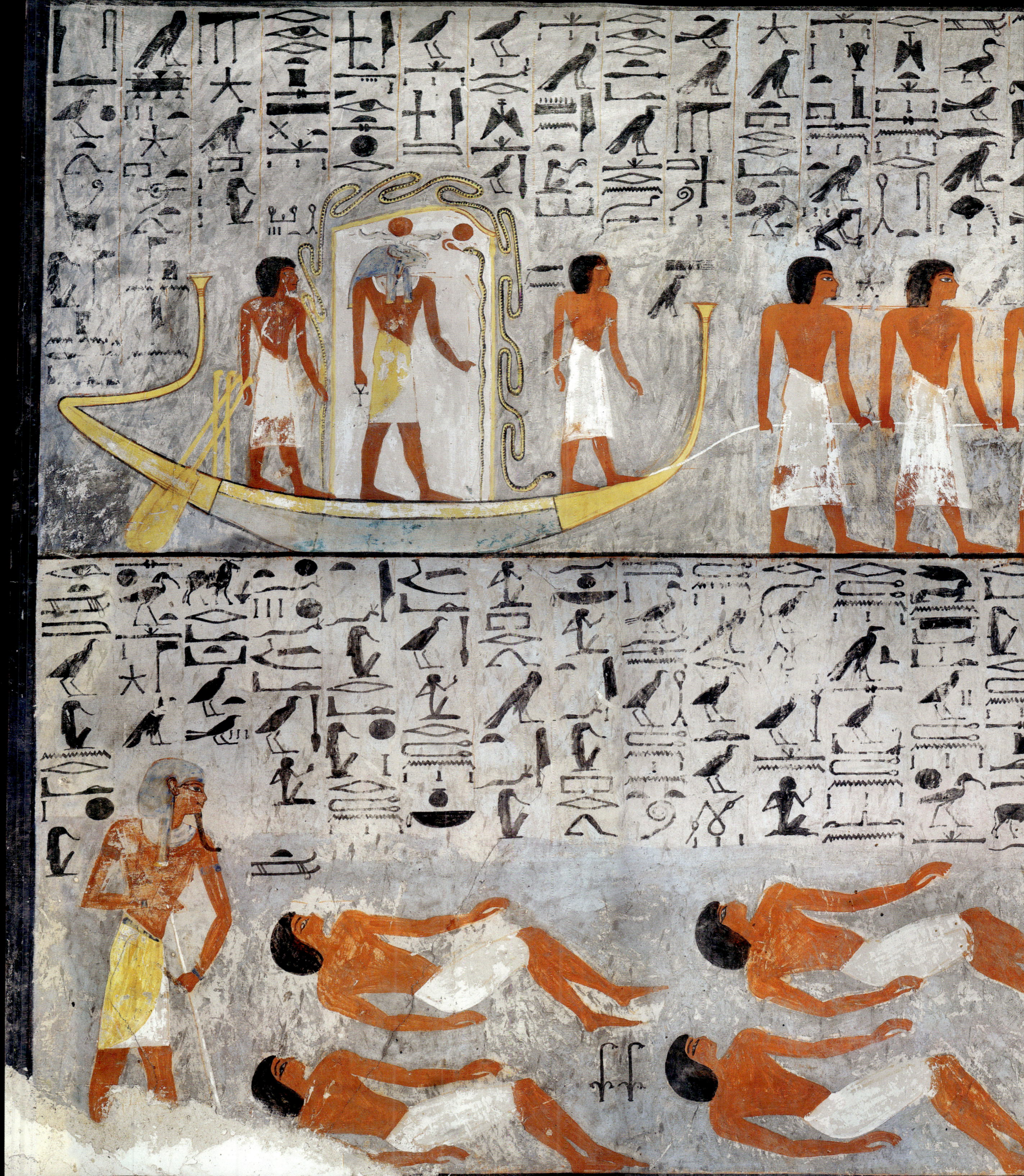

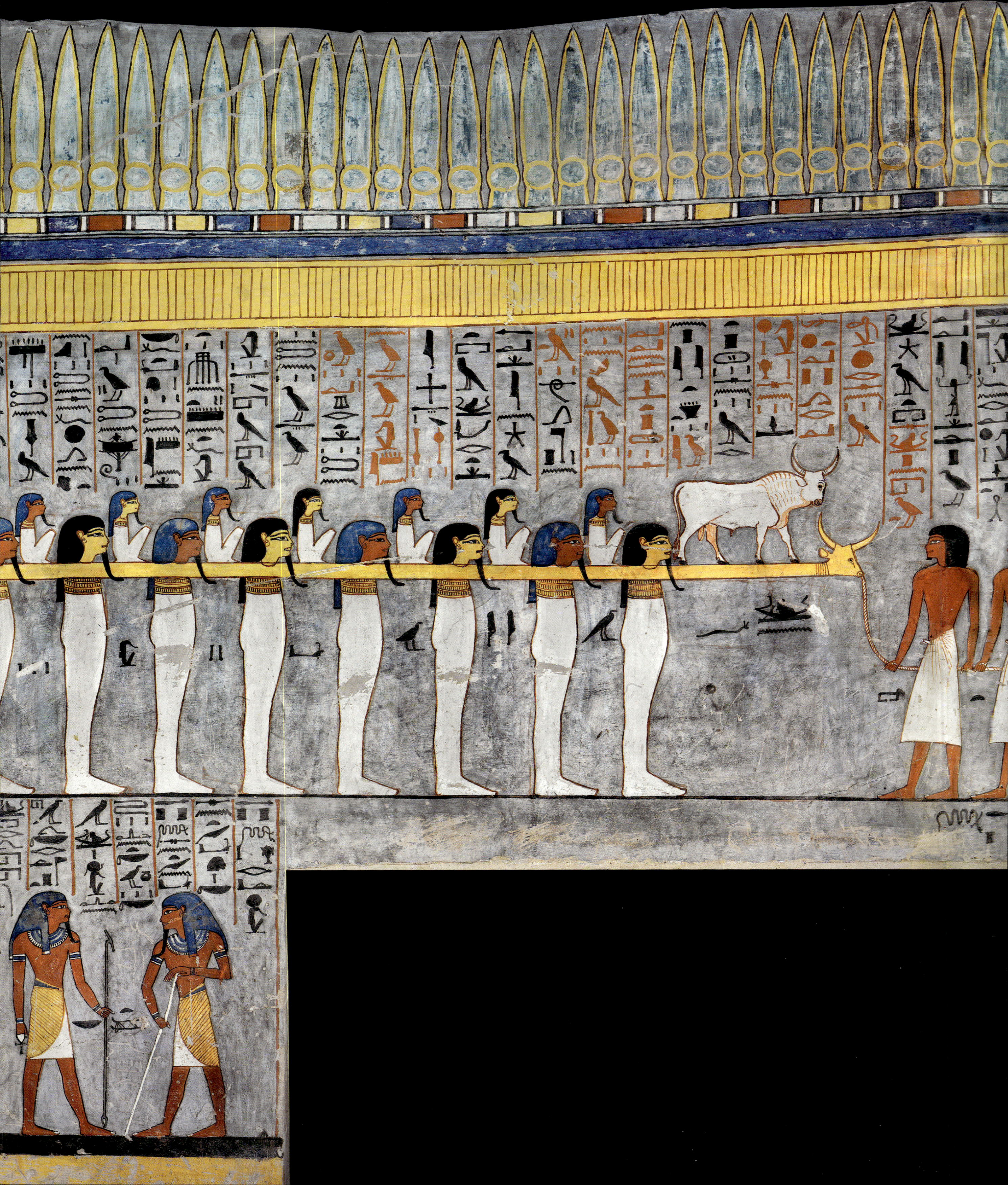

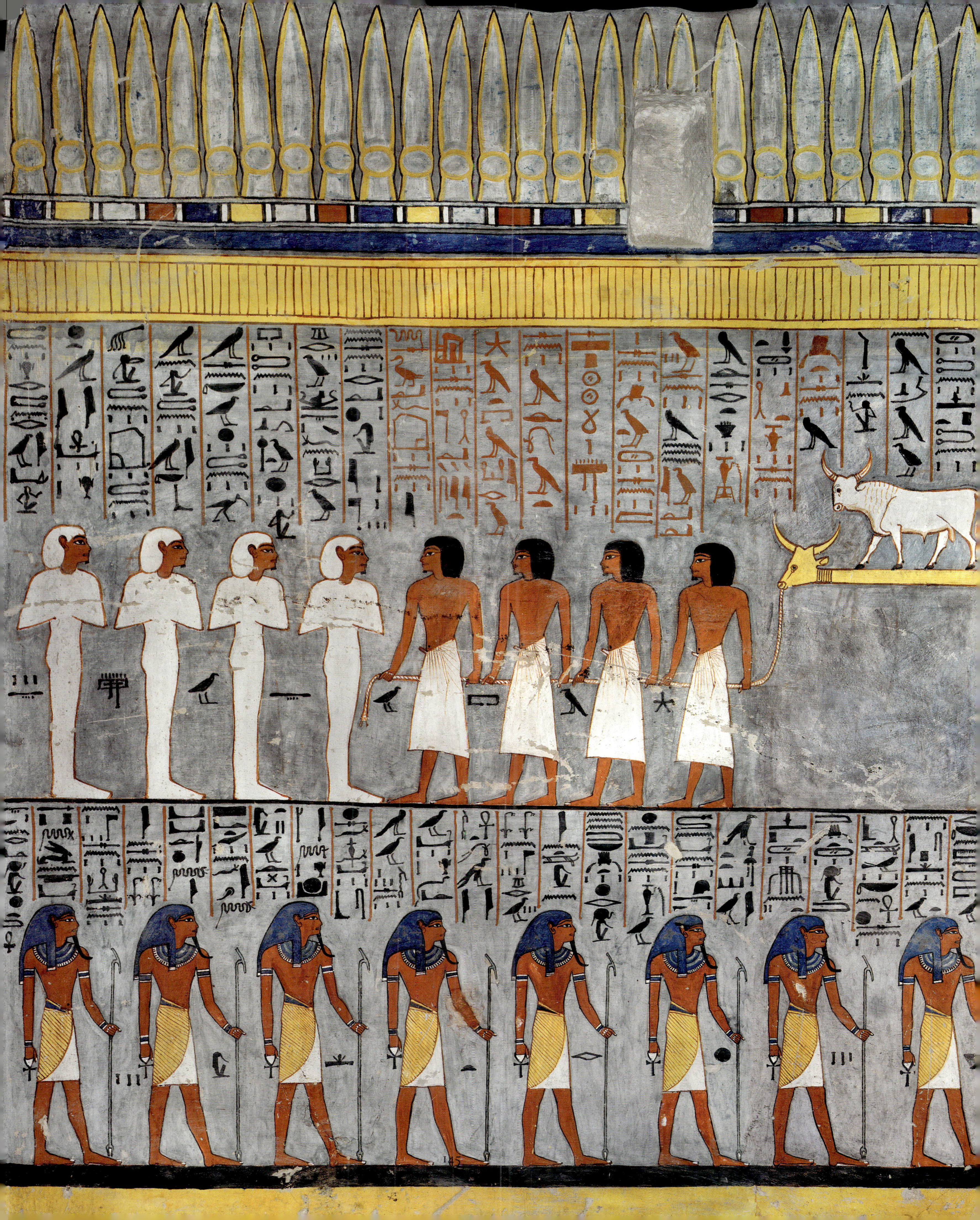

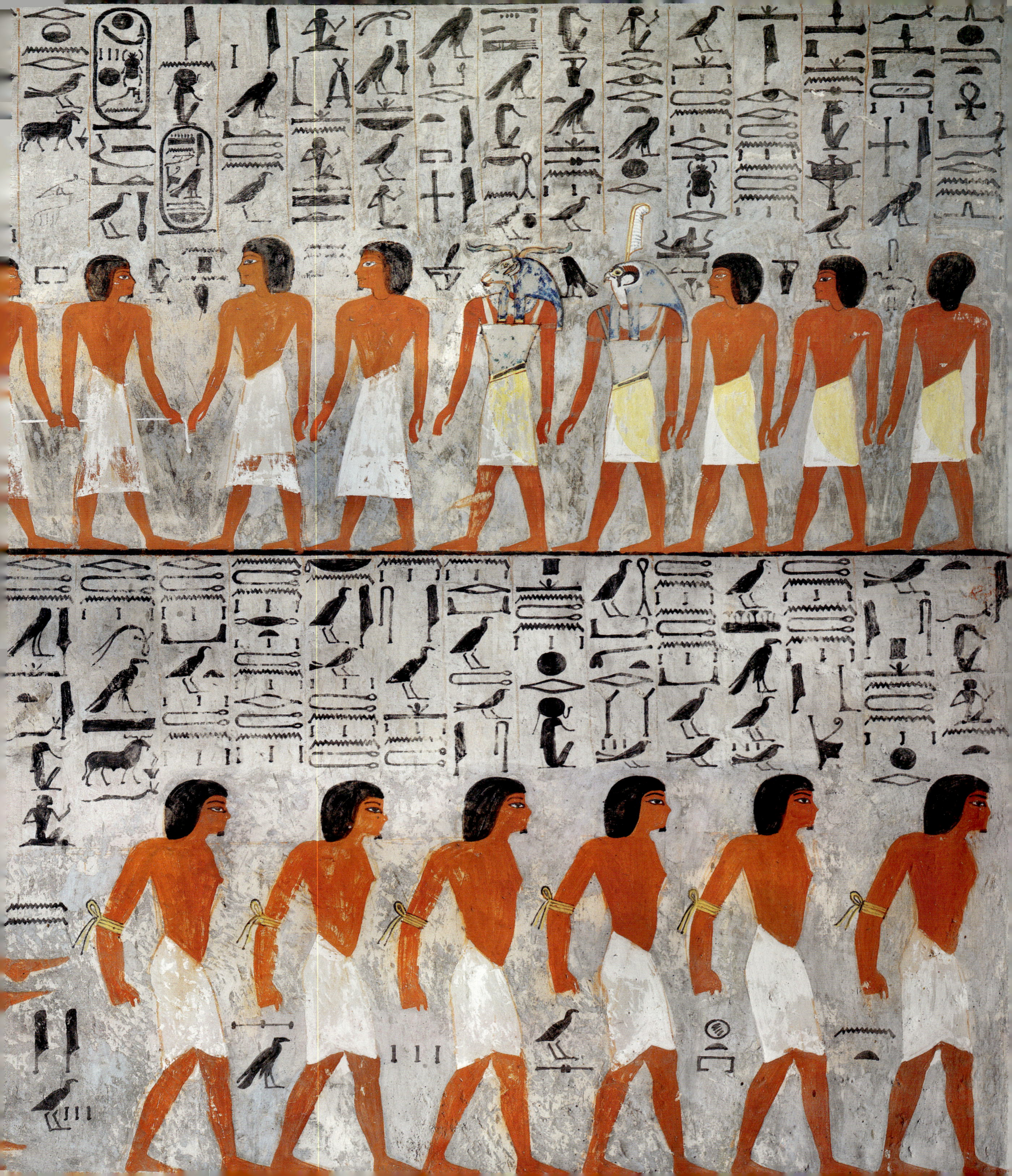

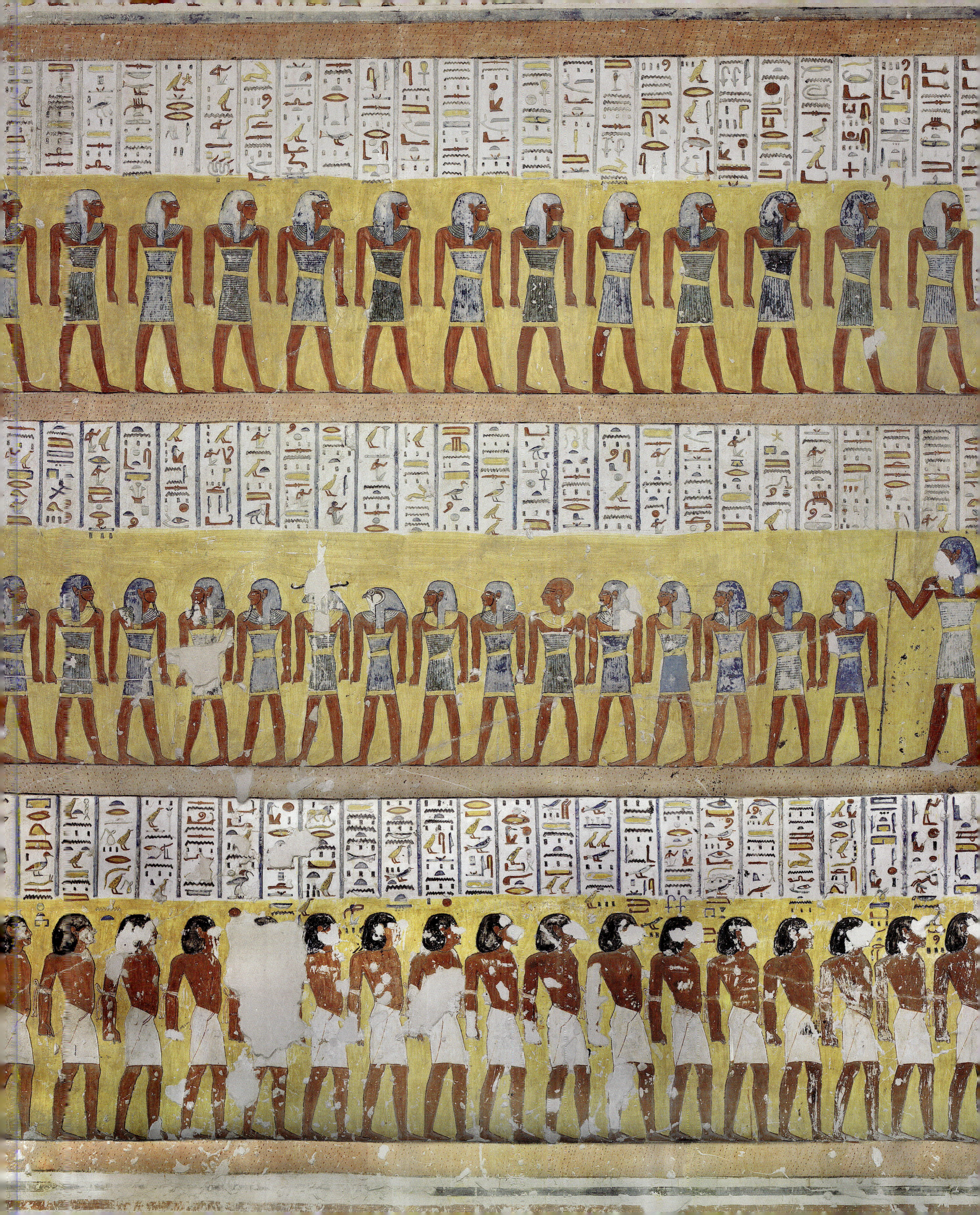

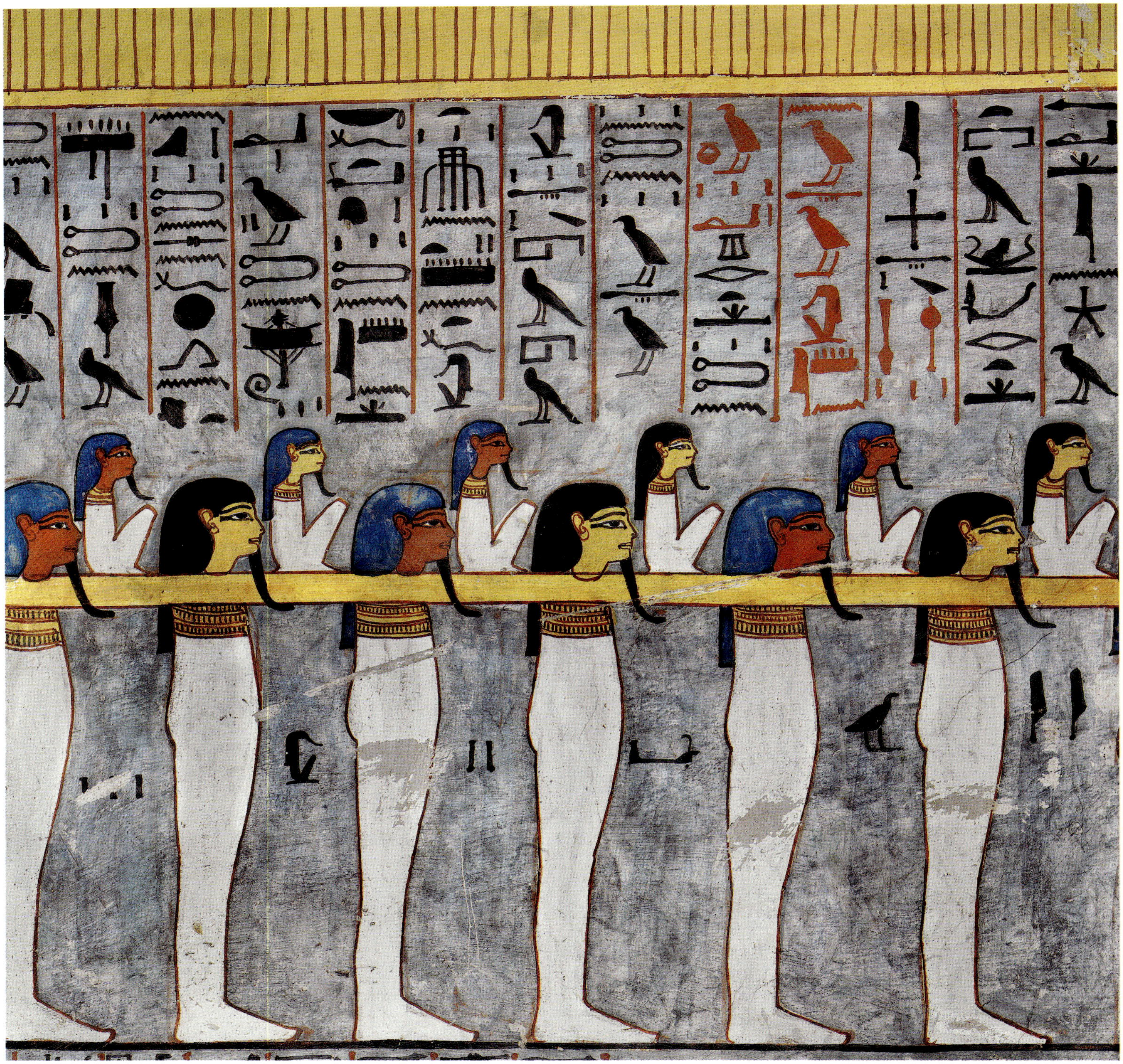

The Third Hour
(left and above)
In this image from the tomb of Ramses I (arranged opposite to the usual orientation), the tow rope of the sun bark is attached to a pole with cows' heads on either end, born by mummiform gods. The four figures at the left are linked with providing clean linen for the deceased. In the lower register, the god Atum leans on his staff and faces the snake of chaos, Apophis.

The Second and Third Hours
(Following pages)
Parts of both the second and third hours are seen here, with the gate separating them in the middle. In both hours, the sun bark is in the central register, the blessed dead appear in the top register, and the damned and the enemies of the sun god appear below, their arms tied behind their backs.

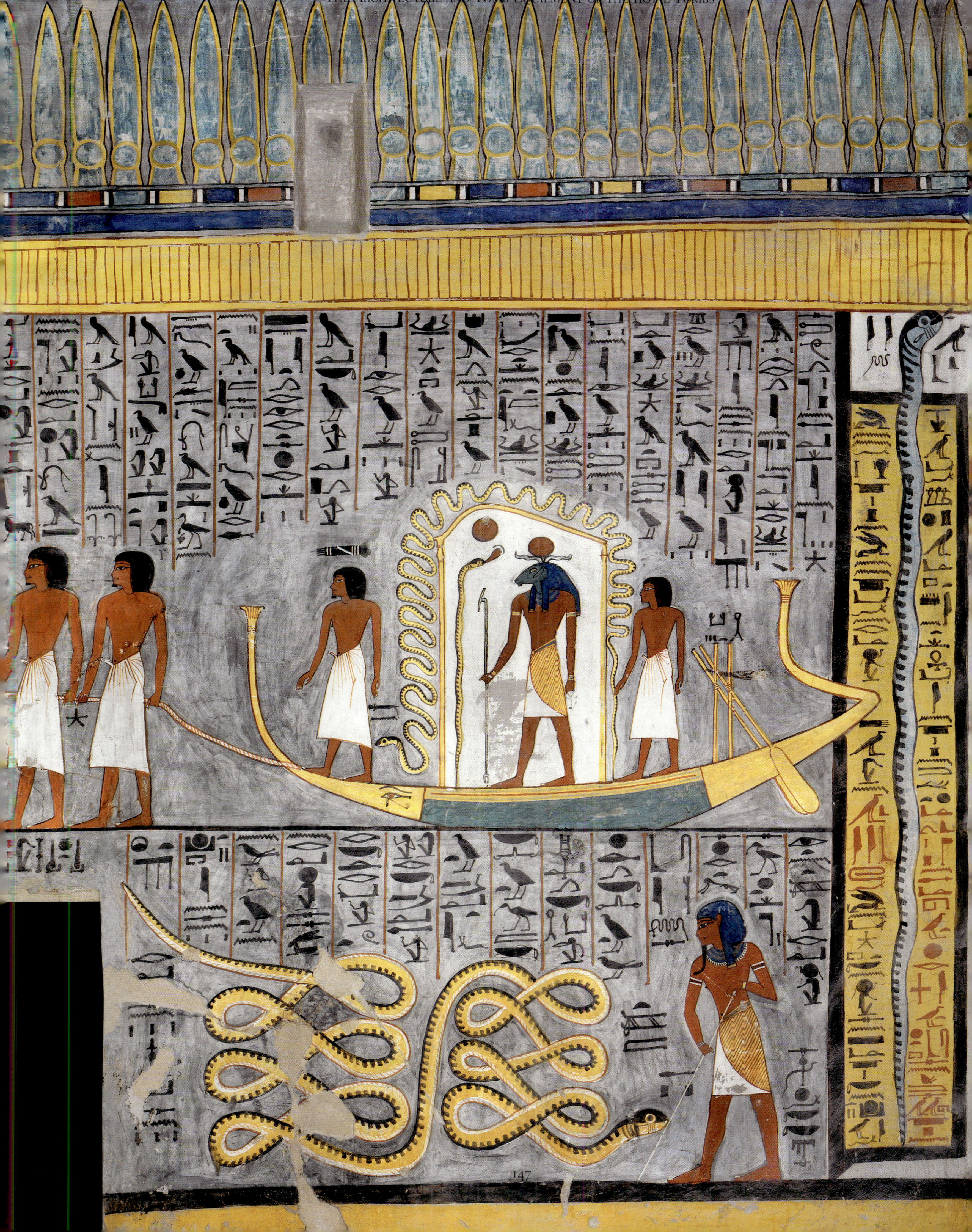

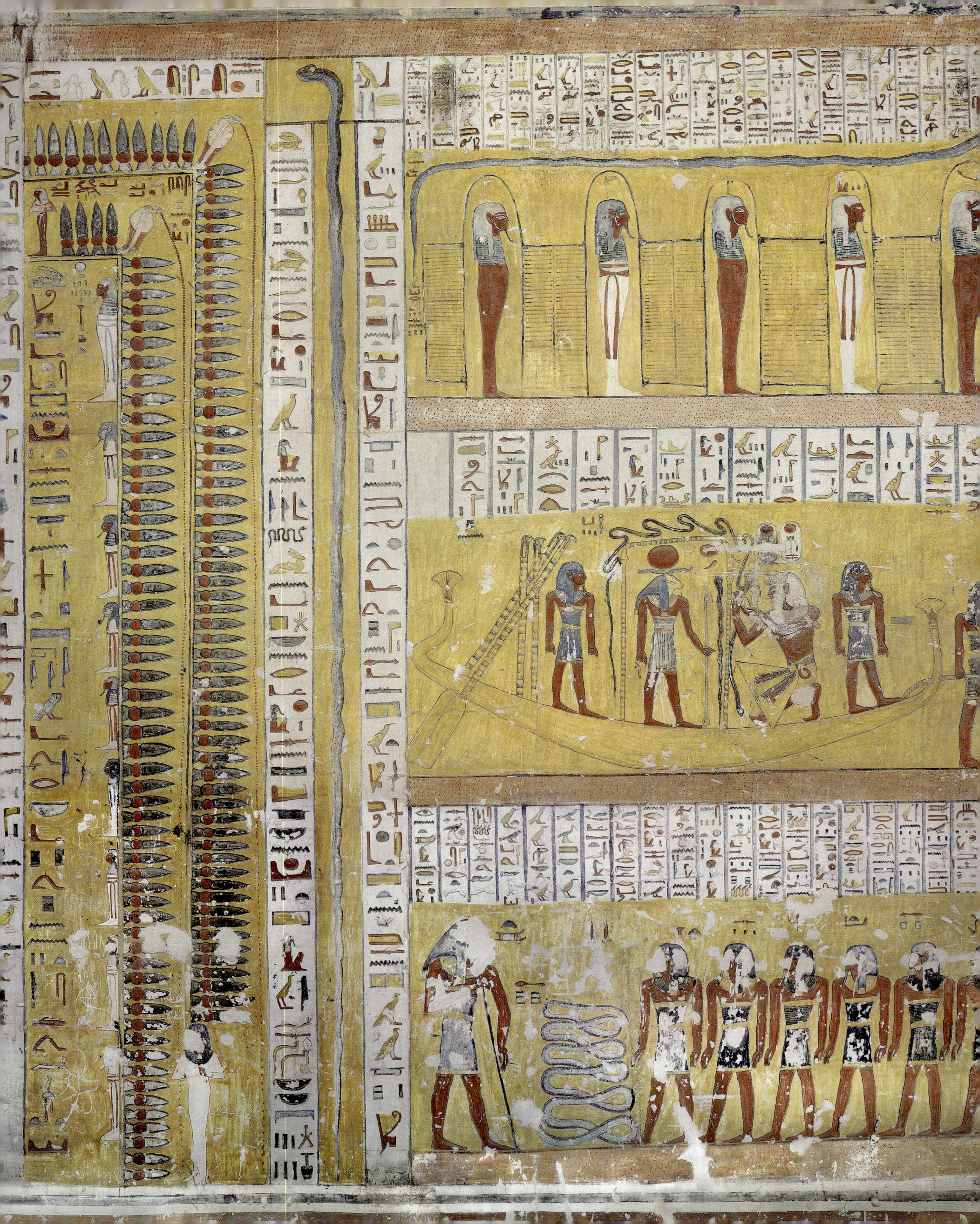

Hour Three

One of the most commonly depicted hours, the third hour continues to delineate the contrasting roles of blessed and damned. The bark is again towed by four figures, and the rope tied to a long pole with cows' heads at back and front held on the shoulders of eight mummiform figures. A cow stands on each end of the pole, on which sit seven deities. The tow rope continues at the far end of the pole, and is pulled by an additional four men. Four mummiform figures face this procession; they are connected with the outfitting of the dead with clean linen.

In the upper register, twelve mummies stand within domed shrines, all protected by the outstretched figure of a snake. Before them is the Lake of Fire, in which twelve gods appear, only their wrapped upper bodies visible above the water. Between the gods are sheaves of wheat, symbols of Osiris. As in the Amduat, this Lake of Fire is where the blessed are saved and the damned are destroyed.

The lower register represents the arena in which the struggle between good and evil occurs. To the left is a group of demons headed by the evil snake Apophis, who is shown coiled. Behind them are nine gods with staffs as weapons, led by the primordial god Atum. Atum is shown again at the far left end of the register, as if defending the sun disk from being swallowed by his archenemy. It appears that the defenders of the sun are here under the supervision of Atum. As the sun god passes through this gate, the inhabitants of the Netherworld weep because they cannot go with him, but must stay and face Apophis and the Lake of Fire.

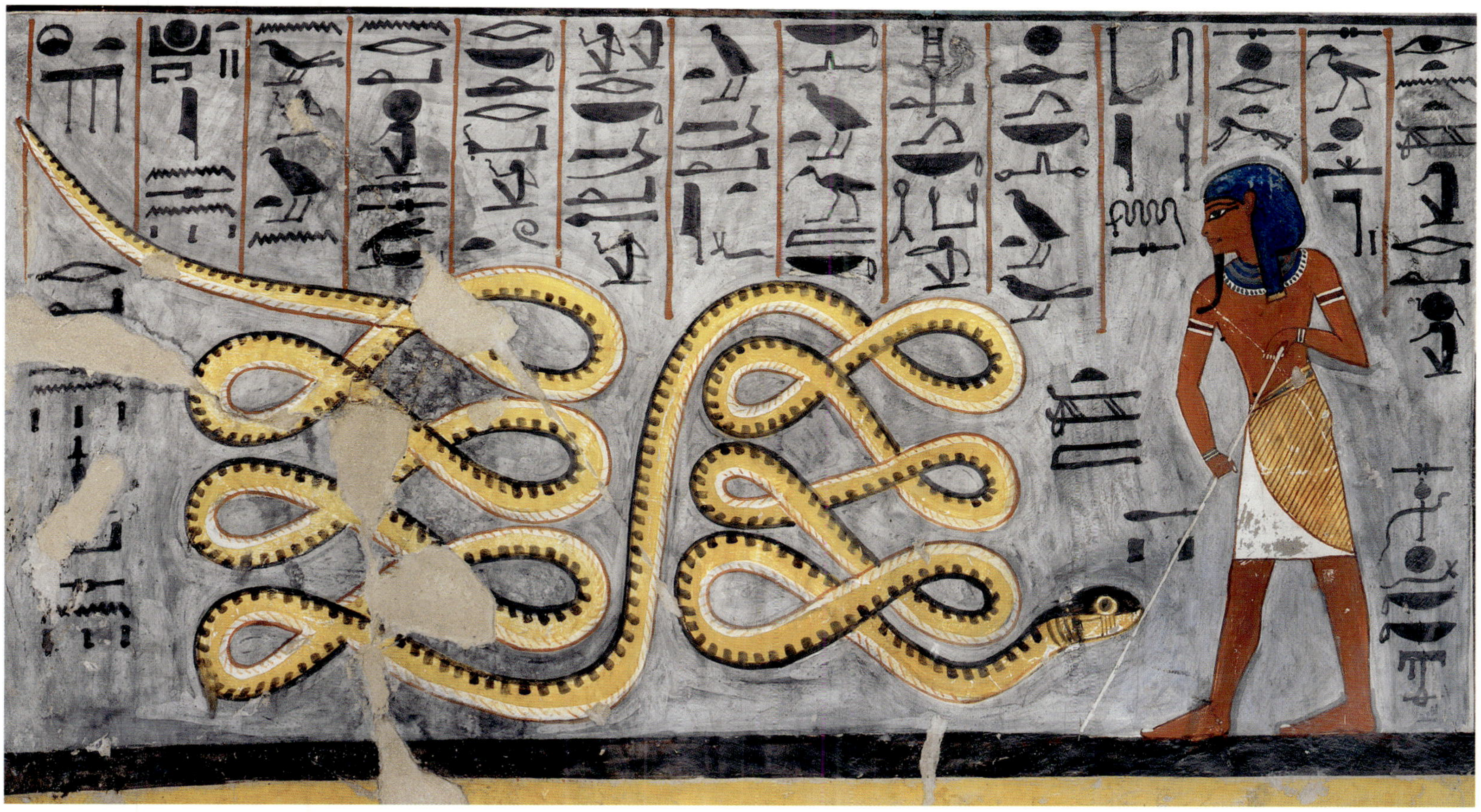

Atum and Apophis
This detail from the third hour shows the god Atum, leaning on his staff, facing the serpent Apophis. Both figures are labeled with their names in hieroglyphs.

The Third Hour
(Following pages)
Another representation of the third hour of the Book of Gates shows clearly the figures carrying the towing pole in the register above and the gods who will join Atum in the battle against Apophis in the register below.

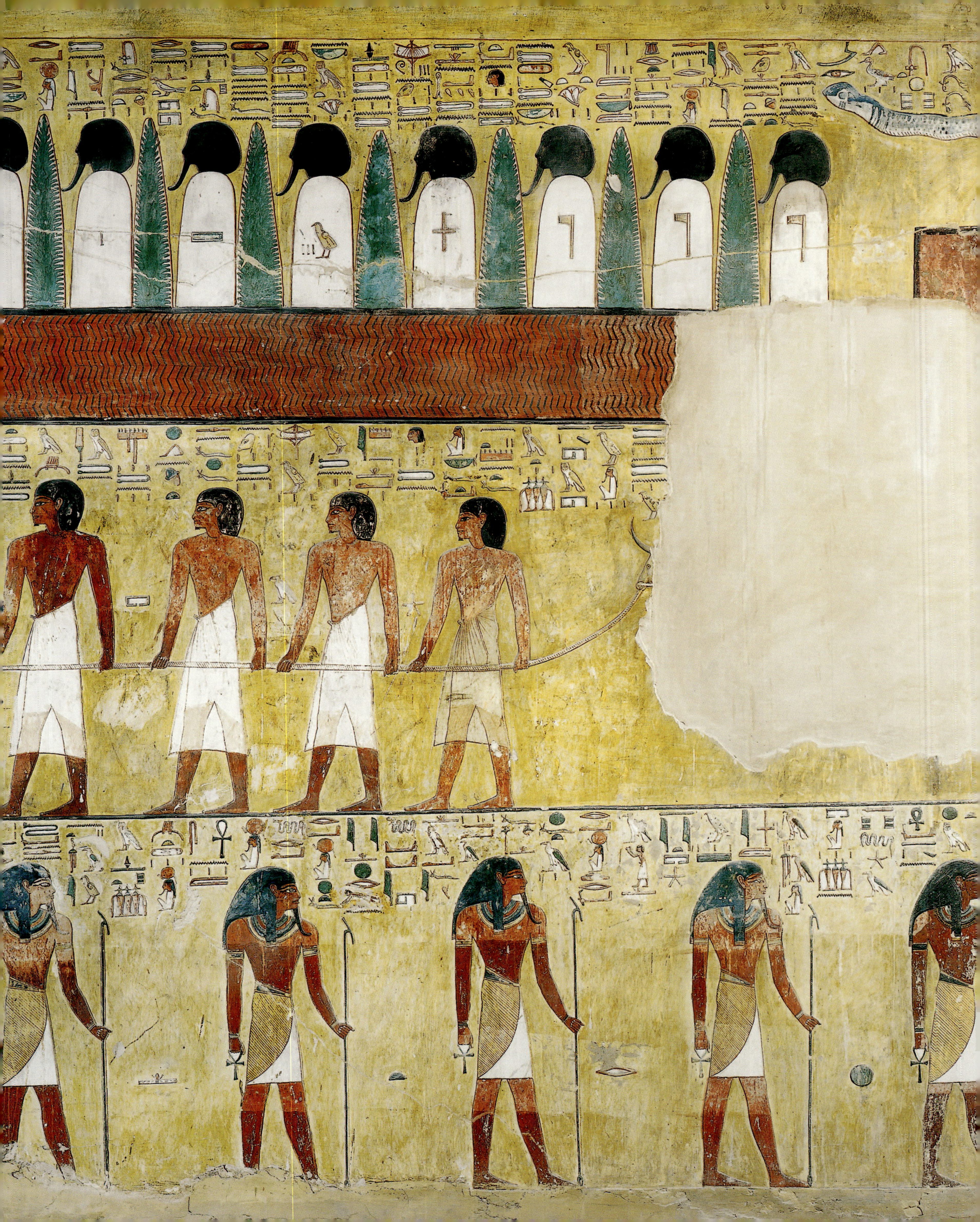

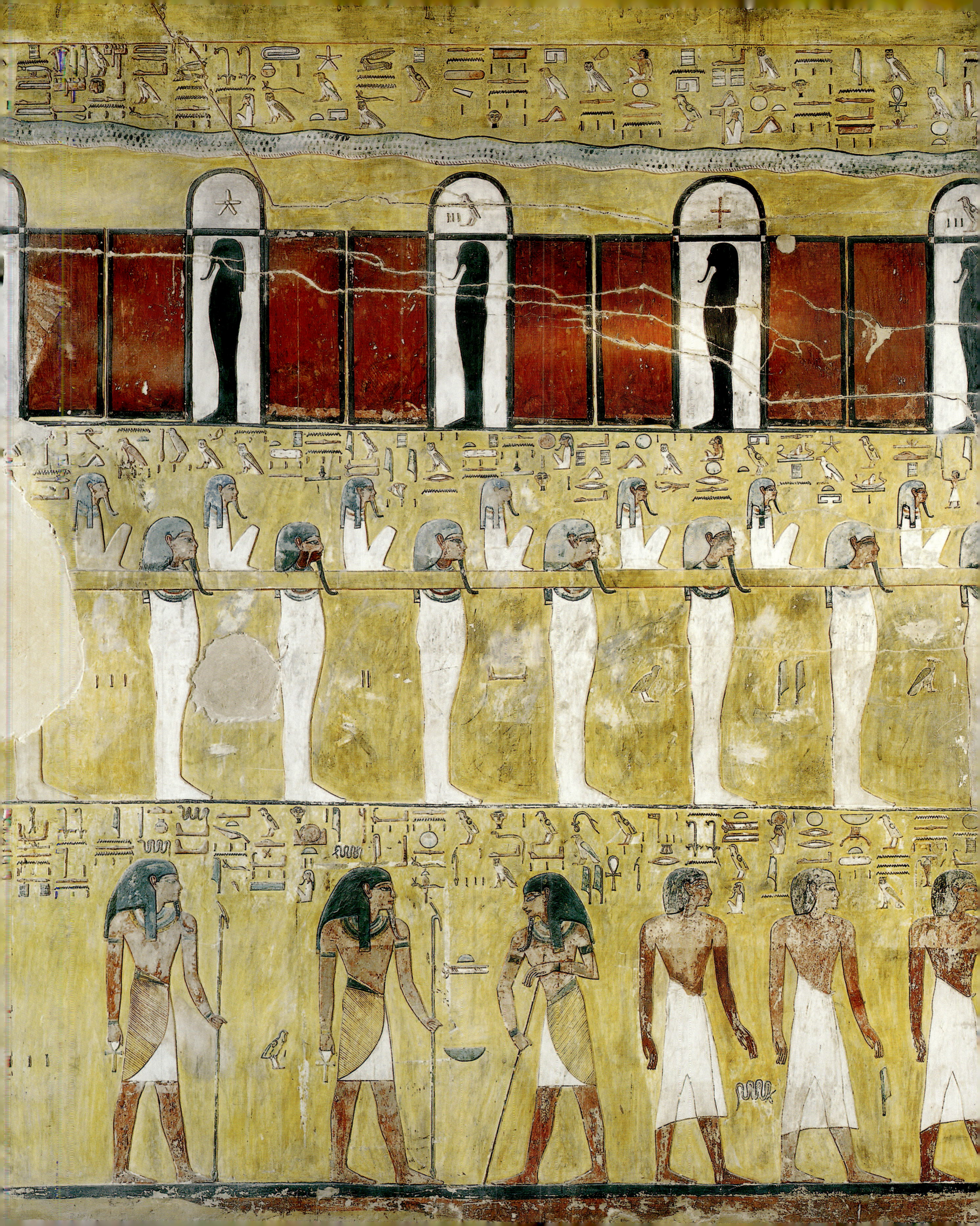

Hour Four

The main thrust of this hour is to proclaim the greatness of Re, who speaks to all the gods and creatures who inhabit this hour. He informs them of their duties toward him as creator god, and guarantees them food. The gods accept, and come to his aid. The images here focus on the relationship between the sun god and his followers, with the various divinities who have come to help Re represented.

In the top register are three series of twelve gods each. First from the right are rearing cobras, seen atop a body of water, probably a variation on the Lake of Fire seen in the third hour. The snakes throw balls of fire at the enemies of Re, but later, when Re is happy, he welcomes all gods, humans, and animals and tells the snakes to cease. The snakes then call Re to come and unite with them. Behind the snakes are twelve jackal-headed humans guarding a second body of water: this is perhaps another incarnation of the Lake of Fire. Last are twelve gods in fully human form.

The solar boat is in its usual position in the central register, and takes the same form as that seen in Hours Two and Three. It is towed by four men. They approach nine mummiform gods who lie prone, still in the sleep of death and waiting to be resurrected, within nine individual shrines or caves. The text identifies these figures as followers of Osiris, here to support Re and protect him from the evil ones. A great snake called Hiririet, representing time, is shown between two groups of six women each, representing the twelve hours of the night.

Below the solar bark is a figure of Horus the Elder (Herwer), leaning on a stick behind eleven human figures that follow a rearing cobra. The entire procession approaches a chapel in which Osiris in the white crown stands on a coiled snake. Walking toward the chapel from the other side are twelve more gods. At the right end of the register are four figures before pits filled with fire. There are conflicting interpretations of these figures: one theory says that the figures are men digging pits in the ground; another believes that they are enemies of the god being punished by fire. A prince holding a scepter and an *ankh* sign supervises this activity.

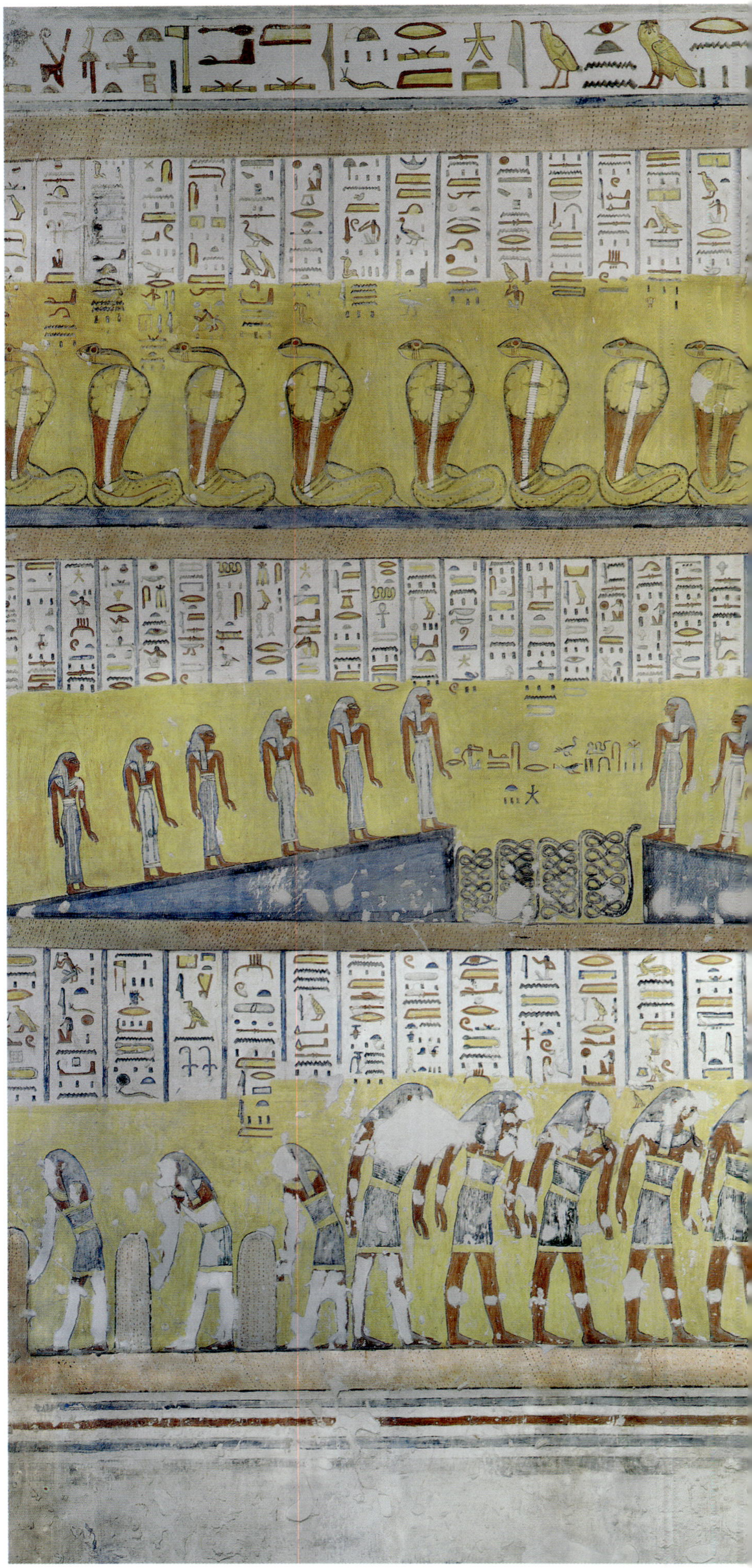

The Fourth Hour
Most of this hour is shown here. In the upper register are two bodies of water, versions of the Lake of Fire, guarded by cobras and jackal-headed humans. Below is the snake of time in a pit, surrounded by water and a mound on which stand the goddesses of the twelve hours of the night, as well as nine followers of Osiris as mummies lying within shrines.

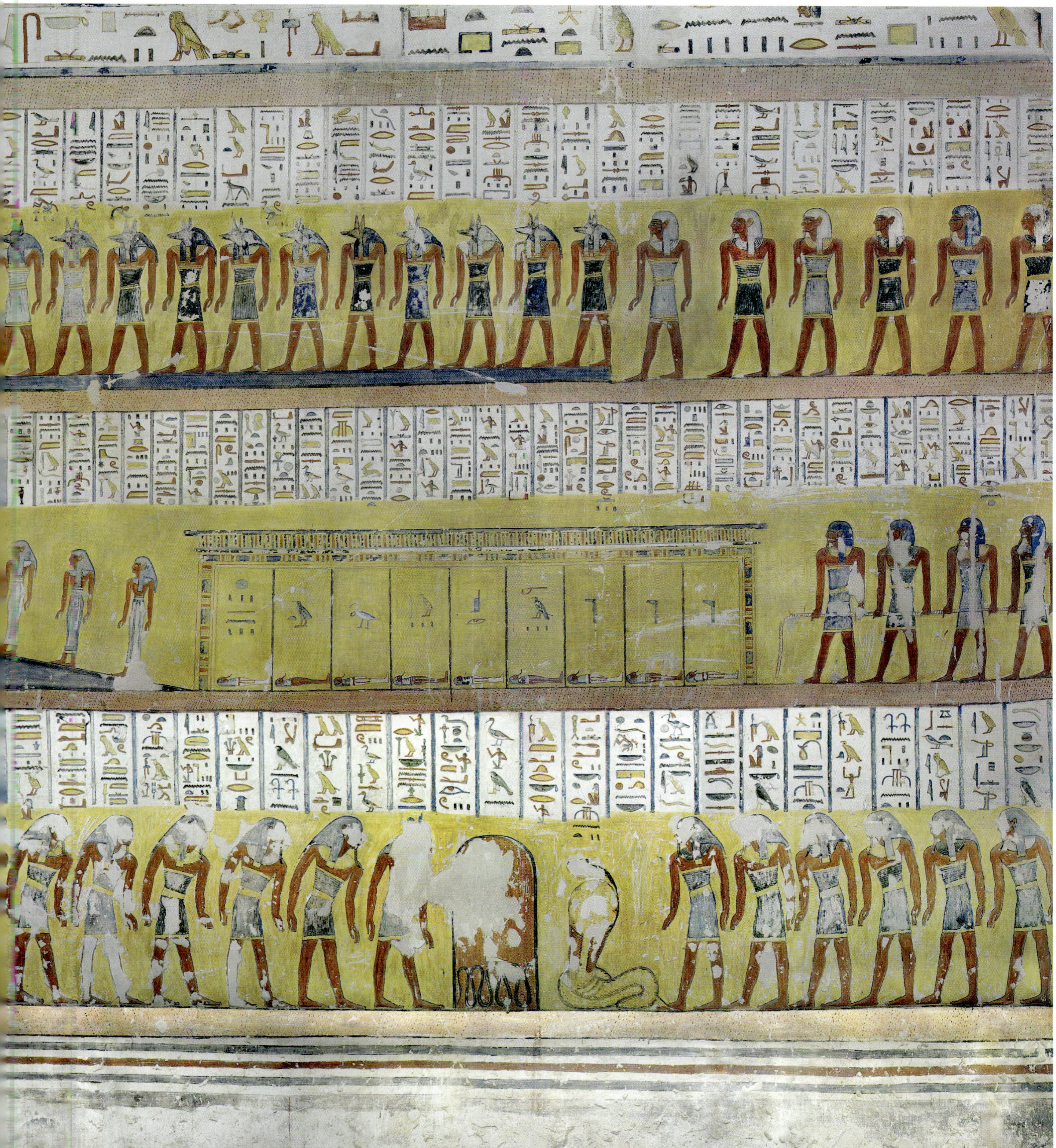

Hour Five

This hour continues to illustrate the popularity of Re, as only his faithful followers appear here. Gods and humans pay homage to the great god, and his priests guarantee that they will reward all those faithful to him. In the first register, we see twelve worshippers leaning forward in an attitude of reverence, followed by twelve figures holding a rope that coils between them. We know that the ancient Egyptians used ropes for surveying and measurement, and it is the job of these men to measure the Fields of the Blessed. Re says to them "Your rule is the secret of the West." Facing these men are four gods holding scepters; they give offerings to Re on earth as he rises in the sky or dwells in his temple. Re promises to give them drink and meat in the West, his most sacred place.

The solar bark in the central register is preceded by nine mummiform gods holding a long, coiled snake, identified as the enemy of the sun, Apophis. These men keep Apophis from attacking the solar bark. The twelve figures (three of whom are ibis-headed) who walk in front of these "holders of the snake" are the souls of men who are in the Duat, whom Re has ordered to tow the boat quickly. Facing them is a god with a scepter, who seems to be supervising the other gods, perhaps calling them to live with him.

The lower register begins with a figure of Horus the Elder leaning on a staff. Before him walk four Egyptians, then three sets of four men, each representing the traditional enemies of Egypt: Asiatics, Nubians, and Libyans. These four sets of figures represent the four races of mankind, here to show that eternal life is available to all. In the speech that accompanies this scene, Re gives credit to Horus, along with Sekhmet, for helping him to create these humans. At the judgment, Horus speaks for the foreigners, since they do not know Egyptian. Another twelve men walk before them, carrying the snake of time, which will measure the souls to be destroyed. This snake is also responsible for assigning the period of time that these souls will stay in the West. Taken together, these figures express the continuity of life. Heading this register are eight men, rulers who were worshipped in the West. Re here rewards all who glorify him, decreeing that they will be given air to breathe and that they will find a place with Ma'at in Rostau.

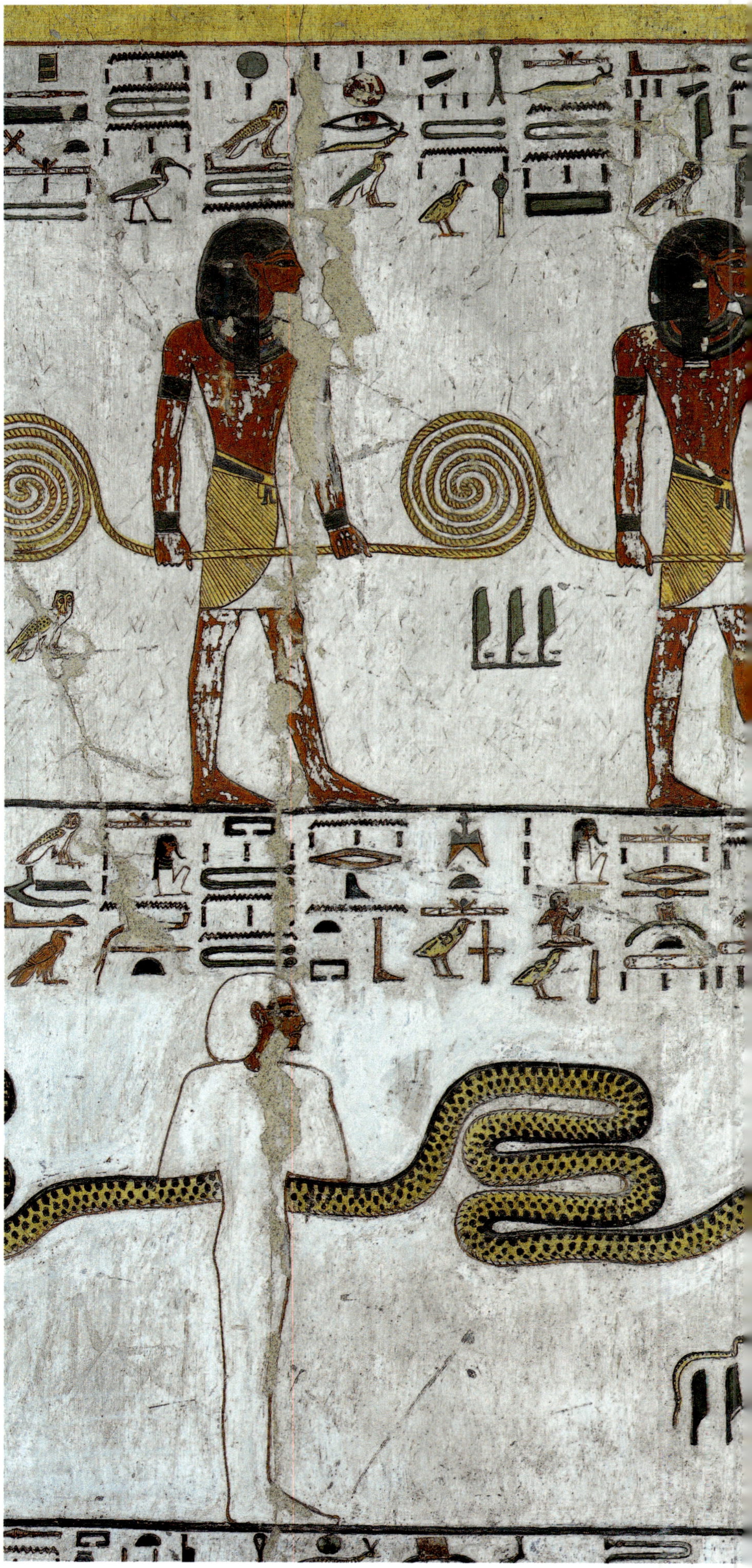

The Fifth Hour
In the top register, male deities hold a rope with which they measure the Fields of the Blessed. Below, mummiform figures hold the snake Apophis, following the souls of those who dwell in the Netherworld.

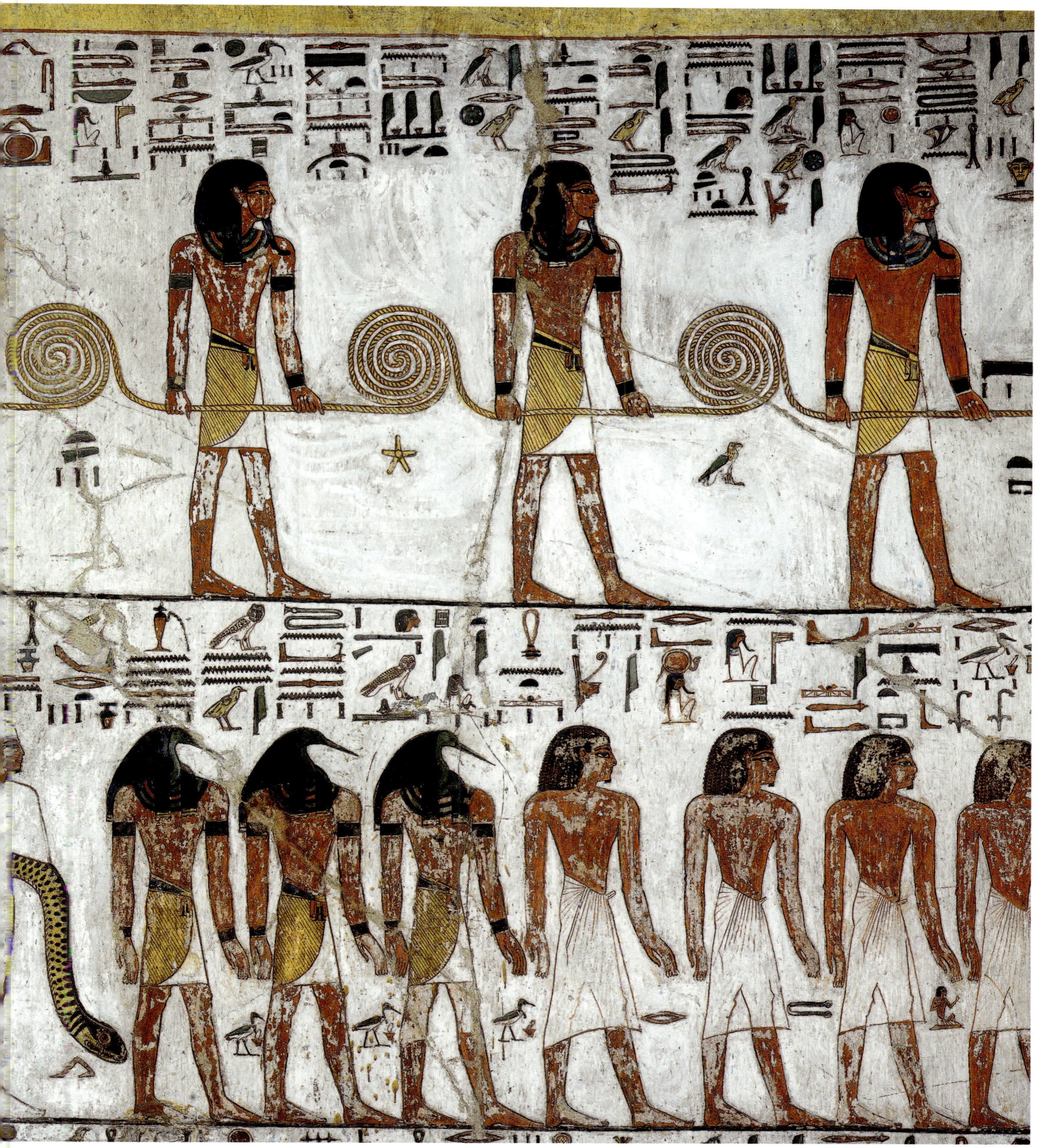

The Judgment Hall

A special vignette showing the judgment hall of Osiris is inserted between the fifth and sixth hours. This is not found at all in the Amduat, but comes instead from the Book of the Dead, seen originally in the tombs and papyri of the elite. The action takes place within a secret chamber protected by a gate. Osiris is shown seated on a throne, wearing the double crown and holding a crook and *ankh*. Before him on his dais is a mummiform figure holding a balance whose pans are empty. Ascending the stairs to meet him are nine of the blessed dead, symbolizing all the friendly souls in the Netherworld. Invisible to the viewer are the enemies who lie under their feet; these enemies have been thrown into the Place of Annihilation. At one side of the scene, two baboons drive away a pig, a potent symbol of disorder: this can be interpreted as Thoth in the form of a baboon defeating Apophis in the shape of a pig. Anubis stands above them, and hanging from the top of the register are four bovine heads, deliberately chosen symbols of disorder.

HOUR SIX

The sixth hour is the deepest part of the Duat, where the *bas* reunite with their bodies. The corpse of the sun is carried in the middle register by a line of twelve gods. However, the body of the sun is invisible, as are the arms of the men who carry it (because they are in contact with the corpse), thus all that can be seen is a line of twelve armless figures, then eight gods with their arms by their sides.

In the top register, twelve men gods carry long, forked poles to keep Apophis at bay. Apophis himself follows, held by twelve men. The heads of twelve people who have been swallowed by the snake appear from his back; these people will now be set free. Leading this register are twelve more figures who hold a twisted rope that is tied around the neck of a mummiform Osiris.

In the lower register, a god called "the one who established the secrets" leans on a staff before twelve mummies who lie on a long snake-shaped bed; they are preparing to participate in the resurrection of the sun. Twelve men in kilts stand before this bed, their arms down in front of them in a gesture of respect. At the right end of the register, two mummiform figures flank a circular image of the Lake of Fire inhabited by a cobra. The solar bark reaches its northernmost point during this hour, and then turns east to enter the seventh hour.

HOUR SEVEN

The focus in the seventh hour is the result of the Judgment of Osiris, with the blessed welcomed to the following of Osiris and the enemies of order condemned to eternal punishment. In the central register, the solar bark is preceded by a figure of Horus leaning on a staff, supervising the punishment of seven pairs of enemies, who are bound to jackal-headed posts known as the Stakes of Geb. These enemies are tormented by demons, a punishment to which Re consents because these men have disobeyed him.

In the upper register are two groups of the blessed dead. To the left are twelve men with baskets filled with grain on their heads; to the right are another twelve men, each bearing the feather of Ma'at, an indication that he has passed the judgment of Osiris, on his head. The caption here tells us that Osiris is welcoming his newly chosen followers. In the lower register, twelve figures work with large ears of grain and seven more hold large sickles, both activities associated with agriculture; these two groups are connected with the feeding of the dead.

HOUR EIGHT

In the eighth hour, the rope of time appears again in the top register, carried by the twenty-four hours of the day and night. In the middle register, the bark is led by twelve "lords of provisions in the West" who are responsible, on behalf of Re, for feeding and clothing the blessed dead and punishing his enemies. In the lower register are twelve mummies who have turned over on their stomachs as the first step towards resurrection. They are protected by twelve judges who will guard them from evil.

THE FOURTH HOUR
(Following pages)
The back wall of the burial chamber of Ramses I is decorated with a number of scenes. To the left, the king is embraced by the gods Anubis and Horus, son of Isis (Harsiese). To the right is the fourth hour of the Book of Gates, with the solar boat approaching nine mummies in shrines who wait to be resurrected, while below the goddesses of the hours of the night stand on a mound surrounding the snake of time.

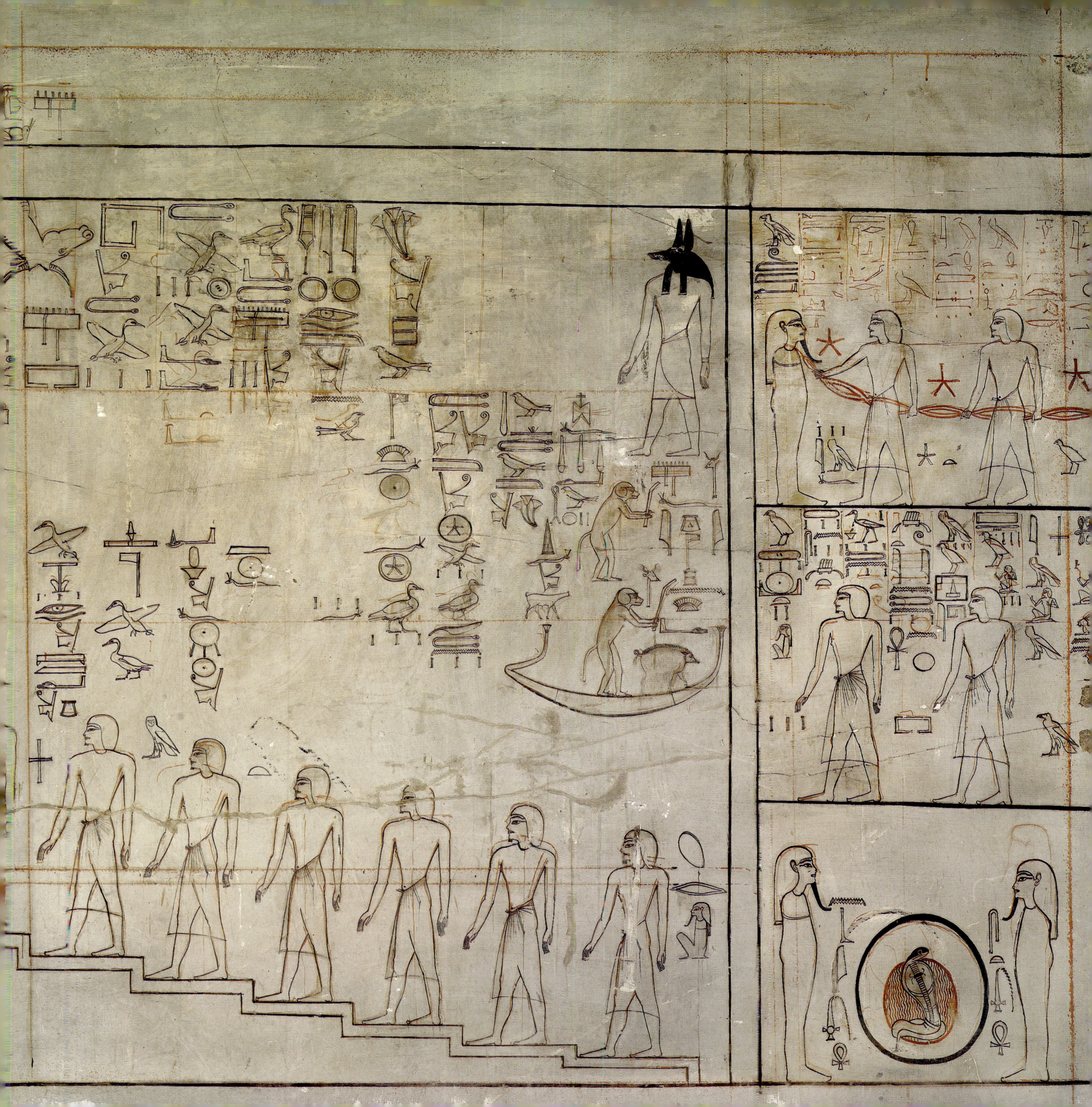

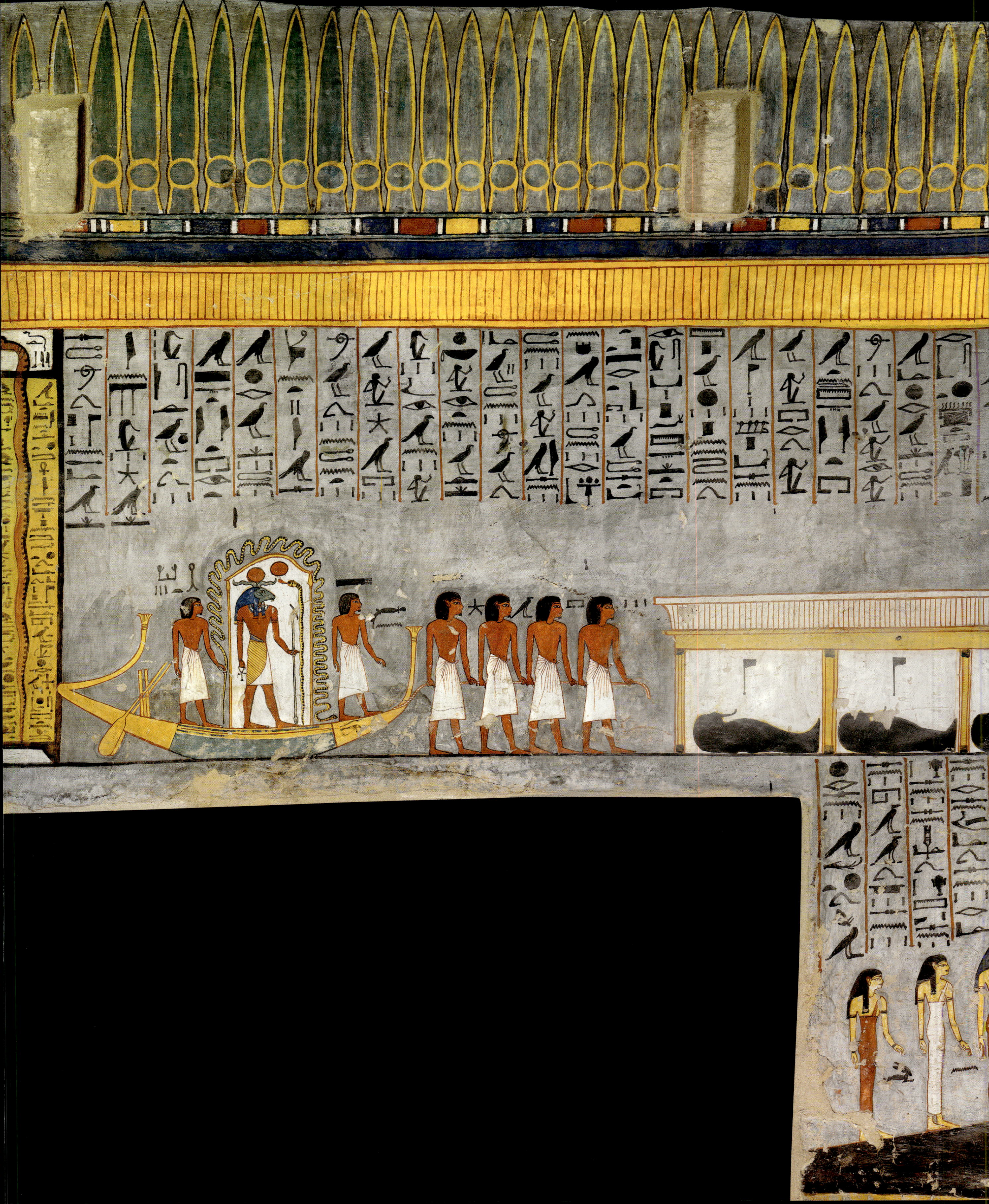

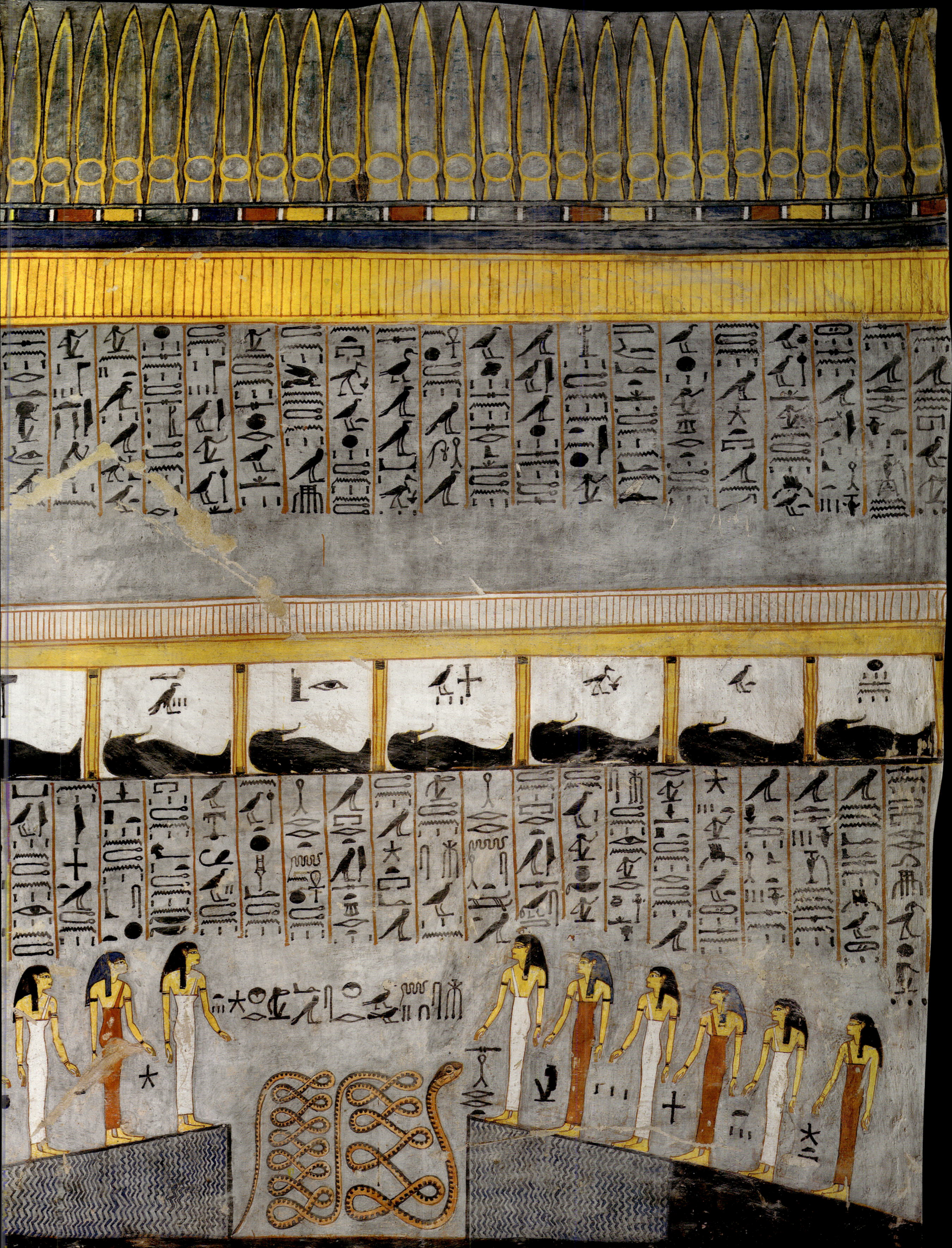

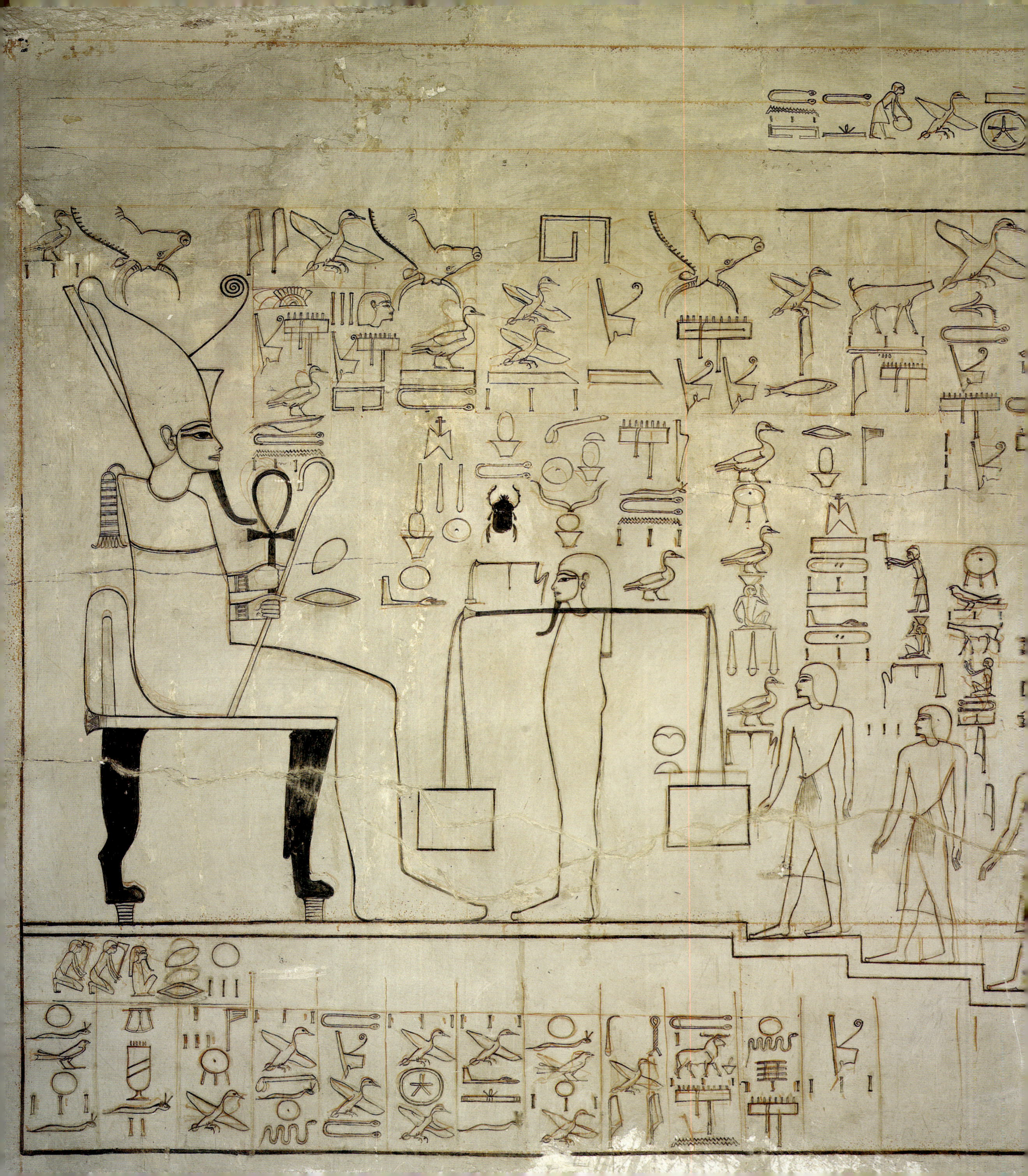

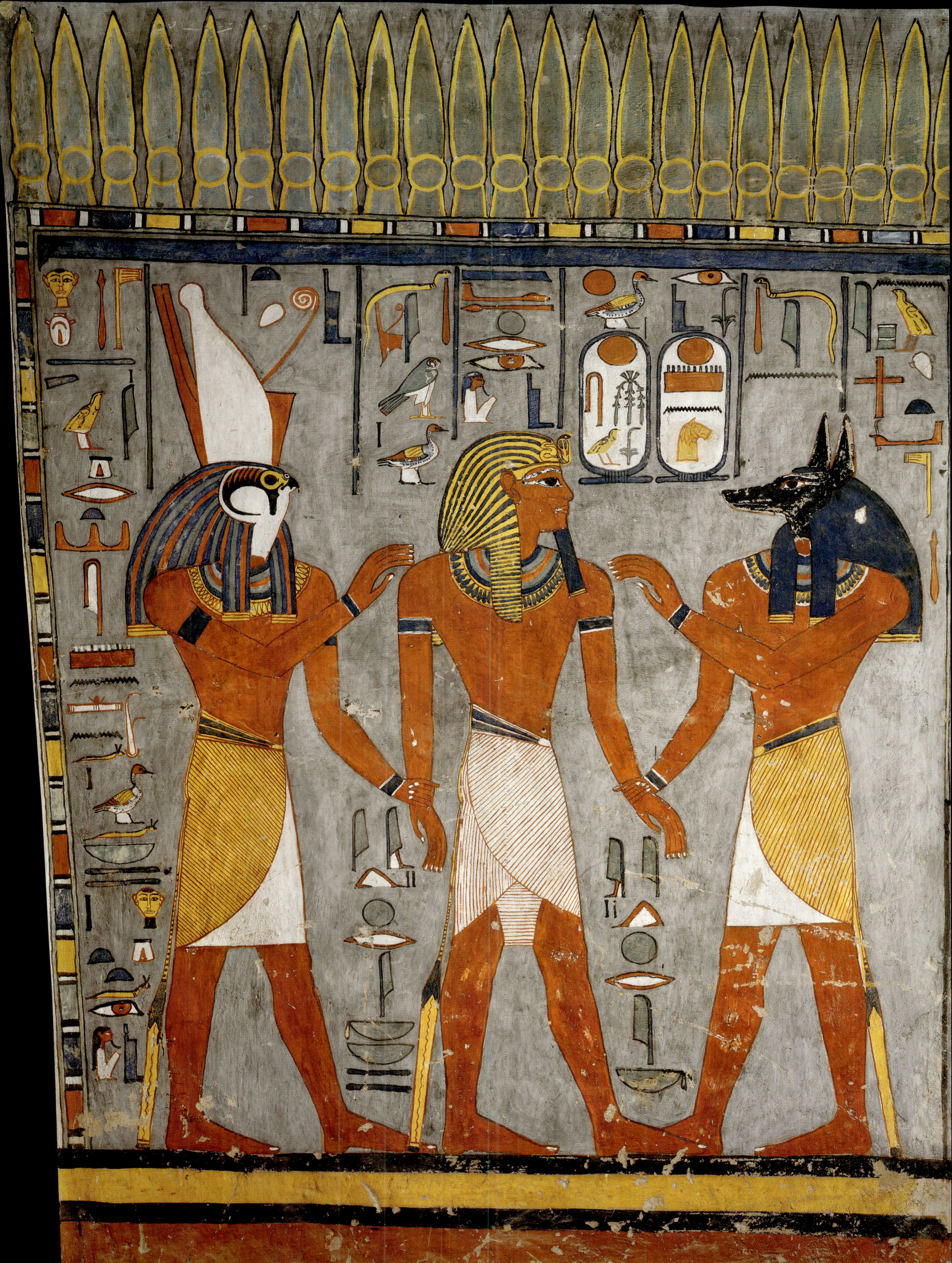

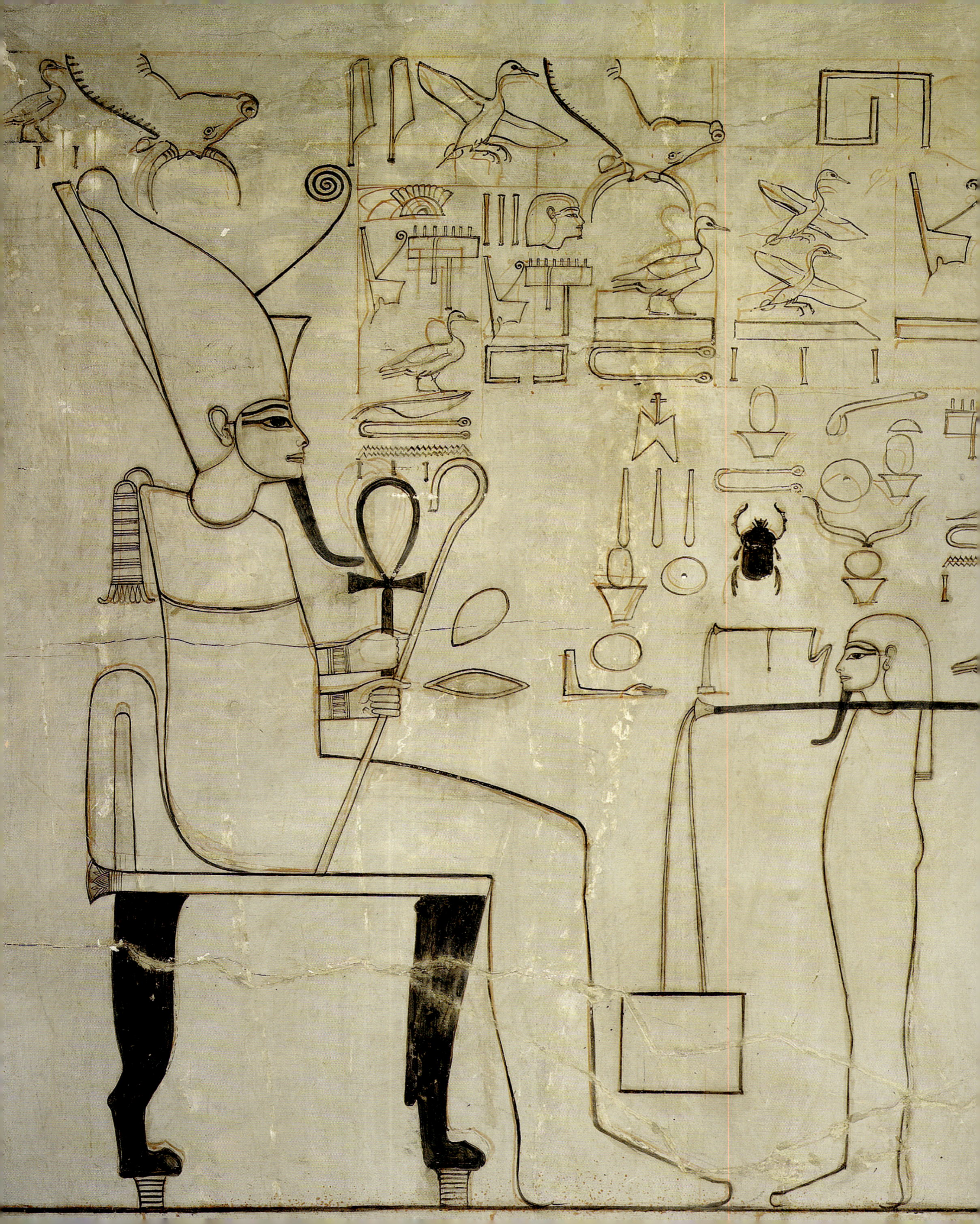

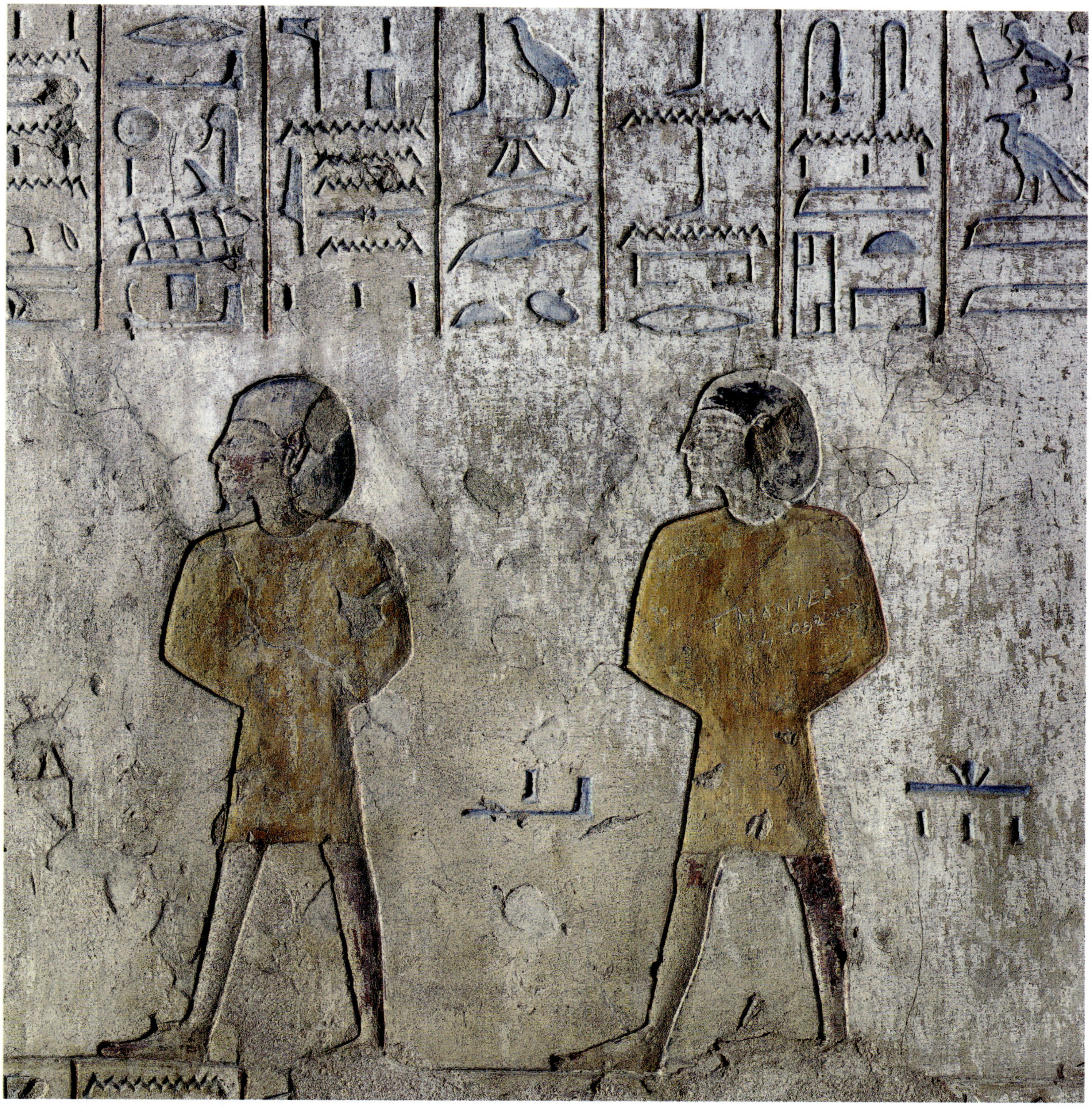

THE BEARERS OF THE SUN

These armless figures from the sixth hour, which is passed in the depths of the Netherworld, are carrying the corpse of the sun god. This corpse and anything with which it comes into contact are invisible at this point in time.

THE JUDGMENT HALL OF OSIRIS

(Preceding pages)

The earliest royal image of the judgment hall of Osiris is found in the tomb of Horemheb. Osiris sits here on a throne, wearing the double crown and holding a flail and an *ankh*. In front of him is the scale on which he will weigh the heart of the deceased. Approaching him, up a flight of stairs, are some of the blessed dead.

Hour Nine

The focus of this scene is a rectangular pool filled with the waters of the Nun, in which four groups of the drowned are shown floating. This is the primeval water, which serves to revive the dead. The souls of nine of the blessed dead appear in the top register in the form of *ba*s, birds with human heads; to their left are rulers, who will offer them food, and the *ba*s raise their arms in worship to Horus, who faces them to the right. In the lower register, enemies are again punished: the Fiery One, a snake named Khety in whose coils stand the bodies of seven mummified gods, breathes destruction at three groups of enemies who have their arms tied behind their backs, with the specific positions indicating the severity of their offenses. The text explains that these men did not respect the power of Osiris, offending him, for example, by destroying images on the walls of temples, and are being punished by Horus at the order of Re.

The power of Re is indicated in the texts, which states that this god gives orders to Horus, deciding who is to be rewarded and who punished. Some scholars take this to show the role of the priesthood of Re in creating this book: Re has power both above and below the earth, while Osiris is important only in the Duat.

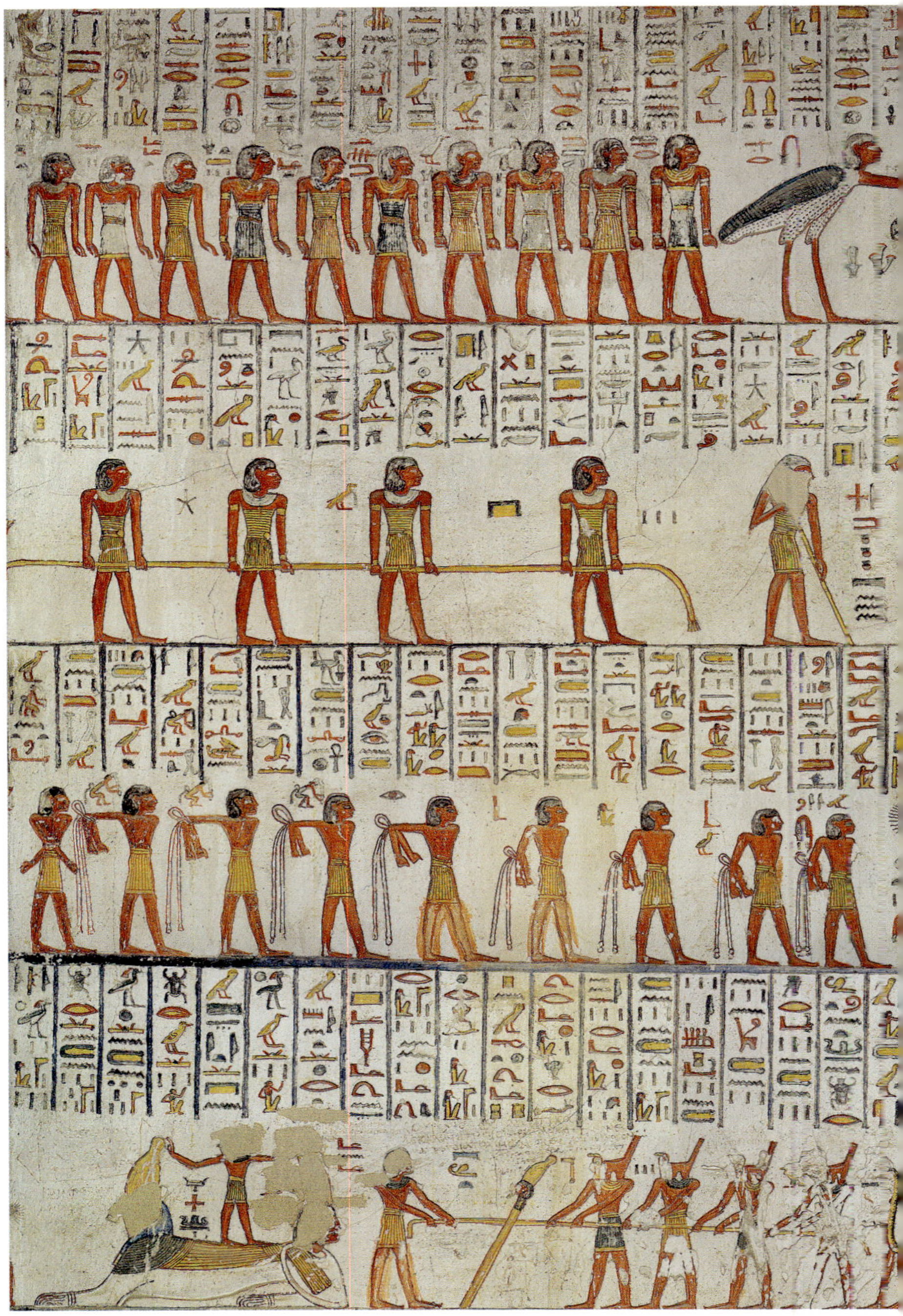

The Ninth Hour
Divided into three registers, the ninth hour of the Book of Gates emphasizes the power of Re. In the top register, Atum faces the *ba*s of the blessed dead. Below is a pool filled with the bodies of the drowned, then the Khety snake who breathes fire at the enemies of the sun god, and finally, in the lowest registers, a variety of strange serpents.

The Pool of the Drowned
The ninth hour of the Book of Gates is dominated by the waters of Nun filled with the bodies of the drowned, a scene that appears in the tenth hour of the Amduat.

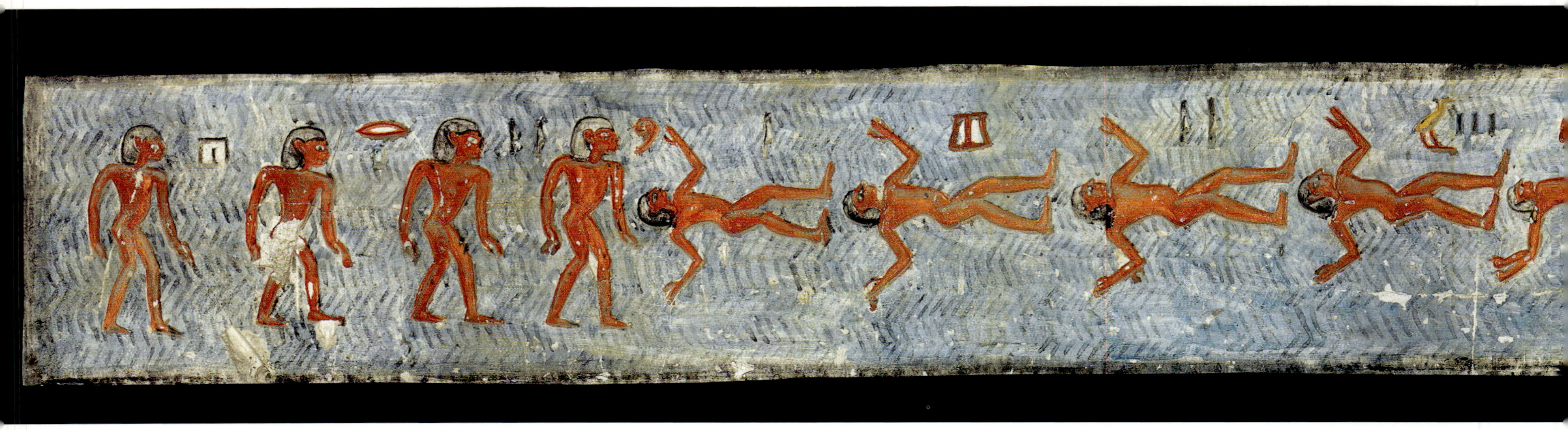

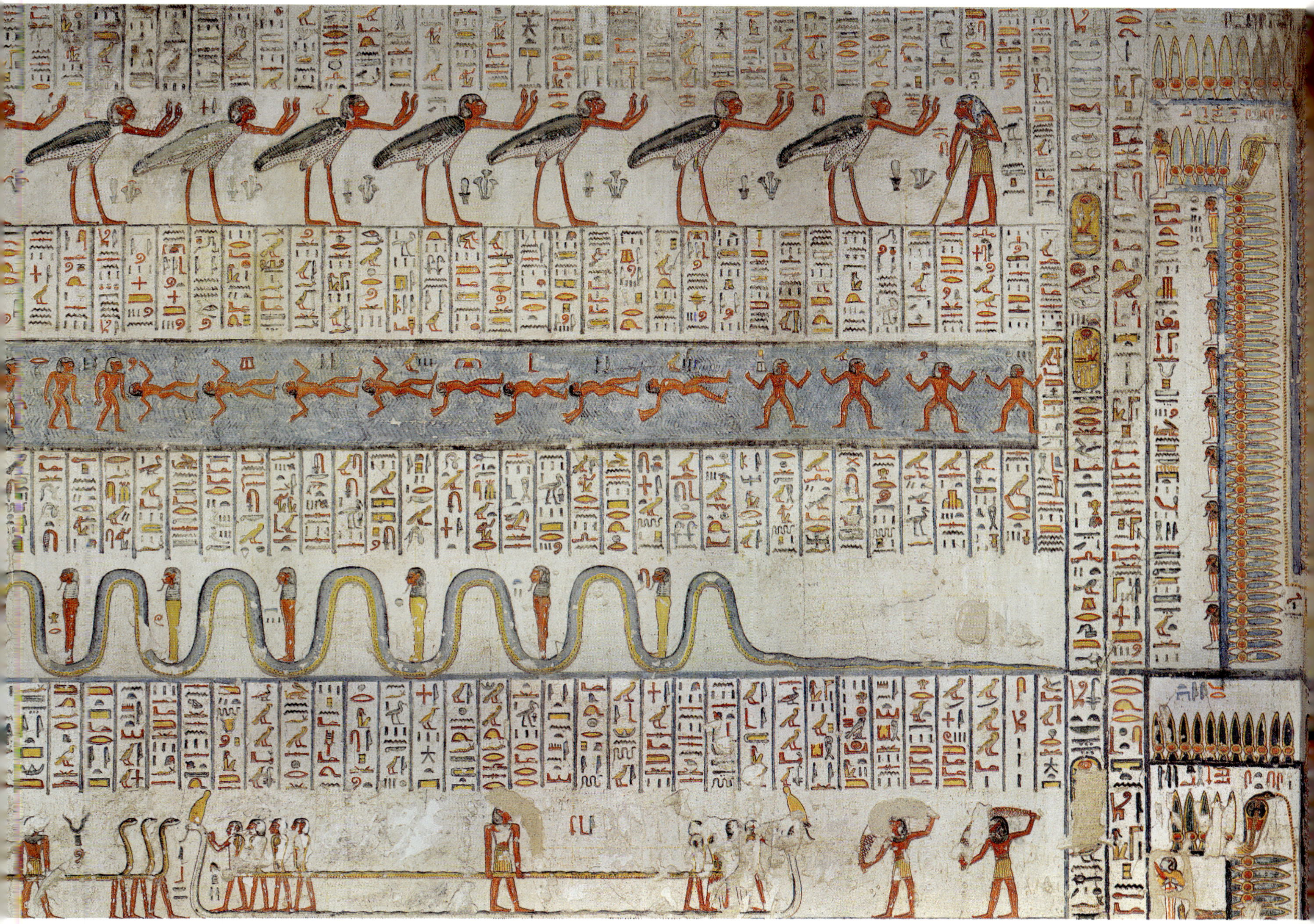

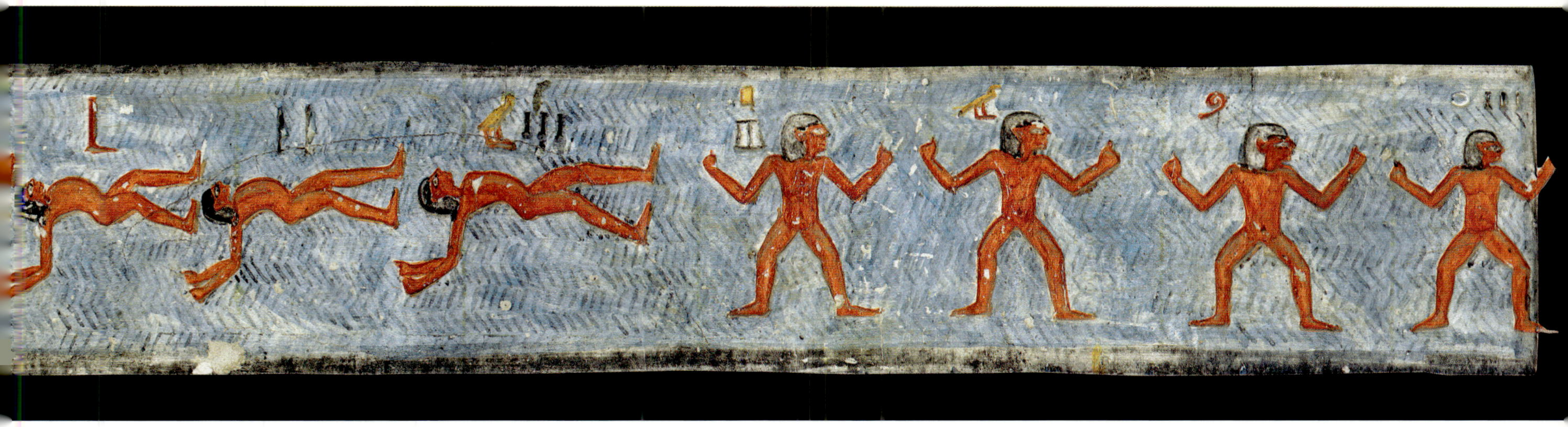

Hour Ten

The battle with Apophis fills the central register of this hour. The great snake lies on the right side, coiled and poised to strike. Above him lies a creature named Sesh-sesh with a snake's head at one end and a crocodile head at the other, another symbol of disorder. The enemies are faced by the Old One (perhaps the earth god Geb), who ties a rope around Apophis's body, and three gods wielding spears. Four goddesses, four apes, and six gods hold nets above their heads with which they throw out magical power to trap the serpent.

In the upper and lower registers are various images of the sun god, along with his protectors. Personifications of the crowns of Upper and Lower Egypt begin the sequence at the top, each raising, with the help of the "chief of the head" and the "chief of the back," a stake topped by a head with the white crown. They flank a double-headed sphinx, with one falcon and one human head, both wearing the white crown. On the back of this sphinx is a figure of the two-headed Horus-Seth god.

To the right are two scenes of struggle between men and serpents: first is the six-headed Shenty, then a strange snake with heads wearing the white crown on each end, controlled by anthropomorphized uraei and a human figure. Below, all the figures are linked with a long rope, carried at the left by four groups of four: the human-headed souls of the West; the ibis-headed followers of Thoth; the hawk-headed followers of Horus; and the ram-headed followers of Re. Next uraei and coiled snakes flank a figure of the sun god as a hawk; then eight gods, the Akhmiu, seen with frontal faces, hold the end of the rope. The texts here tell us that the sun is beginning to emerge in this hour, heading for his day position in the sky.

Hour Eleven

This hour shows the triumph of order: Apophis has been defeated. Sixteen gods stand on his back, holding the rope with which he is bound; this rope is also grasped by a huge fist that emerges from the earth. Apophis is faced by eight gods with knives, four in human shape and four with snakes' heads. Along the front of the rope lies the scorpion goddess Serket, who is the leader of the defenders of Re. Behind Apophis are five snakes controlled by Geb and the four sons of Horus. Khentyimentiu, a form of Osiris, stands at the far end of the register.

The solar bark appears in its usual form and position, but in the center of the same register is a second solar bark, in which a human face called the face of Re appears from the back of a snake; it is here so that the dead can see the god. This bark travels toward the bark in which Re takes his ram-headed form; it is towed by men holding stars to announce the sun's arrival. Before the first solar bark is the god Wenty holding a star, and four seated gods with uraei on their heads. Several strange deities follow the second boat, along with goddesses who raise their arms in worship and another snake on which stands the double-headed Horus-Seth figure. These creatures all lead Re to his rising.

Continuing this theme, the twelve star-crowned goddesses of the hours, time, and energy, are in the lower register, along with twelve oarsmen and a group of four gods in various forms, They face two standards, one topped with a baboon (perhaps the representation of a Syrian god), and the other by a *wedjat* eye, symbol of knowledge and healing, and of the victory of light over darkness.

Hour Twelve

This hour is filled with divinities announcing the arrival of the sun god to the final gate. In the upper register are gods who carry sun disks in their hands, and other gods with the stars that appear before sunrise, along with various inhabitants of the West and eight goddesses seated on coiled cobras. In the center register, the solar bark in its usual form is preceded by gods with knives and staffs who face the fettered Apophis. Four baboons, announcing the arrival of the god in the eastern horizon, and three additional deities lead the procession to sunrise. More groups of gods and goddesses, many linked with the crowns of Upper and Lower Egypt as symbols of power, fill the lower register. These crowns are meant to be worn by the king when he emerges from the Duat. The text here says that these divinities are responsible for justice in the chapel of Re and for measuring the time various creatures must stay in the Duat and the sky.

The last gate is guarded by Isis and Nephthys as uraei. The final scene fills all three registers, and shows the solar bark, with the sun in the form of the beetle Khepri pushing the solar disk before him, being lifted from the rejuvenating waters of the primordial cosmos by the arms of Nun himself. With Khepri in the bark are deities, including Isis and Nephthys, who embrace him and help to lift him. The god Osiris, arched into the form of a circle and symbolically surrounding the world, raises the figure of Nut toward the solar disk to welcome him to the sky.

The Serpent Shenty

This six-headed serpent with twelve legs (*above*) is named Shenty; he is caught by a man named Webu, and is used for protection against Apophis.

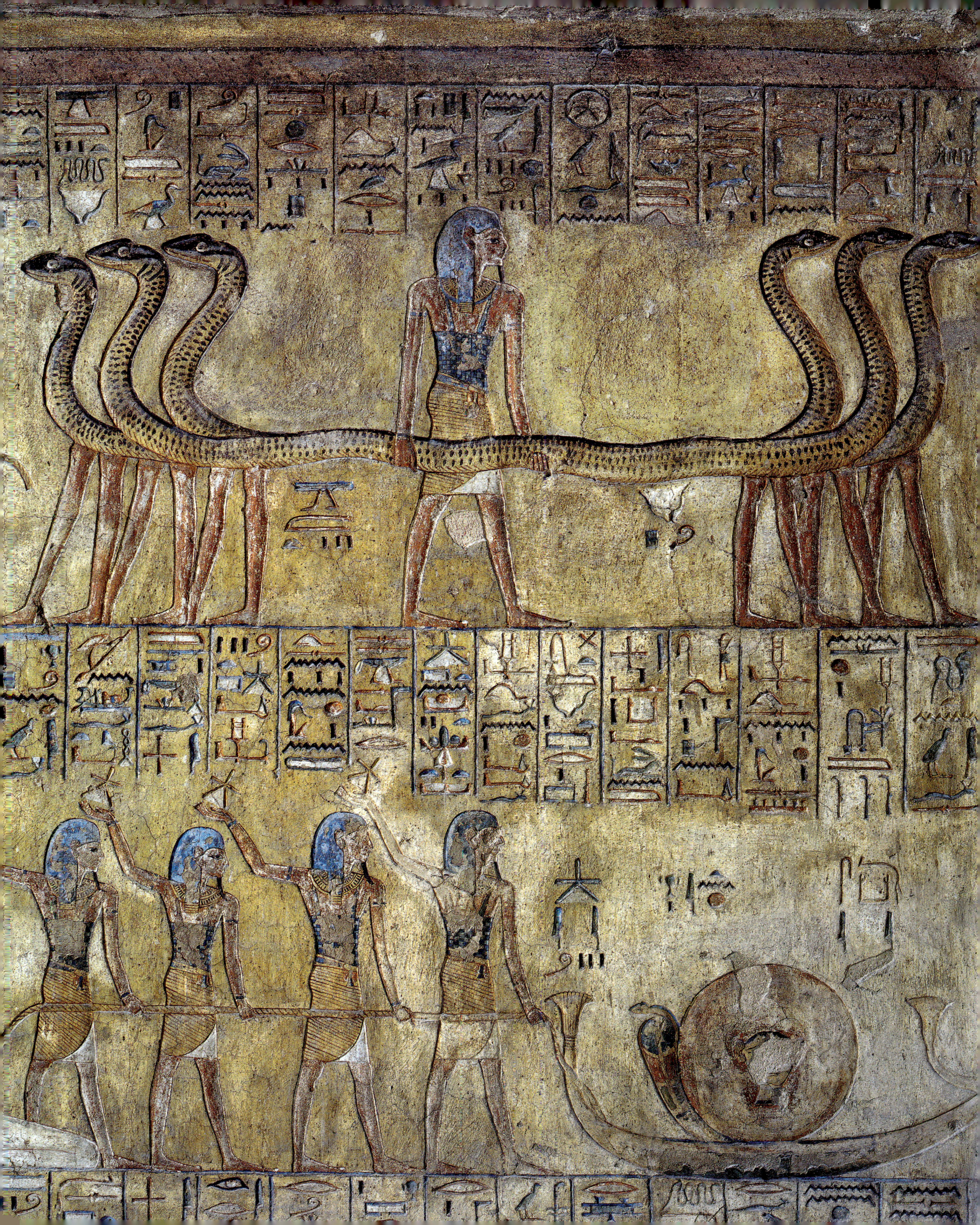

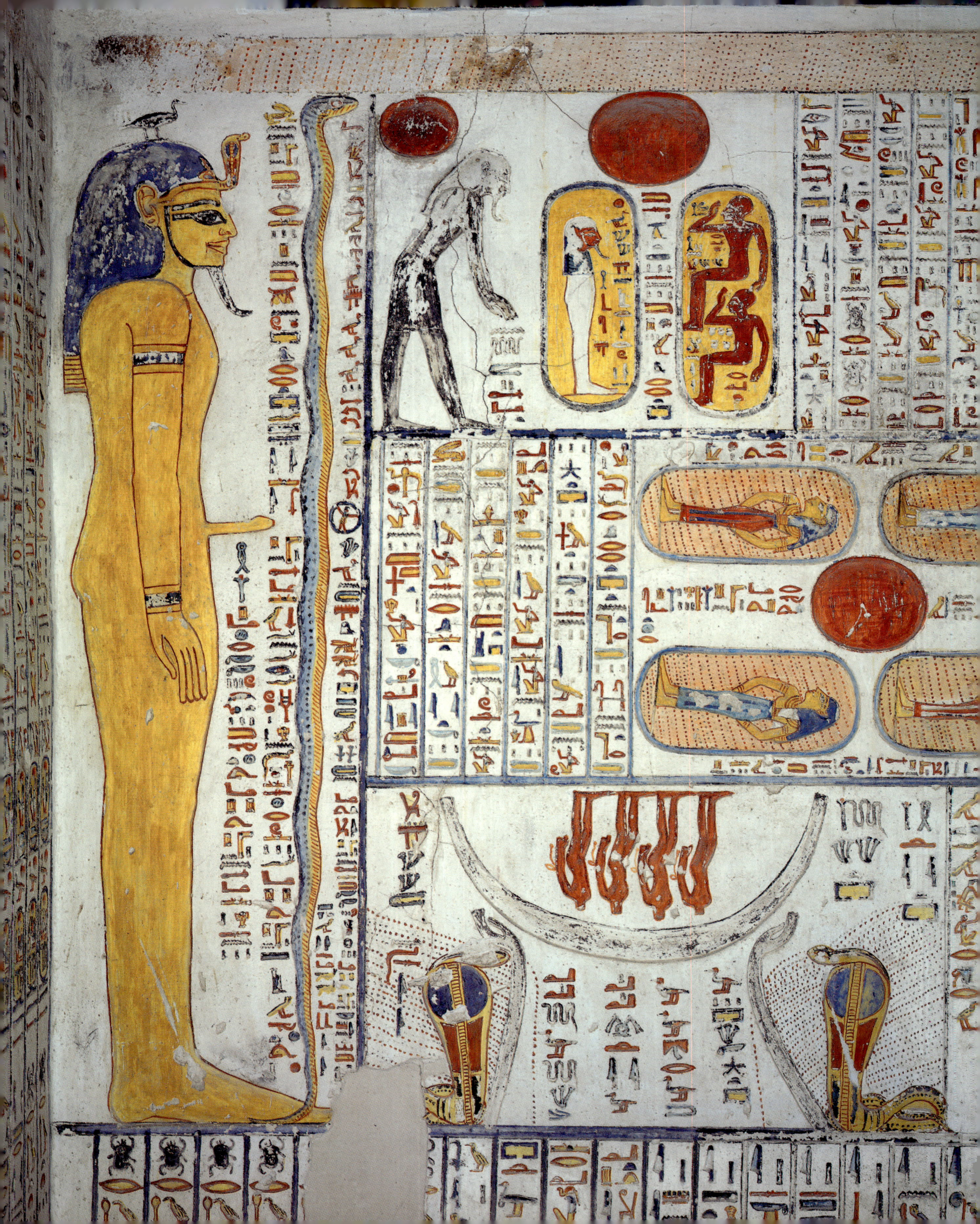

Chapter 5

The Book of Caverns and the Book of the Earth

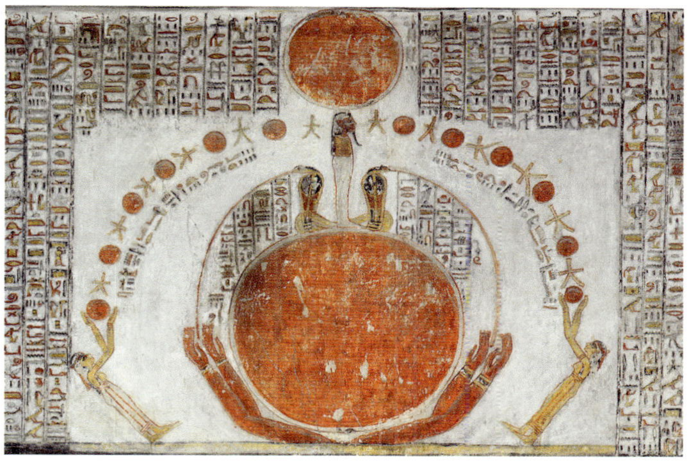

The Book of Caverns

The Book of Caverns first appears in the Osireion of Seti I, in decoration added by Seti's grandson, Merenptah. Merenptah was also the first to use this composition in the Valley of the Kings, choosing the fourth, fifth, and sixth chapters for the walls of his first pillared hall. In the tomb of Tausert and Sethnakht, excerpts from the Book of Caverns are found in the burial chamber, and in the tomb of Ramses III, parts are seen in the lower passage and burial chamber. In the tomb of Ramses IV, it replaces the Amduat in the third corridor. The fullest version is found in the tomb of Ramses V/VI, and there are scenes from this book in the second passage of the sepulcher of Ramses VII, where a new vignette appears. Ramses IX took excerpts from the first four chapters for his first and second corridors, and added selections from chapters five and six to the decoration in his burial chamber.

The ancient title of the Book of Caverns is not known; the name is modern, and refers to the six caverns through which the sun, appearing here in the form of a disk that illuminates the world of the blessed dead, travels. Caverns were seen earlier, in the eighth hour of the Amduat, but here they replace the hours of the night as the defining structure of the composition, which is thus divided into six chapters, grouped into two principal sections marked by two large figures of the sun god in his ram-headed form. In contrast to the Books of the Amduat and Gates, the solar bark is found here only in the concluding scene. The principal deities of the Book of Caverns are again Osiris and Re, but here they are seen as complementary aspects of one god. An important focus of this book is the complete destruction of the enemies of the sun god, who generally occupy the lowest register of the wall.

Osiris from the Book of Caverns
This image from the fifth chapter of the Book of Caverns is dominated by an ithyphallic figure of Osiris, with his *ba* represented as a bird on top of his head. In front of him are mummies within sarcophagi; in the lowest register, the damned are burned in cauldrons.

An attempt is sometimes made to organize this composition into the standard three registers, but modifications are often made, as for the Amduat and Gates, for reasons of space. In chapters one and two, the text (which comprises a monologue delivered by the sun god) and images are kept separate; the remainder of the composition integrates scenes and inscriptions, although chapters four to six include separate litanies.

Chapter One

The Book of Caverns is introduced by two vertical bands that occupy the full height of the wall. In the first band is the sun disk; in the second is Re in his ram-headed guise, who moves forward to enter the Duat so that he can protect Osiris and defeat his enemies. In extant representations, this chapter is divided into five registers. At the top, three coiled serpents guard the entrance to the Duat. Behind them are two groups of nine deities: first nine rearing cobras, then nine cow-headed gods.

The register below begins with nine oval shrines (probably to be interpreted as both sarcophagi and eggs from which rebirth will occur) containing gods who face in various directions; eight of these are prone and the ninth is standing. Behind them are nine jackal-headed figures who bend forward, their arms before them in gestures of respect. A god and goddess, each holding a sun disk above his or her head, completes this register. In the third horizontal band are eleven figures—ten gods and one goddess, who assume the pose seen above in the jackal-headed followers of Anubis. Osiris appears in this register, standing in his usual costume of mummy bandages and white crown within a rectangular shrine surrounded by the protective Mehen snake. Four gods in oval sarcophagi precede him, and four goddesses follow him.

Below are nine goddesses, nine more gods in oval shrines (eight prone, and the ninth, who is Horus with a falcon's head, standing), then two pairs of figures (two gods and two goddesses) facing each other. A crocodile-headed god brings up the rear. The lowest register is reserved for the enemies of order. The three guardian snakes again begin the sequence. Behind them are sixteen bound captives, eight with heads and eight without. These enemies are damned to eternal non-existence by Re.

Chapter Two

The second cavern is guarded by an abridged form of a gate: one snake standing on its tail, followed by four horizontal serpents. The top register is filled with gods and goddesses in oval sarcophagi: first twelve of the followers of Osiris, four with mummy bandages in lieu of heads and eight with animal heads; then seven goddesses. Between the two groups stand two hawk-headed gods; at the end of the register is another god in fully human form.

The second register begins with a crocodile-headed god, drawn like the ones in the sarcophagi above. He is approached by nine gods who tug on locks of hair that they hold in front of their faces. Twelve mummiform figures in ovals follow, worshipped by a ram-headed figure.

In the central register, the principal action focuses on the coffer of Osiris, seen in the middle. The corpse of the god is stored here, surrounded by six gods who lean forward and raise their hands in gestures of worship; five more gods face forward, worshipping the ram-headed figure of Re that introduces the register. Beyond the coffer are two groups of four stakes each: four are topped with ram's heads and the other four by jackal heads. These are already familiar from the Book of Gates.

Register four is filled with gods in oval sarcophagi: at one side are twelve mummiform figures of Osiris, shown vertically; to the other is a group of nine images of Re, eight prone and one vertical, all with rams' heads. Each group is flanked by other deities: the mummiform figures are offered respect by a hawk-headed figure and worship by a human; the ram-headed dead are worshipped by additional ram-headed gods.

The lowest register is again filled with the captured enemies of the sun. Four are headless, with their heads represented before them. Four more are shown in a vertical line, and the final eight are shown upside-down, their feet on the register line above them and their hearts torn out of their bodies. All the enemies are naked and bound, and threatened by four knife-wielded guards with horns. The text here has Re informing Osiris that he will enter the cavern of Aker.

Chapter Three

This cavern corresponds with Hour Six of the Books of the Amduat and Gates, where Osiris and Re join and the journey toward rebirth begins. The top of three registers begins with two snakes and a sun disk surrounding the deceased king as Osiris in an oval sarcophagus. Next, a long snake stretches its body over seven gods with the heads of catfish; these are associated with the earth god Aker. Two images of the corpse of the sun god follow, lying face down within half-circles. All of these vignettes are topped by sun disks, which illuminate the action here. At the opposite end of the register, Osiris stands within his shrine in the "cavern of Osiris—Foremost of the Westerners," protected by snakes and surrounded by thirteen gods in various forms within oval sarcophagi.

A figure of the ram-headed Re as the Elder One leaning on a staff introduces the central register. He faces four faceless figures of Osiris, whom he addresses as "Lord of the Duat." In the center of the register is the double-headed Aker sphinx, the prone figure of the god, and the Khepri beetle in an oval sarcophagus, a variation on the scene familiar from the sixth hour of the Amduat. Three gods and four goddesses, members of the primeval Ennead of nine gods, stand on the forelegs of Aker.

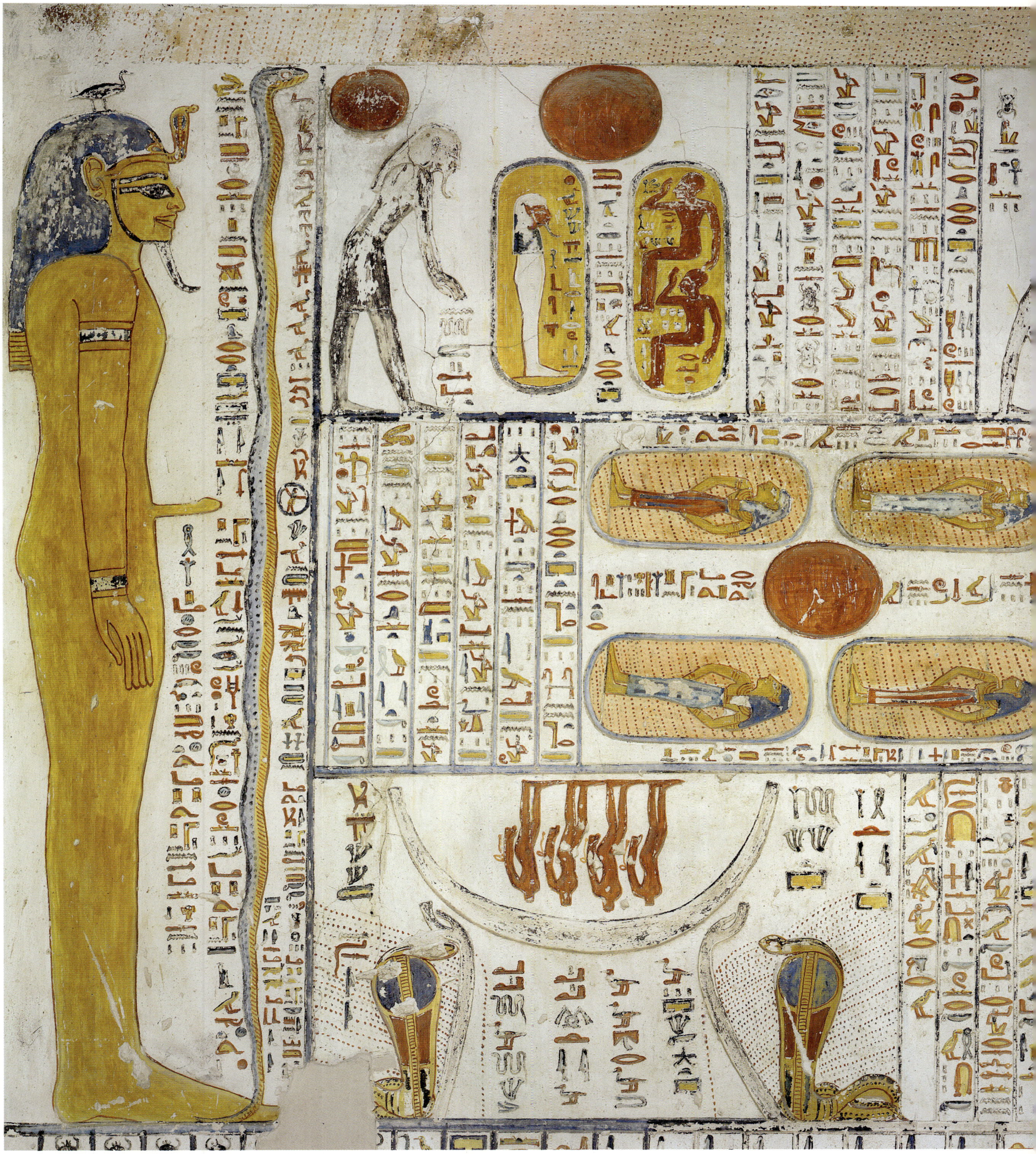

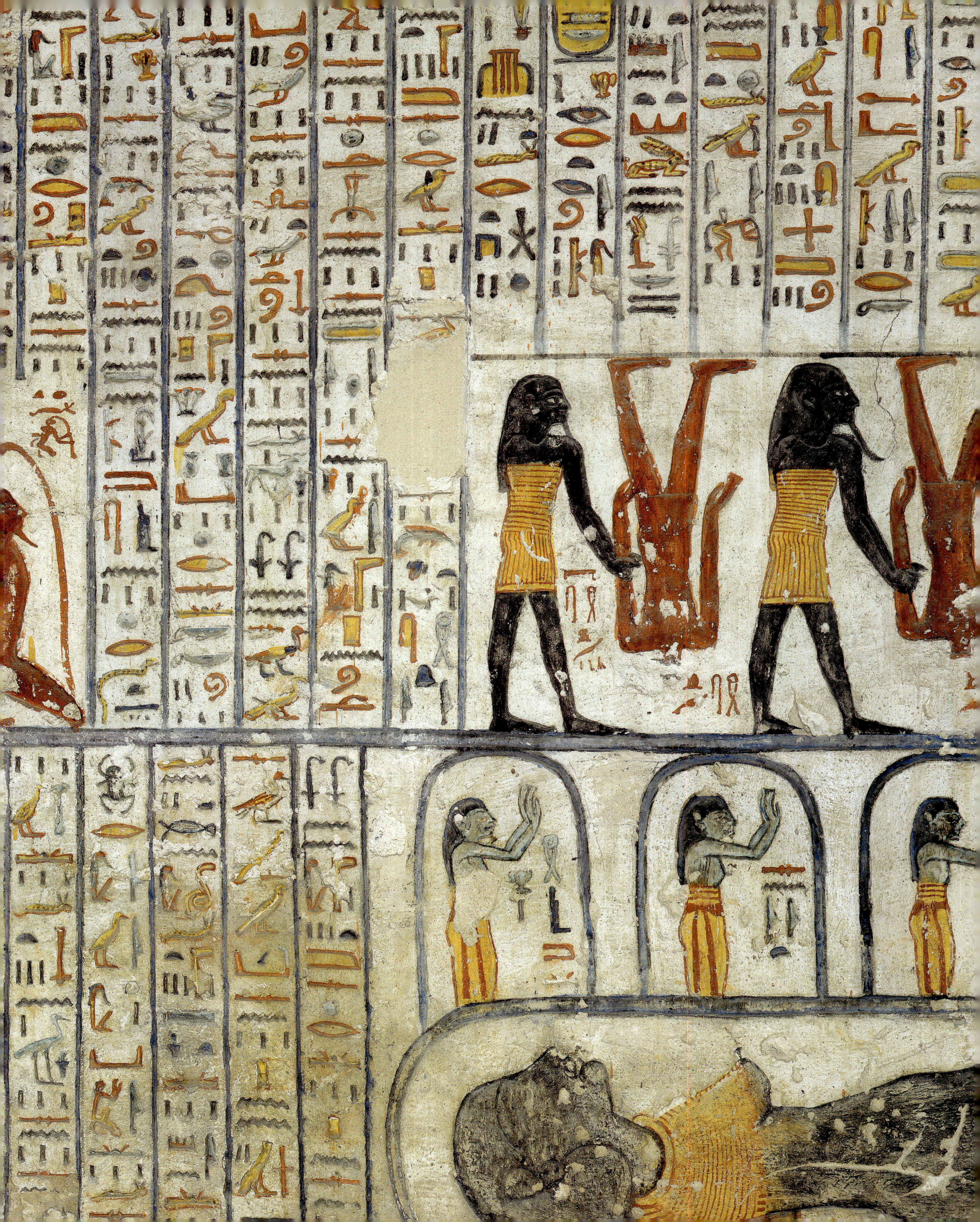

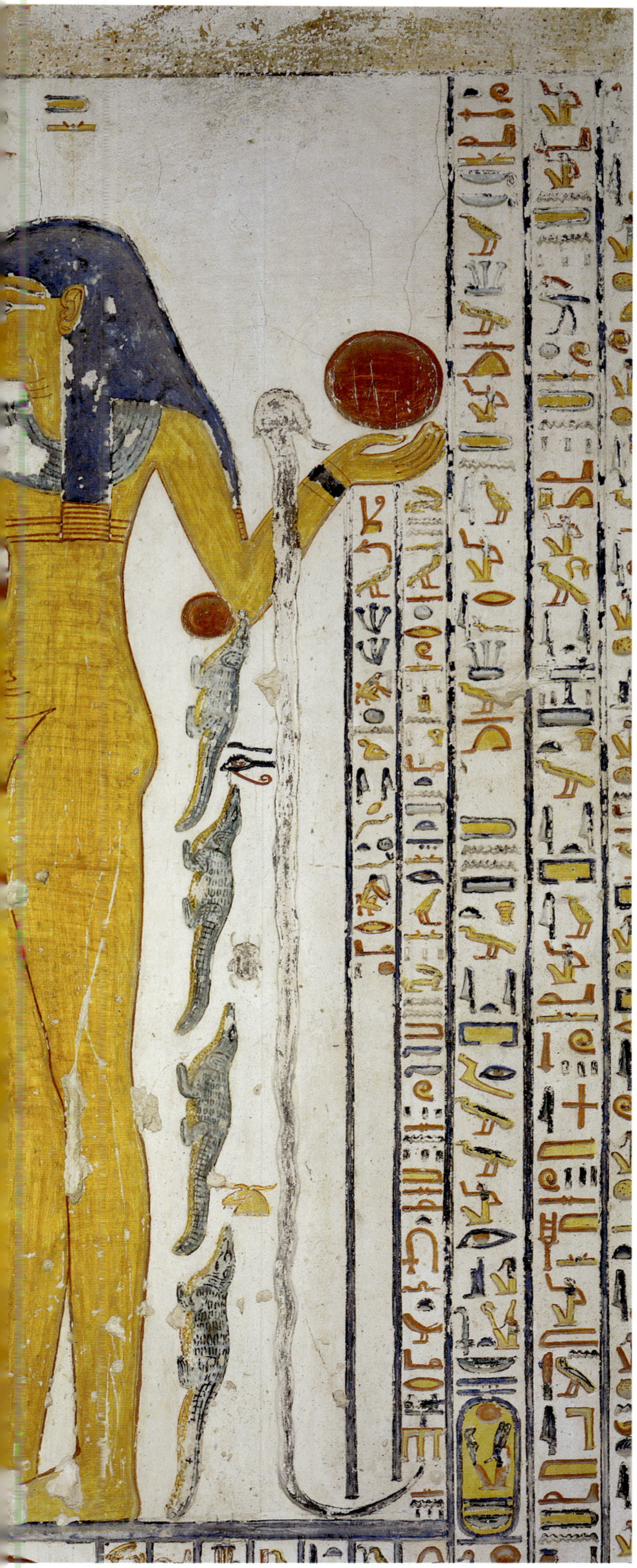

Book of Caverns, Detail of Chapter Five

In the upper register here are two sarcophagi, one of which contains two figures of Re as a child, and the figure of the earth god, Tatanen. Below are more sarcophagi holding the mummies of those to be resurrected; in the lower register, the damned are punished in a fiery cauldron.

Book of the Earth, Section D

(Following pages)

The lower register of this section, located in the "Place of Annihilation," focuses mainly on the punishment meted out to the enemies of the sun god, seen bound and decapitated or being burned in cauldrons. In the center is the "corpse of Shetit," a personification of the land of the dead. In the right of the upper register is the solar disk and the Khepri beetle; in the left of the lower register, Osiris is flanked by the corpses of Geb and Tatenen.

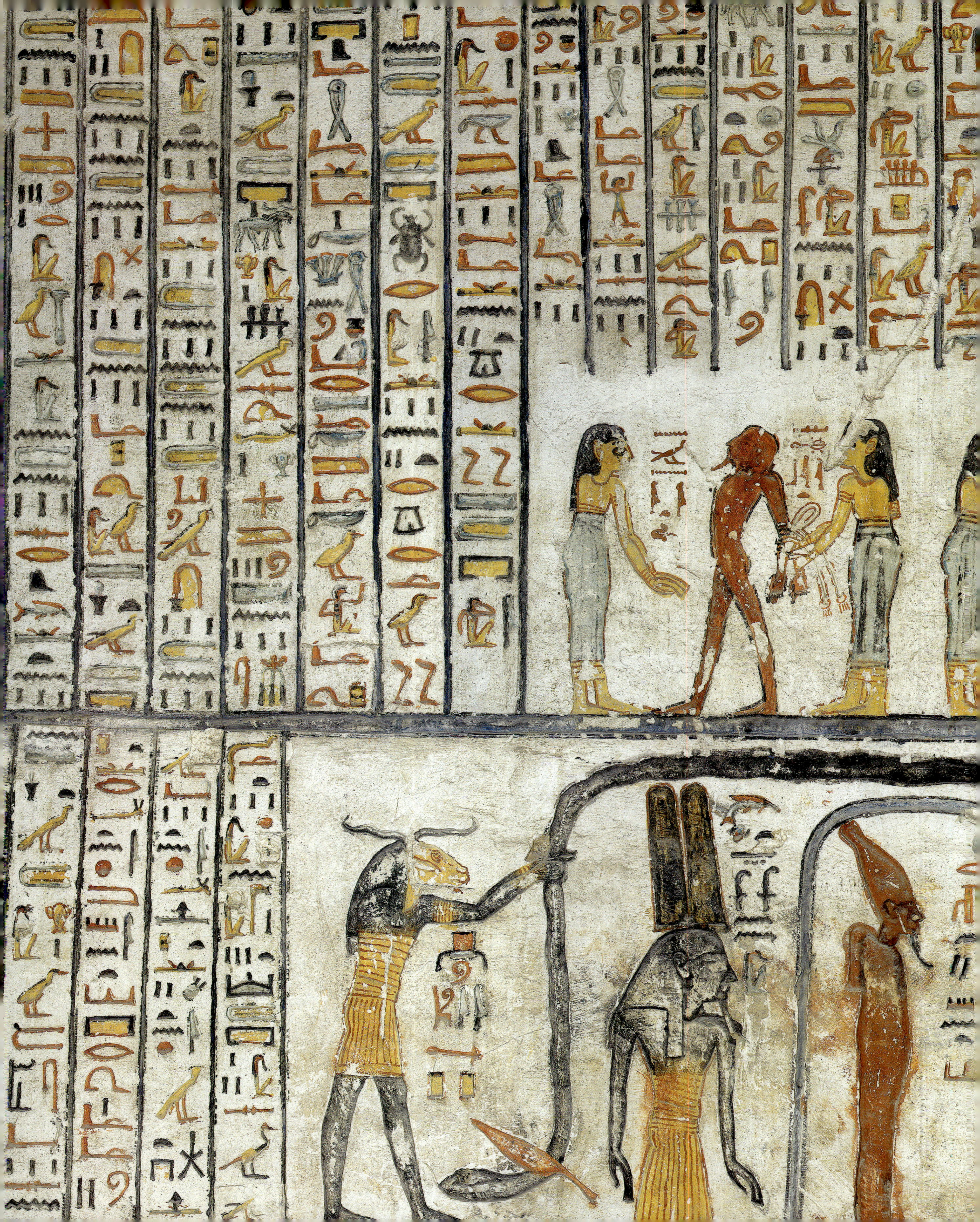

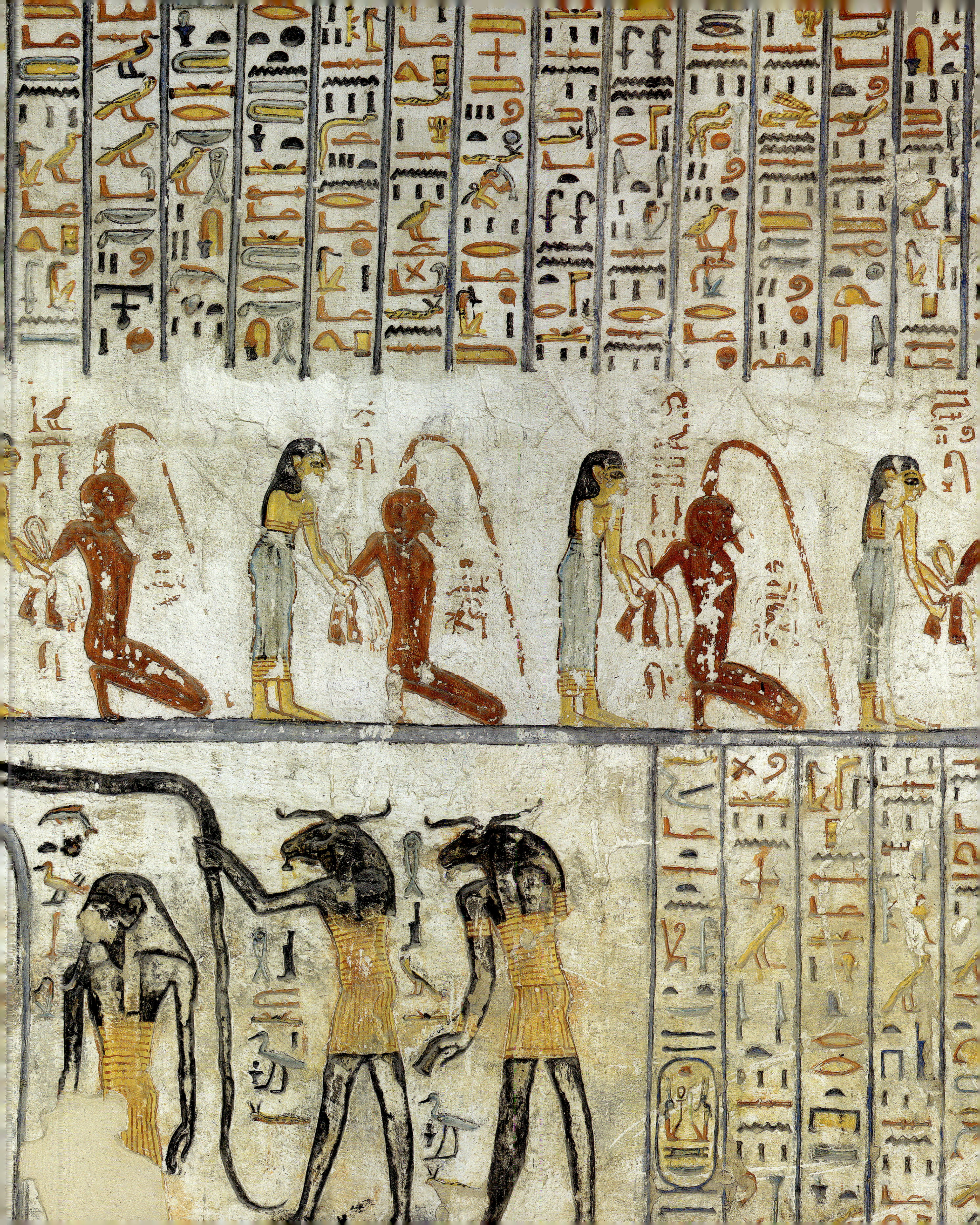

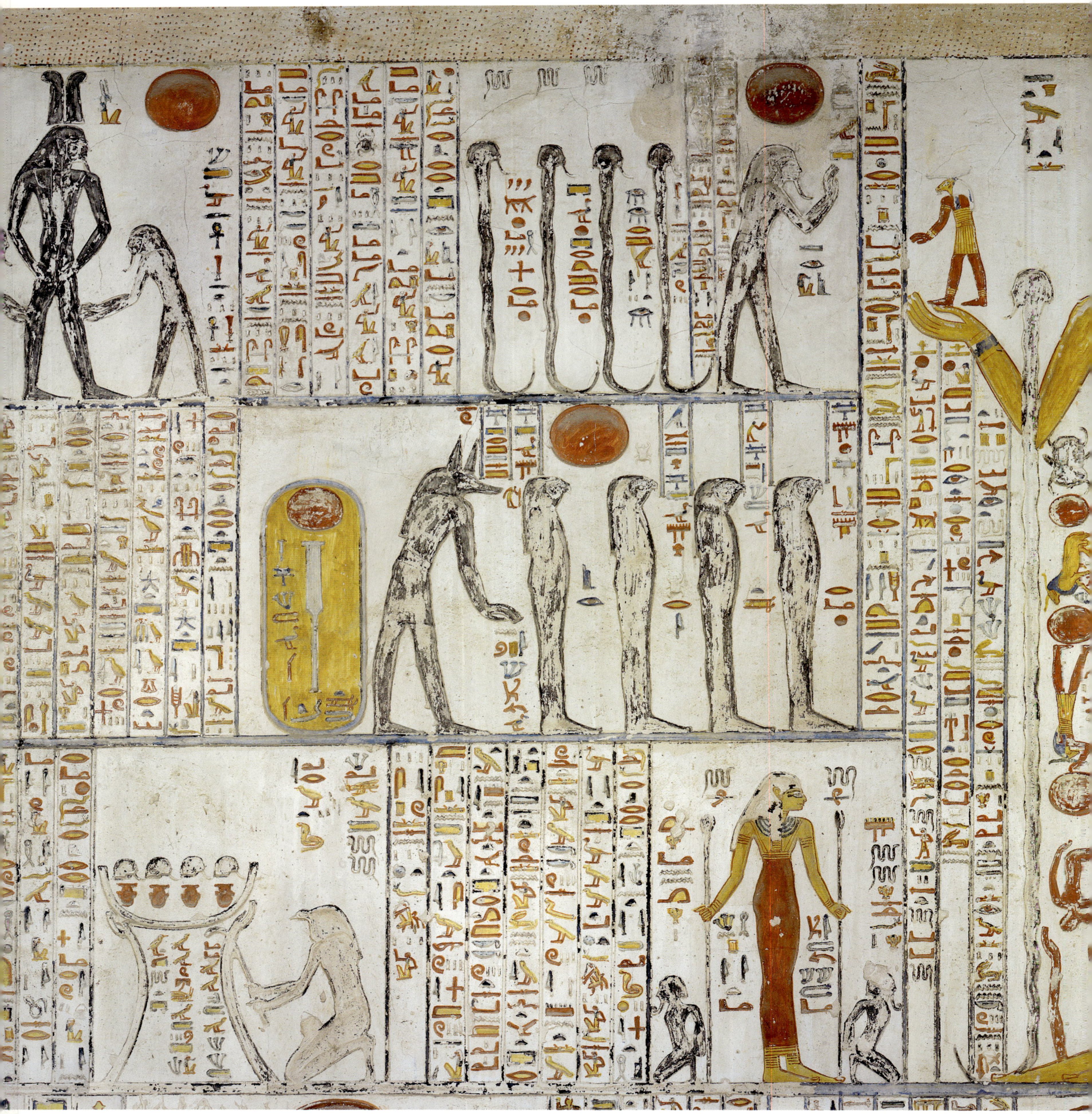

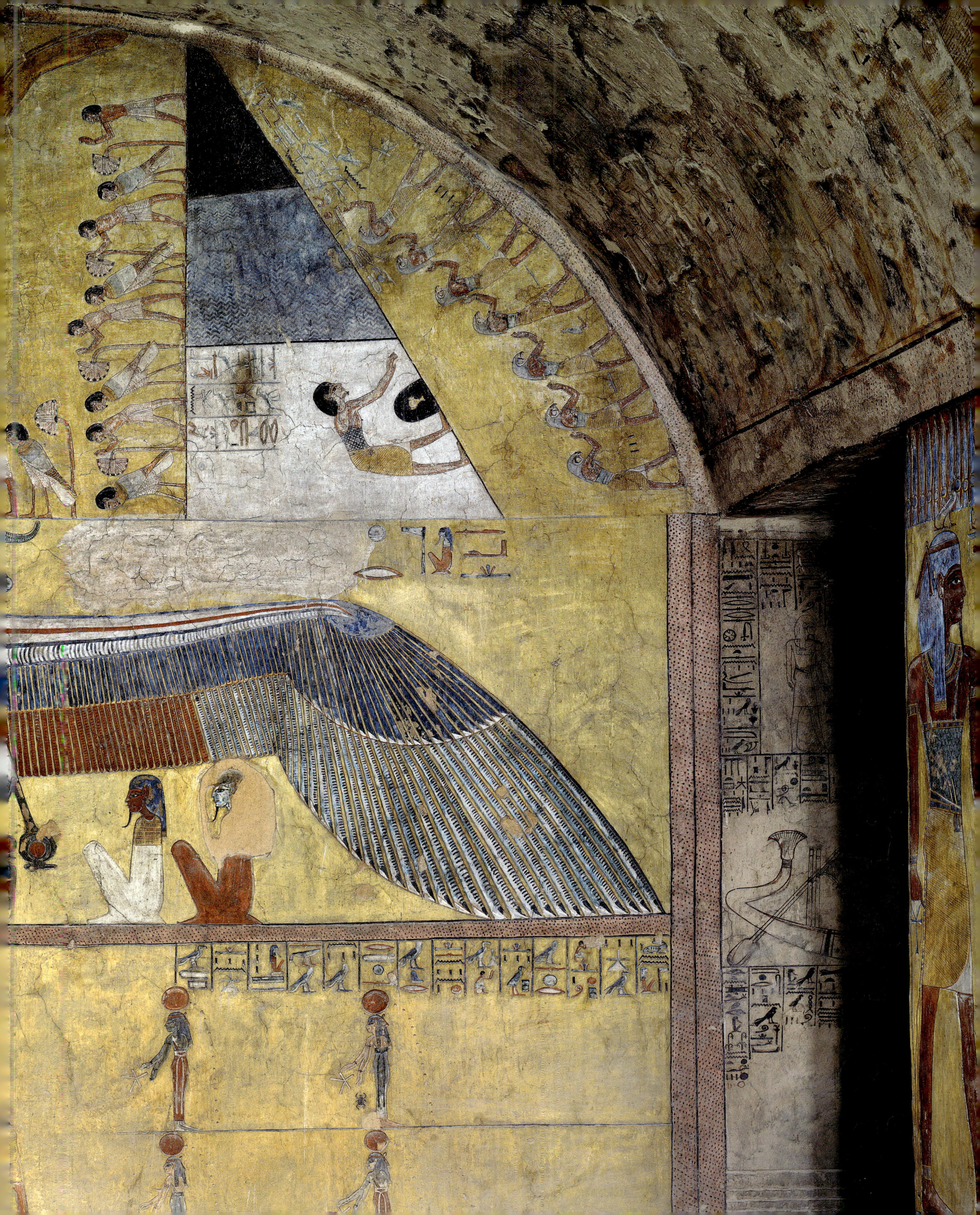

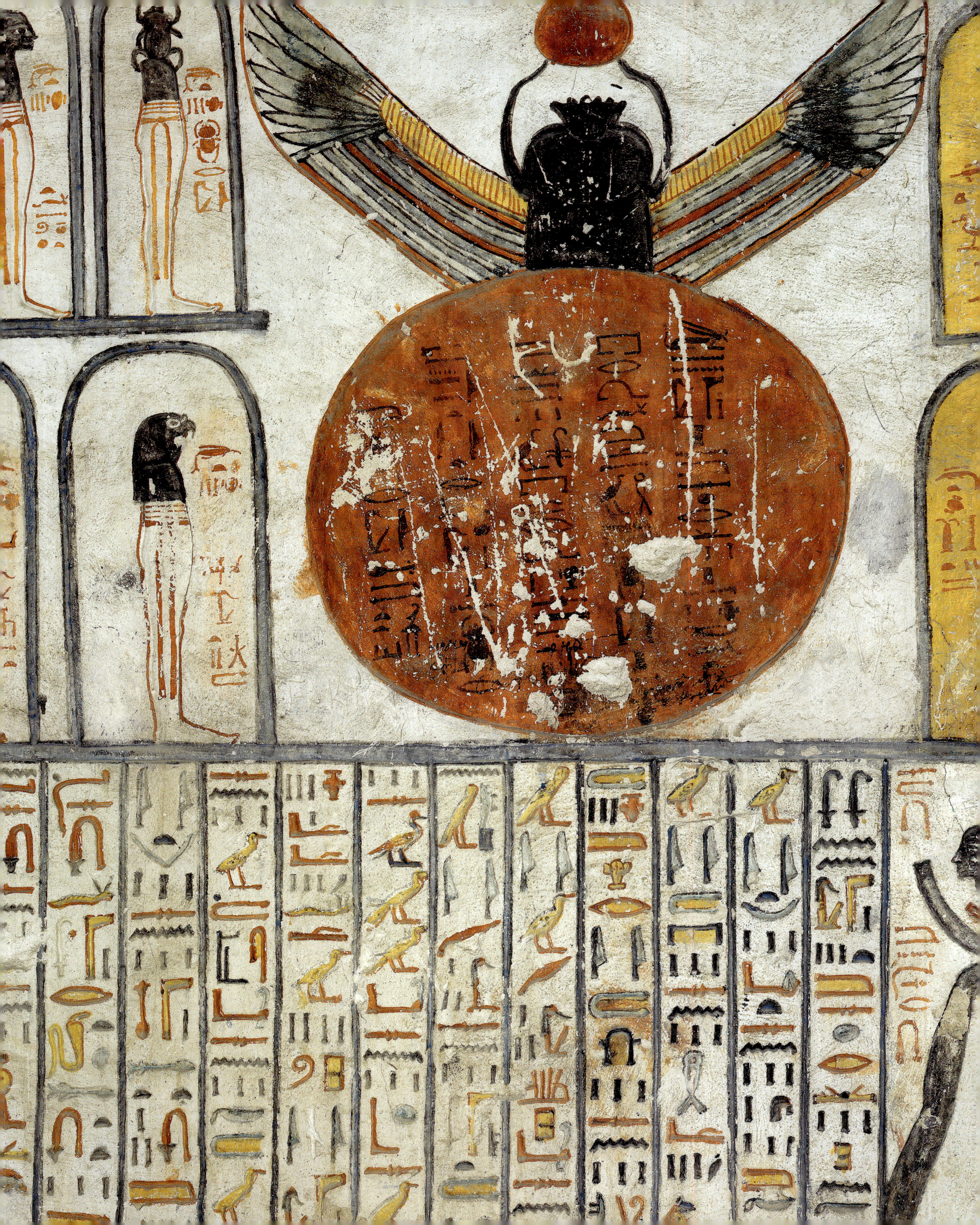

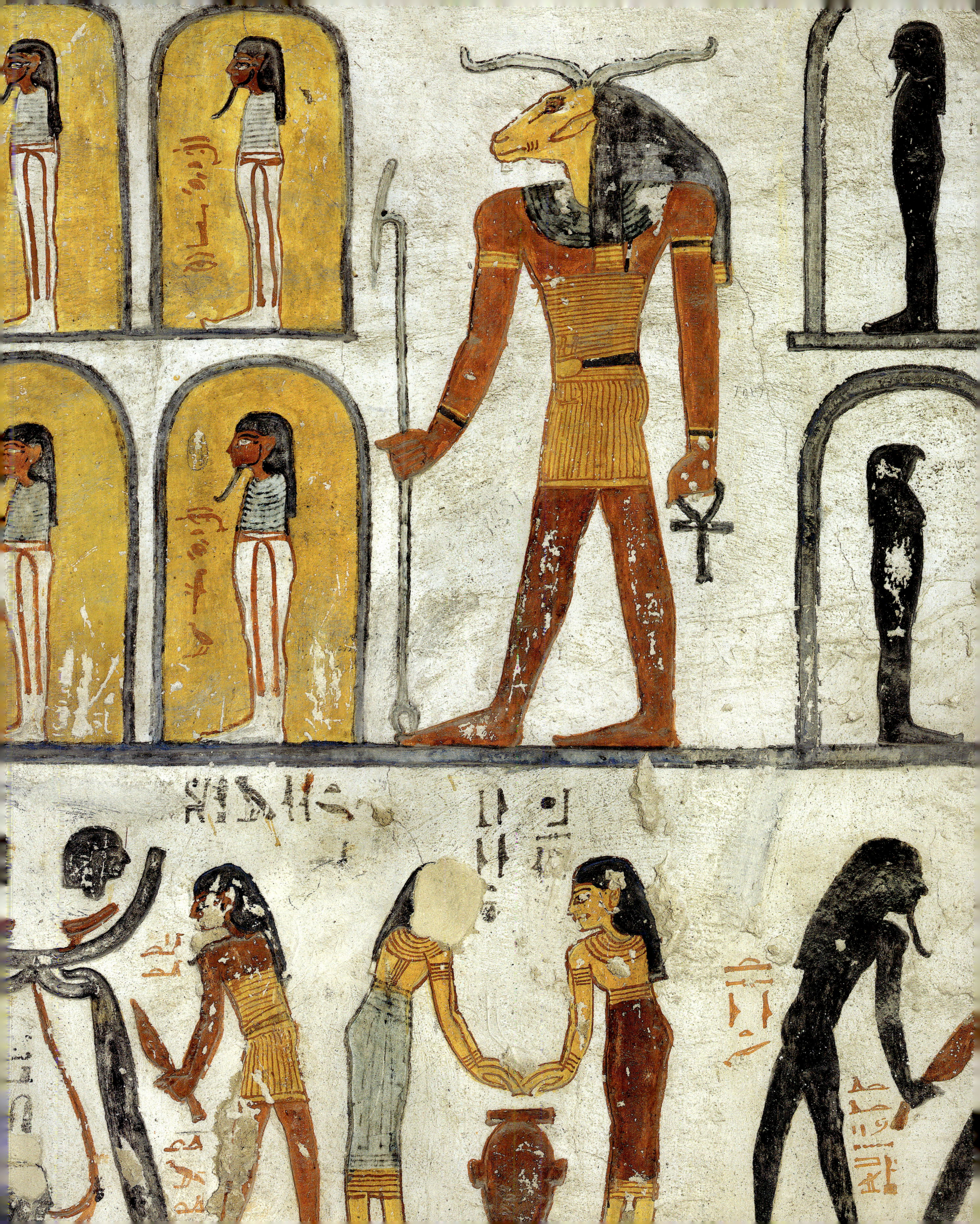

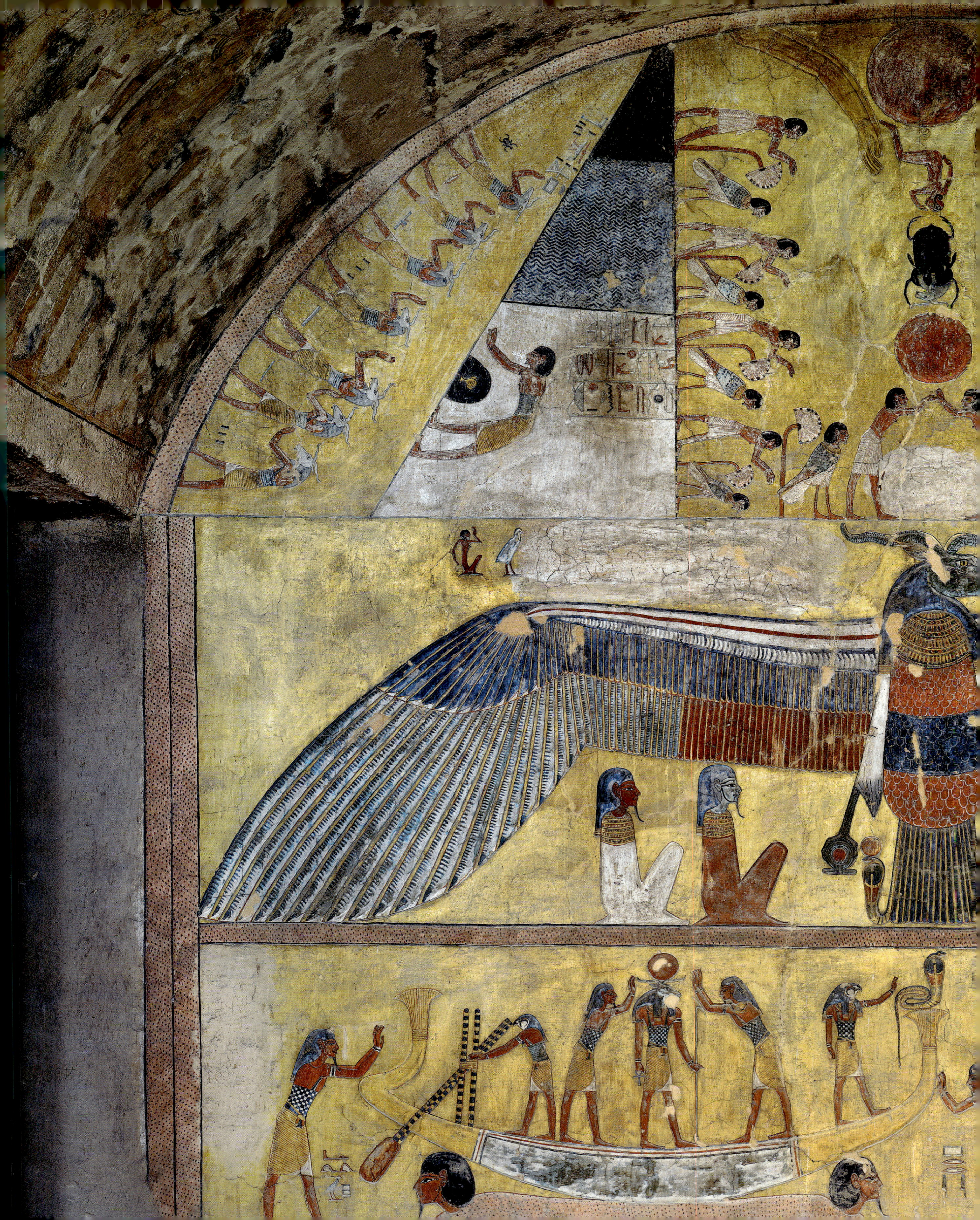

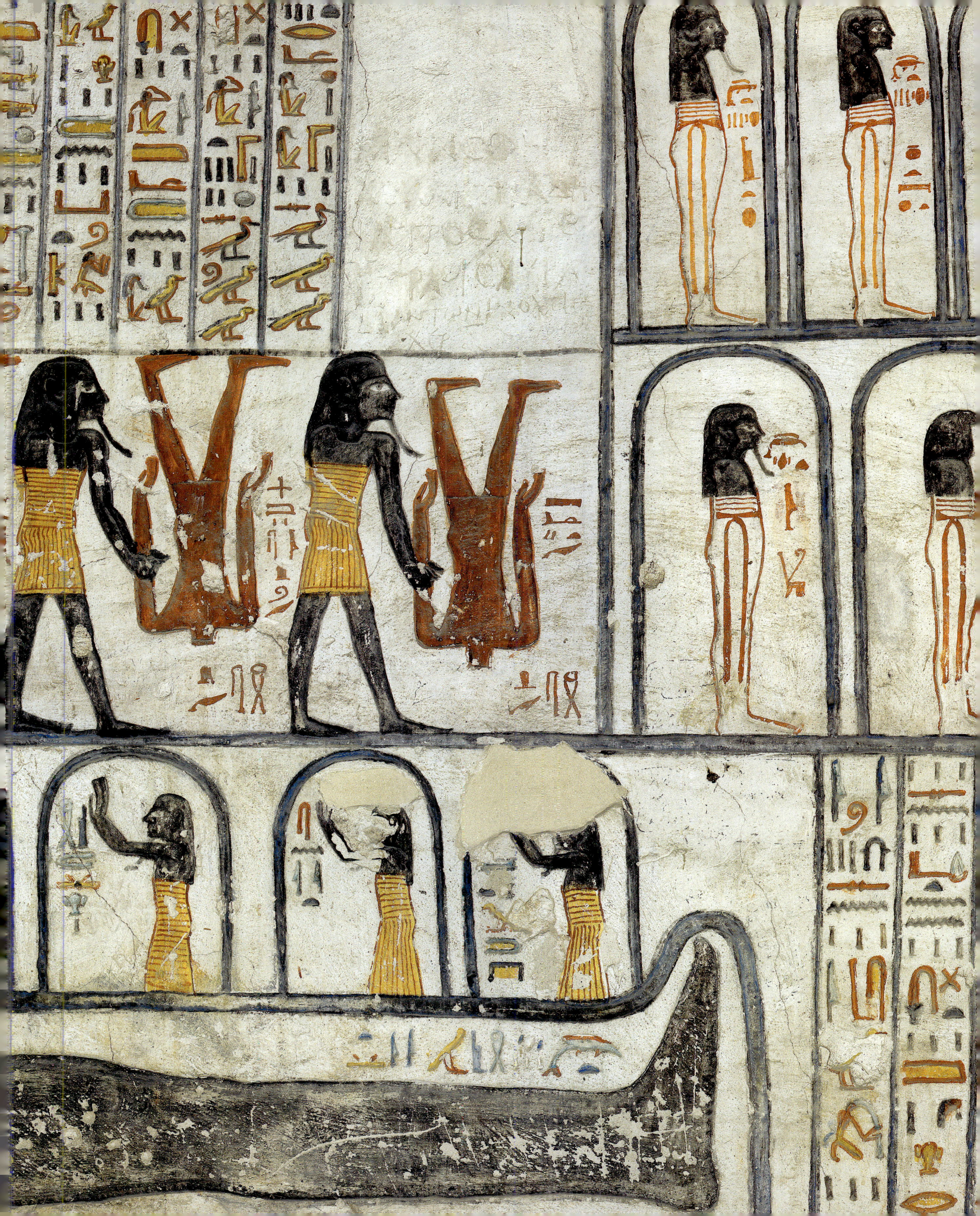

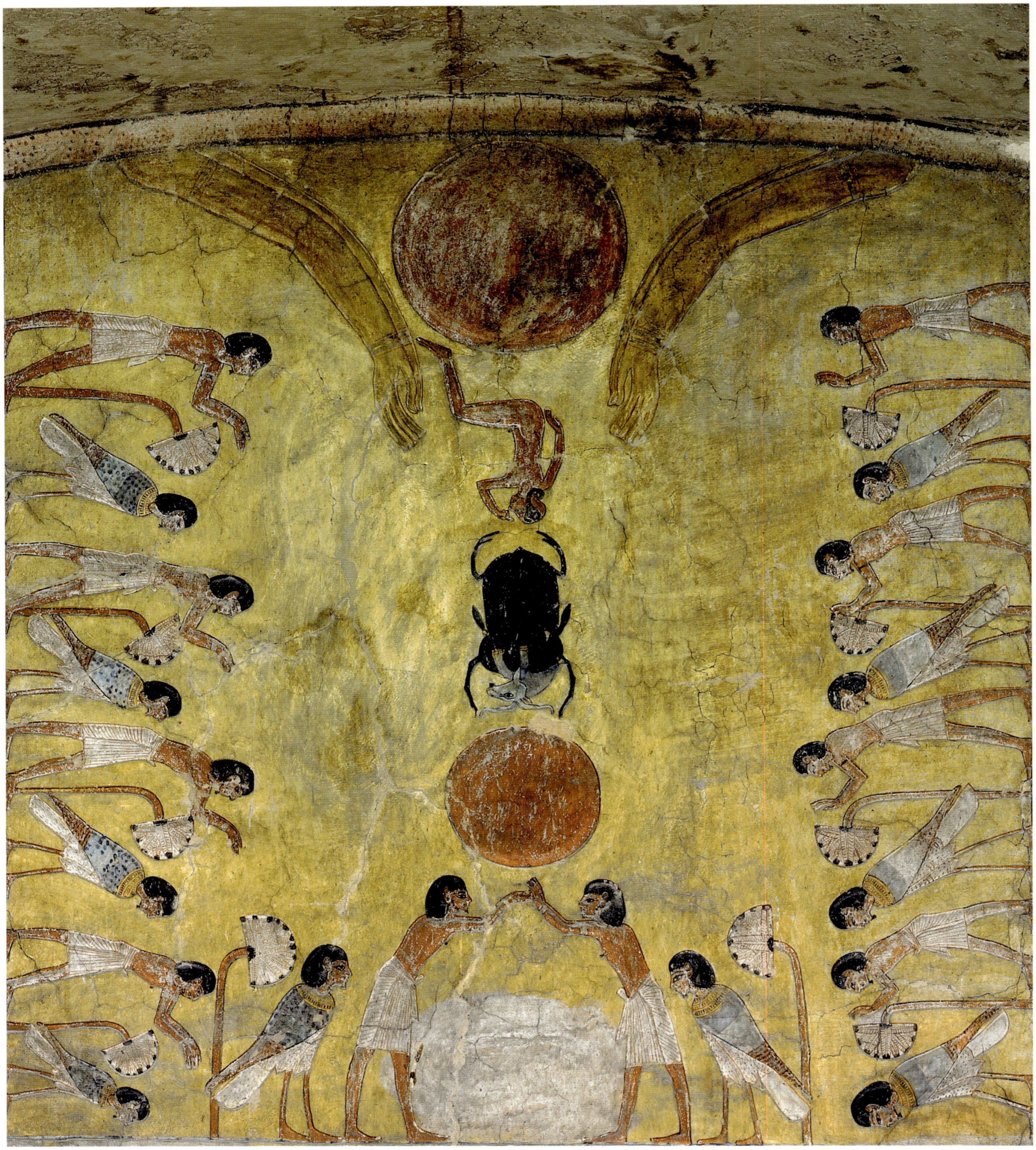

BOOK OF CAVERNS, FINAL SCENE
The Book of Caverns ends, like most of the Netherworld books, with the rebirth of the sun at dawn. Dominating the scene is the winged *ba* of the ram-headed sun god, preparing to rise between two mounds of earth. Above him can be seen the sun in various other forms: as a disk, a scarab beetle, and a child.

Osiris's corpse, a ram's head, and the eye of Re, each in its own sarcophagus, come next, within a rectangle formed by a snake which grasps its tail in its mouth. This image, expressing the amalgamation of Osiris and Re, is worshipped by four male gods. The register ends with two male deities paying homage to a crocodile-headed figure, perhaps also to be understood as an image of Osiris, who stands on a snake.

The action in the lower register is mostly topsy-turvy, with the majority of the figures standing on the upper register line. There are various enemies, for the first time both male and female, an ithyphallic figure of Osiris within the body of a snake, and eight bound enemies. At the far end of the register are the *ba*s of these enemies, also turned upside-down.

Chapter Four

The second half of the Book of Caverns begins with the fourth chapter. It is separated from the third section by two vertical bands similar to those that introduced the composition; in this case, they are occupied by a snake that stands on its own tail (named the "Great One on his Belly") and a figure of ram-headed Re set at the top of the band and crossing into the upmost register of the three that follow. The rebirth of the sun begins here, and continues in the two chapters that follow. The text comprises litanies praising Re, along with promises that Re makes to Osiris and his followers.

The top register begins with figures of Isis and Nephthys, their arms outstretched, with Osiris the king as a child with a sun disk arched between them. The second vignette in this register shows Osiris again, flanked by Horus and Anubis. Finally, a cow-headed god, Osiris as "bull of the West," raises his arms before two oval shrines with a sun disk between them. In the top oval is a mongoose; in the lower is a heart flanked by two sun disks.

Re as an elder appears again in the second register, leaning on his staff and facing three forms of Osiris that bend toward him in a gesture of protection. In the center of the register are two prone corpses of Osiris in oval sarcophagi, with a sun disk and snake between them, protected by Horus. At the end of the register is Anubis and a figure of Osiris with his *ba*. The lower register is occupied again by upside-down enemies, punished by the cat-headed "one from whom there is no escape."

Chapter Five

The fifth chapter begins with an image, occupying the height of the wall, of the goddess Nut. She lifts Re in the dual forms of the ram-headed god and the sun disk toward the horizon. She is surrounded by images that represent the course of the sun: to the right, traveling downward, are a beetle with the sun disk, a ram, then a god with a head of a ram. Two arms from the baseline emerge to receive the god Re as a child. To Nut's left are four crocodiles, moving upward.

At the beginning of the first row, Osiris worships a figure of Re held by Nut; above him is the sun disk, behind him are four human-headed snakes standing on their tails. The earth god Tatanen follows, protected by the corpses of Atum and Khepri, then two children and Osiris within oval sarcophagi. Below are four hawk-headed Horus mummies protected by Anubis, and a coffin containing a *sekhem* scepter with a sun disk, the staff of Atum. Next, four goddesses lie prone in oval sarcophagi, surrounding a sun disk.

The lowest register here contains three vignettes: a goddess holding stakes to which are tied captives; two arms emerging from the earth, supporting a cauldron in which are placed hands and hearts; then another pair of arms holding a cauldron, this time filled with the four enemies from which the hands and hearts were taken. This last image is flanked by two uraei who fan the flames of punishment.

The three registers are interrupted again in this chapter by another image that fills the height of the wall. In this band is an ithyphallic figure of Osiris, his *ba* above his head in the form of a bird, with a snake stretched out vertically in front of him. The three registers behind him continue the themes seen before: on the top, two gods holding an oval containing bits of meat representing the flesh of Osiris between them; in the middle, a ram-headed god and the goddess Tayt face one another below a sun disk; then two gods, one human and one hawk-headed, praise the sun disk, which rises above a ram-headed stake. At the bottom, two arms raise a cauldron containing the flesh, *bas*, and shadows of the enemies of Re and Osiris.

Chapter Six

Between Chapters Five and Six are thirteen litanies in which Re speaks to the inhabitants of the Duat, both friendly and inimical. The cavern here takes the oval shape seen at the end of the twelfth hour of the Amduat, with an oval boundary at the far end from which the sun disk will emerge. The three registers here are filled with deities protecting oval sarcophagi containing the bodies of those who will be resurrected. An important vignette here appears at the beginning of the middle register: the scarab beetle brings the sun disk out from between the "two mysterious caverns of the West," in which Re and Osiris are inherent. The disk is met by four standing gods. The accompanying text tells of the resurrection of the god, but informs us that first the great serpent, seen in the next vignette, must be defeated; two gods in oval sarcophagi cast a spell to cut the snake into pieces.

The enemies of order are again punished in the lowest register. Both males and females appear here, some decapitated already, and two with their hearts removed. The text tells us that their *ba*s and shadows will also be annihilated. Two more groups of enemies follow, then two cursed individuals disappear head-first into the depths of the Place of Annihilation while Osiris rises, protected by a large snake.

The solar bark appears in this chapter for the first time, at the end of the central register. The ram-headed god is accompanied here by the Khepri beetle, and the boat is towed by twelve deities, four human-headed, four with rams' heads, and four with the heads of hawks. In the prow of the boat, a bird stands on an egg or a mound.

The concluding scene of this chapter, spanning all three registers, has the solar bark passing between the two mountains of the horizon. The beginnings of two triangular shapes, half black and half filled with blue water, which symbolize the entire journey and end at the eastern horizon, are marked by two mounds over which gods bend protectively. The rising sun is represented in three forms: as a disk, as a child, and as a ram-headed beetle. Fourteen gods raise their arms in praise as the sun slips into the day sky.

THE BOOK OF THE EARTH

Found in several tombs, often on a wall opposite from the Book of the Caverns, is the Book of the Earth (one of several modern names given to this text). Several scenes that later become part of this composition are seen singly in tombs of the 19th and early 20th Dynasty, specifically in the burials of Merenptah, Tausert, and Ramses III. Scenes from this book were used in the decoration of the burial chambers of Ramses IV, Ramses VI, Ramses VII, and Ramses IX. Scholars have not been particularly successful in terms of organizing this book into an exact sequence, although it does seem to be divided into two halves. There is not, however, an obvious beginning or a clear end. Egyptologists refer to it in sections A through D, with some individual vignettes included in a section E. The book has been given its modern name because of the importance given to the principal gods of the earth.

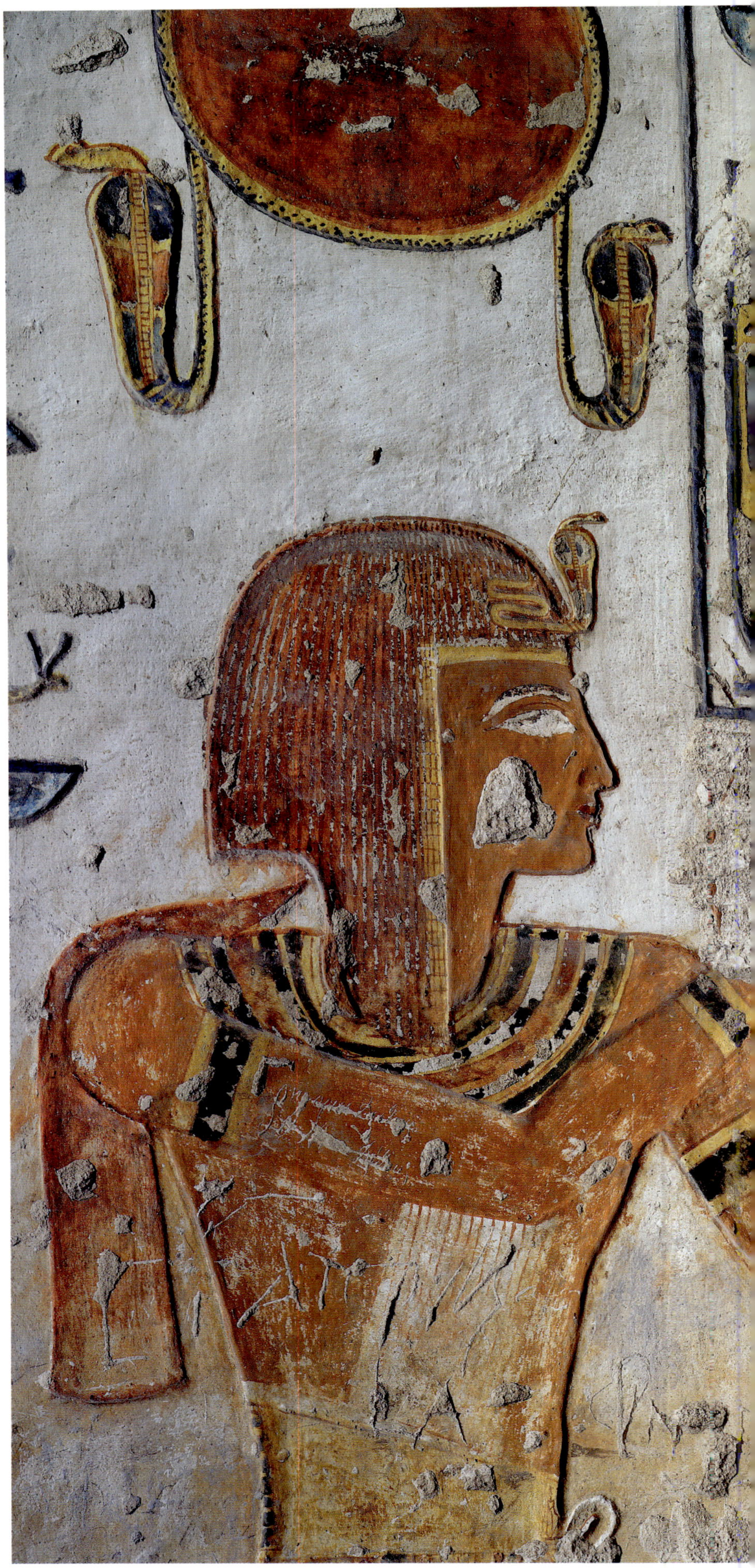

THE BOOK OF THE EARTH, SECTION D
The first section (D) of the Book of the Earth can be seen here on wall of the burial chamber of Ramses V/VI, on this page beyond a pillar bearing an image of the king, and on the following page in full. Prominent here is the sun disk rising from the depths of the Nun in the upper register, the resurrection of the sun in the form of a scarab beetle rising from a sun disk, a large corpse representing the realm of the dead, and a line of decapitated enemies.

THE BOOK OF THE EARTH, SECTION D
(Following pages)
Although scholars are not certain about the exact sequence of the scene groups that comprise the Book of the Earth, this unit, known as Section D, is thought to come first, and represents the entire realm of the dead.

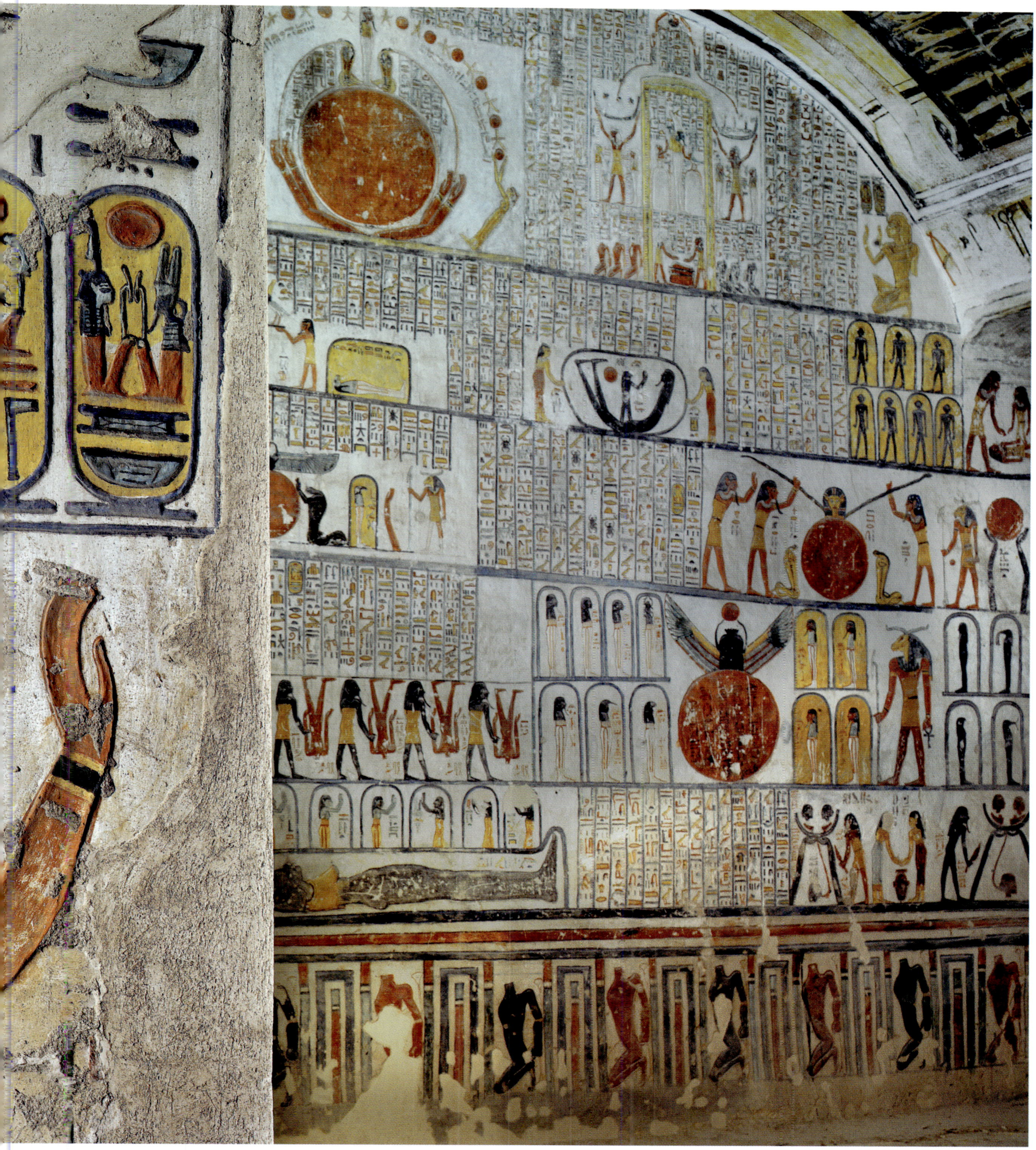

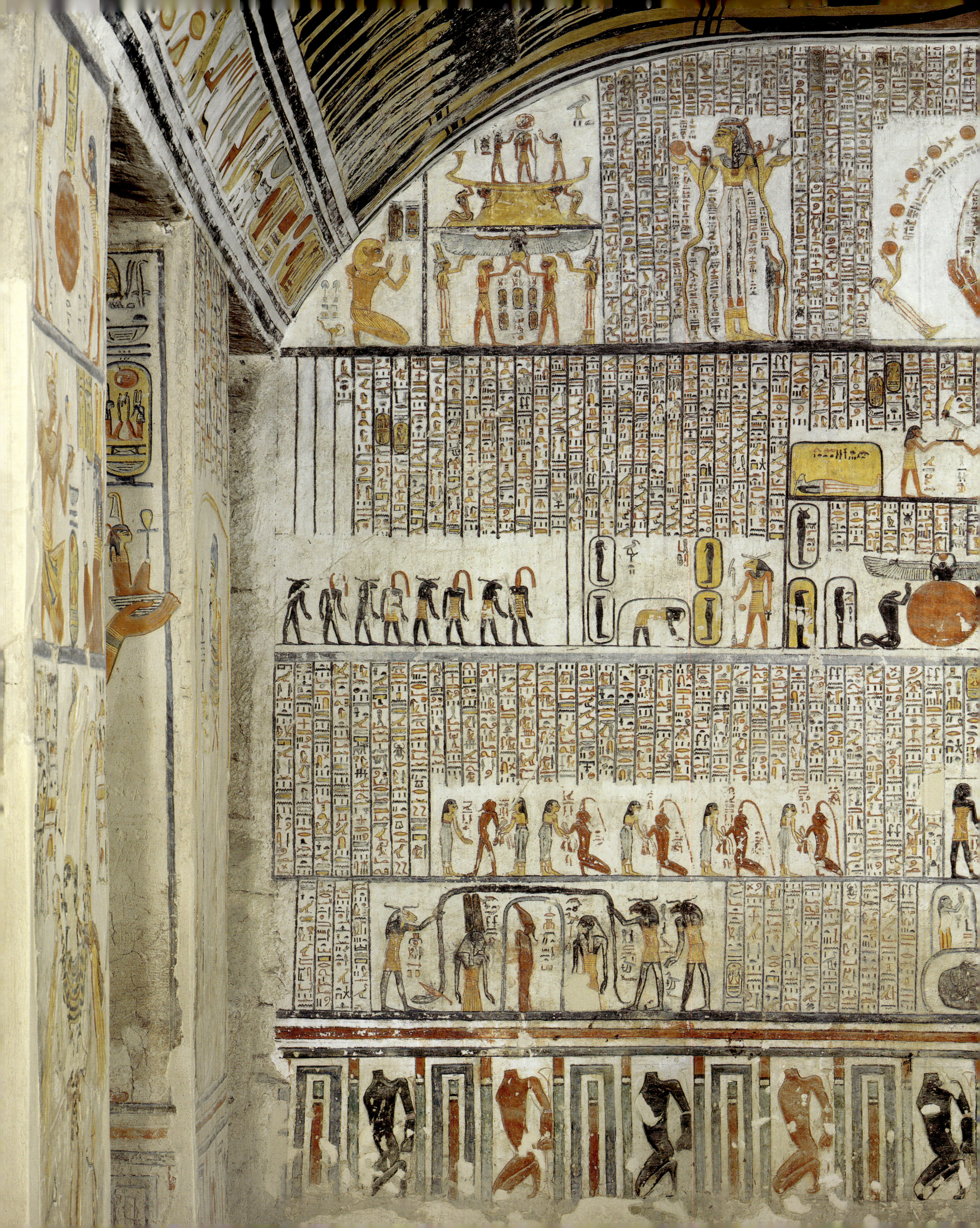

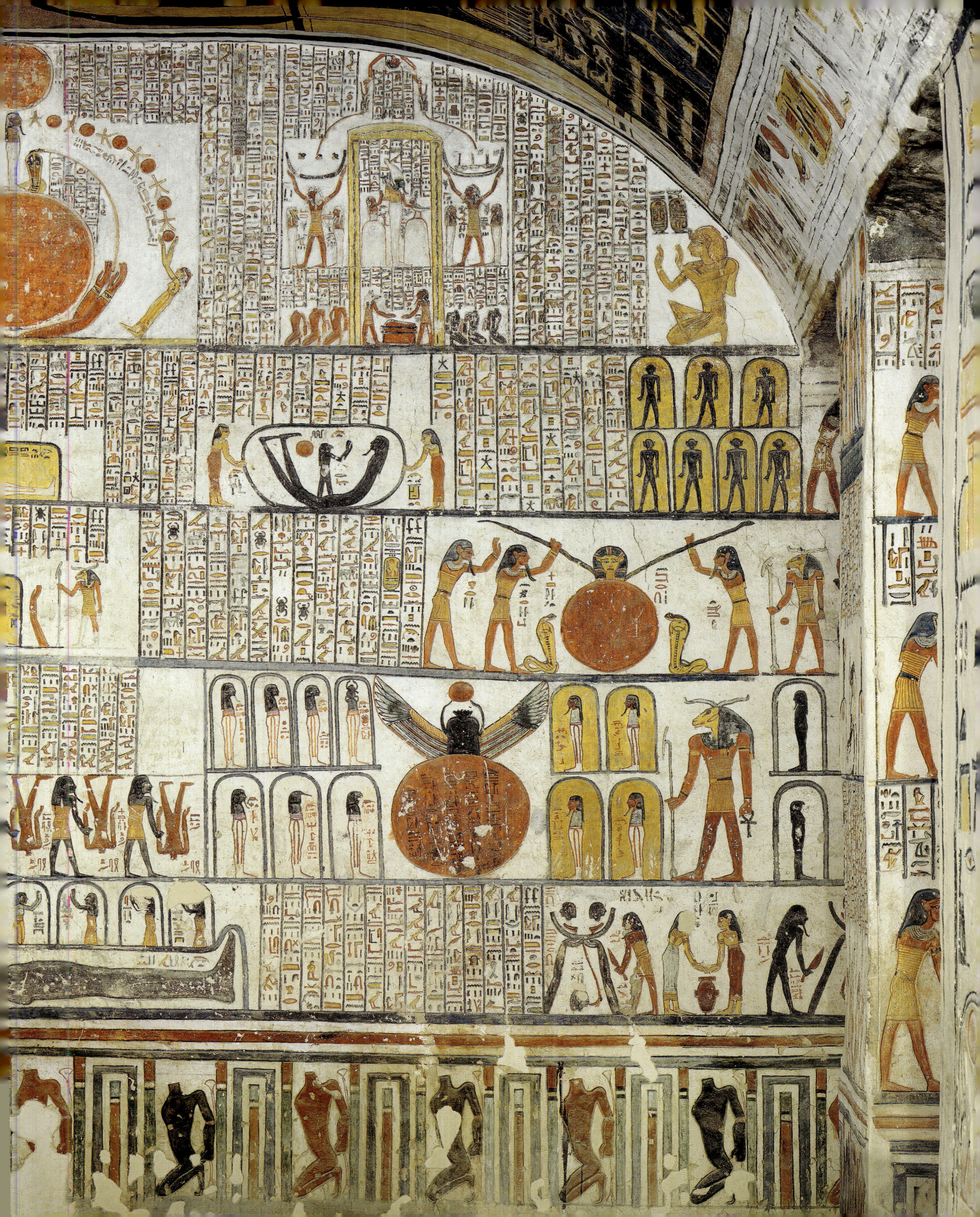

As was the case in the Book of Caverns, the solar bark is absent from most of the scenes of the Book of the Earth. Solar disks are evident in many scenes, providing light for the Netherworld and serving to represent the sun god.

The principal gods who feature in this composition are the earth gods Aker, Geb, and Tatanen. Aker was, as we have seen, represented as a double-headed sphinx. He can also be seen as a narrow band of earth with a human or lion's head on each end. One head always faces west toward the sunset; the other east to the sunrise. These heads also guard the entrance to and exit from the Netherworld.

Geb, whom we have also met previously, is the primordial god of the earth, born from the union of Shu and Tefnut. According to one creation legend, Geb was sad because his father Shu had separated him from his sister-wife Nut: from his tears came the first humans. Geb was considered the creator of kingship, and gave his earthly power to Osiris, then to Horus. The human king was known as the heir of Geb.

One of the earliest earth gods, worshipped from the earliest times at Memphis, was Tatanen, depicted in the form of a bearded man wearing a two-plumed crown. One of Tatanen's titles was "Lord of time."

Section D

This group of vignettes appears to come first, although again, no sequence can be securely determined. In the upper register are four individual scenes surrounded by hieroglyphic texts. First is an image of the sun bark on the back of a figure of Aker; in the bark, the ram-headed Re is worshipped by Khepri and Thoth. Aker is held aloft by four figures: Isis, Nephthys, and two kings. In the next scene, in an abbreviated version of the large-scale figure seen in the Book of the Caverns, Nut is shown as the "mysterious one," holding the sun god in the form of a ram-headed man and a sun disk aloft on her palms. The next scene shows two pairs of arms emerging from the Nun, embracing a sun disk on which the mummy of the sun god stands between two uraei, who spit fire. A necklace of twelve stars and twelve sun disks held by two goddesses indicates the passage of the hours.

The key scene here focuses on an image of the mummy of Osiris within a tomb guarded by two snakes. He is worshipped on one side by his *ba* and on the other by the mummy of Geb. Beneath him, Anubis and a deity known as the "Mysterious One" protect the chest in which his recovered body has been placed. To each side are cauldrons for the punishment of enemies above the bound figures of headless captives.

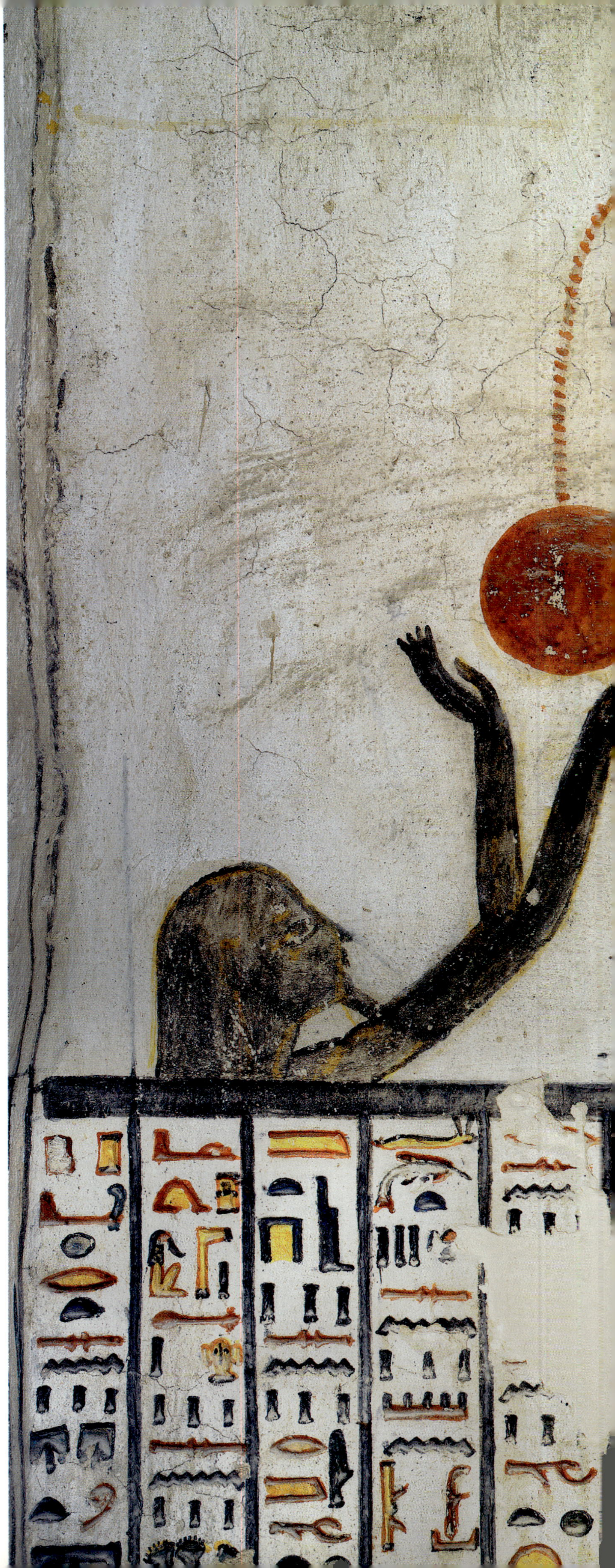

THE BOOK OF THE EARTH, SECTION C

This image from Section C shows four figures of Osiris, each wearing the white crown, haloed by the light of a sun disk that is supported by a pair of hands that emerge from the invisible Nun below.

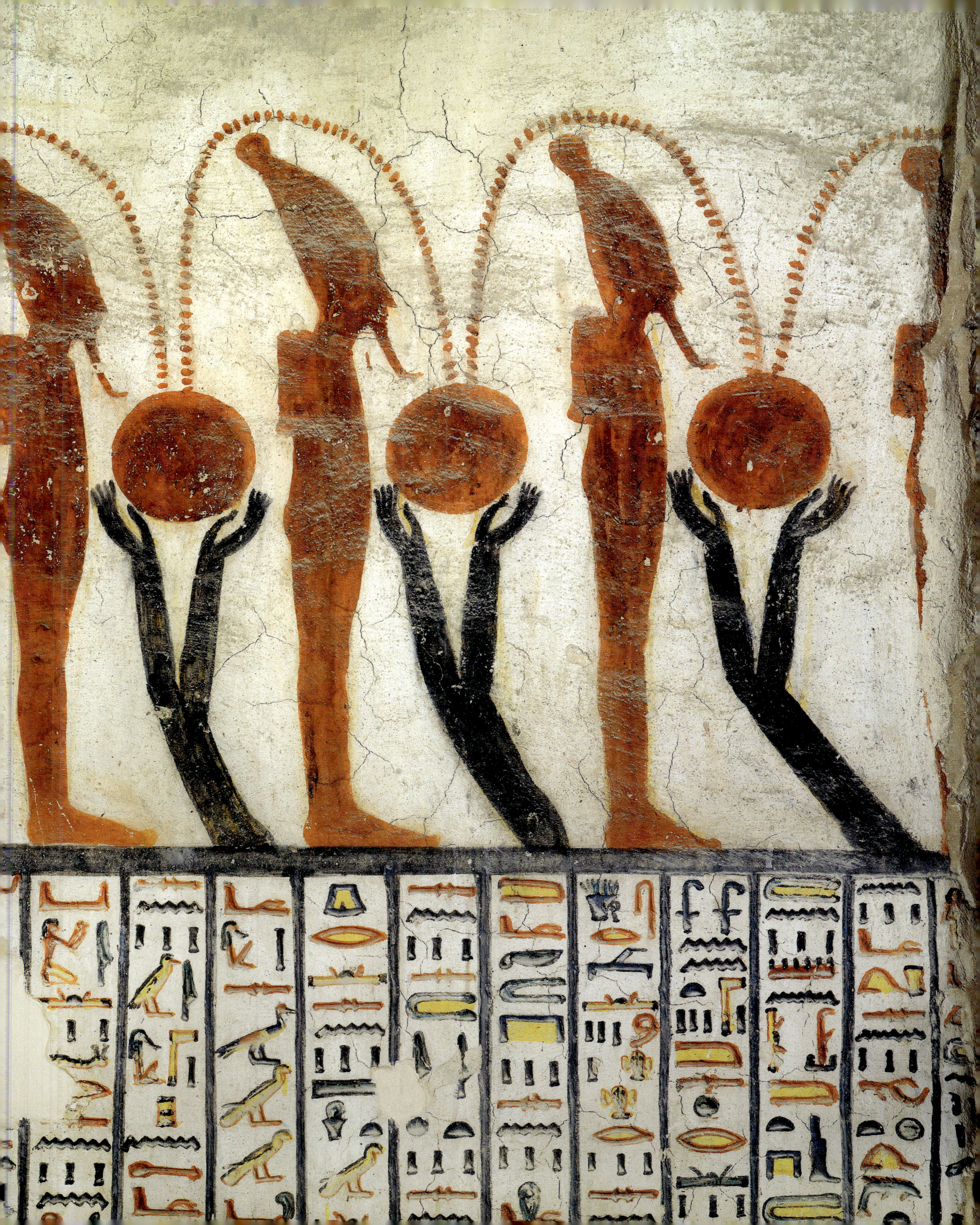

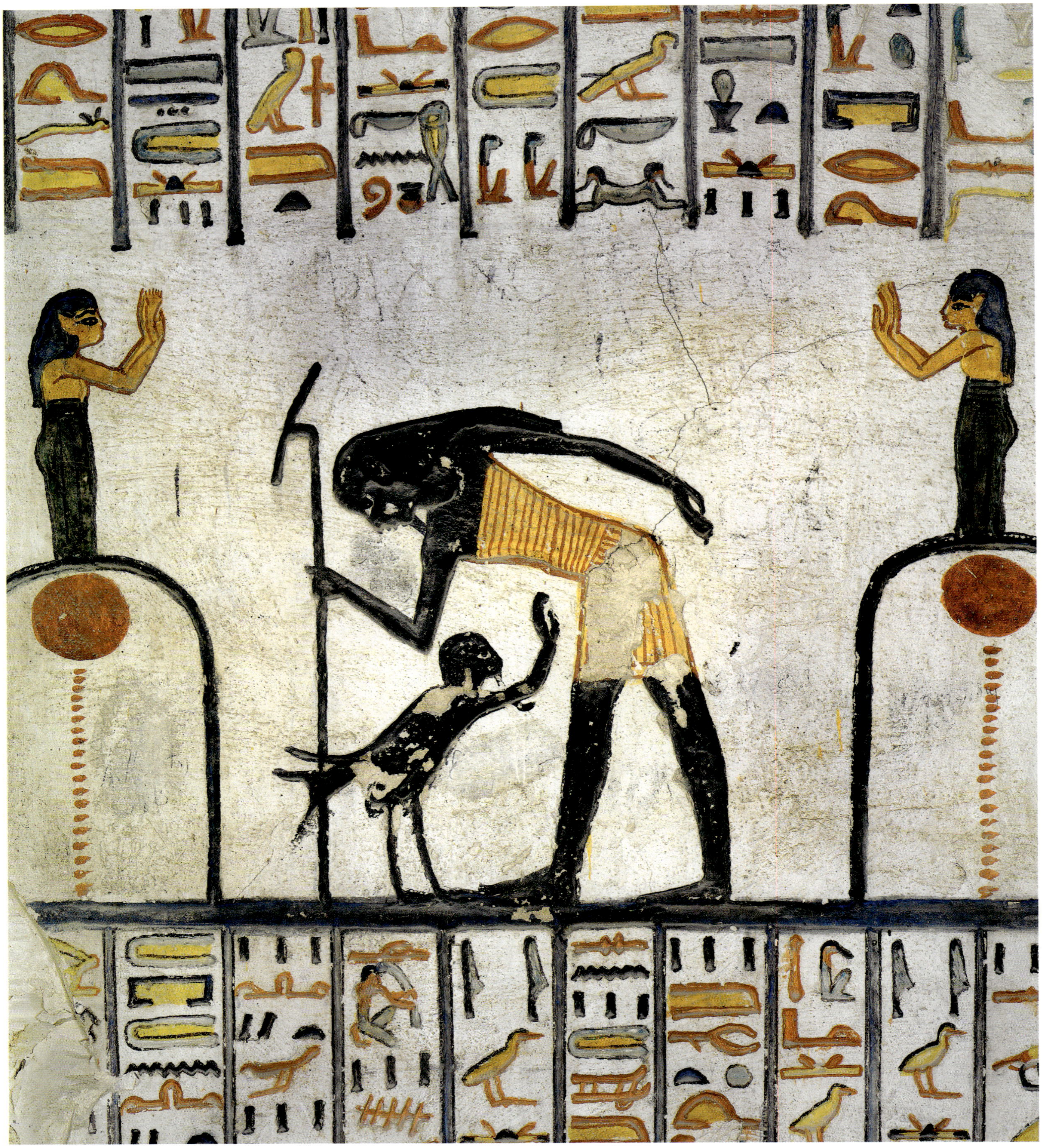

THE BOOK OF THE EARTH, SECTION C
Another scene from this section depicts the corpse of the earth god Aker bending over a figure of his own *ba*.
He is flanked by burial mounds containing sun disks, each surmounted by a praying goddess.

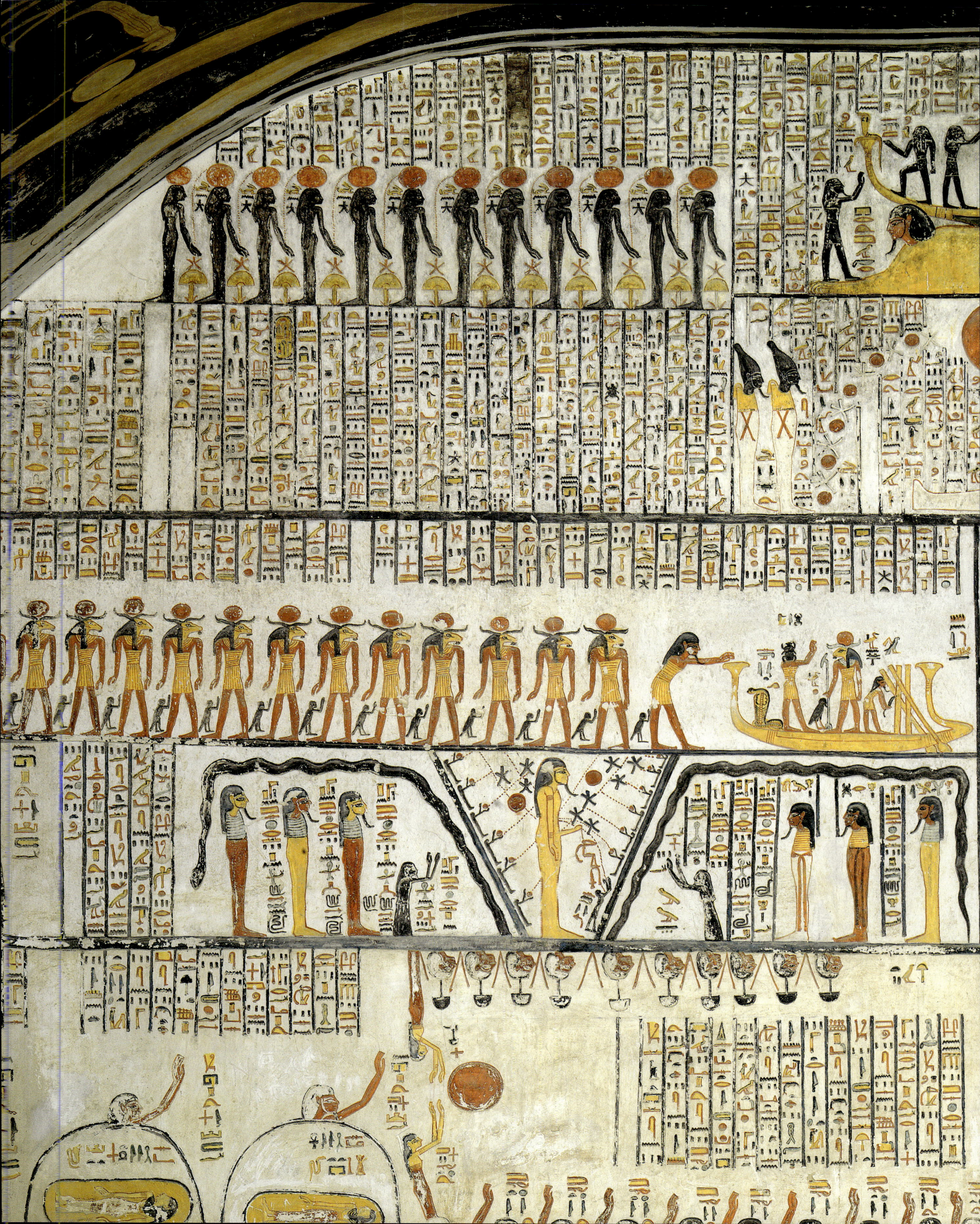

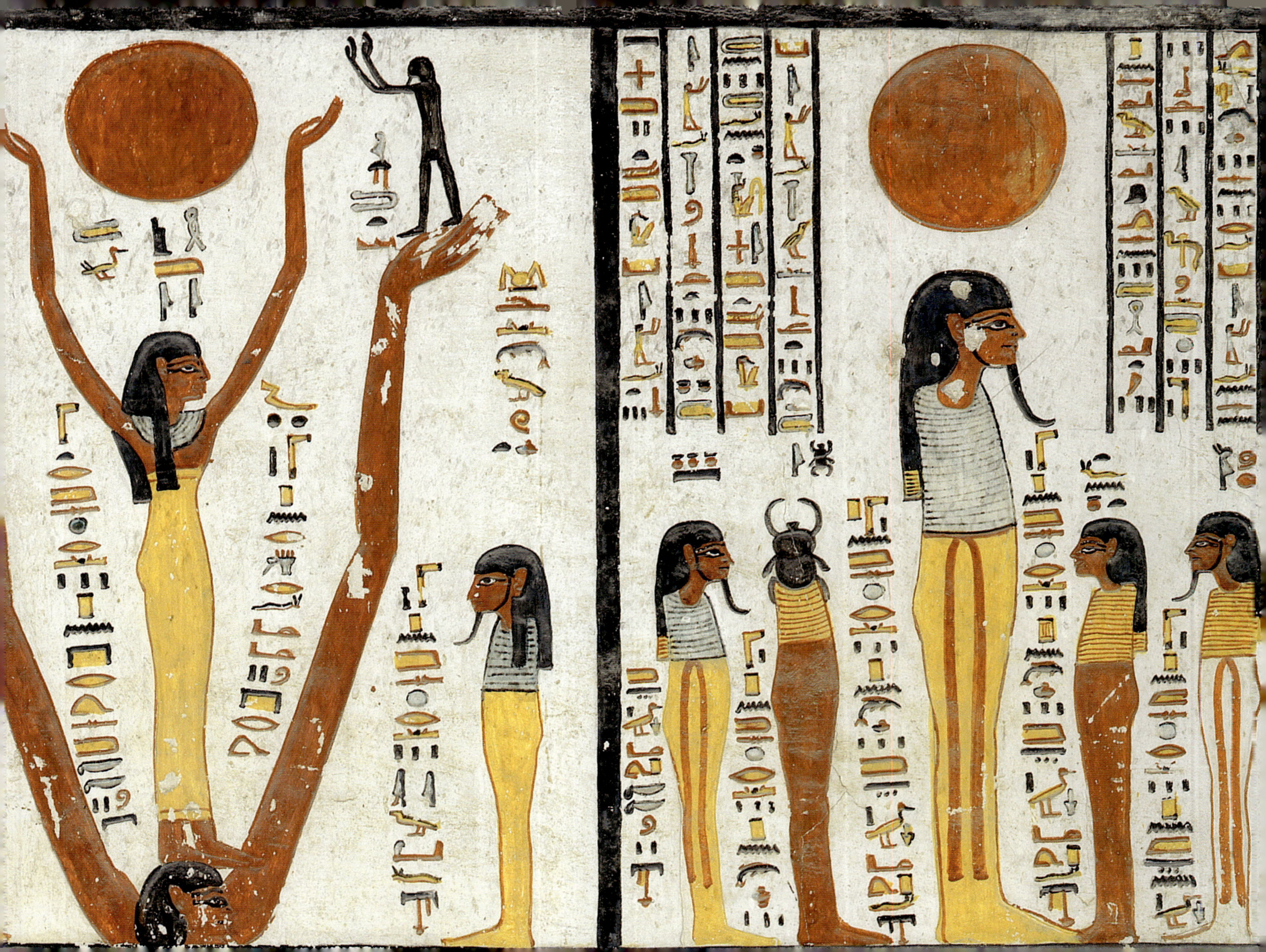

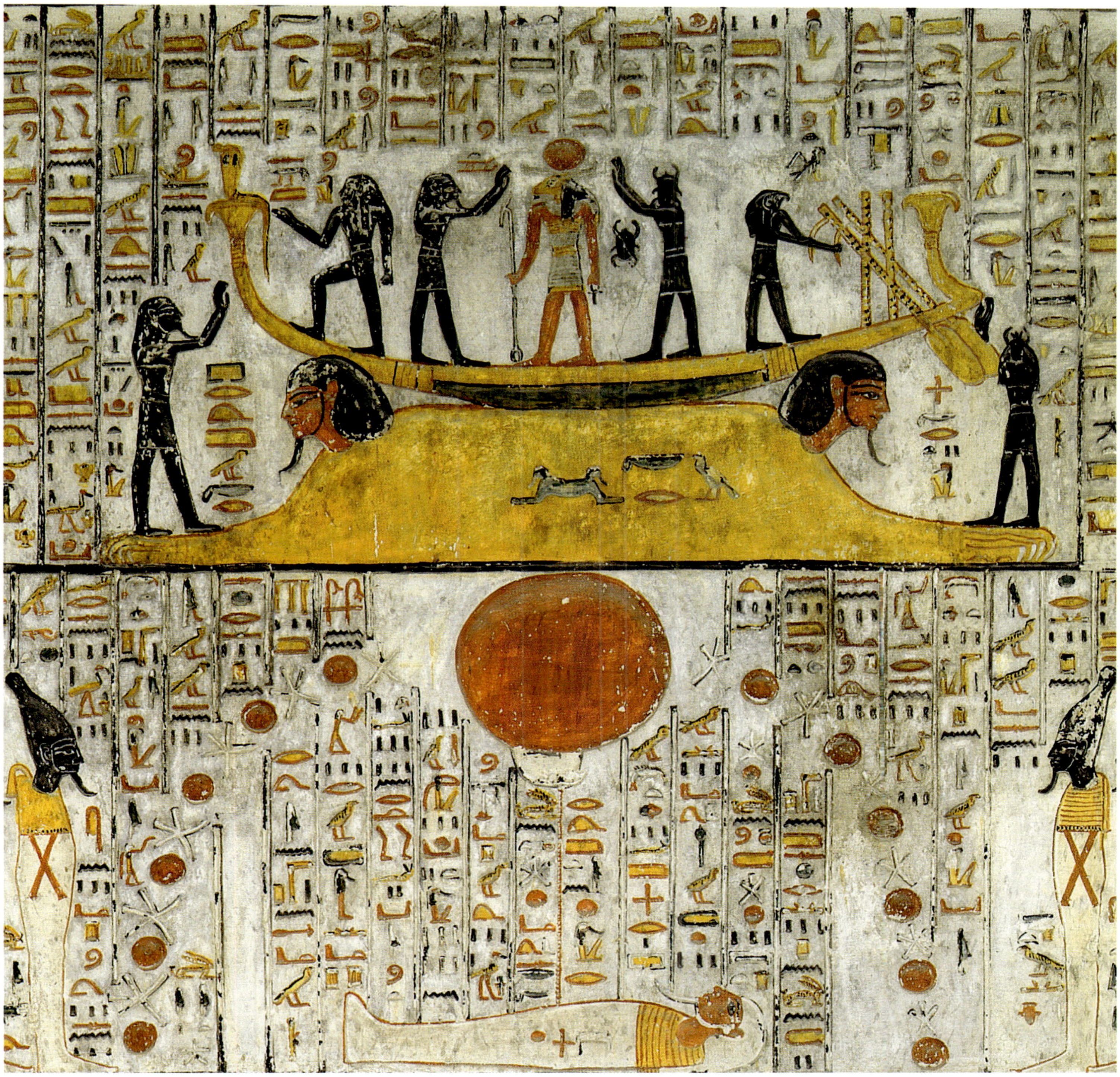

THE GOD AKER
In this detail from Section A of the Book of the Earth, the earth god Aker is seen in his form as a double-headed sphinx, with the solar bark on his back. His name can be seen written in hieroglyphs on his body. The mummy in the register below represents the united Osiris and Re.

THE BOOK OF THE EARTH, SECTION A
(Preceding pages)
The complex images and texts of Section A of the Book of the Earth fill this wall from the burial chamber of Ramses V/VI. In the center of the upper register is the key scene, showing the god Aker as a double-headed sphinx, the solar bark resting on his back and oriented so that its stern faces the exit of the Duat. Below are various scenes connected with the rebirth of the sun and the blessed dead.

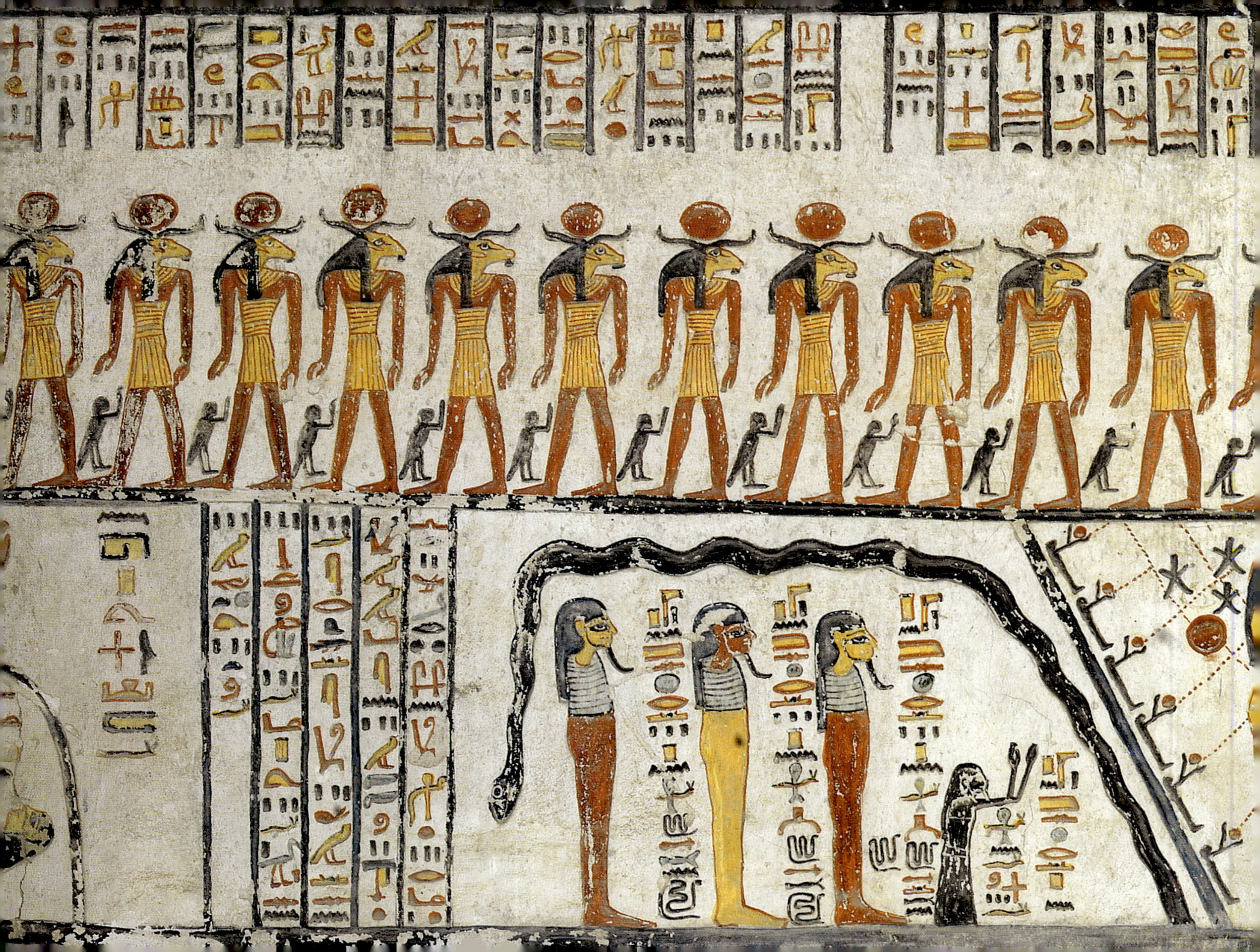

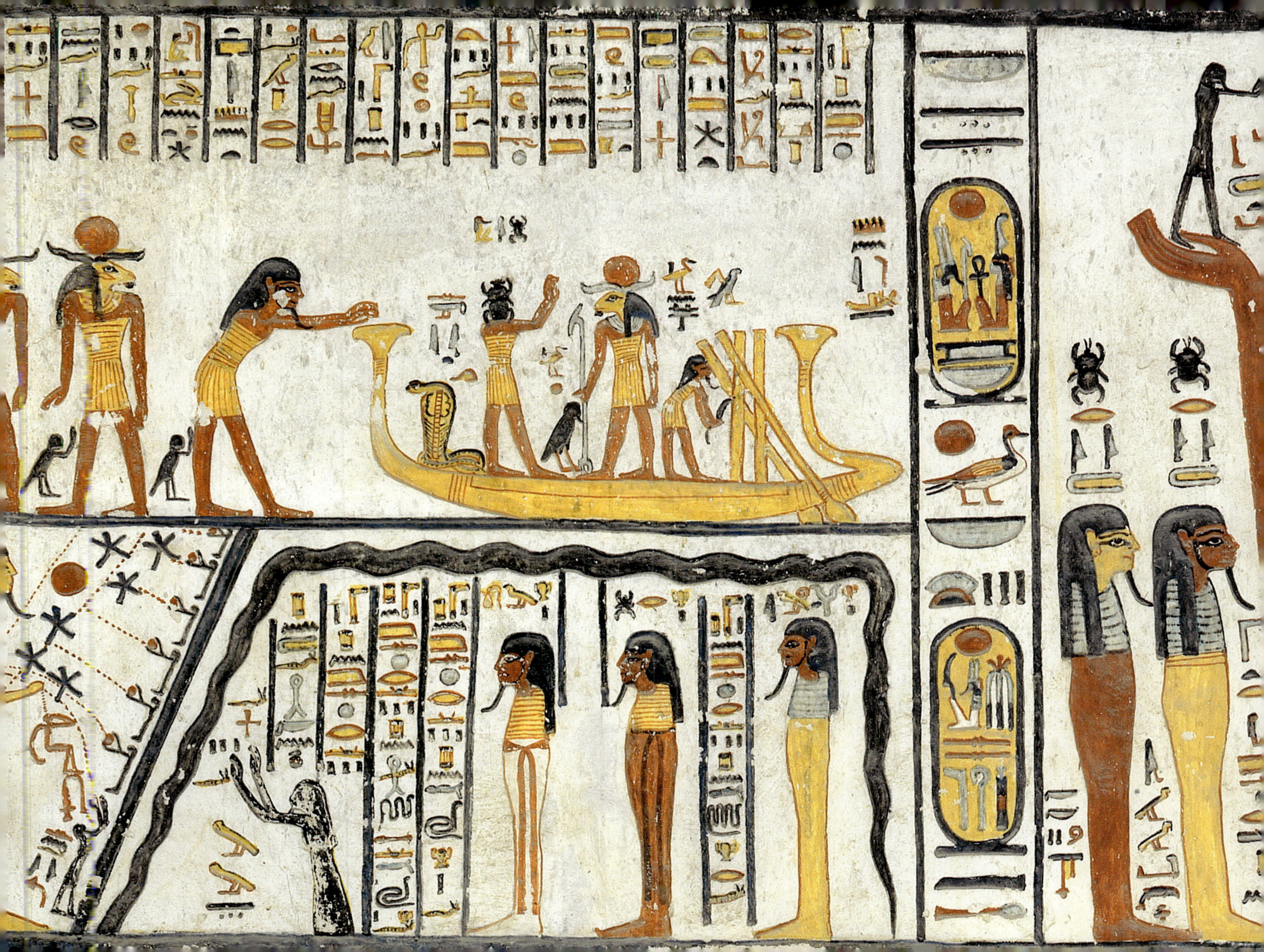

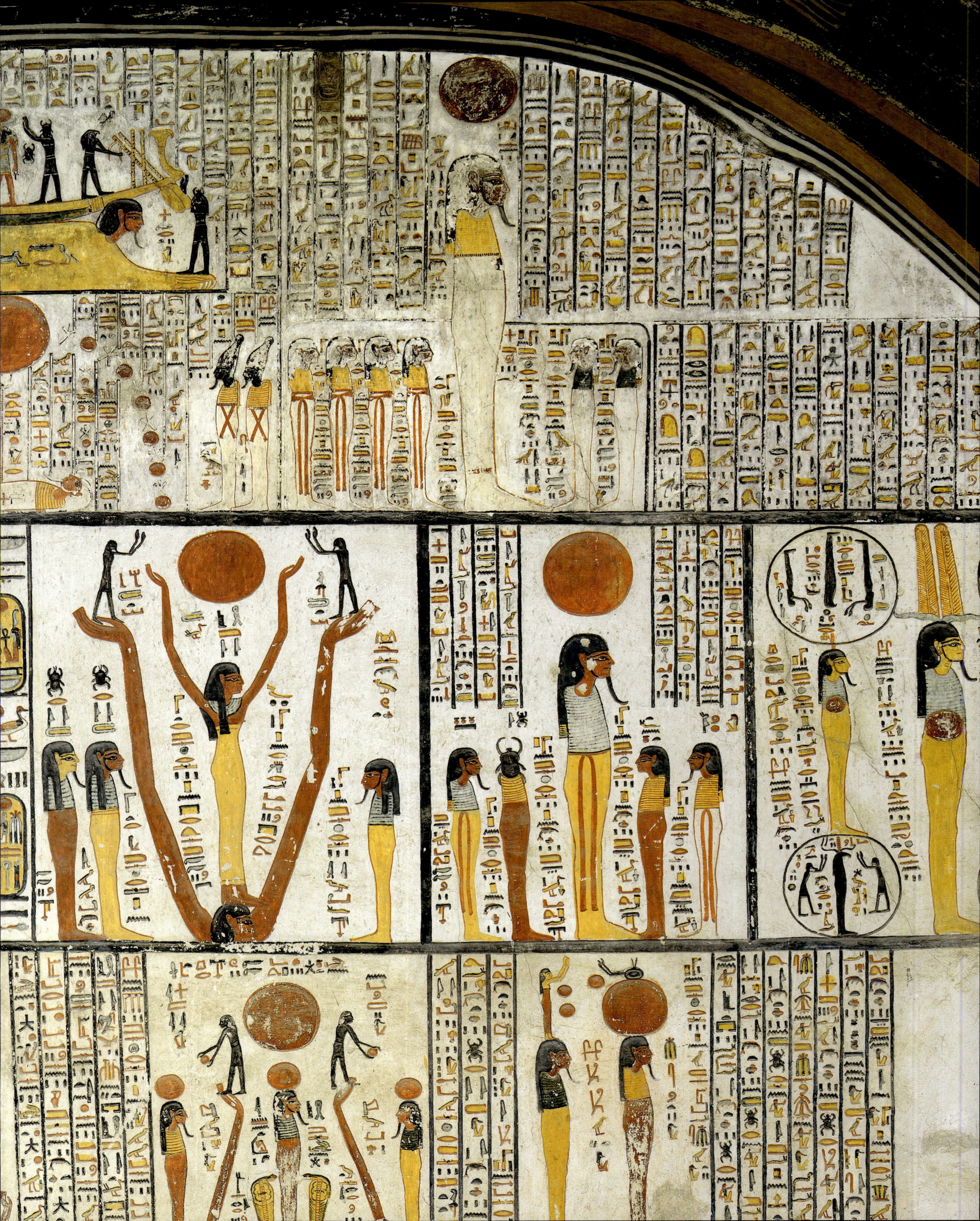

In the central register, the most interesting scene symbolizes the posthumous conception of Horus. The body of Osiris is shown here within a modified oval, flanked by Isis and Nephthys. Horus stands atop his father, worshipping him; the scene is illuminated by a sun disk.

To one side are two ram-headed mummies within tombs, with two gods between them holding the *ba* of Osiris in the form of a bird wearing the white crown. In the scene beneath this a winged scarab, flanked by mummies in ovals (including Osiris as the Bull of the West), emerges from a sun disk. Beside this are seven shrines containing gods; the register ends at this side with the birth of Horus, who is protected by Atum. Beneath this the sun disk appears, held by the arms of Nun. After a figure of the ram-headed Re appears a second sun disk, from which the heads of Hathor and a serpent emerge; this is flanked by gods and uraei.

In the lower registers, as was the case for the Book of Caverns, the principal theme is the punishment of enemies. In the center, Osiris lies inside a burial mound. To one side, the motif of scarab with sun disk emerging from a larger sun disk is repeated; this is flanked by deities who are prepared to join in the resurrection of the sun god within sarcophagi. The enemies are punished here in a variety of ways, mainly having to do with burning. Apophis is subdued by ram-headed gods.

Sections B and C

The themes of the rebirth of the sun god and the punishment of enemies repeat in these sections. Again, the sequence is confusing, and although B and C are represented together, it seems that B is linked more with Section A.

Section C is divided into three registers. At the top, the sun as a scarab beetle, his *ba* above his head, sits atop a figure of Apophis protected by Atum and Shu. This *ba*, and a second on top of a pyramidal perch, raise their arms in homage to the sun god as a disk and a ram-headed man. In the central register, Re with a ram's head and Horus with a hawk's head guard a sun disk, from which emerges the head of Horus of the Netherworld. Beside this, the corpse of Aker in human form bends over his own *ba*, flanked by burial mounds topped by goddesses. At the far end of this register are four Osiris figures with sun disks.

The sequence in the lower register is led by a god and goddess, then four gods holding posts with human heads. Next are three gods who have tied the arms of captured enemies behind their backs; and finally mounds on which lie mummies who have turned over, ready to be reborn.

Section B is divided into four scene groups. In the first, guarded at the top by an outstretched snake, are four sarcophagi containing mummies, and then four burial mounds in which the mummies have begun to turn over. The second group is filled with images of a mummiform god with a sun disk inside his body. In front of him, a pair of arms lifts a god and goddess; behind him, a second pair of arms lifts ram- and jackal-headed stakes and a full-size crocodile. In the third section are more sarcophagi containing mummies on which stand their *bas*, some with the hieroglyph for shadow (another important aspect of the human being, alongside the *ka*, *ba*, body, and name) on their head. Beneath these are two barks in which the corpses of Osiris and Horus of the Netherworld lie. The last group repeats these themes.

Section A

The action here flows from register to register, and much reference is made to the depths of the Nun that lie beneath the world visible on the walls The solar bark appears a number of times. In the central register it is towed by fourteen ram-headed gods, each accompanied by his *ba*, above an ithyphallic representation of "he who hides the hours." Beneath his phallus is seen a child, and he is surrounded by a snake that emerges from the depths on both sides.

A number of mummiform figures are seen here, and various pairs of arms and heads to rise from beneath the register lines. This section is dotted with sarcophagi and burial mounds containing the blessed dead.

The central scene is in the top register. Here a mummy lies beneath a sun disk from which the head of a falcon appears. Light from this head falls onto the corpse, which represents the united Osiris and Re. A necklace of stars and suns surrounds this corpse, which is flanked by mummies. Above is Aker in the form of a double-headed sphinx, with the solar bark on his back. This bark, whose direction has been reversed so that the stern of the boat faces the way out, is flanked by personifications of the entrance and exit of the Duat.

A second image of Aker occupies the center of the lowest register, in a scene that symbolizes the full course of the sun. Three representations of the solar bark are included here. To the left, the bark is occupied by a scarab beetle and the ram-headed Re and is towed by seven *bas*. As it travels over one head of Aker, it is received by Tatanen, then is raised again over the second head by Nun. Fourteen uraei tow the bark out of the Duat so that it can begin its journey through the day sky anew.

Book of the Earth, Section A
(Preceding pages)
The central register of Section A of this composition includes a number of complex images. At the left is the solar bark, towed by ram-headed figures accompanied by their *bas*. Within the cave underneath is an ithyphallic god named "he who hides the hours." To the right, two more vignettes linked with the birth of the sun are visible.

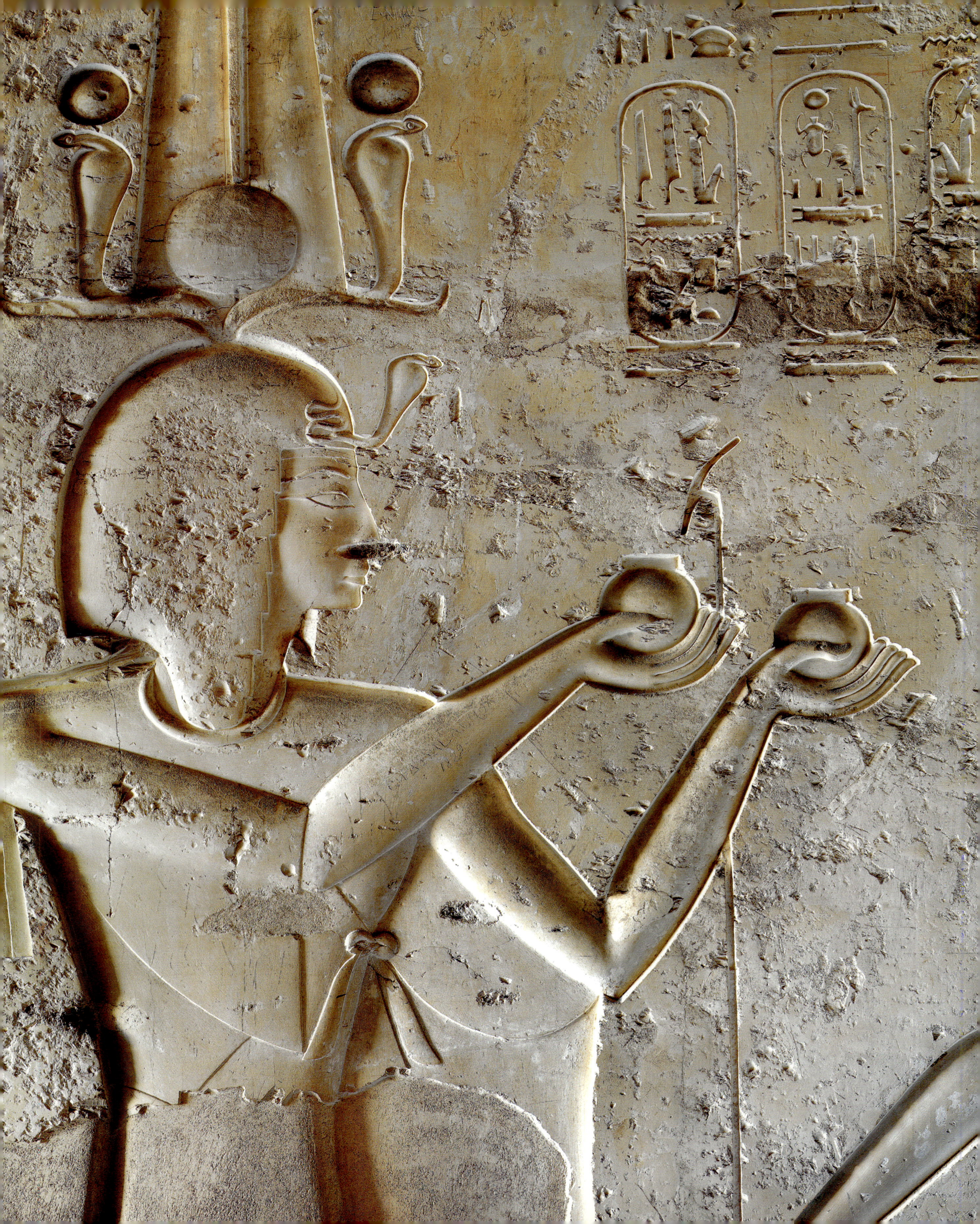

CHAPTER 6

THE LITANIES OF RE

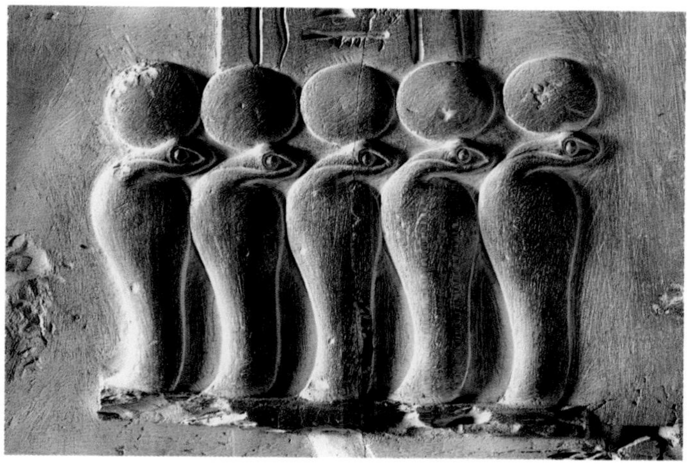

The sun was one of the most important natural features dominating the world of the ancient Egyptians. Its rising and setting defined their daily lives, and they noticed how it brought hot days in summer and kept the world warm in winter. They saw it as essential not only as a source of light and heat but also as a font of life. The ancients worshipped the sun in the form of Re, who was one of the chief gods in their pantheon.

The sun and its god were given many forms, depending on the occasion; we have already met many of these in the previously discussed Books of the Netherworld. In the morning, he was given the form of the scarab beetle, Khepri, who pushed the sun disk before him into the sky. In the middle of the day, he was Kamutef, "bull of his mother," who impregnated his mother so that she could bear him again the next morning. In the evening, he was shown as an old man, Atum, leaning on his staff. In a parallel conception, the Egyptians imagined the sky as a woman, Nut, whose child was the sun who grew up during the day as Re, died at sunset, was hidden in the Netherworld overnight, and was reborn each morning. As discussed earlier, the center of the sun cult was ancient Iunu or On, known by the Greeks as Heliopolis, the "city of the sun." This remained the principal center of sun worship throughout Egyptian history, even into the Greek and Roman periods.

Re stood at the head of the Heliopolitan Ennead, a group of nine gods. Syncretized with the great creator god, Atum (also the sun's evening form), as Atum-Re, he was the one who "made himself by himself"; and was given no mythical parents. It was he who stood atop the pyramidal mound, surrounded by the waters of the Nun at the moment of creation, and brought the world into being. With him in his Ennead were his direct descendents, all of whom we have already met: Shu, Tefnut, Geb, Nut, Osiris, Isis, Nephthys, and Seth.

Although there is some evidence for On as Re's cult site dating back to the 3rd Dynasty, the great rise of the sun god began in the 4th Dynasty. The change from step to true pyramid seen during the reign of the first king of the 4th Dynasty, Sneferu, has been linked to the increased importance of the solar religion. The title "son of Re" is first attested for

THE KING (AND THE SUN GOD)
Seti II makes offerings to the sun god in his falcon-headed form (*see next page*) in the entrance corridor of his tomb in the Valley of the Kings. This image of king with god at the beginning of the tomb became standard in the Ramesside Period.

the son of Khufu, Djedefre, and immediately became an essential part of the royal titulary. The sphinx, first seen in the reign of Djedefre and then expressed in colossal form during the reign of Khafre, was a potent solar symbol. The kings of the 5th Dynasty paid particular homage to the sun god, building, as we have seen, temples to this god in the Memphite necropolis, and maintaining close links to the priesthood of Re.

In the New Kingdom, a local Theban god named Amun rose to prominence, threatening to displace Re as the king of the gods. The Egyptians dealt with this problem by amalgamating the two gods, creating the syncretized Amun-Re. The Amarna period saw the rise of a new form of the sun, the anthropomorphized disk called the Aten. Although the new philosophies developed during this time continued to affect the development of Egyptian religion, this particular brand of what amounted to monotheism did not survive the reign of Akhenaten.

Re is mentioned in the Pyramid Texts, and appears in a variety of myths and legends, such as the Destruction of Mankind (see above, Chapter 2). He was imagined to travel in a boat built by the other gods. The world became populated by the enemies of the sun, who had to be defeated by the followers of the god.

Developing out of hymns to the sun that can be traced back to the Old Kingdom, the Litanies of Re became an important part of the decoration of the royal tomb during the Ramesside period. The first of these, the Great Litany, is actually one of the earliest compositions to appear in the Valley of the Kings, as portions of it were painted on the pillars in the burial chamber of Tuthmosis III. The entire text of the book, without illustrations, is seen on a shroud from the same era that was buried by Amenhotep II with his father. The book then disappears, and is not seen again until the reign of Seti I. From this point forward, the Litanies of Re occupy the walls and ceilings of the first and second corridors of the majority of the royal tombs. Their importance during the Ramesside era is demonstrated by the fact that Seti II had the Litanies of Re in the tomb of Amenmesse (KV 10), who usurped his throne and was later defeated, hacked from the walls.

The Litanies of Re is not a Netherworld Book in the same sense as those we have studied so far. It is not a guide through the Netherworld, and it makes no reference to the twelve hours of the night, although the number twelve does feature prominently within it. Instead, it describes the various forms of the sun god, beginning by listing his seventy-five names, and specifically identifies the deceased king with Re and his *ba*, linked with Osiris. The principal purposes of these texts were the symbolic union of Re and Osiris and the identification of the deceased king with this integrated being, in whom is inherent the power of resurrection.

In this composition, in contrast to the books reviewed so far, the text and images are separate. The organization is very clear, and generally consistent. The litanies, of which there are nine altogether, begin with the title, "Book of Praying to Re in the West, Praying to the United One in the West." From the reign of Seti I on, a title illustration is inserted between the title and the first section, which is known as the Great Litany. After the Great Litany, which lists the seventy-five names of the sun god, come eight smaller litanies, each composed of a group, varying in number, of double verses. In the second litany, the deceased king claims that he now knows the names of the nocturnal forms of the sun god, and is one with this deity and his *ba*. He then asks that the route through the Netherworld be opened for him and his *ba*. It is important to note that the deceased king speaks here; this is in contrast to the other Netherworld books, in which verbal communication is only between the sun god and the inhabitants of the Netherworld. In the remaining litanies, the identification of the king with Osiris and Re is completed and his deification ensured. The texts are balanced between mourning and rejoicing, with death and rebirth both playing prominent roles. Also key is the sun god's responsibility to provision the blessed dead and punish the damned.

The Frontispiece

The first illustration of the Litanies is the "frontispiece," a large image that fills the wall between the title and the Great Litany. Here is found a sun disk (really a globe, shown in two dimensions), within which is carved the scarab beetle, Khepri, and a ram-headed god—the dawn and night forms of the sun god. Above the disk, upside-down, are a serpent and the head of an antelope; below is a crocodile and another antelope's head. The standard interpretation of these figures is that they are enemies of the sun god, fleeing before his power. However, a recent reinterpretation by American Egyptologist John Darnell suggests that they are defenders of the sun god, sent out to protect him from his enemies.

The Sun God (and the King)

Completing the illustration seen on the previous pages is this figure of the falcon-headed Re-Horakhty, the day form of the sun god. He is offered wine by the king as part of the standard opening image of the tomb.

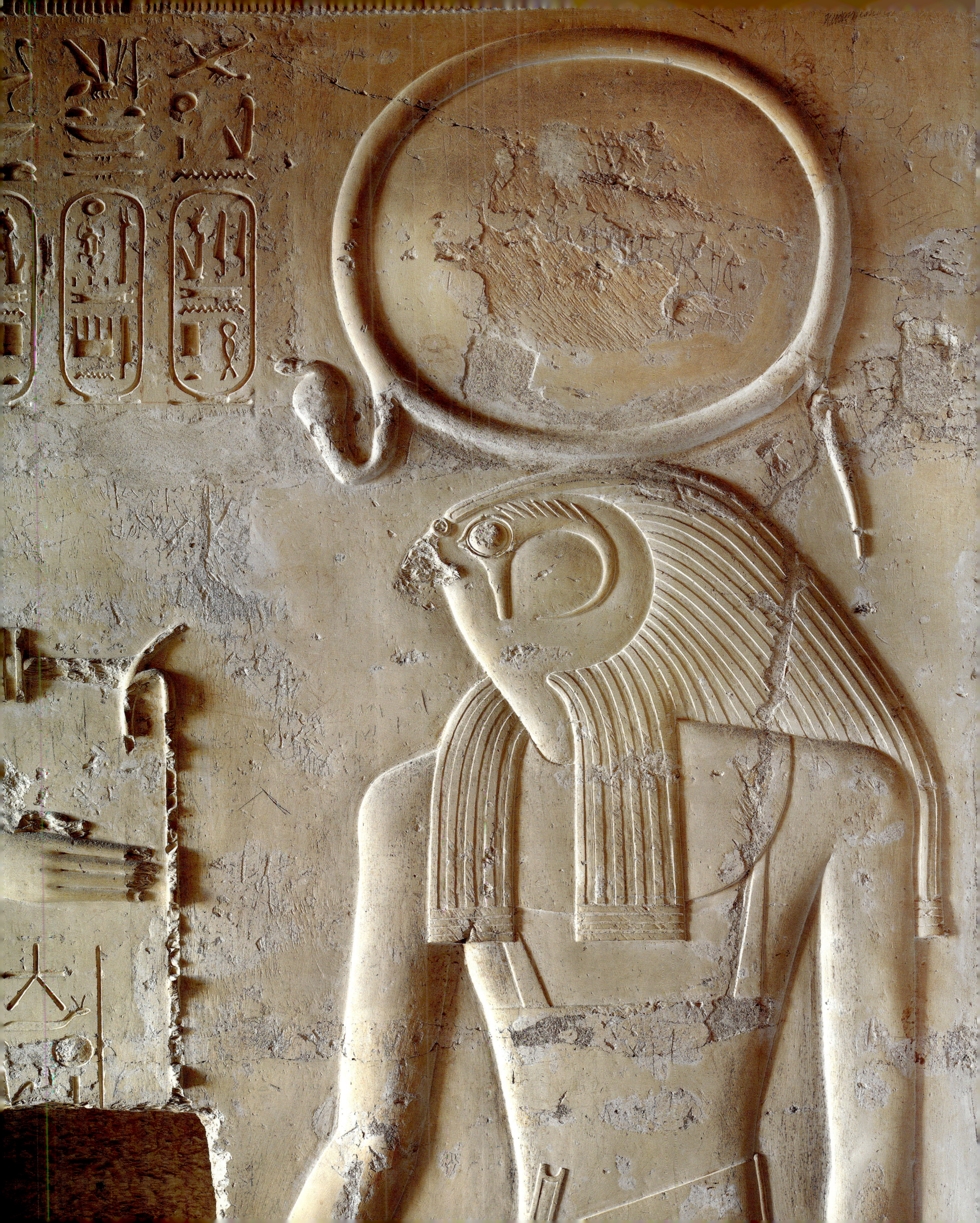

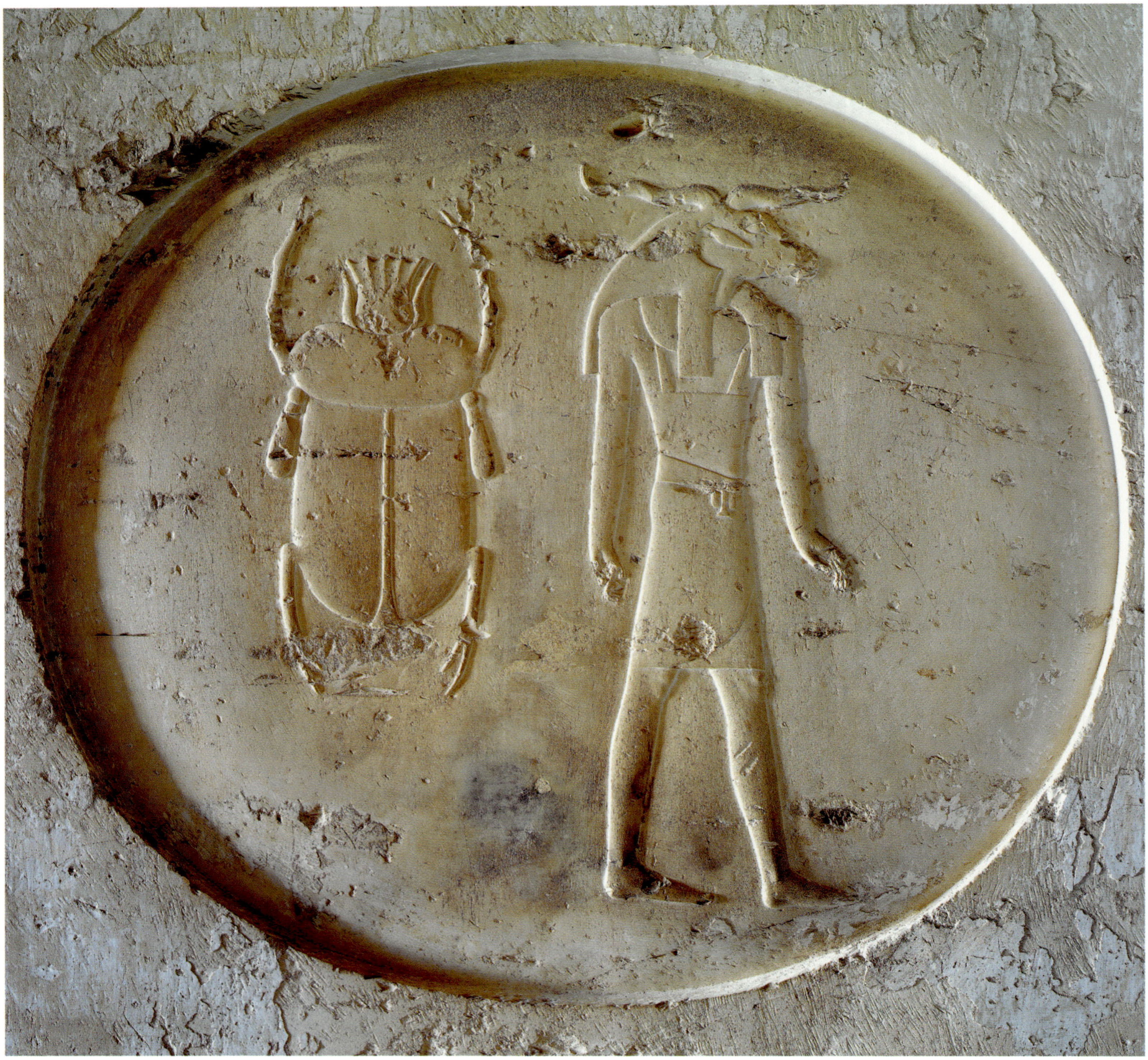

FRONTISPIECE
(*Following pages*)
The central image of the title illustration associated with the Litanies of Re is shown here. It is composed of the globe of the sun, inside which are carved the sun god in two of his guises: his dawn form—Khepri, the scarab beetle, and his night form—the ram-headed Re.

THE TITLES OF THE KING
In his guise as a priest, the king often wore a sporran with a leopard's head at the top, such as is illustrated here. Some of the titles of the king are clearly legible here in a vertical band: King of Upper and Lower Egypt, Lord of the Two Lands, Userkheperure-meryamun (the throne name of Seti II), Son of Re.

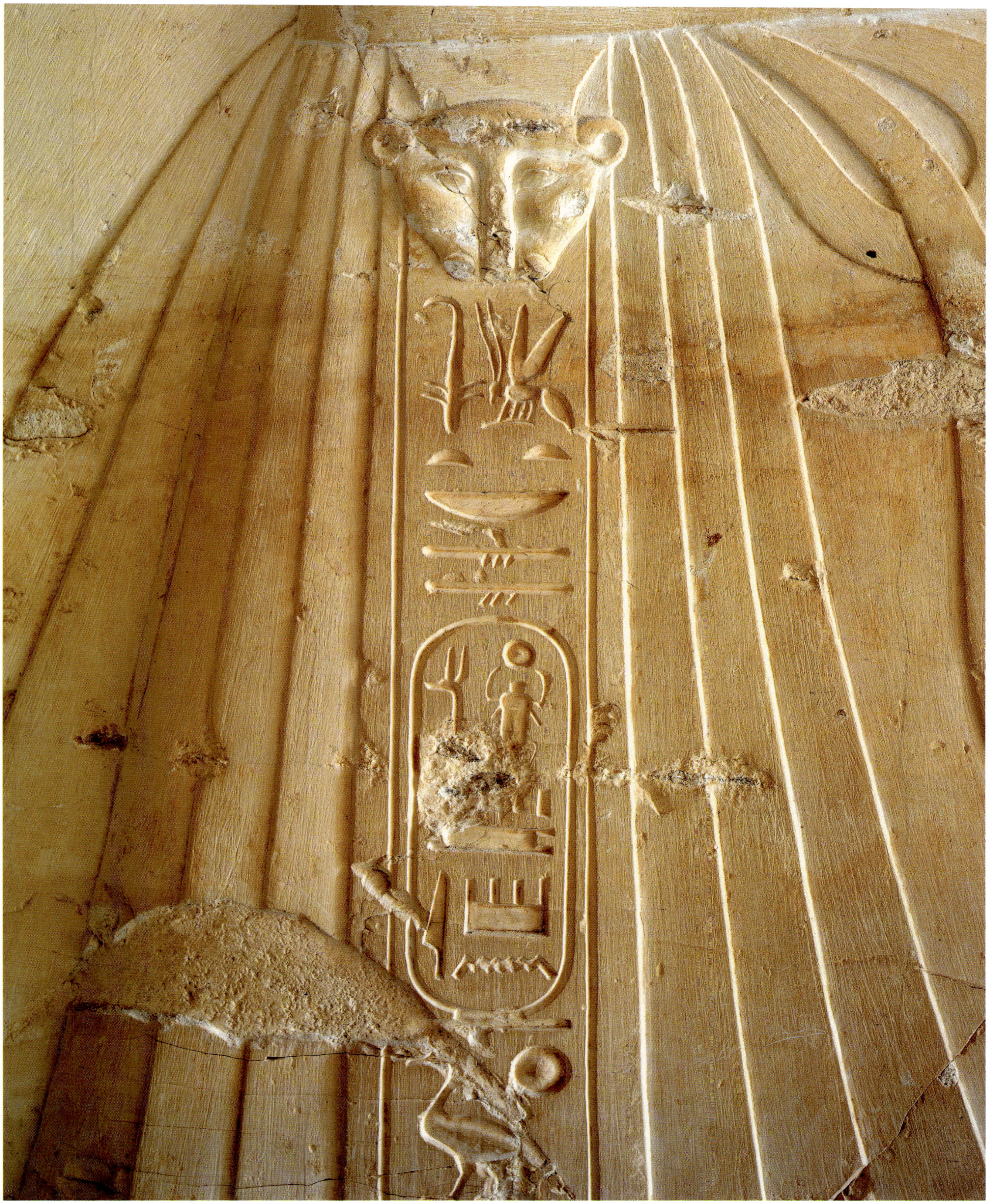

The Great Litany

The Great Litany is comprised of 75 texts invoking the sun god in his various guises, each illustrated by a figure of the god in a particular form. A seventy-sixth figure, of a ram's head within the red sun disk, follows; this is the *ba* of the god. Texts and images are separate: from the reign of Seti I on, the text fills the walls of the first corridor (sometimes spilling over into the second corridor), while the images are placed on the walls and ceiling of the second corridor. It is interesting to note that in the tombs of Seti I and his son Ramses II the hieroglyphs and figures face inward, so that they would be read from the interior of the tomb out; from the reign of Merenptah on, this is reversed, so that the text would be read as the viewer progressed into the tomb.

The form of the text is relatively straightforward. Each invocation is introduced by the phrase: "Praise to you, O Re, great of power"; this is followed by a descriptive name such as "the one who is upon the road of the soul," or "master of the souls." The figures that illustrate the litany are divided into two groups, with one group on each wall. For the first 50 prayers, the figures of the litany (each of whom is labeled with his name) are organized very regularly, with the odd numbers on the left and the even numbers on the right. Fifty-one and 52 are on the left, and 53 and 54 on the right, then the sequence continues in reverse order with the odd numbers on the right and even numbers on the left. There is no clear division of themes: everything relates to the identification of the sun god in the Netherworld and the union of Re and Osiris.

Most of the figures are mummiform, with various heads. Some of these are human, mostly wearing divine beards; many also wear crowns. There are animal-headed mummies, with for example the heads of falcons, cows, rams, or cats. Figures of animals, such as the scarab beetle (which appears three times, in different guises), the cat, and the ram, also appear. The figures with whom Re is identified include his Ennead, but with Seth replaced by his nephew Horus, and the primeval gods Nun and Tatenen. Osiris is shown in his guise as the Foremost of the Westerners.

Re appears in this text as a migratory bird, emphasizing his role as a cyclical traveler through the beyond. In the final prayer of the Great Litany, he has become a dweller in the caverns of the Netherworld. At the end of this text, the deceased king addresses the inhabitants of the Netherworld, informing them that he knows the names of the unified Re-Osiris, and is one with him.

The Second and Third Litanies

In the second litany, the blessed dead are ordered to prepare a place for the king within the following of Re. The third litany begins with the words: "May you lead me to the roads of the West." In this text, the deceased king is equated with Nun, then Re, then the *ba* of the sun god, then the solar cycle. This speech is interrupted by one more invocation, this one to the sun as the "one who shines among those in the Netherworld." A ceiling text that forms part of this litany invokes the unified Re-Osiris, identifying the king as both the *ba* and corpse of this being. The king announces that he is now one of the gods who rule in the West, sharing in their triumphs over the enemies who dwell in sky and earth.

The Fourth and Fifth Litanies

The fourth litany is a short text of only three double verses, which addresses Osiris as Re and praises the sun god. In this litany, Osiris and Re meet, and Re's *ba* uses his power to light the dark Netherworld so that its denizens can see. The deceased king asks that his vision be renewed and his heart returned to his body. Eight double verses comprise the fifth litany, which is generally concerned with care of the god. The deceased prays to be saved from the fiery ovens, cauldrons, and traps set by the enemies of order.

The Sixth and Seventh Litanies

In the sixth litany, sixteen double verses long, the god appears in the form of his *ba*. The deceased king prays that Re will come to him and guide him and appears in splendor as the god. Care of the deceased is addressed here through the appearance of the pelican goddess. The five double verses of the seventh litany result in the complete exaltation of the deceased king, including the deification of his various limbs.

The Eighth and Ninth Litanies

In the eighth litany, there is general rejoicing. The ninth and final litany concludes with the ultimate identification of the deceased king as Re and a prayer to the blessed realm of the West. The *ba* is given over to the sky, and the corpse is consigned to the earth.

Frontispiece

Below the sun disk in the title illustration of the Litanies of Re are a crocodile and an antelope, traditionally assumed to be fleeing from the forces of order.

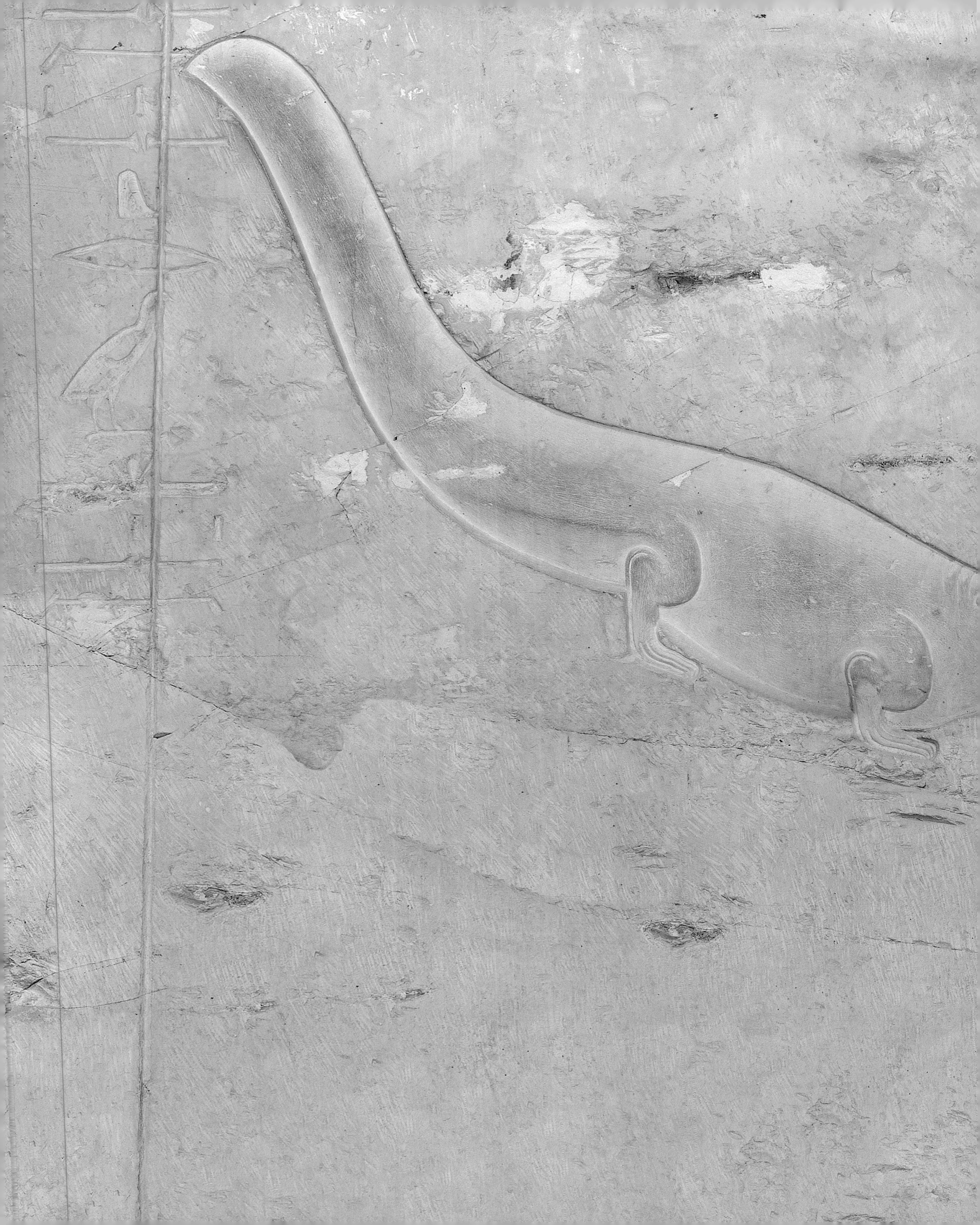

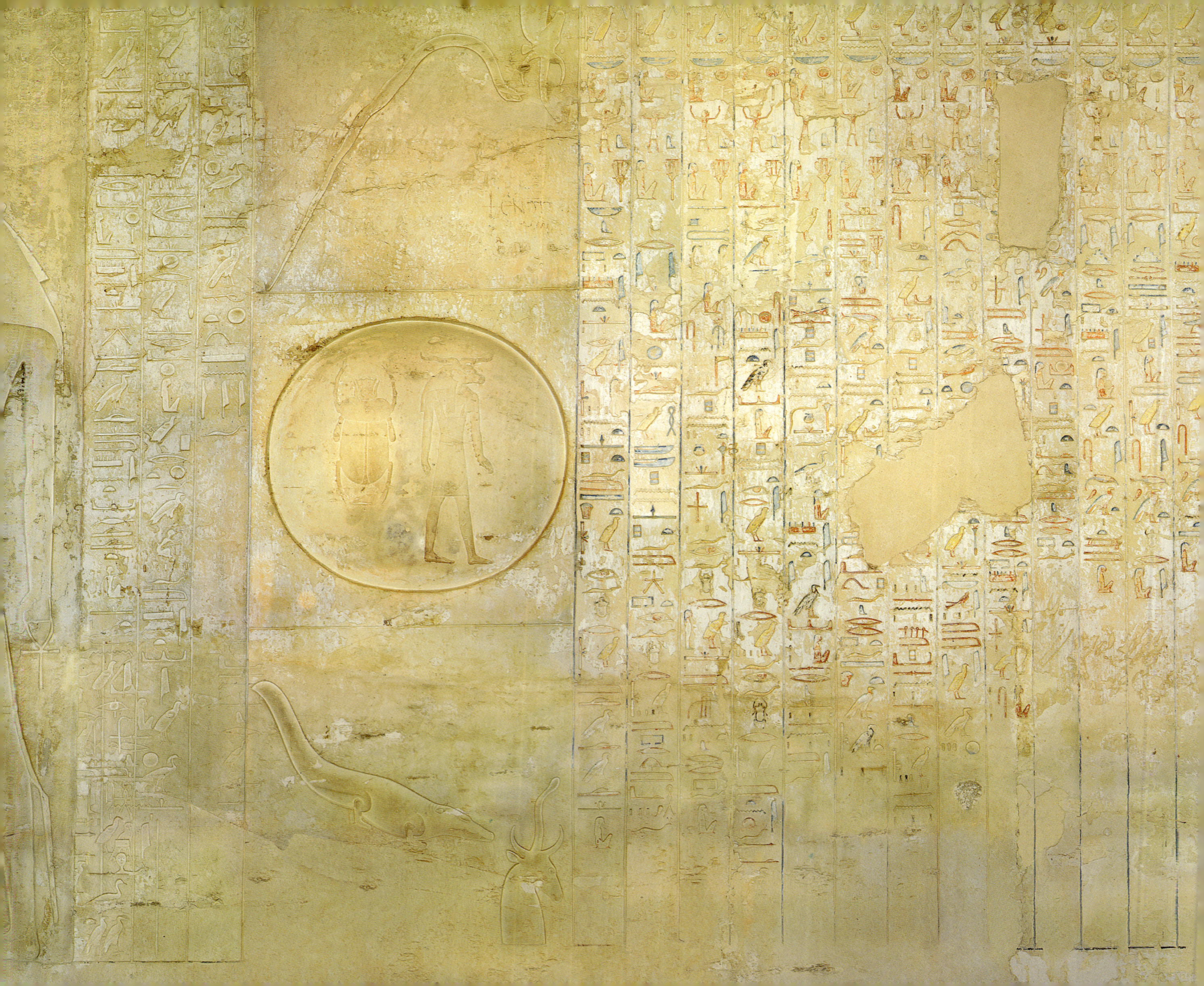

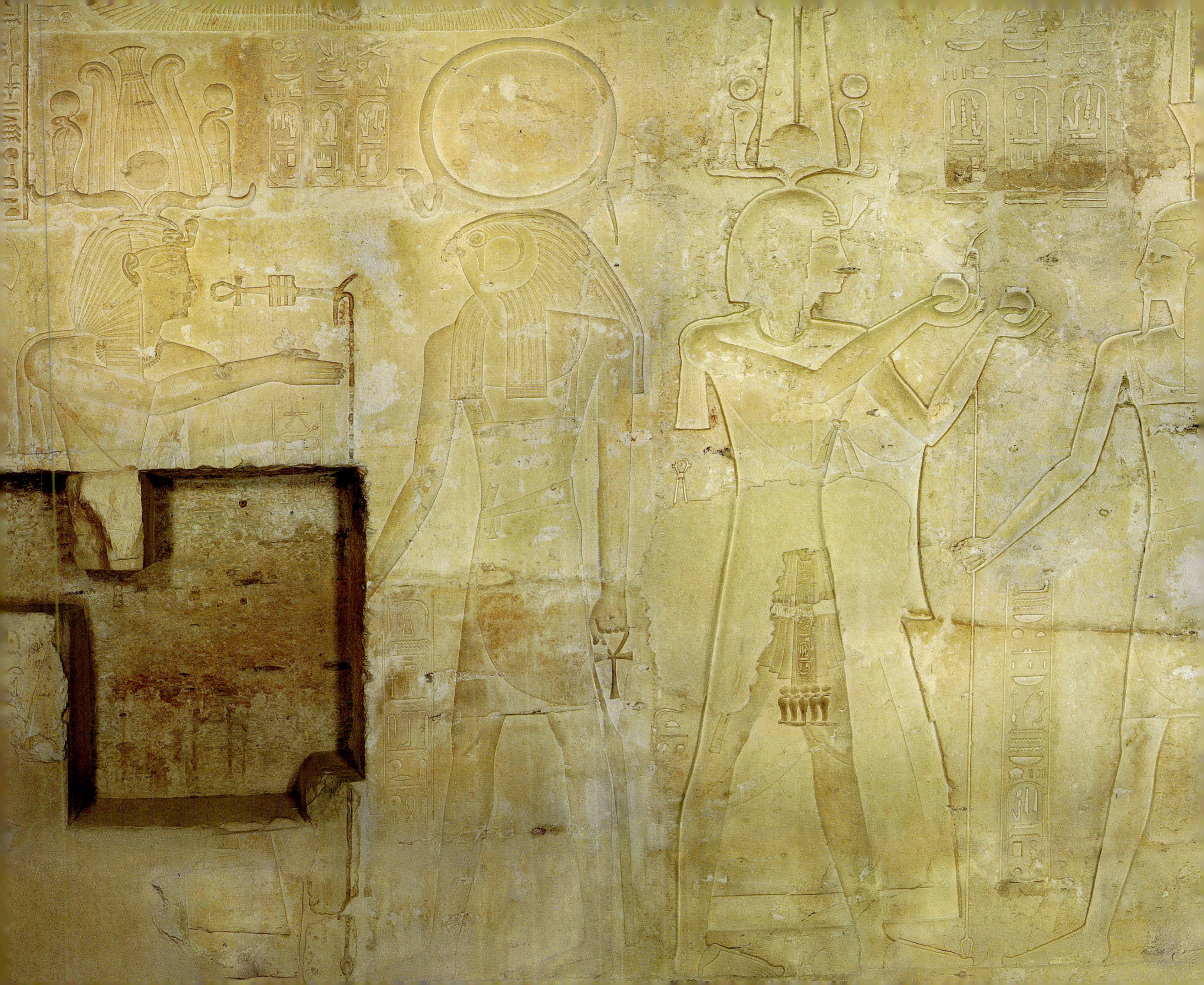

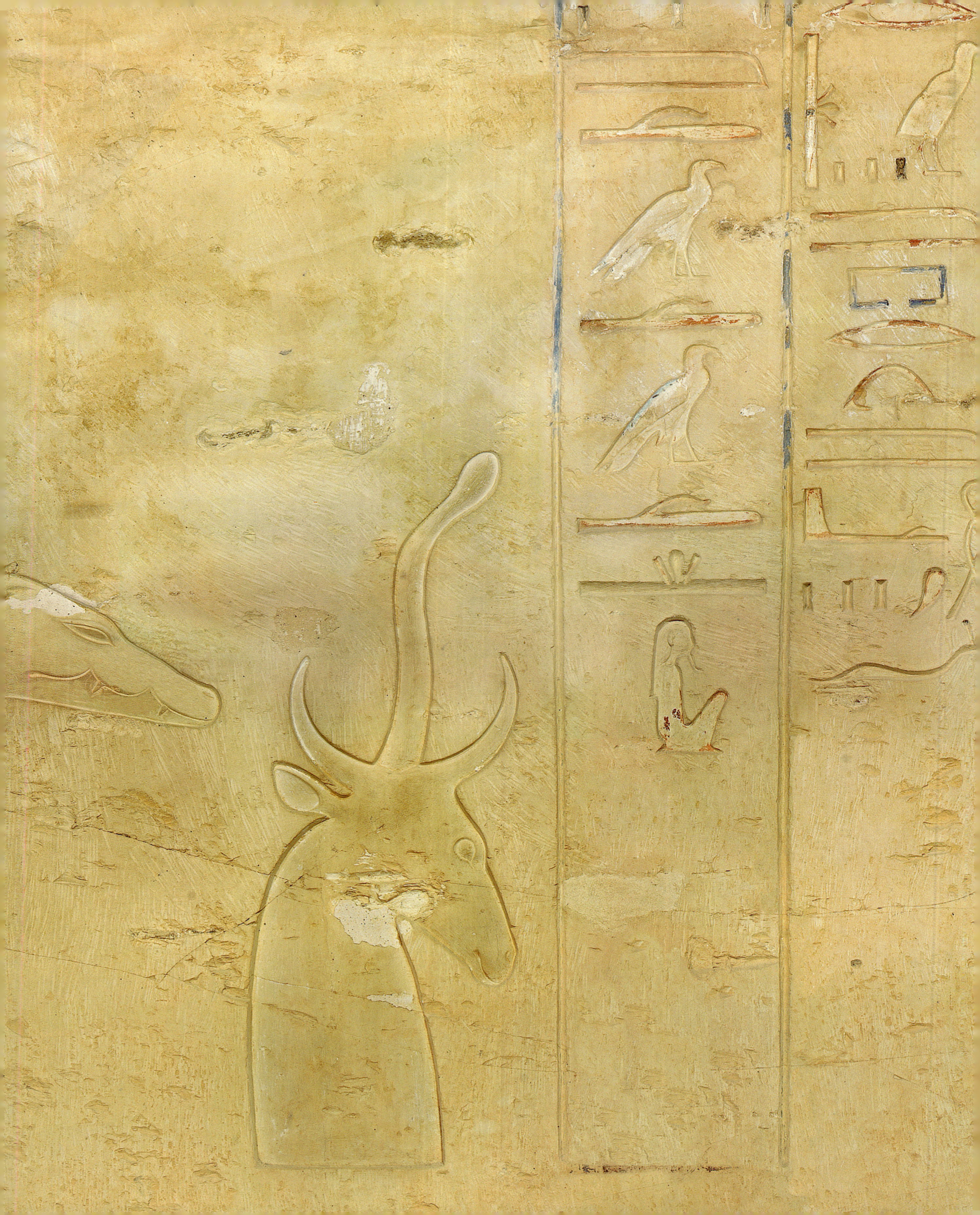

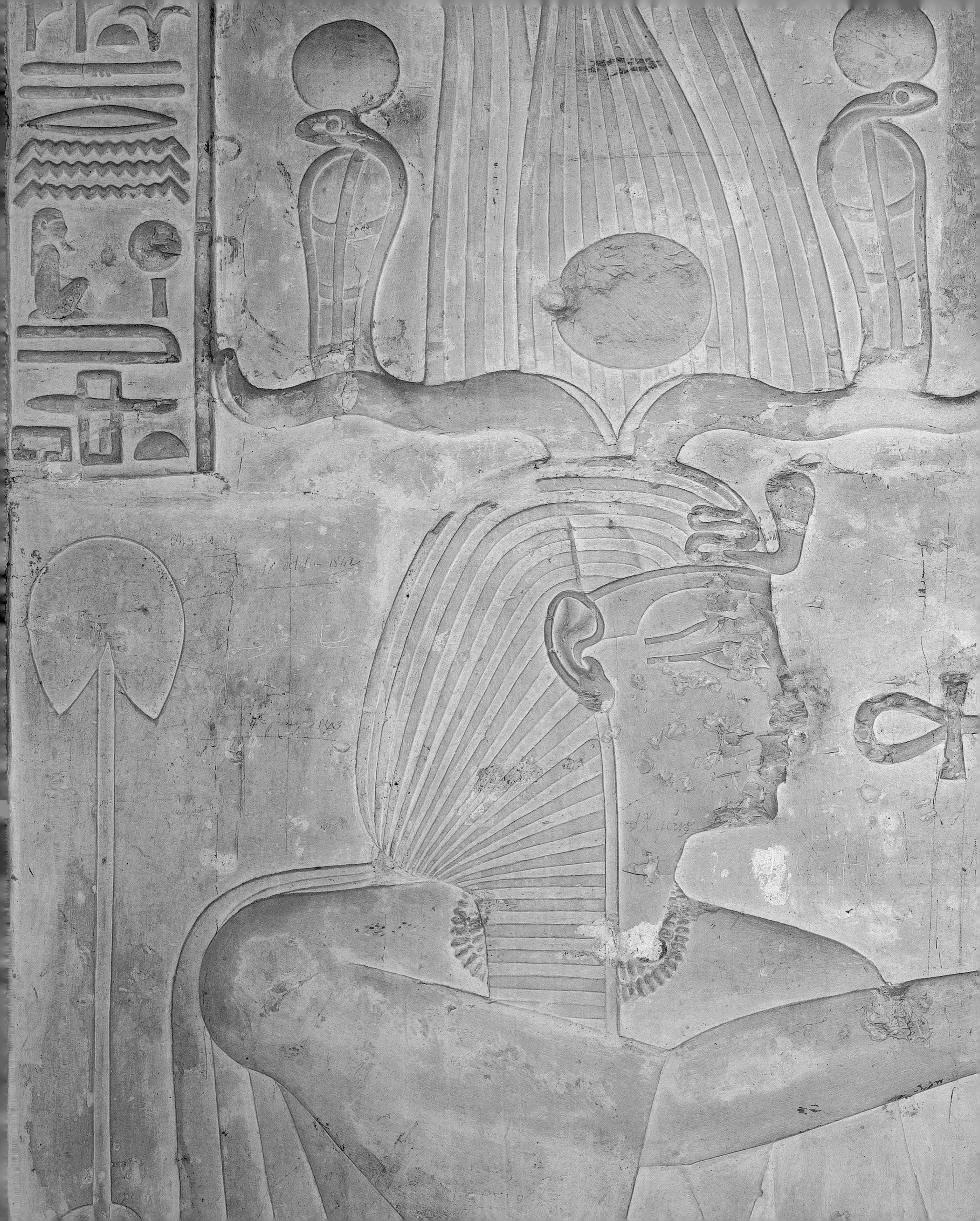

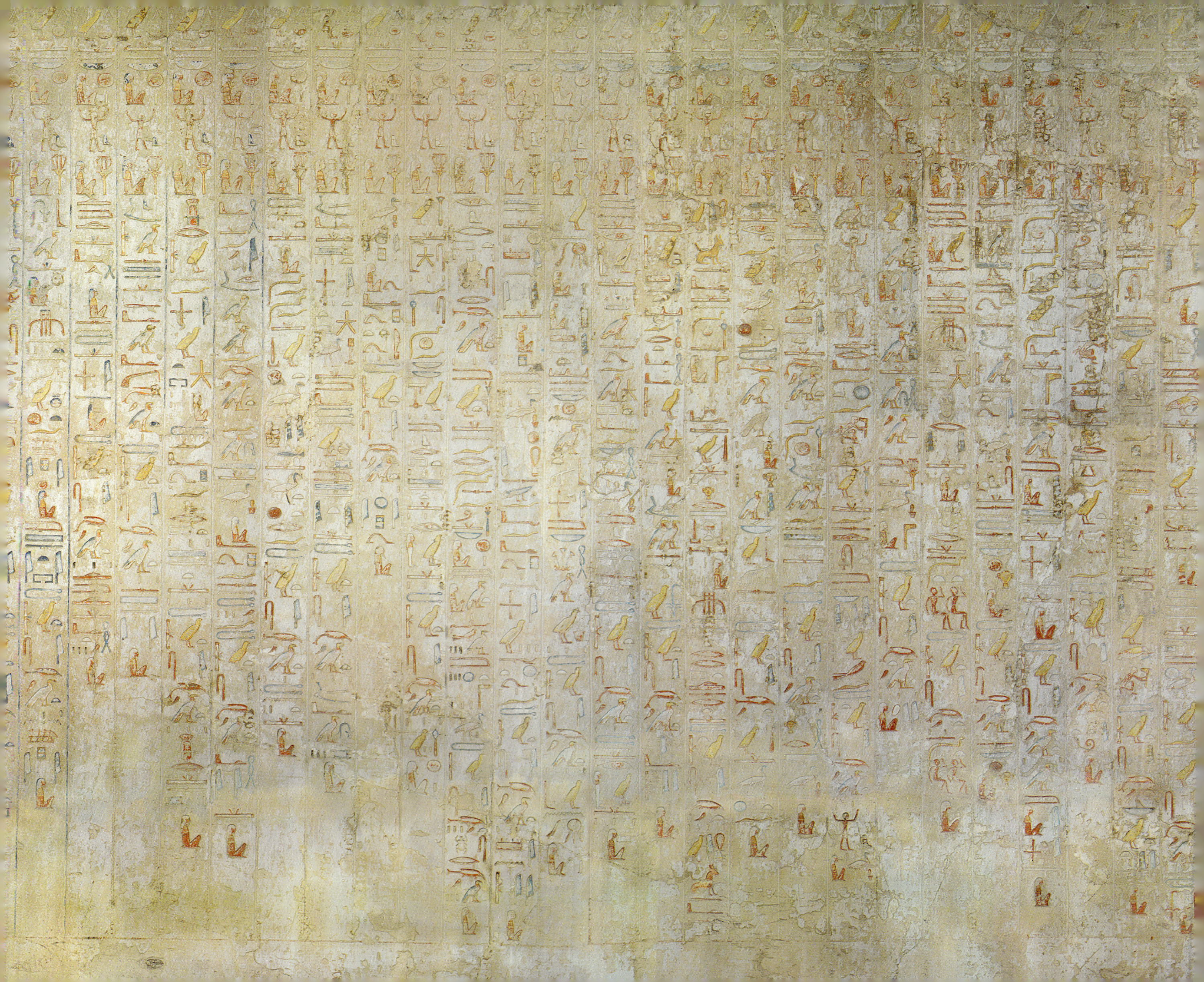

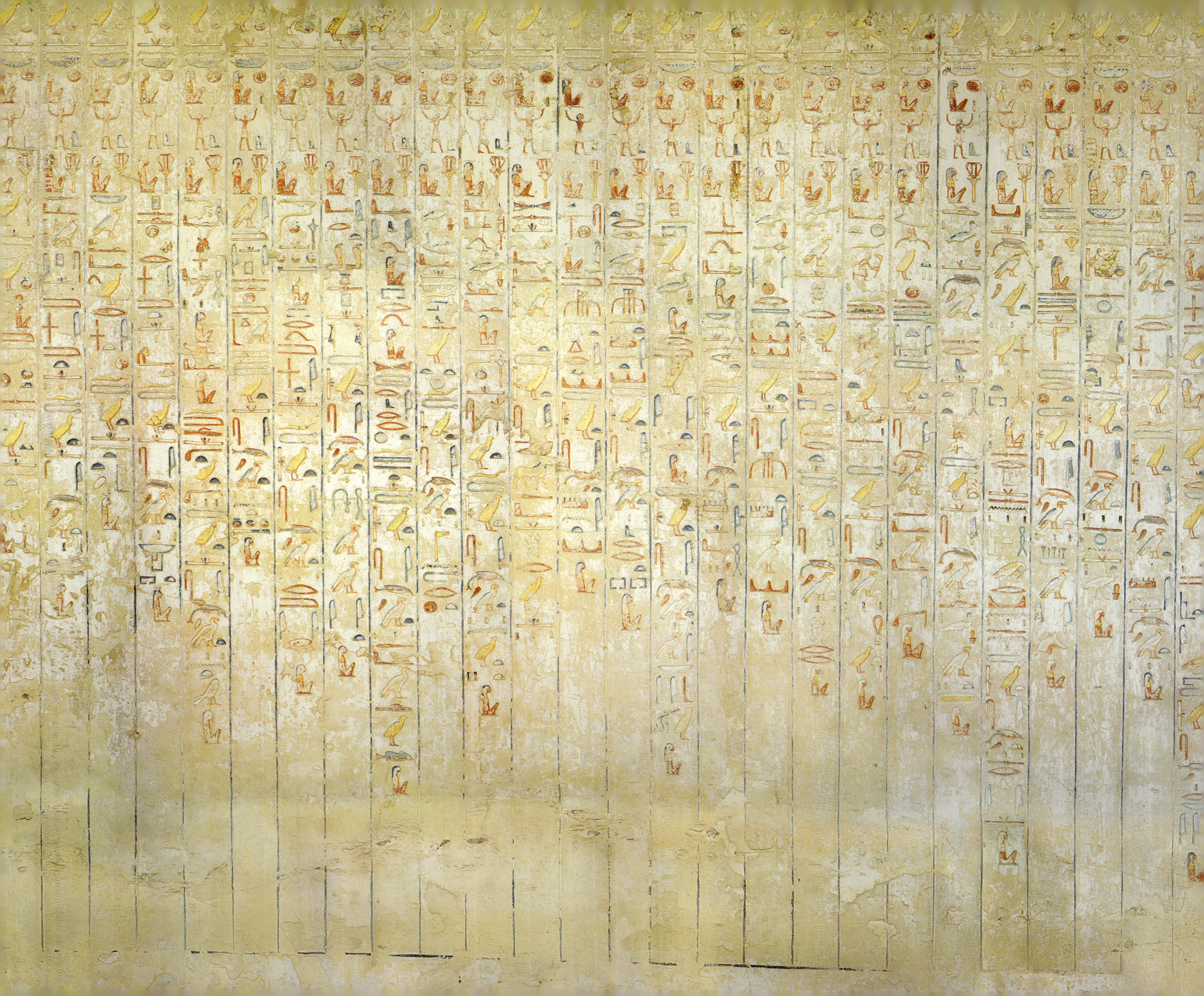

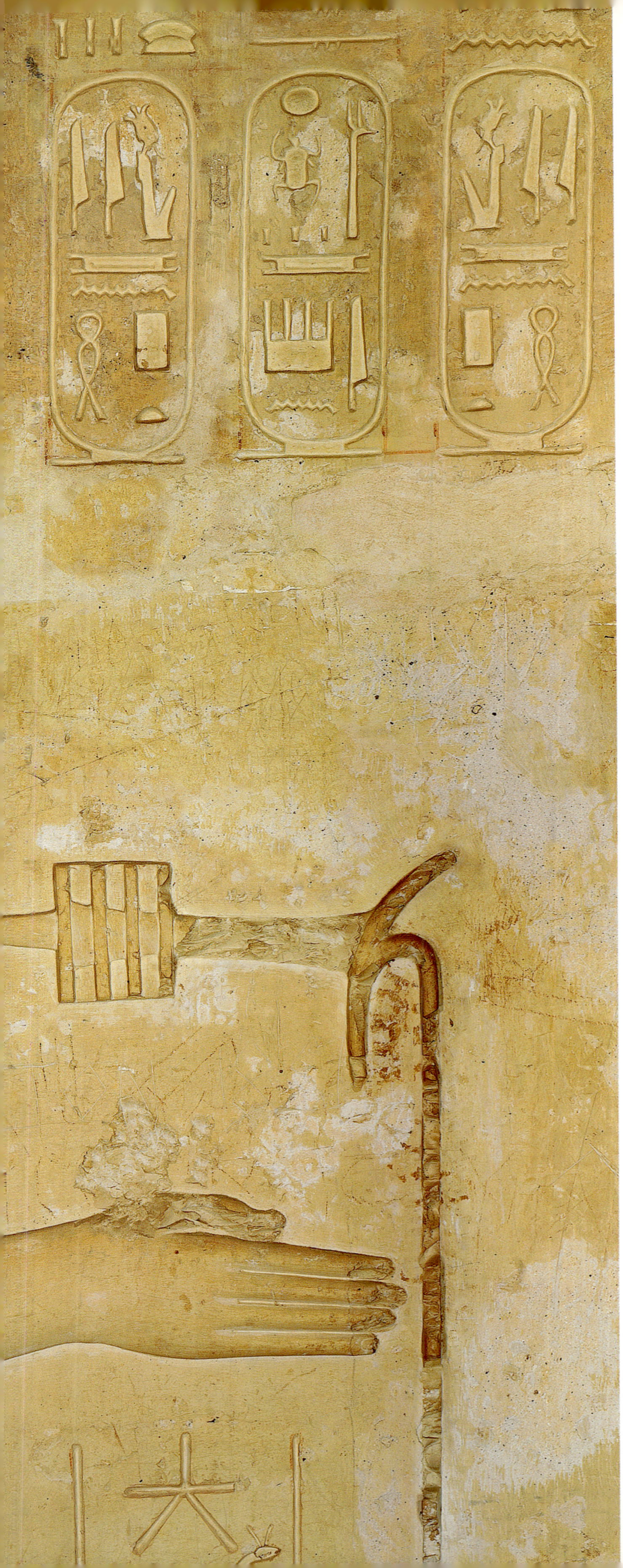

THE LITANIES OF RE
(Preceding pages)
During the Ramesside Period, it became standard to put the Litanies of Re on the walls of the entrance corridor of the royal tombs.

THE KING RECEIVING LIFE
In one of the images from his entrance corridor, Seti II is shown here receiving the signs for life, stability, and dominion from a god.

THE GOD NEFERTEM
(Following page)
Another incarnation of the sun at dawn was Nefertem, depicted as a god with a lily or lotus flower supporting double plumes on his head.

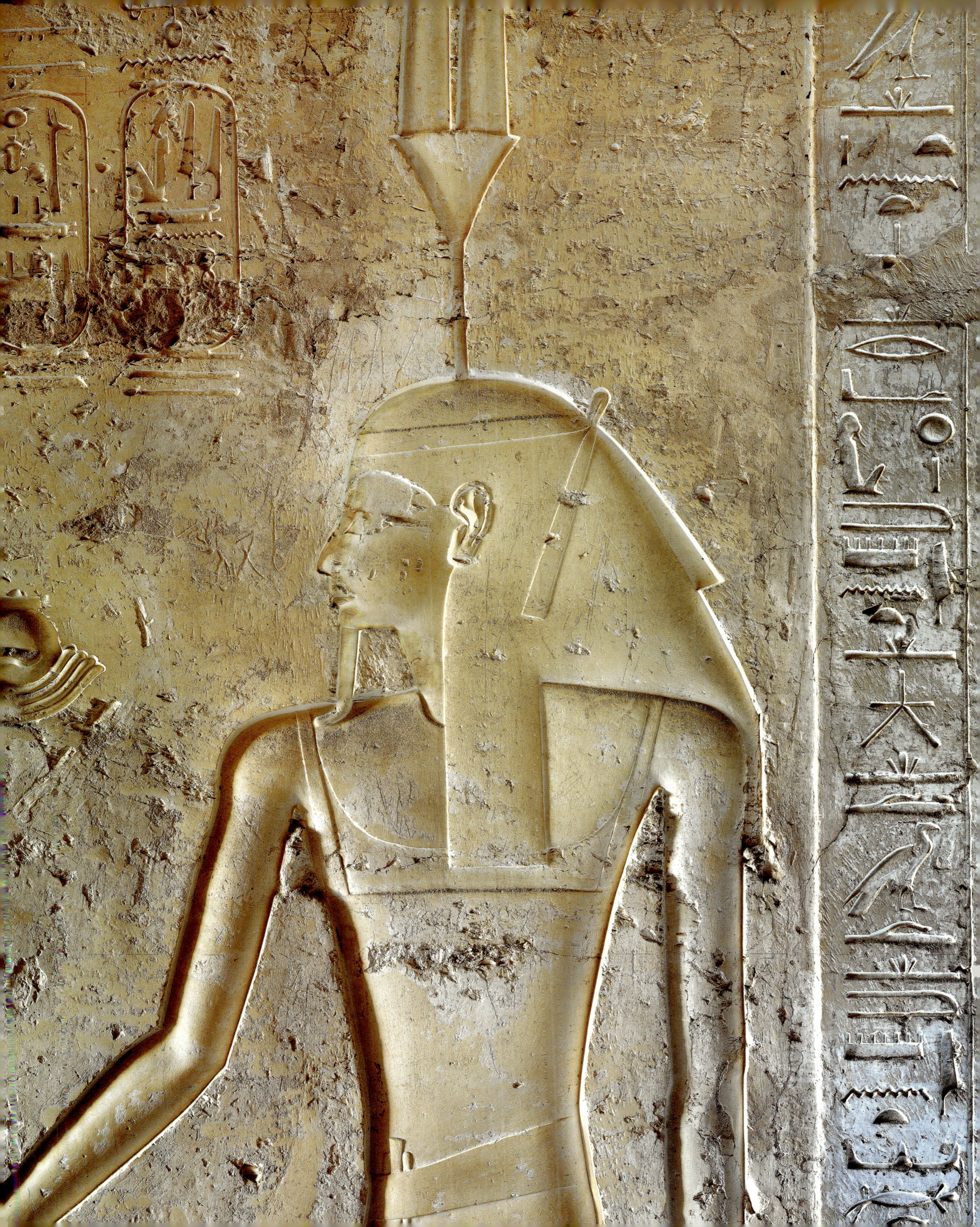

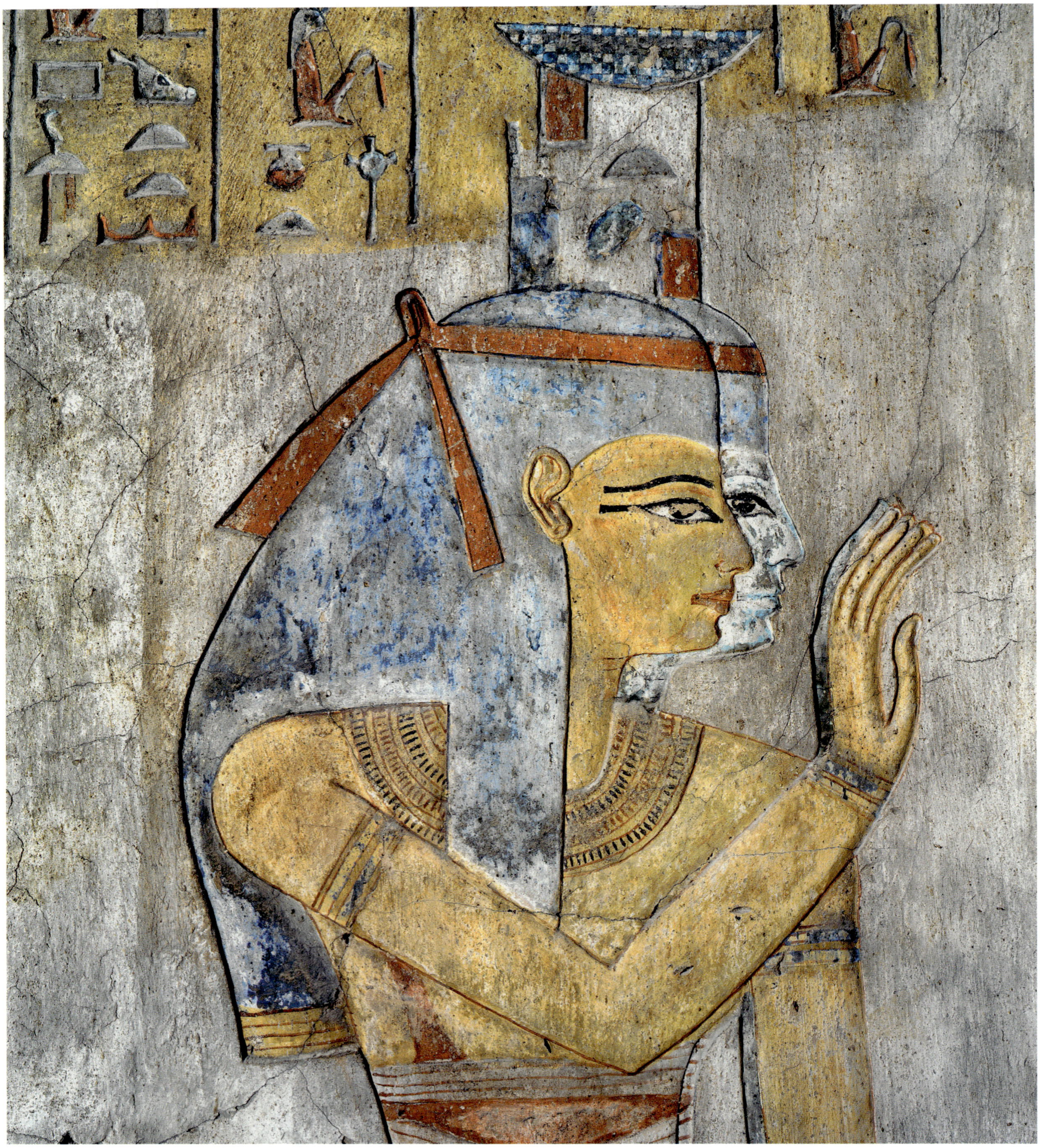

Isis and Nephthys
The goddess Isis and her sister Nephthys, both daughters of Geb and Nut, stand side by side making identical gestures of praise.

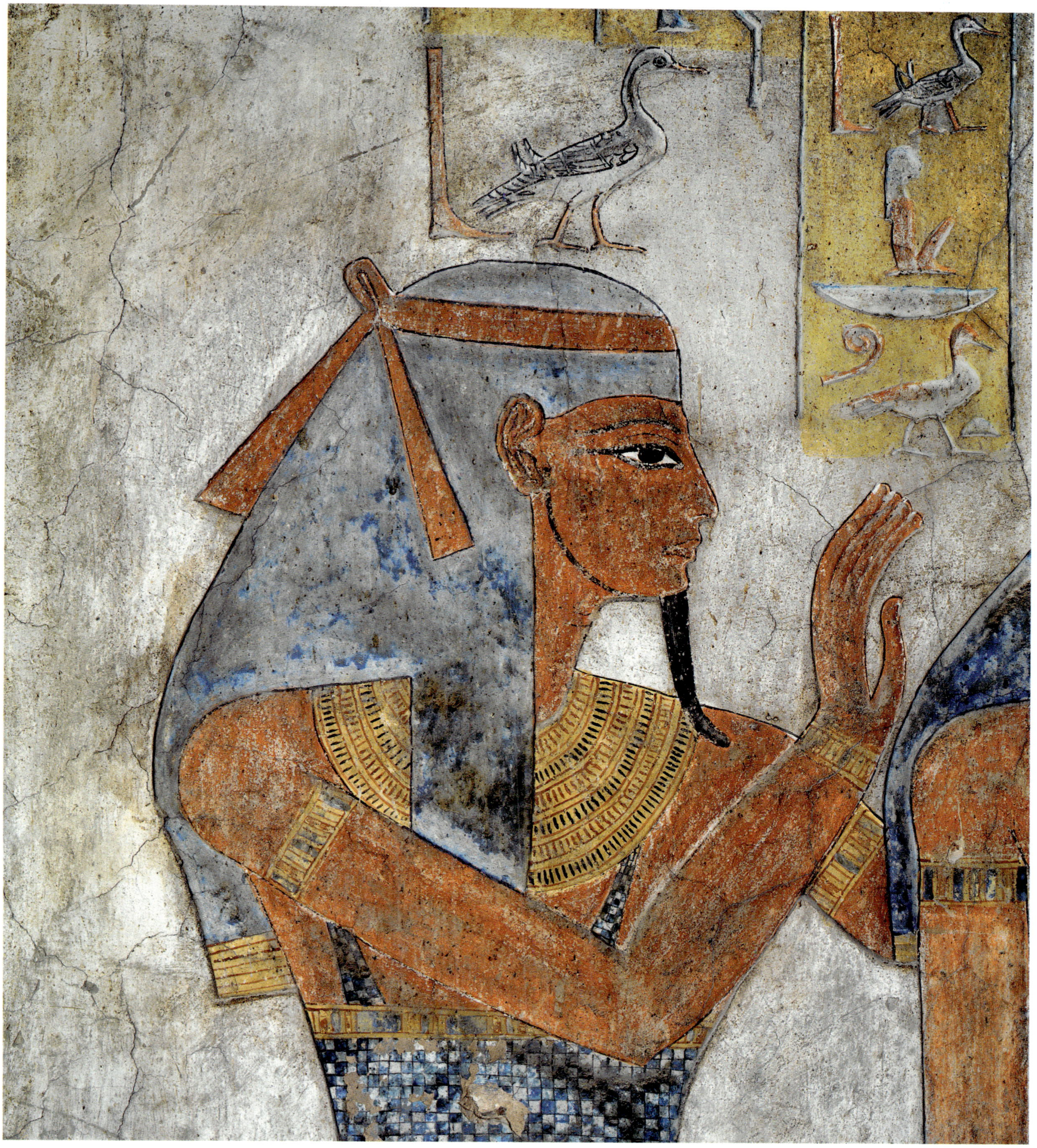

THE GOD GEB
God of the earth, Geb is shown here with his name, written with the figure of a goose, above his head.

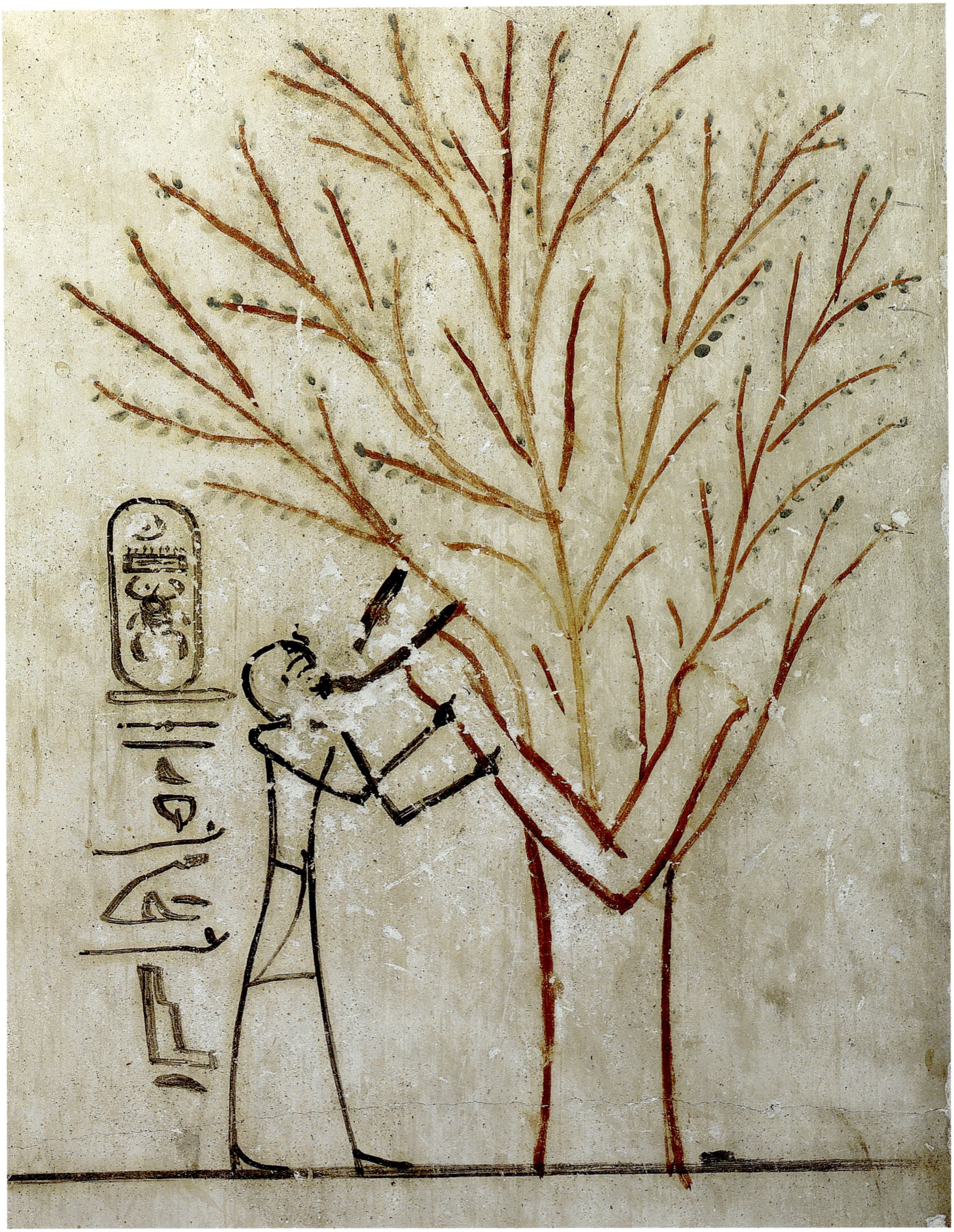

TUTHMOSIS III AND ISIS
(Preceding page)
In this scene from a pillar in his burial chamber, King Tuthmosis III nurses at the breast of a tree goddess, identified in the inscription as Isis. The tree goddess is normally associated with Hathor; in this case, she is labeled as Isis because this was the name of the king's mother.

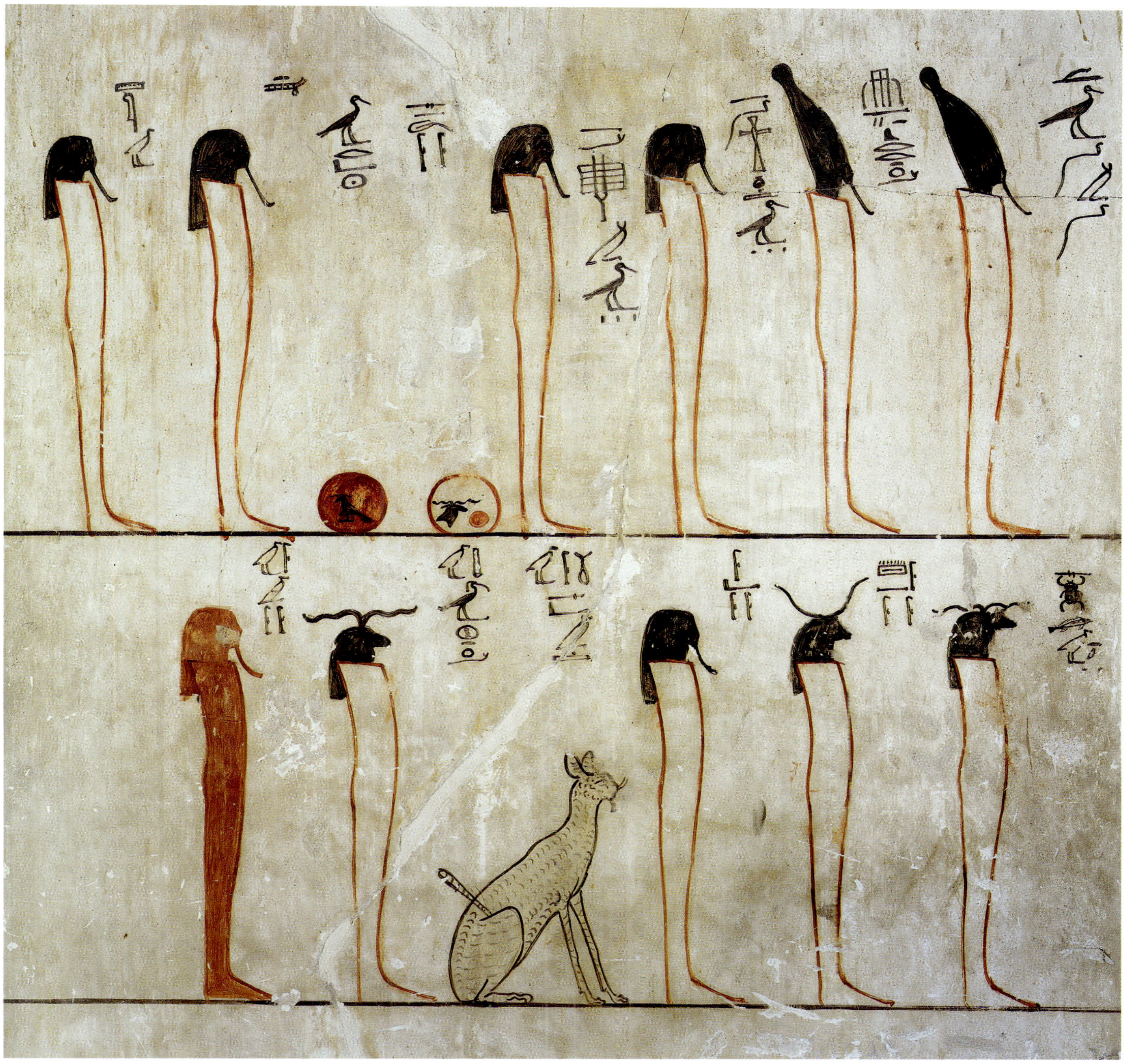

THE GREAT LITANY
The first appearance of the Great Litany is on the pillars of the burial chamber of Tuthmosis III. Fourteen of the seventy-five forms and names of the sun god are visible here.

THE LITANIES OF RE
(Following pages)
Six more of the forms of the sun god from the Great Litany can be seen here, along with an extensive text that comprises an abridged form of the Book of the Amduat.

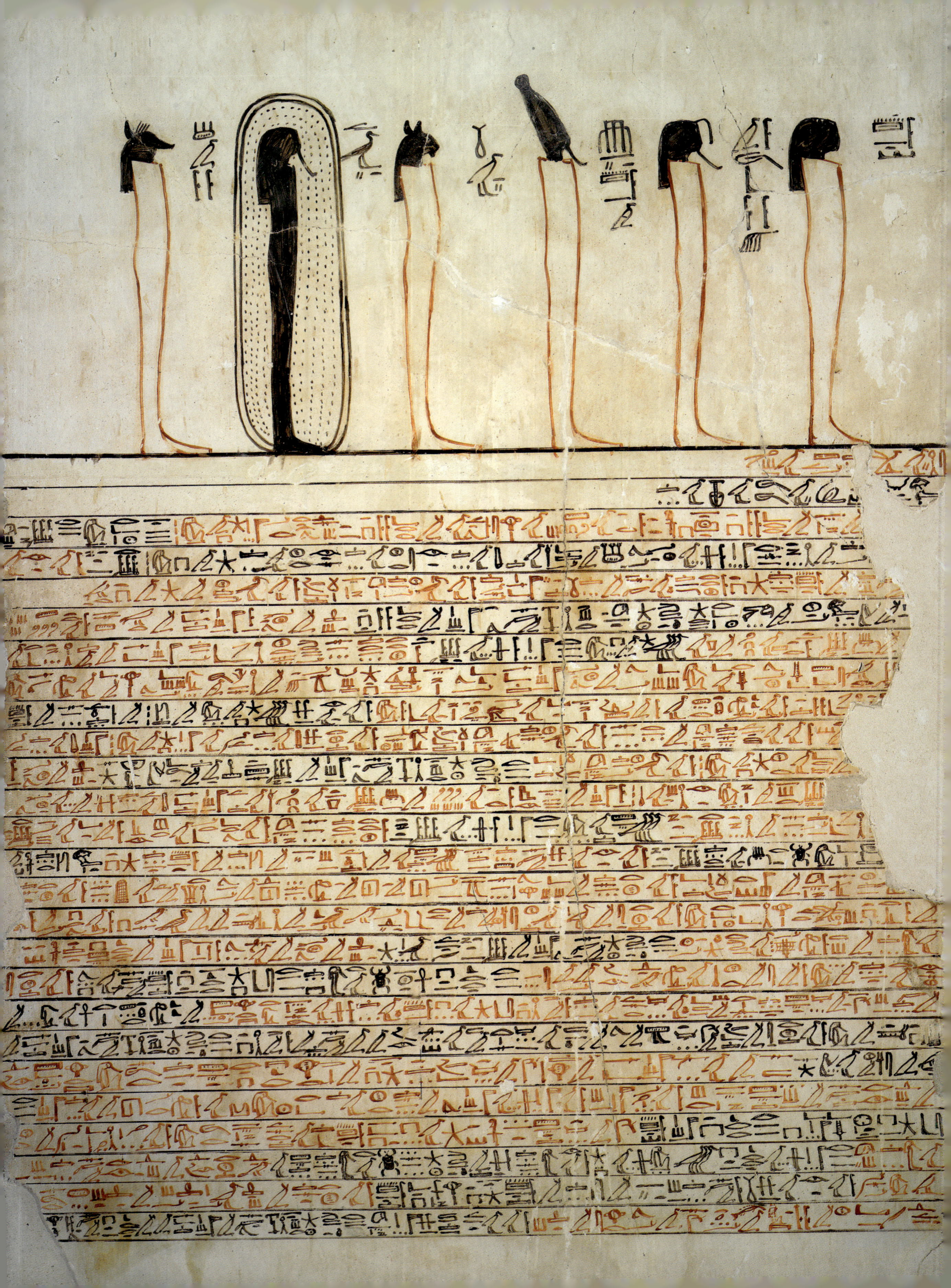

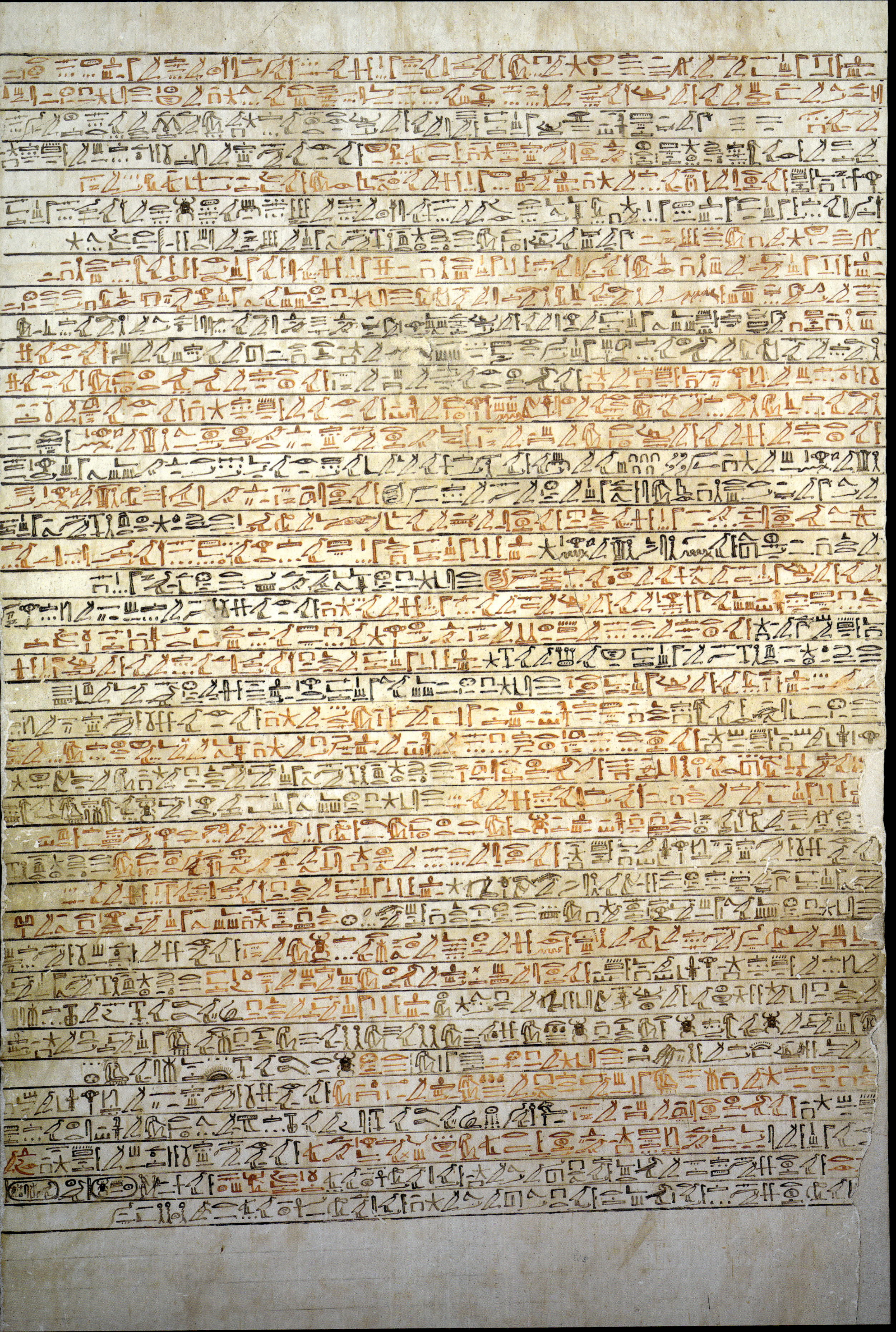

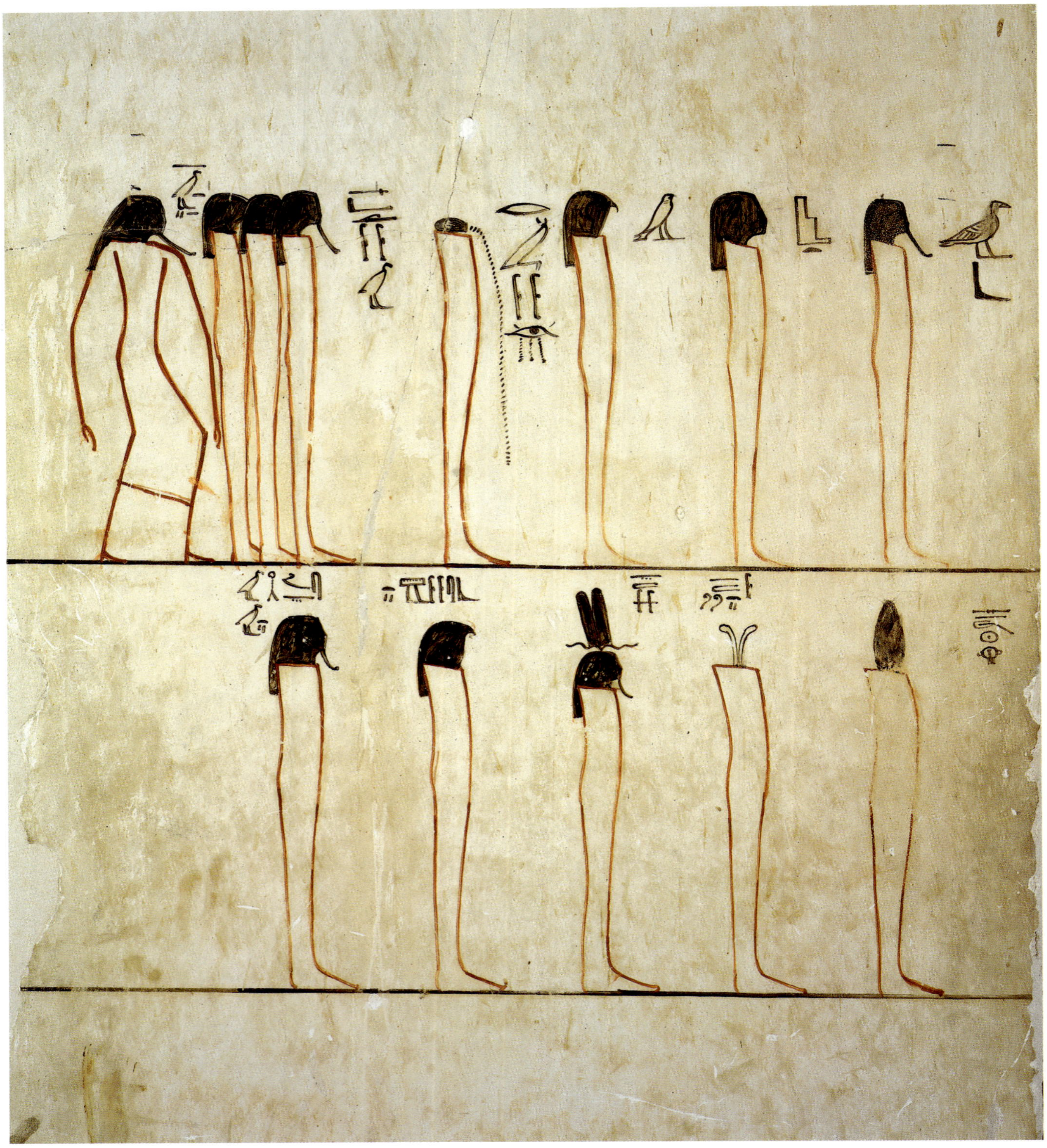

The Great Litany

The Great Litany continues on this pillar from the tomb of Tuthmosis III, with two more registers of gods, including mummified forms of Geb, Osiris, and Horus.

The Great Litany

(Following pages)

Here the sun god is depicted and named in thirty-five additional guises. He is seen in his dawn form as a scarab beetle three times in this sequence; his additional shapes include his fully ram and ram-headed and baboon-headed forms.

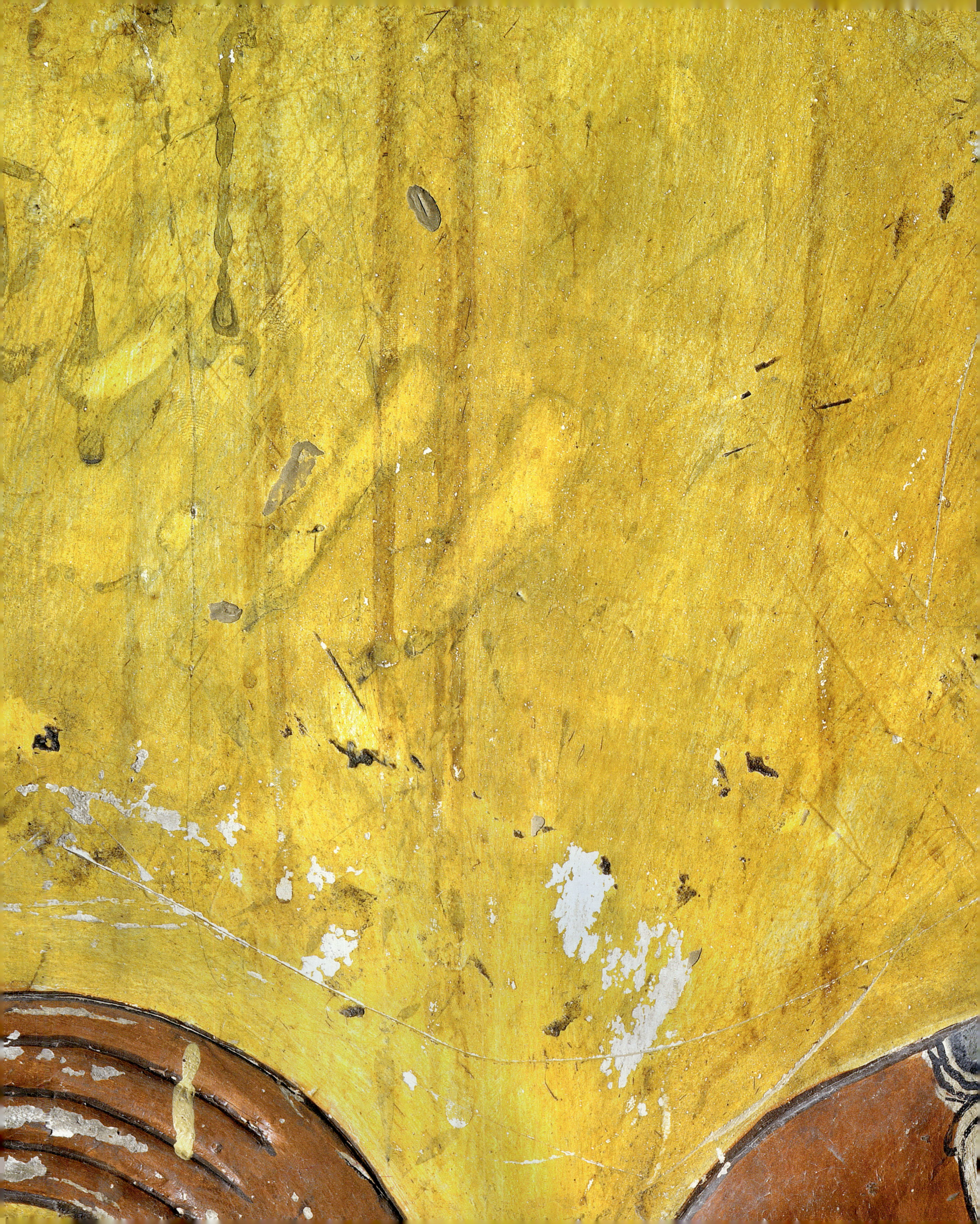

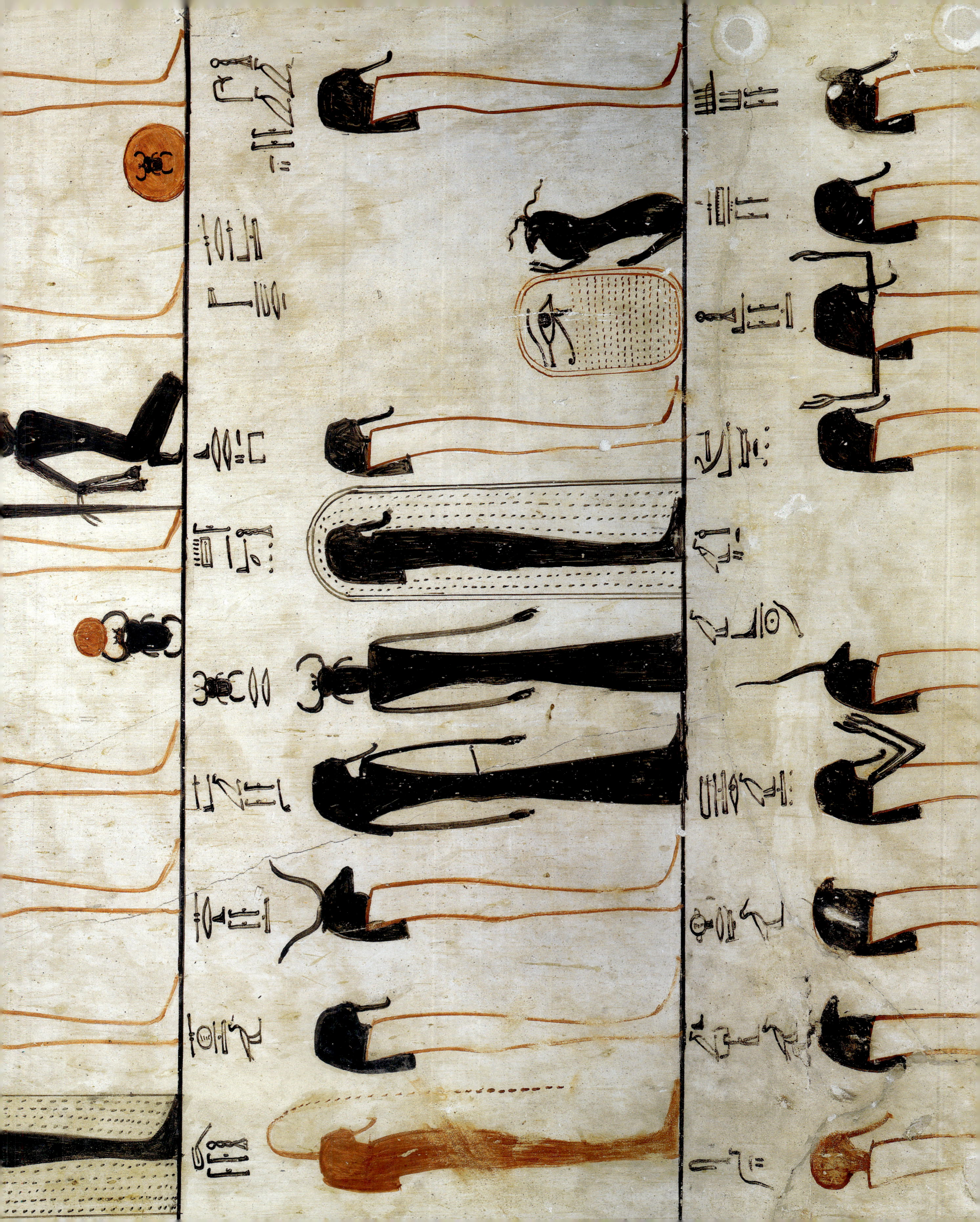

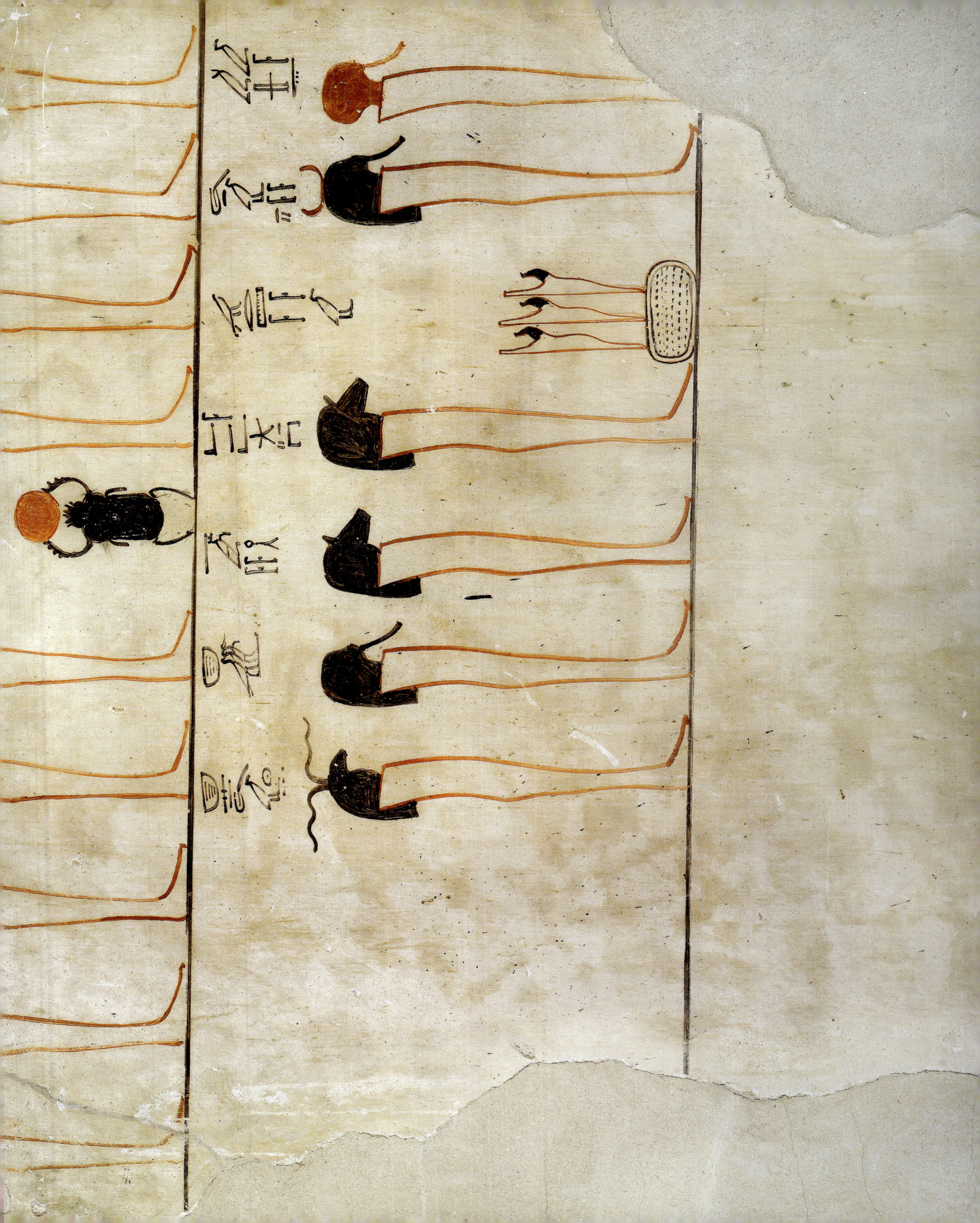

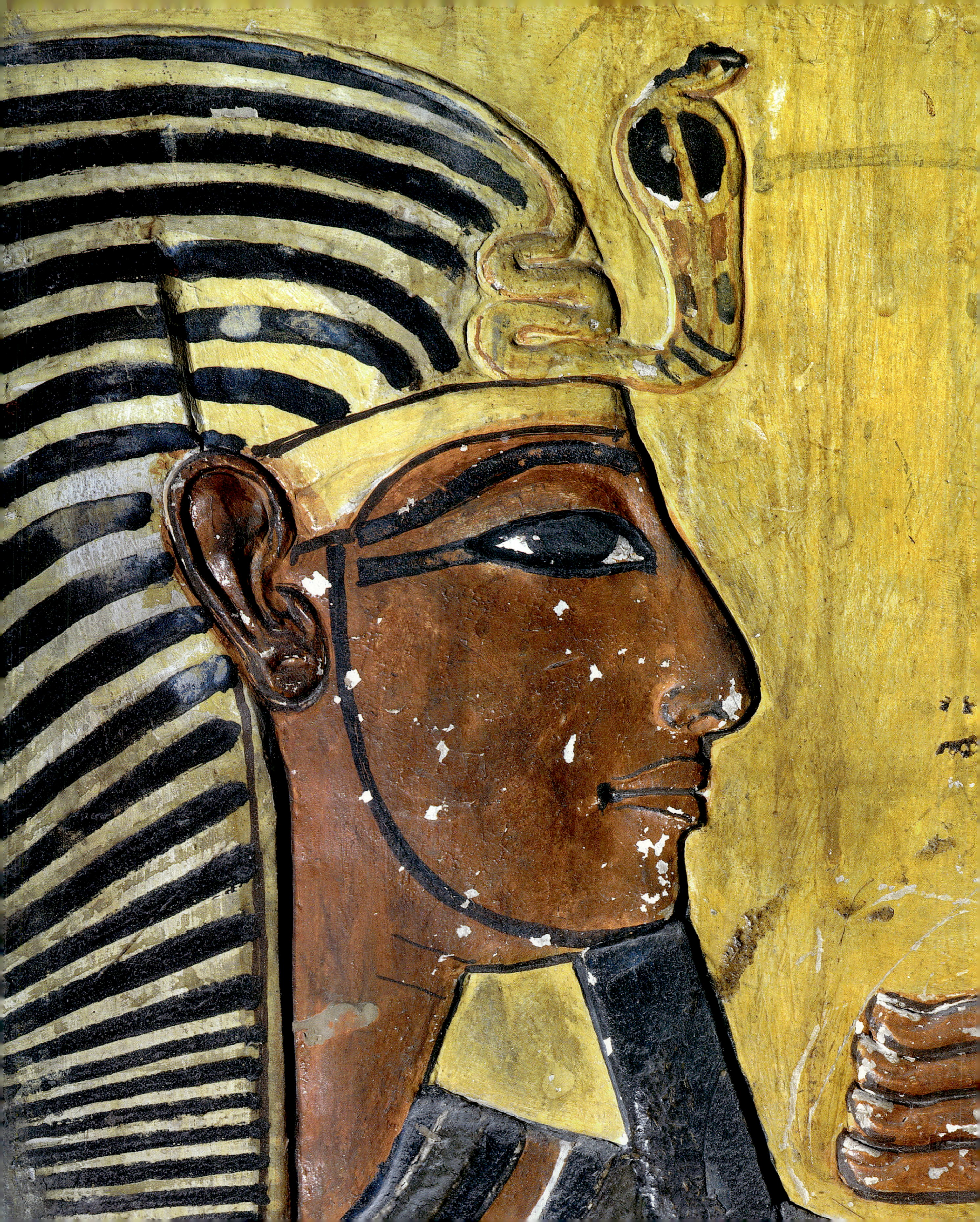

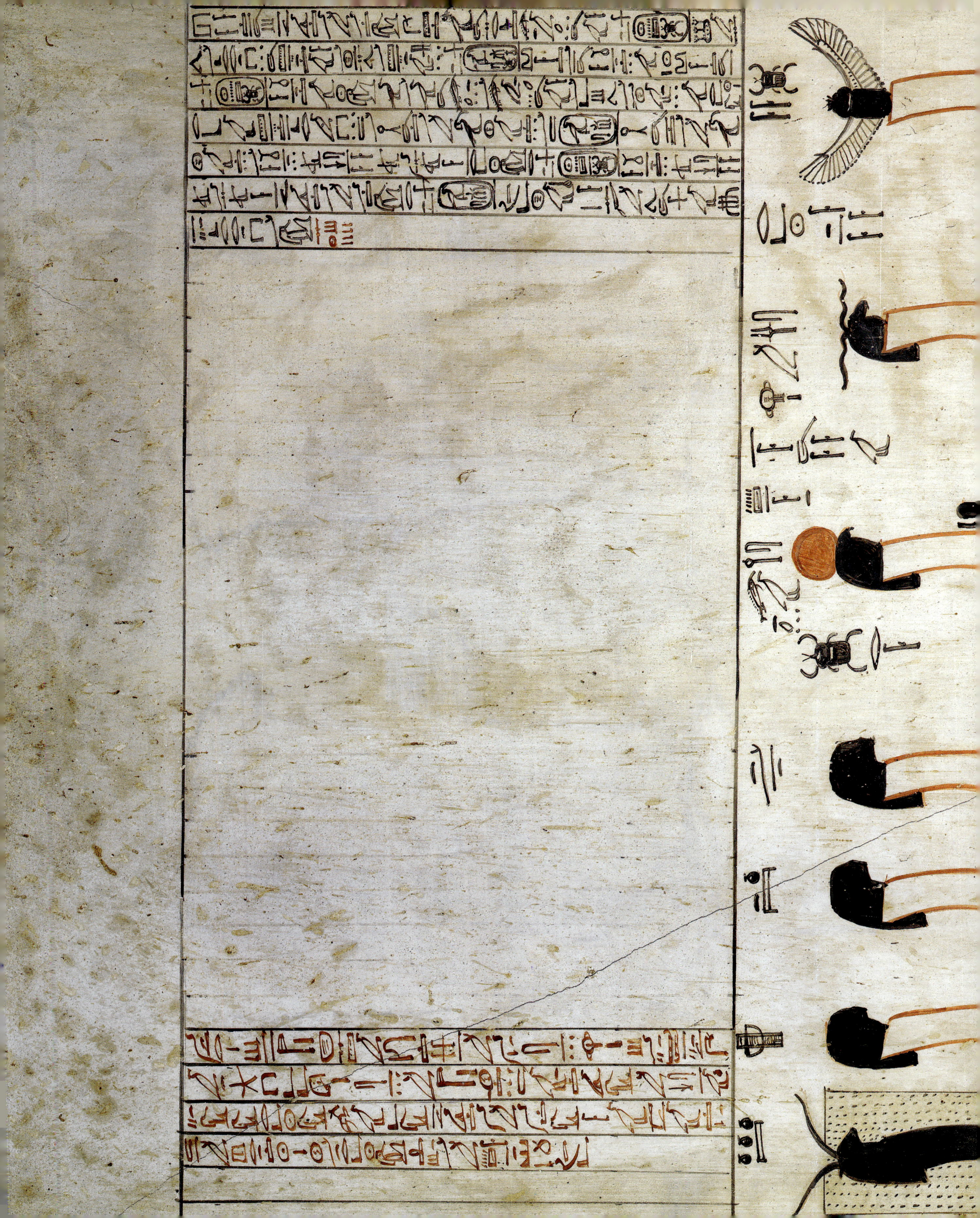

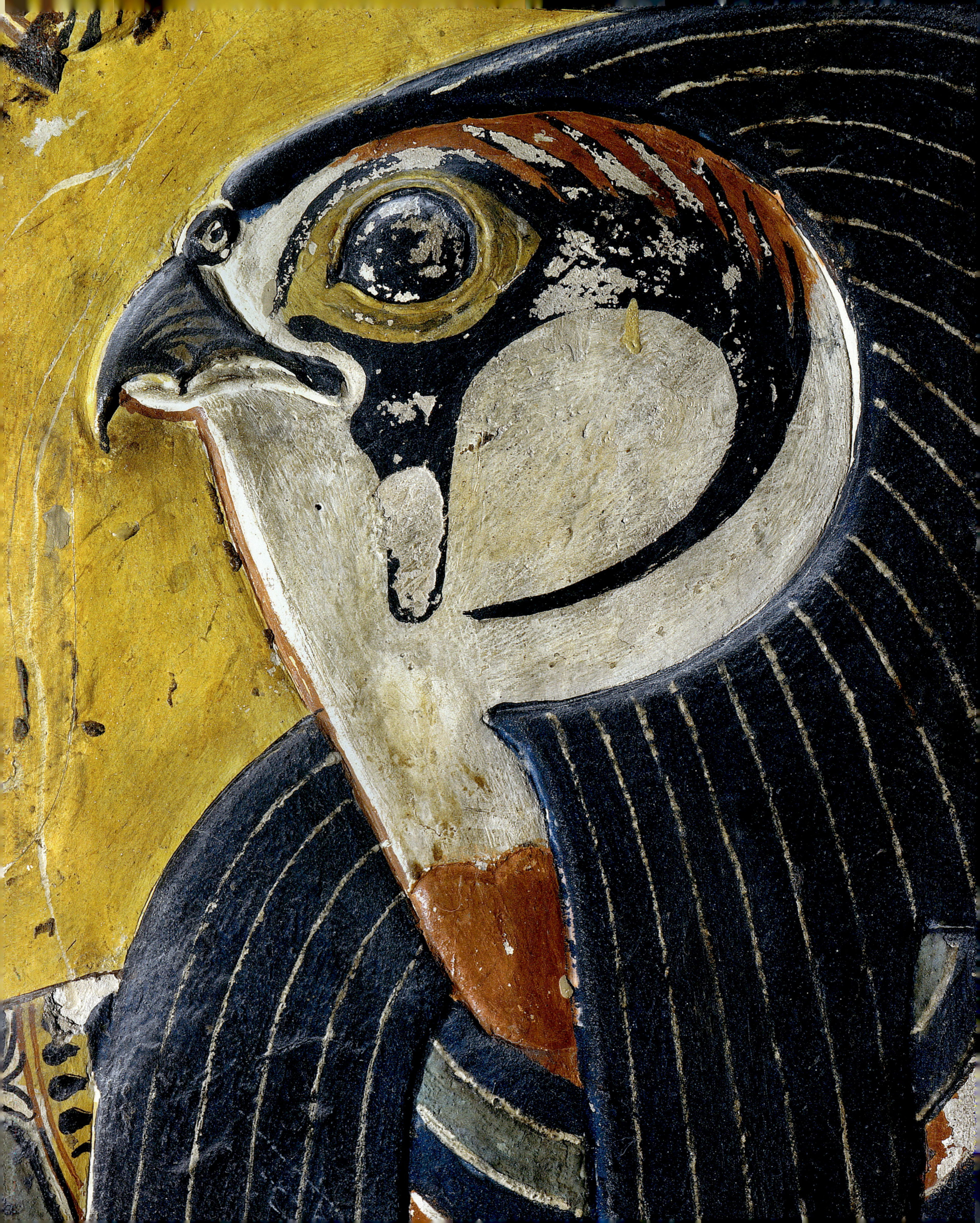

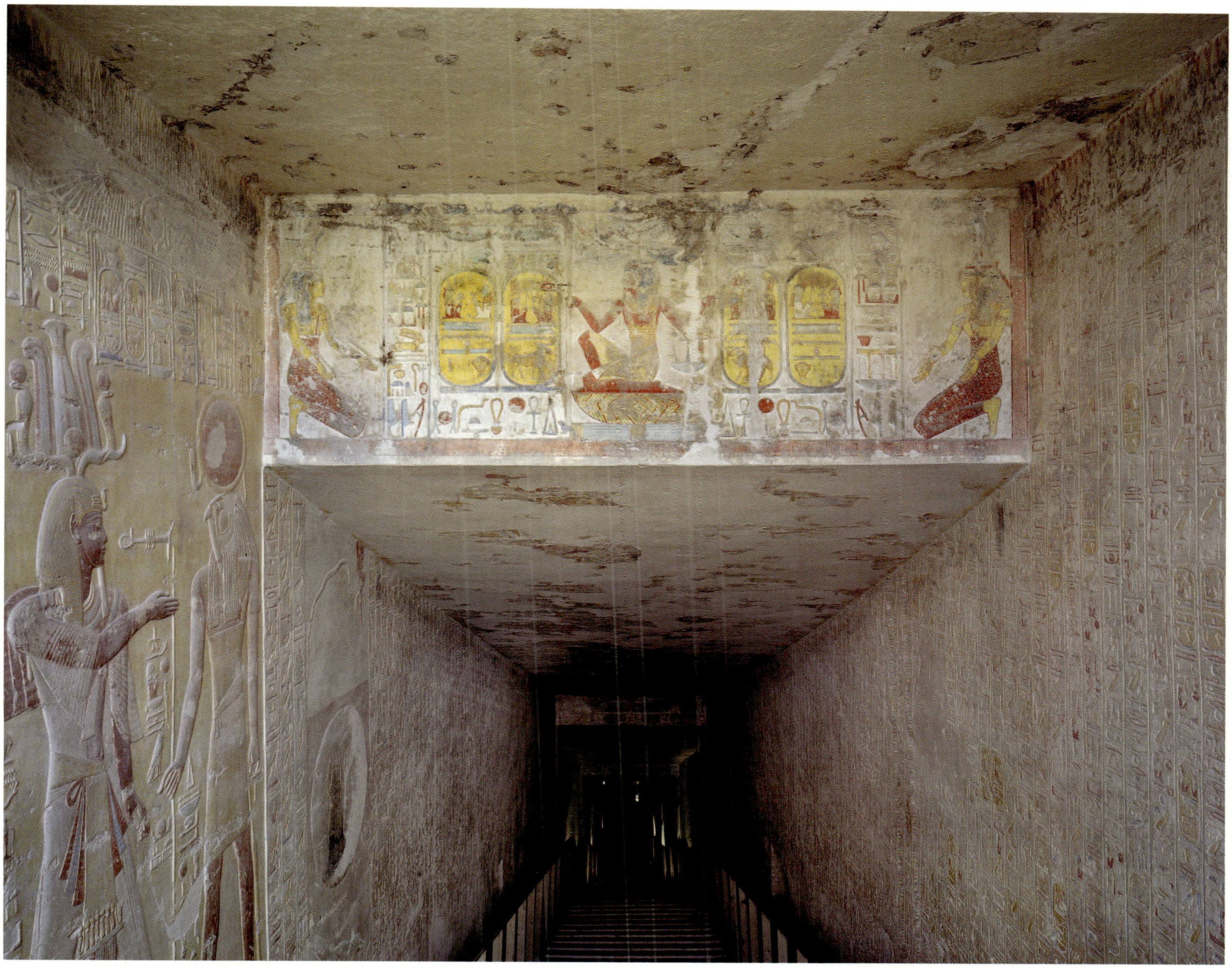

Entering the Netherworld

This view into the tomb of Merenptah shows the arrangement of the Litanies of Re, along with other images common at the entrances to Ramesside royal sepulchers. On the architrave, the cartouches of the king flank a figure of the god Heh, the entire composition protected by images of the goddess of the west. On the viewer's left is the king with Re-Horakhty, then the title illustration to the Great Litany; on the right is part of the text of the litanies.

Seti I and Re-Horakhty

(Preceding pages)

This detail from the the tomb of Seti I depicts the king in the *nemes* headdress, his distinctive Ramesside profile evident, being embraced by the falcon-headed sun god, Re-Horakhty.

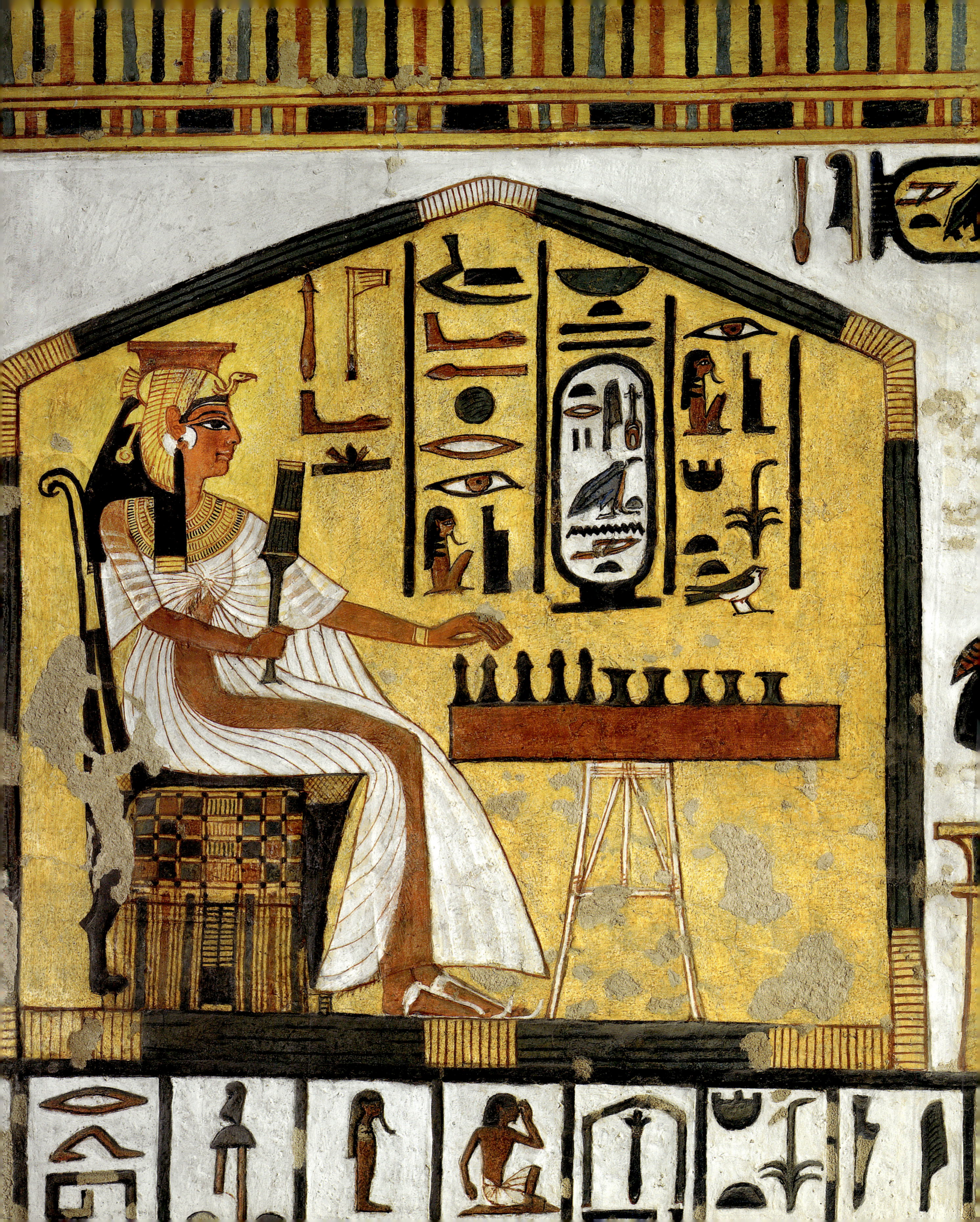

CHAPTER 7

THE BOOK OF THE DEAD

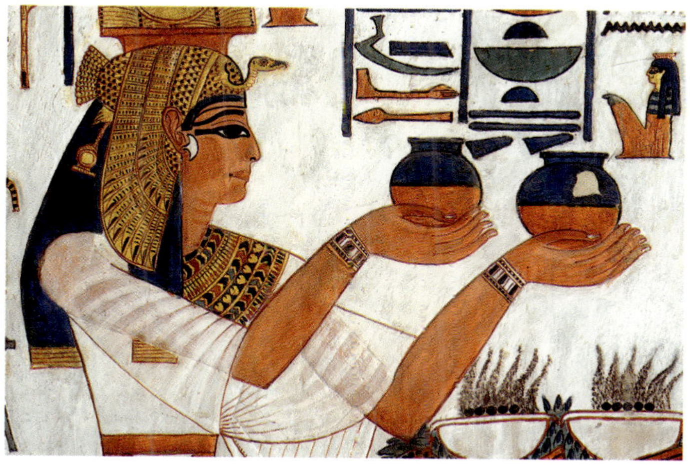

The Book of the Dead was one of the most popular funerary texts used in the New Kingdom, and is seen in both private and royal contexts. Its origins can be traced to the Coffin Texts of the Middle Kingdom, which were in turn based on the Old Kingdom Pyramid Texts. The earliest examples of spells from the Book of the Dead are found on coffins of the 17th Dynasty; in the New Kingdom, excerpts from this book are seen first on mummy shrouds and coffins of the early 18th Dynasty. Known to the ancients as the "Spells for Coming Out by Day," this composition, really a collection of spells, is found most often on papyri, written in a form of cursive hieroglyphs that falls halfway between full hieroglyphs and hieratic. The language in which it was composed, as is the case for most of the Netherworld Books, was classical Middle Egyptian. The full corpus of the Book of the Dead counts close to 200 spells; most examples include only a subset of these. Before the Ptolemaic Period, there was no set order, although there were a number of standard variations. The spells vary in length, from a few verses to over 400.

The papyri seen most often in elite burial assemblages were originally put into coffins so that they could be held by the deceased and thus would be easily accessible to them on their hazardous journey. Beginning in the Ramesside period, such papyri were often placed inside hollowed-out statues of Osiris. Some of the elite also included images and texts from the Book of the Dead in the decoration of their tombs, and selected spells were used also on *shabtis* and heart scarabs.

This composition, like its predecessors the Pyramid and Coffin Texts, are primarily concerned with guaranteeing the safe journey of the deceased to the other world. The texts are not descriptive, but are instead magical formulae to be recited, guaranteeing the deceased safe travel through the Netherworld, allowing him to join the sun god so that he too can travel through the darkness protected by light and continue through to rebirth and the day journey. His goals are to leave the tomb with each sunrise and "go forth" into the sky and to traverse the paths to the Fields of the Blessed, where he will join Osiris.

Some spells allow the deceased to take on new forms, such as birds or animals, so that he can move more easily through the darkness of night and death. Others help the deceased to avoid losing parts of his body to decay, and others are hymns

NEFERTARI PLAYS SENET
On the wall of her antechamber, Queen Nefertari is shown playing the game of *senet*. This was a real game, but it also had ritual overtones: by winning, the deceased would gain passage to the Netherworld. *Senet* is also mentioned in Spell 17 of the Book of the Dead.

to various gods. An important focus of these spells was the proper behavior of the deceased and the protection and provisioning of the dead; reunion with beloved family members was also important.

The earliest occurrence of the Book of the Dead in a royal context is seen on a shroud that Amenhotep II dedicated to his father, Tuthmosis III. In the tomb of Amenhotep II himself, the oldest copy of Spell 186, a hymn to the goddess Hathor, was found written on a papyrus. Certain *shabti*s from the tombs of these two kings bear versions of Spell 6, instructing the *shabti* how to answer if the deceased is called to do agricultural work in the afterlife: "I am doing it, I am here, you should say."

Beginning with Tuthmosis IV, some royal tombs were also equipped with magical bricks, sets of four unbaked clay bricks topped with figures of Osiris, Anubis as a jackal, a reed torch (the "pedestal of the magical flame"), and a *djed* pillar (the hieroglyph for stability) placed in niches in the walls of the burial chamber. These bore excerpts from Spell 151, protecting the king from various dangers. The Osiris brick of Tuthmosis IV, for example, was inscribed with a passage that assures the deceased and his tomb that anyone who came to grab or attack him would never be allowed to do so; in fact, it would be the protector who would do the grabbing and attacking. It ends by saying: "I am the protection of the Osiris, King Menkheperure, Son of Re, Tuthmosis, justified."

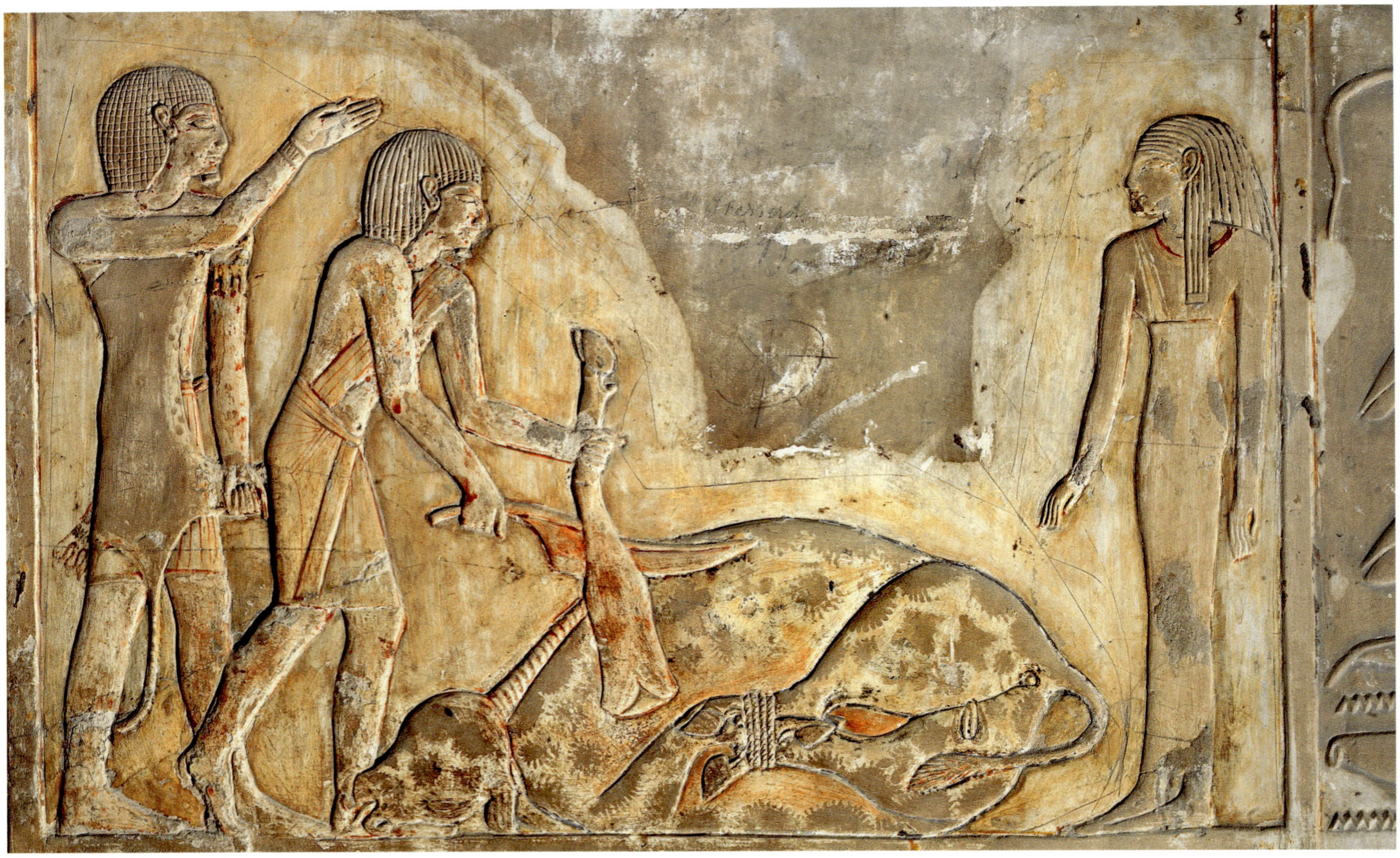

Cutting the Foreleg

An essential part of the funeral ceremony was the cutting of the foreleg of a sacrificial ox. This was necessary for the Opening of the Mouth, a ceremony that enabled the mummy and other images of the deceased to function in the afterlife.

King Seti I

Seti I is shown here in an image from his tomb. Living here for eternity, he was protected and guided through the Netherworld by its decoration, which included a number of spells from the Book of the Dead.

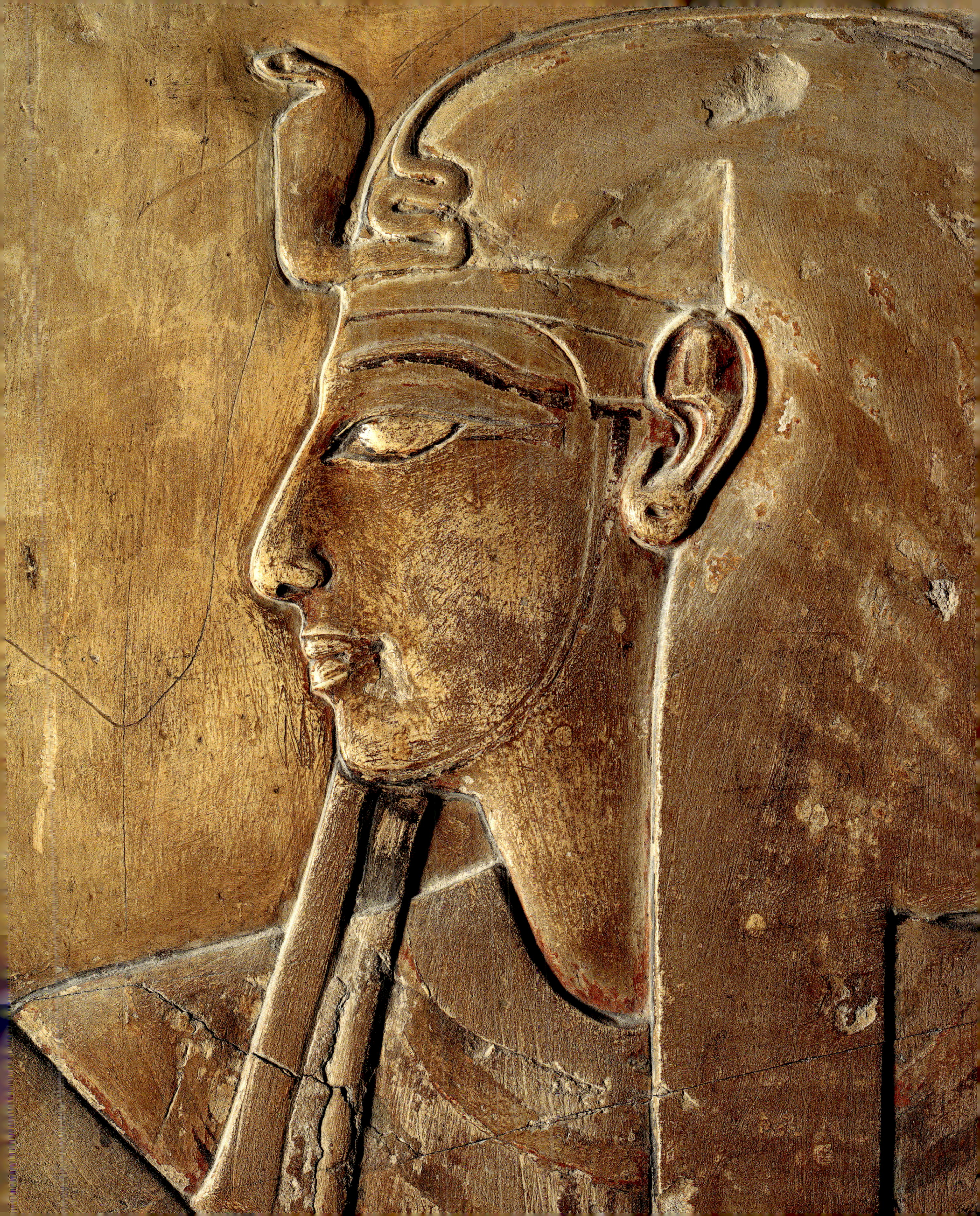

There are no instances of the Book of the Dead from the Amarna Period, but a number of objects in Tutankhamun's tomb are inscribed with excerpts from the Book of the Dead. His heart scarab, found in a chest in the Treasury rather than on the mummy, was inscribed with Spell 30B, which asks the heart not to bear witness against the deceased in the Hall of Judgment and give the pure of heart offerings. Spell 1, to be spoken on the day of the funeral, is referenced in an image of the funeral procession on the east wall of his burial chamber. The Opening of the Mouth, a set of rituals that magically revived the mummy—or indeed any image of the deceased, is painted on the north wall; this illustrates Spell 23, the words to be spoken at this ceremony, which ask that various gods open the mouth of the deceased so that he can speak and eat in the Afterlife. On the south wall of Aye's burial chamber are Spell 130, to be recited on the birthday of Osiris in order to make the *ba* live forever with Re, and Spell 144, which gives the names of the guardians of seven roads. There are also images from Spells 141 and 142, both of which help the deceased to become an excellent spirit, know the names of various gods of the Netherworld, and successfully go out by day.

Spells from the Book of the Dead become a more common element of tomb decoration in the Ramesside period, although the repertoire remains limited. Spell 151, the protective spell seen earlier on magical bricks, which in its entirety includes the major elements of the funeral, is found in the tomb of Seti I, as is the Opening of the Mouth (Spell 23). Several additional spells are inscribed on this king's massive sarcophagus. Ramses II includes Spell 151 in his tomb decoration, and introduces several additional spells. One of these is Spell 125, the Judgment of the Dead. In the first part of this spell, Anubis asks the deceased if he knows the names of the doors he must pass through to enter the Hall of Justice, where the Judgment of the Dead will be carried out. The second part of this spell comprises the judgment itself, including the "negative confession," in which the deceased swears to a panel of divinities that he has acted properly during his life: "I have done no wrong… I have not stolen… I have not killed… I have not told lies… I have not been angry unjustly… I have not committed adultery," and on through a long list of evils that he has not committed. Ramses II decorated the walls of one of his side chambers with Spell 110, the first of the texts connected with the arrival of the deceased into the Fields of the Blessed. Merenptah also chose Spells 125 and 151 for the decoration of his tomb; Seti II used Spell 125 and Spell 110; and Siptah selected Spell 151.

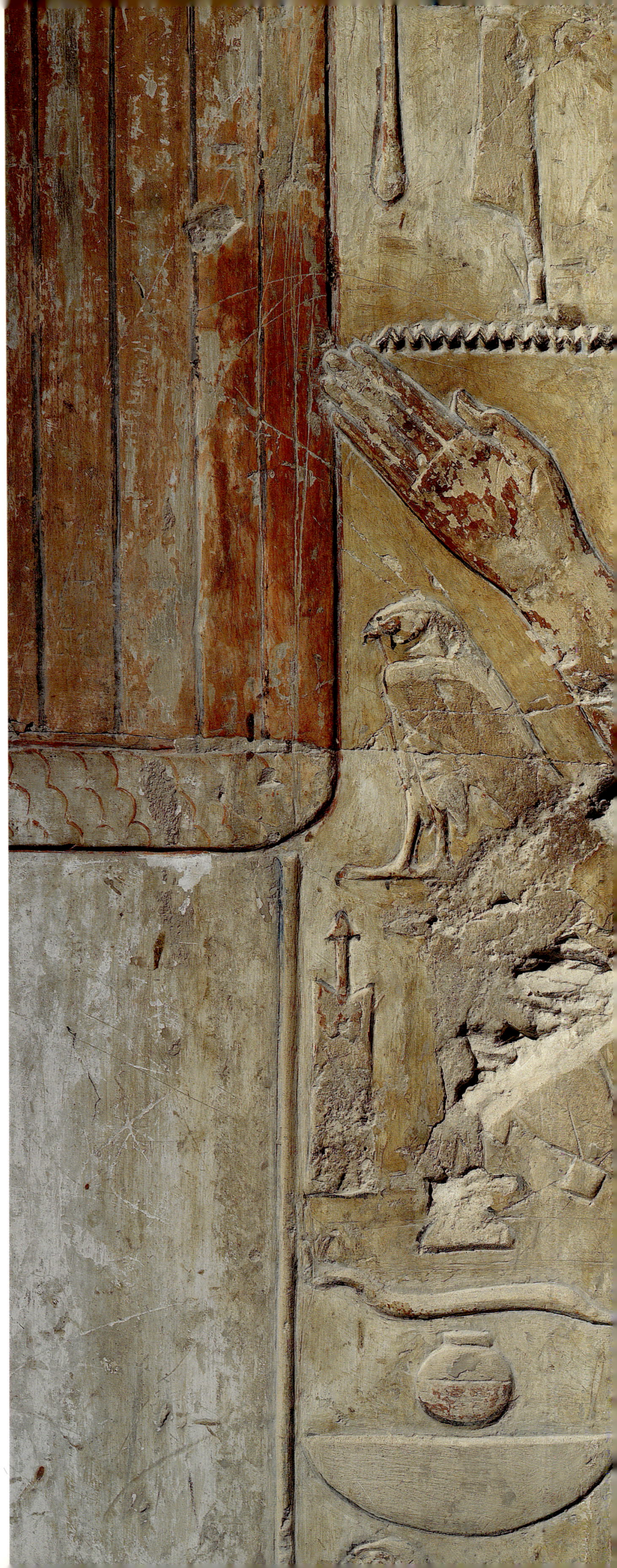

The Iunmutef Priest

Representing the eldest son of the deceased, the Iunmutef (literally "pillar of his mother") priest, shown here in his traditional panther skin and sidelock of youth, was responsible for the proper celebration of the funeral ceremonies.

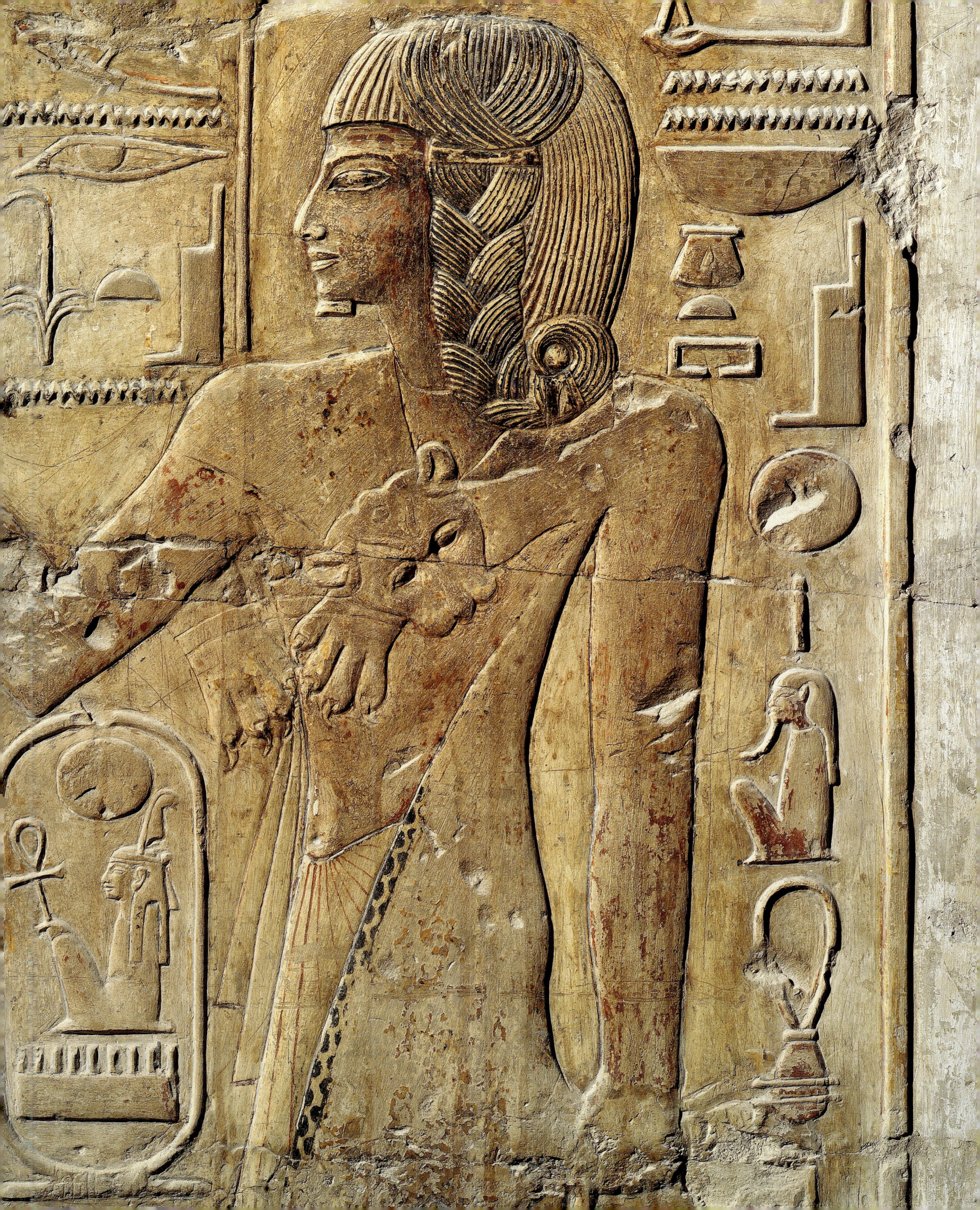

In the tomb of Tausert and Sethnakht, Spell 151 appears again, along with two new spells: 145 and 146. Spells 145 and 146 are extensive texts in which the deceased passes through a set of gates guarded by various deities, whose names he must know, in order to pass safely into the domain of Osiris. These are similar in some ways to the Book of the Gates.

The kings of the 20th Dynasty used mostly the same repertoire of spells, but added several more. The tomb of Ramses III is decorated with Spells 151 and 110, and adds Spell 148, praising Re and asking for offerings of bread and beer. In the tomb of Ramses IV, Spell 125 is joined by Spell 123, in which the deceased claims to have built his tomb and behaved well; Spell 124, preparing the deceased to enter the Hall of Judgment; and 127, part of the Litany of Re, permitting the deceased to join the sun god in his solar bark. Ramses V and VI again include Spells 125 and 127, adding 126, in which the Lake of Fire (known from the Books of the Amduat and Gates, appears) and 129, a spell to make a man excellent and allow him to join Re in his bark. The preserved decoration in the tomb of Ramses IX includes Spells 125 and 126.

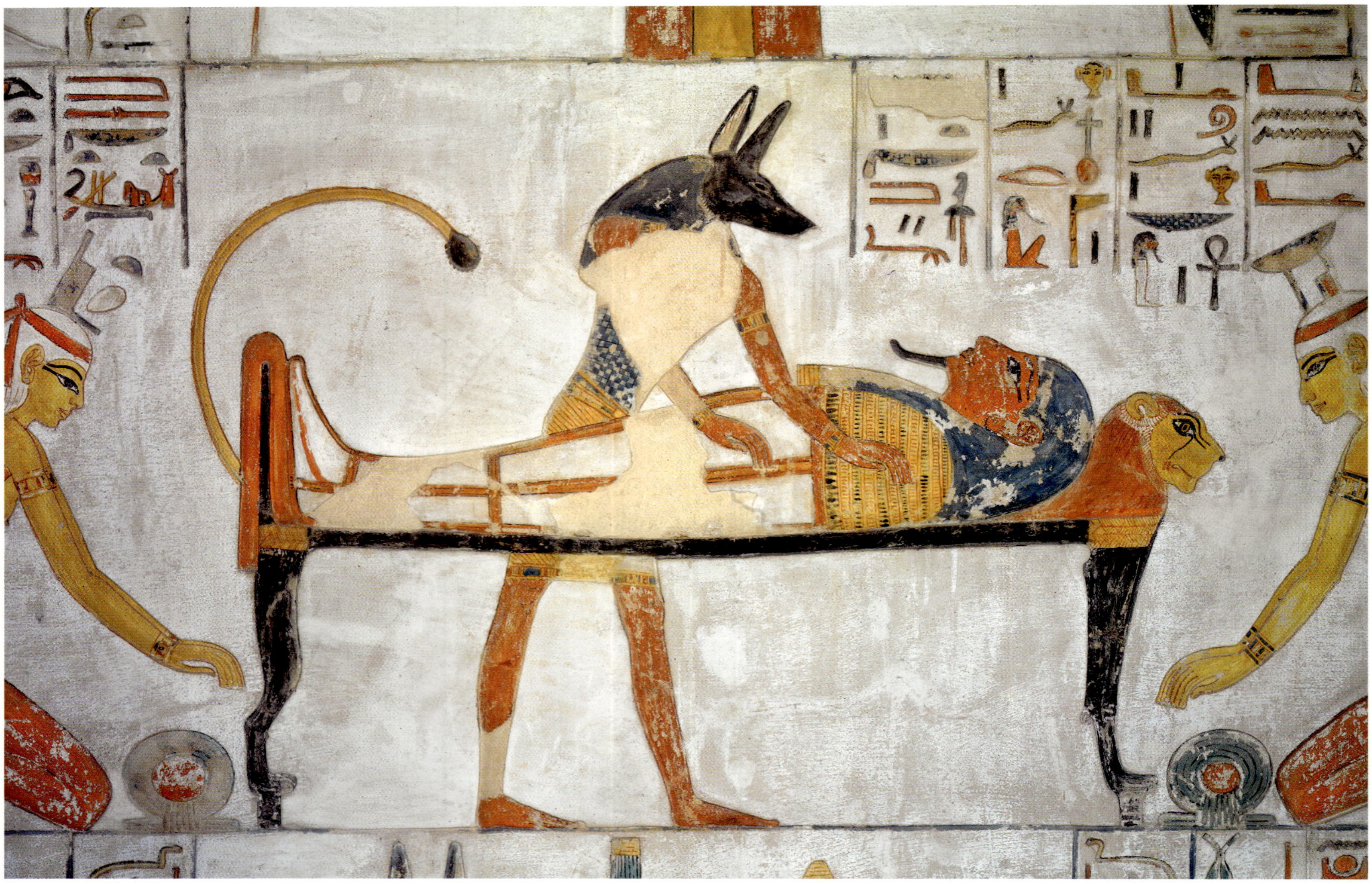

Embalming the King
One of the many vignettes associated with Spell 151 shows Anubis tending to a royal mummy that lies upon a leonine bed, with Isis and Nephthys standing by.

The Tomb of Aye
The south wall of Aye's burial chamber is inscribed and illustrated with spells from the Book of the Dead (Spells 130, 141, 142, and 142). Above are two boats: in front is Nephthys and the solar bark bearing the Ennead of nine gods (Re-Horakhty, Atum, Shu, Tefnut, Geb, Nut, Osiris, Isis, and Horus); behind is a bark containing two falcon standards, with a reed mat hung at the prow.

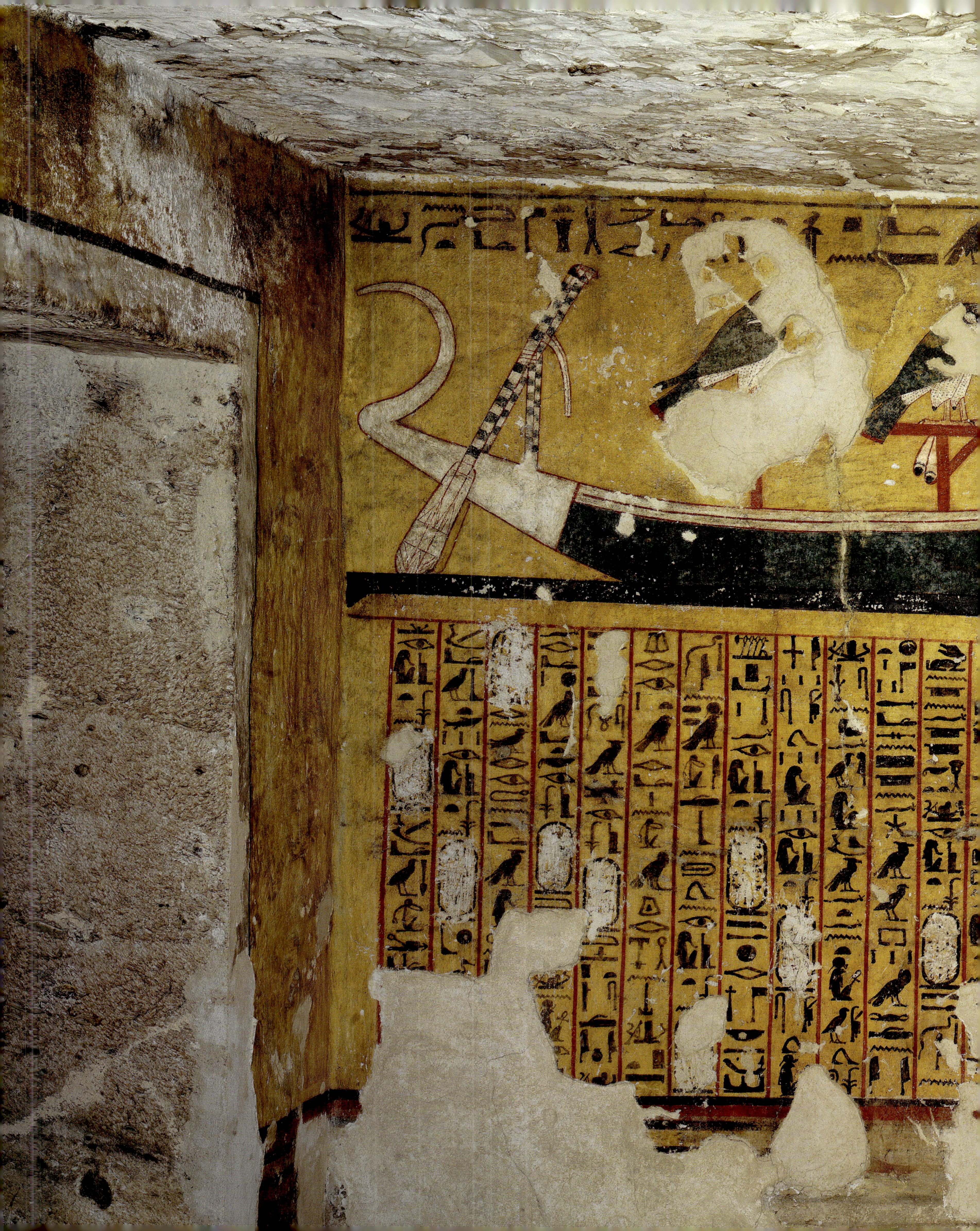

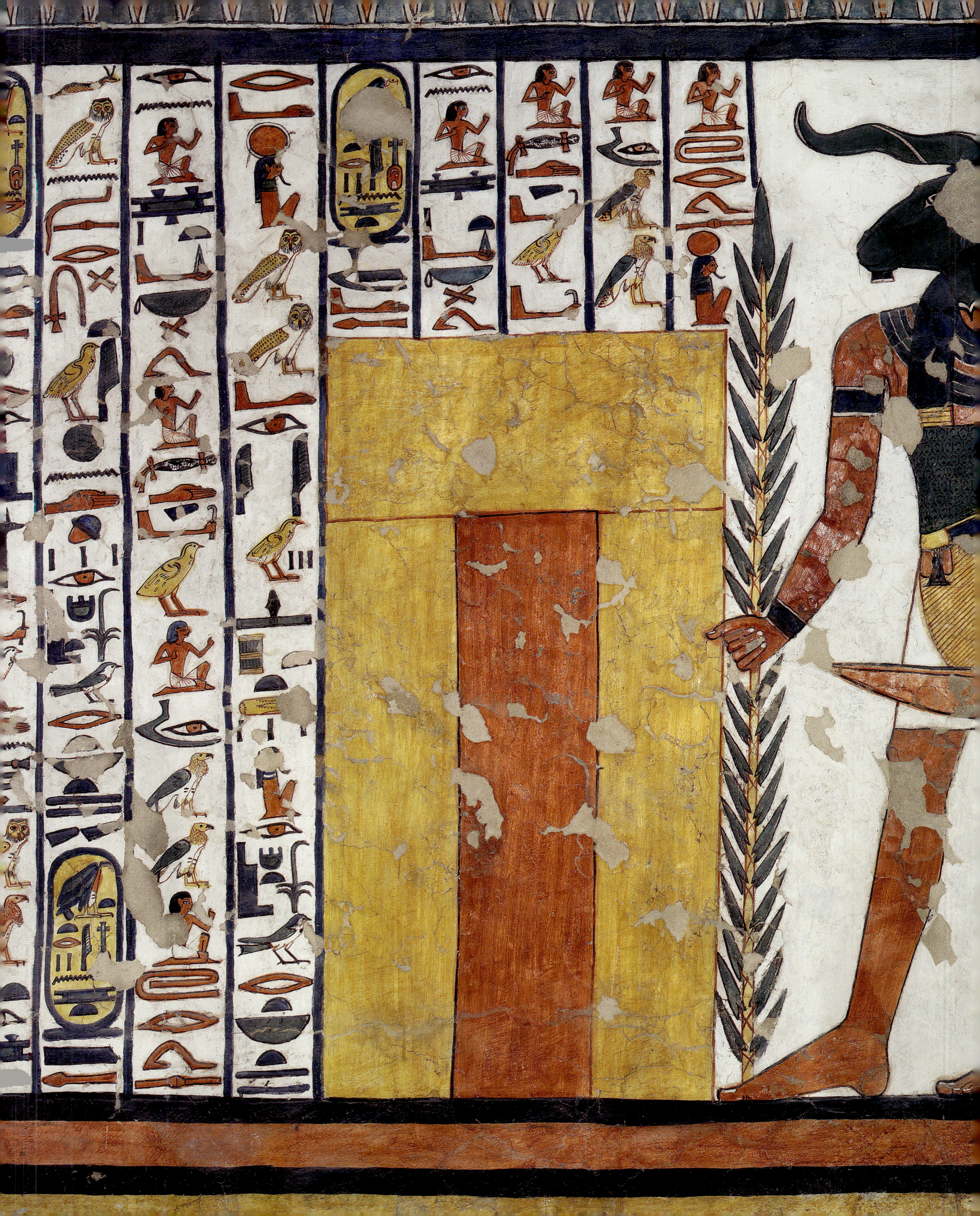

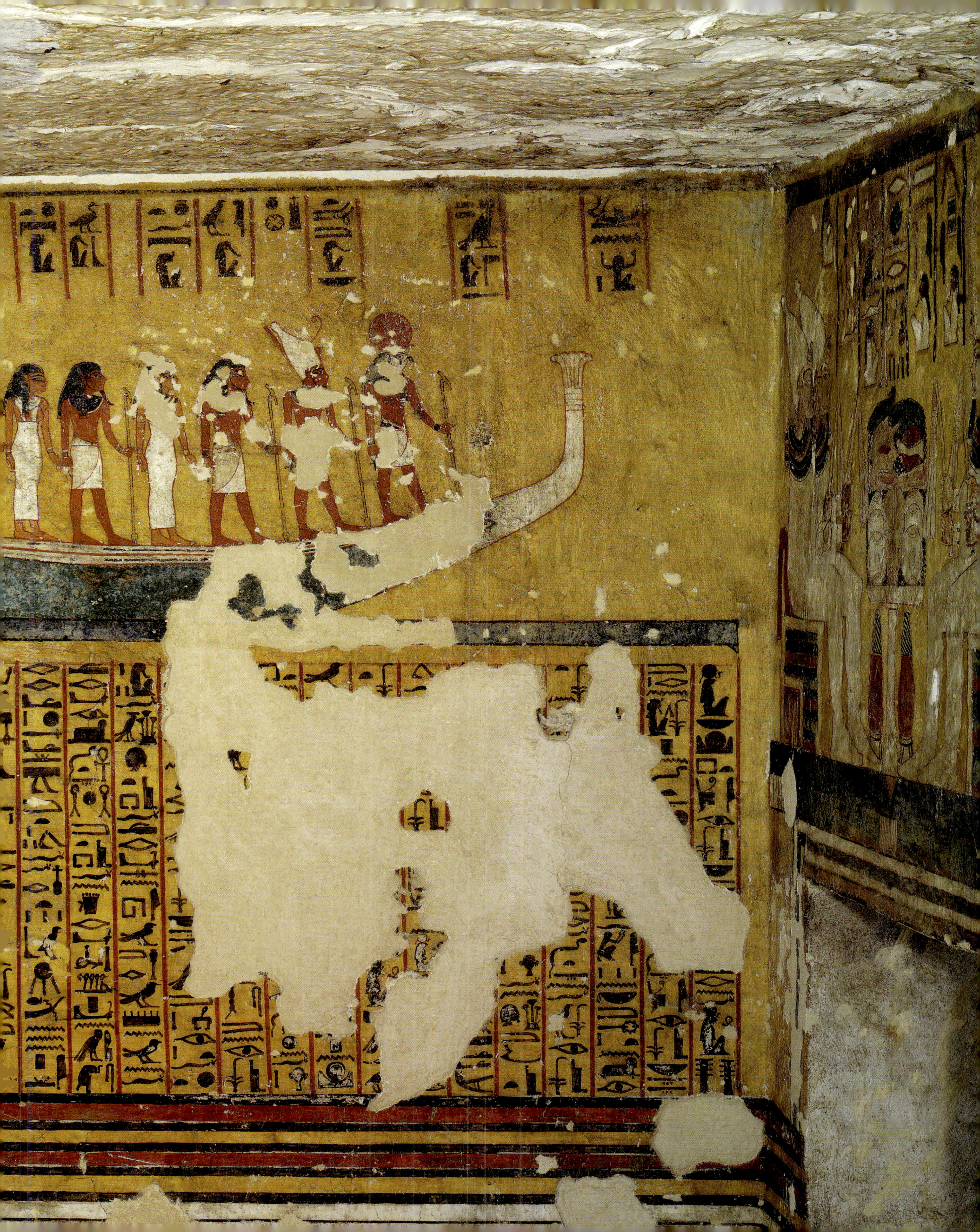

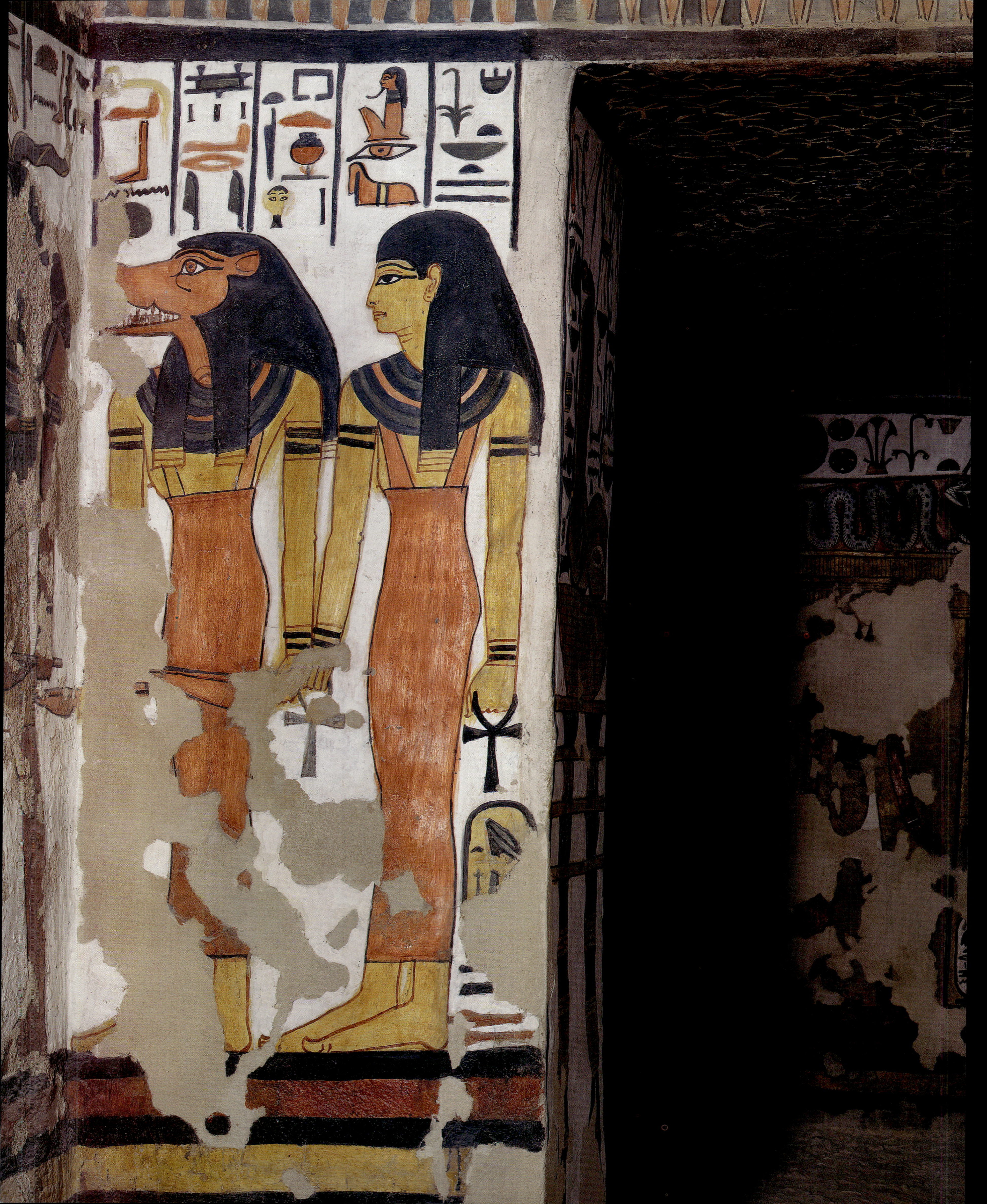

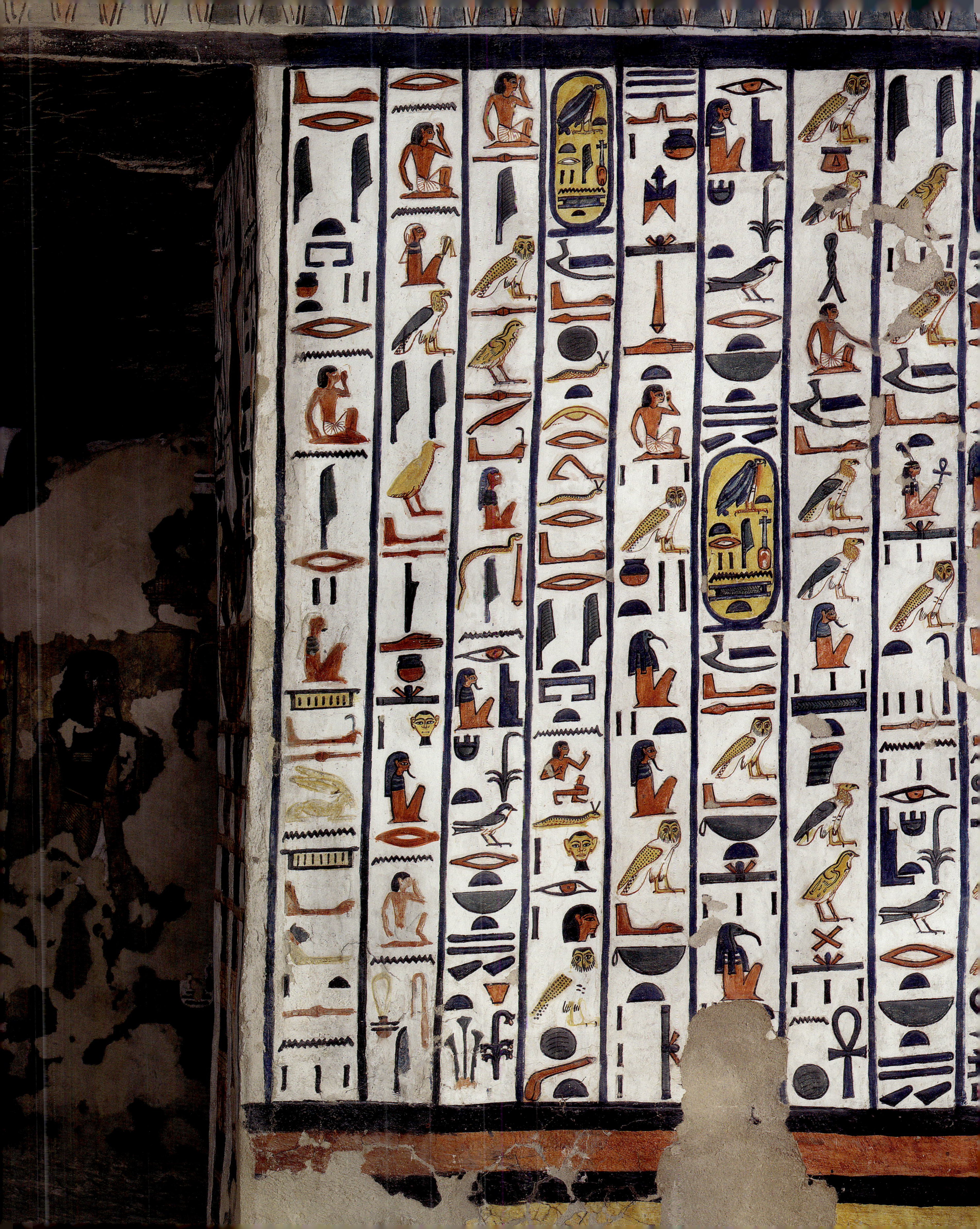

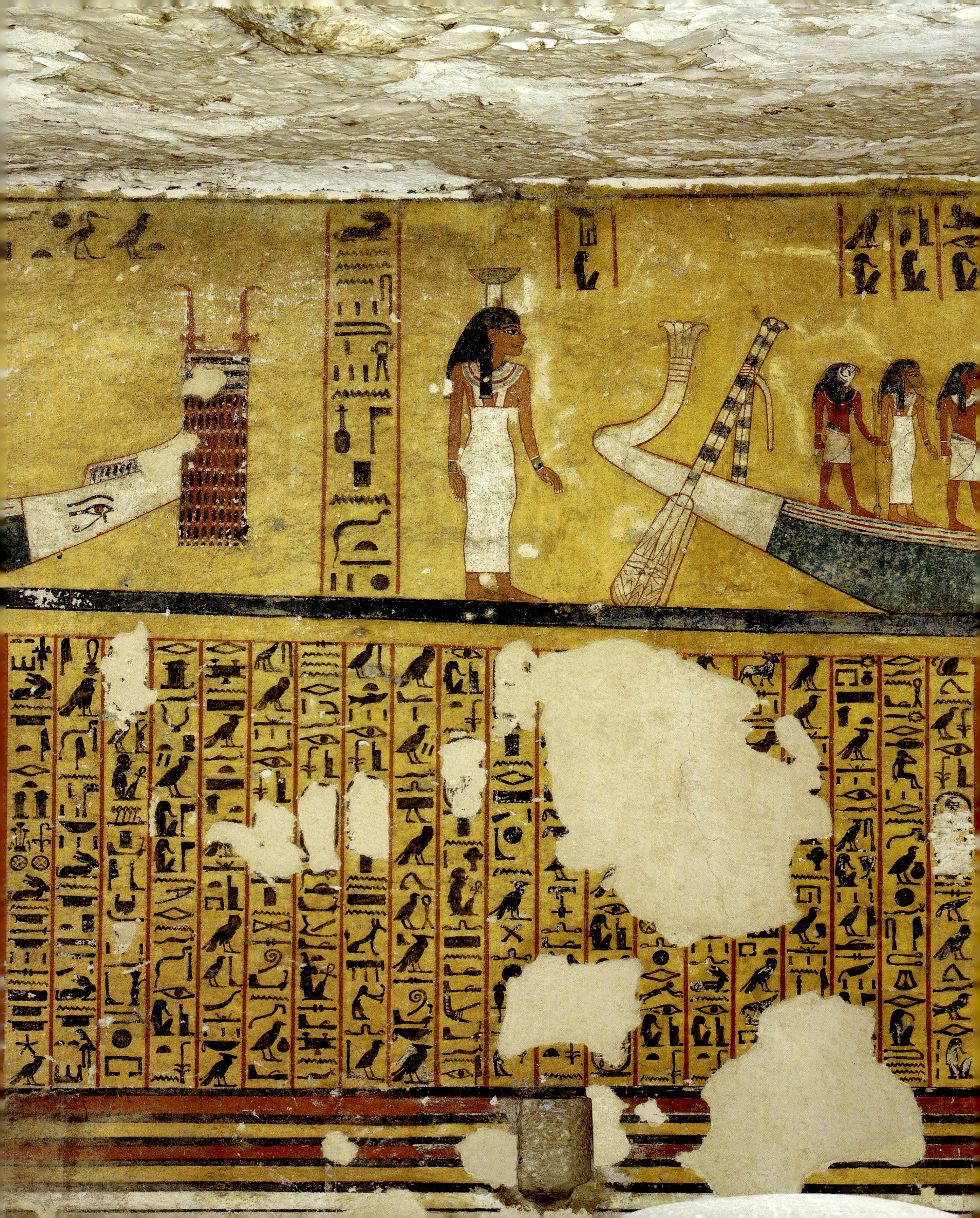

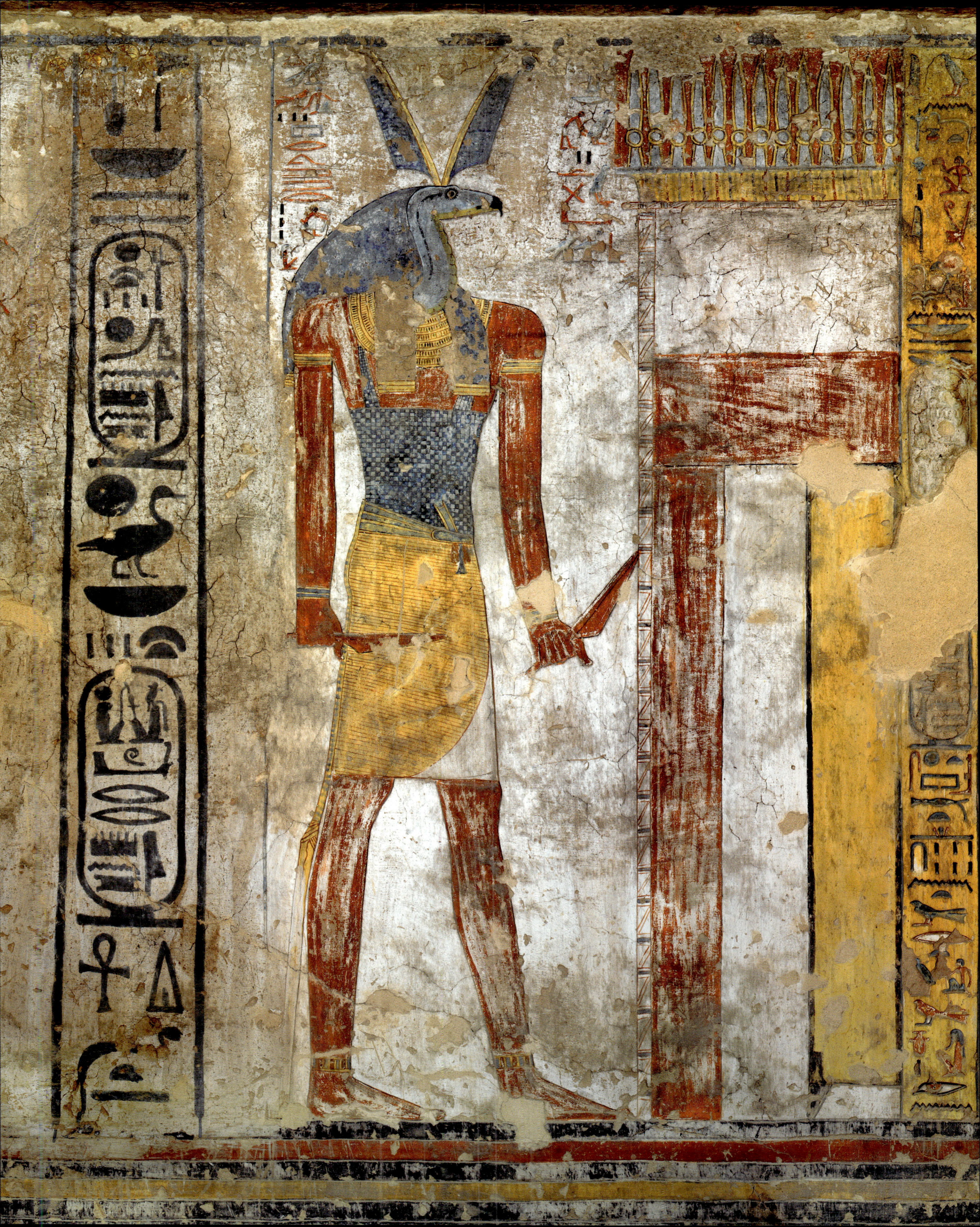

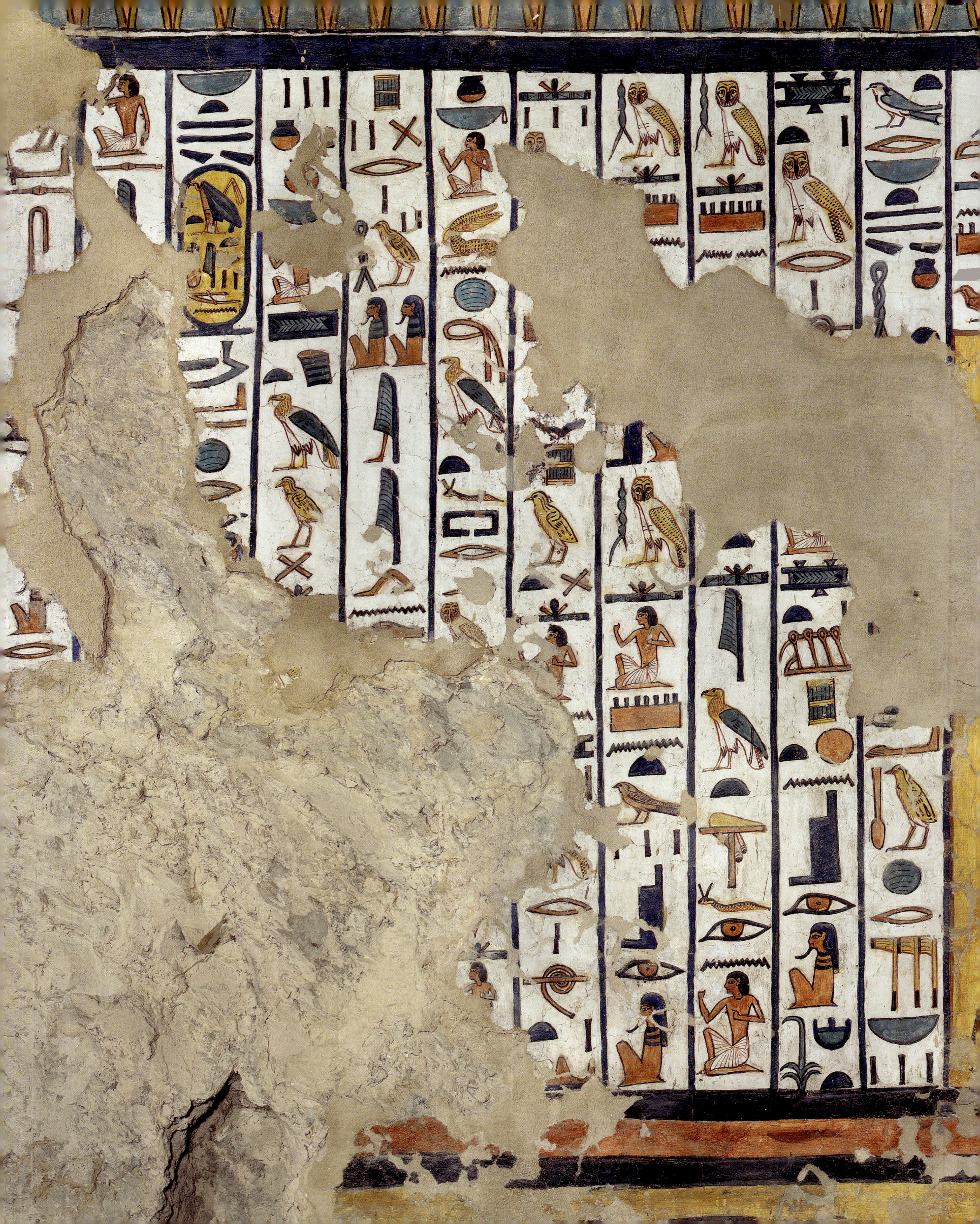

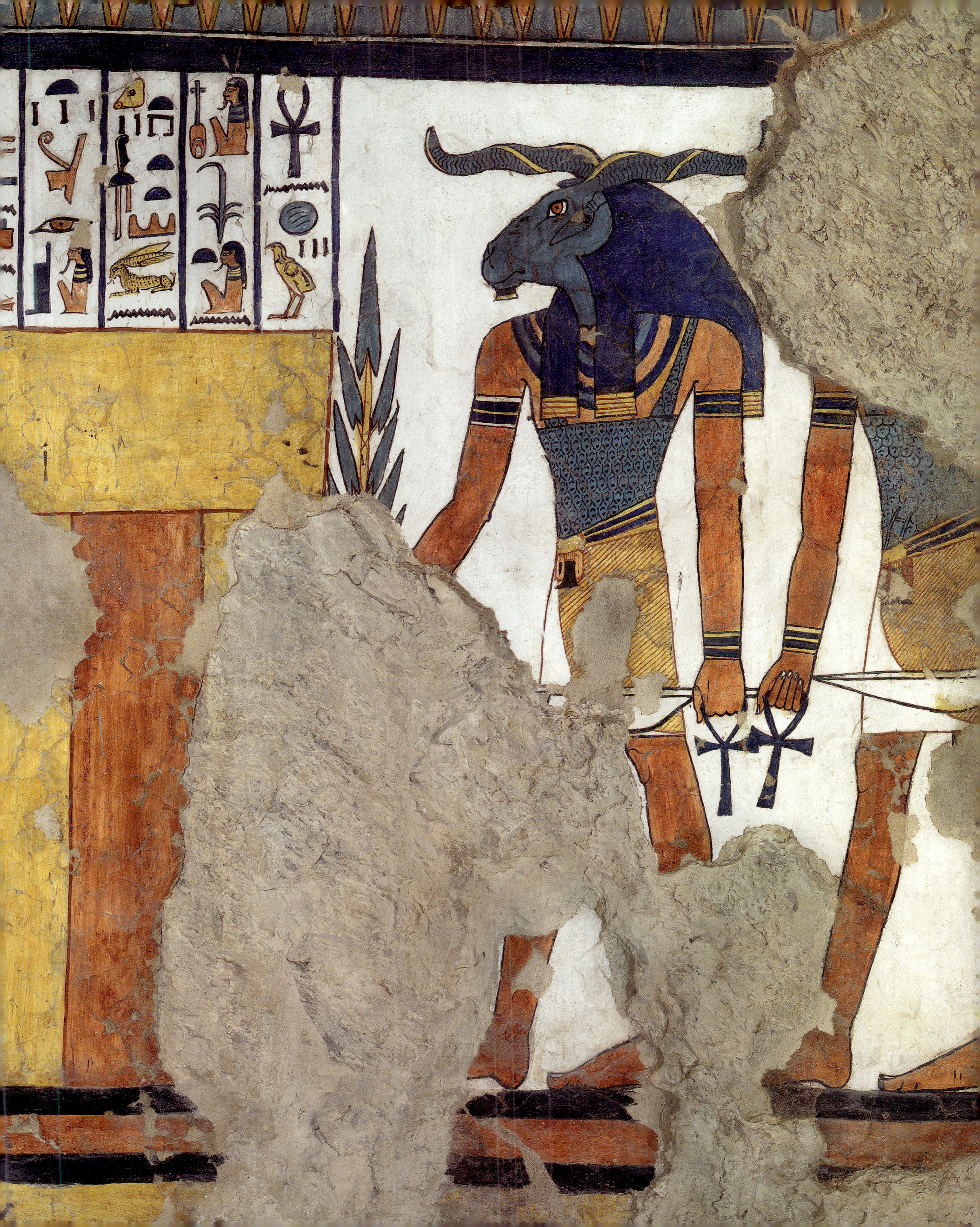

GUARDIANS OF THE GATES

(Preceding pages)

Groups of otherworldly deities are shown here on a wall from the tomb of Nefertari. Taken from Spell 144 of the Book of the Dead, they were the keepers of the gates of the Netherworld, menacing the enemies of order with their sharpened knives. In the center we see the three guardians of the first gate.

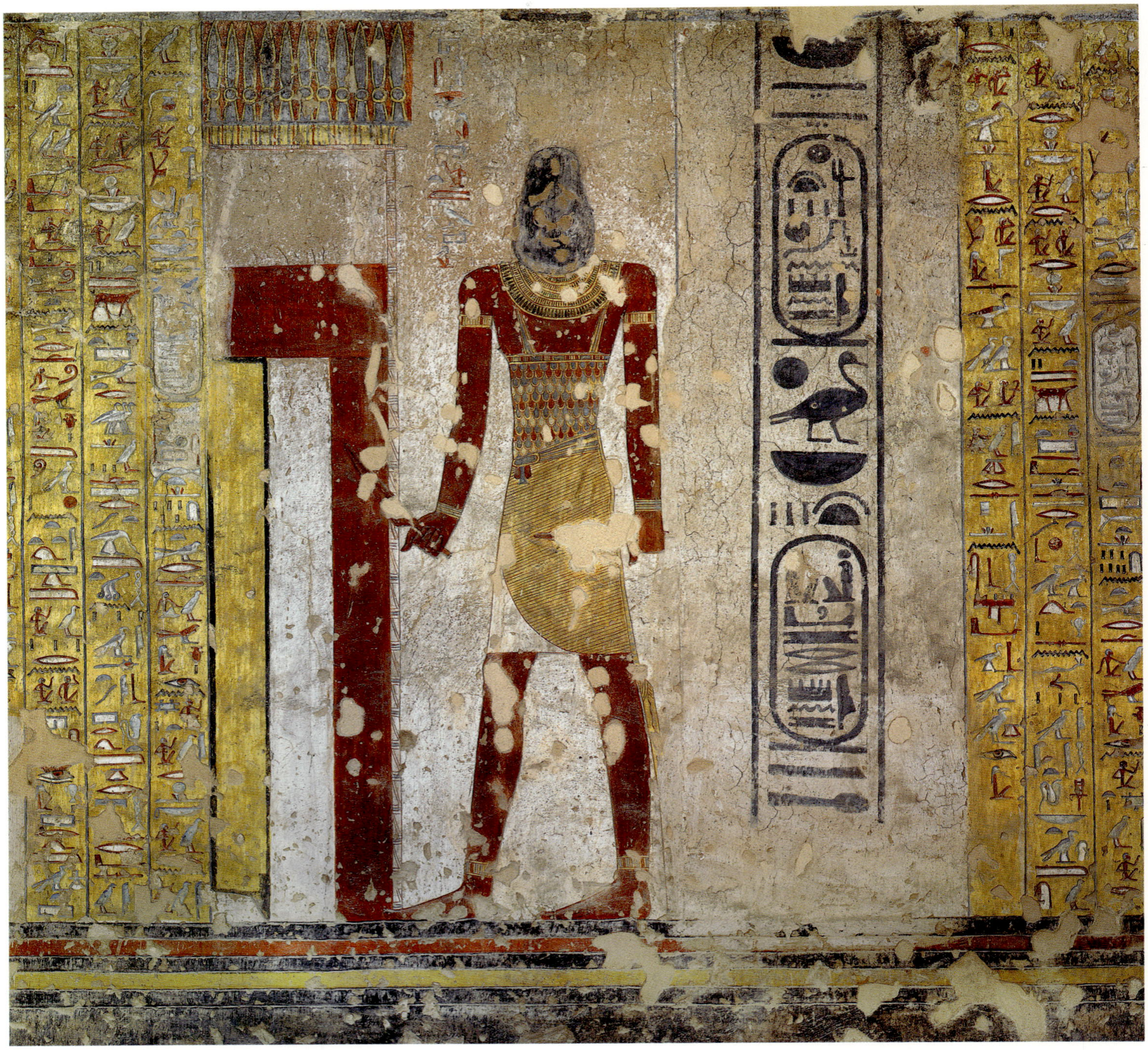

GATEKEEPERS OF ETERNITY

These two images illustrate several of the strange beings who guarded the gates of the Netherworld from Spell 145 of the Book of the Dead, standing in front of their respective gates and wielding knives to keep the enemies of the sun god away. On the left is the keeper of the fifteenth gate; on the right are the keepers of the fifteenth and sixteenth gates, with King Sethnakht standing between them.

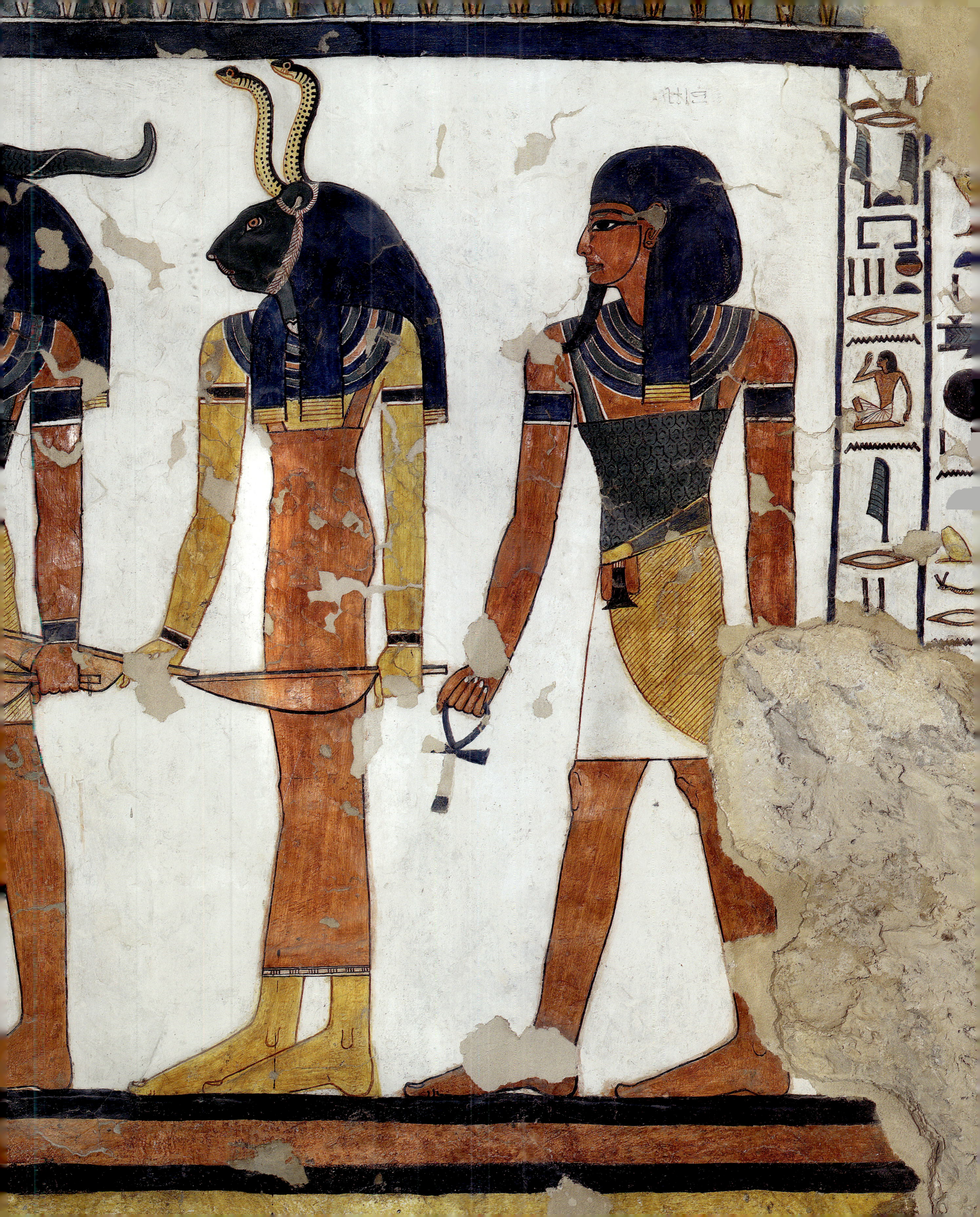

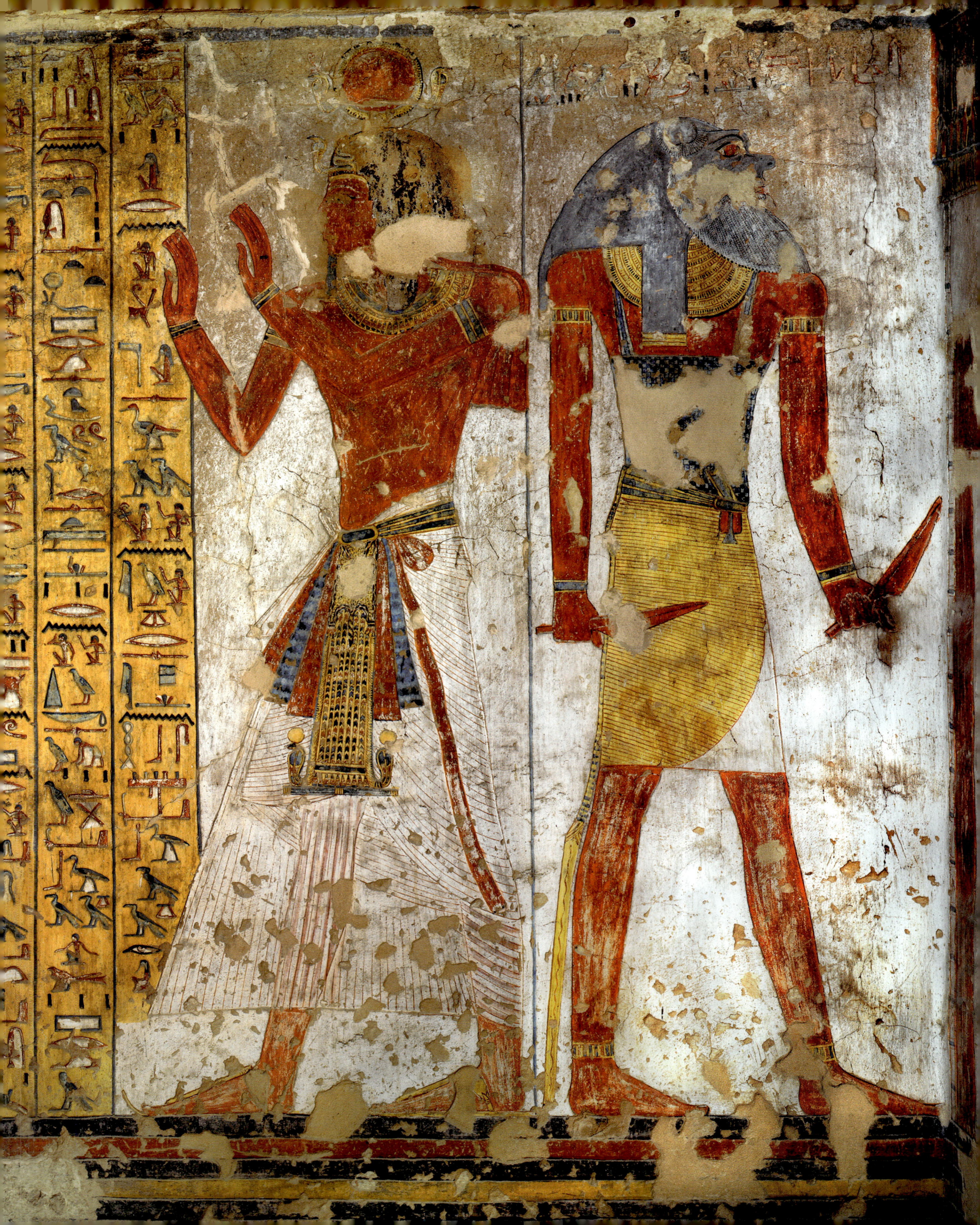

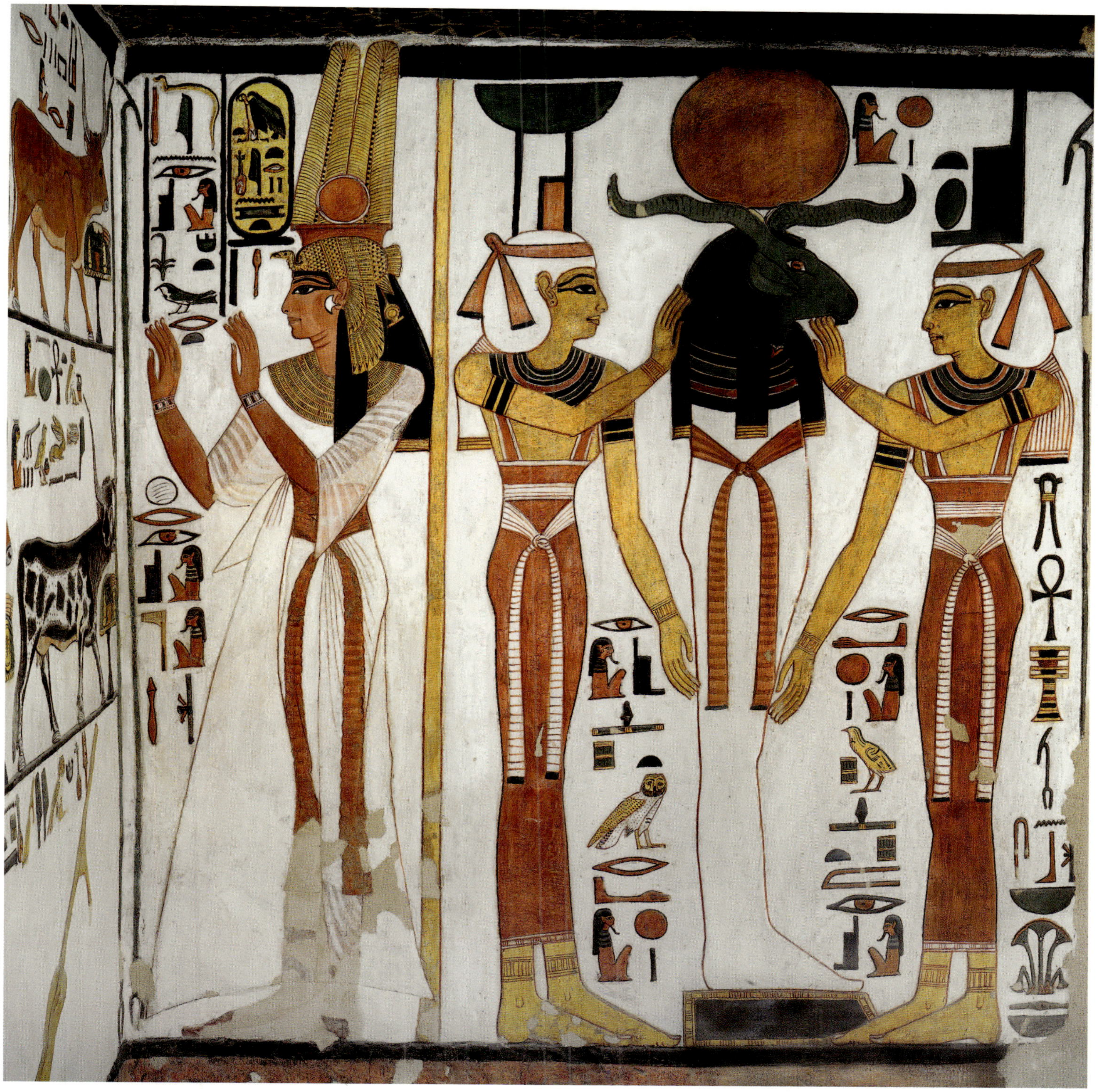

UNION OF RE AND OSIRIS
This image from the Litany of Re shows the unified Re and Osiris, tended by Nephthys (*left*) and Isis (*right*).

THE CELESTIAL CATTLE
(*Following pages*)
In this illustration of Spell 148, Nefertari (visible on adjacent wall) worships seven heavenly cows and one sacred bull. Beneath the cattle are four steering oars, each representing one of the four corners of the sky. The spell itself deals with the provisioning of the dead.

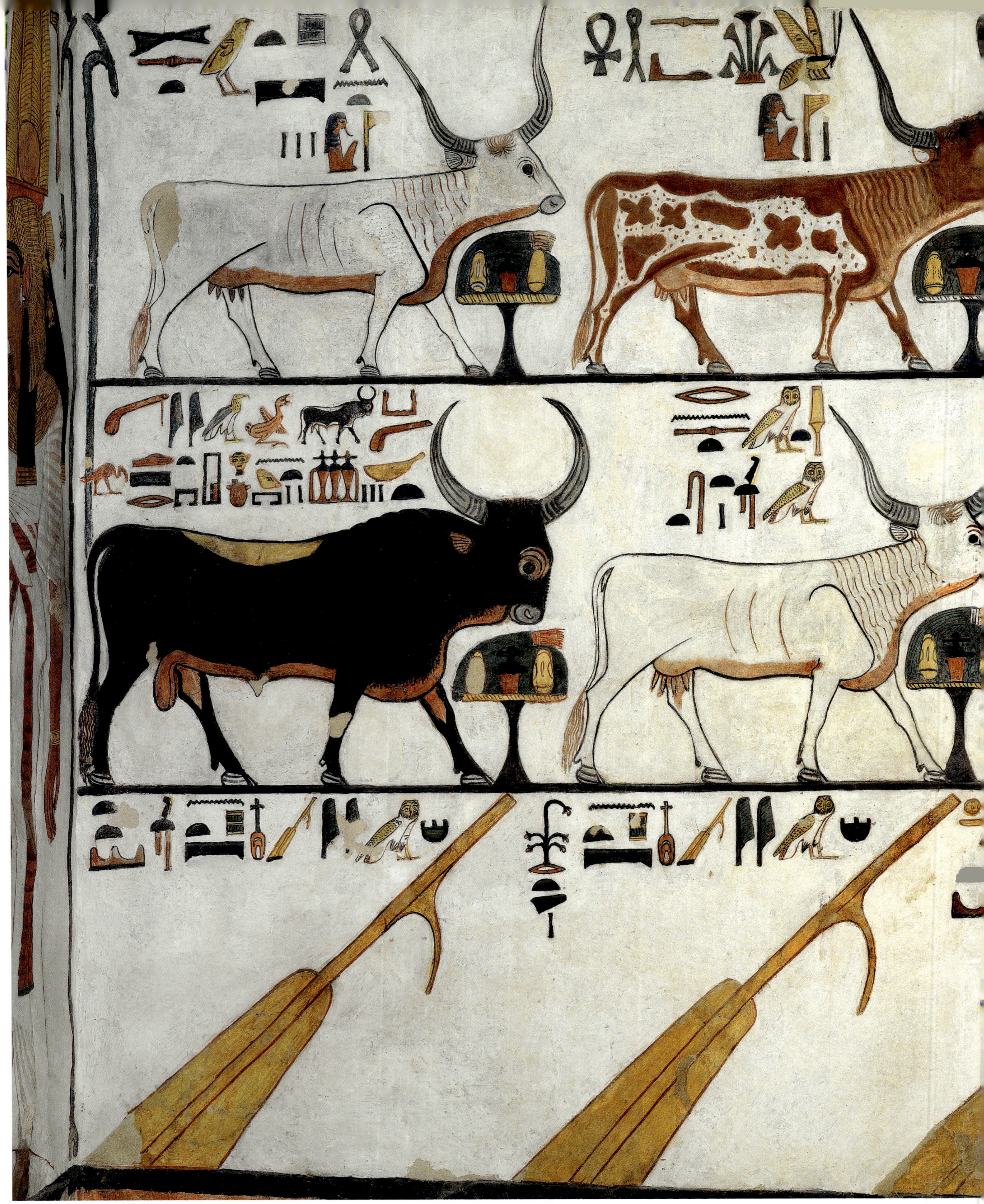

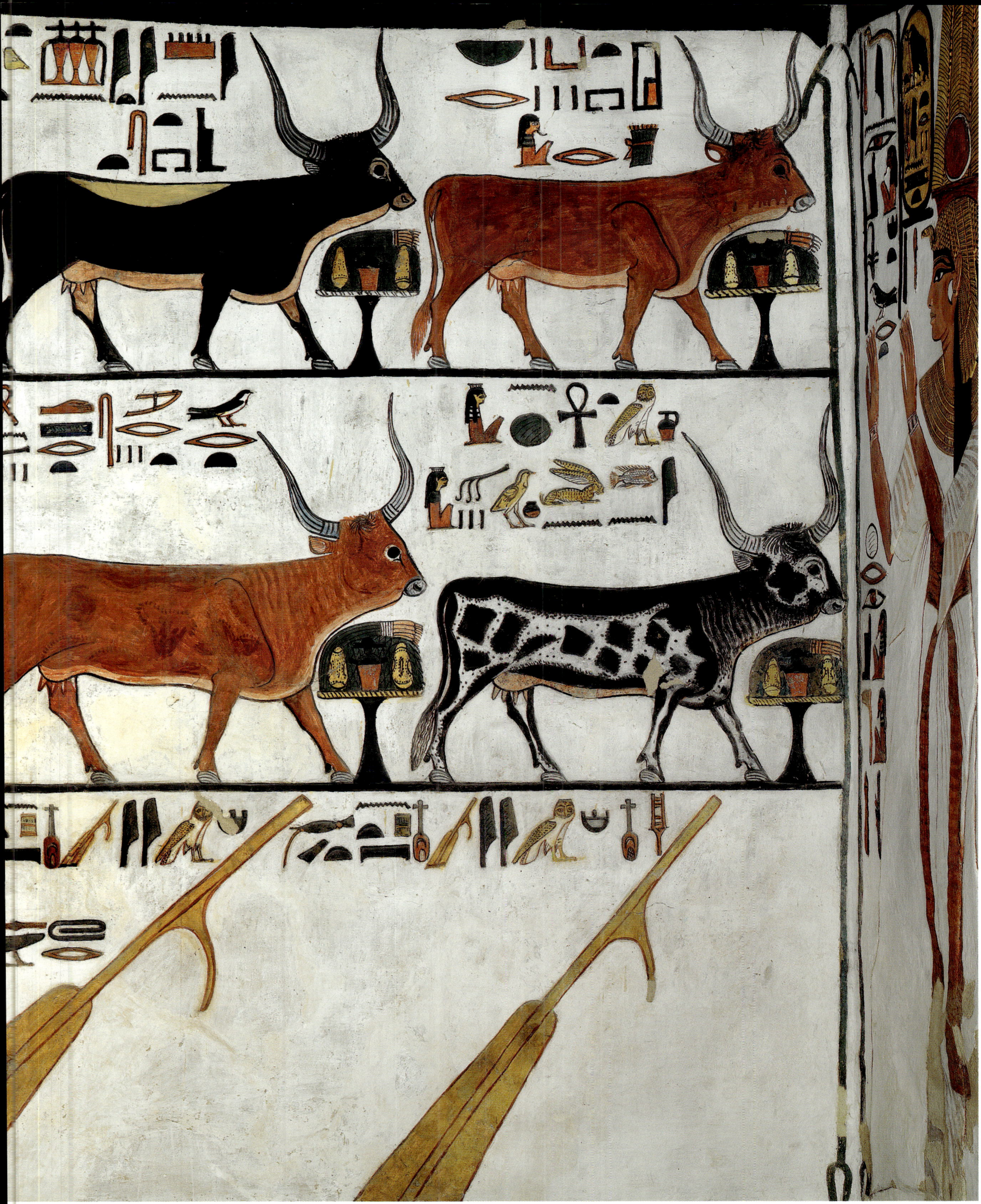

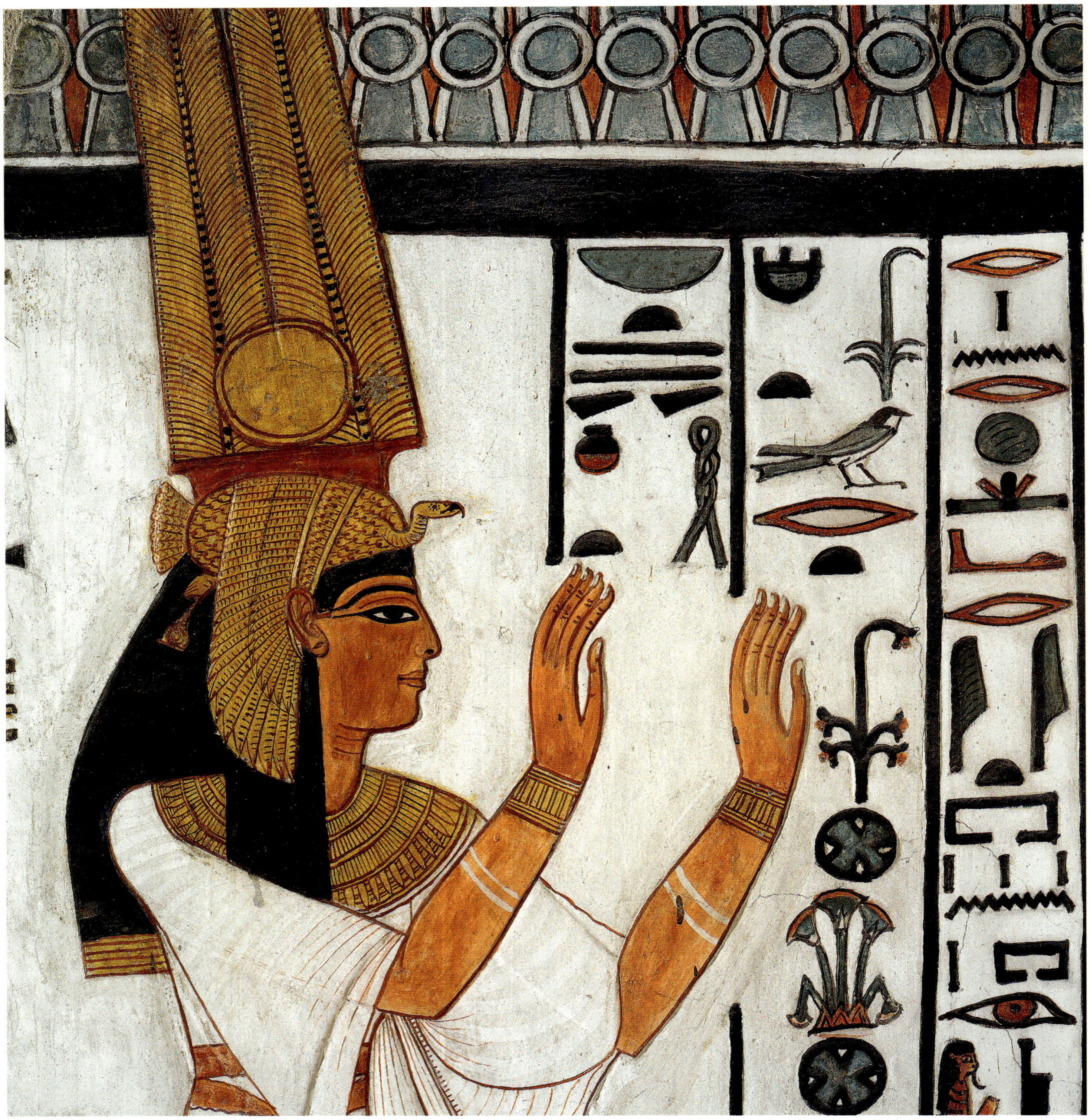

NEFERTARI WORSHIPPING
In another beautiful vignette from her exquisite tomb, Nefertari is shown raising her hands in an attitude of adoration.

NEFERTARI AND THOTH
Spell 94 of the Book of the Dead ensures that the deceased will know the mysteries of Thoth in the Afterlife. Here Nefertari is shown with the ibis-headed patron god of scribes, the water-pot and palette from a writing kit shown on the stand between them, along with a frog that represents eternity.

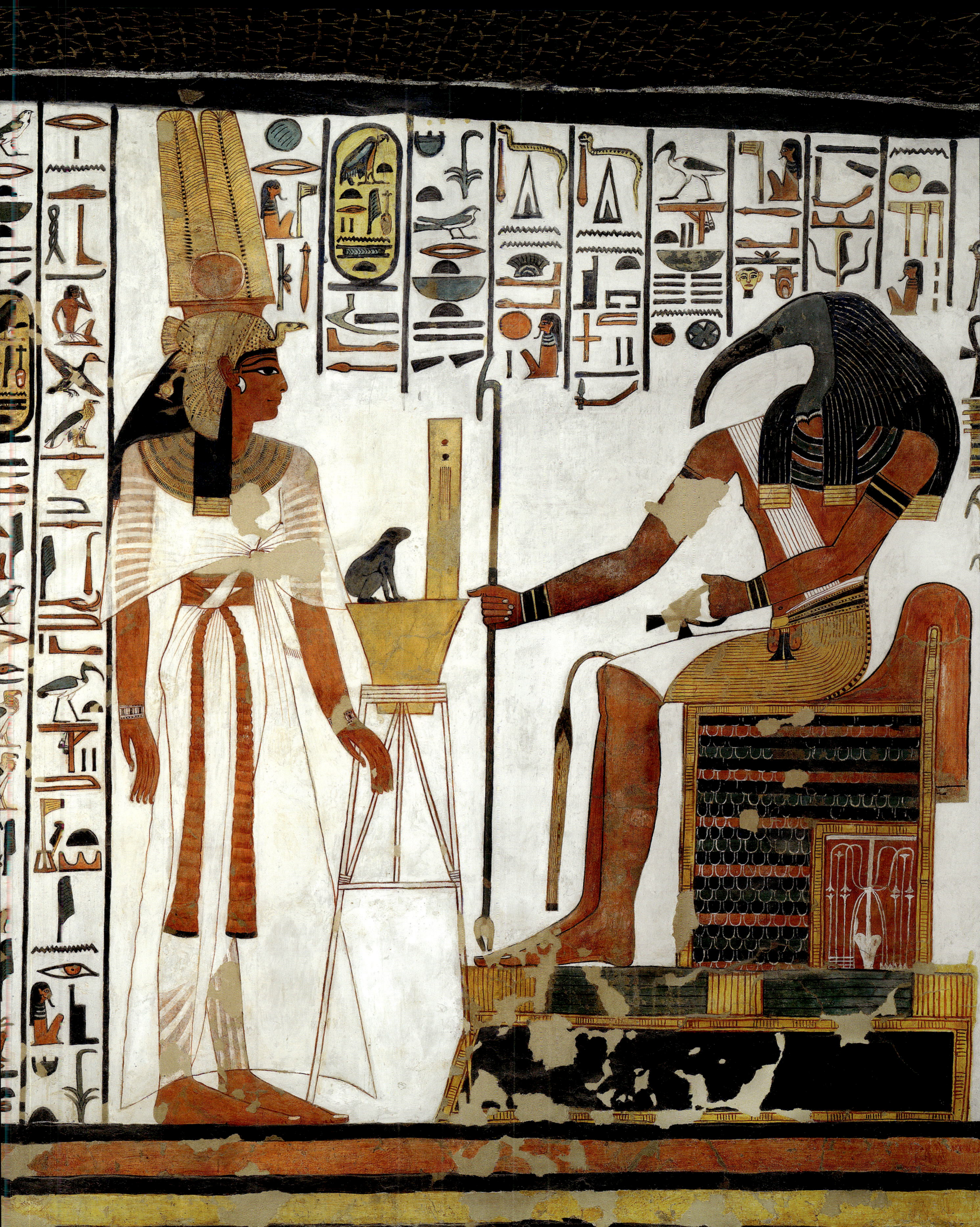

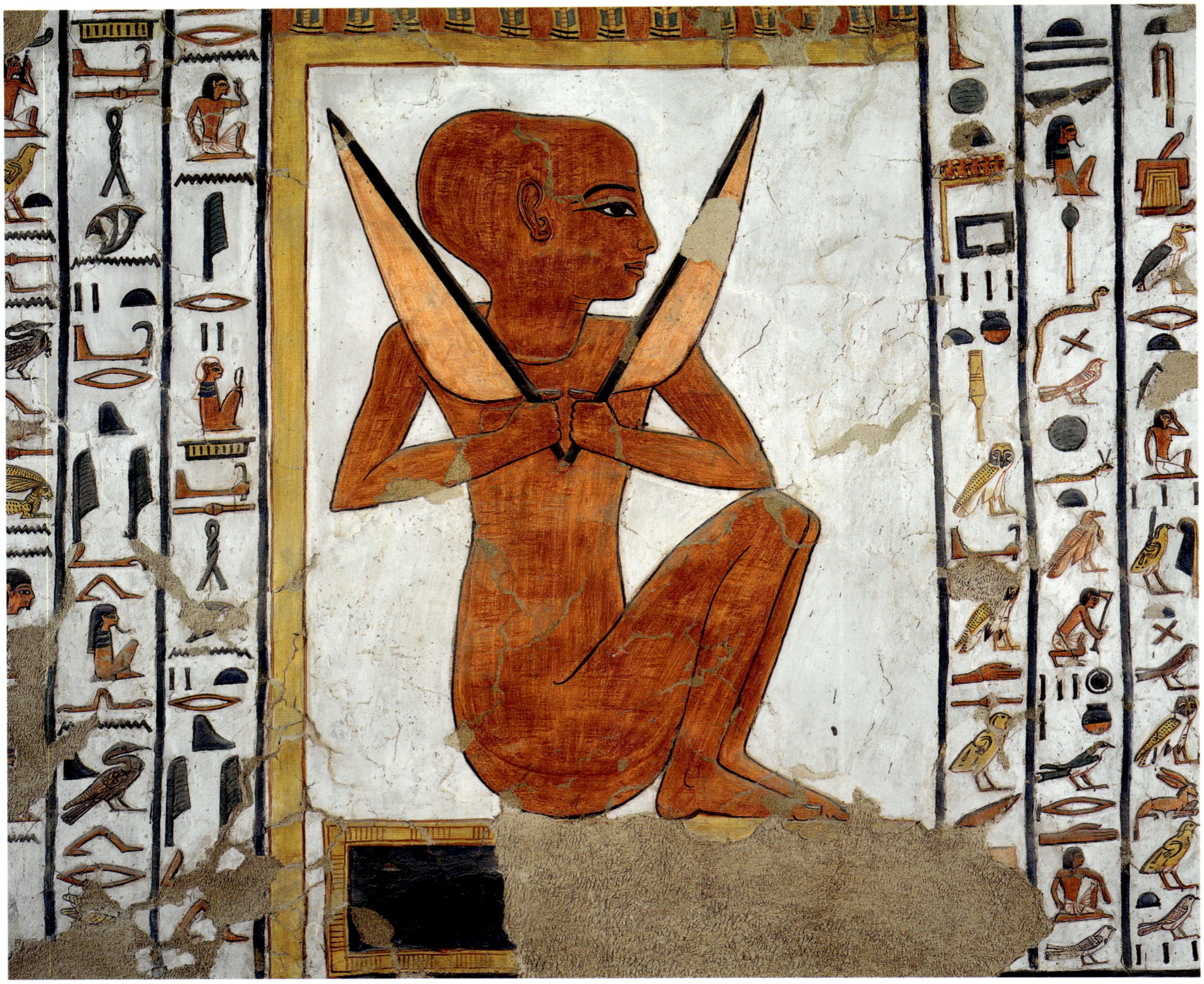

The God Henty-Reky
Another of the guardians of the Netherworld gates (in this case the fifth, from Spell 146) was this child god named Henty-Reky ("he who drives away the enemy"), seated and holding two knives. In order to pass these gatekeepers and enter the Fields of the Blessed, the deceased had to know their names.

The Goddess Serket
One of the goddesses who kept watch over the body of the deceased was Serket, the scorpion. Her primary duty was to guard Qebehsenuef, the god who protected the intestines of the deceased.

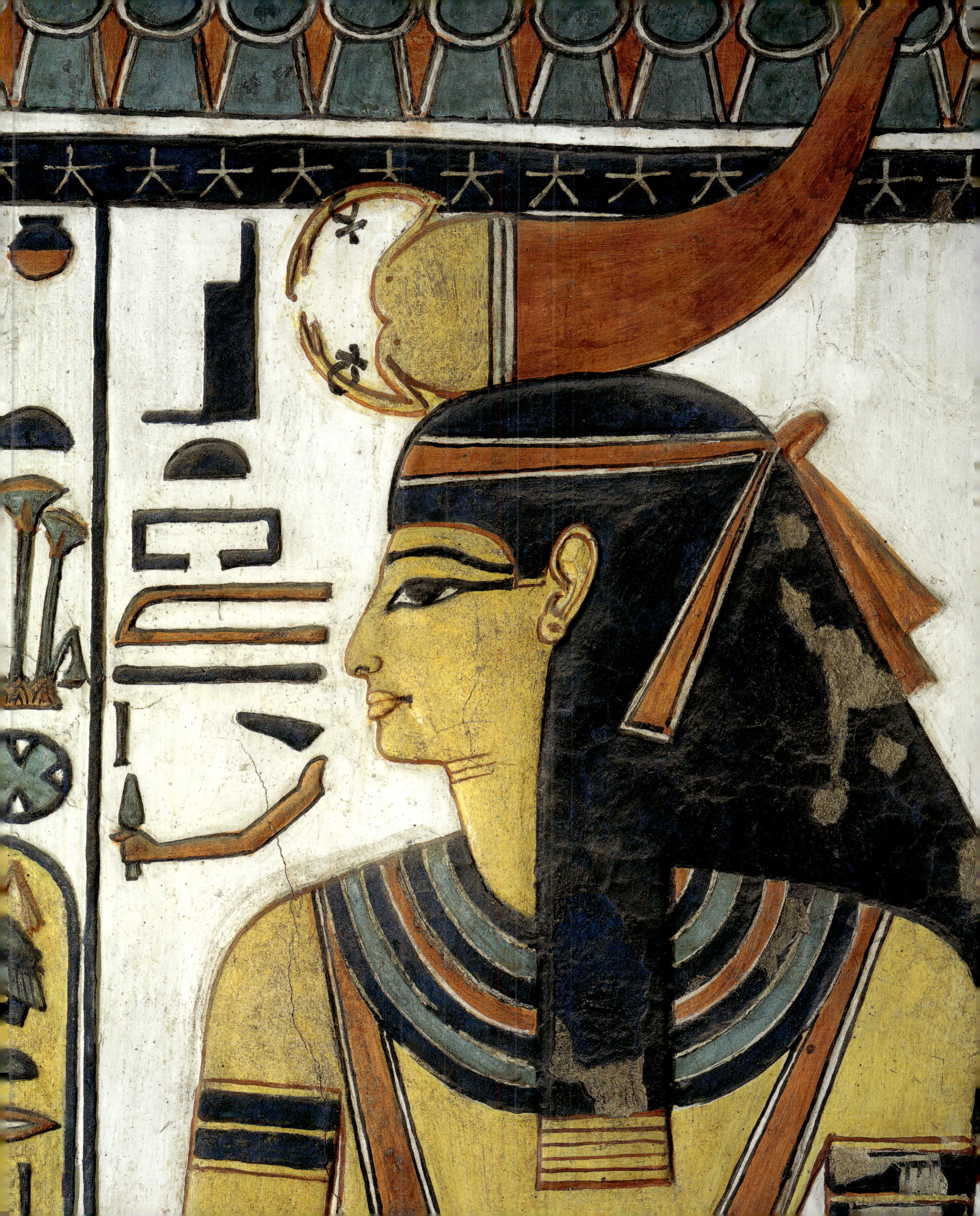

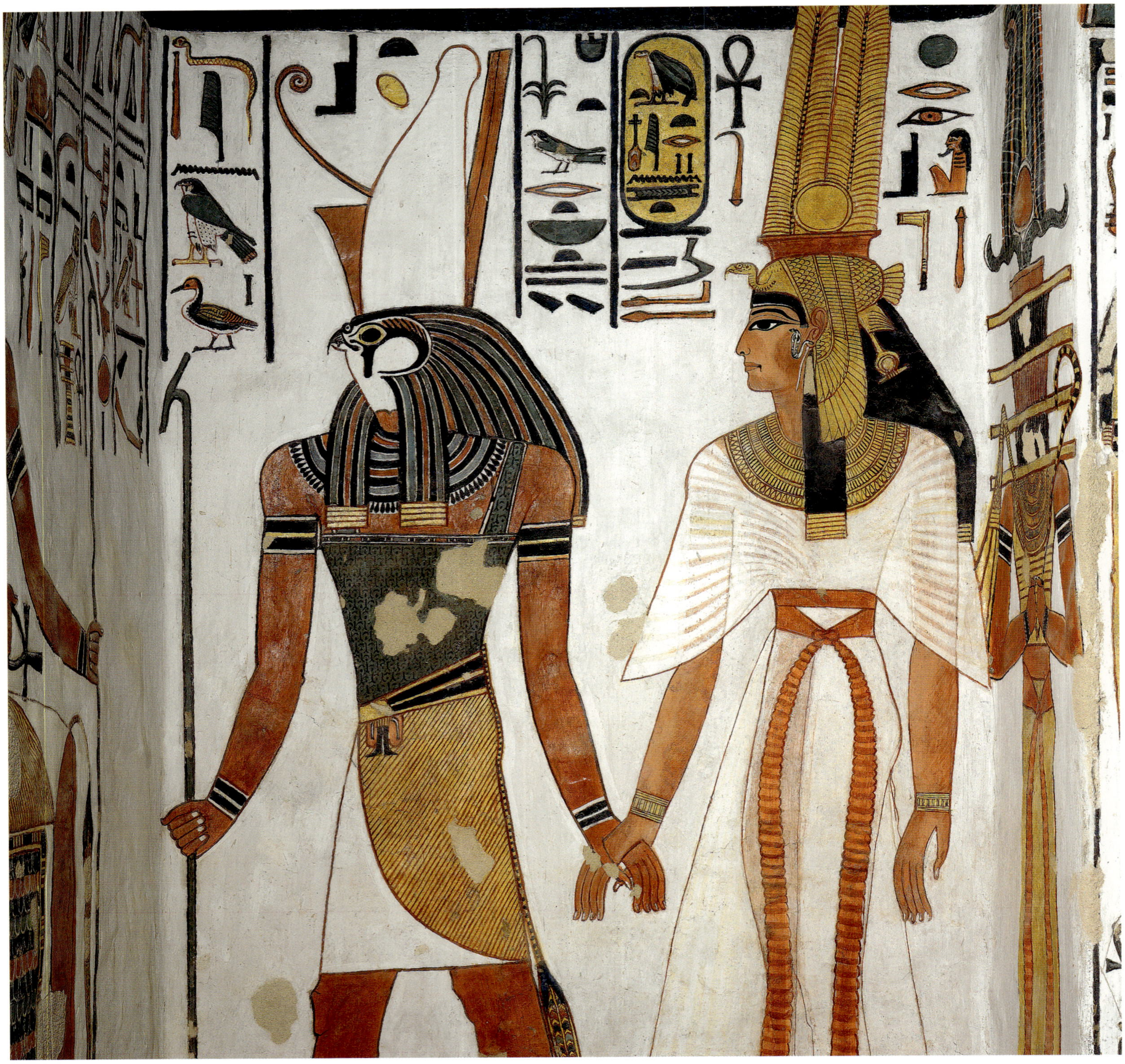

NEFERTARI AND HARSIESE
Horus, son of Isis (Harsiese in ancient Egyptian), is shown here leading Queen Nefertari to meet Re-Horakhty and Hathor, Mistress of the West, who are seated on the adjacent wall (not visible here).

SPELLS FROM THE BOOK OF THE DEAD
(*Following pages*)
These two vignettes from the tomb of Ramses V/VI illustrate Spells 126, 127, and 129 from the Book of the Dead. On the left, the king (here Ramses VI) raises his hands to worship Ma'at; on the right, the king worships baboons who sit encircling the Lakes of Fire.

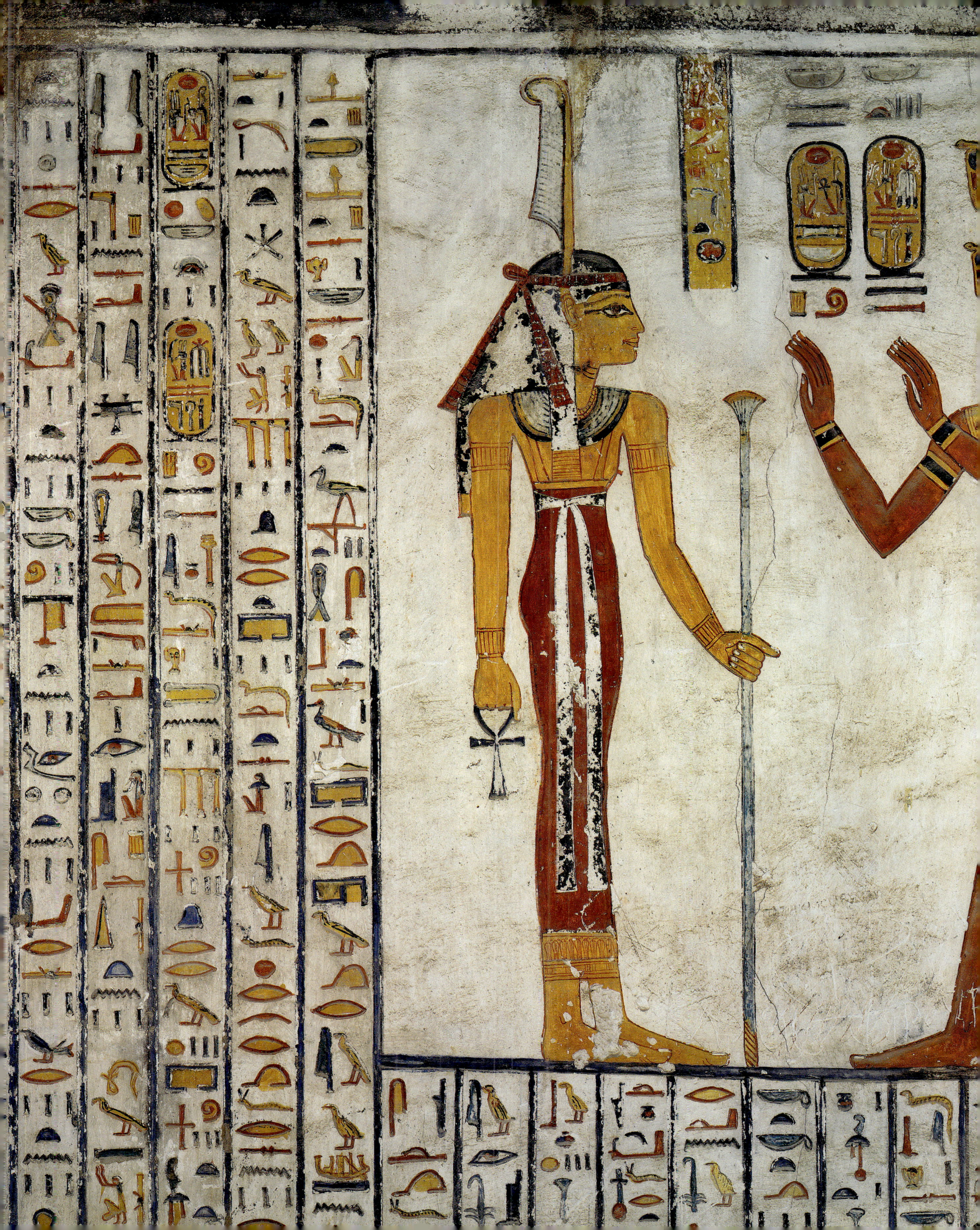

NEFERTARI AND HER BA
(Preceding pages)
To the right of the vignette in which Nefertari plays *senet*, Nefertari's *ba* stands on a shrine; in the final image here, the queen kneels and raises her hands in an attitude of worship.

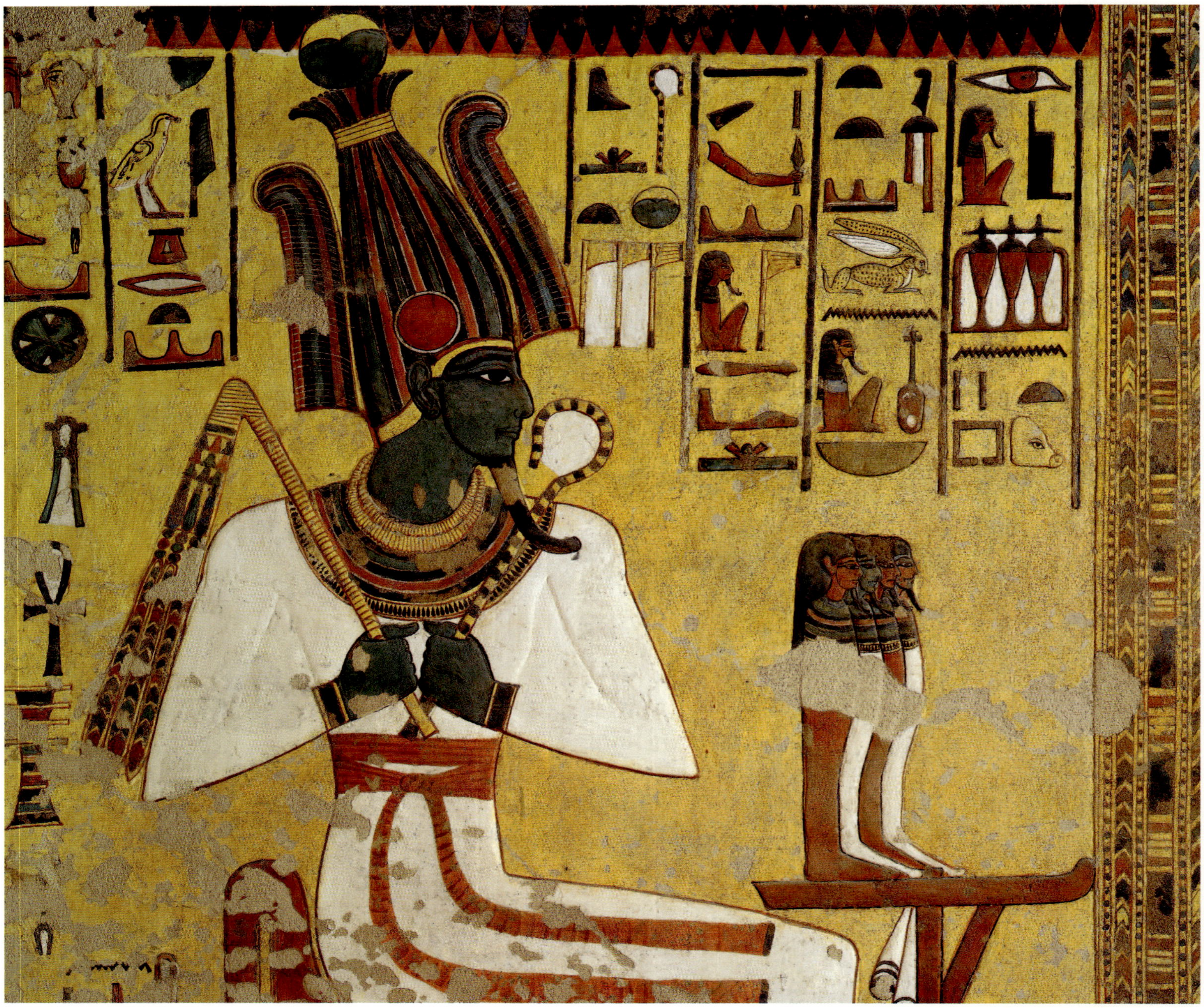

OSIRIS AND THE SONS OF HORUS
In this image from the tomb of Nefertari, Osiris is seated on a throne, his plumed *atef* crown brightly striped. Around his waist, like Nefertari herself in the images to the left, he wears a red sash. Before him, on a standard, are the four sons of Horus, all with human heads.

HIEROGLYPHS
(Following page)
In the center of this inscription from the tomb of Queen Nefertari is her name within a royal cartouche, preceded by her titles: "Great royal wife, Mistress of the Two Lands, Nefertari, justified before Osiris."

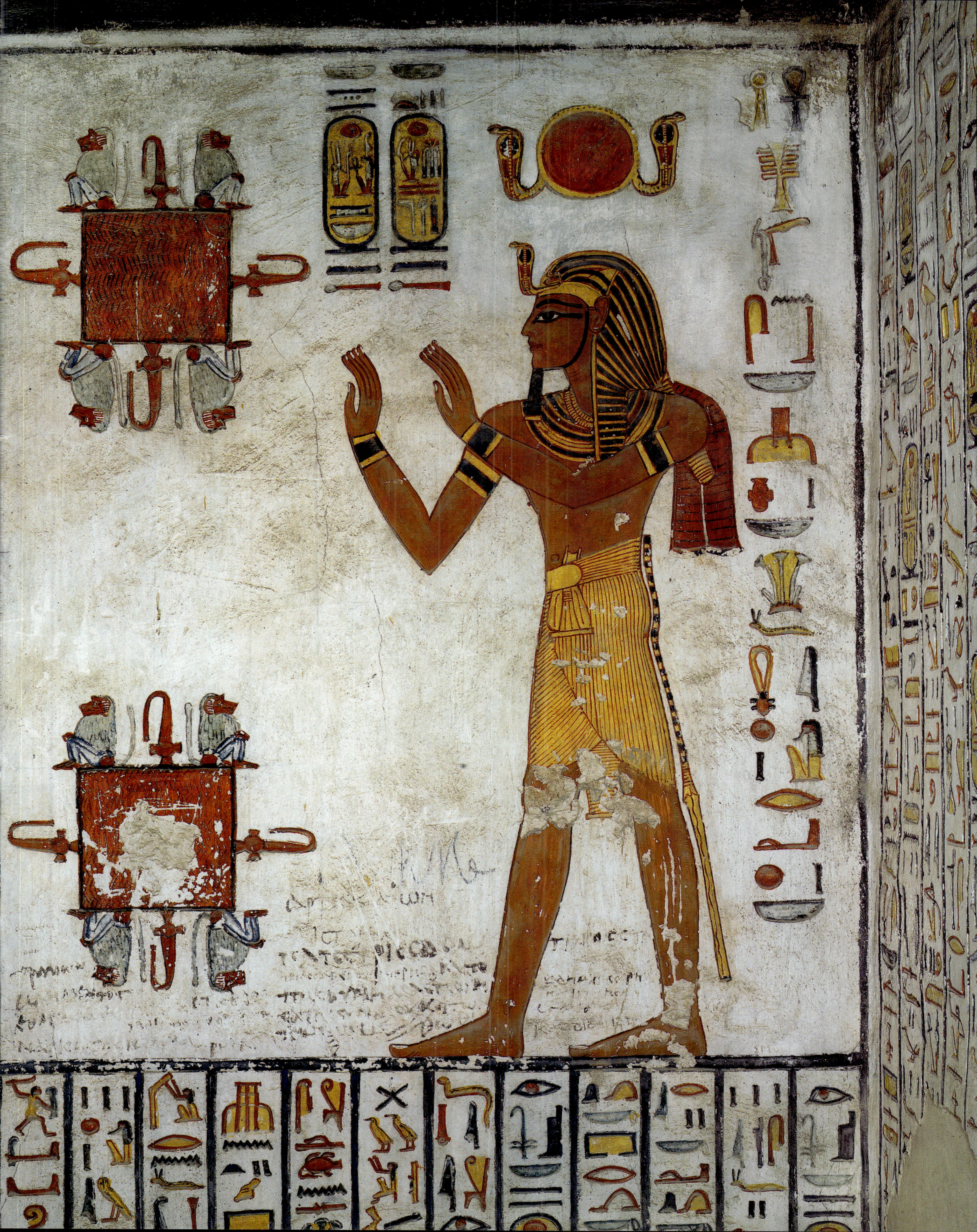

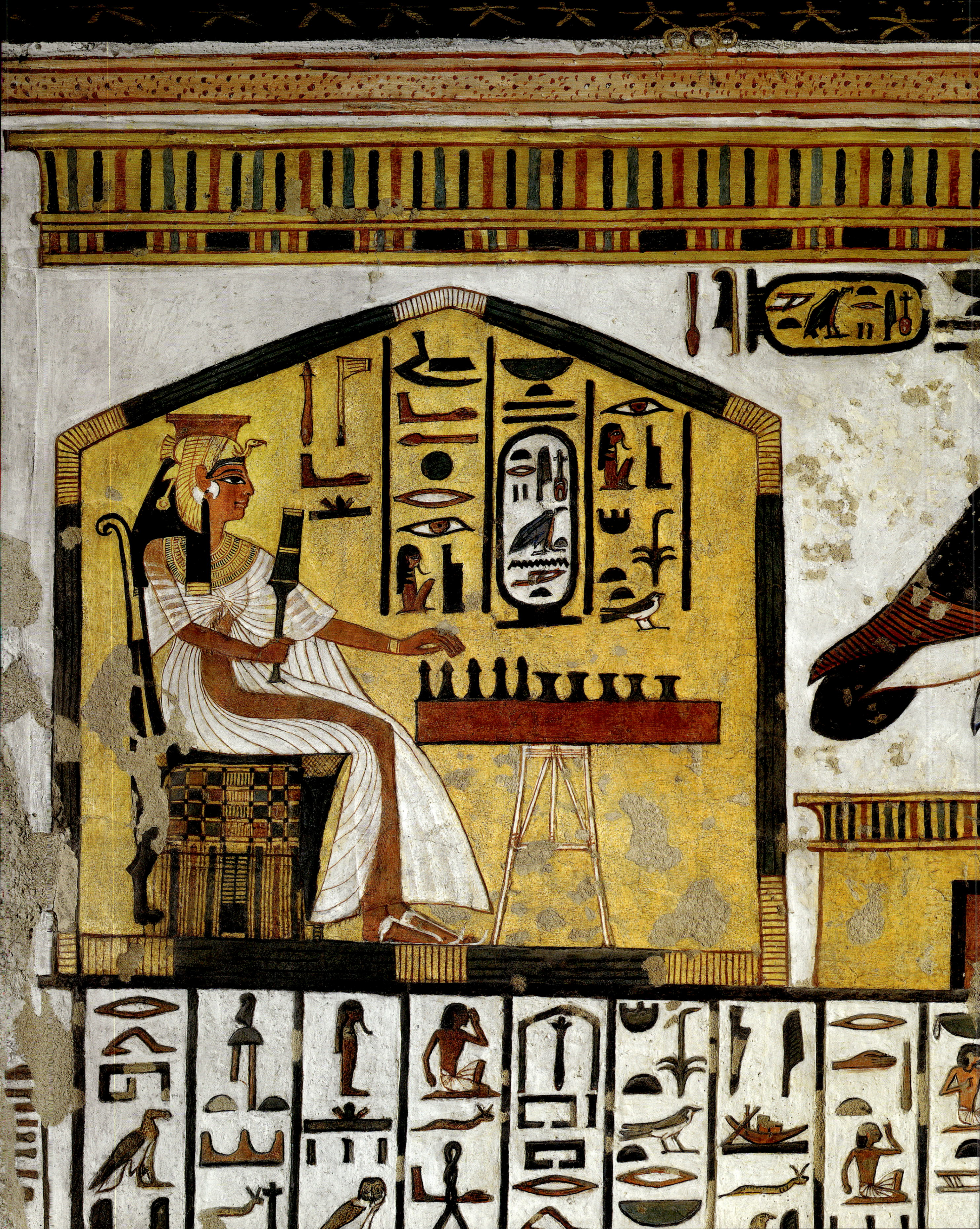

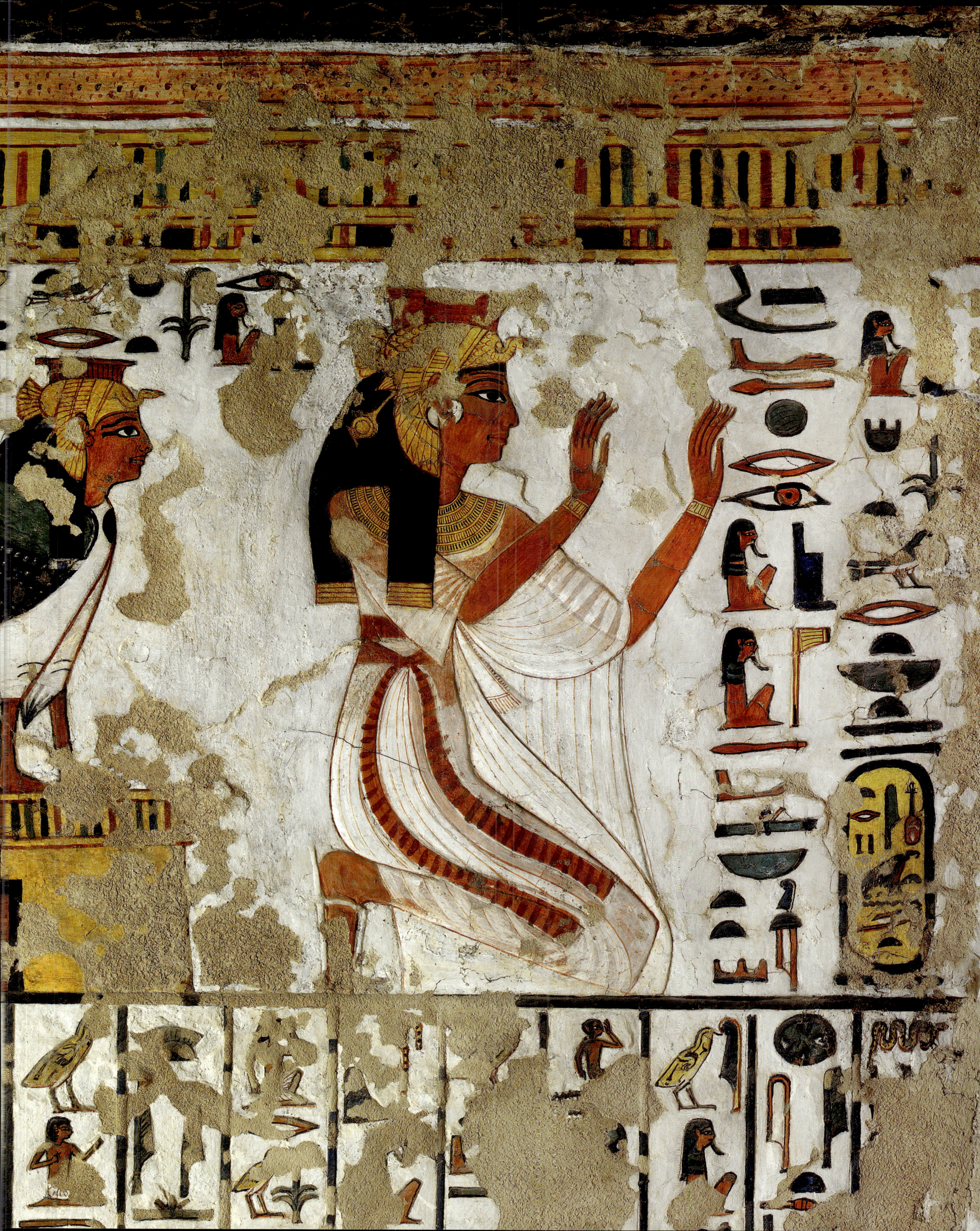

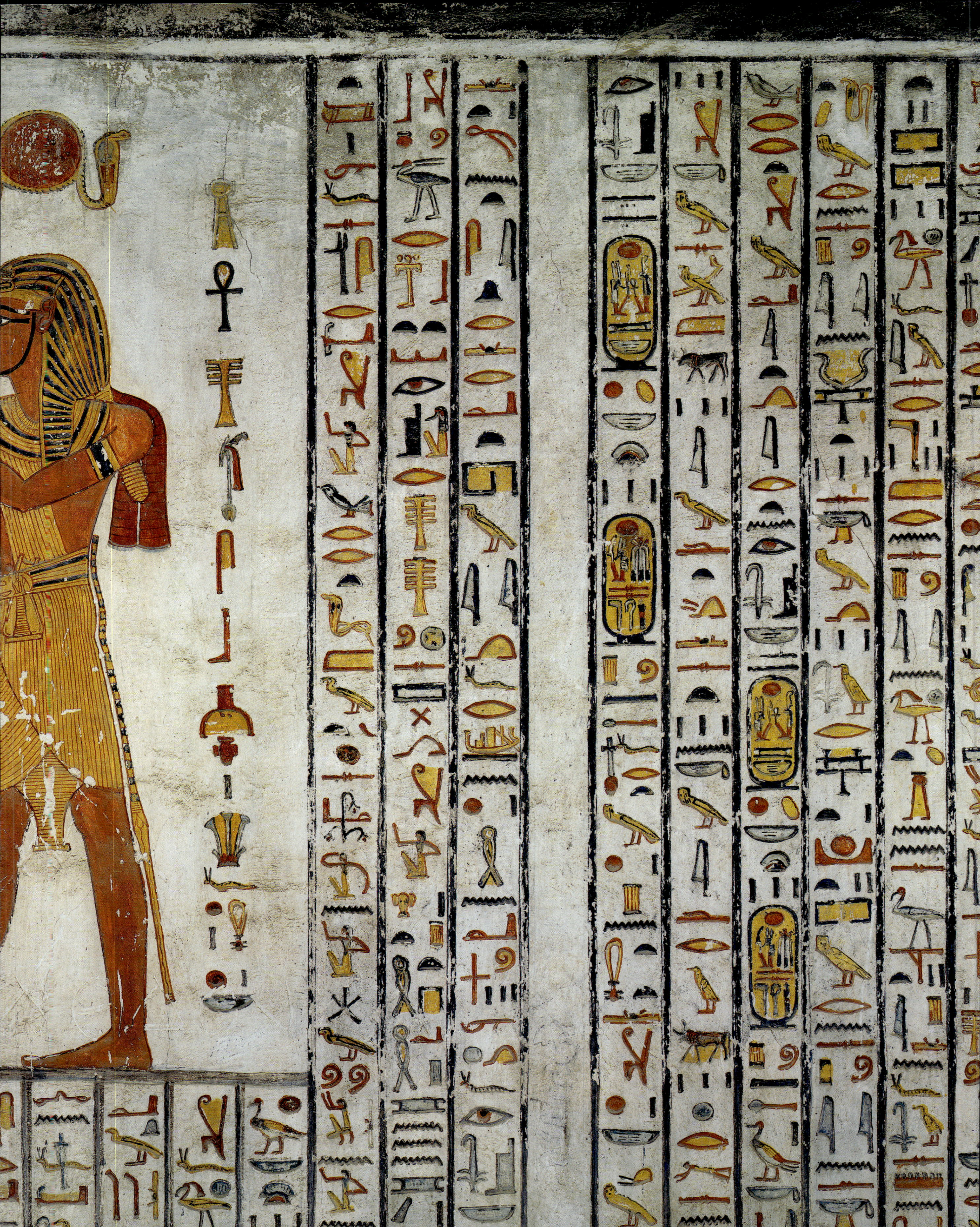

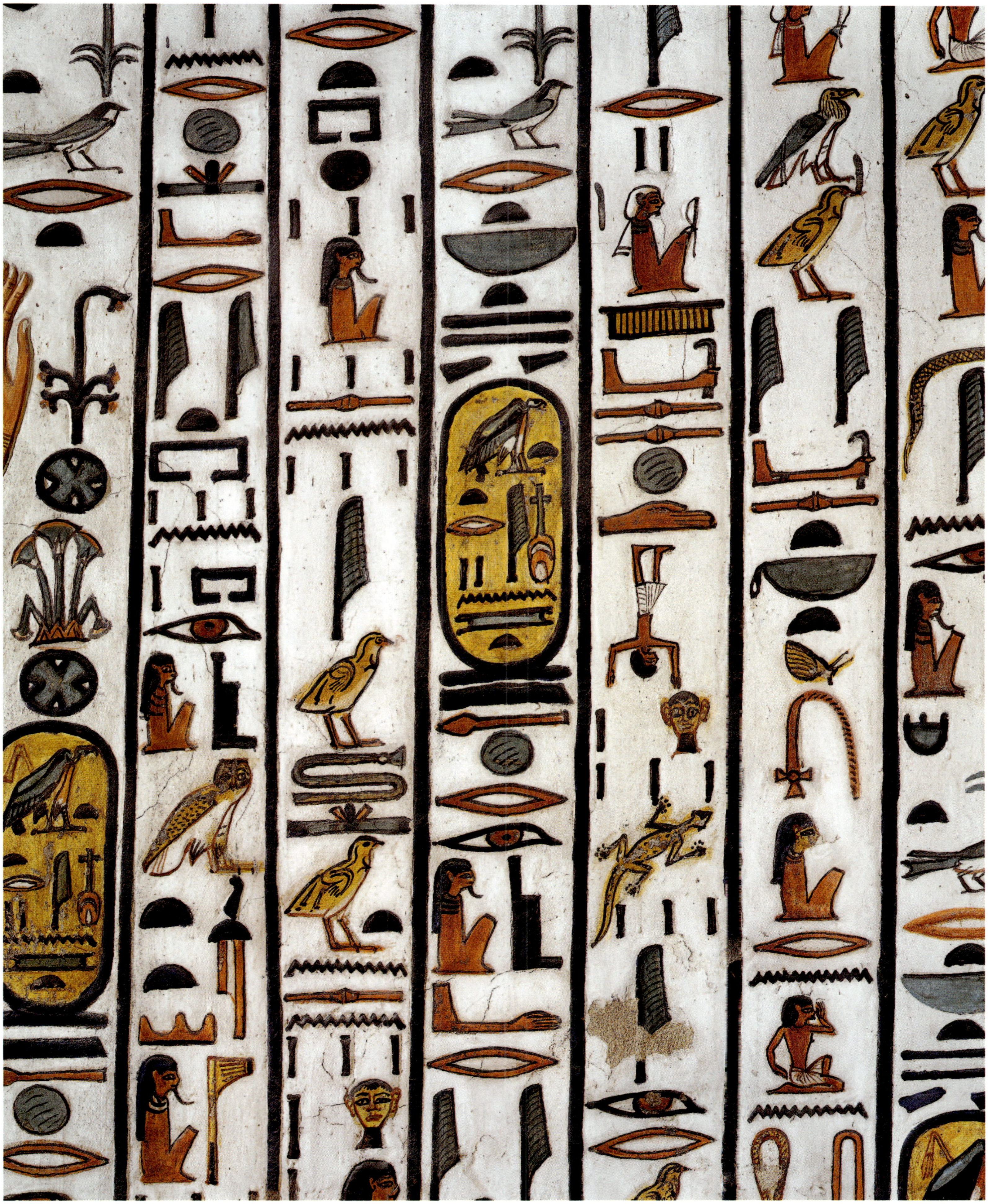

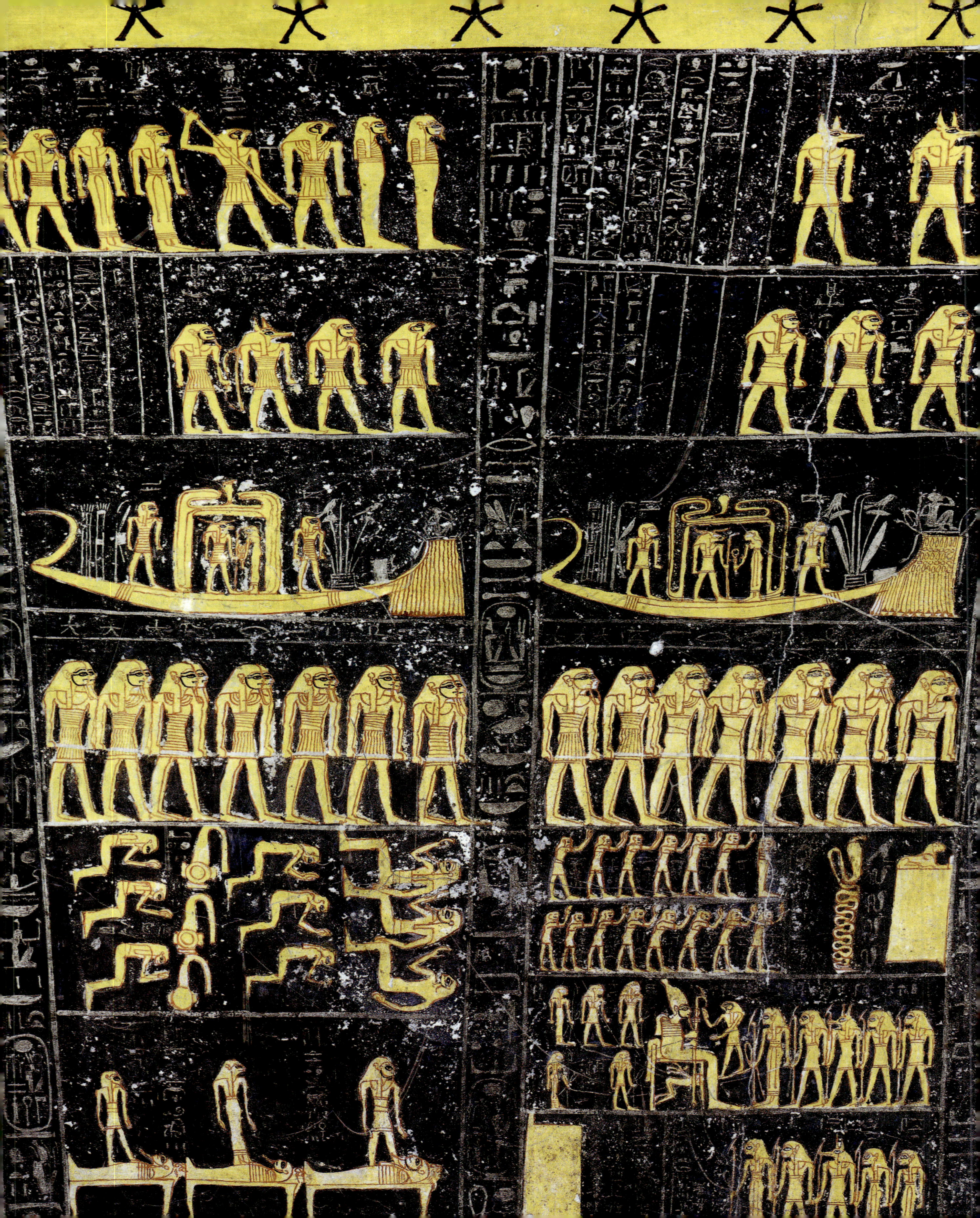

Chapter 8

The Books of the Heavens

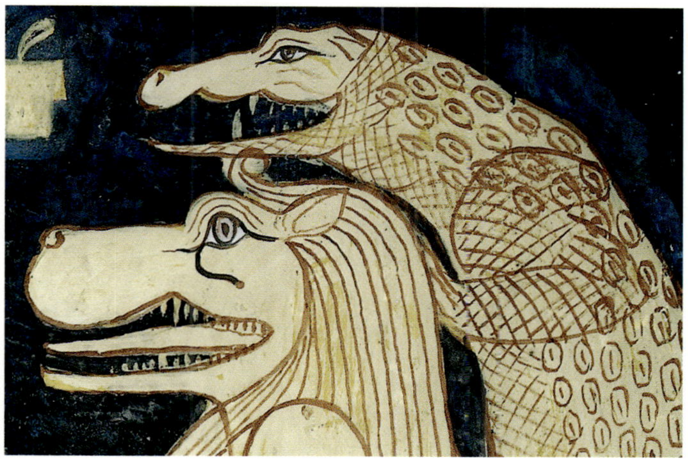

In the later New Kingdom, several new Afterlife Books, which shifted the focus of the night journey away from the Netherworld, entered the repertoire of royal tomb decoration. Rather than concentrating only on the world of the Duat, the new compositions describe the journey of the sun through the sky. This represents a different but parallel conception of the cosmos, in which the landscape through which the sun travels at night was a mirror of his day setting. Many of the elements seen in texts such as the Book of the Amduat and the Book of Gates are still present, although in altered form, but other concepts of the cosmos also come into play. The goddess Nut, embodiment of the sky, is present on the lids of coffins, where her outstretched body, sometimes with wings, protects the king. But it is in these later texts that Nut's role as the "mother" of the sun, the body in which the god gestates and the womb from which he is born, is made explicit in the decoration of the royal tombs. The repertoire of images on the tomb walls expands to include the heavens as well as the Duat, and the entire cycle of day and night: thus the full cosmos (both earthly and other) is illustrated.

Various compositions have been included in the corpus of the Books of the Heavens. Here the focus will be the Books of the Day and Night (often found together as a unit and thus treated as such in this chapter), the Book of the Heavenly Cow, and the Book of Nut.

The Goddess Nut

As the original sky goddess, one of the third generation of the Heliopolitan Ennead, Nut appears in many forms and is given numerous epithets over the course of Egyptian history. Daughter of Shu and Tefnut and sister-wife of Geb, she was the mother of Isis, Osiris, Nephthys, and Seth and grandmother of Horus. Nut is attested often in the Pyramid Texts, but it is not until the New Kingdom that her role was fully conceptualized and illustrated. Represented in the form of a woman, most often seen stretched out naked above the earth with her hands and feet touching the eastern and western horizons, Nut could also be shown dressed, sometimes with a round jar (the hieroglyph for her name)

The Books of the Heavens
The Books of the Day and Night, each bounded by an elongated figure of the sky goddess, Nut, are arranged back to back on the ceiling of the burial chamber of Ramses V/VI.

on her head. The other guise in which she commonly appears is that of the divine cow, probably the very earliest form of the sky goddess conceptualized by the Egyptians. As the embodiment of the heavens, Nut was imagined to create thunder through her laughter and rain with her tears. She did not have a specific cult center, in part because she was merged with other great goddesses such as Hathor.

It has been suggested that the image of a cow or woman in the sky is linked to the appearance of the Milky Way, or perhaps just its faint outer arm, as it stretches across the night sky. In this conception, Nut's head would be formed by the constellation Gemini, and part of the shape of Cygnus would be her legs. The brightest star in the latter constellation, Deneb, has been identified as the exit of her birth canal.

Glowing faintly, Gemini falls below the western horizon at the vernal equinox; some Egyptologists imagine that this could have been seen by the ancients as the moment just after Nut has eaten the sun—the moment of conception. Two-hundred and seventy-two days later, at the winter solstice, the lower half of the goddess's celestial body would have reached the point where a great circle tracing a path through the northern heavenly pole and Deneb intersects the eastern horizon at just the point where the sun rises. Egyptian women gave birth squatting on bricks, and we can imagine that the ancients saw this as the moment of the sun god's annual birth. Support for this admittedly theoretical reconstruction of the thinking of the ancients can be found in the fact that the period of time between the "conception" at the vernal equinox and the "birth" at the winter solstice corresponds to the nine months of a normal human pregnancy.

According to some versions of the Heliopolitan myth, Geb and Nut were physically connected to one another until Nut became pregnant, at which point the patriarch of the family, Atum, ordered that they be separated by their father, Shu. This separation of the anthropomorphized earth and sky by the air is a commonly illustrated motif, with Geb (earth) lying on his back, his penis erect, Nut (sky) as either a woman or a cow arched above him, and Shu (air) between them, holding them apart. This is a wonderful personification of the world: Geb, the fertile earth, lies below, with Nut, the sky, above and Shu, embodiment of light and air, between them.

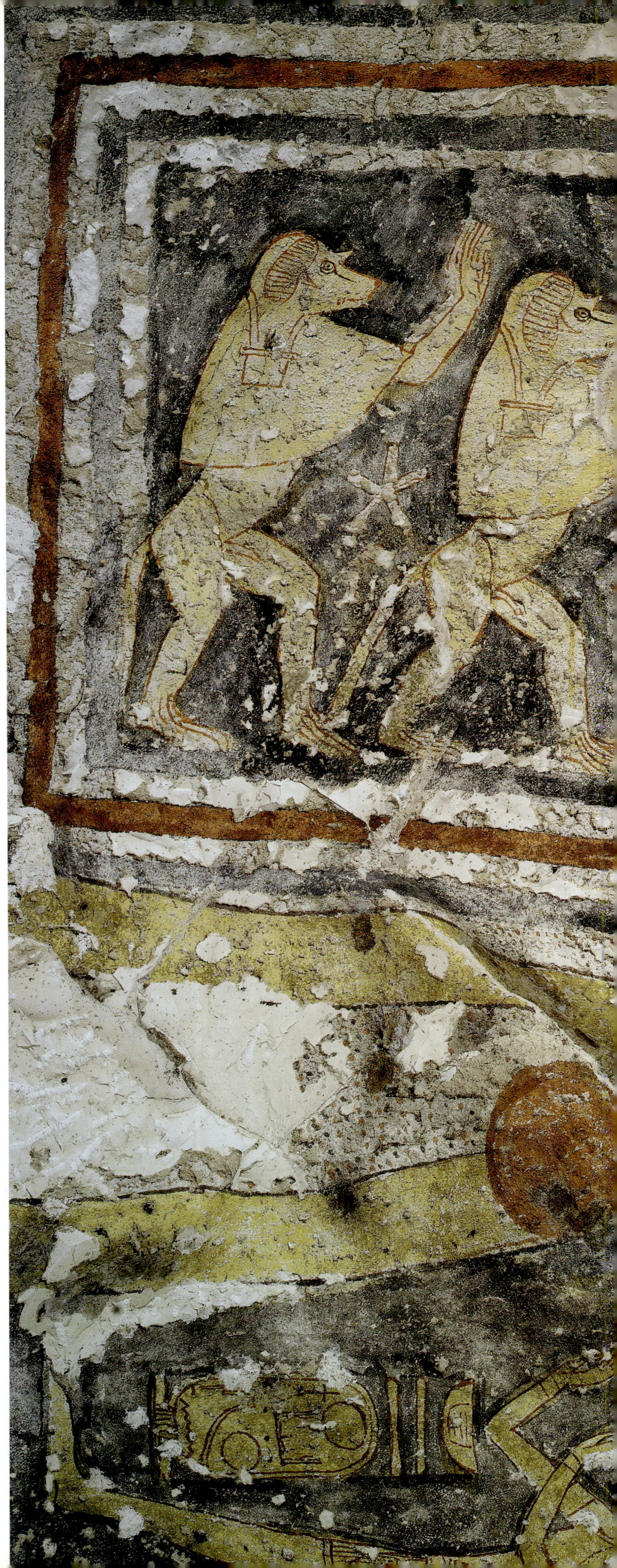

Praising the Sun

Two heads of Nut are visible here, below a vignette showing the ram-headed sun god within a sun disk flanked by adoring baboons.

The Books of the Day and Night

(Following pages)

The burial chamber of Ramses IX is decorated with back-to-back images of the Books of the Day and Night.

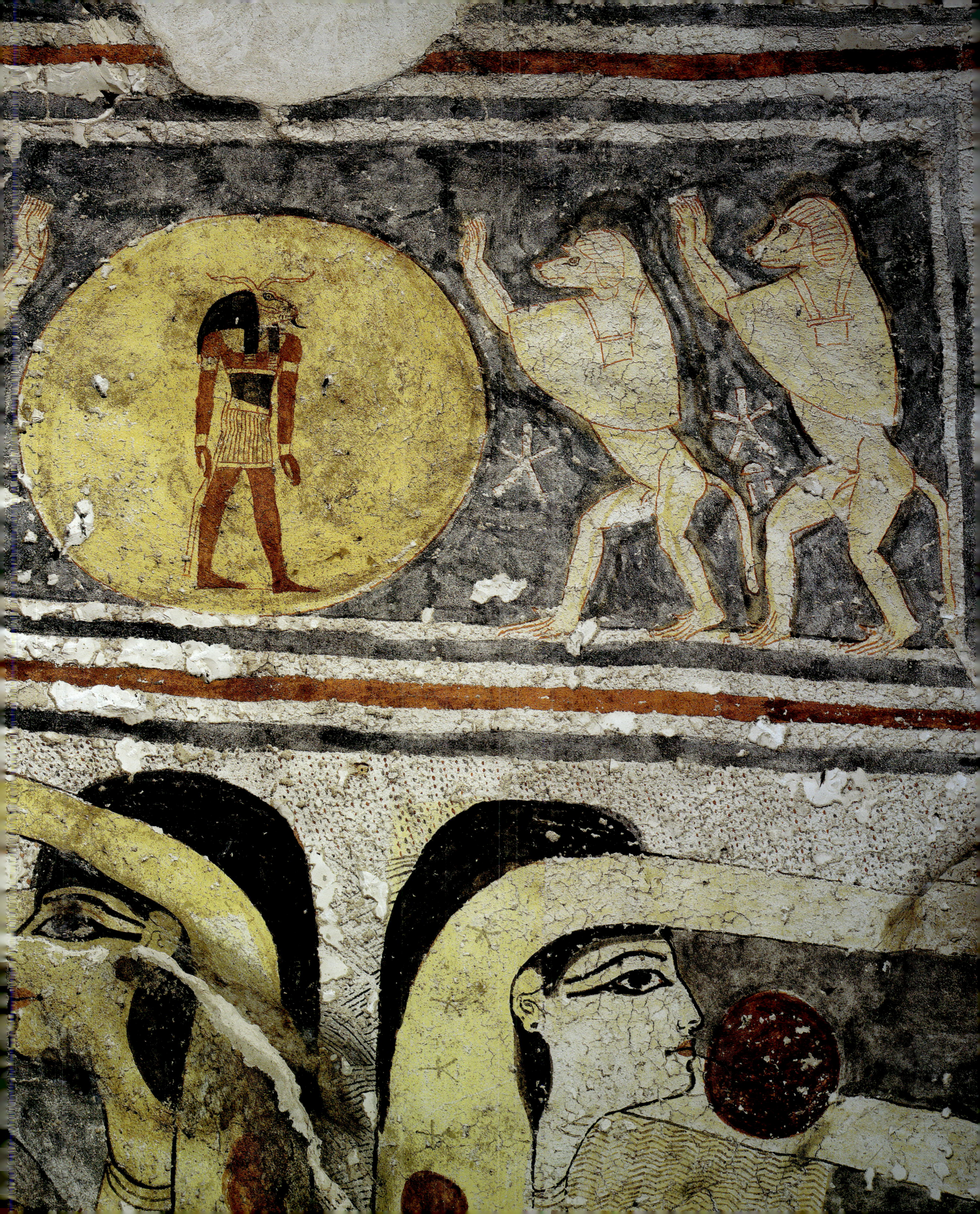

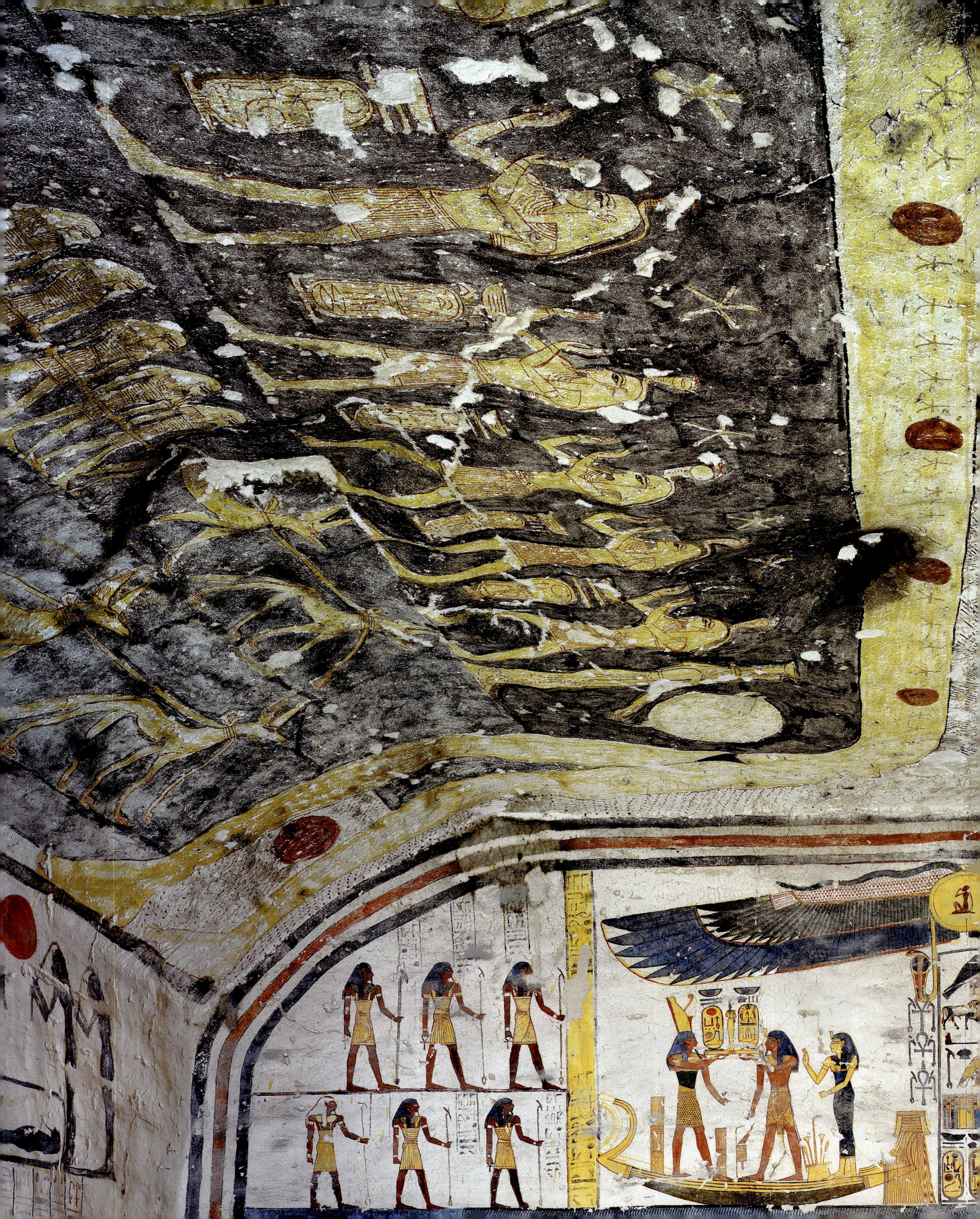

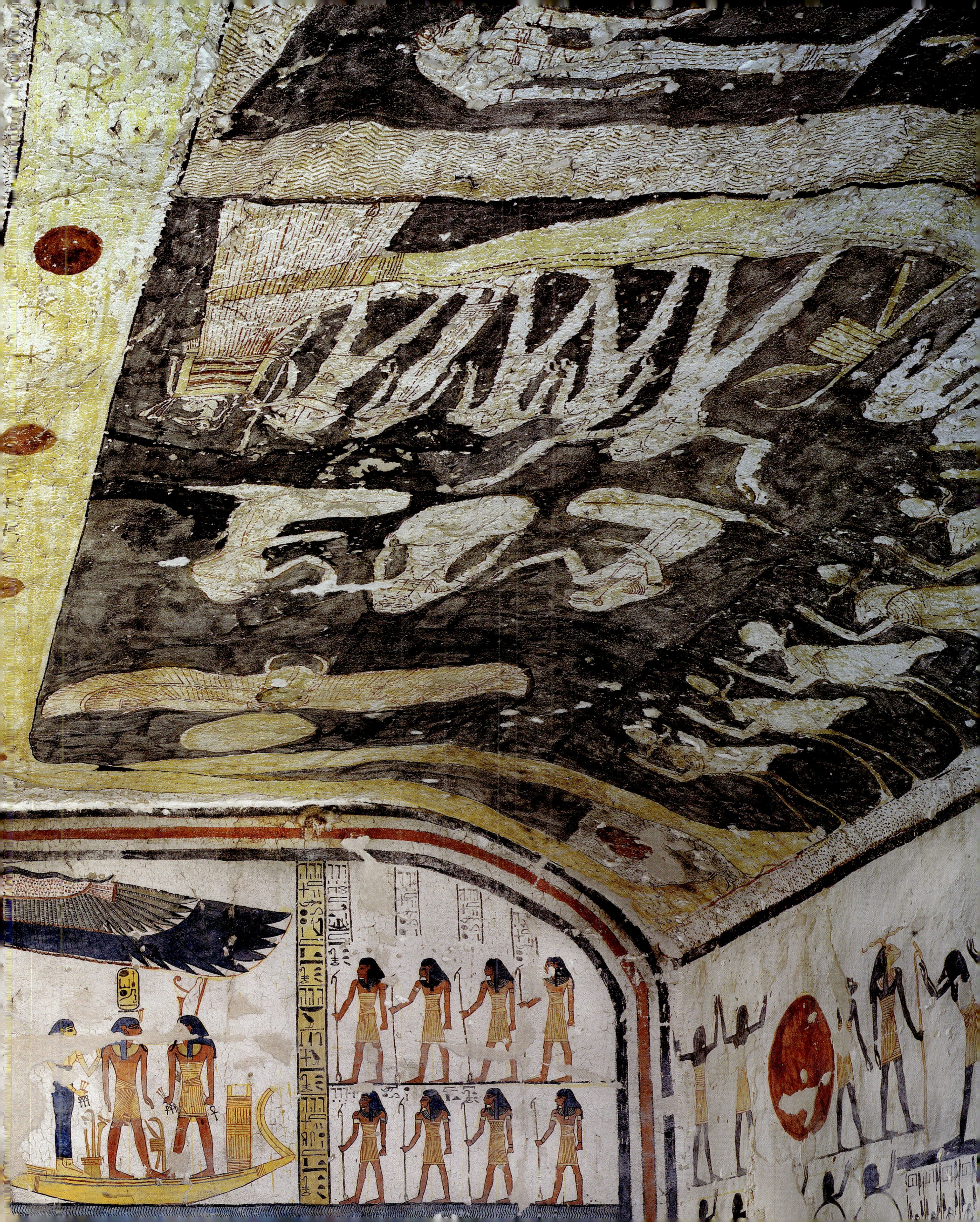

In one version of this myth, Shu could not continue to hold the body of Nut in her bovine form alone, and so asked his father for help. Atum responded by creating eight gods to act as the pillars of the sky, each pair supporting one part of the divine cow.

Nut was considered the mother of the sun god, as she swallowed him each evening and gave birth to him again each morning. The stars were also thought to travel along the river that flowed through her body during the day to reappear each evening (or at other regular intervals), in some cases towing the bark of the sun. These myths gave rise to one of Nut's many epithets: "she who eats her children."

Astronomical Ceilings

The ceilings of the earlier New Kingdom royal tombs had, like the pyramid chambers of the Old Kingdom, been covered with golden stars on a field of blue. In the tomb of Seti I, a new trend began, of using constellations to decorate the ceilings of the royal burial chambers. This is closely connected with the appearance of the Books of Heaven, which also make their debut during this reign.

Astronomy was essential to the Egyptian world-view. Interest in and attention to the sky is associated with some of the earliest monumental structures from the Nile Valley, namely stone megaliths aligned in various formations clearly related to astronomical observations found at Nabta Playa in the Nubian Western Desert. The importance of sky-watching continued throughout Egyptian history.

Many Egyptian myths, as we have seen, were based on observation of specific celestial bodies. The ancient Egyptians founded much of their civil and religious lives on the movements of these bodies, which allowed them, for example, to predict the annual flood and choose the best time to plant and harvest their crops. Their calendars were organized around the orbits of the earth and the moon. Egyptologists believe that two cycles were originally used in constructing two different calendars, which were later merged.

The first cycle, created in Lower Egypt very early in Egyptian history (or perhaps even late in its prehistory), was based on the 365-day cycle from one winter solstice to the next (the moment when the sun made a full circuit and rose again from the same geographical point, the solar "birthplace"), thus the period from one annual birth of the sun to the next. It has also been suggested that the "mouth" of Nut was almost due west at this moment, and that this westerly point was identified as the entrance to the Duat. In this system, months were either 29 or 30 days in length, and extra days had to be added every two or three years.

Another important astronomical marker was the heliacal rising of the star Sirius, identified with the goddess Isis, who was considered in some contexts the daughter of the sun god Re. Once a year, this star disappeared below the horizon for seventy days; the moment when it appeared again marked New Year's Day for the Upper Egyptian calendar. This became the basis for the civil calendar, with twelve 30-day months. Each year, five "epigomenal" days were intercalated after the end of the last month. When Egypt was unified, it is thought that these two calendrical systems were merged.

The ancient Egyptians did not use the same constellations as the ones we identify today; our constellations are based on Hellenistic and Babylonian models that were adopted in Egypt during its later history; it is not until the Ptolemaic period that the twelve constellations of the zodiac we still use today were introduced. In fact, astronomers and Egyptologists still have not succeeded in correlating most of the ancient Egyptian star clusters with actual star groups.

Among the heavenly bodies crucial to the Egyptians were the circumpolar stars, which neither rose nor set. Clustered around the north pole, these were identified in the early periods with the spirits of the deified kings, and were later grouped into constellations. By the New Kingdom, this area had become the location of the Fields of the Blessed.

Also important to the Egyptians were the "Decans," a series of stars located in a band south of the ecliptic. There were 36 of these, each of which dropped below the horizon for a seventy-day period before rising again in the night sky. The principal Decan was Sirius. Each of the 36 Decans marked one "hour" (actually only 40 minutes long) of the night for a period of ten days: each night used 18 of the Decans to count the passage of the night—three for the twilight, and 12 for the hours of darkness. Of the ancient Decans, only Sirius, called Sopdet in ancient Egyptian, has been reliably identified, although the constellation Sah has been shown to correspond with our Orion, and the seven stars of the Big Dipper were identified by the ancients as the hind leg of an ox (named Meskhetiu), associated with Hathor.

Tables listing the Decans first appear on a series of coffins from the 9th and 10th Dynasties, at which time the passage of the stars was the best way to mark time. This type of observation required two men: one faced north and sighted through a notched palm rib; the other looked toward the stars themselves. In the New Kingdom, the water clock—a calibrated vessel filled with water from which a carefully controlled flow trickled at a steady rate—provided another reliable way to count the hours. Stellar observation continued to be used, however, and certain New Kingdom tombs, most famously those of Senenmut (dating to the early 18th Dynasty) and King Seti I of the 19th Dynasty, provide us with star and constellation charts. Additional charts of this type are found in the tombs of Ramses V/VI, Ramses VII, and Ramses IX. These latter represent the last era in which heliacal rising was used for time-telling; in later periods, focus moved to stars that were transiting the meridian and adjacent celestial sight lines.

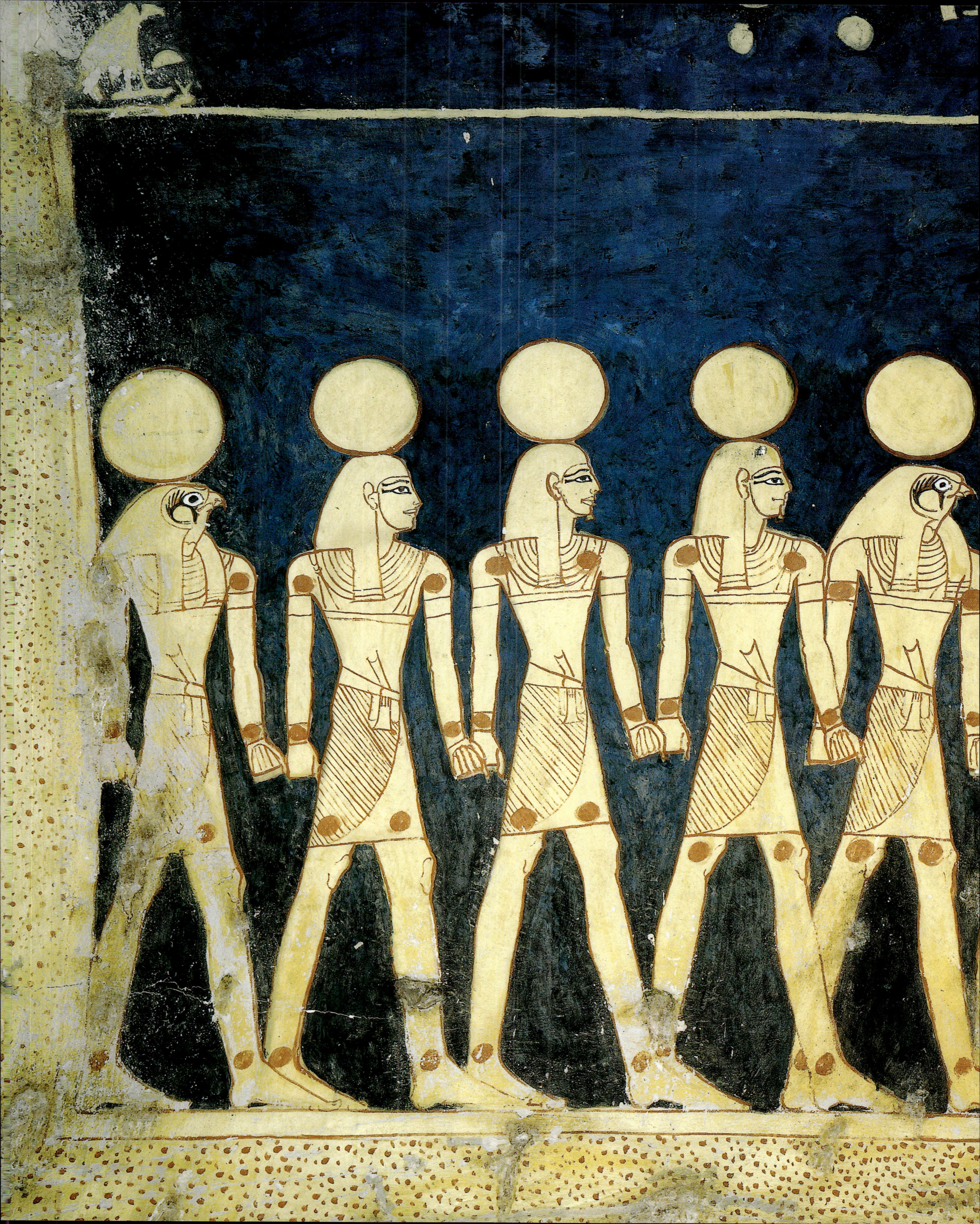

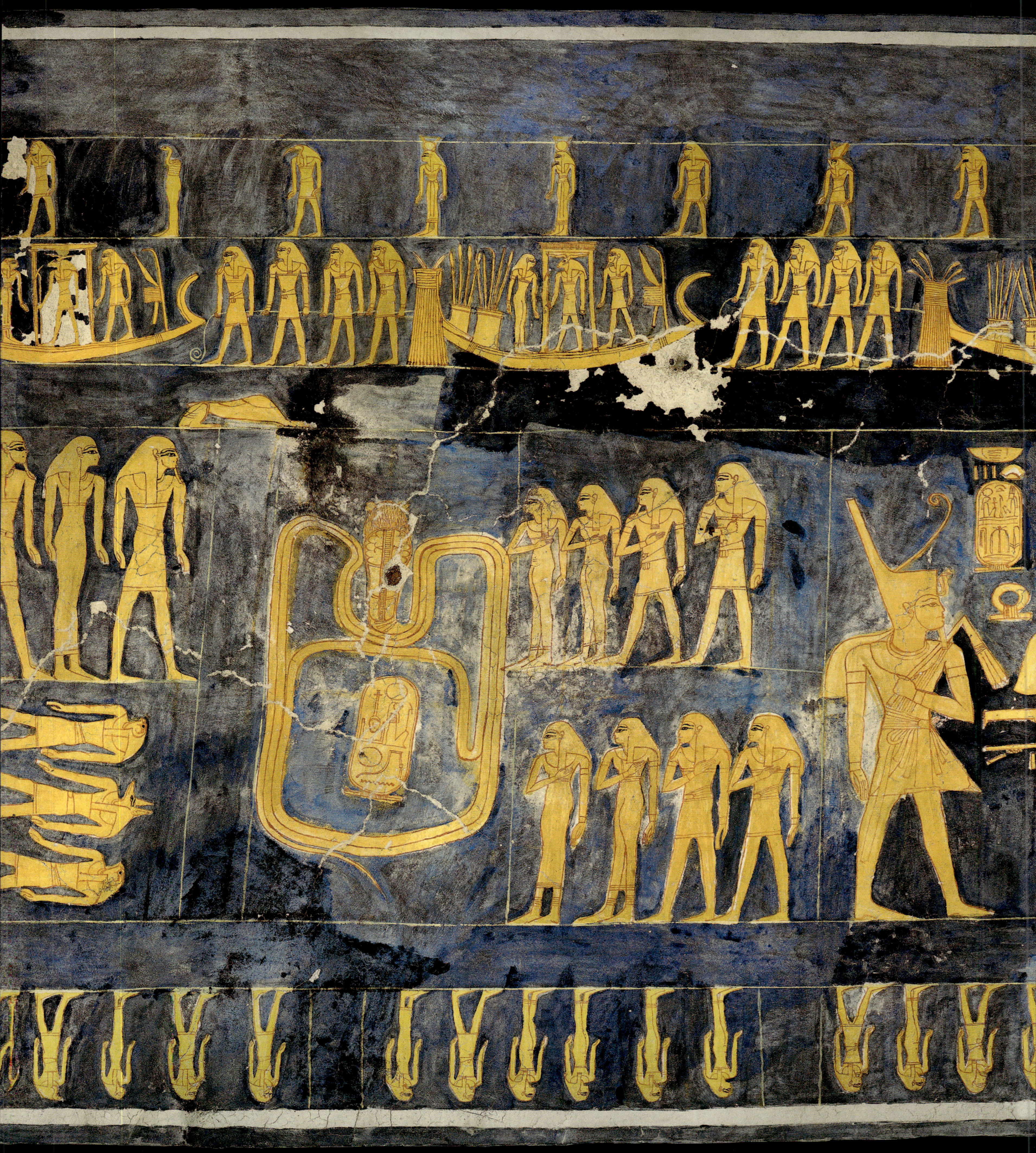

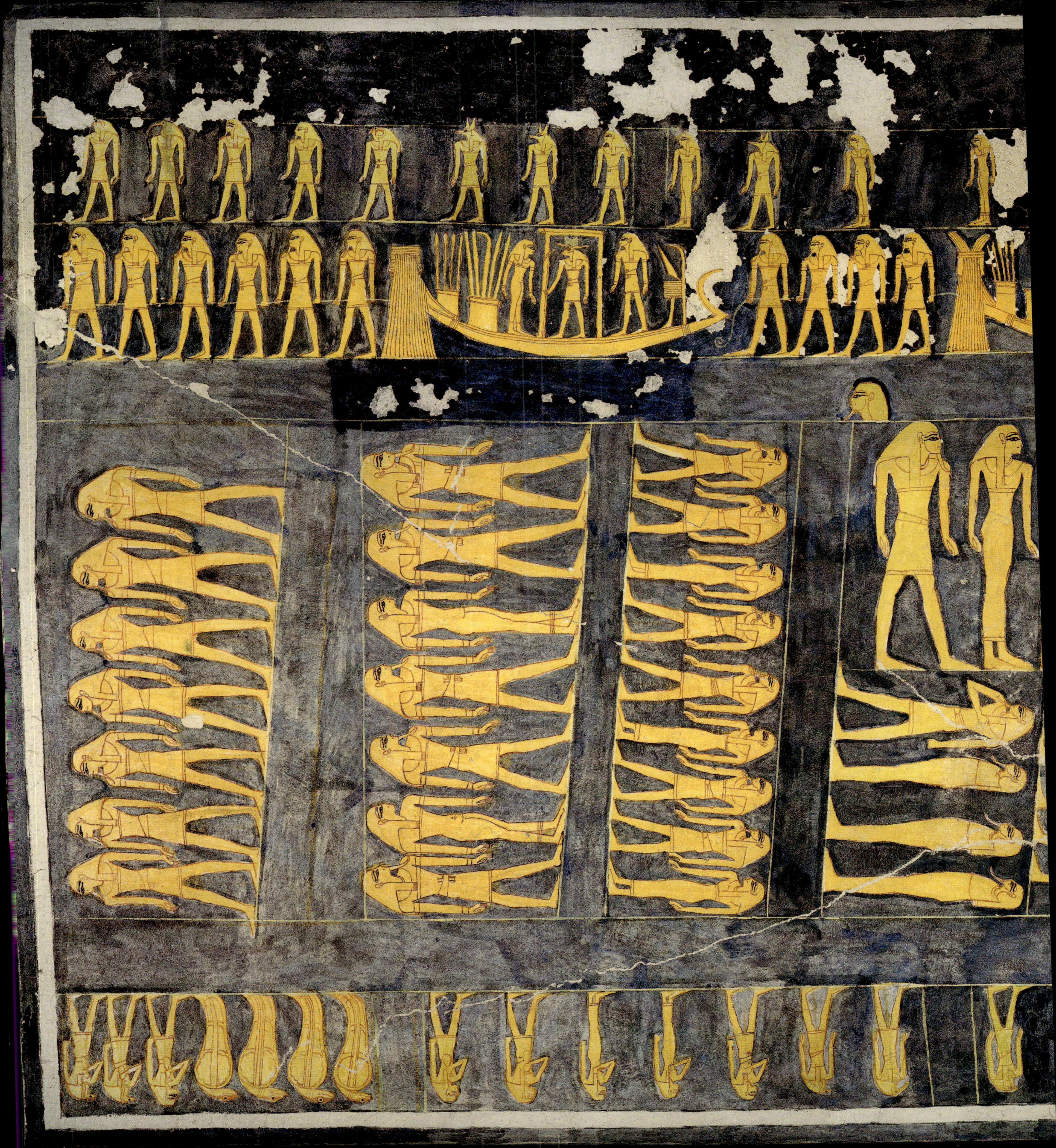

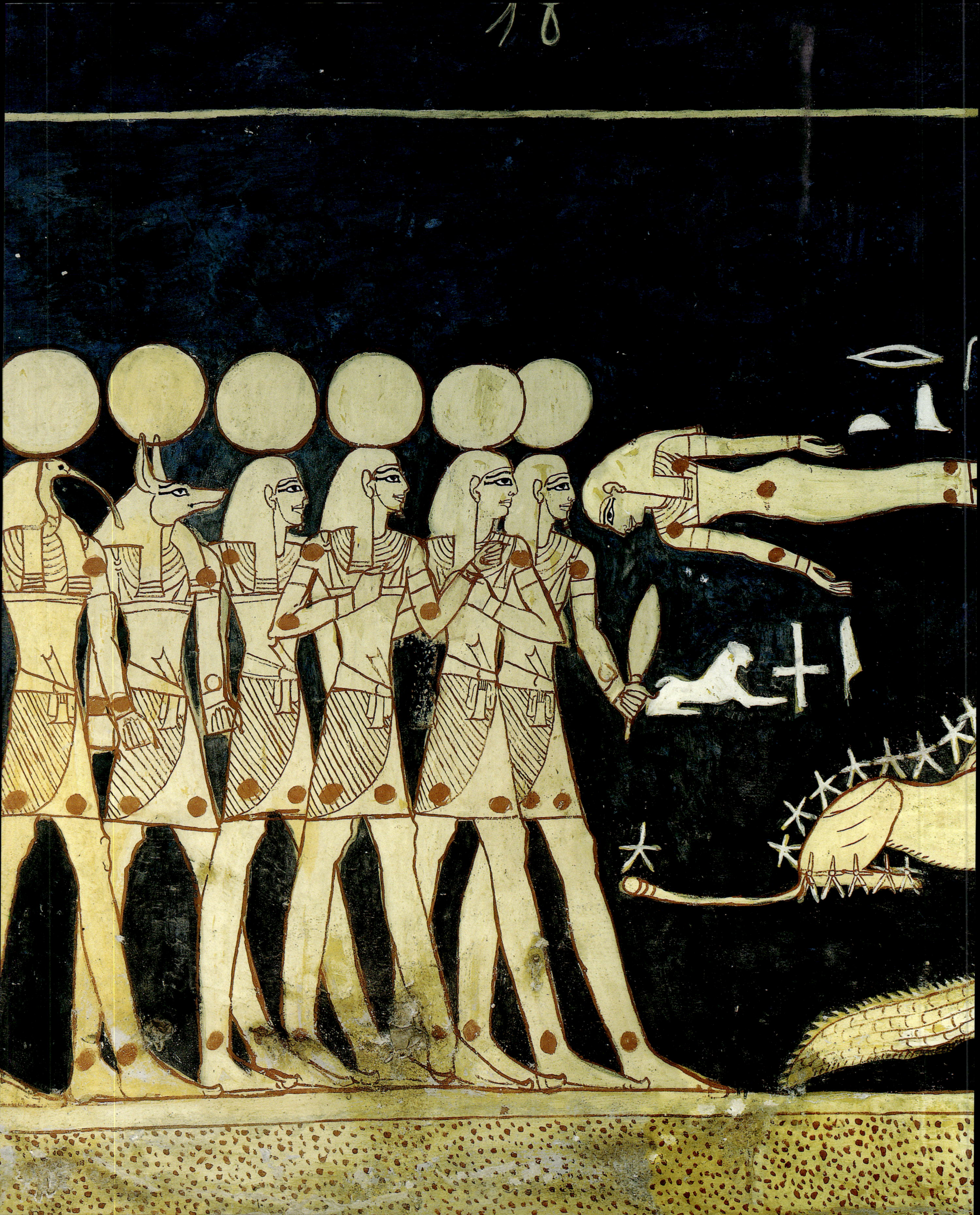

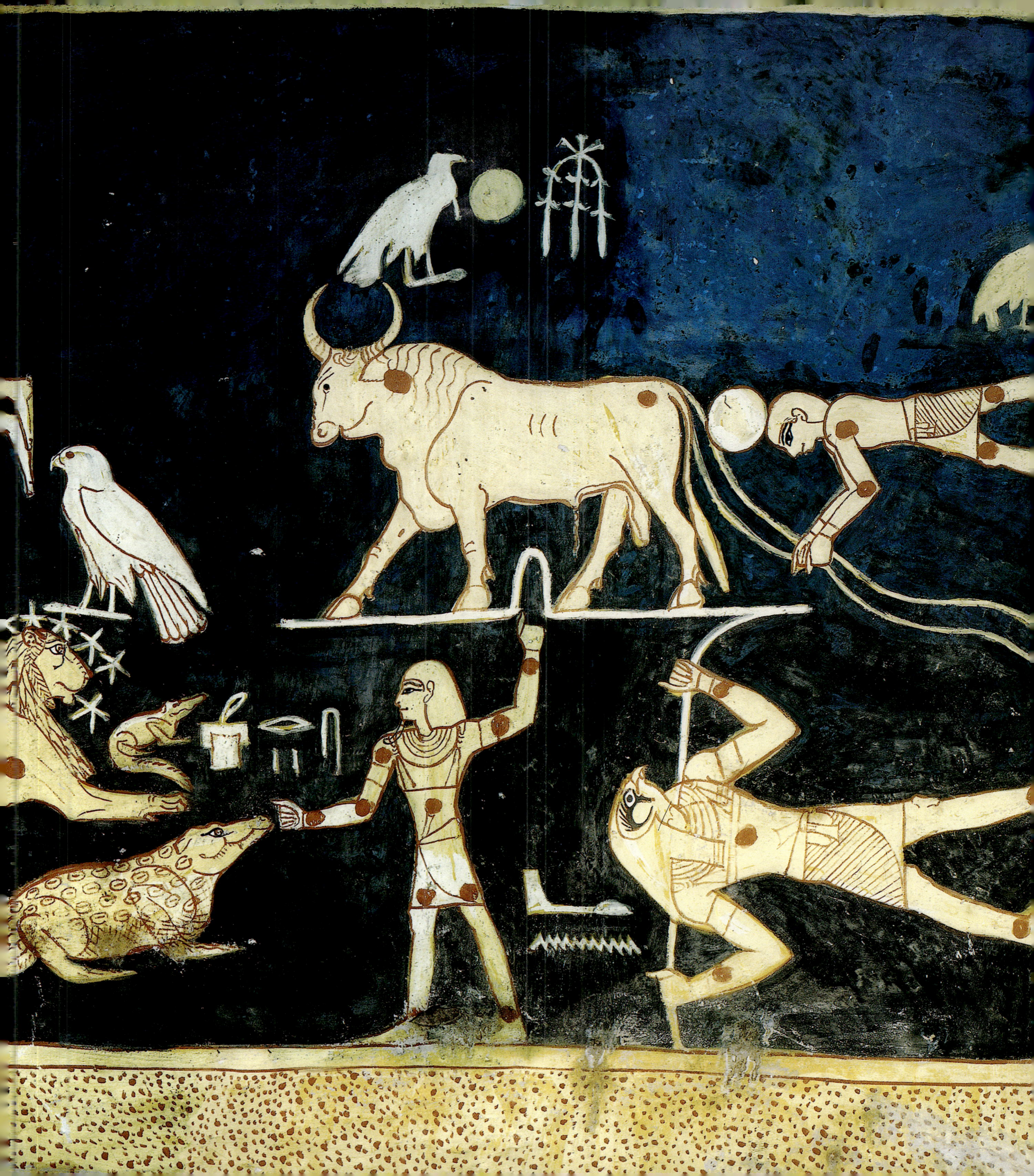

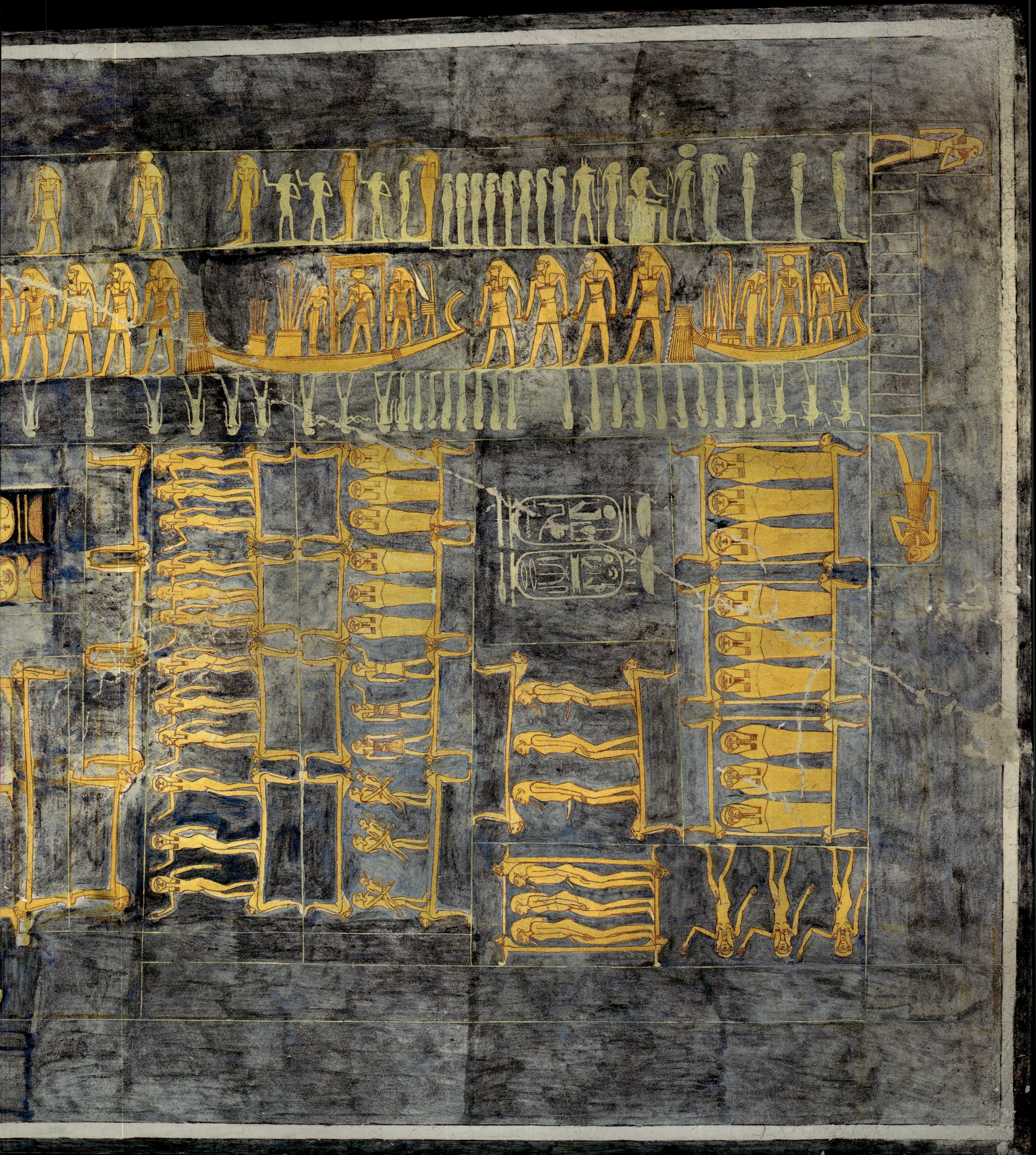

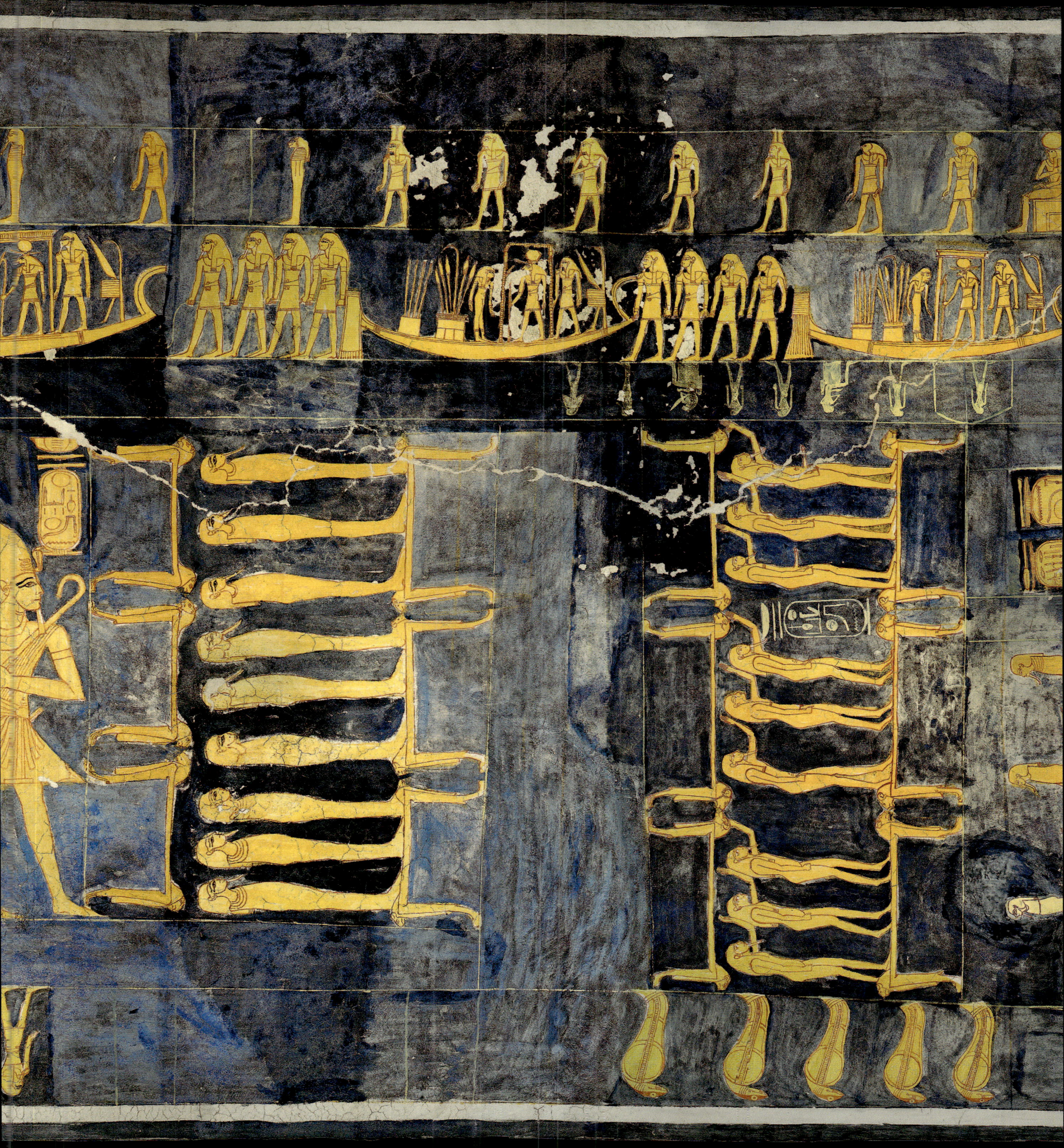

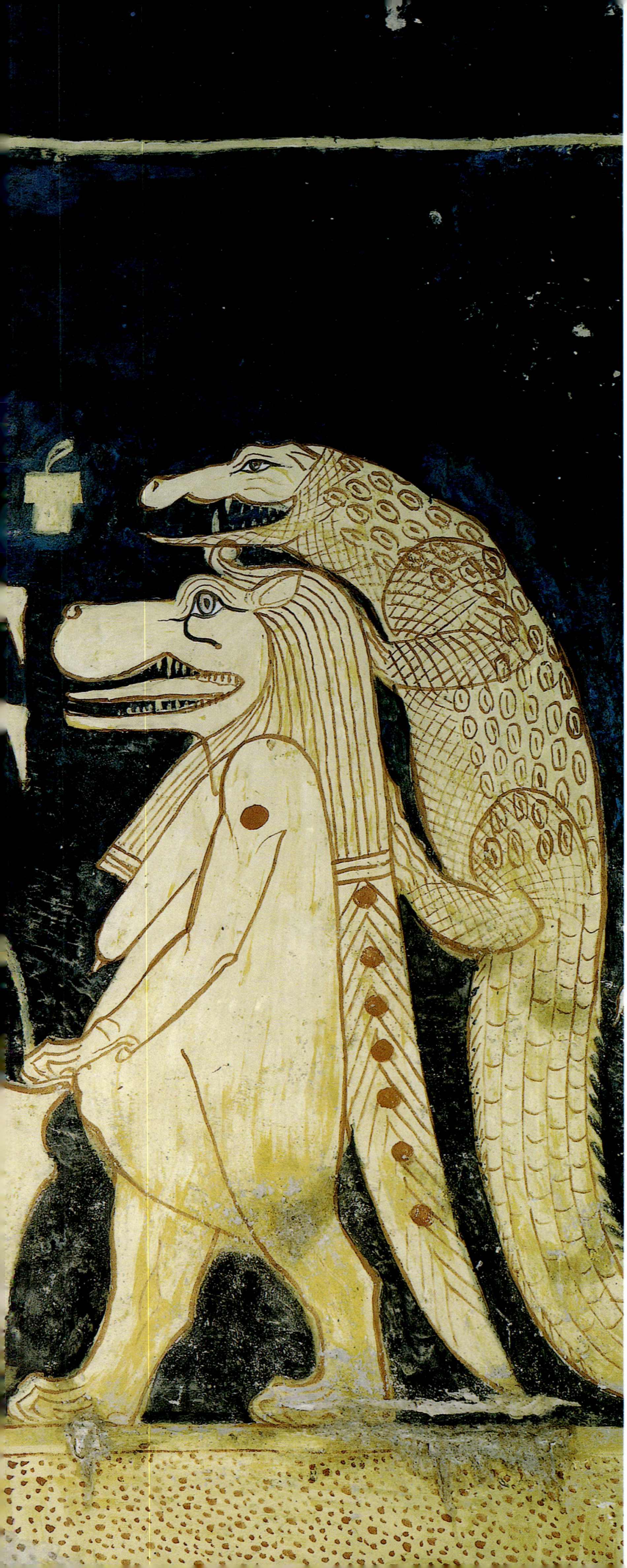

Ancient Constellations

(Pages 271–272)

Eleven of the Decans, personified as striding gods with human, animal, or bird heads, can be seen in this detail from the astronomical ceiling of Seti I. To the right the circumpolar stars, including a cluster identified with the goddess Serket, are partially visible.

The Circumpolar Stars

In ancient Egypt's northern sky was a group of stars that circled the north pole, and neither rose nor set. Some of these stars are visible here, grouped into named clusters such as Samut (the goddess Tawaret with a crocodile on her back), and An (a falcon-headed figure).

The Ceiling of KV 6

(Pages 273–276)

The ceilings of the corridors leading into the tomb of Ramses IX are decorated with a variety of images, including the solar bark at various stages of its journey and the blessed dead in the process of being resurrected from their funerary beds, from the Book of the Night. In the center are larger-scale images of the king in the crowns of Upper and Lower Egypt, and a Mehen serpent, its coils encircling and thus protecting the cartouche of the king.

The Books of the Day and Night

Found on the ceilings of later New Kingdom royal tombs, the Books of the Day and Night describe the journey of the sun through the body of Nut during the 24-hour daily solar cycle. The first appearance of these books is in the Osireion at Abydos, where the first nine hours of the Night are found. In the burial chamber of Ramses IV, the Book of Nut (see below) and the Book of the Night up to the fourth hour are placed back to back on the ceiling. The tomb of Ramses V/VI contains both the Book of the Day and two full versions of the Book of the Night, while the Book of the Night alone is included in the decoration of Ramses IX's tomb. All of these representations are on the ceilings of the burial chambers and corridors. Additional astronomical images can accompany these compositions.

The Book of the Day

The Book of the Day is always framed by a large figure of Nut. The twelve hours of the day begin at her vulva, since the sun is born from her womb, and end at her head, where she swallows the sun (thus symbolically conceiving him anew) so that he can begin his night journey. The sun god appears during the hours of the day with the head of a falcon, in contrast to his ram-headed night form.

The hours are generally arranged horizontally into five registers, with no distinct divisions between them. There is an introductory text at the beginning, and a conclusion at the end. We do not know the original title of this book. In terms of orientation, it is interesting to note that most of the figures in the scenes of this book face Nut's head.

During the day, seven solar barks (each representing one of the day hours) sail on the river that flows through

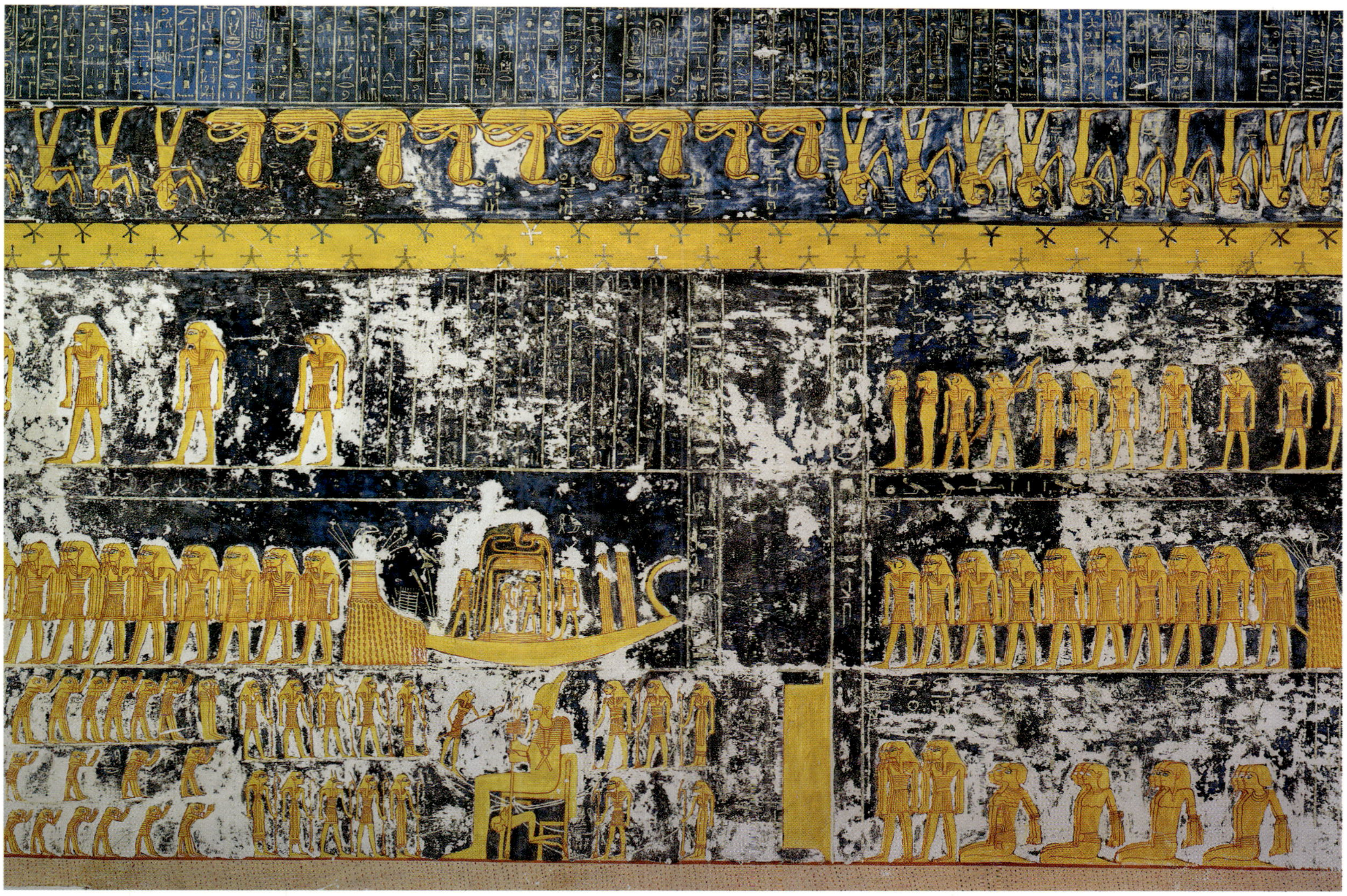

The Book of the Night
The pillared chamber of the tomb of Ramses V/VI is decorated with images from the Books of the Day and Night. In the central section, illustrated here, a line of stars separates the two books, stretching above the eleventh and twelfth hours of the Book of the Night.

(actually beneath, in a typically Egyptian artistic convention of conveying maximum information) the body of Nut. Groups of gods occupy the banks that lie on either side of this river, accompanying the sun on his journey through the sky. Within Nut's actual body are twelve solar disks—one for each hour, flanked by lines of stars.

The day begins at the exit of the birth canal, directly in front of Nut's genitals. Here we find a sun disk, a winged scarab beetle (the sun at dawn), and a smaller figure of Nut, supported in this case by Isis and Nephthys, who gives birth to the sun in the form of a child. Shu stands in the register below to assist. The sun disk is accompanied by the cartouches of the king, showing that the monarch was identified with the sun god and participated in this rebirth.

The following hours are given over for the main part to lists of deities and hymns to the various hours. Key scenes include the defeat of Apophis, and some actions take place in a heavenly version of the Fields of the Blessed. Many of the deities here can be recognized from the Netherworld Books, but here are given duties in the day sky.

The book ends at the head of Nut, which is surrounded by zigzag lines that represent water. The sun disk lies at the end of the heavenly river, ready to enter the mouth of the great goddess and thus the hours of the night, during which it will gestate in preparation for its rebirth the next morning.

The Book of the Night

The Book of the Night begins where the Book of the Day ends, when Nut swallows the disk of the sun. The twelve hours of the night take place in a sort of heavenly Duat that is, like the celestial realm, surrounded by the primeval Nun. During this time, the sun god appears in his ram-headed form, as was usual in the earlier Netherworld Books. Re travels again in his bark, protected by the Mehen snake and accompanied by the gods Sia and Hu, as he does in the Book of Gates. Ma'at is also shown aboard the divine bark, which is towed by a long line of men called the "untiring ones"; these are probably to be understood as stars. In some of the hours, they are led by a figure to be identified as the king himself.

The Book of the Night is divided into twelve sections, the first of which lies between the arms of the goddess, and then eleven more set off from one another by vertical lines of texts that serve as gates, with the legs of the goddess serving to mark the final division. The vertical texts introduce each hour, with additional inscriptions serving as captions.

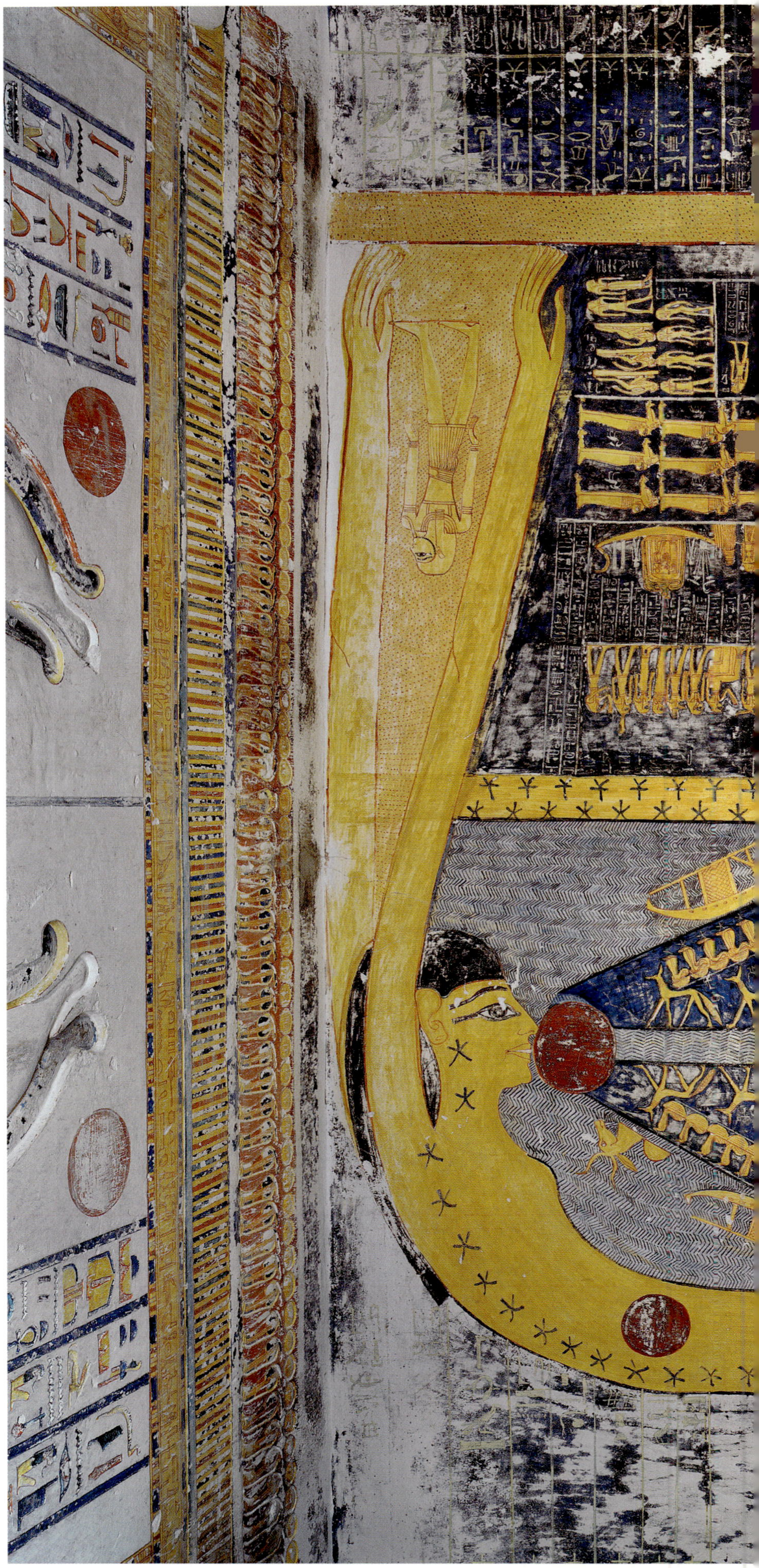

The Books of the Day and Night
This image shows a large section of the ceiling of Ramses V/VI's pillared chamber. The goddess Nut can be seen stretched over both books, her body along the top of the Book of the Day and her arms reaching down to form one boundary for the Book of the Night. At the lower left, Nut swallows the sun at the conclusion of its day journey.

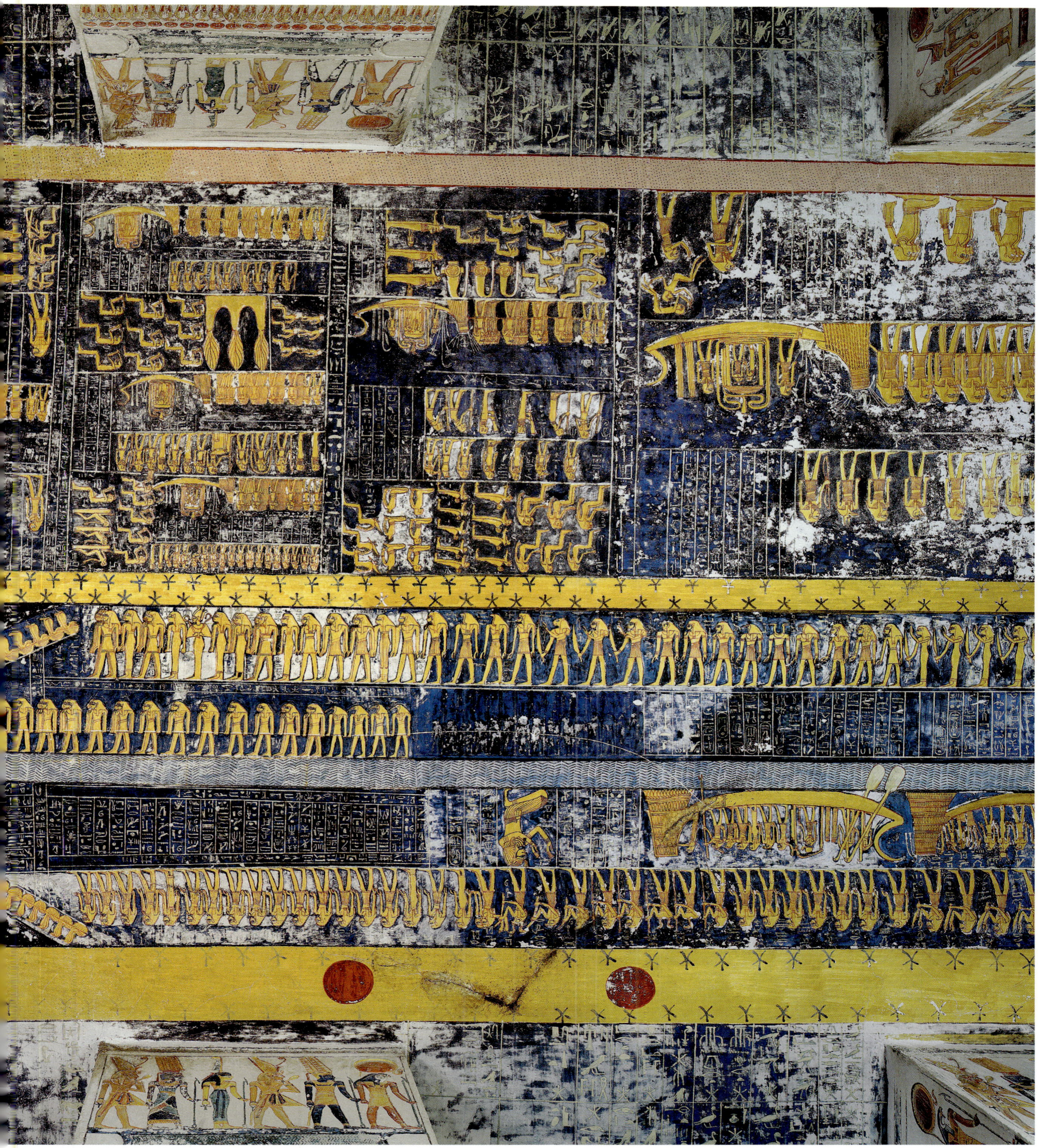

Although all of the action is conceptually thought to take place inside Nut's body; as in the Book of the Day, the hours are illustrated beneath so that they can be seen. Many of the personalities and motifs found here are known from the Netherworld Books. The goals of the journey are similar as well: caring for the blessed dead, judging the evildoers, and preparing for the morning rebirth of the sun.

In general, the scenes are arranged in three registers, with the sun bark in the center. In the upper register are the gods of the night hours, with both the blessed dead and the damned in the lower register. There is no water shown here; instead, the action seems to take place in a desert landscape, perhaps a wadi, with Re and his entourage traveling between two mountainous areas. Another difference between this book and the Netherworld compositions is that there is no reference to the union of Re and Osiris. In addition, instead of the serpent Apophis, it is the god Seth who is defeated.

The first image in this composition depicts Nut swallowing the sun. The king is visible here, holding an *ankh* sign to guarantee eternal life. The denizens of the succeeding hours include the anthropomorphized forms of the four cardinal points, the *ba*s of the cult sites of Buto and Hierakonpolis, the Enneads, the earth god Tatanen, Horus, and the souls of both Egyptians and foreigners. The regeneration of the sun begins to become evident in the seventh hour, paralleling the earlier Netherworld Books. In the lower register of this hour, a scene from the Book of the Gates appears, in which Horus intercedes on behalf of both Egyptians and foreigners. Osiris comes to prominence in the eighth hour, where he is shown victorious over an enemy later named as Seth. In the ninth hour, Sia announces the results of the final judgment and proclaims the fates of the dead. The damned then disappear, dying forever, and in the tenth hour, only the blessed appear.

The action of the twelfth hour looks toward the conclusion of the journey and the rebirth of the sun. Four jackals, identified as the Western *ba*s, join the towmen; these jackals appear at the beginning of the Book of the Day, emphasizing the unity of the two compositions. The stars appear to light the world of the dead, and the sun god is transformed before Nut into his morning forms of scarab beetle and child, each guise protected by a kneeling god. The birth of the sun is represented a third time in a scene centered on an altar atop a sledge. On top of the altar is a scarab; to the right is a sky sign with a scarab beneath and an infant above.

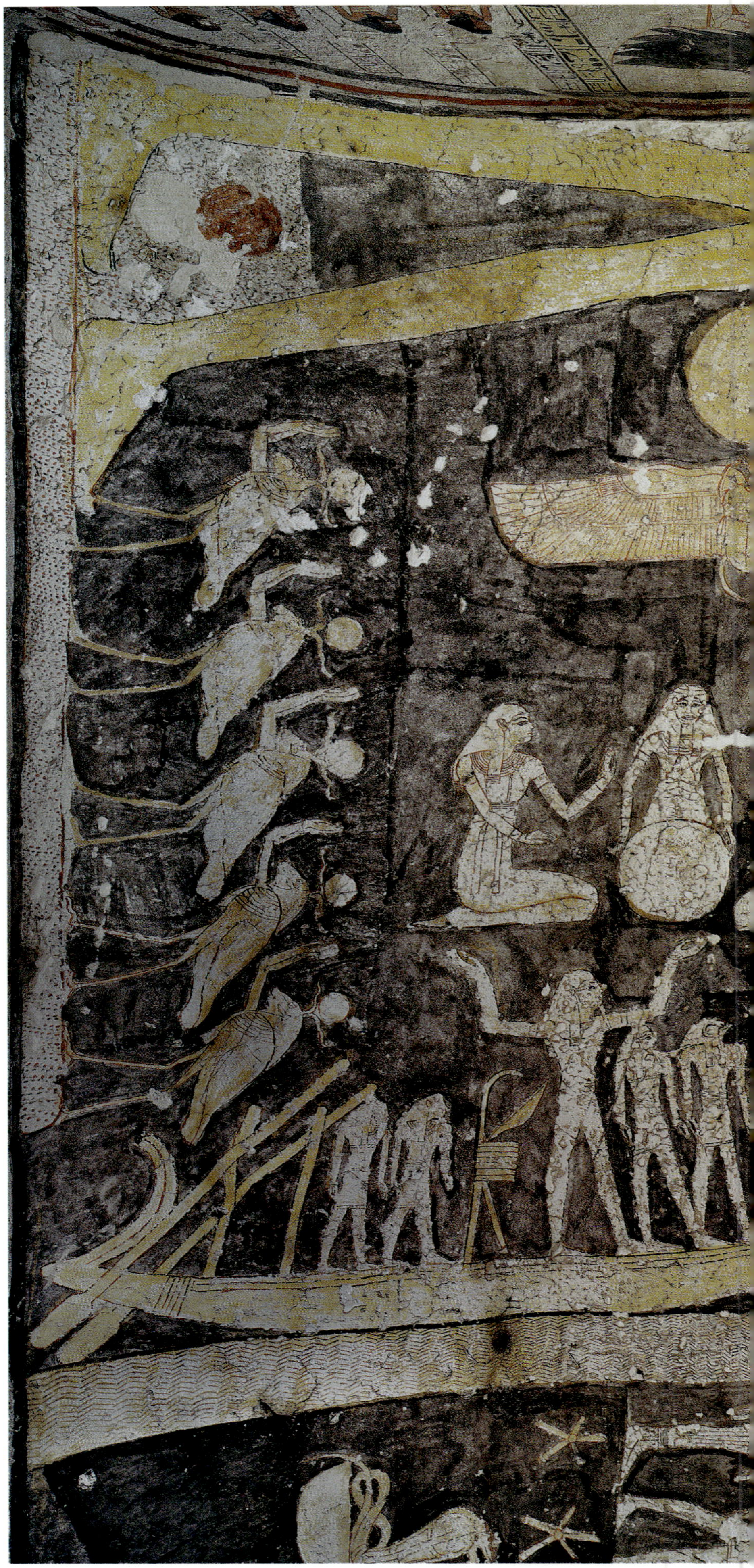

The Rebirth of the Sun
The birth of the sun is depicted on the left, in the scene that opens the Book of the Day. The sun appears directly below Nut's genitalia in the forms of a winged scarab and a sun disk. Beneath this a smaller figure of Nut, flanked by Isis and Nephthys and supported by Shu, again bears the sun.

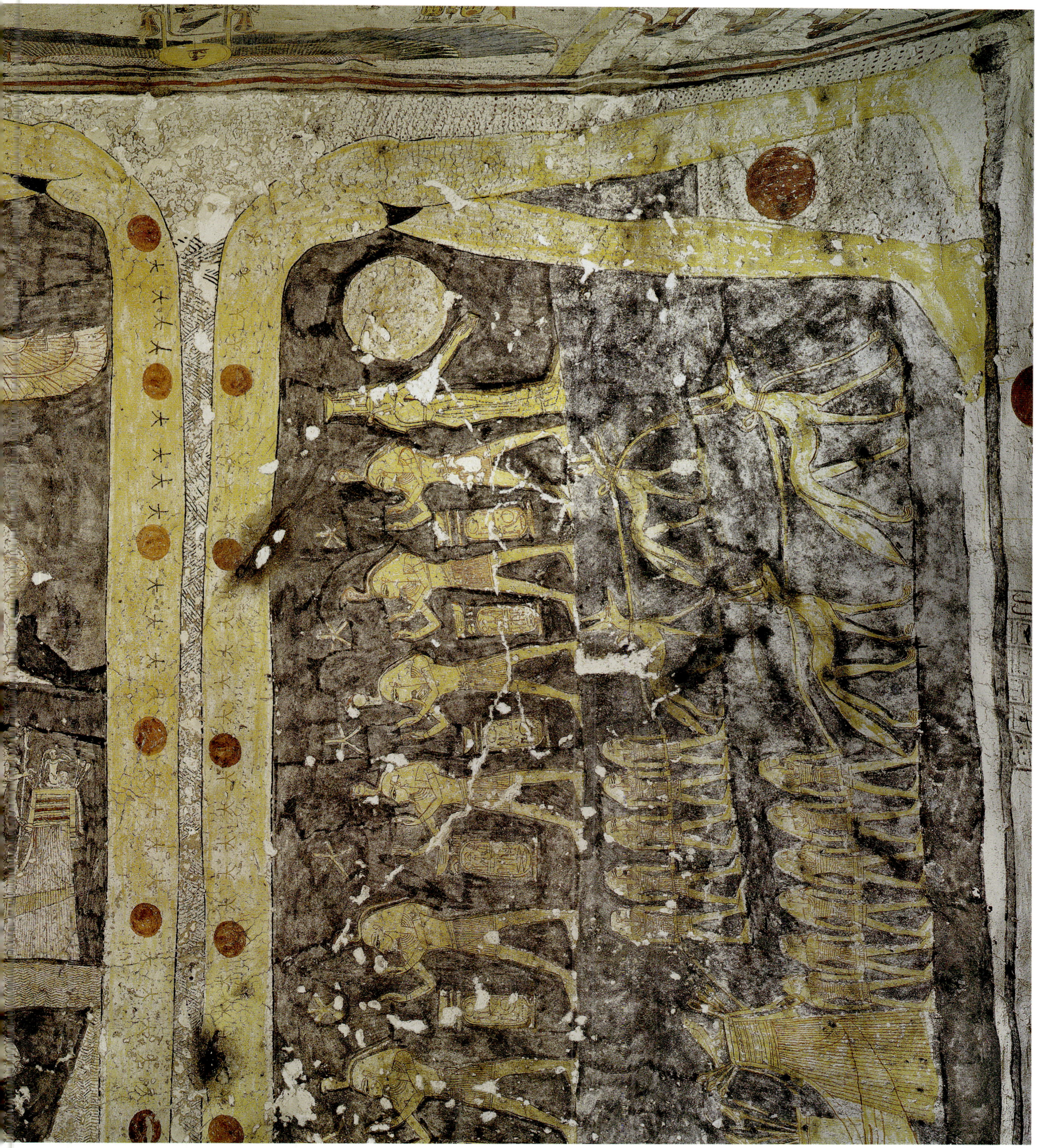

Finally, we see Isis and Nephthys raising the sun disk into the sky. The text here announces the birth eloquently: "Leaving the Duat in peace in the morning bark, traveling on the Nun to the hour of Re, 'He who Sees the Beauty of his Lord,' becoming Khepri, raising himself toward the horizon, entering the mouth, going out from the womb, rising in the mouth of doors of the horizon, to the hour 'The One who Raises the Beauty of Re' in order to make the people live." [after Piankoff]

The Book of the Heavenly Cow

Appearing first in a royal context on the golden shrines surrounding Tutankhamun's sarcophagus, the Book of the Heavenly Cow does not become part of the wall decoration of the royal tombs until the reign of Seti I, in whose tomb it is seen decorating one of the side chambers. Ramses II followed the example of his father, but then the composition is not seen again until the tomb of Ramses III. After this it disappears from the repertoire, with the exception of excerpts found in the tomb of Ramses V/VI.

According to this legend, Re was unhappy with the earth, and especially with the humans that lived on it. Nut, in the form of the Celestial Cow, took him up onto her back and carried him to the sky. There he sailed in his bark through her body, away from the anger of mankind.

The Book of Nut

The Book of Nut is the least common of the Books of the Heavens, found only in the Osireion of Seti I at Abydos and, in a short form, in the burial chamber of Ramses IV. This composition, consisting of one illustration with captions, is dominated by a large figure of Nut arched above the ground, upheld by Shu, but without a figure of Geb.

The focus here is on the topography of the sky; with captions giving details about the heavens and the daily course of the sun, the activities of the sun god, and other divine figures. The Decans are listed and their duties described. The farthest reaches of the sky are seen here as limitless, stretching into the lightless primordial darkness and water from which the universe was created: "The distant regions of heaven lie in perpetual darkness; Their borders unknown to the south, north, west, and east."

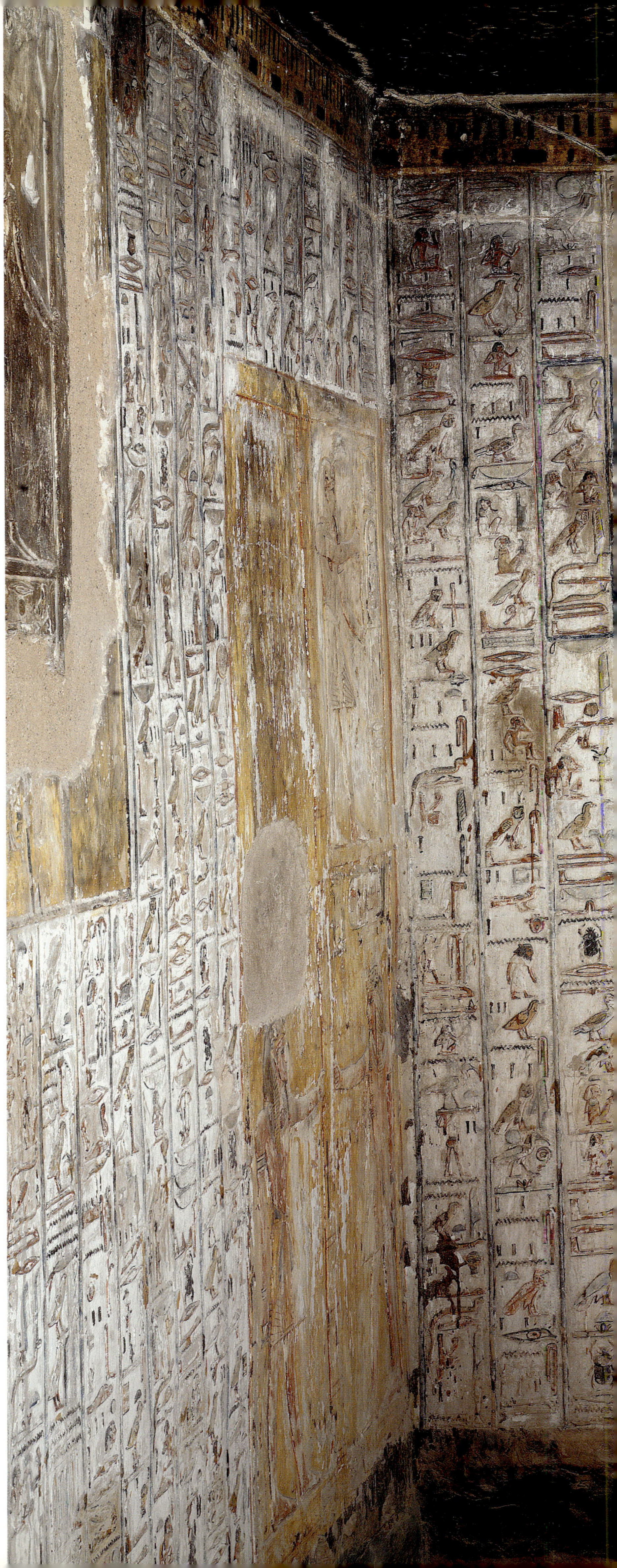

The Celestial Cow

The myth of the Celestial Cow is illustrated here in a scene from a side chamber in the tomb of Seti I. Here the sun god is angry at humankind, so the heavenly cow takes him on her back and carries him to the sky. The god Shu and the Heh gods of Hermopolis help to support the sky goddess.

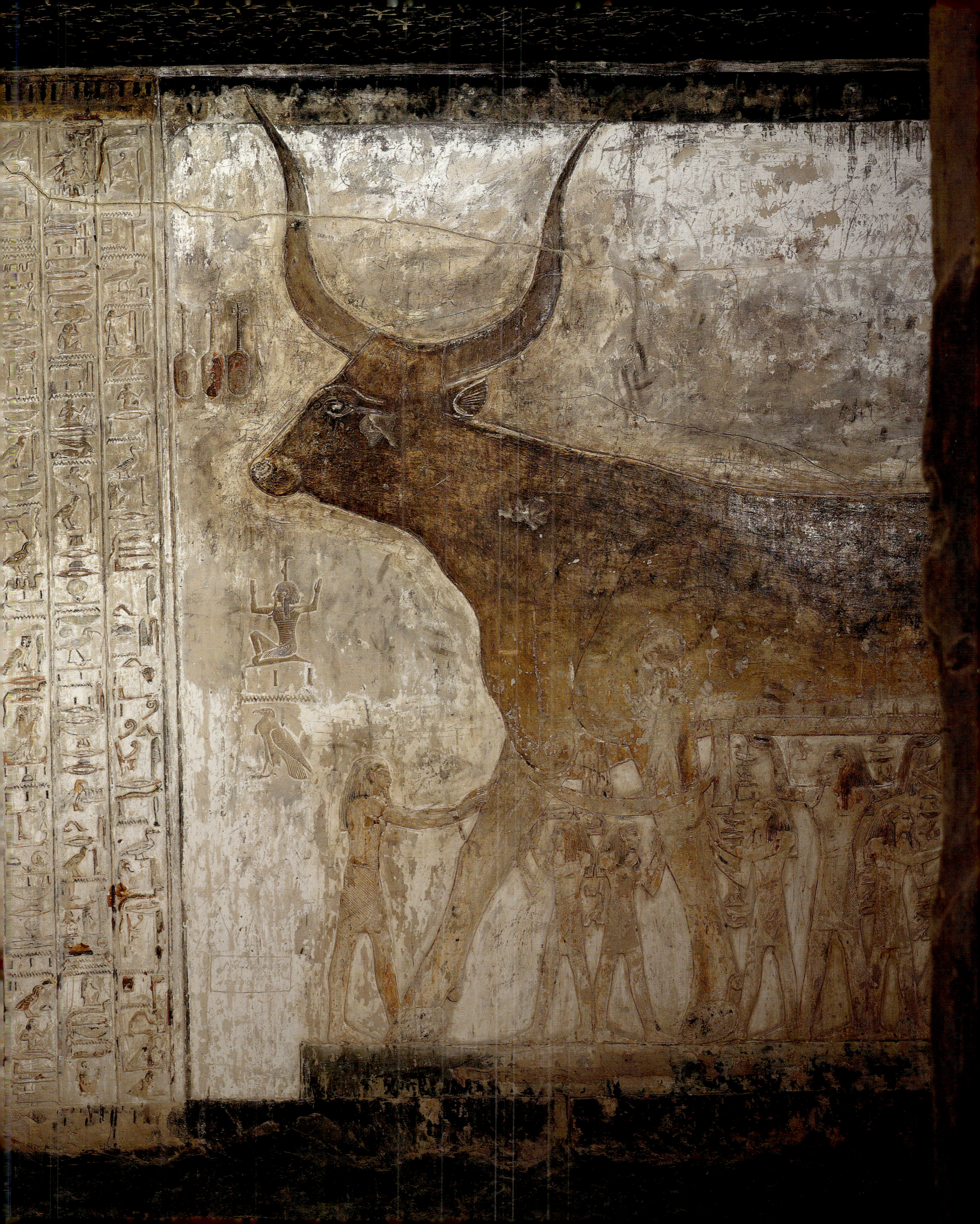

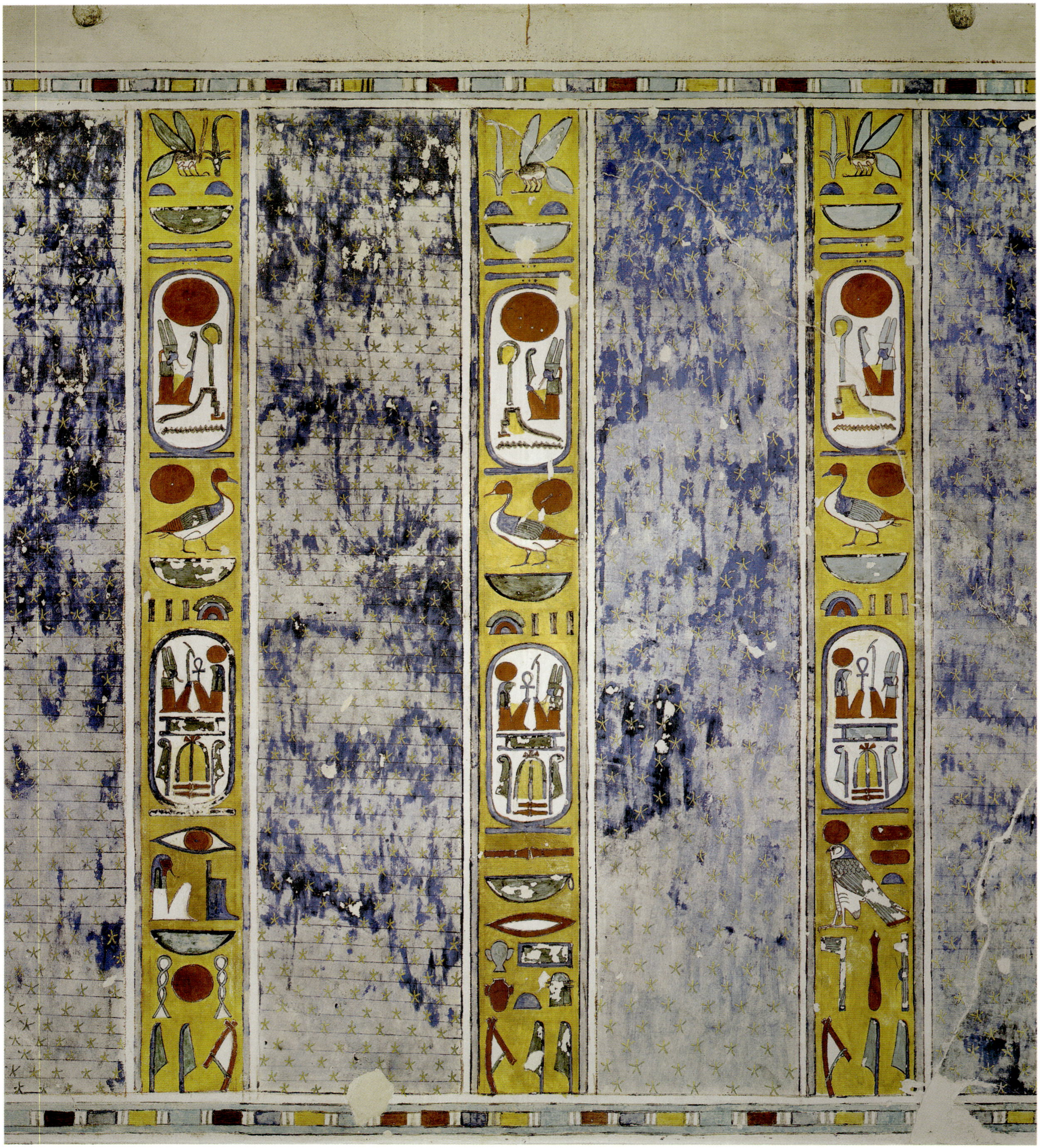

Cartouches of Ramses IV
The ceiling of the well chamber of Ramses IV's tomb is decorated with the king's names and titles in bands of yellow over a pattern of stars.

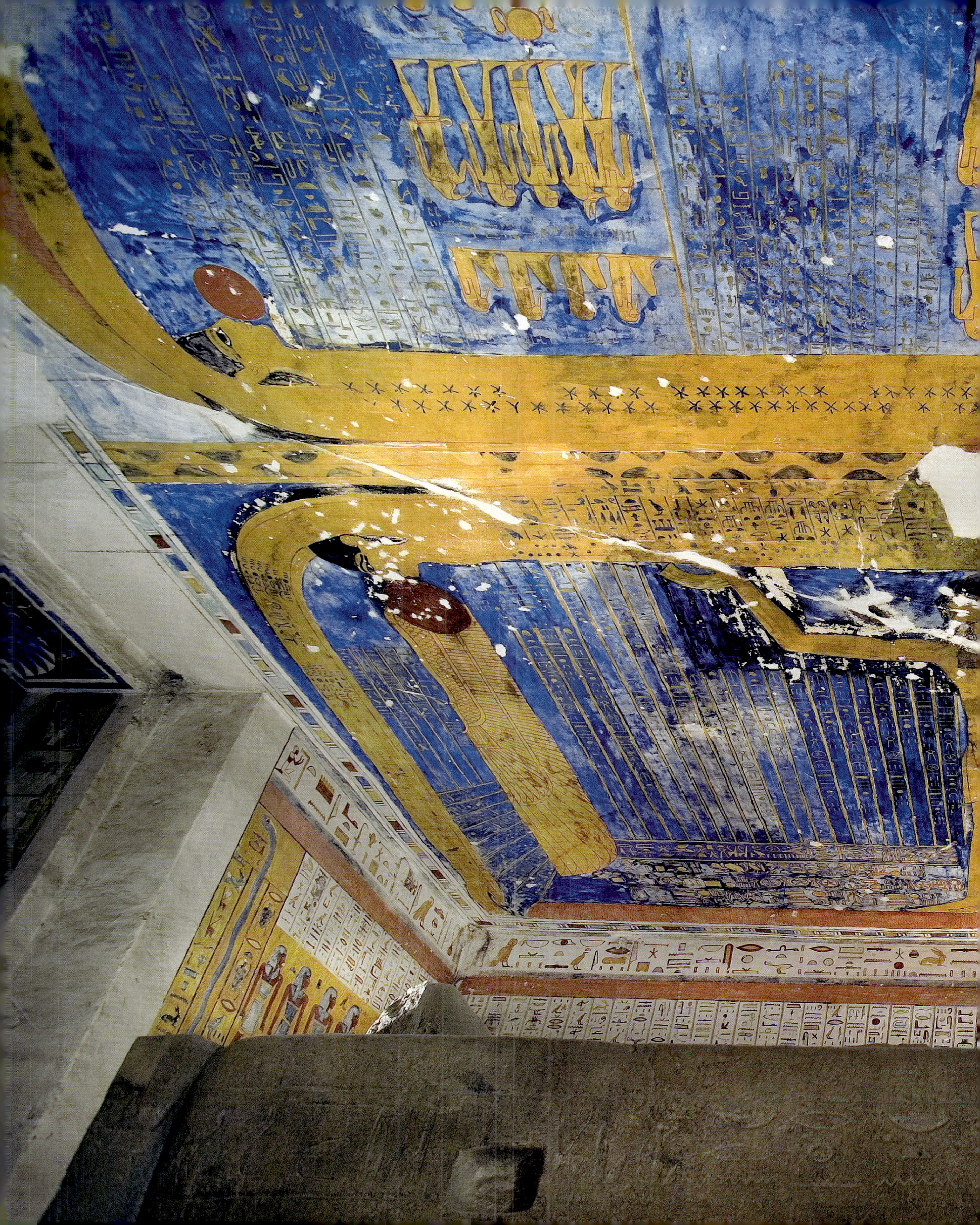

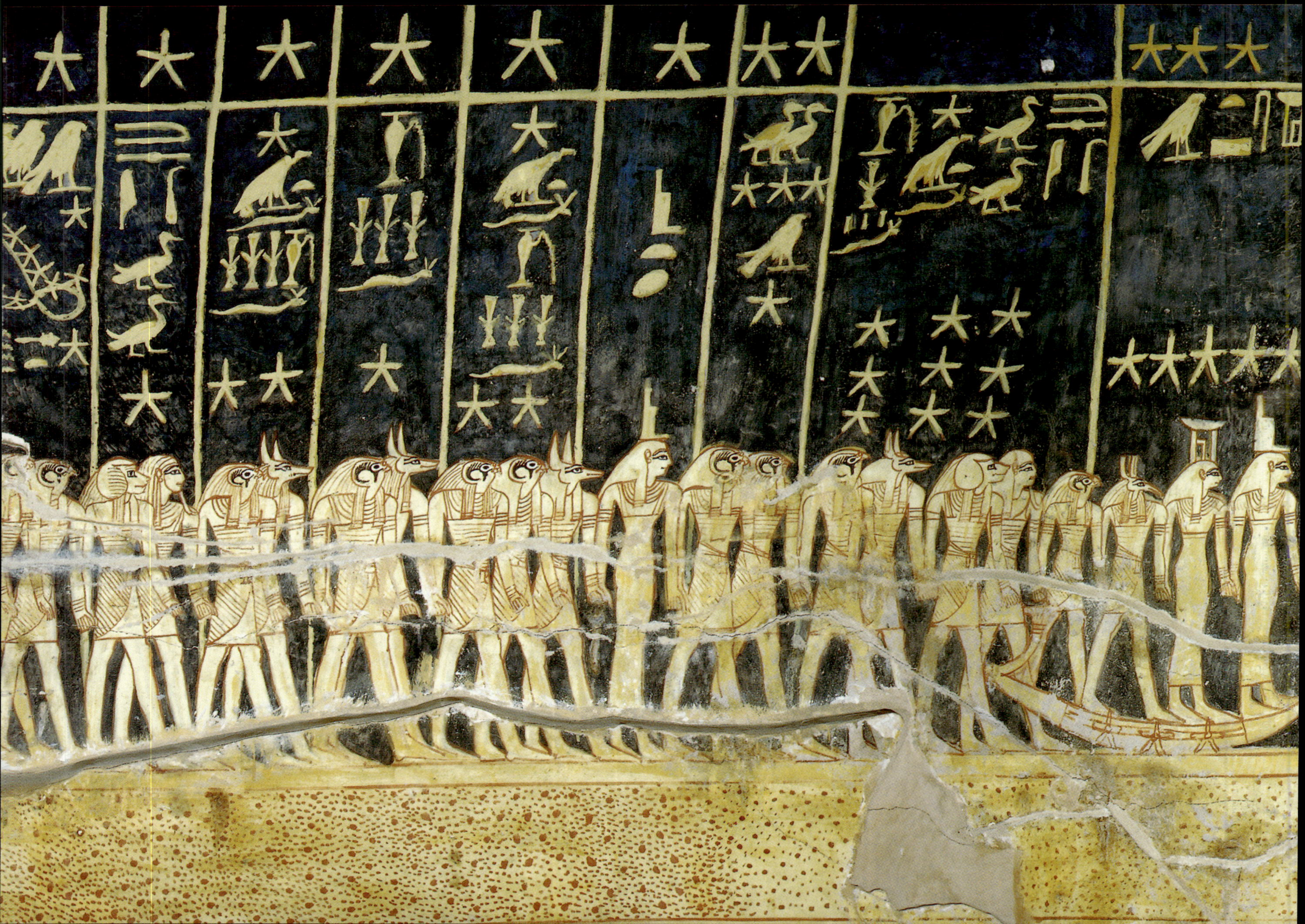

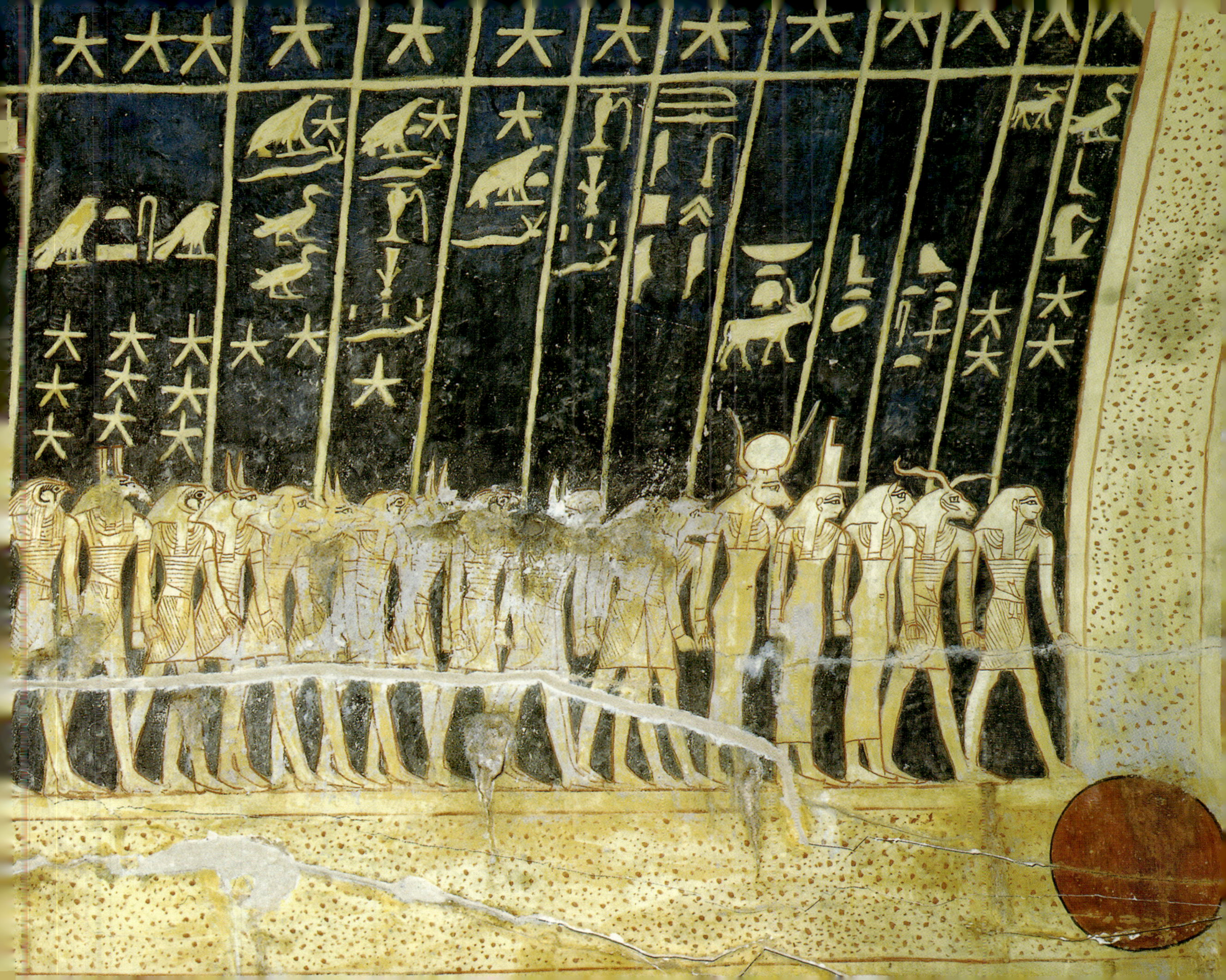

THE SOUTHERN SKY
(Preceding pages)
One half of the astronomical ceiling of Seti I depicts the stars of the southern sky, grouped into anthropomorphized clusters comparable to our modern constellations.

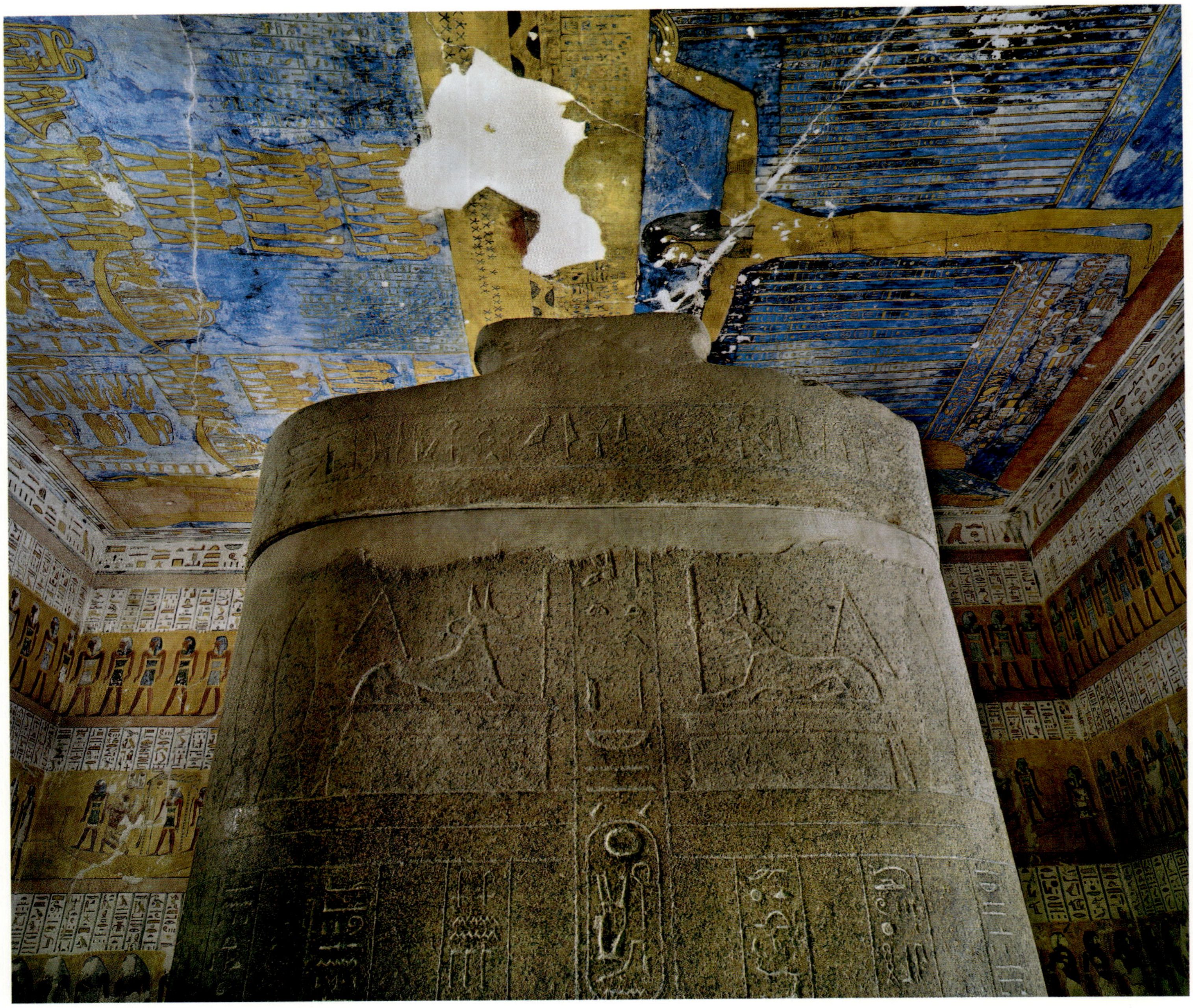

THE BURIAL CHAMBER OF RAMSES IV
The king's sarcophagus can be seen here, filling the center of the burial chamber of the tomb of Ramses IV.

THE BOOKS OF THE NIGHT AND OF NUT
The flat ceiling of Ramses IV's burial chamber is adorned with two figures of Nut, back to back, framing the Book of the Night (foreground) and the Book of Nut (background). In the Book of Nut, Shu can be seen supporting the sky goddess, standing on a flat strip of ground representing the earth.

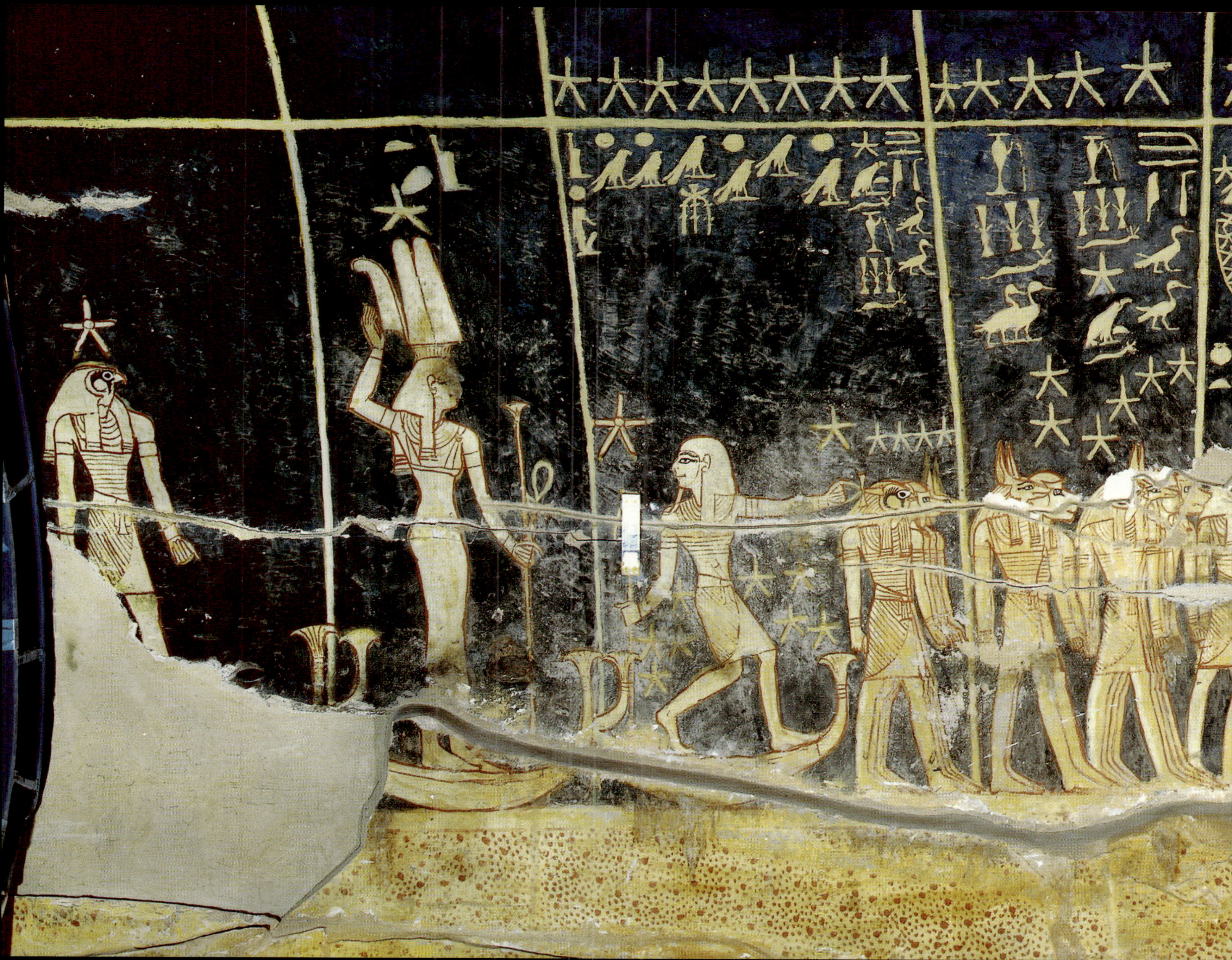

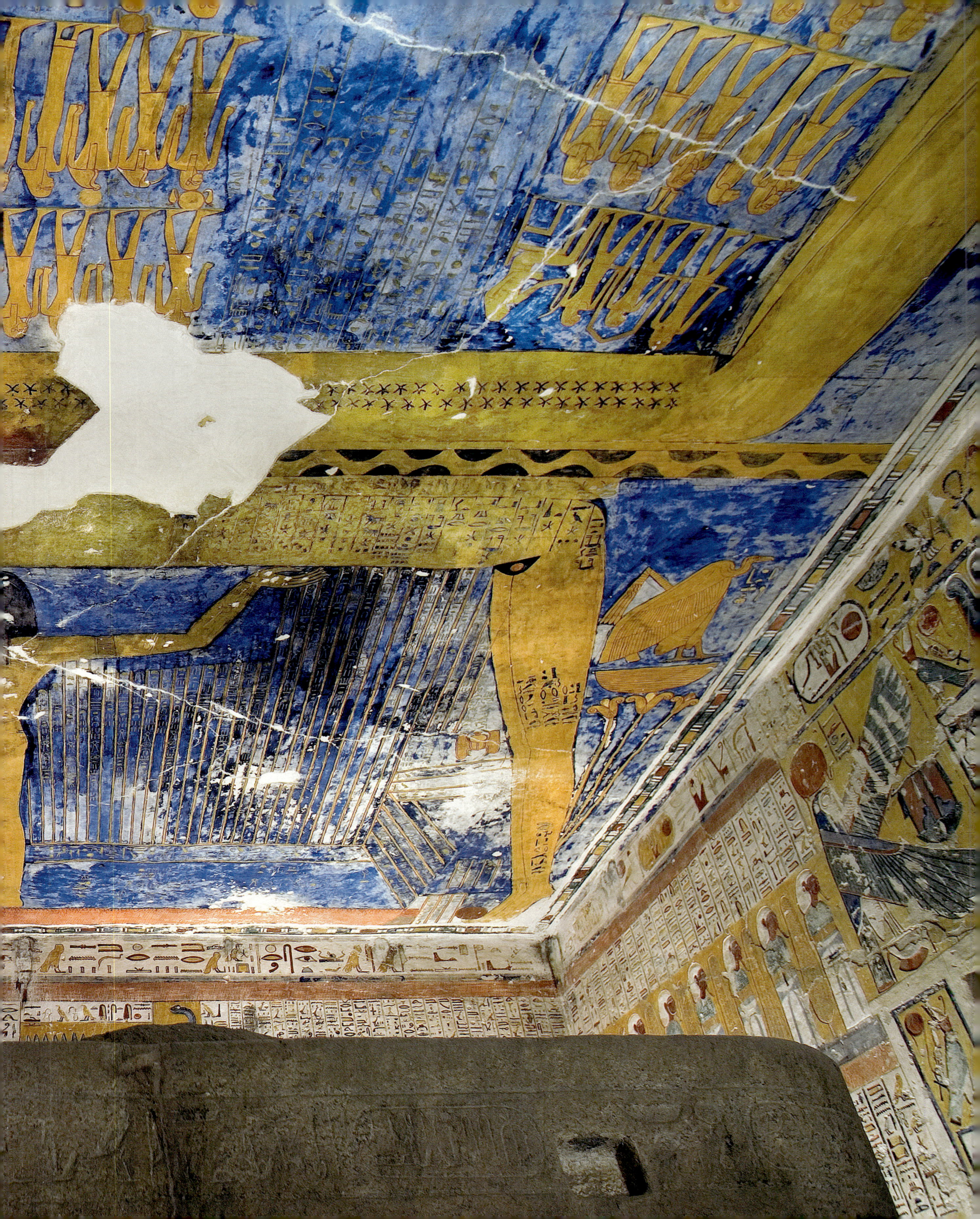

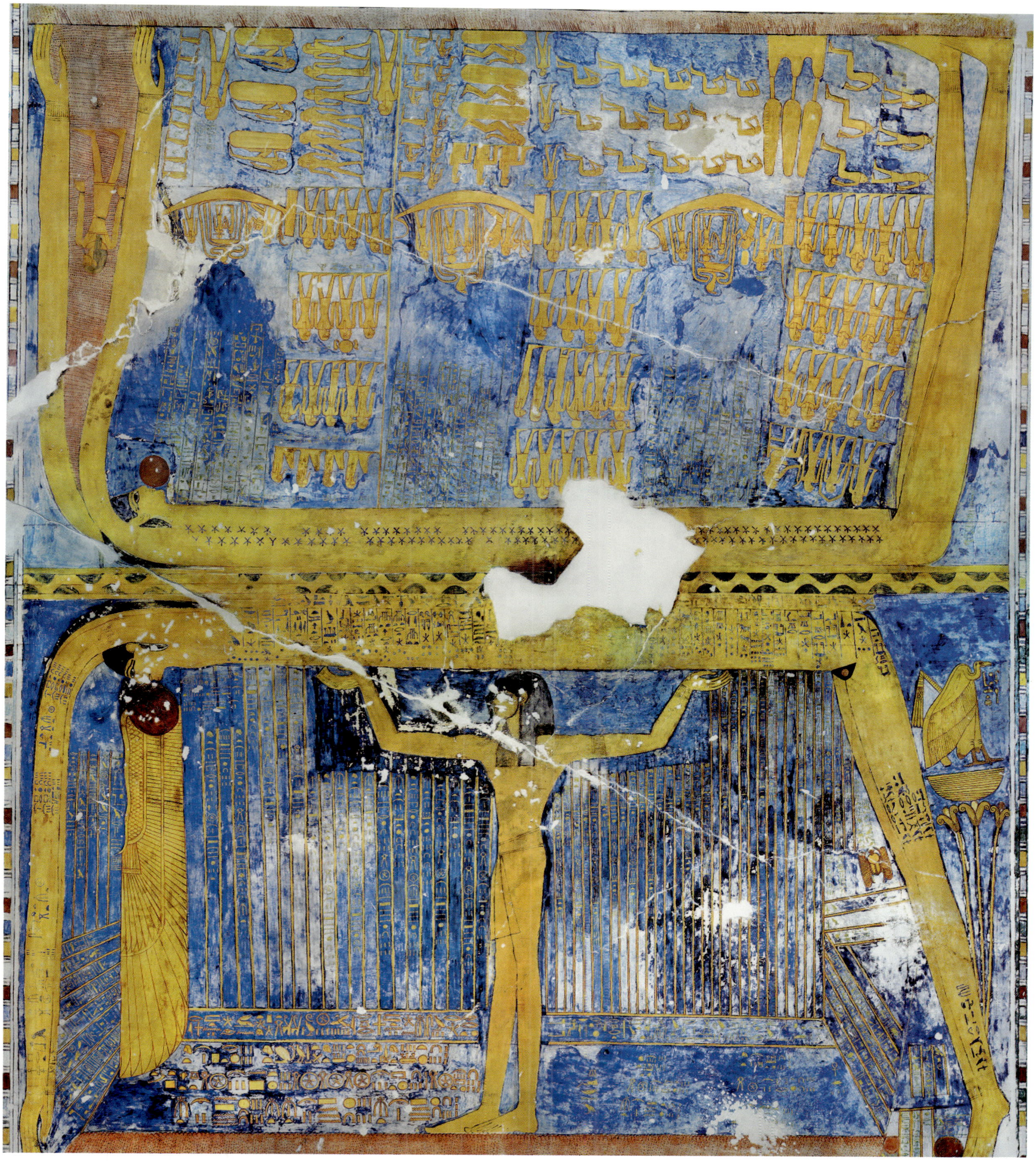

THE BOOK OF NUT
In a rare example of this composition, the sky goddess, arched above a simple, non-anthropomorphized strip of earth, is held up by the god of the air, Shu. The captions here give detailed information about the heavens and the daily course of the sun.

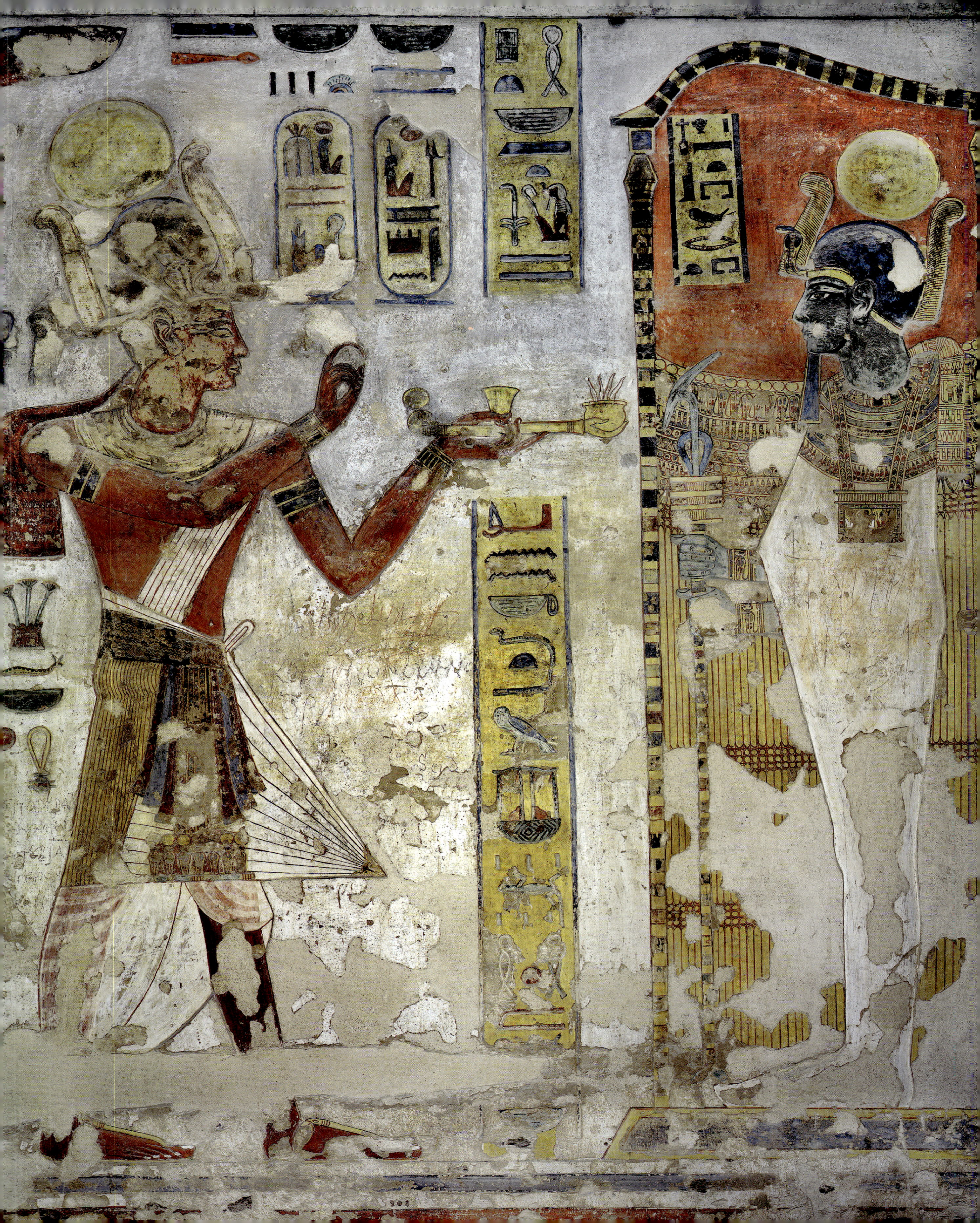

Conclusion

Saving the Valley of the Kings

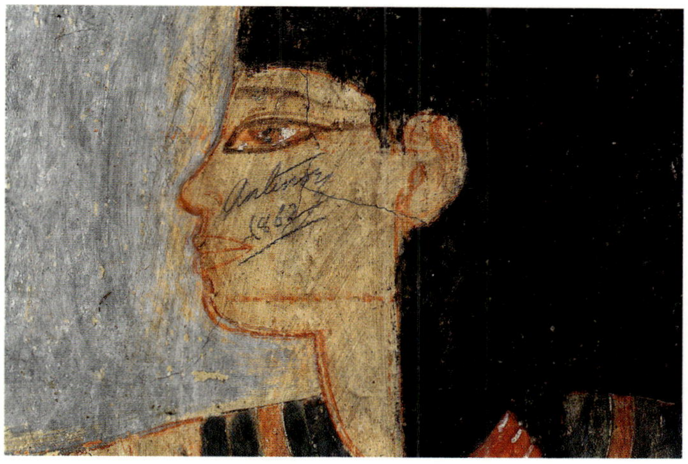

The Valley of the Kings has been neglected for a long time. For many decades, only a few of the royal tombs were open to the public, so that the burials of kings such as Tutankhamun, Seti I, Ramses VI, Horemheb, and Tuthmosis III were visited by thousands of tourists each day. These visitors have done great damage to these tombs, most inadvertently, some through carelessness, and some through ignorance. Many people are not mindful—they crowd into the tombs with their backpacks, and scrape against the walls when they turn around. Some, including many tourist guides, do not know how much destruction is caused by the human touch, which leaves behind oils and salts, and rub their fingers across the paintings. Tour guides also stay inside the tombs for a long time, explaining the decoration. And even those who are respectful and care for the ancient monuments cannot keep from damaging the walls, as their breath contains moisture, which brings the salt out from the underlying stone and destroys the scenes.

For a long time, there was no system in place for managing the cars that brought the tourists to the valley. Anyone could drive right up to the entrances, creating both fumes from their exhausts and sight pollution. Add to this the natural hazards, such as periodic flooding caused by torrential rains (which had already, over the millennia, ruined the decoration of the tomb of Ramses II), and you have a recipe for disaster. If nothing is done, the tombs will be gone within a century.

Over the past few years, we have begun a site management program to save the Valley from destruction. The most important aspect of this program has been to control the flow of tourists and their cars, but we are also including plans to keep floods from washing through the tombs.

To begin with, we have closed some of the tombs in the greatest danger, such as Seti I and Horemheb, and opened additional tombs to take the pressure off the most-visited sepulchers. We have put a rotation system in place, so that tombs will be closed according to a regular schedule for

Ramses III and Ptah

This scene from the tomb of Ramses III, depicting the king offering incense to the god Ptah, displays the ravages of time, with much of the painted plaster having fallen from the walls.

cleaning and restoration. Signs have been put up in front of each tomb, showing its plan and highlighting the most important scenes, so that tour guides can (and must) give their explanations outside. This lessens the time tourists spend inside the delicate corridors and chambers and clears up some of the problems caused by large groups crowding around to hear their leaders.

In cooperation with the Japanese government, we have built a visitors' center a few kilometers from the Royal Valley itself. A short film by National Geographic will play here, to orient tourists before they continue to the tombs themselves. There will also be archival images displayed in this center, and other materials that will help educate the interested visitor. The visitors' center will include facilities such as shops and a cafeteria. We have built a new parking lot and put in electric trams, so that tourists arrive at the mouth of the Valley itself without creating air or sight pollution. The SCA has recently announced a competition for a new transportation system to ferry the tourists to the Valley and back; this should be suitable to the site and non-polluting.

The Valley will be lit so that tourists will be able, for the first time, to visit the tombs at night. There will be three shifts each day: one in the morning, one in the afternoon, and one in the evening. Only a certain number of tickets will be sold, in advance, for each of these shifts. Visitors will be able to make reservations to see specific tombs ahead of time. This will also help the tourists: one complaint we get is that people arrive at the Valley without knowing which tombs are open, then have to go back down to the ticket office again.

An important project has been carried out by the American Research Center in Egypt (ARCE), which will help save the valley from flooding. Studies have been done of the geology of the area, and plans made for concrete barriers that will deflect the flow of the water. Within the tombs themselves, we are carrying out studies to see how best to save them and protect them for the future. One project currently in the works is a ventilation system.

The guards at the Valley of the Kings will be educated so that they understand its importance better. They will begin to enforce new rules, such as no photos with flash and no large bags in the tombs. The inspectors here will also

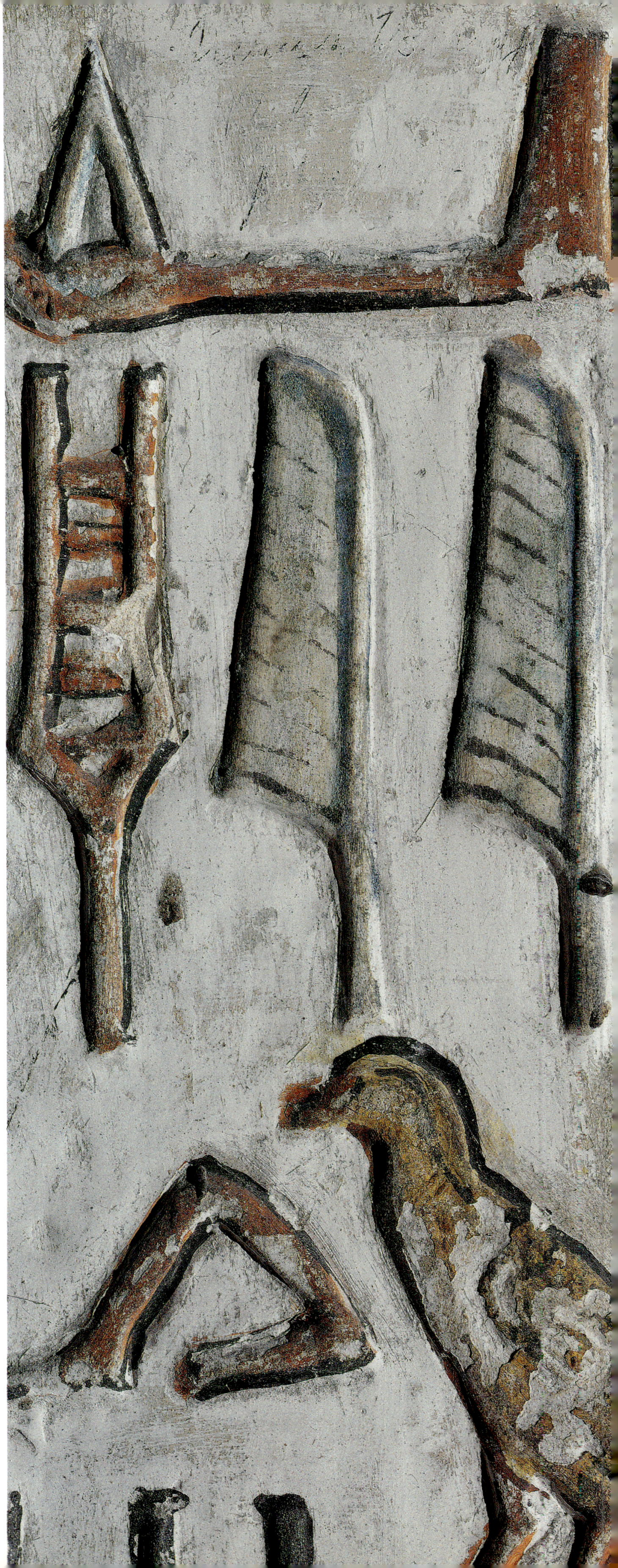

Ancient and Modern Writing

This bearded god from the tomb of Seti I has lost much of his paint. He is surrounded by ancient hieroglyphs, but the image is also marred by modern graffiti, scratched by some thoughtless visitor.

Victorian Visitors

(Following pages)

Victorian visitors, such as this "P.T." from 1870, sometimes recorded their passages through the royal tombs, to the great detriment of the wall paintings.

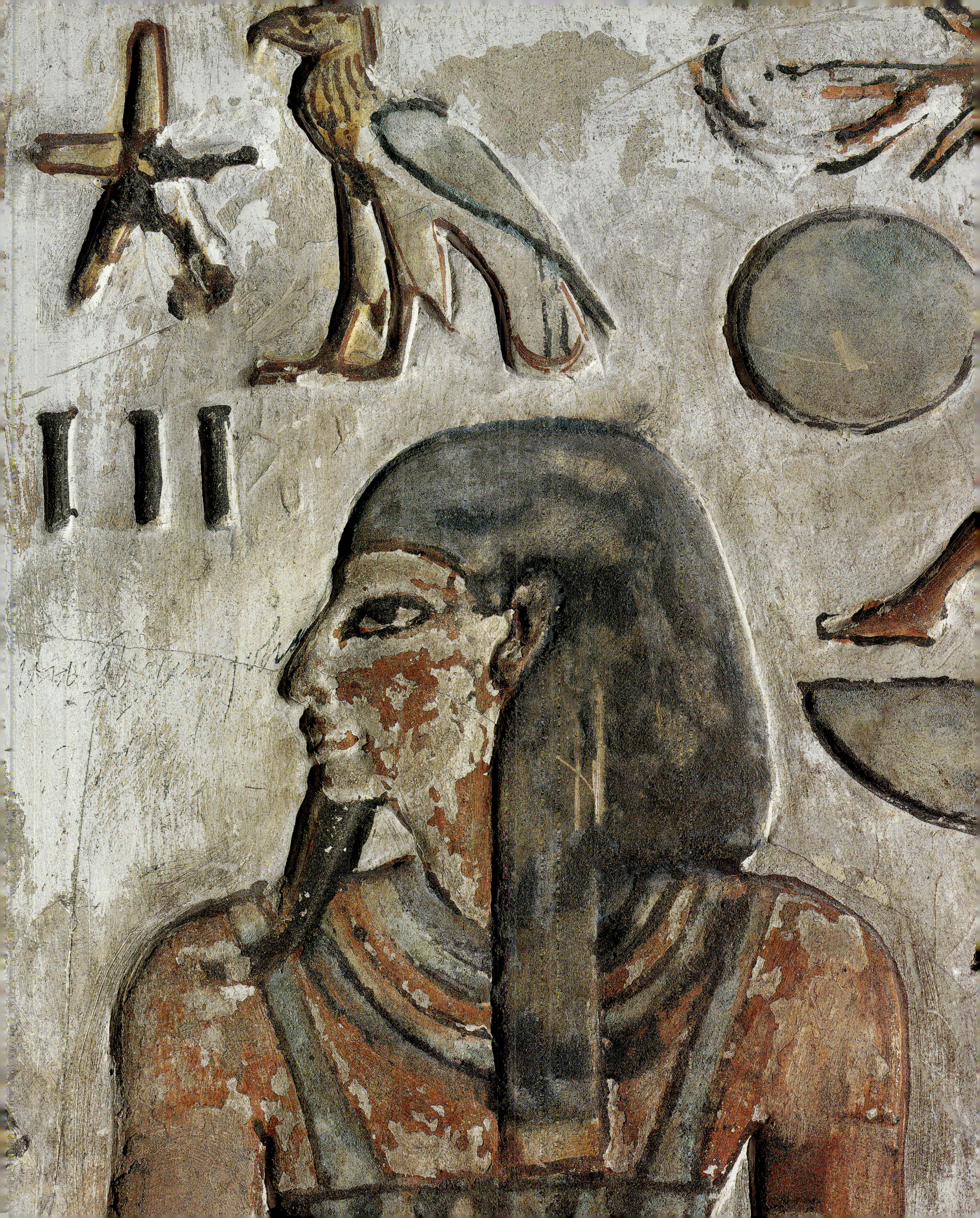

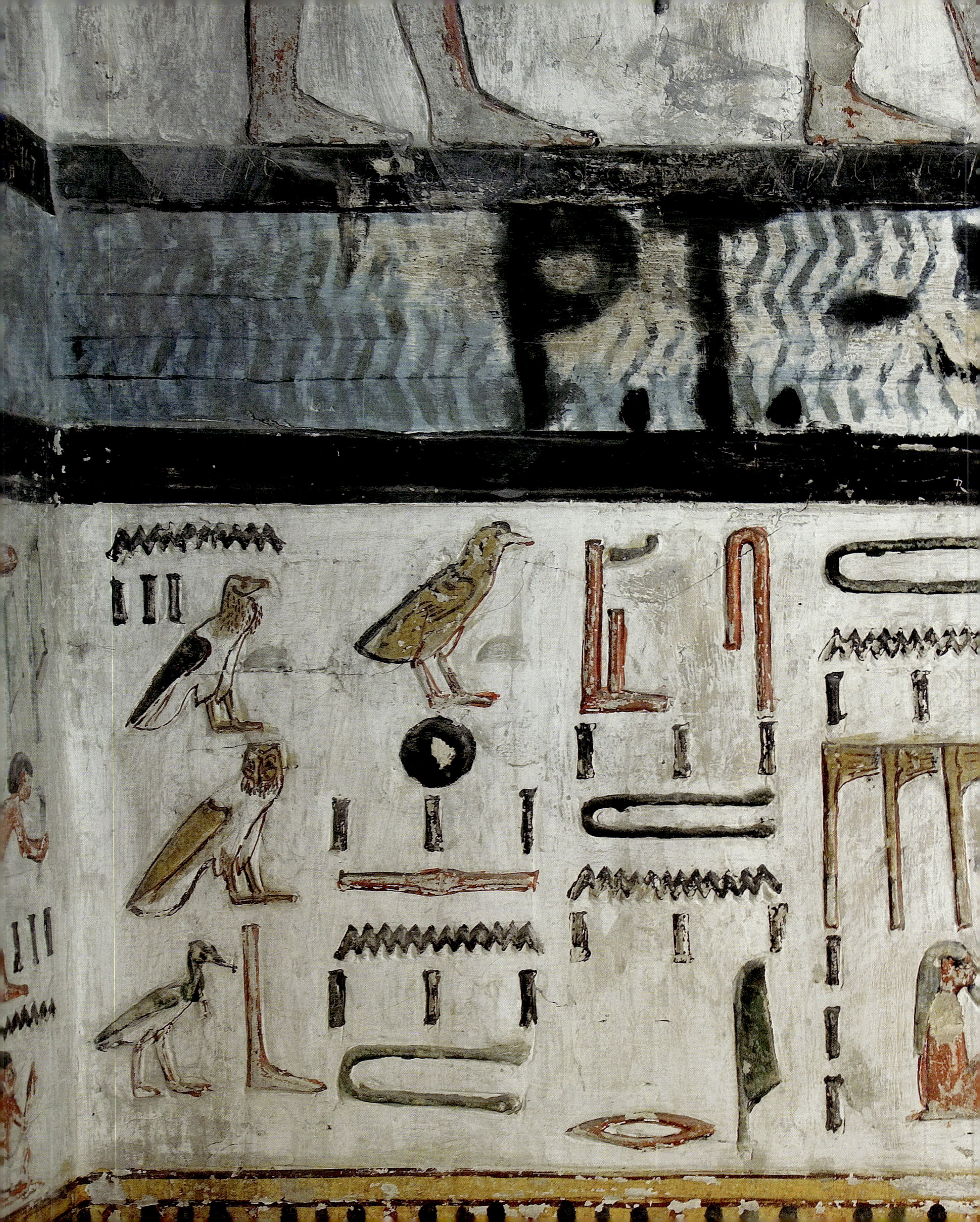

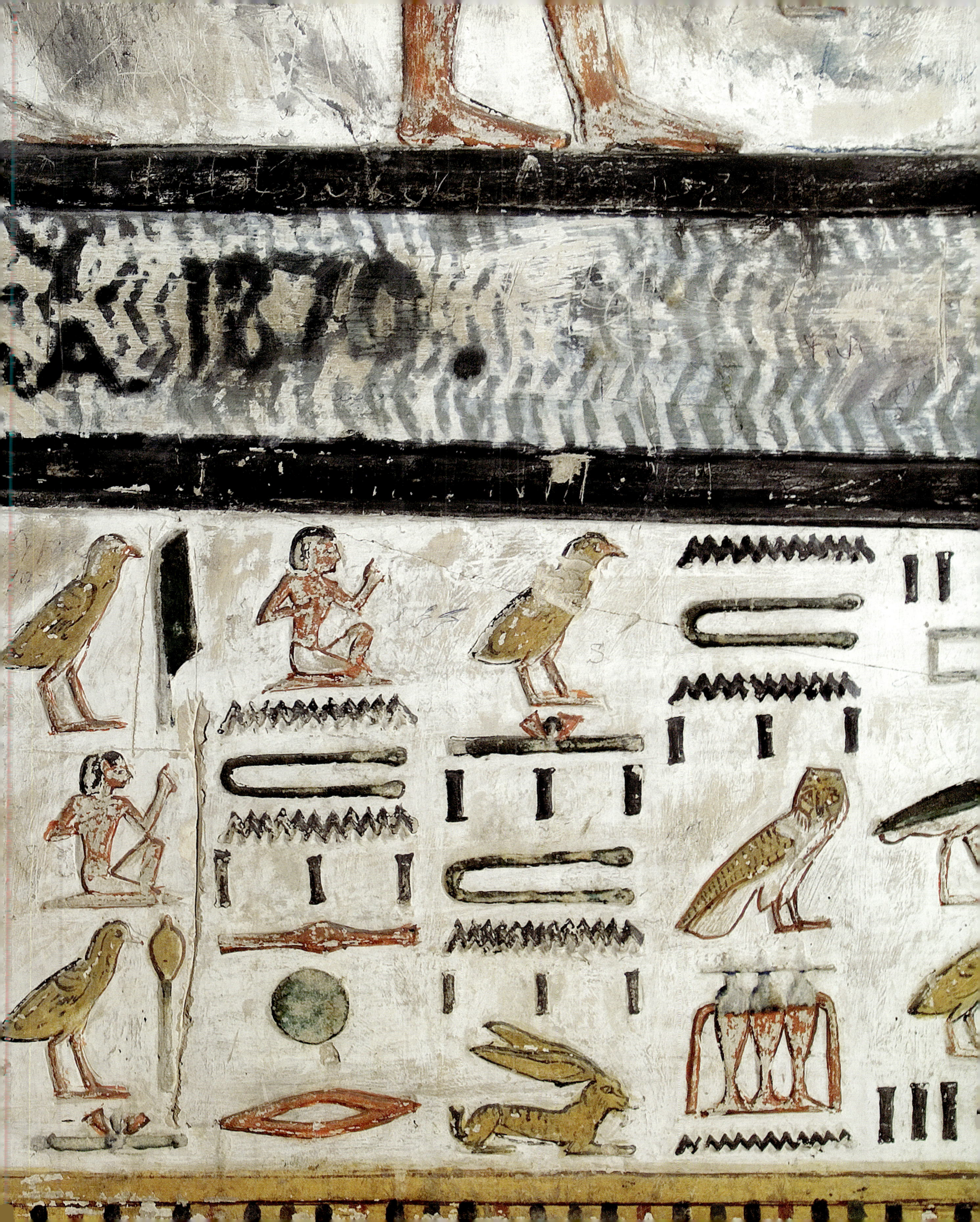
1870.

receive additional training, and will be given instruction in conservation and site management. ARCE has already initiated one such training program, which is teaching many young archaeologists the basics, as well as giving further training in dealing with archaeological and conservation issues that arise at the site to senior inspectors. Foreign missions will work more closely with the SCA, and with one another, to coordinate their efforts. A conservation lab will be built in the Valley of the Kings that will be ready to deal with preservation and restoration issues as they arise.

We are still considering whether or not it will be safe to reopen some of the recently-closed tombs after they have undergone cleaning and restoration. For example, the tomb of Seti I will be closed permanently to most visitors, to save it from complete destruction, but the tomb of Horemheb might be reopened on a periodic basis. The visitors' center will provide information to tourists about which tombs are open, and when.

I do not think that there is any place in the world that has the magic of the Valley of the Kings. Even with their bodies gone, the ancient kings still travel, through the magical images on the walls, on their eternal journey to the beyond. It is up to us to preserve these priceless treasures, to save them so that future generations can enjoy and learn from them.

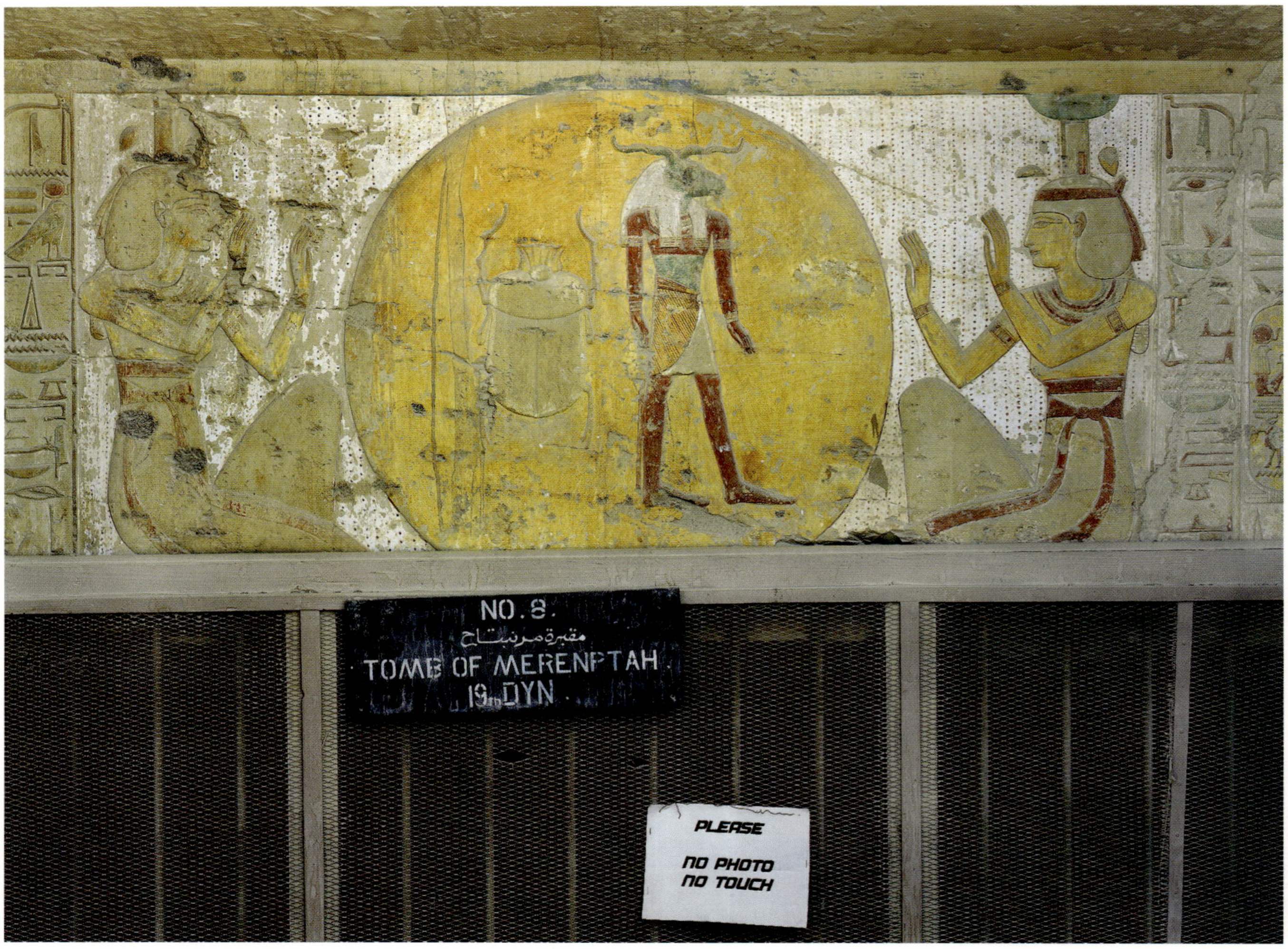

Site Management

Our new site management plans include new signs for the tombs, to replace the old, sometimes barely legible ones in place today. Large panels outside each tomb will provide a place for guides to lecture, significantly decreasing the traffic inside the corridors and chambers.

Wear and Tear

(*Following pages*)

Centuries of weathering, and decades of heavy tourist traffic, have chipped much of the paint off the walls of this royal tomb. We are currently using a rotation system to close each tomb in turn for restoration and conservation, and keeping the most fragile, such as the sepulcher of Seti I, off-limits for tourists.

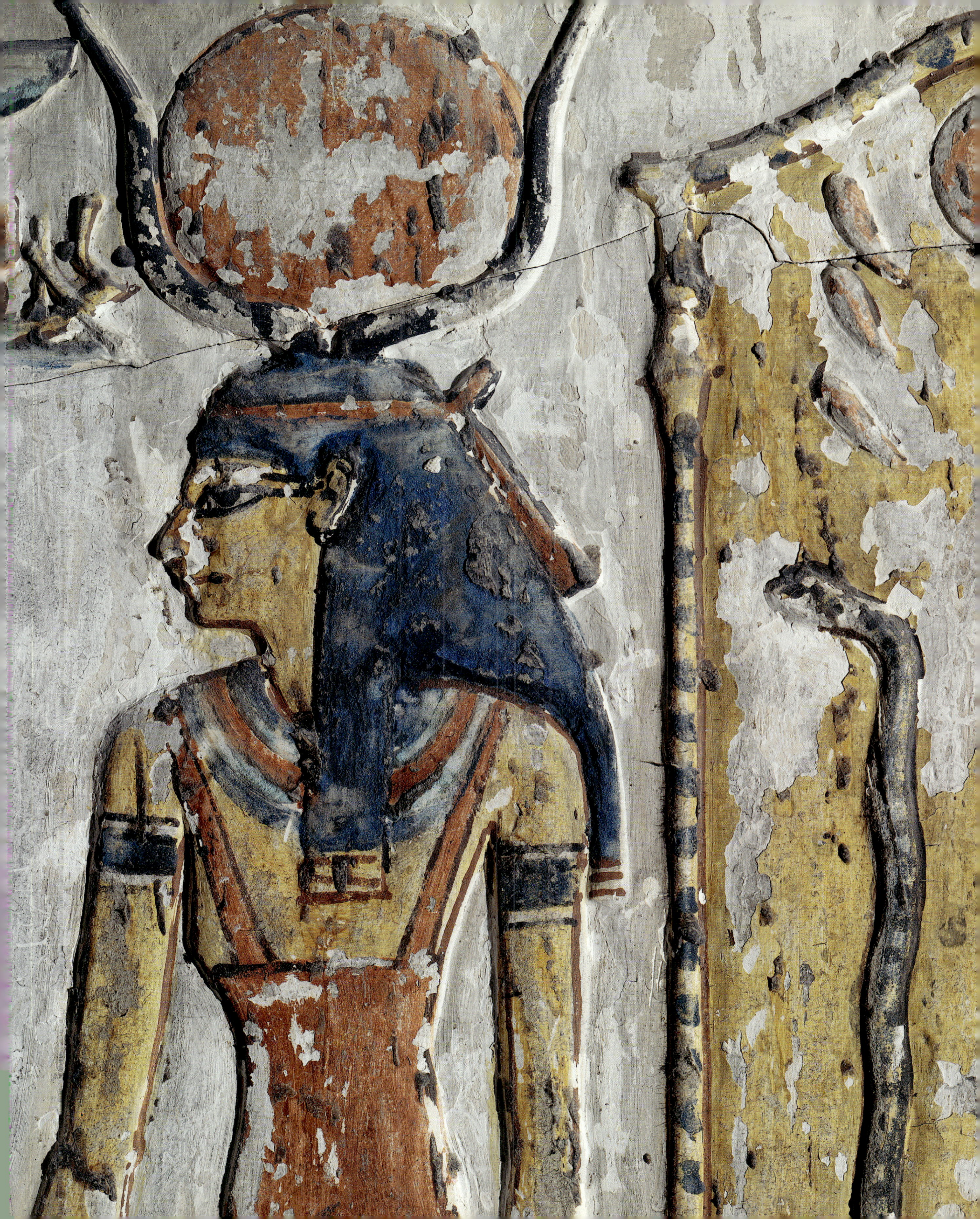

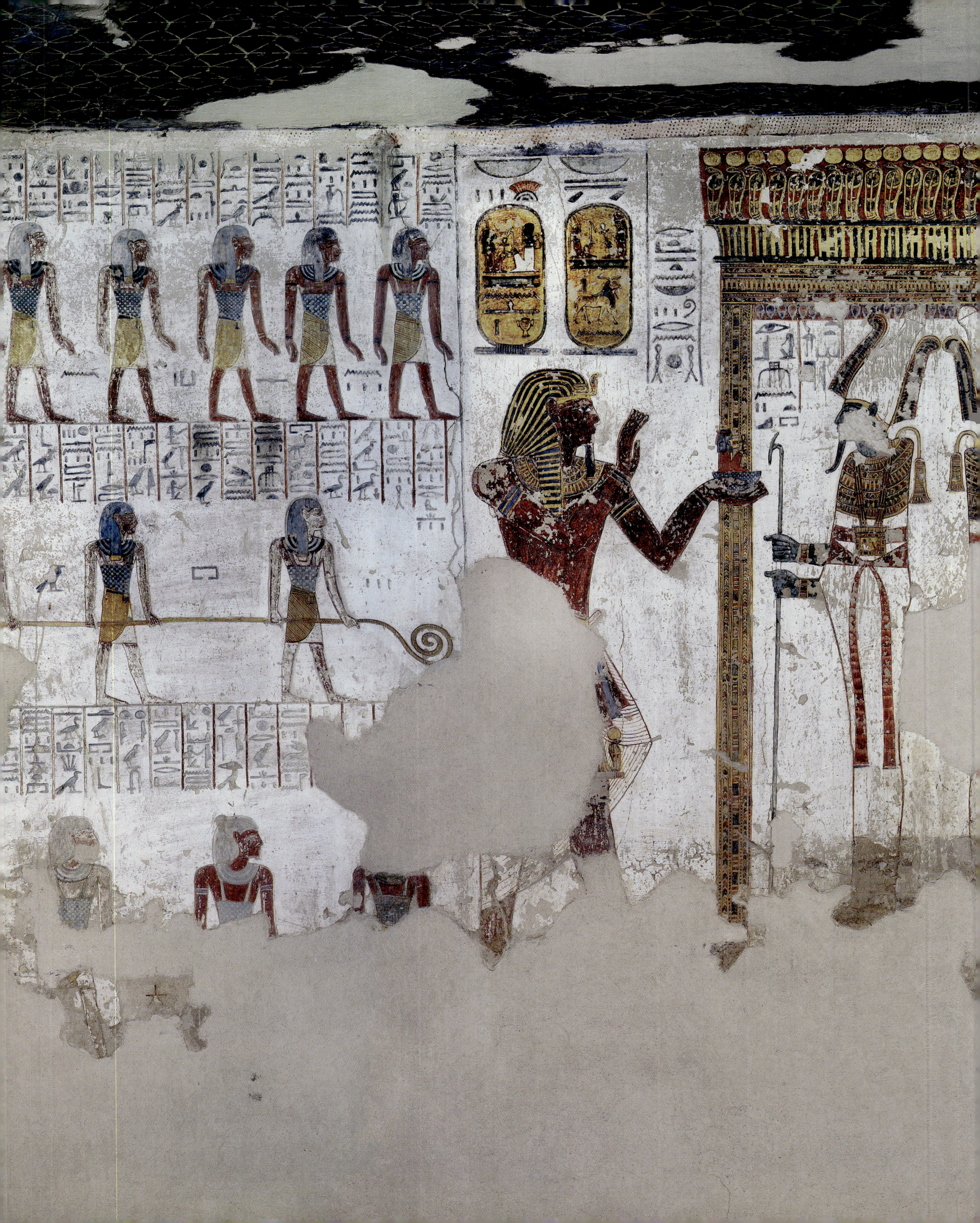

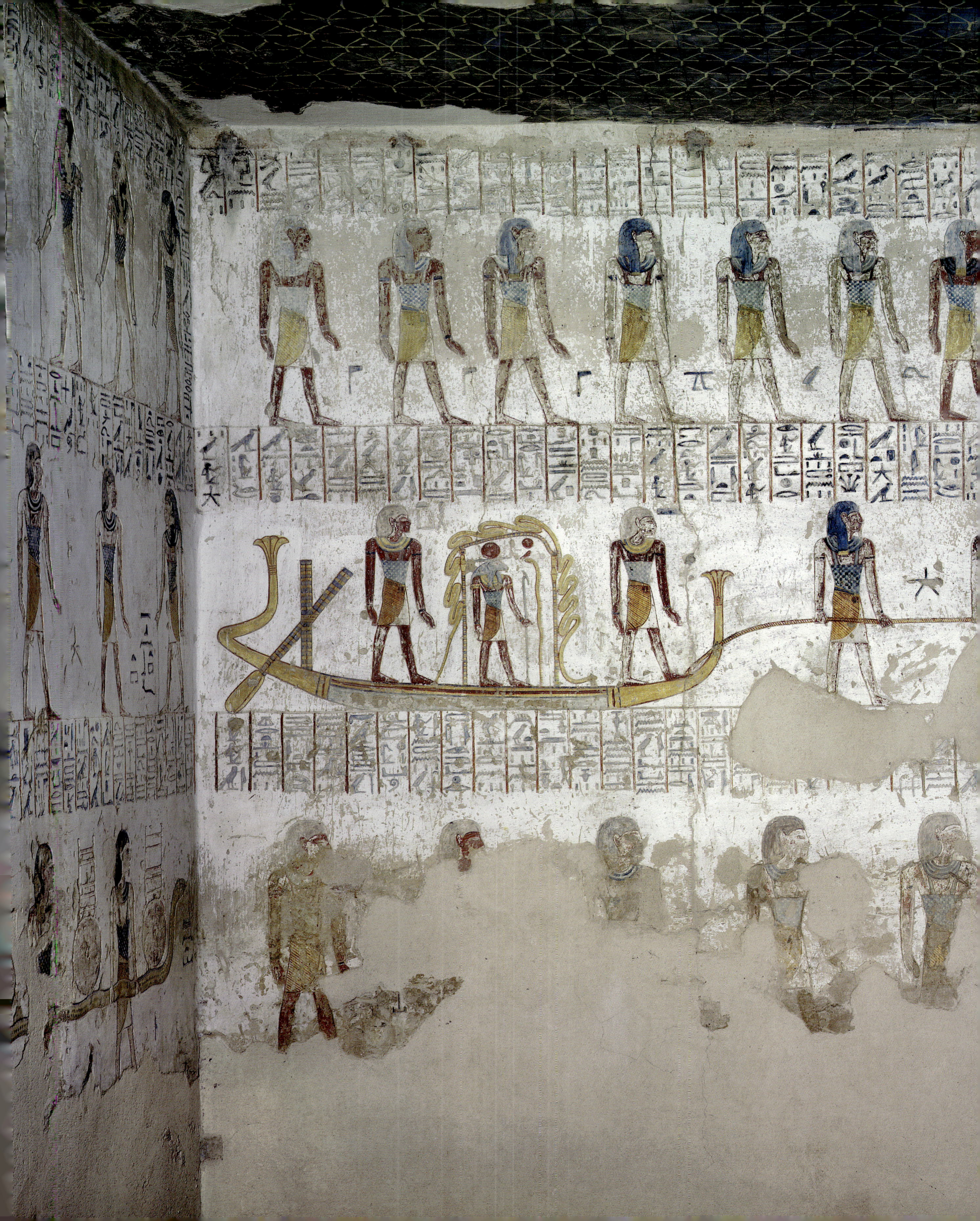

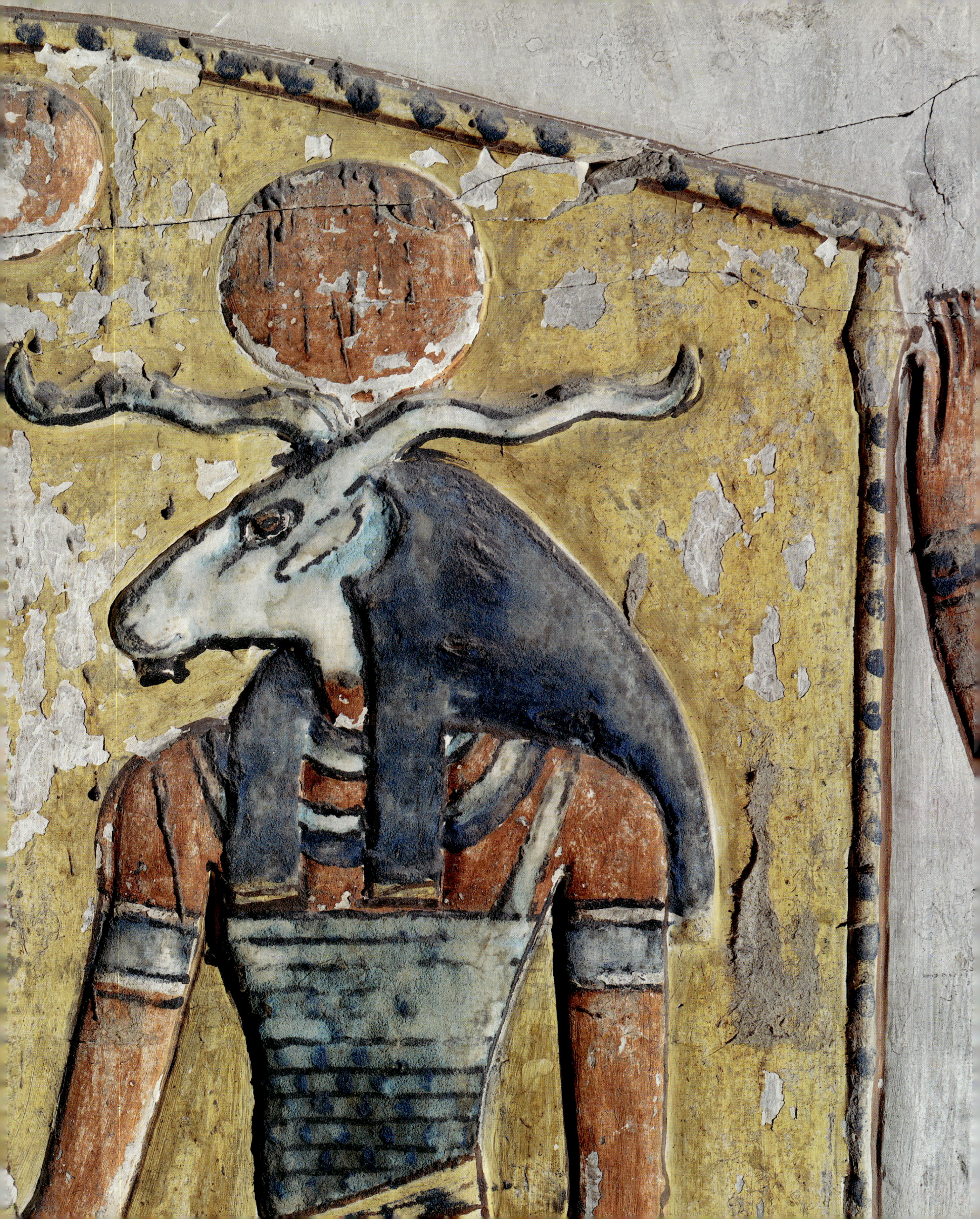

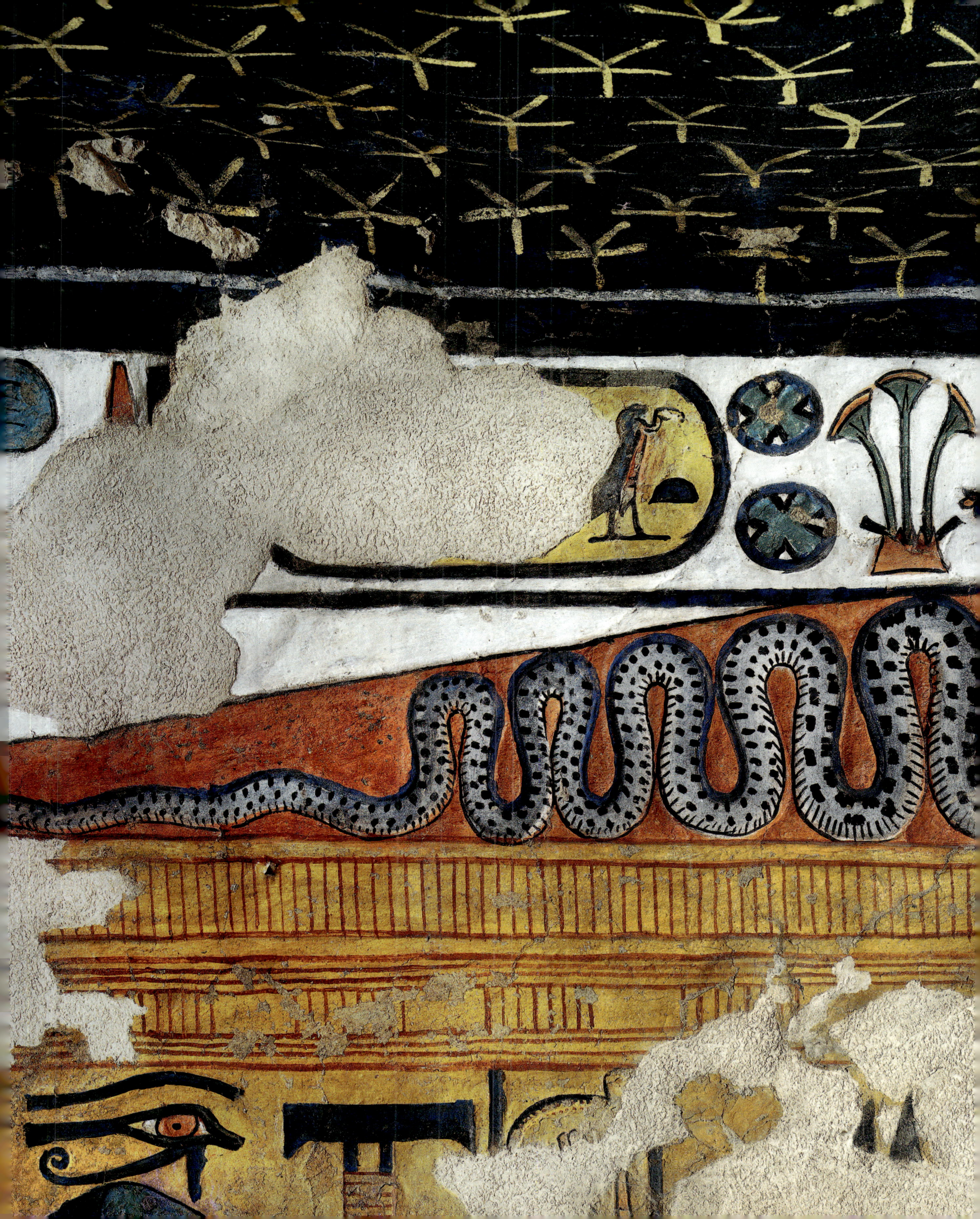

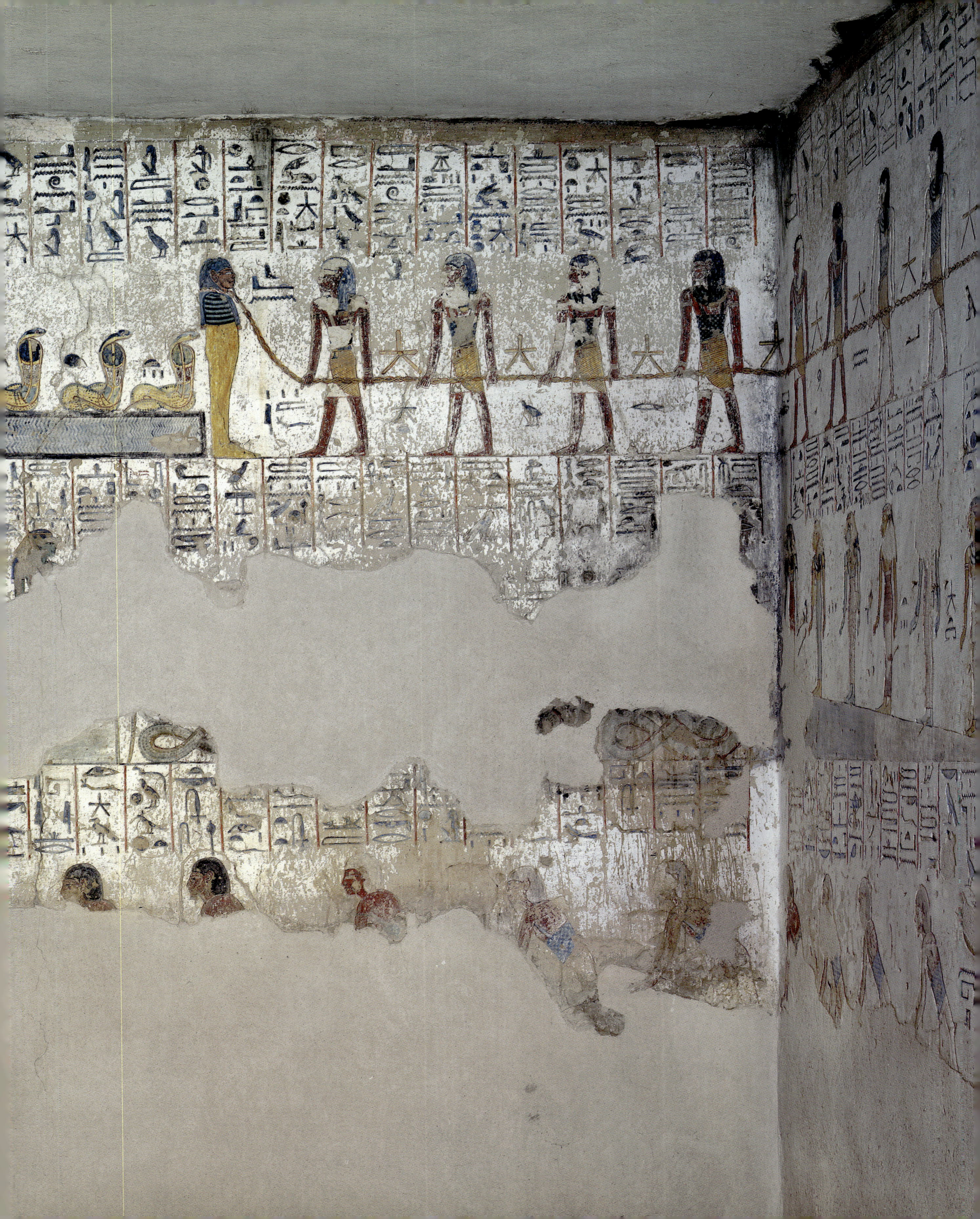

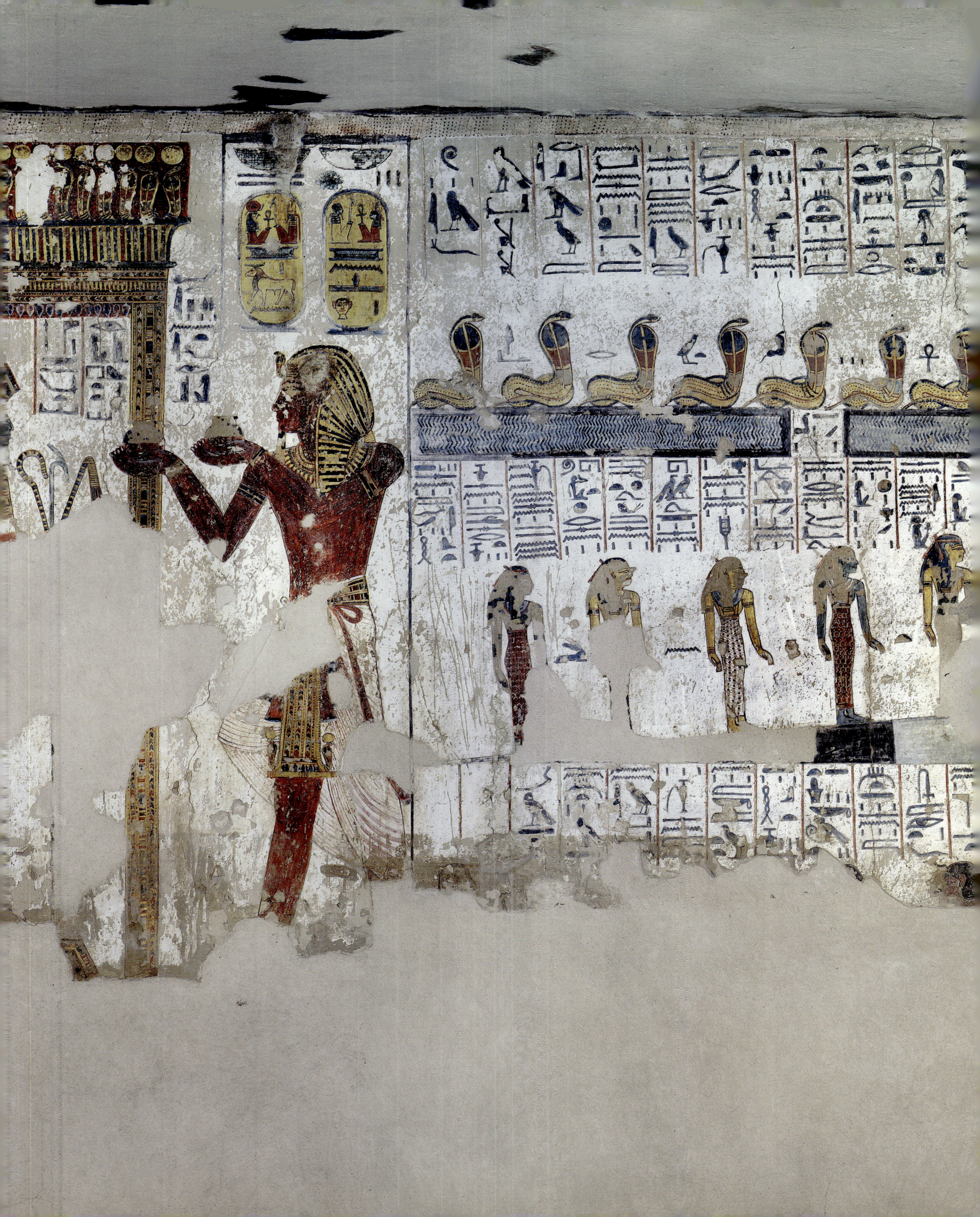

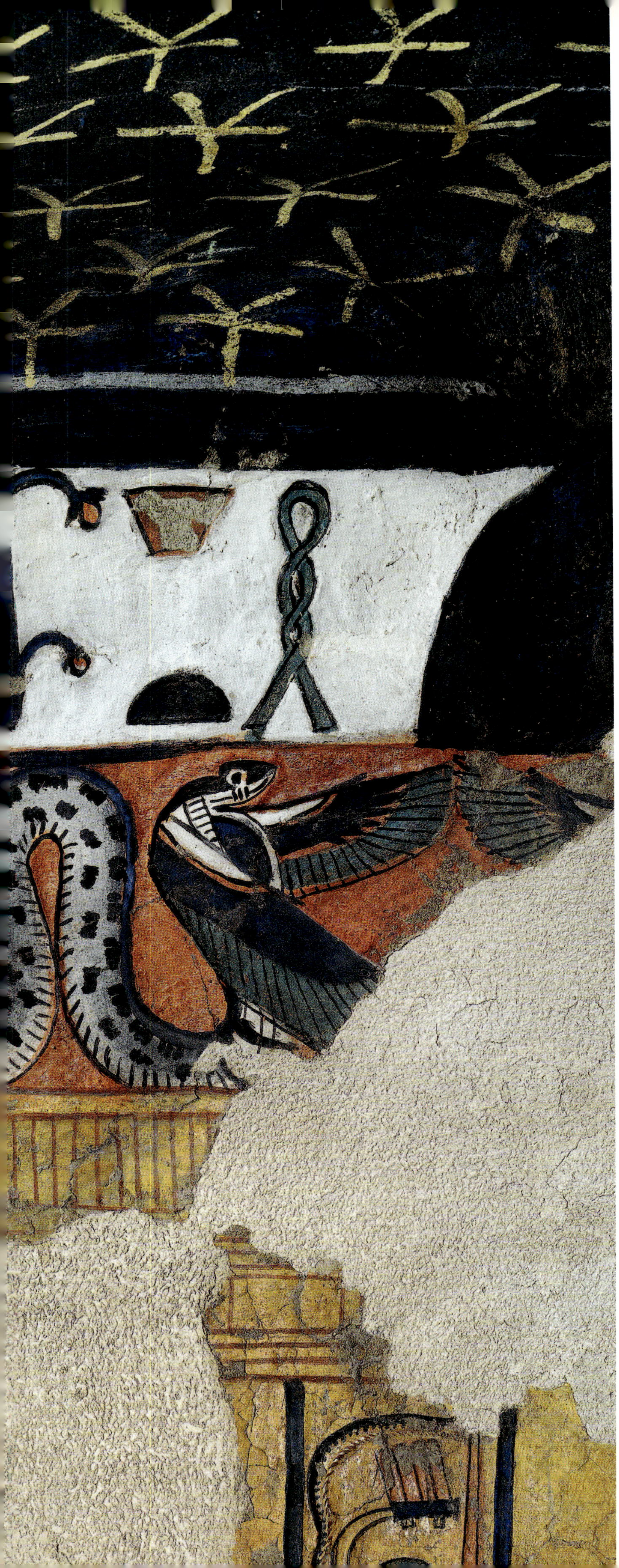

Merenptah and Osiris

(Pages 303–306)

This wall from the pillared hall of the tomb of Merenptah has been badly damaged, most likely by flooding that left a residue of debris behind which then pulled the painted plaster from the walls. The untouched parts of the paintings, which show the king making offerings to Osiris, are still rich and vibrant.

Nefertari in Danger

Even the newly conserved tomb of Queen Nefertari shows the effects of millennia of wear and tear. This priceless jewel of Egyptian art was in great danger from floods of tourists, and is now closed to the public. Recent conservation work has stabilized the paintings for now, but we must constantly be vigilant to prevent future damage.

Damnatio Memoriae

(Following pages)

In addition to the patches of paint and plaster that have fallen by accident, this wall from the tomb of Aye displays the work of agents of the early Ramesside kings, who tried to destroy the memories of Akhenaten and the kings who came after him. These men have erased the monarch's name from his cartouches, visible at the upper right.

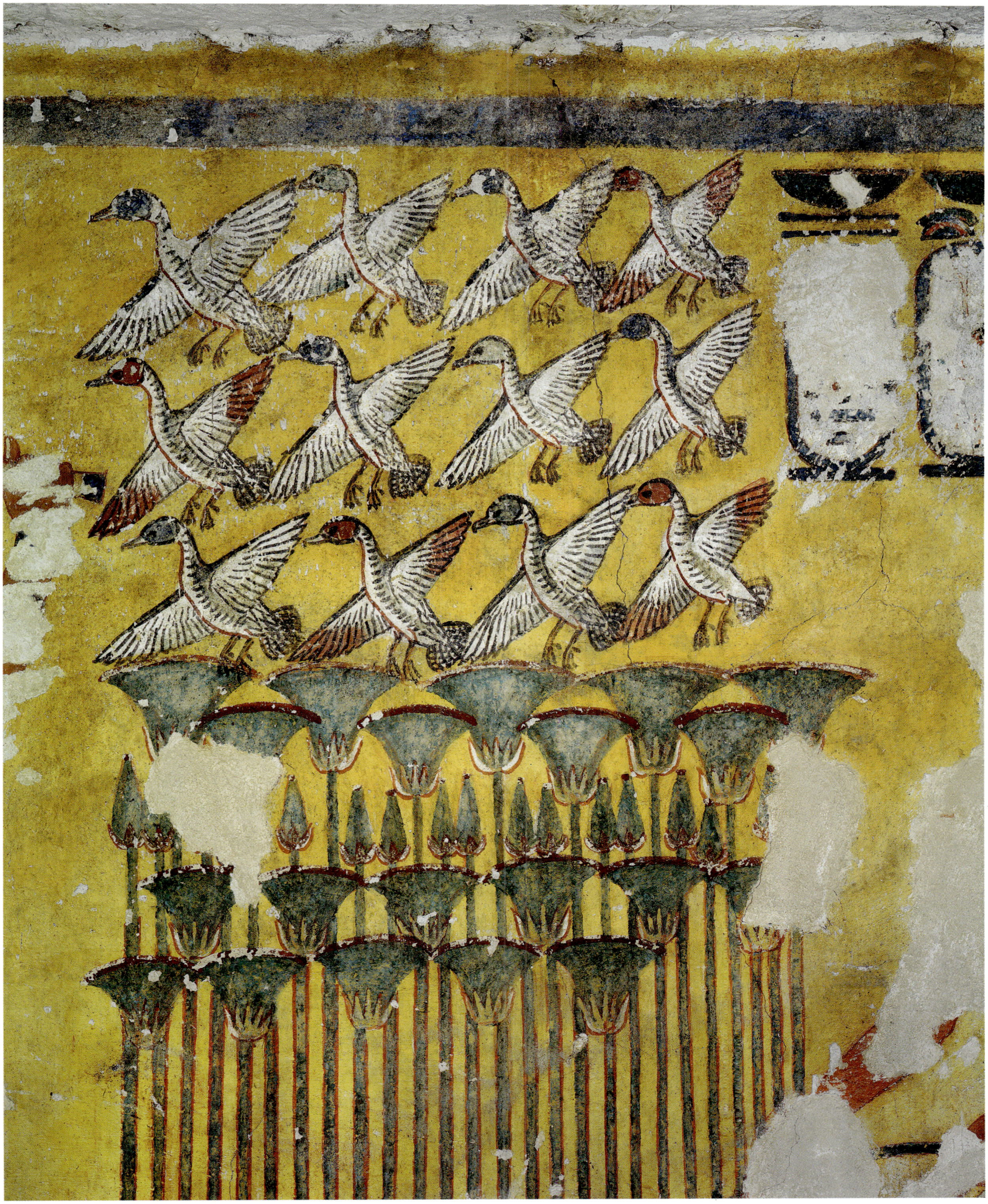

GLOSSARY

Aker. An earth god responsible for the eastern and western borders of Egypt, Aker was said to open the gates to the Netherworld for the deceased king. Originally represented as a strip of land with heads at both ends, he later became depicted as a two-headed sphinx.

Amun. A local Theban god, Amun rose to prominence in the 11th Dynasty, when Theban princes reunited the country at the end of the First Intermediate Period. His name means "The Hidden One"; he was represented in human form, wearing a corselet and a low flat crown with plumes on top.

Ankh. The hieroglyph for life; thought perhaps to be an image of a sandal strap.

Anubis. God of embalming, Anubis was represented in the form of a black super-jackal. He had major cult centers at Assiut and Abydos.

Apophis. The principal representative of chaos in the Duat. Seen in the form of a great serpent, Apophis tried to stop the journey of the solar bark by swallowing the sun god and his entourage.

Aten. The globe of the sun, selected as the principal god, and then transformed into the only state god, by the "heretic" Akhenaten during the late 18th Dynasty.

Atum. The creator god of the Heliopolitan cosmogony, Atum appeared on the primeval mound to bring the Egyptian cosmos into being. He was the progenitor of the Heliopolitan Ennead: Shu, Tefnut, Geb, Nut, Osiris, Isis, Nephthys, and Seth.

Ba. One aspect of the soul, seen in art as a human-headed bird.

Bes. A household god, protector of women in labor and children, Bes was shown in the form of a grotesque dwarf.

Canopic Jars. The four jars in which the viscera (lungs, liver, stomach, and intestines) were stored.

Cartouche. Expanded version of the *shen* ring, in which kings' names, and later the names of queens as well, were written.

Chthonic. Of the earth. Gods such as Aker, Tatanen, and Geb are considered chthonic.

Cosmogony. An understanding of how the world came into being.

***Djed* pillar.** Originally a vegetal motif, the *djed* pillar became identified as the backbone of Osiris and a symbol of fertility.

Duat. The ancient Egyptian word for the Netherworld, this was the realm beyond the earth where the dead carried out their eternal existence.

Ennead. Group of nine gods, usually used to refer to the Heliopolitan pantheon.

Four Sons of Horus. Duamutef, Qebehsenuef, Imsety, and Hapy were the four deities, known as the four sons of Horus or sometimes of Osiris, who protected the viscera of the deceased.

Geb. Son of Shu and husband of Nut, Geb was the anthropomorphized earth.

Hathor. Both daughter and wife of the sun god Re, Hathor was one incarnation of the primeval "great goddess."

Heka. Powerful god of magic, Heka was one of the sun god's principal companions in the Duat.

Heliopolis. Ancient Iunu, or On, Heliopolis (in Greek, "city of the sun") was the center of the sun cult from the Old Kingdom through to the end of the pharaonic era. It is located on the outskirts of modern Cairo.

Horemakhet. Literally "Horus in the horizon," this was a form of the sun god. By the New Kingdom, the Great Sphinx at Giza was called by this name.

Horus. One of the original sky and sun gods, Horus took the form of a falcon. He was the son of Isis and Osiris, and considered the incarnation of the living king.

Hu. Often found in conjunction with Sia, Hu was linked with the Memphite idea of creation and personified the concept of magical utterance.

Isis. Daughter of Geb and Nut and sister-wife of Osiris, Isis was another of the great goddesses.

Iunmutef. Represented as a priest in a panther skin, the Iunmutef (literally "pillar of his mother") stood in for the eldest son, responsible for presiding at the funeral ceremonies.

Ka. The lifeforce of the person, his or her "double."

Khepri. The sun at dawn, Khepri was depicted in the form of the scarab beetle.

Ma'at. Representative of the abstract concept of the proper order of the Egyptian cosmos, Ma'at is shown in the form of a woman with an ostrich plume, the hieroglyph for her name, on her head.

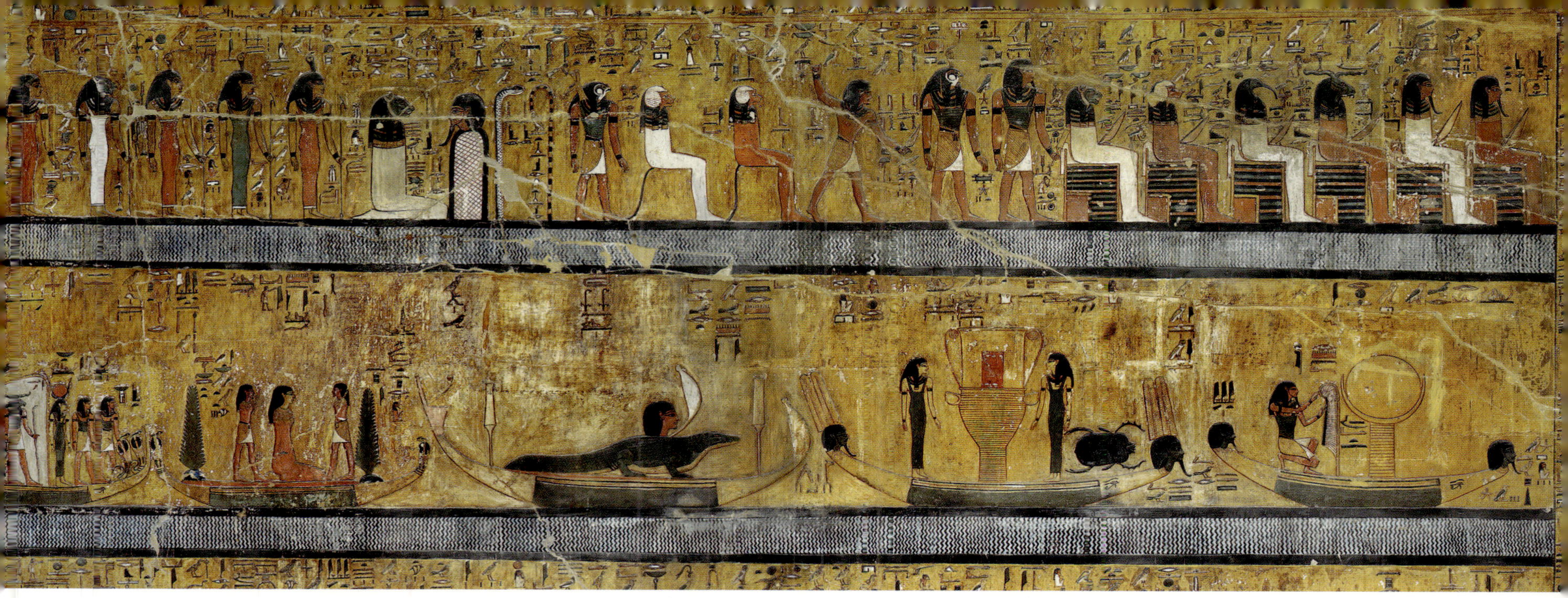

Mehen. The coiled snake that protected the front of the solar bark in many representations from the Netherworld Books.

Nefertem. Another form of the sun god at dawn, Nefertem is usually depicted as a young man with a lotus flower on his head.

Neith. Goddess of warfare, Neith was also one of the goddesses who protected the viscera.

Nephthys. One of the offspring of Geb and Nut, Nephthys partnered with her sister Isis to bring their brother Osiris back to life; she was an important protector of the deceased.

Nun. Incarnation of the primordial waters that preceded the creation of the cosmos.

Nut. Daughter of Shu and Tefnut and wife of Geb, Nut was the goddess of the sky, shown stretched out across the heavens so that the sun and stars could travel through her body.

Ogdoad. Group of eight gods; in Egyptian mythology, the gods of Hermopolis.

Osiris. Ruler of the Duat and king of the dead, Osiris was the son of Geb and Nut and husband of Isis. Murdered by his brother Seth, he was brought back to life by Isis, and fathered Horus.

Ptah. Creator god in the Memphite pantheon, Ptah was the patron of artisans. He was depicted in the form of a mummy wearing a tight skullcap.

Re. The principal solar deity of the Egyptian pantheon from at least the Old Kingdom, Re had his main cult center at Heliopolis.

Re-Horakhty. A syncretized version of the Heliopolitan sun god, Re, and the sun and sky god Horus of the Horizons.

Sed Festival. Festival of rejuvenation, celebrated by each king after his first thirty years of rule and then at more frequent intervals thereafter.

JOURNEY THROUGH THE DUAT
This detail from the second hour of the Book of the Amduat shows the solar bark and its companion vessels as they travel through the waters of the Wernes.

Sekhmet. Lioness goddess, daughter of Re, who had both fierce and protective aspects.

Serket. Serket, often referred to as Selket, was the scorpion goddess, one of the four protective female deities assigned to guard the viscera.

Seth. Brother of Osiris and husband of Nephthys, Seth was considered the god of chaos. In later periods especially, he was seen as the incarnation of evil.

Shabti. Funerary figurine. By the end of the New Kingdom, a full complement was 413 *shabtis*: one for each day of the year; 36 weekly overseers; and twelve monthly supervisors.

Shen. Circle of rope, tied at one end, that represented the circuit of the sun.

Shu. God of the air, Shu was the son of Atum and the brother and husband of Tefnut, goddess of moisture.

Sia. Paired with Hu, Sia was the personification of perception, and traveled with the sun god through the Duat.

Sokar. An earth god from the Memphite region, Sokar was syncretized with Ptah and Osiris.

Uraeus. Hooded cobra that protected the king by spitting fire at his enemies. Many goddesses were represented in this form.

Tatanen. Also an earth god, Tatanen, often merged with Ptah as Ptah-Tatanen, was a local Memphite deity, associated with the primeval mound.

Thoth. God of wisdom and writing, Thoth was shown as ibis, baboon, or human with the head of an ibis.

***Wedjat* Eye.** The sacred eye of Horus, the *wedjat*, healed by Isis, became a symbol of protection and health.

List of Illustrations

Selected Bibliography

Friedrich Abitz, *Statuetten in Schreinen als Grabbeigaben in den ägyptischen Königsgräbern der 18 und 19 Dynastie. Ägyptologische Abhandlungen* 35, Harrassowitz, Wiesbaden 1979

Friedrich Abitz, *König und Gott: Die Götterszenen in den ägyptischen Königsgräbern von Thutmosis IV bis Ramses III. Ägyptologische Abhandlungen* 40, Harrassowitz, Wiesbaden 1984

Friedrich Abitz, *Baugeschichte und Dekoration des Grabes Ramses' VI. Orbis Biblicus et Orientalis* 89, Universitätsverlag, Freiburg 1989

Giovanni Battista Belzoni, *Narrative of the Operations and Recent Discoveries Within the Pyramids, Temples, Tombs and Excavations in Egypt and Nubia,* John Murray, London 1820

Alessandro Bongioanni and Mario Tosi, *Uomini e dei nell'antico Egitto,* Maccari, Parma 1991

Peter A. Clayton, *The Valley of the Kings,* Wayland, Hove 1995

Anna Maria Donadoni Roveri, *La Vallée des Rois,* Atlas, Paris 1982

Dennis Forbes, *Tombs, Treasures, and Mummies: Seven Great Discoveries of Egyptian Archaeology,* KMT Communications, San Francisco 1998

Zahi Hawass, *The Golden Age of Tutankhamun: Divine Might and Splendor in the New Kingdom,* American University in Cairo Press, Cairo 2004

Zahi Hawass, *Tutankhamun and the Golden Age of the Pharaohs,* National Geographic, Washington DC 2005

Erik Hornung, *The Valley of the Kings: Horizon of Eternity.* trans. David Warburton, Timken Publishers Inc., New York 1990

Erik Hornung, et. al. *Immortal Pharaoh: The Tomb of Thutmose III,* Factum Arte and United Exhibits Group, Madrid 2005

Salima Ikram and Aidan Dodson, *The Royal Mummies in the Egyptian Museum,* Zeitona, Cairo 1997

Salima Ikram and Aidan Dodson, *The Mummy in Ancient Egypt: Equipping the Dead for Eternity,* Thames & Hudson, London 1998

Christian Jacq, *La Vallée des Rois: Histoire et découverte d'une demeure d'éternité,* Perrin, Paris 1992

Christian Jacq, *La Vallée des Rois: Images et mystères,* Perrin, Paris 1993

Robert B.Partridge, *Faces of Pharaoh: Royal Mummies and Coffins from Ancient Thebes,* Rubicon, London 1994

Alexandre Piankoff, *The Tomb of Ramesses VI,* Pantheon Books, New York 1954

Alexandre Piankoff, *The Litany of Re,* Pantheon Books, New York 1964

Nicholas Reeves and Richard H. Wilkinson, *The Complete Valley of the Kings: Tombs and Treasures of Egypt's Greatest Pharaohs,* Thames & Hudson, London 1996

Nicholas Reeves, *The Complete Tutankhamun: The King, The Tomb, The Royal Treasure,* Thames & Hudson, London 2000

Catharine H. Roehrig, *Explorers and Artists in the Valley of the Kings,* American University in Cairo Press, Cairo 2002

John Romer, *Valley of the Kings,* William Morrow, New York 1981

John and Elizabeth Romer, *The Rape of Tutankhamun,* Michael O'Mara, London 1993

Alberto Siliotti, *The Valley of the Kings and the Theban Tombs,* American University in Cairo Press, Cairo and New York 2000

Elizabeth Thomas, *The Royal Necropolis of Thebes,* Princeton 1966

Kent R. Weeks, *The Lost Tomb,* William Morrow, New York 1998

Kent R. Weeks, ed., *The Treasures of the Valley of the Kings: Tombs and Temples of the Theban West Bank in Luxor,* American University in Cairo Press, Cairo 2002

Kent R. Weeks, *The Illustrated Guide to Luxor: Tombs, Temples, and Museums,* White Star, Vercelli 2005

Acknowledgments

I would like to thank many people who participated in this book. First, I would like to express my gratitude to Antonio Scuderi of DeAgostini for encouraging me to write this book. Also, my thanks to all those who have participated in bringing this book together: Davide Bernardini, Barbara De Spirt, Valeria Camaschella, and the designer, Adriano Tallarini. Of course, this book would not have happened without the great photographs of Sandro Vannini. The new techniques he has developed have allowed him to produce exceptional, never-before-seen images.

I would like also to thank my colleagues and assistants at my Cairo office, who collected some of the published data for me, especially Heba Abdel Moneim, Wisam Mehrez, and Nagwan Edward. Finally, I would like to thank my friend and colleague, Janice Kamrin, for editing this book.

Zahi Hawass,
Cairo, 2006

A photographic work such as this requires the contributions of many people. I would therefore like to thank everyone who helped to make this project possible. First and foremost Ali el Asfar, who led the investigation team on the West Bank at Luxor, and Mansour Boraik, with whom I have worked for many years, for their invaluable advice. Thanks are also due to all the staff at my studio, Eraldo Gabrielli, Daniele Vita, Massimo Luciani, Nico Piazza, and to Piero Lucchetti, for his assistance in the field, as well as the irreplaceable Hamdy Hamdan at Luxor. I also would like to acknowledge all the supervisors who put themselves out for me during the many months of work, taking turns to follow the most tedious shoots. It would never have been possible to put together this book without the bright ideas of Zahi Hawass, who always believed in my work. And finally, last but not least, thanks to my wife Maria Rita, without whom I may never have been a photographer for all these years.

Sandro Vannini
Viterbo, 2006

First published in the United Kingdom in 2006 by
Thames & Hudson Ltd, 181A High Holborn, London WC1V 7QX

www.thamesandhudson.com

First published in 2006 in hardcover in the United States of America by
Thames & Hudson Inc., 500 Fifth Avenue, New York, New York 10110

thamesandhudsonusa.com

British Library Cataloguing-in-Publication Data
A catalogue record for this book is available from the British Library

Library of Congress Catalog Card Number 2006901536

ISBN-13: 978-0-500-51322-4
ISBN-10: 0-500-51322-8

Printed and bound in Italy